COALITION DIARIES
2012–2015

Praise for *Coalition* by David Laws

'Definitive and forensic ... This is an impressive work. A lucid, engaging mix of anecdote and forensic detail, it has a fair claim to become, at least for the foreseeable future, the definitive account of the UK's first postwar experiment in coalition government.'
CHRIS MULLIN, *THE OBSERVER*

'A crisply written chronological look at the ins and outs of policymaking during 2010–15 ... Laws is a wry, thoughtful observer ... *Coalition* is a deadpan version of *The Thick of It*.'
THE TIMES

'Packed with remarkable verbatim accounts of the arguments between the men at the top: David Cameron, George Osborne and Nick Clegg.'
DOMINIC LAWSON, *SUNDAY TIMES*

'This book makes the politics of coalition come alive. It is well written, with a great deal of humour and a nice eye for detail ... This is an important work that goes a long way towards explaining our contemporary political predicament. I cannot recommend it too highly.'
PETER OBORNE, *NEW STATESMAN*

'Brilliant ... This is the real thing: page after page of first-hand accounts of rows, feuds and cover-ups ... If, like me, you think plots and personalities are as important as policies in understanding the way we are governed, this is the book for you.'
SIMON WALTERS, *MAIL ON SUNDAY*

'These memoirs are terrific ... Everyone should read them.'
PETER HITCHENS

'David Laws has written what deserves to become the definitive account of the 2010–15 coalition government. It is also a cracking good read: fast-paced, insightful and a must for all those interested in British politics.'
PADDY ASHDOWN

'There are few – even from within my own party – whose inside story of the 2010–15 coalition I would trust more than David Laws's.'
MATTHEW PARRIS

COALITION
DIARIES
2012 – 2015

DAVID LAWS

Biteback Publishing

First published in Great Britain in 2017 by
Biteback Publishing Ltd
Westminster Tower
3 Albert Embankment
London SE1 7SP

ISBN 978-1-78590-232-1

10 9 8 7 6 5 4 3 2 1

A CIP catalogue record for this book is available from the British Library.

Set in Sabon

Printed and bound in Great Britain by
CPI Group (UK) Ltd, Croydon CR0 4YY

MIX
Paper from
responsible sources
FSC® C020471

For 'Bugs'

CONTENTS

'Cameron has a classic nose for political survival.
He ducks and he weaves. He always believes that he can
get himself out of a tight corner. One day, he won't.'
NICK CLEGG, 23 MARCH 2015

PREFACE

These diaries are written for those interested in politics, and in particular in the innermost workings of the 2010–15 coalition government. Here are described, for example, the forces and considerations which caused David Cameron to take the biggest gamble of his career, and one of the most important decisions of any postwar British Prime Minister, by announcing a referendum on the UK's future in the European Union. We are still living with the momentous consequences of that and other key decisions of the coalition era.

In early 2012, in anticipation of a return to government, I started a diary. This was recorded on an irregular basis until the September 2012 ministerial reshuffle, when I was appointed as both Minister of State for Schools and Minister of State in the Cabinet Office. I joined the Cabinet, and sometimes attended the 'Quad' of the most senior members of the government. From then until May 2015, I recorded a daily diary in some detail. This was usually dictated at the very end of the day, at around midnight, or the following day, at around 6 a.m.

My positions in the Cabinet, on numerous Cabinet committees, as a minister in the Education Department, and in the Cabinet Office at the heart of the government – brokering deals between the coalition parties – meant that I had a rare vantage point from which to help shape and record the work of this Cameron–Clegg government.

I decided to keep my diaries both for my own reference and in order – in time – to be able to record the political history of what was arguably Britain's first real coalition government.

To help ensure that the Liberal Democrat role in the 2010–15 administration was not underplayed, neglected or distorted, I used my diaries and other records to publish an account of this period of government in *Coalition*, which was published in early 2016. Those who want a historic account of the policy challenges facing the Cameron–Clegg government, with each major issue dealt with in a distinct chapter, will find that volume more easily accessible than these diaries.

I decided, however, after encouragement from my publisher, Iain Dale, to release this edited selection of key excerpts of my diaries, for two main reasons. Firstly, those interested in the politics and operation of government often find diaries both more readable and more revealing than formal accounts carefully written months or years later. Emotions are more raw when recorded in the heat of the moment, and usually in a state of tiredness at the very beginning or end of each day. And in diaries, the overlapping pressures and challenges of government are reflected more accurately than in later historic accounts, in which particular issues can be carefully dealt with in individual, hermetically sealed, chapters. In government, there are often many balls to be juggled at the same time – which may be why so many are dropped.

Secondly, my diaries run to a couple of million words, and it was impossible to record or even summarise all of this information in one volume. I was aware that this meant leaving much material out which might be of interest to political obsessives, historians and those interested in the detailed evolution of policy – particularly in areas such as education, where I was intimately involved in most major debates.

So this volume is for those who are intrigued by politics, who want to understand more about how it works in practice, and in particular for those interested in the inner workings of the coalition government.

I should add one important qualification about political diaries: what we select to record each day, and what we later decide is of interest to readers as we edit down the extensive text, often tends to be biased in favour of the controversial, the errors and disasters, the disagreements and animosities. That may make for more interesting reading than hearing about all the areas of policy consensus, all the decisions that were taken cooperatively and implemented successfully, and all the policies effectively delivered.

However, there is a risk that some readers of this diary will conclude that government is only about rows, controversies, backstabbing and disasters. In fact, I am proud of much that the coalition government achieved, and in general of the way in which agreement was secured. Our record in restoring economic confidence, significantly reducing the deficit, reforming our education system, putting in place the foundations of a better system of mental health, legislating for equal marriage, delivering on our responsibilities to the poorest nations on the planet, and seeking to tackle some of our major environmental challenges is one which I think both coalition parties can be justly proud of.

In telling this story, I have erred on the side of openness in revealing what really went on behind 'closed doors', except where issues of national security are involved or where individuals – particularly civil servants – are entitled to anonymity.

Diaries record a 'warts and all' account of those who appear within them, and inevitably there will be individuals who would rather amend or obscure some of the information recorded about them in this book. But most of the 'major players' can expect to find in these pages sections which reflect well on their work and motivations, as well as those more critical at other times, and I have sought to be fair to political friend and foe alike. It was my experience that most of the senior members of all three major political parties were people of integrity, whose purpose for being in politics was to serve their country rather than themselves.

Standing alongside my earlier volume, *Coalition*, I will let these *Coalition Diaries* speak for themselves. I will now, however, diverge from this discipline in one respect.

Since *Coalition* was published, there has been one major development in UK politics which is difficult to ignore – the June 2016 referendum, in which the public decided by a narrow majority to leave the European Union. This led immediately to the resignation of David Cameron, and indeed the departure from government of many of the Conservative 'big beasts' of the coalition era – including George Osborne, Michael Gove and Oliver Letwin.

In defending his decision to trigger a referendum, Mr Cameron has argued that a public vote on the European Union was not only inevitable but had been delayed by the 'political elite' for too long. Arguably, both propositions are accurate. But what I think is revealed, both in these diaries and in *Coalition*, is the tactical, short-termist and risky way in which the decision over the referendum was taken by David Cameron. This eventually led, entirely predictably in my view, to a referendum taking place after a short and rather superficial 'renegotiation', at a time when the UK had little real bargaining power to extract significant concessions from other member states, and with very little time or attention having been committed to a serious process of winning over wavering voters. That is the real indictment of Mr Cameron's risky and ultimately failed strategy.

In *Coalition*, I recorded my thanks to many of those who assisted me over my political career.

On this occasion I can therefore be a little more concise. I wish particularly to thank Claire Margetts, who had the dubious privilege of transcribing my late-night, lengthy tapes – and who did so without complaint and with complete discretion.

I would like to thank my private office staff in the Cabinet Office and the Department for Education, who did so much to support my work in government; Wilhelmina Blankson, Lydia Bradley, Philip Cattle, Samuel Cook, Jonathan Crisp, Laura De Silva, Nick Donlevy, Tom Dyer, Becci Fagan, Camilla Frappell, Katie Harrison, Samuel Kelly, Suzanne Kochanowski, Georgina Manley, Natalie Perera, Ursula Ritz and Daniel Sellman.

I would also like to thank my Yeovil and Westminster office staff of Sue Weeks, Claire Margetts, Sarah Frapple, Sadye McLean, Alec Newton, Theo Whitaker and James Mole. Together, I hope that we delivered a timely and responsive service to many thousands of constituents, even while I was heavily occupied by ministerial work.

Tim Leunig, Matt Sanders, Chris Paterson and Julian Astle were my education policy advisers, and all four made a major contribution to better government and a more effectively functioning education system.

My thanks also to those ministers I worked most closely with in government, and who necessarily find themselves at the centre of the narrative of these diaries. I must particularly single out a few: Nick Clegg, whom I greatly admire as a person of integrity and decency, and whose contribution to providing stable and grown-up coalition government was in my view greater than any other individual; Sir Danny Alexander, who ranks as one of the most effective Chief Secretaries of the last fifty years, and whose endless lectures on the importance of fiscal prudence, when all I wanted was a bit more money for education, I now forgive; Sir Oliver Letwin, a thoroughly honourable and unassuming person, whom it was a genuine pleasure to work with; and finally Michael Gove, who occasionally drove me to distraction, but who was also a clever, amusing and loyal friend, and a passionate and radical education reformer.

Finally, I am grateful to the small but very dedicated team at Biteback Publishing, who do so much to ensure that our political history is recorded and accessible. I must particularly thank Olivia Beattie, my patient and hard-working editor.

David Laws
London
July 2017

DRAMATIS PERSONAE

LORD (ANDREW) ADONIS – Labour, former Minister of State for Education

DANNY ALEXANDER – Lib Dem, Chief Secretary to the Treasury 2010–15, Treasury spokesman 2015

DOUGLAS ALEXANDER – Labour, shadow Foreign Secretary 2011–15

LORD (PADDY) ASHDOWN – chair of the Lib Dem general election committee 2012–15, former Lib Dem leader

JULIAN ASTLE – Lib Dem, special adviser to Nick Clegg 2011–15

NORMAN BAKER – Lib Dem, Under Secretary of State for Transport 2010–13, Minister of State for the Home Office 2013–14

JOHN BERCOW – Speaker of the House of Commons since 2009

NICK BOLES – Conservative, Under Secretary of State for Communities and Local Government 2012–14, Minister of State for Skills 2014–16

PAULINE BOOTH – Lib Dem, volunteer, local party activist and campaigner

JEREMY BROWNE – Lib Dem, Minister of State for Foreign Affairs 2010–12, Minister of State for Home Affairs 2012–13

PAUL BURSTOW – Lib Dem, Minister of State for Care Services 2010–12

LIAM BYRNE – Labour, shadow Secretary of State for Work and Pensions 2011–13

SIR VINCE CABLE – Lib Dem, Secretary of State for Business, Innovation and Skills, president of the Board of Trade 2010–15

DAVID CAMERON – Conservative, Prime Minister 2010–16

MENZIES ('MING') CAMPBELL – former Lib Dem leader

ALISTAIR CARMICHAEL – Lib Dem, government deputy Chief Whip of the House of Commons 2010–13, Secretary of State for Scotland 2013–15

MARK CARNEY – Governor of the Bank of England since 2013

DOUGLAS CARSWELL – first elected MP of the UK Independence Party

KEN CLARKE – long-serving Conservative MP, Secretary of State for Justice Lord Chancellor 2010–12, Minister without Portfolio 2012–14

NICK CLEGG – leader of the Lib Dems 2007–15, Deputy Prime Minister 2010–15

RYAN COETZEE – Lib Dem strategy director 2012–14, general election director of strategy 2014–15

TIM COLBOURNE – Lib Dem, special adviser to Deputy Prime Minister 2012–13, deputy chief of staff to Deputy Prime Minister 2014–15

GRAHAM COLE – chairman of AgustaWestland

SAM CRABB – Yeovil Lib Dem councillor and David Laws's election agent

DOMINIC CUMMINGS – special adviser to Michael Gove 2010–14

ED DAVEY – Lib Dem, Secretary of State for Energy and Climate Change 2012–15

HENRY DIMBLEBY – British cookery writer and a co-founder of the Leon Restaurants fast food chain

NICK DONLEVY – private secretary at the Cabinet Office

NADINE DORRIES – Conservative MP since 2005

PAMELA DOW – principal private secretary to Michael Gove 2012–14

IAIN DUNCAN SMITH – Conservative, Secretary of State for Work and Pensions 2010–16

MICHAEL FALLON – deputy chairman of the Conservative Party 2010–12, Minister of State for Business and Enterprise 2012–14, Minister of State for Energy 2013–14, Minister of State for Portsmouth 2014, Secretary of State for Defence since 2014

TIM FARRON – president of the Lib Dems 2011–15, Lib Dem spokesperson for Foreign and Commonwealth Affairs 2015

LORD (ANDREW) FELDMAN – chairman of the Conservative Party 2010–16

DON FOSTER – Lib Dem, Under Secretary of State for Communities and Local Government 2012–13, Comptroller of the Household 2013–15, government deputy Chief Whip in the House of Commons 2013–15

SAM FREEDMAN – adviser to Michael Gove 2009–13

NICK GIBB – Conservative, Minister of State for Schools 2010–12, Minister of State for School Reform 2014–15

TIM GORDON – chief executive of the Lib Dems 2011–17

MICHAEL GOVE – Conservative, Secretary of State for Education 2010–14,

Chief Whip of the House of Commons and Parliamentary Secretary to the Treasury 2014–15

CHRIS GRAYLING – Conservative, Minister of State for Employment 2010–12, Secretary of State for Justice Lord Chancellor 2012–15

JUSTINE GREENING – Conservative, Secretary of State for Transport 2011–12, Secretary of State for International Development 2012–16

BARONESS (OLLY) GRENDER – acting DPM director of communications and deputy director of government communications 2012

ANDY GRICE – political editor at *The Independent* 1998–2015

WILLIAM HAGUE – Conservative, Secretary of State for Foreign and Commonwealth Affairs 2010–14, Leader of the House of Commons 2014–15, First Secretary of State 2010–15

PHILIP HAMMOND – Conservative, Secretary of State for Defence 2011–14, Secretary of State for Foreign and Commonwealth Affairs 2014–16

MATT HANCOCK – Conservative, Minister of State for Skills and Enterprise 2013–14, Minister of State for Portsmouth 2014–15, Minister of State for Energy 2014–15, Minister of State for Business and Enterprise 2014–15

MATTHEW HANNEY – special adviser to Nick Clegg 2010–15

RUPERT HARRISON – chief economic adviser to David Cameron and George Osborne 2006–10, chief of staff to George Osborne 2010–15

SIR JEREMY HEYWOOD – Cabinet Secretary since 2012, head of the Home Civil Service since 2014

LORD (JONATHAN) HILL – Conservative, Under Secretary of State for Schools 2010–13, Chancellor of the Duchy of Lancaster 2013–14, Leader of the House of Lords 2013–14, European Commissioner for Financial Stability, Financial Services and Capital Markets Union 2014–16

JEREMY HUNT – Conservative, Secretary of State for Culture, Olympics, Media and Sport 2010–12, Secretary of State for Health since 2012

BORIS JOHNSON – Conservative, Mayor of London 2008–16

JO JOHNSON – Conservative, director of the No. 10 Policy Unit 2013–15, Minister of State for the Cabinet Office 2014–15

DAVID JONES – Conservative, Under Secretary of State for Wales 2010–12, Secretary of State for Wales 2012–14

SIR BOB KERSLAKE – Permanent Secretary Department for Communities and Local Government 2010–15, head of the Home Civil Service 2012–15, crossbench peer since 2015

SIR MERVYN KING – Governor of the Bank of England 2003–13

NORMAN LAMB – Lib Dem, Minister of State for Employment Relations 2012, Minister of State for Care and Support 2012–15, spokesperson for Health since 2015

OLIVER LETWIN – Conservative, Minister of State for Government Policy 2010–15, Chancellor of the Duchy of Lancaster 2014–16

TIM LEUNIG – policy adviser, DfE to Michael Gove and David Laws, DfE chief analyst from 2014

ED LLEWELLYN – Downing Street chief of staff 2010–16

STEPHEN LOTINGA – director of communications for Nick Clegg 2014–15

TIM LOUGHTON – Conservative, Under Secretary of State for Children and Families 2010–12

JAMES MCGRORY – DPM press secretary 2010–14, deputy director of communications and DPM spokesperson 2014–15

POLLY MACKENZIE – Lib Dem, director of policy 2010–11, 2013–15

PAUL MARSHALL – hedge fund owner, social entrepreneur and co-author with David Laws of the Lib Dem *Orange Book*

FRANCIS MAUDE – Conservative, Minister for the Cabinet Office 2010–15

THERESA MAY – Conservative, Home Secretary 2010–16

ALAN MILBURN – Labour, former minister for the Cabinet Office

MARIA MILLER – Conservative, Under Secretary of State for Disabled People 2010–12, Minister for Women and Equalities 2012–14, Secretary of State for Culture, Media and Sport 2012–14

MICHAEL MOORE – Lib Dem, Secretary of State for Scotland 2010–13

NICKY MORGAN – Conservative, Economic Secretary to the Treasury 2013–14, Financial Secretary to the Treasury 2014, Minister for Women and Equalities 2014–16, Secretary of State for Education 2014–16

BARONESS (SALLY) MORGAN – Labour, chair of Ofsted 2011–14

LORD (JOHN) NASH – Conservative, Under Secretary of State for the School System since 2013

LORD (MATTHEW) OAKESHOTT – Lib Dem, former Treasury spokesperson

JONNY OATES – Lib Dem, Nick Clegg's chief of staff 2010–15

GEORGE OSBORNE – Conservative, Chancellor of the Exchequer 2010–16

GEORGE PARKER – political editor of the *Financial Times* since 2007

CHRIS PATERSON – DfE policy adviser to David Laws

OWEN PATERSON – Conservative, Secretary of State for Northern Ireland

2010–12, Secretary of State for Environment, Food and Rural Affairs 2012–14

NATALIE PERERA – DfE civil servant and private secretary in the Cabinet Office 2013–15

ERIC PICKLES – Conservative, Minister of State for Faith 2014–15, Secretary of State for Communities and Local Government 2010–15

NICK ROBINSON – BBC political editor 2005–2015

PATRICK ROCK – Conservative, No. 10 special adviser and deputy director of policy 2011–14

AMBER RUDD – Conservative, parliamentary private secretary to the Chancellor of the Exchequer 2012–13, Under Secretary of State for Climate Change 2014–15

MATT SANDERS – special adviser to Nick Clegg and David Laws at the Department for Education, the Department for Culture, Media and Sport, and the Cabinet Office

CHRIS SAUNDERS – senior adviser to Nick Clegg

GRANT SHAPPS – Conservative, Minister of State for Housing and Local Government 2010–12, chairman of the Conservative Party 2012–15, Minister without Portfolio 2012–15, Minister of State for International Development 2015

TOM SHINNER – senior policy adviser to the Secretary of State for Education 2013–16

PHILIPPA STROUD – Conservative, special adviser to Iain Duncan Smith 2010–15

ANDREW STUNELL – Lib Dem, Under Secretary of State for Communities and Local Government 2010–12

JO SWINSON – Lib Dem, parliamentary private secretary to Nick Clegg 2012, Under Secretary of State for Employment Relations, Consumer and Postal Affairs 2012–15

SARAH TEATHER – Lib Dem, Minister of State for Children and Families 2010–12

LIZ TRUSS – Conservative, Under Secretary of State for Education and Childcare 2012–14, Secretary of State for Environment, Food and Rural Affairs 2014–16

JOHN VINCENT – historian, journalist and an author of the School Food Plan

SUE WEEKS – Yeovil office manager

GILES WILKES – special adviser to Vince Cable

BARONESS (SHIRLEY) WILLIAMS – Lib Dem

SIR MICHAEL WILSHAW – chief inspector of schools in England and head of Ofsted 2012–16

CHRIS WORMALD – director general, Deputy Prime Minister's Office 2010–12, Permanent Secretary of the Department for Education since 2012

SIR GEORGE YOUNG – Conservative, Chief Whip of the House of Commons and parliamentary secretary to the Treasury 2012–14

HENRY DE ZOETE – special adviser to Michael Gove

2012

TUESDAY 28 FEBRUARY

Today I am starting a diary, for the first time in my life.

Breakfast with one of Cameron's special advisers at the Cinnamon Club, Westminster. He's astonishingly disillusioned: 'I'd expected to find a Prime Minister who was strategic, modernising and focused on the big issues. Instead, Downing Street is utterly dysfunctional and Cameron is obsessed only with tactics, the media, and opportunistic interventions.'

MONDAY 5 MARCH

Another pre-Budget meeting today with Nick Clegg. We have decided to push for a huge rise in the personal income tax allowance.

Two problems: firstly, Osborne has an utterly crazy idea of cutting the top tax rate from 50 per cent to 40 per cent – a bizarre 'priority' at a time of austerity. Nick and all his advisers are against – apart from Danny Alexander. Even Cameron seems dubious. But George is making it his price for the allowance. Is it a price worth paying?

Problem two is that Osborne keeps blocking our ideas for raising revenue from the rich, to fund the allowance. Instead, the Treasury is pushing a whole series of tax increases on ordinary people – particularly increases in various rates of VAT. Nick thinks they have 'zero political common sense'.

TUESDAY 6 MARCH

Lunch with George Parker, the astute and genial political editor of the *FT*. George asked lots of questions about the 50p rate. Managed to put him off the scent a bit. But this cannot be the 'white rabbit' of the Budget either. The problem now is that unless we allow Osborne a small cut in the top rate, he will scale back on the allowance. Nick still very worried by the politics.

FRIDAY 16 MARCH

Today my article with Tim Farron about a fairer tax system appeared in *The Guardian*, to pave the way for a Lib Dem concession over the 50p rate – now to be reduced to 45p. Unfortunately, somebody has also leaked this to *The Guardian*.

An urgent morning call from Nick Clegg. Apparently Osborne is incandescent about the *Guardian* story – 'Who leaked my bloody Budget?' etc. Nick says he's blaming not only the Lib Dems but me personally: 'I've never known Osborne so angry.'

TUESDAY 20 MARCH

The eve of the Budget. More leaks! BBC *News at Ten* reports that the personal allowance will rise to £9,200, up from £8,100. This will be the largest ever increase, delivering on this Lib Dem manifesto priority.

WEDNESDAY 21 MARCH

Osborne came to the Commons to deliver what was left of the Budget (not much). It went down well in the House. We Lib Dems had been instructed to wave our order papers violently when the increase in the allowance was mentioned, in order to 'claim credit'. The Tory whips had given similar instructions to their MPs, so there was a bizarre moment when George announced the rise to £9,205 and all the Lib Dem and Conservative MPs behind him went competitively berserk. Ming Campbell looked rather disapproving.

THURSDAY 22 MARCH

The Budget coverage is universally ghastly – the worst I can remember. All the good news had been briefed out beforehand. So, the press have all focused on the surprise news – a freeze in the pensioner tax allowance. The *Daily Telegraph* leads with: 'Granny tax hit for five million pensioners'. There is now also a campaign against what's being dubbed a 'pasty tax'. For once, it is Cameron and Osborne taking the flak.

THURSDAY 29 MARCH

Lunch with George Osborne – at his suggestion. A 'clear the air' after he blamed me for the top-rate leak. We met in his extravagantly large Treasury office, overlooking St James's Park.

George looks pretty dented, shell-shocked even, by the ghastly public reaction to his Budget. I made clear that I'd not leaked the 50 per cent cut. George claimed it was the right policy economically, but accepts that it might now be impossible to go any further this parliament.

He is clearly utterly obsessed by political recovery. 'David Cameron and I have "done" opposition, and we don't want to have to go back there ever again. Our main priority now is winning the next election.'

Surprisingly, he asked whether there was an electoral deal that could be done with the Lib Dems in 2015, a sort of 'coupon election' – where we stand down in some key Tory/Labour marginals, and where they stand down in some of our seats.

I said that I thought this was incredibly unlikely, as the Lib Dems would fight the next election as an independent party, and if we had some kind of 'pact' with the Conservatives then effectively it would mean that we were no longer a serious force in all of the seats in the country that had Conservative MPs – half the seats in total. George looked rather disappointed.

He also talked about party funding reform and said that he thought that we ought to devise a package that would 'stuff the Labour Party and stop the unions diverting funding into our seats and yours ... I'd much rather have Ed Miliband on TV every night defending his links with the unions than talking ad infinitum about my 2012 Budget fiasco!' Has there ever been a more political occupant of No. 11?

Our meeting lasted an hour and three quarters. George is always interesting, and he has a very shrewd sense of the internal dynamics of other parties and what motivates people. You may not like his politics or his political brutalism, but he's an engaging, amusing, candid and often self-deprecating individual. A good person to have a private dinner with, provided you bring a very, very long spoon.

FRIDAY 30 MARCH

The government seems to be making a complete balls-up of the threatened strike by tanker drivers. Francis Maude, the Cabinet Office Minister, has been going around saying that people should panic-buy petrol in 'jerry cans'. Certifiable.

SATURDAY 31 MARCH

The 'fuel fiasco' has taken a nasty twist. Yesterday, a woman suffered 40 per cent burns when petrol ignited as she was pouring it from a jerry can into a jug in her kitchen. Francis Maude, our 'jerry can man', faces calls to resign.

WEDNESDAY 18 APRIL

Dinner with Nick Clegg at Quirinale restaurant in Westminster. We drove there in Nick's bomb-proofed Jaguar, with doors so heavy I could barely close mine. His Metropolitan Police protection officers came in and sat at one of the nearby tables. They were hardly inconspicuous – two huge burly men sitting uncomfortably together at a tiny table, as if they were auditioning for the role of Britain's least likely gay couple!

Nick has quite an appetite and we went through three courses in rapid order. He raised for the first time whether or not he should fight the next election as party leader. It's clear that he feels pretty battered and bruised, and also that he wants to do the right thing for the party – 'I mustn't outstay my welcome'. I told him that he was more than capable of emerging by the next general election as a leader who was respected for what he'd done in government, even if he is no longer the fresh-faced boy of 'Cleggmania'.

Nick is surprisingly disenchanted with Cameron – 'very bright but incredibly tactical ... a traditional shire Conservative, who doesn't think very hard and who is intellectually flippant ... he's obsessed by the press and cares desperately about what they say about him. He's in a big panic about Leveson, the Budget, the economy, Europe, Boris Johnson...'

Nick was more generous about Osborne and even Theresa May: 'Yes, she's naturally secretive, unbending and an "Ice Maiden", but I have grown to like and respect her. When she sees a road block she will try to steer around, rather than crashing right into it.'

He feels that pressure for an in/out referendum on the EU is going to grow, and that the risk of leaving the EU is getting quite high. Talks of a 'defining moment' in the next parliament.

THURSDAY 17 MAY

Nick met Cameron last night to discuss a compromise on Lords reform – first elections for, say, 100 new Lords would go ahead in 2015, with a referendum in 2017 before further elections. In exchange, we would vote through the new Commons boundaries and the cut in MP numbers.

Nick said Cameron's reaction was 'too clever by half'. I'm not surprised. I can't see how we could possibly argue that a referendum should come after the first elections!

THURSDAY 21 JUNE

The newspapers suggest that the Tory rebellion on the Lords is over 100 MPs – enough to kill reform.

In addition, massive coverage of a new and unapproved 'plan' by Michael Gove, to abolish GCSEs and go back to O-levels – with less intelligent students taking simple 'CSE' exams that would allow them to 'do things like reading railway timetables'. Unbelievable! It all sounds like a 1950s rewind.

Nick is in Brazil. I received an angry email from him, describing the Gove stuff as 'a complete bounce – totally unacceptable'. Ed Llewellyn claims that the Prime Minister 'knew nothing about it'. Cameron is said to be 'outraged'.

Some are speculating that this is Michael preparing for a future Tory leadership fight; others are suggesting a new form of Tory 'differentiation'. Either way, this will not improve the already bad relations between Michael and Nick.

THURSDAY 28 JUNE

Nick announced the House of Lords reform plans yesterday – but the support from the PM was lukewarm. Rumours are that the Tory whips are not being very hard on their MPs. Spoke to Jonny Oates this morning – said I thought that we need to be preparing for the failure of Lords reform. It would be a disaster if we tried to force this through over many months, when all that would happen is a referendum obligation would be inserted and we'd end up losing the referendum if it was held in this parliament or not being able to implement the changes until 2020 if the referendum was held on Election Day 2015.

I argued that if we lose the programme motion, then Nick is going to have to kill the Commons boundary changes – kicking the whole constitutional reform agenda into the long grass.

This afternoon I spoke to Lord (Andrew) Feldman, the Tory Party chief executive. He was candid: 'David has problems with four different groups of Conservative MPs – those who hate Lords reform on principle, those who hate Cameron on principle, modernisers who want a different type of reform, and those who want to "retire" to the Lords via party patronage.' He feels there are probably eighty to ninety MPs in danger of voting against.

Andrew said that the problem is that without the boundary changes, the Conservatives' chances of winning an outright majority in 2015 are 'pretty limited'. I said that I thought Nick would torpedo boundaries if the programme motion fails.

On party funding reform, where the cross-party talks trundle on, Andrew said that he'd had discussions with Cameron and Osborne. He said the Conservative Party would lose about £20 million in an election year with a £10,000 donations cap, and would lose about £10 million in a non-election year. He said the response of the PM and George had been 'rather dismissive' – they think that our emerging reforms would simply 'bung additional public money at the Labour Party', while preventing the Conservatives accessing large donations 'for ever'.

MONDAY 2 JULY

Yesterday's *Sunday Telegraph* led with an extraordinary story – that David Cameron is considering calling a referendum in the next parliament on whether the UK should stay in the EU. It's all being written up as a desperate attempt by Cameron to unite his own party and see off the UKIP threat to his right flank.

Spoke to Nick. Interestingly, Cameron apparently phoned him up on Saturday afternoon to warn him the story was coming out. He sounded nervous. Nick was staggered when Cameron told him what he was proposing, and warned him that it was very dangerous to think he could successfully exploit/control Euroscepticism. He told Cameron the whole thing made him 'look weak and pandering to his backbenchers', and that if we held an EU referendum, other nations would not feel obliged to give the UK an attractive deal in order to bail us out.

Cameron was apparently pretty feeble and unconvincing and said he felt that he might have to offer a referendum in order to 'keep the Tory Party controllable'. He also babbled on about how the media had recently misreported some of his utterances as too pro-EU, and he now needed to 'recalibrate' things.

It all sounds highly panicky and ill-thought-out. Of course, Cameron is under a lot of pressure on the economy, Leveson (which apparently is causing blind panic in No. 10), the Lords/boundaries row, and with people like Boris Johnson on manoeuvres. But winning an EU referendum would be a massive challenge and it all feels like a dangerous roll of the dice. As Nick said: 'Short-term gain for monumental long-term risk.'

TUESDAY 3 JULY

Nick told me that yesterday he sent a letter to Cameron warning him that we will torpedo the parliamentary boundary changes if there isn't a majority for Lords reform when the programme motion is debated on 10 July.

Nick's adviser, Julian Astle, has advocated a very simple message to ensure the Tory leadership is clear where we stand – what he calls a 'Kitty gets it' strategy. 'Just tell Cameron: "Here is Kitty. This is essentially the boundary changes. Here is a revolver. If the House of Lords programme motion doesn't get voted through, then the revolver and Kitty are going to experience a coming together which will not be wholly to Kitty's advantage."' It's certainly simple.

WEDNESDAY 4 JULY

Walked with Nick to Prime Minister's Questions. He is uncomfortable about us having to vote down the boundary changes. Frankly, he is sometimes too decent a person for politics. I told him we needed to be brutal. It's all the Tories understand.

In the afternoon, we were due to meet Maude and Feldman, as well as the Labour representatives, for talks on party funding. When we got to the meeting, neither Maude nor Feldman turned up. I was spitting blood. We are supposed to be in coalition together.

The fact is that the Conservative Party has made all these undertakings at the last general election and in the coalition agreement on party funding and Lords reform, and it's now quite clear that they haven't the slightest intention of implementing any of it. I am determined we will vote down boundaries unless they deliver. They have to understand that if they are going to put their narrow interests first, then that has a price.

Apparently the Prime Minister and George met this afternoon to consider the 'Kitty gets it' letter. Ed Llewellyn has told Julian A that Cameron is 'furious' and doesn't accept the link between Lords and boundaries. His position is going to be that 'if any Lib Dem minister votes against the boundary reform then they will have to leave the government'. A laughably feeble threat! If Lib Dem ministers were sacked, this would end the coalition – and probably Cameron.

THURSDAY 5 JULY

Spoke to Nick this morning – he mentioned that Cameron was now getting very difficult and aggressive with him, acting like the 'Flashman' bully he is. 'The problem with Cameron is that he's clearly worried about his position, and fears that if he loses the boundary reforms he may lose the next election and cease to be Leader of the Conservative Party.' His problem, not ours!

I said to Nick that I'm sure that if the Conservatives were in our shoes they'd behave exactly as we are – except that they would probably be tougher and find an excuse to torpedo boundaries anyway.

Spoke to Julian Astle. Nick has asked Julian's views on whether what we are doing is 'legitimate' and 'honourable'. Julian told him that it absolutely was.

This afternoon I saw Michael Gove for what was supposed to be a thirty-minute meeting. It lasted one and three-quarter hours. We started by discussing 'middle-tier accountability' – what sits between the DfE and schools. Michael seemed to be far more positive about my proposals than before, though I wondered whether this was related to his desire to make progress on 'O-levels'.

Also present were his special adviser, Dominic Cummings, who has a reputation as somebody with very sharp elbows, and his other adviser, Sam Freedman, who is very bright and decent, and only interested in the serious policy issues.

Michael is clearly sensitive about the criticism that his plans would result in a two-tier system – with an O-level for bright people and CSEs for everybody else. However, his suggestion to deal with this is a rather bizarre one, since he seems to be suggesting that everybody is going to have to take O-levels in English, maths and science, with the 'slower' learners taking their O-levels at age seventeen or eighteen.

He also argued that even though he was going to make English, maths and science exams much more challenging, exactly the same number of people would pass them. I told him that I thought that this was completely ridiculous. His advisers looked uncomfortable. I said that while we Lib Dems wanted to build stretch into exams, we didn't want a system that was simply designed around the needs of the top 10 per cent.

SUNDAY 8 JULY

Jonny Oates fixed a conference call for 7.30 p.m. I was at Nice Airport, when 'Switch'* called. Went out into the area outside the restaurant, with panoramic views across Nice and the surrounding countryside – it was all very beautiful, with the sun going down on a perfect day.

Nick started by saying that he'd been at the Wimbledon final and had bumped into David Cameron, who said that Lords was looking 'very difficult' and shrugged his shoulders.

Nick's view is that if we lose the vote by a small margin there is a case

---

*   The Downing Street switchboard.

for bringing another programme motion back in September, but the real issue is what we do if we lose by a big margin.

To my frustration, Alistair Carmichael, Danny Alexander and Jo Swinson all said we should fudge things a bit and that it would be terribly difficult if we immediately torpedoed boundary reform.

I said that I thought that if there was a massive Tory rebellion then this was the best possible time to kill boundaries – as people would see we were doing it in response to the Tories having voted down a part of the coalition agreement. Although the immediate row would be serious, it would actually be better for the coalition to get this out of the way.

MONDAY 9 JULY

The normally moderate Nicholas Soames MP, grandson of Winston Churchill, was in the *Telegraph* saying that he'd only voted against his party twice – and this would be one of the occasions. Ominous.

Spoke to Richard Reeves this morning. Richard is no longer a Nick adviser but is still close. He said he wasn't surprised by the wobbling over the Lib Dem position on Lords – 'this tends to happen before every big decision'. He named the 'worst wobblers', who he said then undermine Nick. He said he'd seen the same happen over tuition fees, NHS reform etc.

Julian said that he'd spoken again to Ed Llewellyn – and the Tories are getting incredibly worked up. Ed said that he sat in the negotiating room and that the boundaries were clearly linked to the AV referendum, so he can't understand why we're threatening to torpedo boundaries just because the Tories aren't going to deliver Lords. This is complete rubbish – the idea that the Conservative Party can simply dump any coalition policy that they don't like, but assume that we won't touch boundaries is naïve twaddle. What they don't like is that we are no longer being walked all over.

TUESDAY 10 JULY

Flew down to the Farnborough Air Show with Graham Cole, the superb chairman of AgustaWestland. Met Geoff Hoon, the former Defence Secretary. Geoff seemed incredibly happy and relaxed – until I mentioned that I'd recently been reading the memoirs of Alastair Campbell, including on Iraq. His face dropped: he said that he hadn't read the diaries and didn't want to.

Jonny Oates called, asking me to join a conference call at 11.45 a.m. Nick opened by saying that he'd just spoken to Cameron, who is predicting defeat on the programme motion. Nick clearly spelt out to him that we would then withdraw the Lords Bill and torpedo the boundary reforms.

Nick said that the PM pleaded for 'more time'. Nick said that he could anticipate the type of objections Julian Astle and I would have to this, particularly that we might enter the 'swamp' of parliamentary debate in which we might be 'drowned', for example by MPs insisting on a referendum. But Nick pointed out that it would be very difficult for him not to give Cameron 'a few more weeks'.

The whole call was very difficult, because I was on a mobile phone, standing outside, next to the Farnborough runways. Every time somebody was about to say something particularly important, either a helicopter would fly noisily overhead or one of the RAF's new Eurofighter aircraft would take off. We eventually came to a sensible conclusion: more time, but not much!

WEDNESDAY 11 JULY

Le car crash est arrivé! A massive rebellion on Lords reform – with ninety-one Tory MPs voting against and an estimated fifty abstaining.

Spoke to Andrew Adonis. Andrew claimed that the view in the 'senior civil service' is that the coalition isn't going to last beyond the autumn of 2013. I don't buy this. It's not in the interests of Nick or Cameron to go to the country in 2013.

Spoke again to Richard Reeves. He was commendably robust. He said that the problem that he's seen in the past is that we're inclined to take a position, 'and then give 5 per cent and then another 5 per cent and another 5 per cent and suddenly our position has changed'. We have to resist this. We have to make clear that Lords reform and boundaries are in lock-step.

This evening spoke to Nick. He's very pissed off with Cameron: 'The problem with him is that he got elected as Conservative leader on a super-ficially modernising agenda, which has never fed down to the roots of the Conservative Party. Cameron doesn't really know what he stands for, and he's being found out in government. The Tories are absolutely panicked that because of the weakness of their agenda, they can't win a general election in 2015 without the boundary changes.'

Bad coverage for Cameron today – about a row he had with Tory rebel Jesse Norman after the vote yesterday – where he let his well-known temper get the better of him and jabbed Norman in the stomach.

A useful 'Coalition 2.0 dinner' at Paul Marshall's offices on the Embankment, where pro-coalition Tories and Lib Dems meet for food and talk. We had a very frank discussion about Lords and boundaries. I think both sides now understand where the other is coming from.

MONDAY 16 JULY

Julian Astle spoke with Ed Llewellyn on Friday. Ed said that after the Lords car crash, David Cameron had 'slept on it' and come down the next morning, having decided more than ever that what he now wanted to do is 'to make the coalition work – and pull back towards the centre ground', rather than conceding territory to his right wing.

Cameron seems to have realised that as one of the architects of the coalition, he's going to stand or fall by its success. He's also figured that he cannot buy off his right wing – and even if he won the next election with a modest majority, he'd be totally in hock to them, which would arguably be a lot more unpleasant than being reliant on the Lib Dems!

THURSDAY 26 JULY

Yesterday I held the last of our villages advice centres, in Yeovil constituency, in the best and sunniest weather of the year – temperatures touching 30° Celsius.

We had a particularly pleasant last stop in the beautiful village of Combe St Nicholas. There I met a former Conservative district councillor, who recently contacted us as he was suffering from a terminal illness and needed some drugs, which had been denied to him on the NHS. He'd come to thank us for 'saving his life'. It was certainly a day on which to celebrate being alive.

The news on the economic front is considerably gloomier than the weather. The economy shrank in the second quarter of 2012, at a much larger than expected 0.7 per cent – the third successive quarterly decline.

Lord Oakeshott, the Liberal Democrat peer, has called for the Chancellor to be sacked and replaced by Vince Cable. He even referred to Osborne as the 'work experience Chancellor'. This is all part of Matthew Oakeshott's plan to undermine the coalition, undermine Nick Clegg, and get Vince as leader. Matthew started his career in the Labour Party, as an adviser to Roy Jenkins, and it must be very uncomfortable for some of these people to suddenly find themselves in coalition with the Conservatives.

Later in the day, did a note to Nick Clegg proposing using the profits from quantitative easing to boost investment. We've apparently got £20 billion plus sitting in a bank account doing nothing.

This evening had a meeting with Nick. Sounds as if the reshuffle is going ahead on 2 September, and Nick still wants me to go to the Cabinet Office, with a second job at Education. Leaving the Lib Dem side of the government would be Sarah Teather, Nick Harvey, Paul Burstow and Andrew Stunell.

On the economy, Nick is planning to write to the Prime Minister with Lib Dem proposals to support growth. We need more proactive monetary policy, and a fiscal easing to be announced for a limited period – this could involve bringing forward the increase in the personal allowance to £10,000; extra capital investment; or capital allowances to incentivise investment.

By now, we were expecting economic recovery to be in place. But Eurozone chaos and the huge spike in inflation have hammered real incomes and confidence.

At the end of the meeting there was some joking about Vince Cable. In an *FT* interview last week, he wouldn't rule himself out as the next Lib Dem leader, and today he's refused to rule himself out as the next Chancellor. 'Tomorrow, he'll probably refuse to rule himself out as the next Pope,' Nick said, only half in jest.

Vince wants to tear up the economic strategy and just borrow to invest. We need to be cleverer about pushing new policies that stand a chance of winning cross-coalition backing.

FRIDAY 27 JULY

Today Jeremy Hunt had a near miss when he rather over-enthusiastically rang a hand-held bell to mark the beginning of the Olympic Games. The bell then flew off the handle and over the back of his head and landed on a young lady a few metres away. He was lucky that he didn't knock her out.

An impressive opening ceremony, the highlight of which was a film of 'James Bond' going to Buckingham Palace and then airlifting the Queen to the Games by helicopter – from which it was made to seem that both the Queen and James Bond were parachuting into the Olympic Stadium! We watched at home and roared with laughter.

Boris Johnson is getting a lot of coverage. Nick thinks that both Cameron and Osborne are 'intimidated and frightened that he will one day challenge one or both of them to be PM'. He says they see him as 'playing by his own political rules'.

Olly Grender said that she bumped into Cameron yesterday, who was moaning about Lord Oakeshott: 'The problem with that man is that although he's a pain in the arse he has a very good way with words and his sound bites really hit the spot! George hates it: "Work experience Chancellor!" Ouch!'

MONDAY 30 JULY

Met up for lunch today with Michael Gove at a restaurant called The Providores in Marylebone. Not sure MG is a great fan of Boris, from what he said, but he offered the view that Boris should not be underestimated as a potential future Tory leader or even PM! Quite extraordinary! I always assumed Boris was an amusing, clever buffoon.

I asked MG whether he would ever stand to be Tory leader/PM. He claimed that he wasn't suited. He said he didn't think he could take all the pressures involved, and he also didn't think that he looked the part. I think Michael was being rather self-effacing. What isn't entirely clear is whether he's serious or wants to leave his options open. I'm minded to think the latter. When I said to him that people had never expected John Major to be Prime Minister, I thought he looked rather taken aback by the comparison, probably regarding himself as a few notches above Major. If that's really his view, could he resist a run at PM one day?

Michael pressed on me in a rather unsubtle way his hope that the Lib Dems might want to take over the further education portfolio in the reshuffle. I assume he would rather we did FE than schools. FE is less of a priority for MG and it sits half in the Business Department and half in DfE.

WEDNESDAY 1 AUGUST

There's a piece in the *Daily Telegraph* today about how well Boris Johnson is doing, and how he's lining himself up to take over from Cameron. I've never taken this possibility seriously, but perhaps after yesterday's lunch with MG I should do. I can't imagine Boris in charge of a whelk stall, let alone the economy and nuclear weapons!

FRIDAY 3 AUGUST

Andrew Feldman called me on the party funding talks. Andrew said that he'd been unable to get Cameron and Osborne to sign off on his proposals, and he said that if the boundary reform went down then it was even less likely that they would be cooperative. He said that George is interested in some sort of funding deal which would just 'stitch up the unions'. Classic George!

I talked about the implications of some of party funding reform for UKIP – knowing how sensitive the Conservatives are about UKIP's threat. Andrew said that he thought that the impact of any deal on UKIP would be trivial: 'Without some kind of promise by us on an EU referendum, we will be totally hammered by UKIP in 2014 anyway...' More confirmation that Cameron is now tempted to offer a referendum in order to protect his right flank.

SUNDAY 5 AUGUST

Nick phoned to confirm that he will be announcing tomorrow that he's withdrawing the Lords Bill and Lib Dem support for the enactment of the boundary changes. 'A deal has been broken by the Tories, so we must amend the terms of the deal and move onto other things, etc...' Good. We have held the line.

MONDAY 6 AUGUST

I wrote to Nick and Danny on the economy. Growth is weak or non-existent. Our borrowing projections will soon be even higher than those left by Alistair Darling in 2010. With growth and borrowing targets being missed, people will say, 'It's hurting, but it's not working.'

Spelt out that we need to acknowledge clearly that the economic headwinds are much stronger than expected in 2010. The sensible thing to do is to moderate the near-term tightening. Sorting out the government's finances is rapidly turning into a ten-year project.

If we are to ease fiscal policy in 2013/14, I think we need some credibility-enhancing policies. The obvious approach is to set out future tax and welfare reforms that will raise money from 2015 onwards.

I again proposed that we should transfer the net interest earnings from quantitative easing to the Treasury. We could use this £20 billion windfall to fund the easing of fiscal policy, without borrowing more.

TUESDAY 7 AUGUST

This evening I met with Andrew Feldman at his club near Marble Arch. Was relieved that Andrew picked up the bill – two glasses of wine and two tomato juices cost £78! Andrew started with his normal spiel about how the Conservatives didn't accept the connection between Lords reform and boundaries. I just laughed.

Andrew showed me the quite detailed paper he'd prepared for Cameron and Osborne on party funding. The paper seems to be along the lines that we'd previously discussed of a two-stage deal, with some reform and extra money before 2015, and then with the caps and reforms to union funding coming in from 2017/18.

Andrew said that the Conservatives' real problem here is that it just looked like we were 'bunging money at the Labour Party', while taking away the Conservative Party's ability to raise money from rich donors.

Andrew said that the Labour Party would then be in 'a very good place', in that it would be able to rely on the trade unions and the taxpayer for all its funding. Andrew said that he simply didn't think he could sell a £10,000 cap to the Prime Minister or the Conservative Party. It would need to be £50,000.

WEDNESDAY 8 AUGUST

In the evening I went to the Olympic Games in the main arena. A fantastic experience – and great weather. No British winners, but good to see Usain Bolt – the world's fastest man – easily win his 200-metre semi-final.

FRIDAY 10 AUGUST

Out in France. Beautiful weather. Swapped emails with Nick. He said he was irritated by Gove's unilateral announcement on lifting the requirement to employ qualified teachers in academies.

Yesterday evening we went out for dinner. We'd been sitting down around half an hour when a family came in and asked for a table. I glanced round to see the back of Chris Grayling, the Tory Welfare Reform Minister – and not a great friend of the Lib Dems. Fortunately, the restaurant was completely booked up. A very close shave!

SATURDAY 11 AUGUST

Nick phoned today, while I was out enjoying the sun. He recounted a relatively unproductive dinner last night with Cameron, Osborne and Danny. On the economy, the Conservatives have agreed to rewrite the second fiscal rule [which requires debt to be declining as a share of the economy] so that we don't have to tighten again in this parliament, but predictably they're incredibly defensive about our plan for a £10 billion fiscal boost. They're not prepared to increase borrowing as they think this will undermine their entire narrative. 'If we did that, we would be dead,' said Cameron, gesturing with his hand across his throat.

They were, however, willing to consider using the profits from quantitative easing to fund a fiscal boost – Osborne said he'd raise this with the Governor of the Bank of England. My fear is that the Treasury and the Bank will be incredibly cautious and we won't get anywhere.

On party funding, Nick said that both Cameron and Osborne had said that they're not prepared to make any further progress. Instead, they want an anti-trade union Bill that would require a higher threshold of turnout before strikes, as well as measures to prevent 'third-party campaigning' by the unions etc. Nick said they asked him to support that 'in exchange for dropping the proposals for regional pay in the public sector'.

I said that I didn't think this was a very good trade, and that my strong view is that we should tell the Tories that we won't support union reform unless party funding reform goes through.

On education, Cameron is up for giving me a big role in schools policy, but they want Liz Truss to have control of childcare, in order to pursue a 'deregulatory approach'.

Nick said he raised two other areas for action, one of which was further education. He said he was rather cheesed off when neither Cameron nor Osborne seemed to have the slightest interest in FE. Nick said they both felt it was an area of not much interest to 'our people'. He said that he really is 'pretty cheesed off with Cameron and his rather elitist approach'.

TUESDAY 28 AUGUST

My first full day in the constituency after the break in France was marred by a meeting with my stalwart local party activist and friend Pauline Booth. Pauline told me that she's suffering from terminal cancer. She probably only has a few months to live. Shocking and stunning.

Pauline has been an incredibly loyal friend in good times and bad over the past thirteen years, and it's a tragedy that somebody who relishes life so much is going to lose what ought to be another twenty or twenty-five years of living. She has been present in every single set of elections. Campaigning will never seem quite as fun again.

THURSDAY 30 AUGUST

Had a text message from Sarah Teather drawing my attention to a *Daily Mirror* poll that says that she and I are the most popular Lib Dems to be promoted in the reshuffle. Felt uncomfortable as I texted her back, knowing that she's already scheduled for the chop and I'm replacing her at the Department for Education.

That egomaniac Matthew Oakeshott has given an interview to the *Today* programme which basically puts Nick Clegg 'on notice' and implies that Vince should take over. What Matthew is saying is probably what Vince is thinking, magnified by 500 per cent. Paddy has written an article for tomorrow's *Guardian*, defending Nick.

FRIDAY 31 AUGUST

Oh dear! *The Guardian* has splashed with a story about Paddy Ashdown 'begging' party members to be loyal to Nick Clegg. Spoke to Paddy. He said that he'd talked to Nick and knows Nick's concerns about whether he's the right person to lead the party into the next general election. It's a commendable aspect of Nick's character that he's thinking only about what's best for the party.

Paddy said: 'My advice to him was to focus on putting in place a convincing forward strategy – you deal with these issues not by saying that you're going to go on for ever, but by mapping out a path forward so that people want you to go on for ever.'

Paddy said that he feared that Vince Cable might want to make a move for the leadership shortly, based on his age and current popularity. I said I thought it was far too early, and that the real risk point for Nick was autumn of 2013 – after three and a half tough years in coalition, and before the final run-in to the general election.

Had lunch with Jeremy Hunt in the National Portrait Gallery. Unfortunately, it turned out that the gallery has about three different restaurants and I went first to the two that Jeremy wasn't in – so he was looking a little bit lonely and fed up when I turned up fifteen minutes late.

He's an extremely nice person, and has obviously had a horrible time over the whole Leveson Inquiry. He's keen to stay at Culture, but he doesn't really know what's going to happen in the reshuffle.

We then discussed the coalition and Jeremy said that the loss of boundary reform was a huge blow, including to Tory support for coalition: 'It's one of the few things that George Osborne mentions when defending the coalition to sceptical Tory MPs.'

Jeremy said that we need to focus on making the coalition a positive experience for the next two and a half years, and we have to make sure that even if this is only a one-term government, we are proud of what we achieve.

He asked whether there could be some kind of coalition ticket at the next election, where we each stood down in the other's constituencies. I said that this would be extremely difficult for the Lib Dems, as effectively it would align us with the Conservative Party. Jeremy said it would also be very difficult for the Conservative Party – but he clearly wants to see the coalition run for a full ten years.

Jeremy is a Conservative moderniser, though I wouldn't say he's in David Cameron's inner circle. He said that he doesn't socialise with Cameron and has never been to his home, and he said he was taken by surprise by the extent of the connections between Cameron and News Corp during the Leveson Inquiry.

Met Olly Grender this afternoon to talk about next week's reshuffle. There is a 'care package' being put in place for the ministers who will be leaving – Andrew Stunell, Nick Harvey, Paul Burstow and Sarah Teather. None of them are expecting the chop.

SUNDAY 2 SEPTEMBER

The *Sunday Times* has dragged up some of the greatest nonentities in the party to 'prove' that Nick is suffering a crisis of confidence. Firstly, there is that prime-time lightweight Adrian Sanders MP, who has apparently accused Nick of 'bumbling'. To be accused of bumbling by Adrian really is something! Then there is a peer called Lord Smith of Clifton. Never heard of him. Spoke to Paddy Ashdown, who's still in France, writing a book. Paddy said that the only people criticising Nick are 'madmen and minnows'.

MONDAY 3 SEPTEMBER

I have a mixture of excitement and fear over the reshuffle – excitement about taking on such important roles, and fear about going back into the shark-infested waters of government.

The *Sunday Times* yesterday had some hints that Sarah Teather is going to be removed, along with Nick Gibb. I feel quite guilty about both. Sarah is a good person and I like Nick Gibb, who's a low-key but conscientious individual, passionate about schools and obsessive about phonics!

Reshuffle fever is sweeping Westminster.

TUESDAY 4 SEPTEMBER

Reshuffle day has finally arrived. Most of the newspapers confirm that I will be going to the Department for Education as Michael Gove's deputy as well as having a roving cross-Whitehall brief in the Cabinet Office.

The Conservative side of the reshuffle is far more extensive than expected. Ken Clarke leaves Justice to take on a rather non-role of Minister without Portfolio.

Andrew Mitchell leaves DfID to become the new Chief Whip, replacing Patrick McLoughlin. There is a pretty awful decision to move Chris Grayling, the very right-wing Welfare Reform Minister, to become Justice Secretary. Andrew Lansley is demoted from Health to Leader of the House – a pretty big fall.

Jeremy Hunt is promoted to Health Secretary. This is a huge surprise – to Jeremy as much as to anyone.

Julian Astle phoned through before noon to say that the reshuffle had encountered a few problems. Apparently David Cameron wanted to move Iain Duncan Smith from the Department for Work and Pensions to Justice, but IDS said no. Cameron blinked and IDS has ended up staying at DWP. Iain is not thought of very highly by Osborne and his team. George basically sees the Department for Work and Pensions as a cash cow that he can milk in order to tackle the deficit, whereas IDS sees policy through the social justice prism. In addition, George views Universal Credit as a massively complex scheme that relies on expensive IT and is bound to go wrong. Iain thinks it can save the world. So clearly Osborne wanted rid of IDS – but I guess Cameron concluded that it was too great a risk.

David Jones is confirmed as the new Welsh Secretary – frankly I've never heard of him, but his surname seems to be a step in the right direction for the Tory Party in Wales! Maria Miller is appointed as the new Secretary of State for Culture, Media and Sport, confirming Cameron's tendency to put women in the least important jobs in Cabinet. Grant Shapps (think ambitious used-car salesman), the young and rather right-wing Tory MP, is promoted to be the new Tory Party chairman. Apparently No. 10 have invented a new job and title for Baroness Warsi as the 'Senior' Minister of State at the Foreign Office, attending the Cabinet!

Finally got the call to meet Nick Clegg for the photo opportunity to mark my return to government. Olly Grender ordered me to set off on a ludicrous route through Portcullis House, along the river, past the Ministry of Defence building and back onto Whitehall, where we met James McGrory from Nick's press office. We then strolled down Whitehall to the Cabinet Office, where Nick was waiting with the snappers.

In the afternoon, I had a telephone call from Switch. Could I find time to speak to the Prime Minister? Cameron was put through about forty-five minutes later. He confirmed my two new roles and said: 'Education under Michael has been one of the more radical and successful areas in the government and I hope that this work will continue with you there.' He also said that we now needed to have a period in coalition with the two parties working effectively together, and he hoped that in my Cabinet Office role I'd be able to work to facilitate that.

At around 4.30, I walked across Parliament Square to the Education Department, where I was met by Chris Wormald, the Permanent Secretary: 'Congratulations, Minister. After the Secretary of State, you are now the second longest-serving minister in the department.'

'I can't be,' I replied, 'I've only been here for ten minutes.' But it was true.

Much to my shock, I discovered that not only were Nick Gibb and Sarah Teather leaving, but Tim Loughton, the Parliamentary Under Secretary for Families, had been sacked, and John Hayes, the FE Minister, was moving. In addition, Lord Hill, the other Schools Minister, wants to leave voluntarily.

The DfE staff were very welcoming, but there was a bit of a sense of shell shock.

It seems a little bit odd that David Cameron told me earlier that he thought the Department for Education had been one of the best-performing departments – if so, why axe or move 80 per cent of the ministers?

WEDNESDAY 5 SEPTEMBER

Today was my first, chaotically busy, day back in government. It started with a visit to Mulberry School in Tower Hamlets, an absolutely brilliant school with a fantastic head and very confident children – one of whom wants to be Prime Minister!

Later, we held a political meeting in Portcullis House. There is a problem that the political balance of the Cabinet has changed. Cameron has decided to put some ministers, who he was basically demoting, into the Cabinet to keep them quiet – Ken Clarke and Baroness Warsi. Jonny Oates implied that he and Nick were discussing with the Prime Minister whether we should have somebody else in the Cabinet, and he glanced at me.

Went back to my DfE office and wrote a proposal about the division of ministerial responsibilities. I want to take all funding issues, all accountability issues including Ofsted, pupil premium, teacher issues, teacher pay etc. Michael's being incredibly helpful, and it looks like I'm going to get another adviser in the department. This will be Tim Leunig, who is a really very brilliant brain. Michael and I are going to get on very well, I hope.

Later, while I was meeting with Michael, a private secretary came in and told me that I was now being required to attend Cabinet – in ten minutes. A pile of paperwork was shoved into my hands. I leapt into the back of Michael's car and the two of us drove into Downing Street. I made sure that I was seated on the famous No. 10 door side of the car, so I could hop out quickly and not be seen by the media.

Unfortunately, Downing Street was absolutely bursting full of journalists, including Adam Boulton from Sky News. I leapt out of the car and made for the door, but before I could get there, Michael said, 'I do think this is a bit of a coalition moment.' He stopped me and we turned round while the snappers got the picture they wanted.

George Osborne opened Cabinet by drawing attention to the 'very good news' of an 'upgrading' of growth. He then mentioned that the upgrading of growth amounted to the economy contracting at 0.5 per cent in the last quarter, rather than at the original estimate of minus 0.7 per cent. Nick Clegg and I exchanged amused glances.

I noticed that IDS kept on chipping in loyally and mentioning George Osborne in a helpful way. The Chancellor didn't even bother to look up – it's clear that there's no love lost there.

Towards the end, Michael Gove gave a sparkling commentary on education reform. He turned a very dull briefing into something that had everybody chuckling enthusiastically. He said that education policy is rather like the Yalta Summit between Stalin, Roosevelt and Churchill. He then proceeded to describe how the Stalin bit was the five-year plan, with lots of new academies and free schools, the Roosevelt bit is something to do with the New Deal, and frankly I've forgotten what the Churchill bit was about.

Later in the day I had a meeting with Matt Sanders, our education adviser. Michael Gove has finally capitulated on O-levels/CSEs, and has agreed to reform the existing GCSEs, with a single new qualification with an entirely new name. Progress!

THURSDAY 6 SEPTEMBER

My first serious day as minister, and with two departments to work in, it starts pretty early, at 6.30 a.m. My new roles mean that I will be doing everything from brokering major agreements at the very top of government to doing all the rather dull, low-grade duties of a junior minister. I will certainly have a very full diary.

An unhelpful article in *The Times* this morning from that newshound and grade-A mischief-maker Sam Coates, claiming that Michael Gove is deeply irritated by having me in his department. This is an odd thing to write when Michael and I are good friends. On the other hand, Michael did try to persuade me to take a role in BIS running FE instead, so maybe he does see my arrival as Nick Clegg putting 'tanks on his lawn'.

Later on, I attended a meeting with Michael about introducing a fairer funding formula for schools. Cameron has taken to calling this 'Michael Gove's plan to lose me the next general election'.

FRIDAY 7 SEPTEMBER

Throughout the day I was fielding endless emails and telephone calls about the GCSE reform paper, which is supposed to go from Michael Gove to the Home Affairs Committee of Cabinet for approval. At the last minute, Michael ended up revising his letter, not with a few tweaks here and there but by putting a red line through about 30 per cent of the text!

I'm concerned about the slapdash policy-making procedures this highlights – I've asked very obvious questions about why we're only proposing to replace GCSEs in the key academic subjects, after Dom Cummings has gone out to trash the entire GCSE brand. However, in spite of the fact that this is supposed to be launched in just a few days' time, nobody can tell me what we're going to do with the remaining GCSE qualifications, or even the name of the new qualification! One assumes that the UK government would have a Rolls-Royce policy operation and that all this stuff would be sorted out well in advance. Sadly not. We are talking about the exams being taken in future by millions of students. We should not be rushing this.

SUNDAY 9 SEPTEMBER

Had an email from one of the officials in the No. 10 Policy Unit, saying that a whole series of names had been considered for the replacement GCSE qualification – including 'World Class Qualifications', the name that Michael Gove's people have been using. The chance of a new qualification being called WCQ doesn't seem high, as it's rather open to parody.

A list of possible names that the advisers and officials had brainstormed was circulated. The normally sensible Julian Astle has suggested that GCSE should be replaced with DCSE – but I felt that this was bound to be dubbed as a 'dumb' version of the GCSE.

Other names are: School Certificate, School Diploma, Standard Certificate of Education, Standard Certificate of Secondary Education, General Certificate of Education Standard Level, International Certificate of Education, International Certificate of Secondary Education, Baccalaureate, General Baccalaureate, General Certificate of Skills and Knowledge. I decided that 'Standard Level' would be best, as it needs to be something that sounds very solid, British and credible.

MONDAY 10 SEPTEMBER

Civil servants showed me my new home in the Cabinet Office – and I had the choice between a rather posh office on the fourth floor or a tiny dingy cupboard on the ground floor, but much closer to Nick Clegg. I chose the smart office, and I noticed that it was already being prepared for me – so I don't think they had any doubts what I would choose. My private secretary told me later: 'Ministers always choose plush offices over proximity to power. With civil servants, it's usually the opposite.'

We had a very long meeting on exam reform with Michael and with his special advisers – the thoughtful and reasonable Sam Freedman, and Dom Cummings, who was initially vetoed from coming into the government by Andy Coulson, because of his allegedly chaotic and disruptive behaviour. Dom has a fairly fearsome reputation for playing the man, the ball and everything else, and he's believed to be the person who recently leaked the proposals on O-levels. He tends to sit at the back of meetings, a scruffy and brooding presence, looking generally unimpressed. Dom said he wanted the DfE to control the media announcement: 'No. 10 always bugger everything up, and they're absolutely useless. Clueless half-wits. We don't tell No. 10 anything, as they always make a mess of it and leak it out in a half-baked way.' Dom says that he wants to have a good run-in to all policy announcements so that they can be announced in a coherent way. That would be a very pleasing contrast to the launch of the housing policy last week, where it was being agreed between the Chief Secretary and the Chancellor at 1 a.m., for a 7 a.m. launch by the Prime Minister and Nick Clegg. But if Dom believes all this, why did he spin out the O-level story with no consultation whatsoever? Double standards?

TUESDAY 11 SEPTEMBER

At Cabinet today, we discussed the Olympics. An immense amount of tedious self-congratulation. You would have thought we'd put a man on Mars, rather than organised a few races.

Everyone was worried about the economy. Everyone, that is, but Ken Clarke.

Ken was in great form, holding forth in his wonderfully laid-back way. 'Some of you are getting rather wobbly on growth. I'm not. I'm entirely unsurprised that the economy has gone into a double-dip recession and frankly I've been expecting this all along.' He said that it was clear that the economy was 'bouncing along the bottom' and said, 'We should really be rather grateful for this ... bouncing along the bottom is a great achievement, you know.'

I'm not sure he convinced us all, but he certainly cheered us up. He should be bottled and exported.

Having been out of government for two years, it's interesting to see the Cabinet dynamic again. Cameron is business-like, always very eloquent, a good chair of the meetings, and very much on top of the issues. Never wrong-footed. Never any doubt that he's in charge.

Nick is very definitely next in the pecking order – a genuine Deputy Prime Minister. He always comes in to speak straight after the PM. He is extremely eloquent and impressive, respected and authoritative. Vince

Cable is listened to carefully, though with a sense that he's the 'grumpy old man' of the Cabinet. Michael Gove crackles and sparkles in a way that no other minister manages – he cannot say anything without saying it in an amusing and interesting way, and people always listen to him. Sometimes there's a risk that his flamboyance and style submerges the serious messages.

Iain Duncan Smith speaks often, but not usually memorably. Ken Clarke sits there in the centre of the Cabinet, on Nick Clegg's left, a true representation of coalition values in action. He's been sitting around this Cabinet table for decades and gives every impression that he's seen it all before. He's charged up with common sense, and willing to dispense it in his genial and blunt manner.

George Osborne comes alive when he's dealing with the bits about the economy, but goes into deep thought when others are speaking, often giving the impression of not being altogether interested. When Justine Greening was speaking today, I could tell that he was thinking what I was thinking – why does she keep going on about transport issues when she's now supposed to be the International Development Secretary!

Theresa May is economical with her interventions, but makes them when necessary, and in an authoritative way.

But it's quite clear that this is not remotely a serious decision-making body, and all the big decisions are made outside – in the Quad and in bilaterals between David Cameron and Nick Clegg.

After Cabinet, I met with the irrepressible Liz Truss, the new Parliamentary Under Secretary for Childcare. Liz is mind-bogglingly ambitious, and has Duracell-like reserves of energy. I will need to keep an eye on her!

WEDNESDAY 12 SEPTEMBER

In the evening, there was a Coalition 2.0 dinner at the offices of Marshall Wace at the Adelphi building. These dinners have been very positive and constructive, and they've gone on in spite of the ups and downs of coalition relationships.

Paul Marshall is an excellent host, and there's always good conversation. This meeting was again well attended by the Conservatives, with Nick Boles – the new Planning Minister – there along with Michael Gove, Matt Hancock, Amber Rudd and Greg Clark.

On our side, we had Norman Lamb, along with Julian Astle, Tim Leunig, and Jo Swinson. We had an excellent discussion on the mid-term review.

Matt Hancock said he thought our differentiation strategy had been a 'disaster', and that we simply had to work very closely with the Conservatives. Michael Gove accepted that being a small party in coalition is like 'being in bed with an elephant', and there's a real chance of getting crushed. The smaller party is therefore going to try to differentiate more, and this will lead to some tensions.

THURSDAY 13 SEPTEMBER

Met Michael Gove, who told me he had thought of a good name for the GCSE replacement: 'It's not O-level, is it?' I joked. He said that he had come up with the idea of the 'English Baccalaureate Certificate'. I said that I thought it sounded fine, and that Liberal Democrats would like it, as it was both European-sounding and fresh! Michael Gove likes it because 'Baccalaureate' sounds high-quality, and he said that it would also allow him to give the impression that when he introduced the English Baccalaureate measure around a year ago he was thinking ahead and planning the whole thing through, in terms of the replacement of GCSEs.

FRIDAY 14 SEPTEMBER

There is now a 'Quad Plus' away day at Chequers on Monday, and what's planned is a six-hour meeting on the mid-term review and some other key issues. Apparently the Tories are going to get there on Sunday night, and wanted us to come down too, for dinner. Jonny Oates thought that was risky. Nick eventually vetoed a Lib Dem 'sleepover': 'Uncle Jonny is advising against it. He's probably right. Our activists would go nuts if they heard about it.' As a consequence, we are going to turn up at 9 a.m. on Monday. Sensible, but a pity.

SATURDAY 15 SEPTEMBER

Busy advice centres in Ilminster and Crewkerne. Then back up to London for Olly Grender's fiftieth birthday party. Had a telephone call from Henry de Zoete, Michael Gove's media adviser. He told me that the *Mail on Sunday* has 'unfortunately got the entire story about GCSE reform'. Hmmm. Suspicious.

SUNDAY 16 SEPTEMBER

At 11 a.m. there was a knock on the door and my first ministerial red box turned up. I was rather hoping not to have to bother with red boxes at the weekends. The Department for Education might have been up for that, but the Cabinet Office certainly isn't. Firstly, they're obsessed about security, and they're not willing to have me wandering around the country carrying secret papers. Secondly, they are strongly of the view that I'm going to have quite a bit of reading to do at weekends.

This afternoon I read a copy of a letter from the Cabinet Secretary to the Prime Minister and Deputy Prime Minister on proposals for trade union reform. Jeremy Heywood has been asked to do an 'objective' analysis of a paper by Danny Alexander and George Osborne, exploring a large number of very politically tricky trade union reform proposals. I thought this was a bit sensitive for a civil servant.

Sir Jeremy goes through them all carefully, line by line. At the end there is a wonderful 'civil service' conclusion: 'The arguments for and against moving ahead with these reforms immediately are finely poised and could be used to support action ... or the status quo.' Sir Humphrey Appleby would be proud!

MONDAY 17 SEPTEMBER

Danny Alexander arrived in his ministerial car at around 7.20 a.m. We headed off to Chequers, while Michael Gove and Nick Clegg went to a school in west London to launch the replacement for the GCSE.

I expected Chequers to be quite an impressive house, but we entered along a relatively inconspicuous driveway, and then through a gap between some large stone walls and into a gated courtyard. There is a low-key entrance to the house, with a few steps, and then in to a large reception room with sofas and some coffee laid out. Down a corridor, we could hear chortling and muffled voices – the Conservatives, who had arrived the previous night, were having breakfast. There was a newspaper rack, but all the papers had disappeared, with the notable exception of the *Daily Mirror* and *The Independent*.

Eventually, Nick Clegg arrived. We went upstairs and sat down around a large table, which appeared partly modelled on the Cabinet table.

In the middle, on the far side looking out over the gardens, was the Prime Minister, with Oliver Letwin on his left and Ed Llewellyn on his right. Opposite the Prime Minister was Nick Clegg, and to his right sat George Osborne, with me on George's right. On Nick Clegg's left was Danny Alexander.

We started on the Autumn Statement, and George said that obviously the situation was going to be much tougher because of the growth slow-down. There might be a need for further cuts of £6 billion in 2015/16 and £10 billion in 2016/17.

To my great surprise, Cameron floated the idea of moving away from real protection of the NHS budget, to a freeze in NHS spending in cash terms. Extraordinary, as this would be both risky and a clear breach of Conservative and coalition pledges. I thought Sir Jeremy Heywood looked a bit sceptical and I said I thought that by 2015/16, after five years of a real-terms freeze in the NHS budget, there was a big risk that moving to a cash freeze might cause the quality of the NHS to deteriorate sharply.

George then raised the issue of whether we could delay our commitment to achieving the 0.7 per cent GNI target on overseas development assistance. The Prime Minister looked pretty dubious. 'Is it really worth all the political hassle of being seen to go back on a pledge, particularly if all the charities are really upset and we end up with a great big campaign against?'

Cameron also made it clear that he's not interested in reopening discussions about pensioner allowances such as the winter fuel allowance or free TV licences: 'I made my pledges on that very clear in the election and, as I said before, I'm not going to have one of those "split-screen moments" where the TV people put up what I said in 2010 and how it's all different now.'

George raised the possibility of cutting, or delaying the introduction of, Universal Credit. He said that we needed to achieve a lot more in terms of welfare savings, possibly by freezing the value of benefits in cash terms. Nick said he wasn't very keen on this and I argued that freezing benefit levels was the equivalent of a real cut in the incomes of some of the poorest people. I said I didn't really see how that was consistent with our coalition pledge to protect those on the lowest incomes from the impact of austerity. Cameron looked displeased. Nick then said: 'It's just not acceptable for the next stage of austerity to be delivered on the backs of the poor. There has got to be a tax contribution from those on higher incomes.'

George Osborne rolled his eyes: 'Nick, there just aren't enough Russian oligarchs in London.'

Nick said that he was thinking of some kind of wealth tax, possibly the mansion tax. Cameron said that he felt that we'd 'already been round this circuit before', and that he wasn't interested or attracted by a mansion tax.

We'd made precious little progress in filling our Budget 'black hole', so we went on to discuss other policy areas.

Oliver Letwin seems to have invented an utterly bizarre policy, in which people who are self-employed could get tax-incentivised shares in their own businesses, provided they gave up all their own employment rights. It sounded hare-brained in the extreme – a fairly desperate way of the Tories getting somewhere near the 'Beecroft solution' of businesses being able to sack without reason or notice. Even David Cameron looked puzzled.

Cameron then pursued a similar theme by saying he 'wanted some action to tighten up on the unions'. I said that anything on the unions needs to be tied into party funding reform. They didn't like that at all. Cameron got rather irritated and said: 'I don't understand the connection between trade union reform and party funding, and this is a completely new idea that you are raising.' He claimed he hadn't seen any proposals on party funding, which I know to be nonsense because Andrew Feldman told me that he put a note into David Cameron's weekend box.

I interrupted to say that Feldman had made clear to me that he was happy to do a deal on party funding, and thought this was sellable to the Conservative Party. I said that we were pretty much prepared to sign up to the Conservative position on party funding reform, including a high cap. They were definitely not expecting this. Cameron flushed red, and said to Nick, 'Sorry, this is all new stuff as far as I am concerned. I've no idea what Andrew has been saying, but I don't recognise this at all.'

Cameron explained that he wants the mid-term review to include a right for council house tenants to sell their properties in exchange for no further access to housing benefit. He said that this was the 'biggest and boldest' idea he'd heard of for some time, and it would 'set people free'. A number of people around the table, including me, expressed scepticism about the practicalities. The chief objective seems to be to get rid of social housing – an old Tory obsession. Cameron and Osborne simply identify social housing with 'dependency' and voting Labour. I don't think they've remotely thought through the practicalities.

Cameron also observed, as if it were some great revelation (what planet has he been on?) that his recent contacts with the public had indicated that immigration is a top concern, and he said we had to be able to do more about this. He said he'd visited two factories recently and in one of them, 50 per cent of the employees were European migrants and in the other, 60 per cent were. He said we had to be able to 'do something' on this, but Nick pointed out that since most of these people were EU citizens, there wasn't very much we could do. It's quite clear that the pledges that the Conservatives made at the last general election on slashing the numbers of immigrants are simply not going to be met.

Finally, we discussed a package of positive measures on further education, and we made them more attractive to the Conservatives by talking about the 'abolition' of unemployment benefit for 18–21-year-olds. Young people would be 'earning or learning', rather than being on benefit. As Nick had said the previous night, the Conservatives really aren't interested in colleges and FE, but they perked up at the thought of benefit cuts. They are very, very predictable.

Eventually, we stopped for lunch. The conversation then centred on two tricky issues. One was the Leveson Inquiry on press regulation and the other was Europe. On Leveson, it's clear that the PM isn't keen to do anything that would upset the press. He said that he'd recently had lunch with James Harding, the editor of *The Times*, and 'even *The Times*, the most reasonable national newspaper, is apparently against any type of statutory regulation'. Nick Clegg and Jonny Oates both said that people wouldn't understand it if we commissioned the Leveson Inquiry and then did nothing about it.

There was a brief discussion about Ed Miliband. Labour are well ahead in the polls at the moment, but with an underlying sense that Ed won't really cut it as a potential Prime Minister. Oliver Dowden, the arch-Tory special adviser, said that it was terribly important that we should do everything we could to keep Ed Miliband in place. Cameron joked, 'If that's our strategy then we are doing brilliantly – have you seen our latest poll ratings?'

We then went into a long discussion about Europe. Coming down the track at us are two difficult decisions – one on the European budget and the other on European constitutional reform.

We agreed that there was little real upside for either coalition party to constitutional reform in Europe, not least given the extreme position of the right wing of the Conservative Party. But David Cameron is in a real panic about the next EU budget negotiations. The British negotiating position is for a zero real-terms rise in the budget, but most other countries want more than this. We have rather a difficult judgement to make and there has to be a vote on this matter in the House of Commons. But the problem is if we then decide to wield our veto, the European budget would still be set but by qualified majority voting. So in the process of wielding a veto to stop a rise of, say, I per cent in the EU budget, we might end up having larger rises of 3 or 4 per cent imposed on us. It's clear that the EU will go on being a pretty toxic issue in British politics.

TUESDAY 18 SEPTEMBER

Cabinet. A brief update on the dire state of the Eurozone, from George Osborne. We then moved on to discuss the honours system – with a presentation from Bob Kerslake, the head of the civil service. Bob has apparently been asked to 'update' the honours system to get more 'ordinary people' recognised. Hmmm.

I knew immediately that this was an issue on which everyone would have a view – and I had a private bet with myself that the debate would go on far longer than on the Eurozone.

Sure enough, the Eurozone filled fifteen minutes; the honours system forty-five. Everyone, yes everyone, had an opinion.

Michael Gove said that more head teachers should be rewarded. Jeremy Hunt wanted more doctors. You get the picture. A lot of Conservatives said that the honours system was terribly important and that politicians should have more power and influence. A string of ministers complained that they had recommended people for honours but these people hadn't been rewarded, and they'd never heard back. 'An absolute disgrace' etc.

Nick Clegg said that he was very sceptical about honours, and that he tended to think that they were a bit of a waste of time and an obsession of the establishment: 'And even Bob Kerslake must admit that civil servants get far too many honours.' Bob Kerslake glanced up. 'It's "Sir" Bob Kerslake, actually.'

George Osborne interrupted to note that we were spending far longer discussing the honours system than the Eurozone crisis – 'perhaps this is because we have more influence over the honours system than we have over the European economy'. Turning to Nick Clegg, he said that he 'wasn't particularly inclined to bow to the views of the "Lord President of the Council" on the evils of the honours system'!

After Cabinet, I went straight to a meeting on trade union reform with officials from the Business Department. We went very rapidly through the twenty or so Tory proposals on union reform, and it's clear that the BIS officials don't like any of them. Halfway through the discussion, it turned out that the lead BIS official is himself a union member, as is his wife! I cracked a joke about conflicts of interest, but he was utterly po-faced.

A productive meeting with Vince Cable in his office, where we discussed the Business Bank. He said that he was willing to trade this for the 'barmy' employment idea being advocated by Oliver Letwin. Giles Wilkes, Vince's adviser, said that the official BIS advice is unequivocal – that this is a 'fiddly, unnecessary, confusing and "mad" idea'.

WEDNESDAY 19 SEPTEMBER

Attended my first meeting of the Home Affairs Committee – arguably the most powerful of all the Cabinet committees. It takes place in a rather grand-looking 'Conference Room A' in the Cabinet Office. There is a huge square table, in contrast to the long Cabinet Room table. The Home Affairs Committee is chaired by Nick Clegg, with Ken Clarke as the vice-chair. Most Secretaries of State are members.

A paper on fuel poverty was presented by Ed Davey. This questioned whether we have the right definition of fuel poverty and also whether there should be new laws mandating a reduction in 'fuel poverty', as there had been under Labour.

Ed explained that the previous definition of fuel poverty – spending more than 10 per cent of your income on fuel – wasn't actually very sensible. There had been a point in the last couple of years where on this definition it had actually been assessed that Her Majesty the Queen counted as being in fuel poverty, because of the costs of heating the royal palaces!

Ken Clarke then intervened to say that all these 'Brownite' targets were 'an absolute nonsense and a total lot of Labour tosh'. Ken said what we should be worried about is overall poverty, not subsets of poverty. There was a lot of supportive chuntering.

Michael Gove was on mischievous form. He claimed that one measure of poverty which is reliable is the lack of books in a house. He suggested, tongue in cheek, that maybe the government should now derive a measure of 'book poverty', where it would collect statistics on the percentage of households having under a certain number of books. 'We could then pass an Act of Parliament, and the government could deliver large numbers of books around the country to try to reduce book poverty rates!' Ken Clarke and others just chuckled away. Ed fumed quietly.

The Quad. We were the first to arrive. Danny sat on the Prime Minister's side of the table, facing out into the Downing Street garden, with Nick Clegg and I on the other side of the table, facing the Prime Minister.

Cameron and Osborne seemed in a pretty good mood, and the whole occasion was surprisingly relaxed and convivial. Whatever differences there are on policy in this coalition, the two parties actually work pretty closely together.

On the table in front of us were copies of the latest proposed 'deals' on key policy issues that each party wants to announce at its autumn conference. The first of these was a proposed 'deal' in which the Conservatives would get trade union 'thresholds', requiring a minimum percentage turnout to approve a strike, while we would get 'a call for evidence on the issue of decarbonisation'. They must think we are total mugs.

Nick said he really couldn't accept this 'deal', as he thought that the trade union legislation was pretty controversial and he could only consider it for something significant, like progress on party funding.

George Osborne said he thought he was being 'incredibly generous' to the Liberal Democrats, as the call for evidence on decarbonisation would be 'terribly controversial' and would upset Conservative MPs. I chipped in to say that I thought that the trade union threshold issue would run on the front page of every newspaper, while our call for evidence on decarbonisation would do well to get page 48 of the *Financial Times* and page 15 of *Green Energy Weekly*. George chuckled knowingly.

The Conservatives said that they were willing to give Vince Cable a Business Bank with perhaps £1 billion of equity. We then turned to their associated 'ask' of an 'entrepreneurial share-owning employee status company' – the dotty Letwin idea.

George made quite clear that the only reason he's interested in this is to allow the Tory Party 'to throw some red meat to our supporters'. I said that the reason that Vince Cable wasn't terribly worried is that he actually didn't think it would work, and I was a little bit worried that this seemed to be the Tory view of the Vince Cable Business Bank. Was it the case that we were both signing up to things that the other party wanted on the basis that we didn't think they would work?

We looked in detail at the list of 'Conservative Party conference asks' and came to a proposal from Chris Grayling to strengthen the rights of homeowners to protect themselves against burglars by introducing the right to use force unless this was 'grossly disproportionate'. George Osborne whispered to me: 'This has been announced and re-announced at every Conservative Party conference for the last fifteen years!'

We considered a small Lib Dem proposal to remove the word 'insulting' from Section 5 of the Public Order Act. The Home Office had apparently cleared this a few days ago, but they have now got cold feet. David Cameron said he was 'pretty sceptical right now'.

THURSDAY 20 SEPTEMBER

Nick's team pre-briefed the media about his party political broadcast next week, apologising for breaking our pledge on tuition fees. Vince Cable went on *Newsnight*, but didn't do a very good job, saying that he had been 'sceptical' of the fees policy before the election. Nick texted: 'Vince is making a total pig's ear on Newsnight, completely departing from the agreed line. We'll need to clean up behind him.'

SATURDAY 22 SEPTEMBER

There's still a lot of very negative media coverage about the extraordinary situation of Andrew Mitchell, who was apparently leaving Downing Street on Thursday on his bike when he was stopped by the police officers and told to dismount. A great row ensued, which ended up with Mitchell allegedly saying, 'Don't you know who I am? I'm the Chief Whip. We're the people running the country, not you lot.' He then is alleged to have called the officers 'plebs'!

Of course, the irony of all this is that it was only on Wednesday that we were meeting David Cameron for a Quad, where the first item on the list of Liberal Democrat asks was for an amendment which would have deleted the word 'insulting', hence allowing people to insult the police. Thank goodness we decided not to proceed!

MONDAY 24 SEPTEMBER

Party conference, Brighton. Julian Astle tells me that Nick is rather down about his extraordinarily negative personal poll ratings. Nick told Julian that the history of party leaders who are viewed in this way is not a good one, as they usually don't manage to overcome the negative stereotype of them.

I did an interview with the *Westminster Hour*, and was forced to listen to an incredible lot of twaddle from Linda Jack, some nonentity who's ended up on the party's Federal Policy Committee because only three people and a dog ever vote for its members. She came out with the biggest load of tosh I've heard for a long time, including how we'd achieved nothing in government and how Nick Clegg was useless. It might just as well have been a party political broadcast for the Labour Party.

WEDNESDAY 26 SEPTEMBER

The weather has been absolutely miserable all week.

The conference has gone smoothly from a leadership perspective, with no serious votes lost – and a crushing victory against the left wing over a half-baked motion on the coalition's economic policies.

There has, in my view, been far too much publicity about mansion taxes, green taxes and taxing the rich. There is a risk that the Lib Dems get defined by unpopular policies, such as Europe and higher taxes, instead of our popular policies on education, cutting the tax burden for low- and middle-income families, and improving the pension system.

The only person who seems to me to have had a good conference of the future leadership contenders is Tim Farron, who is entertaining and distinctively non-Conservative, but also manages to remain loyal and supportive of the leadership. Tim is an upgraded and more reliable version of Simon Hughes, and he needs to be taken very seriously as a contender when Nick eventually steps down. However, he really is from the more left-wing/oppositional part of the Liberal Democrats.

Nick's conference speech went well. There weren't many jokes in it, and there wasn't much applause – apart from the announcement that Paddy Ashdown will be coming back to chair the 2015 general election campaign.

Halfway through, during a particularly 'worthy' section on the environment, Danny Alexander suddenly leaned across. He shouted to me that I needed to wake Simon Hughes up. Gave Simon a sharp elbow. He hadn't quite gone to sleep, but appeared to be falling into a trance and his head was gradually drooping forward. Got to him just in time, before the snappers could get the shot they wanted.

THURSDAY 27 SEPTEMBER

Had a ministerial meeting with Michael Gove. Michael talked about the Conservative conference. He said that he is going to be speaking in the same session as Boris Johnson and Jeremy Hunt, and he suggested as a consequence that this particular morning's proceedings might have a banner up saying: 'Sponsored by Rupert Murdoch'.

MONDAY 1 OCTOBER

Off to the Cabinet Room in 10 Downing Street for a meeting of the Enterprise Committee, chaired by the Prime Minister. Cameron has an impressive and commanding style, and some interesting hand gestures. He has a tendency to hold his hands out in front of him, palms facing downwards and with fingers outstretched, with hand movements which appear to be pushing the air or some invisible person (Boris Johnson?) away from him. It's a sort of alpha male thing to spell out his dominance in the meetings, and it sends a subliminal message which is all about wanting things done, being in charge etc.

THURSDAY 4 OCTOBER

Wrote a note about my educational priorities: implementation of the pupil premium; improving school accountability and intervention; and developing a school capital and revenue funding programme.

I met Sir Michael Wilshaw, the Chief Inspector of Schools, along with Baroness Sally Morgan, chair of Ofsted. Sir Michael is excellent and objective, and he certainly doesn't believe that free schools and academies are going to automatically solve all the problems of the education system. Like me, he believes in a strong accountability system and strong intervention and support where schools are failing. It's clear that Ofsted is going to get tougher on local authorities and academy chains, and is going to make them more accountable. This is in line with my own thinking, and will allow me to strengthen the case for a robust 'middle tier'.

In the evening I had dinner with Nick Gibb, my predecessor as Schools Minister. He's a genuinely nice individual who didn't deserve to lose his job. Nick is a Conservative moderate, though he's also very much into a 'back to basics' approach to education. He can, at times, seem a little obsessive. I told him that there was no reason why he couldn't, one day, return to the DfE – and suggested that Cameron might have second thoughts. He looked dubious, but hopeful.

Julian Astle came to see me to recount a meeting that he'd been in earlier on in the day about the Autumn Statement. It seems as if Danny has been 'got at' by Treasury officials, who are now 'advising' him that the net interest earnings from quantitative easing can only be used to pay down the deficit, and there are 'legal reasons' (I think that this is complete twaddle!), meaning we couldn't actually spend this money on additional capital expenditure or time-limited tax cuts. Total balls and incredibly frustrating!

FRIDAY 5 OCTOBER

Ed Miliband has made a conference speech 'without notes', which for some reason is supposed to impress us. He's also tried to claim the mantle of 'One

Nationism' from Disraeli, and the media seem to have gone wild – not least because their narrative at the moment is all about how awful Cameron and the coalition are. I'm unconvinced. Speaking for an hour without notes is hardly a serious qualification to be Prime Minister. Comedians can do as much. And what if you forget something crucial?

In the evening, I headed to Devon to stay with some friends. Arrived at 1 a.m. in very heavy rain.

SATURDAY 6 OCTOBER

Woke up at 7 a.m. and to my surprise heard the sound of splashing outside the window. Thought I was dreaming. Tried to go back to sleep. But it turned out that the house had flooded overnight (it's a mill!) and we all had to go downstairs to help bail out. We seemed to be fighting a losing battle, but eventually the fire brigade arrived.

Late on Friday evening, Nick had forwarded me the front page of the *Mail on Sunday* with the headline 'Osborne: my tax gift to middle England'. The strap line is 'Chancellor pledges no Mansion Tax, no Wealth Tax – and a freeze on Council Tax'.

SUNDAY 7 OCTOBER

Danny said that we should be relaxed about the briefing of Osborne's speech – he interprets this as the Tories' negotiating position. I'm a bit dubious. I think Danny is a little naïve about their willingness to contemplate a mansion tax, and it seems to me unlikely they will agree to higher council tax bands either. Later, Nick Clegg sent me a copy of Osborne's speech. This not only rules out the mansion tax but goes on about targeting £10 billion worth of welfare savings. Nick is pretty angry. Emailed him to say that I think the £10 billion proposed cuts are not deliverable.

TUESDAY 9 OCTOBER

Met with Paul Kirby from the Downing Street Policy Unit about proposals on social housing, which we are told David Cameron is 'incredibly keen on'. These are mind-bogglingly ambitious, and quite controversial – e.g. bringing market rents to social housing.

We then had an 'Earn or Learn' meeting – another policy idea for the mid-term review, to help support 18–21-year-olds into training or work. I'm very enthusiastic about this and think there's an opportunity for a marriage of Lib Dem and Conservative principles.

WEDNESDAY 10 OCTOBER

In the early afternoon I had a meeting with Jeremy Browne, now at the Home Office. Jeremy was sent to the Home Office with a clear instruction from Nick to sink the Communications Bill. This proposal is essentially to extend existing snooping powers to other forms of communication, so that the security services can keep up with changing communications pathways. The problem is not only that there are many ways around this, but also that the controls to protect law-abiding citizens are remarkably light – and there seem to be over half a million cases of intercepted communications in the last year alone!

In the evening, I went to Danny's house in Balham. We ordered a curry and some wine. Spent most of the evening discussing the Autumn Statement. Danny went through his list of potential welfare cuts, which was even larger than the total cuts that George Osborne has said he wants. George has said that he wants £6 billion of cuts in 2015/16 and £10 billion the year after. Danny has identified £10 billion of cuts in 2015/16, and £11.6 billion in 2016/17!

THURSDAY 11 OCTOBER

At 8 a.m. Switch put through Norman Baker. Norman is concerned about the Conservative plans to 'privatise' the Highways Agency and all the trunk roads and motorways – alongside a new system that would charge people for using these roads. He's right. What on the earth are the Tories thinking? Political insanity of the first order.

At 1 p.m. we went to Nick Clegg's office for the first serious meeting on the Autumn Statement. Danny led with a fairly bland overview, and then went on to the issue of welfare cuts: 'We need to start off with as high as possible a target for savings, given that we have to fund things like the increase in the personal allowance, the cancellation of fuel duty increases, and policies from the mid-term review.'

Nick suddenly interrupted somewhat impatiently and said, 'Look, let's be absolutely clear about this. I'm fed up with being bounced into these types of cuts, and I want a full analysis of what cuts such as this would mean and how much they would impact people on very low incomes. I've made clear that we ought to start off by expecting a contribution from people on high incomes. Regardless of what the Treasury wants to do, I'm simply not going to accept £10 billion worth of cuts.'

Went to dinner with Michael Gove – Olivo's in Eccleston Street. Michael said that the Prime Minister had been asking whether he thought the Lib Dems would stay in coalition for the full five years – he replied that he thought we would.

Michael talked about the issue of Europe and the European referendum, and he seemed to imply that the Conservatives would eventually find it impossible not to sign up to a referendum. He said he thought that towards the next European elections the Conservative Party would say that there would be EU constitutional reform at some stage in the next parliament, and that at that stage the Conservatives would push for a devolution of powers in the European Union, followed by a referendum.

This is designed by Cameron to get the Conservative Party off its short-term hook in 2014, with the risk of UKIP doing extremely well right now. However, I pointed out that the risk of advertising a referendum as a short-term device to protect against UKIP was that in the longer term it could actually end up splitting the Conservative Party – as it would separate the sensible people in the Conservative Party who want to stay in the EU from those people whose basic agenda is to leave. Also, there is no guarantee we would get what we wanted from a new constitutional settlement, and could we even be sure when this opportunity would arise?

Michael also revealed that his strong preference is to stay at the Education Department for the whole parliament. A pity, as I was hoping that this would be one of the departments that the Lib Dems might 'take over' in any future reshuffle.

SUNDAY 14 OCTOBER

Having originally been told that they wouldn't need to send out a red box on Sunday, at 10.30 a.m. I had one delivered which turned out to be full to overflowing. Hidden away at the bottom, after five hours of other paperwork, was a submission on employment law. This started off in a low-key way, but then halfway down the page suddenly turned into a massive anti-union rant, concluding with the suggestion that the Secretary of State for Education should write to all Cabinet colleagues proposing draconian anti-union legislation.

This is clearly politically inspired, and I suspect they were simply hoping I wouldn't notice. I wrote a particularly rude note on the submission, saying that I wanted to see the official who had written it. This will put the wind up somebody.

MONDAY 15 OCTOBER

At 8.30 a.m. I had a briefing on immigration. The Home Office admitted there is an estimated 'stock' of between half a million and 1 million people in the UK illegally. This is a stunning figure, which they seem to be doing little about.

Theresa May has a tough reputation on immigration, but she is going for the easiest targets, which aren't the real problems. She seems to be targeting a reduction in foreign students rather than those overstaying their visas.

Our system of monitoring who is in the country and who is overstaying their visas is still pathetically inadequate. You would have thought this would have been sorted out ages ago. Better to tackle this than getting rid of real students and skilled workers.

How we can let hundreds of thousands of people enter the country and yet not effectively monitor whether they are leaving is quite beyond me. No wonder people have so little confidence in our immigration system. You'd assume a Conservative Home Secretary would be clamping down in this area very robustly.

To Nick Clegg's government business meeting. There was some discussion of a *Mail on Sunday* article alleging that Michael Gove wants Britain to leave the European Union. I don't think that's really Michael's view. Or is it? Reflecting back on our dinner, I don't think he made his own position very clear!

Walked back to the Department for Education, where I had a chat with our new policy adviser, Tim Leunig. Tim has already made an impact, with his very sharp brain and his fearless approach to giving advice. There are some new English and maths tests being introduced for trainee teachers. When Tim saw the test drafts, he did what few special advisers or politicians would do, and actually looked at the sample questions.

He said that some of the questions were incomprehensible and some of them appeared to have no clear answer. He said that he had asked one of the Conservative special advisers whether they could answer the questions and they couldn't either. We've put the thing on hold.

Tim said bluntly to me: 'My own guess is that our Secretary of State might well fail the maths test. Should we stop clever people like him from teaching, when he might make an excellent English teacher?'

TUESDAY 16 OCTOBER

Had a meeting with officials from DCMS on gay marriage. There have been 228,000 responses to the consultation – the largest ever. Probably mostly a lot of nauseating prejudice from religious groups. Once this is law, no one will remember what all the fuss was about.

Apparently there are still some senior Conservatives who are determined to torpedo the changes. The officials said the people they were concerned about were Iain Duncan Smith, the ghastly Philip Hammond and leading luddite Owen Paterson. My description, not theirs!

We then went into the issue of whether or not we need to define marriage in the Bill. Apparently the current definition of marriage insists that a marriage must be consummated and that adultery can only be committed with the opposite sex! We really don't want to have to put in the Bill a description of how a same-sex marriage can be consummated, and we certainly don't want to get into how we're going to define adultery. The officials think we can get away without amending these parts of the existing law.

A note recording the Prime Minister's recent phone call with Chancellor Merkel. Chancellor Merkel began the conversation by congratulating the

Prime Minister on a successful party conference, although she apparently said: 'I wish there had been a little less Euroscepticism on display!'

On the issue of treaty change, Merkel said that she was coming around to the idea of a growth test for all EU regulations and removing the Commission from certain areas of regulation. She suggested that when the time came for treaty change, this 'growth test' could be written into the treaty, in exchange for British acceptance of the changes that the Eurozone would need.

The Cabinet agenda was pretty full. On the economy, the Chancellor gave a fairly downbeat assessment. IDS chipped in somewhat unhelpfully, saying that more capital spending was needed. He also warned that public comment about not uprating benefits by inflation could be difficult in terms of a legal challenge, and he said 'people' should not get into debating this in public. That was another shot across the Chancellor's bows.

During the afternoon I had a series of meetings on education issues. Apparently Michael Gove is now planning to abolish AS-levels. He's held a consultation, expecting that universities would back the idea, but the consultation was apparently overwhelmingly in favour of keeping them.

The officials seemed rather embarrassed when they briefed me, and they tried to pretend that the Russell Group universities were in favour of abolishing AS-levels. I then glanced down at the briefing, to see that actually what the Russell Group are in favour of is keeping AS-levels and A-levels but getting rid of some of the modular elements. The problem with officials is that they are sometimes petrified of upsetting Michael and Dom, so they don't always volunteer the full truth. But they will never lie directly, so if you ask the right questions you get the truth!

WEDNESDAY 17 OCTOBER

Nick mentioned a meeting with the US ambassador to the UK. He indicated that the US was 'fed up with David Cameron' because they think that he has absolutely no credibility with other European leaders. The US is apparently worried that whereas in the past they were able to influence the EU through the UK, this is now impossible.

Went with Nick to the monthly Home Affairs Committee meeting. Chris

Grayling introduced a paper on freedom of information – the basic thrust was that this is becoming more expensive and burdensome.

Eric Pickles then made a rather strange contribution. He challenged one of the proposals in Chris's paper, in relation to limiting the number of freedom of information requests that any one individual could put in.

Grant Shapps, the Conservative Party chair, who's recently been under pressure for masquerading under a different name while being an MP in order to promote his own business interests, was sitting right next to Eric.

Either completely oblivious to this or relishing the opportunity to embarrass a rival, Eric said: 'I am really worried about this proposal, limiting the number of FOI requests per person. There is a real, real problem with this proposal because we all know that it's very easy for people to take on different names and identities. People can present themselves as somebody who they're actually not. It would therefore be possible for people to put in lots of different freedom of information requests but using different names.'

At this, Grant Shapps flushed a very, very deep shade of red.

I couldn't decide if Eric understood the sensitivity of what he was saying, but others around the table clearly did. A broad smile spread rapidly across the face of David Willetts, sitting opposite me, and he suddenly glanced down to his papers and appeared to take a very detailed interest in something in them.

On the other side of the table, Michael Gove's ears immediately twitched and he looked up, meerkat-like, smiling broadly, and glanced at me across the table. The officials charged with minuting the discussion were struggling, unsuccessfully, not to smirk.

On and on Eric went, while everyone else was thinking the same thing. There was a slightly uncomfortable silence around the room after he had spoken. Grant Shapps, or whatever his name is, said nothing.

THURSDAY 18 OCTOBER

10 Downing Street for a meeting with Liz Truss to discuss the issue of childcare. I like Liz, but she doesn't listen very much, and when people try to make points, she just talks straight over them in a slightly irritating and rather 'deaf' way. Once she's made up her mind, she switches into full auto-drive mode.

While Liz was in the middle of one of her long descriptions of how her policy should work and why it was better than all the other options, I happened to glance up onto the wall behind her, and there looking down on us was a portrait of Margaret Thatcher. Liz Truss is, in fact, like a young Margaret Thatcher on speed, and either she's going to shoot straight to the top of the Cabinet or she's going to overdo it and blow up entirely. I think it will be the former but we'll have to see.

A DfE ministerial meeting at four o'clock. Michael was on typically robust form and launched into full-frontal attack on the Troubled Families Unit, run by Louise Casey. It's one of Cameron's 'big things', but MG is very dismissive. He said he'd been to a meeting earlier in the week where the work of the unit had been discussed, and where it was explained how the target of 120,000 troubled families had effectively been picked out of the air by the Prime Minister on the basis of very little evidence.

Michael clearly thinks the whole thing is some ghastly Gordon Brown-type initiative which is going to fail disastrously, and he had all of us in stitches as he parodied the whole idea. Only Lord Hill sat back in his chair looking rather grumpy, and later he intervened to say that he was very concerned about axing the AS-levels, and felt it was rather disorganised and rushed. Michael looked slightly taken aback.

MONDAY 22 OCTOBER

In the afternoon, I attended the Economic Affairs sub-committee on growth implementation – chaired by George Osborne. The less said, the better. George is keen to go ahead with 'growth-enhancing' changes which mean that anybody can put up a conservatory, without planning consent. Vince Cable relished mentioning that 'Richmond Conservative Party are very opposed'.

George was unimpressed: 'Richmond is hardly ancient Rome.'

TUESDAY 23 OCTOBER

I had a chat with Julian Astle at breakfast in No. 10 and we went through the policies for the mid-term review. A controversial area is the Conservative policies on housing, and some of them are so absurd that Julian and I found ourselves laughing out loud. The Conservatives have one proposal where they are suggesting that somebody should have a right to own their council house, which means that you can simply take over your house from the council in exchange for not claiming housing benefit for five years. The house is then 60 per cent yours and 40 per cent the government's.

Under the Tory proposals, you can then sell off your house and take the money. This seems bizarre, because there's nothing to stop anybody on benefits simply selling the property and using the proceeds to go on an expensive holiday to the Bahamas, or buy crates of champagne. You can then apparently go back on housing benefit. This is an idea from Paul Kirby, in the Downing Street Policy Unit. People say that all the ideas he puts forward tend to end up 'falling to pieces'. Apparently Cameron thinks it's all brilliant. God help us!

THURSDAY 25 OCTOBER

Danny Alexander and I went to the meeting on the mid-term review with Oliver Letwin in 9 Downing Street. I asked Oliver what his answer was to the 'Bahamas question'. Oliver dismissed this with a wave of his hand and said it would be 'easily' possible to think of some sort of solution. Hmmm.

The issue of prisoner voting rights raises its ugly head again. The Law Officers – Dominic Grieve and Jim Wallace – are concerned about public pronouncements, not least by the Justice Secretary and the Prime Minister. It seems that any form of active government support for a proposal that would result in the UK not remedying the current position would be inconsistent with ministers' obligations under the Ministerial Code. It seems that Chris Grayling might be in trouble as active support by him for a non-compliant proposal would be likely to constitute a breach of his oath of office to respect the rule of law. They are clearly firing a shot across the bows for ministers who want to simply ignore the legal niceties of the current difficult situation – that's both Cameron and Grayling. Apparently Dominic Grieve is seriously considering resignation if Cameron ignores the law on this.

MONDAY 29 OCTOBER

Jeremy Heywood has also written on prisoner voting rights, pointing out some of the legal difficulties if we ignore the international courts. In blunt, non-civil service language, this means effectively the Prime Minister has over-reached himself by promising at PMQs not to implement anything on prisoner voting.

A blunt warning to the PM. We now have to hope the legal case goes our way.

TUESDAY 30 OCTOBER

Cabinet. The Chief Whip reported on the Commons amendment which has gone down to cut the European Union budget. So far, twenty-eight Tories have signed. Michael Gove is having to come back early from his trip to Poland. I couldn't help feeling amused, as the Tories normally manage to exploit the European Union as a populist issue, but they're now discovering that the boot is on the other foot.

An update on the economy from the Chancellor, who's clearly pleased by the recent quarterly growth statistics. Vince said that while some people might be inclined to see light at the end of the tunnel, 'the light could well be coming from a train going in the opposite direction'.

George then described the report from Lord Heseltine which is due to be published tomorrow. This proposes giving extra powers to regional bodies and devolving capital budgets from central government to local government and to regional quangos. George gave the coolest possible assessment, describing it as 'a very personal report'. Tongue firmly in cheek, he noted the 'huge effort' that had gone in, and said that we looking 'very carefully' at the details.

The Prime Minister then joked that the report sounded like 'something of a fourth-term priority'. George laughed: 'Yes – a fourth-term priority but for a different government!' Cameron concluded that we should be careful in our response since 'Michael is a very big beast in the political jungle, and upsetting him would be as dangerous as interrupting a silverback gorilla while he's mating'.

Met up with Nick and Danny to talk Autumn Statement. Last week Nick met IDS, who handed over his list of proposed welfare savings. This includes a freeze for three years on all working-age benefits and tax credits, and taxing benefits such as working-age disability living allowance, disability living allowance and attendance allowance. IDS also wants to limit child benefit and child tax credits to families with only two children; introduce a capital limit in pension credit; freeze local housing allowance; limit housing benefit for the under-25s; increase the age at which children should share a room; introduce an under-occupancy for new pensioner applications for housing benefit; and make a shared accommodation rate for housing benefit applicable across the whole of the working age! Extraordinary stuff! All of this raises about £6 billion in 2015/16, and around £9 billion in 2016/17.

However, having discussed this with Steve Webb yesterday, the truth is that IDS doesn't expect many of these savings to be acceptable, either politically or to the Lib Dems. IDS is therefore in the wonderful position where he can put forward these savings knowing that he will never actually need to deliver them!

At 4 p.m. there was a political meeting on the Autumn Statement in Nick's office in the Commons, with all Lib Dem Cabinet ministers.

Vince Cable launched an attack on Danny and said that there was no reason why we shouldn't be spending more on capital investment and just borrowing the money. He said that it was appalling that Treasury officials were suggesting that there should be further cuts to the Business budget. He said that he didn't believe in making any further savings in 2015/16.

When I got back to my office, there was a letter from Vince to Danny. The letter has been copied to the Chancellor of the Exchequer, to the Deputy Prime Minister and to me. The key part of it was the second paragraph, where Vince said that he believes there is an important discussion to be had about the future path of fiscal consolidation and 'pending that ... I've instructed my officials not to engage with their colleagues in other government departments in any discussions about reductions to the BIS budget'. This won't be well received in the Treasury.

At the parliamentary party meeting, Nick announced that a Labour amendment has been tabled in the House of Lords, postponing the boundary reforms to 2018. Of course, behind the scenes we've been talking to Labour about this. Nick pretended that we knew nothing about it. He said that the Tories have already 'gone ballistic' and that David Cameron had made three telephone calls to him within the space of an hour. I'm pleased that Nick is being so brutal about this.

WEDNESDAY 31 OCTOBER

Today was what might be described as a pretty challenging day for the coalition.

Extensive media coverage of the amendment to put the boundary review recommendations back to 2018. The Conservatives have gone absolutely nuts about this, and have now decided to scrap the Lords business today, so that there won't be any vote!

The morning newspapers also cover the further tensions on energy policy. The effervescent and right-wing Conservative MP and minister John Hayes, who was transferred recently to the Climate Change Department, has made a speech in which he has criticised land-based wind farms – 'enough is enough ... I may not be able to create a New Jerusalem but I can at least protect England's green and pleasant land'. This sounds as if it's come straight out of a *Yes Minister* Jim Hacker sketch.

I feel very sorry for Ed Davey, as he's already having his agenda vandalised and undermined in every conceivable way by Osborne.

At 8 a.m. I had a briefing with Department for Work and Pensions officials on the replacement of the disability living allowance by the new personal independence payment. This is basically a plan designed to cut expenditure on disability living allowance by around 20 per cent, but it now turns out that the changes are so aggressive that it's likely that the savings by 2017/18 will be double this. The latest figures suggest savings of £3 billion in 2017/18 out of a total working-age disability living allowance budget of around £9.5 billion. I asked officials whether savings on this scale from a single benefit had been achieved before in such a narrow timescale, and they said no.

What we're now proposing to do would be to unwind all of the problems with this benefit that have built up over twenty years, in just a few years. The losses for people are really quite massive, with 100,000 people experiencing a loss of over £100 per week, and with almost a million people experiencing losses of between £10 and £100 a week.

At 10.30, went to Portcullis House for a meeting with Nick Clegg and Paddy. Nick had been playing tennis with the Governor of the Bank of England. Nick burst into the meeting about ten minutes late to the obvious irritation of Paddy, who is still very military about timings. Nick surprised us all by saying that he'd just had a very detailed discussion about monetary policy and quantitative easing with Mervyn King, while he – Mervyn – was dressed only in his underpants! 'Too much detail,' said Jonny Oates. Mervyn was as cautious as ever about doing anything to support growth.

At 2.30 p.m., when we were supposed to be having a meeting of the full Quad, we ended up just having a Lib Dem meeting. Nick said that Cameron had gone 'completely ballistic' with him today over the Lib Dem support for the Lords amendment on the boundary review. Nick said that he'd never known the Prime Minister to be so angry and that he'd started 'shouting and swearing'. He's also desperately trying to keep control of his own party on the EU budget vote. I went over to vote on this at 7 p.m. and the whips were clearly very much on edge. Sure enough, the result was 307 in support of the amendment and only 294 against. This meant that an amendment in favour of a reduced European budget had been carried. Europe continues to be the running sore of British politics.

Nick said later that he's had another discussion with Cameron about the emerging Tory strategy of having an EU referendum in the next parliament. Nick said to the PM that he felt his strategy on the EU was bound to fail. All Cameron could say in response was: 'Nick, you may well be right!' Nick is finding Cameron to be 'desperate, tactical and flippant' at present. 'This will come back and bite him – mark my words.'

THURSDAY I NOVEMBER

11.45 a.m. The Quad. The mid-term review. Cabinet Room. The external sense of these Quad meetings is that there are just four people in the room – the Prime Minister, Nick Clegg, George Osborne and Danny Alexander. In fact, when there are subjects affecting Oliver Letwin and me, we also both attend, and in addition there's a whole set of advisers at the meeting, as well as the Cabinet Secretary.

The Prime Minister kicked off by saying that he was most grateful to the Liberal Democrats for their 'iron discipline' on the EU vote. No mention of the boundary review.

I started by presenting the childcare proposals, saying that basically these were pitched to the 'squeezed middle'. I then moved on to present the 'Earn or Learn' option. I'm very keen on this, but the truth is that Nick has gone rather cold on the whole thing, as he fears that the measures to reduce the benefit entitlement for young people will prove to be more prominent than the positive measures on training and education. The Prime Minister said that he was keen on the policy, and liked the simple message about earn or learn. Awkward.

Cameron then said that we now needed to turn to the next issue. Oliver said, 'I'll be leading this discussion – on the housing paper.' Cameron leant back: 'Oh, isn't this the mad one?' Paul Kirby looked crestfallen.

I drew attention to the 'Bahamas' problem – what you would do to stop people in social rented properties simply selling their house, taking a large amount of money and going to the Bahamas for six months and getting very drunk. There was a degree of chortling. Nick rubbed things in by saying that he was 'very concerned' that this package would be bad for 'strivers', the word that the Tories are using for their target voter group, as it would involve large windfall giveaways to people in social rented accommodation, while those in private accommodation wouldn't get any benefit at all. Cameron is clearly going very cold on his 'big idea'.

Oliver Letwin then said that we needed to discuss the plan to privatise the trunk roads network. The Prime Minister got up at this point and said, 'Look, I'd love to do this now, but I've got to go and see the President of Indonesia. All I would say about this proposal is that we've just got to do it – it's an absolute no-brainer.'

I said I was worried about the politics of what could be easily painted as a poll tax on motorists. George Osborne said, 'Look, David Laws's test is the crucial one here. If we're going to do this, we need to make sure that the politics work OK.' The Tories haven't remotely thought this through.

MONDAY 5 NOVEMBER

12.45 p.m. Ministerial meeting with Michael Gove. He was in a particularly mischievous mood, 'baiting' Lib Dem Baroness Joan Walmsley. Michael wound Joan up tremendously and then they went on to have a tussle over PSHE education. Mr Chalk and Mrs Cheese!

At 2 p.m. met with Lord Baker, the former Education Secretary, who's pushing a new type of school called university technical colleges. These are 14–18 establishments, where young people do both academic study and vocational education. Michael Gove loathes the idea, but, unusually, they've been imposed on him by the PM and Chancellor.

WEDNESDAY 7 NOVEMBER

Obama has been re-elected as President, to 'finish the job'. That wouldn't be a bad slogan for our coalition in 2015. However, a coalition can't stand for re-election.

At 3.30 p.m. went in to see Michael Gove. I had sent a note to him proposing improvements to school accountability, governance and intervention, and yesterday he seemed to be in favour of the paper, but when we had the discussion today, with all his political advisers present, he was, as ever, far more cautious.

He doesn't really like the idea of any kind of 'middle tier' between individual schools and the department, even if it's a contestable middle tier. His basic vision of schools reform is of a 'schools market', with 23,500 autonomous schools and a small amount of very centralised intervention in the weakest schools. My problem with this is that it leaves a lot of coasting or low-quality schools without effective oversight, as the department simply hasn't got the capacity to intervene in all weak schools.

FRIDAY 9 NOVEMBER

Received a text message from Dom Cummings, saying that 10 Downing Street were putting pressure on the Department for Education to have some kind of press announcement on Monday for the regional cabinet in Bristol, which is being held in a school. Apparently they want to announce either the School Teachers' Review Body proposals on pay flexibility, or a new Education Bill. We're not ready to agree either, and as Dom can't stand No. 10, and says that they always 'screw up' any announcements, he is looking to create an alliance between the Lib Dems and the Tories to block them.

Later we heard that No. 10 have been persuaded to announce instead a 'new initiative' on failing schools – that 400 failing schools would be turned into academies. Dom laughed: 'The No. 10 muppets are too stupid to realise we announced this months ago.'

MONDAY 12 NOVEMBER

Regional cabinet in Bristol.

The government car service took me to Paddington Station. They'd put on a special coach – 'Coach X', for the Cabinet. There was something of an 'in-crowd' of the Prime Minister and his senior officials, who were sitting in the middle of the carriage, and other Cabinet ministers were dotted around.

At Bristol, there were a couple of government Jaguars waiting for the Prime Minister and the Deputy Prime Minister, but the rest of us were loaded onto a coach, as if we were a school football team. There are clearly senior ministers worth guarding, and the rest of us who are probably regarded as 'disposable'.

We eventually arrived at the John Cabot Academy and were ushered into a rather large classroom, where tables had been fitted together to look like the Cabinet table. We were sitting on very small school chairs, which looked a bit odd.

The Chief Whip warned that he'd recently had a private meeting with the Speaker, John Bercow, whom the Conservatives absolutely hate. The Prime Minister in particular clearly detests Bercow and cannot disguise this. Sir George said that Bercow had complained about the poor behaviour of ministers in Prime Minister's Questions, and has warned that if there are any further problems then he is going to suspend them from the Chamber. There was general grumbling, particularly from the Tories, and the Prime Minister asked what would happen if a minister was suspended and refused to leave the Chamber. The Chief Whip reported that there would then need to be a vote of the whole House of Commons, and this thought was left hanging in the air.

Michael Gove then gave a report on schools reform. He was doing rather well until he unveiled some slides on an overhead projector. The Prime Minister asked what they meant, and Michael said that academies were improving faster than other schools. A few ministers then intervened to say that they thought that Michael had misunderstood his graph, and there was a rather confused couple of minutes when everybody around the table tried to give their own interpretation of the slides. There were a few amused glances as it became clear that Michael's interpretation was inaccurate.

In the middle of our discussions, a note was handed to Theresa May – Abu Qatada had won his appeal against deportation to Jordan. The Home Secretary was clearly furious and threw down the paper in a rage.

Had a meeting in the evening with Andrew Lansley to discuss legislation for the third session of Parliament. Andrew and George Young clashed with Oliver Letwin over a number of Bills. I bumped into a grumpy Andrew afterwards in the Members' tea room: 'There is the land which most people occupy and then there is "Planet Oliver"!' he moaned.

THURSDAY 15 NOVEMBER

To the Department for Work and Pensions, to meet Iain Duncan Smith and drive with him to the launch of the child poverty consultation.

I can't quite make out IDS. A lot of the things he's doing make good sense – reforming pensions, introducing Universal Credit, overseeing the Welfare to Work programme. But there's something unconvincing about him.

We had an enjoyably indiscreet car journey. The government car service drivers really must enjoy these occasions, as they pick up an immense amount of gossip. Iain was commenting upon his opposite number in the Labour Party, Liam Byrne, whom he obviously doesn't like. He was also a bit indiscreet about Chris Grayling, who he said 'rather lost his way' in his second year in the department.

After forty-five minutes, we arrived at the Clyde Children's Centre in Deptford. Iain made the first speech and oh my gosh, was he boring. On and on he went. I thought it would never end. The frog in his throat seemed to return, and he croaked his way along.

There were lots of parents in the audience, along with their rather mystified children, aged two or three. After a while, the children began to get bored and started to chatter, scream and shout. Iain ploughed on regardless, and I saw one DfE official desperately sending Post-it notes and other random items round to the various children hoping to occupy them. It's difficult to believe that Iain was once Conservative leader. He was, however, an absolutely wonderful person to follow, since it was impossible to make a speech that would fall any flatter.

At 5 p.m. Nick Clegg and I travelled to the Bank of England. Mervyn King was charming, and he mentioned the tennis match he had with Nick the other day – which Nick beat him in. This is perhaps not surprising as Mervyn is about twenty years older than Nick, and quite a bit larger! Mervyn also seems to play in a cricket team (how does he find time for all this?) and he referred to Danny Alexander being a very good bowler, which I find slightly hard to believe.

The Governor explained that he's pretty worried about the outlook for global growth and fears the UK economy will grow slowly. But he said he didn't think we should loosen fiscal policy.

He seemed terribly worried about yesterday's inflation numbers, which showed a surprise rise from 2.2 per cent to 2.7 per cent – because of higher tuition fees. Even Nick, who would not claim to be the world's greatest economist, pointed out that this type of 'exogenous shock' isn't real price pressure. Mervyn replied that inflation had been well above the Bank's 2 per cent target for a while. I said that I was very surprised by his views, as wage growth is low and there aren't any real inflationary pressures. There is not much we can do about higher energy and world food prices, or tuition fees. I said that I was very surprised if anyone serious really was criticising the Bank for high inflation. The Governor said, 'Oh yes! There was a recent article in *The Spectator*.' God help us!

I think Mervyn is more of a head banger on inflation than I had feared. If it was left to the Bank of England and Treasury, we'd be plodding along at 0 per cent growth for as far as the eye can see.

MONDAY 19 NOVEMBER

In the evening, attended the Lib Dem ministers' meeting on Iran. Nick distributed a numbered paper, which was collected in at the end.

In the evening, popped in to No. 11 to see George Osborne. He said that when he had taken over the Downing Street flat, it was in 'an absolutely ghastly state'. A very direct dig at Gordon Brown.

George said that he felt relatively comfortable about the economic outlook, and sees the Labour Party as on the back foot. He then moved on to Europe. He said that it was becoming a much more difficult issue for the Conservative Party, and thought that Conservative backbenchers are essentially 'unmanageable' on this issue. George said that the problem was that in the past, people like him in the Conservative Party used to argue that Europe was a distraction. But now, not only had the British public moved to the right on European issues, but also Europe was a much more central issue in British politics, given the state of the Eurozone.

George said that he was keen to do some kind of deal on party funding that would 'stitch up' the unions, and that he'd be happy to 'bung the Lib Dems a bit of money' if necessary, provided we didn't ask the Conservatives to do anything that would damage their finances. He nodded knowingly when I said that ruled out any cap on party funding.

George said that he was 'one of the Conservatives who still favoured some kind of pact in 2015 between the Lib Dems and the Conservatives', and he again proposed a 'coupon election', where there would be coalition candidates. We'd discussed that before and I made clear this was not a possibility.

George said he assumed that senior Lib Dems would still want a coalition with the Conservatives after the next election: 'Nick Clegg, David Laws and Danny Alexander won't have much future if there is a coalition with Labour.' He also said that he doubted there would be 'nice chats' like this if the Lib Dems were in coalition with Ed Balls and the Labour Party. A mixture of temptations and threats!

In my box tonight a copy of a wonderfully blunt letter from Michael Gove to the leader of Lancashire County Council.

> Your county's middle-of-the-road performance conceals a darker story of complacency and underperformance ... Lancashire has a number of chronically underperforming schools that have repeatedly failed to give their pupils the education they deserve ... I am grateful for the improvement seen at some schools in Lancashire this year. It would appear that this has been achieved through the hard work of teachers, rather than being driven by the council ... I understand that your officers have refused to identify any schools that are causing them concern. I find this inexcusable ... Your officers are at best content to allow things to continue, and at worst are attempting to frustrate progress...

TUESDAY 20 NOVEMBER

At 1.30 p.m. I had to join the Parliamentary Business Committee to discuss upcoming legislation. The new Bill on Royal Accessions leaves in place the current ban on Roman Catholics becoming the monarch. It appears that the ban only extends to Roman Catholics. I asked whether it was possible for a Muslim to become head of state. A lot of confused faces amongst officials, but it appears that technically it is.

4 p.m. Nick Clegg's office. Nick explained where we are on the Autumn Statement negotiations. The Tories aren't giving way on taxes on the rich. Nick revealed that at the latest Quad he'd threatened we should have 'no Autumn Statement at all this year', and he said that Jeremy Heywood's eyes had almost 'popped out'.

I said that we need not worry. 'It could just be a very minimalist Autumn Statement, with updated growth and borrowing figures.' This is hardly a desirable outcome and would increase the odds of Britain losing its triple-A credit rating.

However, the person who would be most worried about this is the Chancellor of the Exchequer. It would be Osborne who would end up being 'the downgraded Chancellor'. I said we had to stop feeling that we were obliged to keep on tabling endless new proposals on taxing the wealthy. If the proposals we were making were being rejected, we should just sit back and insist that the Treasury came up with its own ideas.

Nick seemed relieved. He said that every time they discussed some tax on the rich, Cameron said that this would be offensive to his donors. Nick said that Cameron is in a very funny place at the current time, 'all over the place on Leveson, and really panicky about the state of the Tory Party on Europe' (probably with good reason).

A brief chat with Vince about the 'Earn or Learn' proposals. Vince is very keen. Giles Wilkes emailed me an extract of a speech that Vince is giving tomorrow. This had a relatively bland line in about improving the offer for people in FE. I said I thought this was fine but it shouldn't be over-spun, as Nick was still cautious and hadn't taken a decision to go ahead.

At 11 p.m. I glanced at my iPhone, only to see that one of the headlines in *The Guardian* is that Vince is backing a new 'Earn or Learn' policy in the mid-term review! Within a few minutes, I had an email from Nick: 'Why on the earth is he going ahead with this when we haven't agreed the policy?'

FRIDAY 23 NOVEMBER

Parliamentary party away day. Depressing hotel off the A1M near Hatfield. At breakfast, I had a chat with Nick. Osborne has spoken to him about doing a deal on two elements of party funding: limits on third-party campaigning, designed to stop the unions doing massive amounts of campaigning, and, in addition, some sort of additional finance for the Lib Dems, possibly through the Scottish system of short funding. I said the problem with that was that if it required legislation we might struggle to get it through the Commons and the Lords, given that neither Tory nor Labour MPs would like it: 'If we're going to do some sort of grotty deal, then it has to be a successful grotty deal.'

SATURDAY 24 NOVEMBER

Spent most of the day ploughing through red boxes, but at 4 p.m. we had a conference call on the Autumn Statement. Nick said that the latest proposals from the Conservatives are for a much more limited set of welfare savings, including a 1 per cent freeze on most benefits for three years. Danny said that what was on offer on taxation was around £1 billion of savings from pension tax, another £1 billion of savings from freezing or limiting the increases in the higher rate tax threshold, freezing or limiting the rises in the inheritance tax and capital gains tax thresholds, and the money from tax avoidance/clamping down on funds held in Switzerland. Looks like we're close to a deal.

MONDAY 26 NOVEMBER

A series of meetings in the morning, including one with Michael Gove over the proposed package of £70 million for school sports. This is absurd gimmickry, with special grants being paid to primary schools to hire PE teachers. I said I thought that the package was the worst type of

'Brownite rubbish'. Michael agreed, but said that the pressure from the Prime Minister to deliver 'something on the Olympic legacy' was overwhelming. He felt that this was 'probably the cheapest way to keep the PM quiet'.

TUESDAY 27 NOVEMBER

Cabinet. Ministers were asked to give an update on speeding up growth. Vince said it was taking quite a long time to get deregulation through the House of Commons on one simple measure, relaxing the alcohol requirements for chocolate liqueurs; they'd taken nine months! No wonder our growth plans are taking so long to get off the ground.

At the end, Cameron said, 'I suppose I ought to give you all an update on the EU conference. I can do so in a sentence: it was very boring – and nothing at all was achieved.'

WEDNESDAY 28 NOVEMBER

Met with Nick to consider the Leveson Report, due out tomorrow.

Discussed how we would deal with the fact that the government would have two different positions. Nick wants to make a separate statement from Cameron in the Commons – pretty well unprecedented. The whips are opposed and think both that the Speaker will resist and that it could go badly wrong. Nick got shirty: 'I simply can't understand why, in a multi-party political system, with a coalition, if there are some really big differences on an issue like this, why can't I make a statement as the Lib Dem leader which is separate from the Prime Minister?'

THURSDAY 29 NOVEMBER

Over to the House of Commons for my first Statutory Instrument debate as Schools Minister. This was on the exciting subject of the 'school premises regulations'. Officials had prepared me an absolutely useless speech – on one page, the same paragraph was repeated in identical form twice. Civil service speeches for ministers always seem to be written by low-grade press officers and they are generally bloody awful. Fortunately, the Labour shadow minister was absolutely useless. We won by ten votes to four, and I felt rather ridiculously delighted.

Later on, I went into the Chamber for the Leveson statement. The PM explained how he was in sympathy with a lot of the Leveson conclusions but he was going to go for a totally voluntary form of press self-regulation. He looked rather sheepish. Nick then made a totally separate statement. Apparently this is the first time this has happened since the 1930s. He came across extremely well. He was right to insist on this opportunity.

SATURDAY 1 DECEMBER

Spoke to Nick. He is worried about the parliamentary by-elections. Particularly horrible was Rotherham, where we came in eighth place – behind Labour, the Conservatives, UKIP, the BNP, Respect, the English Democrats – oh, and even the local vicar, standing as an Independent. God help us!

Later in the day, I spoke to Matt Sanders. He was concerned about some emails that have been leaked to the *Mail on Sunday*. They are apparently about Nick Clegg's involvement in some 'Bookstart' project, where the Education Department wanted to terminate the grant and open it up to a competition, but this was vetoed – it looks like by No. 10. Nick is spitting blood, as the leak tries to draw in his wife, Miriam. It's clear that somebody in the Department for Education has leaked these emails, and the betting is one of Michael's special advisers.

SUNDAY 2 DECEMBER

The lead story in today's *Mail on Sunday* is Bookstart. The Department for Education is being particularly unhelpful – refusing to put out any statement defending the decision or Nick.

Spent a lot of Sunday writing a paper for Michael Gove on schools intervention and accountability. When I read to the end of one of the departmental submissions, I suddenly saw a note from my private secretary to one of the senior education advisers, which had accidentally been attached to the back. The note said:

Susan – you kindly agreed to draft a note for the Minister of State on school accountability. He has had a meeting cancelled tomorrow and I fear that he intends to use the time to think about this himself! Is there any way you would have something ready by 1 p.m. tomorrow?!

Civil servants instinctively dislike it when ministers go off and start having policy thoughts of their own account!

MONDAY 3 DECEMBER

To Michael Gove's office, where there was a meeting with Sir Michael Wilshaw and Baroness Sally Morgan. Sir Michael was describing how he's going to start inspecting local authorities for their school intervention functions, and he also raised the issue of inspecting academy sponsors, which Michael Gove was notably silent on and which he clearly doesn't want. The Conservatives are very ideological and just can't accept that academy chains can ever fail, even though the statistics I've recently seen from Ofsted show that the two worst-performing academy chains are actually worse than any local authority. Michael Wilshaw is very sympathetic to my idea of having some kind of middle tier of accountability.

At 8 p.m. had a private meeting with Sally Morgan in the Commons. She said that she is worried about some of the things going on in the Department for Education, and particularly the influence of Dom Cummings. She said she'd attended a meeting about the new English Baccalaureate Certificate where Dom had made clear that he expected a massive drop in the pass rate and wasn't worried about the implications.

Sally said she was concerned about going back to a system where only a minority of pupils would succeed, and she wondered whether Michael was really committed to social mobility for all children, or only for a small minority who might get in to Oxford and Cambridge.

TUESDAY 4 DECEMBER

The Christmas decorations are now up in No. 10. Met up with Oliver Letwin at 7.30 a.m. in the No. 10 café.

The main subject for discussion was the mid-term review. Oliver said that he thought Dilnot's proposals on social care were 'completely mad' and would cost over £2 billion. He thought that Osborne and the PM agreed, but felt that there was 'a certain inevitability' about us having to sign up to all of this.

On the issue of 'Earn or Learn', Oliver said he was 'waiting to see where the Lib Dems now are'. He said, chuckling loudly, 'I understand that where we are on "Earn or Learn" is that this was a Lib Dem idea put forward by Nick Clegg, who then began to have his doubts, just as the doubts of the Conservative Party began to be satisfied. I understand that the Lib Dems are now uncertain whether they want to proceed with their own idea, except that Vince Cable has now publicly launched it in a speech at the Association of Colleges conference. However, I understand that the Lib Dems still don't know whether they want to support their proposal and Vince's announcement. And we're now waiting for you to come back and tell us!'

As he said all this, Oliver broke into gales of laughter. He obviously finds the whole thing hilarious, and he said if he ever managed to find the time to write his diaries, then this would certainly be one of the amusing stories that would feature.

I said I would in that case need to include the 'shambles' of Conservative policy on the housing and roads proposals in my own diaries!

Have finished my paper on schools reform. This gives the department a lot more power to impose academy solutions on weak schools, in exchange for Ofsted inspections of both local authorities and academy chains, and with a clear role for local authorities in intervening in weaker schools, including 'requires improvement' schools. Local authorities which fail their Ofsted inspections would lose their role in school improvement.

All of this ought to be attractive to any rational person. We'll see.

9.15 a.m. The Cabinet. Came in and saw that my place card was located right at the far end of the Cabinet table, and on the same side as the Prime Minister, which is the worst possible place in the room, as it's impossible to catch his eye. Therefore, before Baroness Warsi came in, swapped my place name with hers, and put her right in the blind spot.

The PM said that the Queen would be attending Cabinet on 18 December. He added that he is waiting for two Cabinet ministers to 'cough up' their £100 towards her present. Cameron said that they didn't know who the two people were who hadn't paid, because 'rather oddly, two of you made payment of your £100 in brown envelopes without any name on'!

We had a discussion about Chinese visas, on a paper introduced by the Chancellor of the Exchequer. This soon turned out to be a full-frontal attack on the Home Secretary for failing to keep a series of pledges about making it easier for people from China to get visas. Theresa May remained very quiet, seething with anger, while the Chancellor, sitting right next to her on her left, launched his scathing attack.

I felt certain that she would come back with a strong response, and she started off sounding irritated and confident. However, she then went on and on, and the more she went on, the more obvious it was that she had very little of substance to say. Cameron got visibly angry and began to go through all the points on the Chancellor's list, one by one. What had happened to this particular deadline? he asked. Why had this particular process not been put in place? Theresa stuttered and stumbled and looked desperately through her briefing notes for the answers that she needed – but without finding any. There was an uncomfortable feeling around the table. Other ministers looked embarrassed at seeing the Home Secretary squirm so badly. At the end of the discussion, Cameron said, 'Look, I really don't want to have to do this again. The Home Office is going to have to get its act together and sort these issues out.' Senior Cabinet ministers aren't usually humiliated in this way, and I doubt Theresa May will forget this.

At 10.45, I met up with the Cabinet Secretary. Jeremy Heywood is a most un-Mandarin-type senior civil servant. He's completely the opposite of Sir Humphrey Appleby, and in fact you get the impression not so much of talking to the Cabinet Secretary as of meeting a middle-rank official in, say, the Department for Work and Pensions. Jeremy has absolutely no sense of pomposity, and he seems to spend his time looking for intelligent and practical solutions to the problems facing us. If we had an entire Cabinet of Heywoods, the country would be very boring but incredibly well governed.

In the afternoon, met with Sam Freedman, Michael Gove's special adviser, about whether or not we should raise the minimum GCSE floor standard for every school to 50 per cent. Special advisers are wary, not least because of the way Ofqual is now interpreting its mandate to maintain standards. This means that they are refusing to allow GCSE results to rise, even if pupils get better grades, unless they can 'prove' these grades are because the children are brighter than before.

WEDNESDAY 5 DECEMBER

The Cabinet heard George Osborne's briefing about the Autumn Statement in subdued silence. To my horror, it turns out that we've wasted £1 billion on reducing corporation tax by another 1 per cent – something that will make precious little difference to the economy, but which uses up the scarce receipts from increasing taxes on the rich and from squeezing welfare.

The basic shape of the package is this: we're spending around £1.5 billion to avoid a 3p increase in fuel duty, and another £1 billion on a further increase in the personal income tax allowance. We're then cutting corporation tax and introducing corporate tax allowances, costing about £1 billion. We've got £1 billion coming in from the restriction of pension tax relief, and the usual few billions from tax avoidance, and then we've got about £1 billion from bringing more people into the 40 per cent rate of tax.

It's quite interesting with Cameron and Osborne that they don't much mind bringing more people into the 40 per cent rate, and they'd much rather do that than hit people who are really, really rich. It's all about protecting their friends and big donors.

George described how he had managed to ensure that borrowing was continuing to fall, though he said this was 'not by very much', at which point he glanced at me and smiled cynically. He's obviously spent an eternity massaging all the figures to make sure that the Labour Party can't say that borrowing is going up between 2012/13 and 2013/14.

The welfare benefit cuts have only amounted to around £3.5 billion in 2015/16, not the £10 billion George wanted. Credit to Nick on this.

The Autumn Statement is politically clever but lacks any imagination on growth. If growth doesn't resume soon, then borrowing is going to get stuck at an uncomfortably high level.

George also described how the government's going to be looking at other energy sources, including shale gas, and he said there would be a new regulator – the 'Office of Unconventional Gases'. As George said, 'A name that's right out of *The Thick of It*!'

THURSDAY 6 DECEMBER

The effects of the Autumn Statement are now clear. The top 10 per cent of the population have had their incomes hit by quite a lot, but the main losers are in the bottom 30 per cent – as a consequence of the reductions in benefit uprating. This highlights the rather bizarre Conservative priority of taking from people at the very bottom, counterbalanced by the Lib Dem determination to squeeze more out of the very top.

Given that George has spent an entire £1 billion cutting corporation tax, it's clear that a large segment of the welfare savings weren't necessary. If we'd got rid of the corporation tax cut and limited the uprating of fuel duty to 1p, we could have reduced the welfare savings by half. Infuriating.

Saw Glenys Stacey, the head of Ofqual. We discussed the English Baccalaureate Certificate. Glenys is amazingly critical and she said she had no idea what the new qualification was going to look like or whether the government really knew what it was going to look like; she had no idea what proportion of people were supposed to be passing it, and no idea what its content should be. Glenys said she didn't think the new qualification could be prepared sensibly in the timescales that were available. She is also very worried by having a single exam board, which she thought was 'disruptive and highly risky'.

At the ministerial meeting, Michael Gove said he felt the DfE had done very well out of the Autumn Statement – 'lots of complimentary press coverage'. He said he felt we had got a lot of political capital in the bank and 'we should think about whether we want to use any of this capital in changing policy in any area'. I said that I was worried about qualifications reform.

At the end of the meeting, I discussed with MG my note on school intervention. He said that he agreed with all of it, except one bullet point about allowing local authorities to intervene in 'requires improvement' academies. It remains to be seen whether Michael will change his mind again. Until we actually have a Bill down in black and white, I won't count on it.

FRIDAY 7 DECEMBER

At 6.30 a.m. I was at the Royal Mail sorting office in Yeovil, for my annual Christmas visit. I took over these visits from Paddy Ashdown. You have to get up early and go round the four Royal Mail sorting centres in Yeovil, Chard, Ilminster and Crewkerne, glad-handing rather exhausted postmen at some unearthly hour.

Sometimes you do meet grumpy people who hate politicians, but the key thing is to pass on rather quickly once you pick up any negative vibes. Although I absolutely dread these occasions, they always go much better than expected, and today the people in the Yeovil sorting office were particularly friendly.

I've found out from Daniel in my private office that there is a planned launch of a new A-level policy on Friday. MG's advisers are apparently trying to keep me in the dark. Because I've found out, they're now saying that they will brief me after Liz Truss meets with the Russell Group universities on Thursday, just a few hours before a launch on Friday. Balls to that.

I'm furious about this. It's the first time that I've discovered the Conservatives being deliberately duplicitous. I'm not going to be bounced into decisions on A-level reform.

SUNDAY 9 DECEMBER

Particularly irritating is a front-page headline in the *Sunday Times*, suggesting that Michael Gove is 'declaring war' on teachers. It doesn't take very long to guess where this story has come from – Dom Cummings. Nick emailed to say:

> I'm incensed by what Gove has briefed into the *Sunday Times* front page – going to war with teachers on pay etc. This completely undermines all our hard work to deliver a reasonable package on teacher pay, as well as insulting a lot of our core voters. I think we should brief out now that this is 'juvenile sabre rattling'.

In the evening, Tim Leunig sent me a note about the new English Baccalaureate Certificates. Tim said that he and Sam Freedman are becoming increasingly worried and feel that the EBC may be something of a policy car crash. He picked up on Michael's comment in the ministers' meeting that this reform is 'keeping him awake at night'. Tim says we should scrap the EBC reforms and simply modify GCSEs, with reduced coursework, reduced retakes and final synoptic exams. Tim said that we could rename them EBCs if we liked, but the change should be as gentle and evolutionary as possible. He also thinks we should scrap the risky move to monopoly exam boards. I agreed on all points.

MONDAY 10 DECEMBER

To Michael's office to have a meeting about the school improvement strategy. Rather ominously, Dom Cummings and Lord Hill were also there. Michael didn't beat around the bush. He said that his thinking on a third-session Schools Bill was rather similar to his fear of flying. A couple of years ago, he was due to make a long-distance flight, and in the run-up to the flight he was getting increasingly nervy and short-tempered but didn't really know why, and then one night his wife suggested to him that they shouldn't go on the holiday after all, and he suddenly felt a huge weight lifted from his shoulders.

He said that the same is true of the idea of having a third-session Schools Bill, and now that he'd taken a decision not to have a Bill, he suddenly felt the load on his shoulders lighten.

I think there are probably two or three reasons why he doesn't want a Bill. The first is that he doesn't want any change that would give local authorities a role in school improvement. The second issue is that he's sceptical about legislation for the sake of legislation, and feels that the department should focus on delivery, which is probably a sensible thing. The third reason is that Lord Hill doesn't want any more work!

I responded by saying that I wasn't obsessed about having a third-session Bill either and this was really the 'ask' of the Prime Minister. What I was far more interested in was the policy issue of how we intervened in weak schools. I pointed out that Sir Michael Wilshaw is now starting to inspect local authorities and is planning to fail those that he doesn't think are capable of carrying out the intervention role. This will therefore require a DfE response. I also said that we were soft-pedalling on accountability for academy chains and that some chains were performing less well than some local authorities. I said we needed to be honest and transparent about local authority and sponsor failure, and we needed to be as tough with bad sponsor academies as we were with bad local authorities.

TUESDAY 11 DECEMBER

I was furious to read an article in the *FT* entitled 'Fears of a Billion Pounds Lost Tax in Share Scheme'. This is about the potential tax costs involved in Osborne's new scheme in which you give up your employment rights in return for shares. The long-term costs are buried in an annexe to the Autumn Statement and show that in five years' time this will be costing around a billion pounds in tax avoidance. Crazy!

The Joint Parliamentary Committee Report on the Communications Bill has now come out and is fairly scathing about how awful the communication intercept measures are. Nick has gone public to say that the Bill is effectively dead in its existing form. Theresa May is absolutely furious and is briefing out outrageous things about Nick 'defending terrorists and paedophiles'!

The Cabinet meeting started at 9.15 with a discussion on immigration. Vince made a rather long intervention, and I glanced at Cameron to note that he was listening with ill-disguised irritation and contempt. Neither the Prime Minister nor George Osborne makes any effort in Cabinet to disguise their views.

George Osborne, William Hague and Michael Gove are clearly the Prime Minister's favourites, and on the Lib Dem side he generally gets on well with Danny Alexander and Nick Clegg and also, to the extent that he notices him, Michael Moore.

Cameron doesn't think much of Iain Duncan Smith, but he treats him with a degree of respect. Owen Paterson, the PM only just tolerates. Most of the women in the Cabinet Cameron has little time for. Only Theresa May is located centrally, on Osborne's right. Meanwhile, Justine Greening, the International Development Secretary, is seated somewhere near the entrance door, well away from the Prime Minister and out of his line of sight. Maria Miller, Theresa Villiers, and Baroness Warsi – the other female members of the Cabinet – are all consigned to the very far end of the table.

We had a brief discussion on the issue of gay marriage. Owen Paterson intervened to say that he wanted to confirm that this would be a free vote for the Conservative Party. Cameron replied impatiently, 'Of course it is, I've made that clear a long time ago.' He added: 'I really don't want this to go on for ever – we must get it out of the way before the summer.' I suspect what he meant is that he wants it out of the way before the Tory autumn conference.

Dinner with Julian Astle at the Cinnamon Club. We discussed Jeremy Browne, at the Home Office. Apparently he doesn't think much of Theresa May and says she is a bit of a lightweight. He's still infatuated with Hague. Theresa is making a speech on immigration tomorrow, but she's refusing to share it with Jeremy. Treats her junior ministers like junior grunts.

WEDNESDAY 12 DECEMBER

Nick told me that Theresa May was absolutely spitting blood over his announcement that the Communications Intercept Bill was being vetoed: 'Theresa has gone completely bonkers, it's really quite extraordinary. The atmosphere is very bad indeed between us.'

At lunchtime, took my private office staff for Christmas lunch, but had to return early for a PM/DPM bilateral on the mid-term review. We met in the PM's office. It isn't a terribly large room – probably no more than 20 ft by 20 ft, with a few armchairs and a sofa and a desk.

Cameron was seated in an armchair, with a big folder on his lap, and around him were Chris Martin, his private secretary, Kate Fall, Ed Llewellyn, Oliver Letwin and Jeremy Heywood. Nick and I sat down on the couch opposite the Prime Minister, and Jonny Oates and Philip Rycroft sat on chairs to our right.

Cameron opened by saying, 'Look, I'm really up for a big coalition agreement on all of this. My worry is that we're just going to have a few Lib Dem-type spending policies, without any really, really radical stuff. For example, on the single-tier pension, you've got to understand that I regard this as a pretty Lib Dem thing. I'm going to get a hard time in the *Daily Mail*. I guess I'm prepared to sort of go along with it, but only if we can do really interesting things on roads and housing.'

Cameron then took us onto roads policy, which he said, bizarrely, was the reform that he's most enthusiastic about. He claimed this would bring in a lot of extra spending for roads. He said that he was open to having something which was 'like a Green Paper or a White Paper' with all the detail filled in later: 'Some people tell me that this is a poll tax on the roads, but I really think we can manage that aspect of it and frankly we have to do something radical.'

I'm amazed that George Osborne hasn't killed this, because it's going to be incredibly unpopular with motorists and with the *Daily Mail/Sun/ Telegraph*.

THURSDAY 13 DECEMBER

There is a row going on about Michael Gove's proposals on A-levels. He's threatening to announce the whole package without proper government clearance.

At 8.30 a.m. I went over to the Department for Education to get briefed by officials on the primary school test results.

The officials all looked very sheepish. I wondered whether the results were awful, or there was some terrible cock-up. No. It turned out that the schools have done far better this year! The more I questioned them, the more genuine the improvement seemed to be. The officials are so used to the political requirement to show 'dumbing down' that they really didn't know how to handle an improvement in results. I finished the meeting by saying, 'Cheer up! And why don't we say something nice about schools for a change? Our criticisms of schools will be taken much more seriously if we say good things when they do well.'

This evening Julian Glover [DfT spad] spoke to me about the roads proposal that the PM is so keen on. The Department for Transport hate the idea. They hope we Lib Dems will 'bury it'.

FRIDAY 14 DECEMBER

At 8.30 a.m. Switch called through with the pre-planned telephone call from Michael Gove. Michael was calling from a motorway service station, so the line was a little crackly. I started off by saying that I was very concerned about last weekend's *Sunday Times* story about 'Gove declaring war on teachers'.

Then moved on to the recent row over A-level reform – said I was very upset that Michael's office had tried to block me from getting policy advice. I also said that I was concerned to hear that an official who deals with A-levels had been moved out of her policy area as a 'punishment' for speaking to my adviser. I said that it was unacceptable for a civil servant to be put in a position where they felt a conflict of loyalty between the two sides of the coalition.

SUNDAY 16 DECEMBER

A Lib Dem conference call on the mid-term review at 10.15 a.m. Nick was out in a park somewhere watching his son playing football. All we could hear was endless screams from children as the match ebbed and flowed up and down the park. At one stage, Danny had to stop speaking because none of us could hear each other.

MONDAY 17 DECEMBER

Another Quad on the mid-term review. Cameron started by saying, 'Look, basically I'm up for a radical mid-term review. But if we're going to have some Lib Dem stuff in the mid-term review, I want some of the things that I'm keen on, such as roads and housing. Are you up for that?' Nick replied rather too bluntly, 'Yes.'

Nick said that he was basically happy with the roads package but he thought it was politically sensitive and therefore there was a strong argument for starting with just a consultation. It was agreed that we'd press ahead with the single-tier pension reform, and we had a brief discussion on the pared-back housing reforms.

Then the Prime Minister said, 'What are we doing on this "Earn or Learn" thing?' Nick said, 'Well, I think we're probably not going to proceed due to some of the policy issues.' Mischievously, the Prime Minister – with a twinkle in his eye – said, 'Oh, I'm really disappointed we're not going to be doing this. We need to send out a clear message about encouraging people from welfare into employment. Why can't we do this?'

Somewhat sheepishly, Nick replied, 'Well, I just think that some of the policies here are very difficult on cutting back on benefits, and the Treasury is worried about wasting money on training for people who would otherwise get jobs.'

We then went onto a long discussion on the Dilnot Report on social care. Danny said that he thought it was 'completely mad' to go ahead with it, and George Osborne also said he wasn't supportive. Nick said he thought that we now were agreed on having a 'cheap' version of Dilnot with a £75,000 cap in 2017/18, which would shift most of the cost into the 2020 parliament. The Prime Minister said that there was in his view a clear rationale for doing the policy, which was to reduce the windfall losses that were suddenly incurred by people if they contracted some very nasty disease late in their lives. The issue was how we funded it. George Osborne said that maybe we should take away benefits from pensioners, such as attendance allowance and disability living allowance – but I pointed out that that would be the equivalent of taking from poor pensioners to give to rich ones! I said that the logical thing to do was to make sure it was the rich pensioners themselves who contributed to this, since they would be the big gainers.

I said that we could either raise money from inheritance tax – at which George Osborne frowned, smiled and raised his eyebrows – or we could take away the winter heating allowance from rich pensioners. The Conservatives were unenthusiastic.

6 p.m. Oliver Letwin's office on the lower ministerial corridor, to go through the mid-term review document. With anybody else, this could have been done in a couple of hours, but it was clear from the very beginning that Oliver was in no rush. By 7 p.m. we'd only covered two pages. Oliver would read each paragraph, for an implausibly long period of time, and sit there thinking. At one stage I thought he must either have fallen off to sleep or be waiting for us to say something – so I asked him whether he was ready to talk and he said, 'Just a couple of minutes.'

We had interminable debates about which road improvement schemes to include in the document, and in particular whether the improvements to the Kettering bypass and the A453 (widening) schemes were worth including.

After one particularly interminable wait for Oliver to rejig the transport section, Julian Astle, Nick Donlevy and I had a barely suppressed laughing fit, which in a small office is difficult to keep from everybody else.

By 10 p.m., four hours later, we were dealing with the section on 'Social Care and Disability'. This started: 'The fact that people are living longer than ever before is a cause for celebration. It gives us all a chance to work longer…'! When I read this bit, I laughed out loud, and Oliver asked me what I was laughing at. I read out the sentence to him, and at the end he burst out laughing with an entire mouthful of Diet Pepsi, which at first he threatened to spray across the room, and then appeared to be in danger of choking on.

Oliver has a very infectious and exaggerated hysterical chuckle, which goes on for a long period of time, and which is very difficult not to join in with.

Eventually got home at 1 a.m. There's a poll with the lowest Conservative support since David Cameron became leader, along with a very high UKIP poll rating. This is going to put pressure on Cameron on his referendum strategy.

TUESDAY 18 DECEMBER

The Quad again. 8.30 a.m. We went into a long discussion about the childcare proposals. It's clear that George Osborne would rather not be doing this at all.

Nick Clegg started a discussion about how we should make work pay for people on lower incomes. This would help, said Nick, to address the problems identified by the Resolution Foundation, under their director Gavin Kelly. George Osborne interrupted: 'Look, Gavin Kelly is just some Gordon Brown acolyte. The idea that we should be fixing policy because of what he says is complete nonsense. We really don't want to go back to fiddling with UC, which will make the whole thing far too complicated.'

David Cameron looked rather puzzled and confused through all of this and it's clear that he hasn't got his head around the details of childcare policy. He's one of those political leaders who is very comfortable on international summits, foreign policy, defence and home affairs. It's clear that he has no idea how Universal Credit interacts with anything else in the childcare system, and isn't really interested in this low-income group.

Cameron went on to say that he thought we really should be 'doing something' on the trade unions: 'Why don't we come back to the excellent proposals that were in the note from Danny Alexander and George Osborne?'

I said we couldn't possibly implement a partial reform of party funding that merely hit the trade unions without doing something to introduce a cap on donations. I also pointed out gently that this was really 'a solution in search of a problem, particularly in the private sector'. David Cameron said, 'Oh no, there really are problems with the trade unions, particularly in the public sector, and with things like the threatened fuel drivers and haulage strikes.'

At 9.45 a.m. the Cabinet started to gather in the Terracotta Room upstairs in No. 10, for the Queen's visit. I chatted with Michael Gove, Vince Cable and Mike Moore until we were ushered next door assembled in two lines facing each other, to wait for Her Majesty. Although all of us are used to meeting major politicians and media stars, there is something special in the air when the Queen visits. She is, after all, one of the most famous people in the world and she has an indefinable 'X factor'.

She arrived, escorted by David Cameron, and he guided her down the line of ministers, shaking hands first with the Cabinet Secretary, then with Baroness Warsi and then with me.

We then went next door for the official photograph. Just as the photographer had finished taking his shots, the Queen suddenly said, 'You can all smile, you know!', which set off a hearty round of laughter. At this point, the photographer suddenly realised that he had an interesting photograph and started clicking away madly. The Queen's comment had the desired effect, giving us an official photograph with everybody laughing – except for the Queen, who remained impassive in the centre of the Cabinet, her eyes focused on the photographer, her face seemingly quite serious, and looking at all times utterly the professional that she is.

Cabinet ministers were then guided downstairs. When the Queen came in, we all stood up and she was escorted to the seat at the middle of the Cabinet table which is normally the Prime Minister's. Cameron introduced the meeting by welcoming the Queen and saying that she was the first serving monarch to attend a Cabinet meeting since 1781, under Lord North's administration. At the time, we were in the middle of a war with the United States of America. The Queen stared, impassively, at the table. I don't think she would have blinked if it had been announced that we were planning a second American War.

Sir George Young described how we are beginning to get legislation together for the next Queen's Speech and the Queen interrupted to say, 'Well, I hope it won't be too long.'

The Queen left after the Afghanistan update and the PM showed her out. When he came back, we asked what present the Cabinet had bought the Queen with our £100 donations. 'Sixty place mats' – I'm sure she was overwhelmed!

SATURDAY 29 DECEMBER

A new version of the mid-term review document. The cover note says that Oliver has asked for a conference call on 'New Year's Day – at tea time'. Very Oliver!

Meanwhile, there has been an exchange of emails over Christmas between Tim Leunig and Michael Gove. Tim said that he thought the new proposed history curriculum is pretty awful, so I suggested he raise his concerns directly with Michael. Tim was as good as his word and sent an email straight off criticising the history curriculum, which he thinks MG has personally dictated.

Very rapidly an email came back from Michael, even though he's currently away on holiday, in the USA.

Dear Tim, I'm out of the UK at the moment – trying to broaden my horizons, but in fact only expanding my waistline. Thank you so much for being so detailed and so candid. Two things I value most in advice – and advisers – are evidence and honesty. It probably won't surprise you to know that drawing up the history curriculum has been the most difficult exercise of all the subjects – for a host of reasons – but perhaps most of all because it is the subject most susceptible to being viewed through a political prism. There may be different Conservative and Liberal perspectives on physics for all I know – perhaps Liberals as instinctive believers in greater pluralism and the virtues of coalition may be more inclined to believe that two different objects can occupy the same space at the same time – but generally the arguments one might have about the physics curriculum tend to be more technical than ideological. The case in point here is the argument you make about the aims of the history curriculum. I tend to the view that the more history one knows – and the better one understands the past – the less likely one is to make – or repeat – mistakes. The case you make that those parts of Germany with an anti-Semitic tradition are more likely to be pro-Nazi does not tell us anything about historical knowledge among Nazi voters per se – it tells us about the persistence of prejudices in particular communities – the same applies in Northern Ireland where I doubt that one in a hundred amongst loyalist rioters has any understanding of why the 1688 revolution might be thought glorious. What they do understand is that they are a tribe – with rituals and antipathies – the membership of that tribe is affirmed by the perpetuation of certain attitudes and prejudices.

On and on the email went. You can disagree with Michael. But you cannot fault his passion and commitment for his education responsibilities.

2013

MONDAY 7 JANUARY

Up at 4 a.m. to prepare for an interview round on the mid-term review.

Met with Nick on Cameron's forthcoming 'big speech' on Europe. Jonny Oates reports Ed Llewellyn saying: 'Expectations of the speech are now far too high.'

Cabinet 11 a.m. Nick spoke about the benefits uprating vote and said bluntly, with Osborne sitting at his right hand, that he didn't like Osborne's language 'demonising' those on benefits.

Afterwards, a briefing in the PM's office to prepare Nick and Cameron for their afternoon press conference on the mid-term review. Party tribalists would be horrified by the bonhomie – sandwiches and cakes passed round to celebrate Nick's birthday today.

I said that the media were focusing a lot on 'what this means for coalition relations'. Cameron said, 'We really have to get away from the coalition being constantly defined as some kind of marriage. Why don't I say that the thing about Nick and me is that we are both married – just not to each other! In fact, why don't I say that the coalition is a 'Ronseal Deal' – what you get is exactly what it says on the tin.'

Pity Cameron's often better at sound bites than policy!

WEDNESDAY 9 JANUARY

The media is dominated by coverage of that prime-time plonker Patrick Rock, one of the Tory advisers in No. 10. He decided to walk along Downing Street yesterday with a confidential briefing note about whether we should publish the annex to the mid-term review, stating which coalition promises we have failed to deliver. The snappers were more awake than Patrick.

THURSDAY 10 JANUARY

Skills Minister and Osborne groupie Matt Hancock turned up late for an ITV discussion at 6.40 a.m. about his new 'traineeships'. These are supposed to give work-related training to young people, including a better sense of disciplines such as turning up on time! He overslept and missed his slot. Bad publicity, but Matt is hyper-ambitious and regards any coverage as great for his career.

4 p.m. DfE ministers' meeting – always relaxed and amusing. They have precious little to do with current education priorities, and they're really an opportunity for Michael to lead a good gossip.

We were joined by (Lord) John Nash, the replacement for Lord Hill. Clever. Posh. No nonsense. Very Tory. He looked baffled as Michael sounded off, including on whether Mary Seacole should be in the history curriculum. This is a black lady who was active in the Crimean War and over recent years she has been taught as part of the history curriculum. Michael was planning to remove her from the curriculum, but there's been a backlash.

Michael then raised the upcoming PM speech on Europe. He shocked the Tory ministers by saying bluntly: 'Surely it's completely barmy to have this speech now? Surely this is a misjudgement, because all it will do is stir up the issue of Europe without actually bringing things to a conclusion? In any case, why are we proposing to speculate now about what might happen in Europe in a couple of years' time, after a negotiation of indefinite length, which might then lead to a referendum, the nature of which is poorly understood? Surely we shouldn't be giving this speech at all? Surely the Prime Minister should drop it?'

MONDAY 14 JANUARY

Cameron's Europe speech is now set for this Friday, 18 January – in the Netherlands. Nick has told the PM that he's got himself in a complete mess.

Discussed with Nick the 2015 leadership debates. Cameron has agreed to do them – sees it as an opportunity to 'wipe the floor' with Miliband. Nick wants them to start as early as possible (January 2015?) to help restore the party's separate identity. Cameron, surprisingly, agrees. Nick also told me: 'Cameron is driven insane by Vince and wants me to move him out of BIS at the next reshuffle.'

TUESDAY 15 JANUARY

In my red box, a Cabinet Office request to amend the 'Succession to the Crown' Bill. Almost a monumental balls-up! They've just discovered that an unintended consequence of the Bill is that if Prince Charles were to marry again without the Queen's consent, then he, Prince William and Prince Harry and all their descendants would be disqualified from the throne! A letter from Minister Chloe Smith: 'Given this unintended consequence we wish to make an amendment.'

Cabinet. Owen Paterson, the DEFRA Secretary, gave a 'ten-point growth plan update'. It's like listening to the man in the pub who's propping up the bar and rehearsing all his prejudices. You don't know whether to laugh or cry. He was later reported back in DEFRA saying the whole thing was 'a great triumph'. Utterly deluded! Mike Moore gave a presentation on the Scottish referendum – we're twenty points ahead. Mike is a pretty low-key guy, but there's something rather solid and dependable about him.

Sent Michael Gove an email, saying bluntly that I thought we now had three options on English Baccalaureate reform – the best option being to scrap the plan and simply reform existing GCSEs.

The feedback from Tim Leunig and Matt Sanders is that many of Michael Gove's advisers agree with me. That's certainly the view of the sensible and grown up Sam Freedman, who's unfortunately leaving the department soon. Dom Cummings and Henry de Zoete both think retreat would be 'impossible', because it would 'upset the *Daily Mail* too much'.

WEDNESDAY 16 JANUARY

In my box, a copy of a September email from Cameron's education adviser to Gove's office, feeding back the PM's views on the English Baccalaureate Certificate: 'The PM's obviously a bit frustrated that once again he hasn't had a proper chance to comment on substance before an announcement'! Amusing to know that we Lib Dems are not the only ones MG tries to bypass.

3.15 p.m. The Quad on the mid-term review. Cameron opened up in his rather vague and general way, saying that we needed to discuss Dilnot first: 'I don't know where you guys are on this. There are various proposals. One is to have a cap of £75,000, another is to have £65,000. I'm not hugely persuaded either way. We've also got to fund all this.'

Nick was insistent: 'I think we should do the Dilnot stuff. It should be funded through inheritance tax or cutting benefits for rich pensioners.'

Cameron looked sceptical: 'The problem is that I've looked into this and benefits for rich pensioners really don't raise very much. Only 5 per cent of pensioners are upper-rate taxpayers, and we'd only save £100 million from withdrawing the winter fuel payment.'

I countered by saying that at least if we did something on this and froze inheritance tax thresholds we would have made a decent contribution towards the costs.

The Prime Minister then said, 'Look, I've got an idea about how we might do this out of the NHS budget.' George then explained his idea of raiding the NHS and social care budgets. Nick and I said we thought this was crazy. The Tories have a complete blind spot on the NHS.

THURSDAY 17 JANUARY

Julian Astle telephoned me to say that the Tories are having second thoughts on funding Dilnot! It's unbelievable how many times they change their minds. Now they're thinking about freezing the inheritance tax threshold, as I suggested.

An urgent afternoon telephone call from Nick. He'd just met ethnic minority representatives and they'd told him they were 'horrified' by the idea of Mary Seacole being removed from the history curriculum. Nick replied, 'That just isn't going to happen.' They've gone straight out and told the media that Nick has 'promised' to veto this. I explained that Mary Seacole isn't actually in the national curriculum; she is in some non-statutory guidance, which Gove wants to drop. I also said that while Michael Gove was previously going to 'name' all the people in English history he thought

ought to be a part of the core curriculum – Churchill, Wellington, Nelson etc. – he has now dropped this. I'm going to have to find a fix, now Nick has 'promised' this!

The situation in Algeria is deteriorating, with Al Qaeda terrorists having attacked an oil terminal. As a consequence of this, Cameron's ill-fated speech on Europe has now been delayed.

Publicity today about President Obama calling Cameron and specifically warning him against the UK becoming divorced from the rest of the EU. This is significant, because if the US is arguing publicly for the UK to stay within the European Union, this could tip the scales. Cameron seems to have got himself in a complete pickle and he's going to end up pleasing no one – and just giving UKIP a lot of publicity.

MONDAY 21 JANUARY

The snow lies thickly on the ground and has turned to ice.

DfE ministerial meeting. We had the usual rather rambling discussion, including on the subject of sex education – which the Liberal Democrat side of the coalition wants included in the curriculum. Michael is totally opposed: 'I'm afraid, David, that we just can't do it. We would unite the Conservative MPs who hate sex with those who hate government inter-ference in the curriculum! I'd never get it through.'

Dinner with Michael Gove in the Churchill Room, overlooking the River Thames. This is probably the nicest dining room in Parliament, and the tables are widely spaced, so you can have a private conversation.

The main agenda item was English Baccalaureate Certificates/GCSEs. Michael has had a complete change of mind, and is finally tempted to bin the EBCs and reform existing GCSEs. I thought it would be indelicate to point out that this was exactly the approach that Nick and I had suggested back in September.

TUESDAY 22 JANUARY

Breakfast with Oliver Letwin at 7.45 a.m. in the No. 10 cafeteria. I secured the last kipper before he arrived, forcing him into ordering sausages – in spite of his diet.

I asked him how he'd managed to lose so much weight: 'I've eaten less.' Very logical, Oliver.

Cabinet. The main item was the 2015/16 Spending Review. A lot of whinging from the Secretaries of State running 'unprotected departments'. Theresa May forged an unusual alliance with Vince Cable to argue that the burden should now be borne by departments spared cuts to date.

I disagreed, as did Michael Gove: 'Prime Minister. We should all reflect on the words of Voltaire, who on his deathbed was asked by a priest, "Do you reject the devil and all his accomplices?" He replied, "This is no time to be making new enemies!"'

Michael's point was that given we had protected Health, Schools and Overseas Aid through most of the parliament, it would be mad to go back on this now.

Dry as dust, dull as ditchwater, charmless right-wing Philip Hammond suggested that welfare should be cut further. IDS replied that it would be difficult to save more, but rather than drawing attention to the big cuts that he's already made and the downsides of hitting people on very low incomes, he used what I thought was the rather cowardly argument that to make further cuts in welfare we'd need legislation, and this would inevitably be 'very difficult because of the need to gain a consensus across the coalition'. It is feeble for him to hide behind Liberal Democrat MPs when he opposes most of these cuts himself.

IDS likes to have it all ways. With some people he presents himself as the defender of the poor, but he doesn't want to damage his credentials with the right, by appearing to be a drag on welfare reform. So he uses the Liberal Democrats as a shield.

Next was a brief update about the 'severe winter weather' from the Secretaries of State for Transport and Energy. From the tone of self-congratulation you would have thought that we had just been experiencing twelve feet of snow and weeks of sub-zero temperatures – instead of some standard winter weather. To be told that we hadn't yet run out of energy was neither a surprise nor a relief. Ministers love to ham up these 'crisis' situations – which offer politicians the opportunity to panic and be reactive, which is what they find easier than developing proactive, intelligent, long-term plans.

Met Sir Michael Wilshaw and discussed his plans to inspect local authorities and academy chains. Sir Michael is taking all of these initiatives without much consultation, which is causing Michael Gove some agitation. MG doesn't want Ofsted trampling all over the academies programme. However, rigorous inspection is clearly right, and I'm going to do all I can to encourage this.

At 4 p.m. over to Parliamentary Business and Legislation Committee. Only one item – the new Bill on equal marriage. Vast quantities of pointless paperwork, including an assessment of the Bill's impact on global warming – 'zero'.

WEDNESDAY 23 JANUARY

8.15 a.m. Sharp-elbowed news hound Andy Grice from *The Independent* came to do an interview, which to be honest I've been trying to avoid. Andy promised to limit the interview to a few subjects, but actually rampaged all over the political agenda. God knows what the headline will be!

Later, a meeting with Nick and Danny on Budget priorities. This got completely sidetracked by a discussion about Vince. Vince is more belligerent than ever about the economic strategy and has said to both Danny and Nick that he is completely opposed to budget cuts in 2015/16. Perhaps more ominously, he's also questioning the whole economic strategy of the government – saying that we must spend more on investment, even if that means borrowing more.

I warned that Vince isn't expressing some kind of 'communist position' on economic policy, but actually is putting the mainstream view of many parts of the economics community and, indeed, the City of London. I said that if we end up with a row over this in the party, then Vince's view would be quite likely to prevail. Also made clear I was very frustrated that we'd missed opportunities to invest more, particularly when we got the QE profits. I said, however, that we had to be realistic and the fact was that there was very little likelihood of the Tories agreeing to a fiscal boost when their entire argument was about the need to borrow less. I concluded that we now have to focus on monetary policy and getting some radical reform of the Bank's mandate.

Cameron made his big speech on Europe today. At PMQs, Ed Miliband appeared to come out against an in/out referendum. Tories delighted.

But for Cameron, this is a high-stakes gamble. It will create uncertainty for the British economy, and if other European countries don't 'play ball' and give Cameron the renegotiation of Britain's position in the EU that he seeks then we could end up having a referendum early in the next parliament, where it would be difficult for the Conservative Party and others to argue for us to stay in the European Union. So a tactical political manoeuvre could propel the UK out of the EU, and Cameron out of Downing Street.

Nick is distinctly unimpressed: 'Cameron may today have sown the seeds of a permanent split in his party over Europe. And if he thinks he can ever win over people like Liam Fox, he must be crazy.'

Nick is now very disparaging about Cameron: 'Never underestimate how short-termist and tactical he can be. He is always thinking of his immediate political problems and never what happens further down the road. For Cameron, this is all about getting through the next few months. He's not thinking beyond that. Basically, he's an optimist who always thinks something will turn up to bail him out.'

Nick has warned Cameron that an EU renegotiation will be very difficult: 'You either end up with something totally flaky and symbolic, like Harold Wilson did, which fools no one. Or you go for a massive renegotiation, without having a strong hand to play.' Cameron apparently just shrugged and said: 'Yeah, Nick. This is difficult. That's why I cannot yet spell out what I want to negotiate on.'

Nick said: 'If I had given the speech that Cameron has just made, the media would say it was rubbish. It's amazing what they let him get away with. Ultimately, I believe Cameron will fail on all this renegotiation stuff. In my view, this makes a second coalition with the Tories not so much impossible as deeply, deeply undesirable.'

THURSDAY 24 JANUARY

The IMF chief economist is on the airwaves today urging the government to slow down the pace of fiscal austerity. This is most unwelcome news to Osborne, a day before the release of growth numbers.

On the way back down from a school visit, I received an email with news reports about an interview given by Nick to *The House* magazine. The main line seems to be that the coalition should spend more on infrastructure and put cash back in people's pockets.

Danny sent a grumpy email to Nick: 'I assume you were referring to the fact that we are putting more money into people's pockets through personal allowance, and we have already put more into capital spending? I will no doubt be asked about this.'

FRIDAY 25 JANUARY

Even Boris Johnson has piled in, suggesting that there should be less gloomy talk of austerity and more capital investment. Who could this possibly be aimed at?

The media is full of photographs of Cameron, Osborne and Boris in an expensive pizza restaurant in Davos, laughing uproariously on the day before the GDP figures. At 9.30 a.m. the growth numbers were published, and were worse than expected – the economy contracted at 0.3 per cent in the final quarter of 2012.

MONDAY 28 JANUARY

Up at quarter past five as usual, and into the office by 6.30 a.m.

Today a 'Regional Cabinet', where we all trek off somewhere to show that we're 'in touch'! Nobody notices.

Today, the purpose of the visit to Leeds was to highlight the launch of plans for High Speed 2. At King's Cross Station I got a cup of coffee and then asked at the information desk where the train for Leeds was, and the assistant volunteered that it was 'Platform Zero'. Wondered if she was taking the mickey, but there is one.

I sat in a compartment with Oliver Letwin, Danny Alexander and Patrick McLoughlin. It turned out that the Transport Secretary had paid £160 for his return ticket, I had paid £155, Oliver Letwin had managed to go online and get his at £39, and Danny Alexander – in charge of public spending control – had somehow paid out £260!

The couple of hours up to Leeds were quite productive. Oliver Letwin was darting around the carriage doing deals with people, and Danny appeared to be holding various bilateral negotiations for the forthcoming

Spending Review. I heard him having some rather blunt exchanges with Philip Hammond and Eric Pickles and laying down the law.

Arrived at Leeds Station – where chauffeur-driven cars were waiting for the PM, DPM and Chancellor. Two minibuses for the rest of us to cram into. Poor Vince Cable ended up sharing a two-seater with Eric Pickles.

After a ten- or fifteen-minute journey, we turned up at Leeds City Museum, entering via a side entrance and completely ignoring a small crowd of 'locals'. We met in a cavernous hall, where a mock Cabinet table had been set up, which was rather longer than usual. The acoustics were so awful that nobody at either end of the table could hear what was being said. All I could pick up was Theresa Villiers, sitting next to me, muttering, 'I can't hear a thing.'

WEDNESDAY 30 JANUARY

8 a.m. Cinnamon Club, Westminster, for a breakfast with Dom Cummings. He arrived ten minutes late and said he didn't want anything to eat. What he did have for me to digest was useful – an email with a suggested 'settlement' on GCSEs/accountability.

Michael has agreed that we will simply reform the existing GCSEs – a huge relief!

Michael is also agreeing to my proposals on accountability, which will get rid of the existing five A*–Cs English and maths accountability measure, and replace it with an English/maths threshold measure, and a best eight GCSEs measure, which will have to include five E Bacc subjects. Also a stronger focus on the progress every pupil makes in their eight key subjects. An excellent result, which will give pupils and schools much better incentives.

We finished the discussion in forty minutes, and I joked that it was 'peace in our time'. Dom replied grumpily: 'More like the Molotov–Ribbentrop pact!' and left me to pay the bill.

Later, I joined a meeting with Nick Clegg to discuss the 2014 European elections. We agreed that Tim Farron ought to be given 'the great opportunity' of chairing the campaign. The election is widely expected to be a disaster.

Ryan Coetzee said he thought this was far too pessimistic. He claimed that some of our messages on the EU chime with voters. 'Not in Yeovil!' I replied. I said we should focus on local elections in 2014, and promote our MEPs as the people 'fighting for you' in Europe.

Nick reacted badly and said that this had been our strategy in previous European elections, where we'd always tried to keep our policies 'a secret'. He said that it hadn't worked. I pointed out that there was no 'counterfactual', as we had yet to discover what would actually happen if we fought on our pro-European policies. 'We might do considerably worse!'

At 4.30 p.m. I discovered that I had a meeting with one of the foreign ministers who has visited for the World Education Forum – the Schools Minister from Saudi Arabia. The meeting was in for a precious hour.

Minutes before the minister was due to arrive, my private secretary came rushing into my office and said: 'Minister, bad news. It looks like the Saudi Minister has brought you a gift. The Foreign Office is in a panic, because it's considered incredibly rude not to reciprocate.'

'What with?' I said. 'We don't have anything.' We searched my spartan office for anything even resembling a possible present. With thirty seconds to go, all we could find was a ghastly print of the London Eye, wrapped in cellophane and with a half-torn £9.99 price sticker on it. This had been left – understandably – by the previous Schools Minister, Nick Gibb.

'It has to be this,' said my private secretary. 'OK,' I replied. 'But only if it's absolutely necessary.'

At that moment, the Saudi Minister arrived, accompanied by various officials. It turned out that we had more in common than I expected, as he explained the high cost of their many small desert schools and how unpopular it was to try to close them.

Eventually the meeting ended, and I thought we had escaped without the need for our 'London Eye' monstrosity.

But at that moment, the minister said: 'Honourable Minister. Thank you for meeting me. I would like to present you with this gift, as a sincere mark of respect for the relationship between our two countries.' Ominously, he passed me a plush-looking green leather box. As I opened it, he explained: 'It is a specially selected gift, formerly in our National Museum, and from one of our most sacred archaeological sites – originally carved 300 years before the birth of Christ.'

At that moment, my private secretary handed to me the cellophane-wrapped London Eye print, with a tear in the back where someone had struggled to remove the price label.

The Saudi Minister looked distinctly underwhelmed. Blushing, I showed him to my door and said goodbye.

THURSDAY 31 JANUARY

A letter today from Owen Paterson, the right-wing head-banger at DEFRA. This proposes to cancel all animal welfare regulations and allow the farming sector to regulate itself. Oliver Letwin and I are going to block this insanity.

Discussed the Heseltine Review with the head of the No. 10 Policy Unit. I said I was assuming that the whole thing would simply be strangled by the Treasury.

'Hmmm. I wouldn't bet on it.'

'Really?' I said. 'Surely the Treasury hate giving up power and Osborne will think localism is just left-wing tosh?'

'Well, the Treasury was sceptical, but it now sees some rather cynical advantages. The Chancellor's view is that money is either wasted in central government or wasted in local government, and it really doesn't matter where. The only advantage, he thinks, is that if we devolve budgets to local government, the Treasury can slice off 10 per cent of the money and no one will be the wiser.'

So wonderfully cynical that I could almost hear George Osborne speaking the words!

4 p.m. DfE ministerial meeting. When I came in, Lord Nash was sitting in his seat and roaring with laughter. He read out the contents of a letter that had recently been sent to Michael Gove. This turned out to be from a head teacher in East Anglia who is very upset about losing out on funding for special needs teaching. She says that she has an unusual idea to raise money. She apparently has some kind of rare breed of dog and she believes that Michael has the same breed – a dog she seems to think is called 'Boris'. The 'Boris' name was apparently a diary column joke.

Anyway, the proposal the lady is making is that Michael should lend her his dog 'in order to impregnate my bitch'. She proposes to sell the resultant puppies to protect her special educational needs teacher. This is certainly the most imaginative proposal for public service delivery that I've yet come across.

At 5.30 p.m. I went down to the fifth floor of the Department for

Education for Lord Hill's leaving drinks. There is a great deal of affection for Lord Hill, because he is a really decent person.

Michael made a very nice speech, and then Jonathan Hill spoke. He told an amusing story of how he was travelling on a train with his female private secretary to visit a school in the north. The female private secretary and Lord Hill were sitting opposite each other, and halfway through the journey Lord Hill received a text message from her which said: 'My darling, I love you so, so much. Looking forward to tonight! With much love and many, many kisses.'

Lord Hill looked at the message nervously, wondering what his wife would think. And then, about a minute later, the same private secretary leaned over the table and said, 'I'm very sorry, Minister, I meant to send that to my boyfriend. Quite obviously it wasn't meant for you!'

MONDAY 4 FEBRUARY

Nick Clegg phoned through, having earlier delayed a call because 'an issue had come up about Chris Huhne'. I asked him whether everything was OK with Chris. 'Actually, no. His trial is due to open in about an hour, but he has told me that he now intends to plead guilty. Terrible for him, and we face a bloody difficult by-election.'*

Nick complained that the history curriculum that MG is proposing is 'utterly ludicrous' and had far too much detail in it. MG has apparently written it himself. Nick thought that Michael insisting on naming Margaret Thatcher in the curriculum, that would be the main story.

At midday I had a meeting with Dom Cummings, Tim Leunig and Matt Sanders. I proposed a new form of wording on the history curriculum which didn't single out Margaret Thatcher as Prime Minister but simply talked about 'recent British governments, including up to the government of Mrs Thatcher'. That put Mrs Thatcher in as an end point of recent British political history, rather than singling her out. I think it's 'peace in our time' again.

---

*   Huhne had resigned from the Cabinet a year earlier when he was charged with perverting the course of justice after his then wife, the economist Vicky Pryce, was alleged to have accepted speeding penalty points on his behalf.

TUESDAY 5 FEBRUARY

My meetings in the afternoon were all moved to the House of Commons as we awaited the vote on gay marriage. The division lobby in favour of reform was absolutely full, including the Prime Minister, senior Labour MPs and most Lib Dems. It soon became obvious that the Prime Minister had not secured the support of the majority of his colleagues.

However, this is a massive step towards an equal society. It's one of the votes that I'm most proud to have taken part in during my time in Parliament. We won by 400 to 175.

WEDNESDAY 6 FEBRUARY

Budget meeting with Nick and Danny. Nick had just met Mark Carney, the new Governor of the Bank of England. He said that Carney 'is a breath of fresh air', who talked about the need to stimulate the economy. At last!

Home rather earlier than usual. Had some text messages from Henry de Zoete and Dom Cummings, saying that the newspapers had 'got hold of' the story about Michael's U-turn on EBCs. Whether this is from the DfE or the Liberal Democrats is unclear. However, the first story I saw was written by Andy Grice in *The Independent*, and it presented the EBC change as a 'humiliating U-turn' for Michael, which Nick Clegg seemed to be credited for. I then saw various other articles in the *Mail*, the *Telegraph* and elsewhere which had much more of a Gove-ite spin on them. A couple of sources were quoted blaming the European Union (what?!) for the potential problems with a single examination board – which is absolute balls of the first order! Cummings's fingerprints for sure.

SUNDAY 10 FEBRUARY

Lots of press coverage of plans for a Dilnot social care cap of £75,000. So is finally launched the government policy that has caused most anguish over the past couple of years, and which probably has least support amongst the leading members of the coalition – hated by Oliver Letwin, hated by Danny Alexander, hated by George Osborne, and to which the Prime Minister is pretty lukewarm. It's only really because of Nick Clegg that this policy is going anywhere, and some credit must also go to Paul Burstow, who pushed this hard when he was a Health Minister.

TUESDAY 12 FEBRUARY

Cabinet. A brief discussion on the Dilnot reform. I did choke somewhat when Philip Hammond took the opportunity to congratulate Oliver Letwin on 'all the work that you've done to resolve this issue'. Philip hasn't got much of a sense of humour, so I doubt he saw the irony. I passed a note to Oliver saying, 'I'm pleased we can now credit you with getting Dilnot implemented!' Oliver scribbled back: 'Alas, not. But at least I do favour the broad thrust!'

The Prime Minister then gave a brief summary of his 'triumph' at the European Council, where Britain ended up leading the charge for a lower budget settlement and, to everyone's surprise, we actually won. There was a generally sycophantic response, though the Prime Minister was strikingly non-triumphalist, and said on this occasion he'd actually found that all he needed to do was 'row in behind the Germans'. He will, nonetheless, have been boosted. Hopefully, it will also make him understand that Britain can be influential in Europe without threatening to exit!

Within fifteen minutes, I was back in the Cabinet Room for a meeting chaired by the Prime Minister on migrants' access to benefits and public services. This committee is normally chaired by Mark Harper, the Immigration Minister, but the Prime Minister had decided to take over to give it some 'impetus' (i.e. he thinks there are votes in it).

Therefore not only were the usual Minister of State team present, but we were joined by the Home Secretary, the Health Secretary and the Local Government Secretary, Eric Pickles.

The Prime Minister was in his 'Why don't we just go ahead and sort all this out' mode, and we had a long list of papers on migrants' access to benefits, tax credits, health, social housing, legal aid and other issues.

Eric Pickles presented a couple of proposals to restrict migrants' access to social housing, which seemed sensible, and then a proposal on private sector landlords which didn't go as far as the Prime Minister wanted.

Cameron wanted every private sector landlord to have to vet their tenants' entitlement to be in the country. Eric rightly pushed back on this and said that it might mean private sector landlords refusing to take on anyone who looked foreign.

Cameron was increasingly insistent, but Eric then dug in and was really quite stubborn: 'Look, Prime Minister, I really don't think we'd want to do this. We don't want to create some kind of underclass that can't get housing.' An extraordinarily rare open tussle, with an increasingly flustered and irritated PM.

This was followed by a discussion on biometric identity cards. Not only did the Foreign Office suggest these would be illegal for EU citizens, but Eric Pickles then chipped in to say how 'appalled' he was by the idea of these 'identity cards'. An example of the card was passed around the table and when Eric received it, he held it between his fingers like something unpleasant he'd picked up off the pavement, and without waiting for his turn to speak, said, 'You must be kidding! Surely this is just an identity card! I thought that we were opposed to these things. This is a terrible, bloody awful idea.'

We finished with a discussion about immigrants who had overstayed their visas by many years. Cameron said he often saw such individuals at his own advice centres: 'We probably need some kind of route to legalise and regularise these people who are never going to go back home.'

There was a gasp around the Cabinet table, and some laughter. Cameron seemed totally unaware that this was exactly the Clegg amnesty policy that he'd opposed so strongly at the last general election. Mark Harper, across the table from me, looked embarrassed, and Norman Lamb and I immediately chuckled and said, 'We tried that at the last election and it wasn't very popular!'

A dreadful paper in my red box summarising the Heseltine Report – thirty pages of completely incomprehensible gobbledegook:

Civil servants based across the country should be brigaded into local growth teams, structured around clusters of LEPs, primarily tasked with joining up government and local partners to facilitate, identify and realise economic opportunities. Ministers and Permanent Secretaries should be associated with individual LEPs, not to advocate individual plans but to add an understanding of place to the existing culture of function. Proposals for the formal collaboration between local authorities will reinforce the importance of the standing of the LEP and enhance the partnership with the private sector across a functional economic market area and should be encouraged and prioritised for government approval. All proposals should be scrutinised by the Prime Minister's Growth Council.

Total balls.

WEDNESDAY 13 FEBRUARY

Breakfast with Oliver Letwin in No. 10. We discussed immigration.

Oliver seems to have a very negative view of Bulgaria and said it was one of the most corrupt countries in Europe and there would be some very unpleasant people who could come here when border restrictions are lifted on 1 January 2014. He wants to do a lot more within Romania and Bulgaria to try to persuade people not to come to the UK!

I suggested to him – in jest – that we should pay to put up posters around the cities of Bulgaria and Romania, with attractive pictures of Spain and Italy, and with the railway timetable details, to encourage their citizens to go to these countries rather than the UK! Warming to the theme, I added, 'How about some posters about the UK too, saying: "Dreadful food, awful weather: give Britain a miss in 2014!"'

I'm not sure Oliver saw the joke, because he turned to his private secretary and said: 'Hmmm. Very interesting. These are the type of ideas we really ought to be taking up with the No. 10 "Nudge" Unit, which has been set up to prompt behavioural change!'

Before I left for Eastleigh, I had a meeting with Dom Cummings. There's been some fairly mad plan in DfE for some time now to reclassify academies as private sector organisations. This is allegedly to help them to borrow money, but I suspect there's a wider agenda here. I said to Dom that I thought this hadn't any hope of getting Lib Dem support, particularly as it would be seen to be 'privatising' education, and would cause a backlash against the important reforms that were already taking place.

THURSDAY 14 FEBRUARY

The latest copy of the left-wing Lib Dem magazine *Liberator* has the headline: 'Laws to write next general election manifesto'. The subtitle underneath says: 'But for which party?'

Went over to the Home Office. We were quickly shown through into the Home Secretary's office. I have to say that I rather like Theresa May. It's quite difficult to make her out, because at times she can seem quite stern and right-wing, but she was, of course, the Conservative who accused the Conservative Party of being 'the nasty party'.

Theresa showed me to the sofa area in her office, and asked me about my new role in the Cabinet Office. She listened very carefully to what I said my interests were on immigration, and she's obviously a bit wary of having a Liberal Democrat involved in this territory. When I told her about some of my constituency cases and my lack of confidence that the UK Border Agency would ever take any action against those people identified as overstaying in the country, she raised her eyes and looked at her officials in a knowing way.

Theresa is also a leading government advocate on women's issues, and she asked me whether there is anything I could do to try to get sex education into the national curriculum. She thinks that it's quite important for girls in particular, but she is well aware that PSHE is one of the things that Michael Gove hates and is determined to bury. Ironically, I might find some common ground with her on this!

MONDAY 18 FEBRUARY

At 8.30 a.m. I had a meeting with Sir Bob Kerslake, head of the Home Civil Service, and Permanent Secretary at DCLG. Bob raised Francis Maude's plans to 'politicise' the civil service. He probably knows that the Lib Dems are not very attracted to it.

We also discussed the proposed mid-term review package on housing. I pressed him on the issue of 'garden cities', which are important to Nick Clegg. Apparently Eric Pickles's view is that he doesn't mind the garden city concept provided this is a 'bottom-up' proposal from local areas. Sir Bob referred to the Treasury's enthusiasm, which he acknowledged seemed to be based very heavily on George Osborne's desire to impose large garden cities in two particular constituencies – one of which is the constituency of Nadine Dorries, the Conservative MP, who referred to David Cameron and George Osborne as 'two posh boys who don't know the price of milk'. George's other proposal is to put a large, sprawling garden city in the constituency of John Bercow, the Speaker, who is absolutely despised by both Cameron and Osborne!

WEDNESDAY 20 FEBRUARY

Started the day in Eastleigh, at the by-election. We have a well-organised local party, a good solid local candidate, and a Tory opponent who is both right-wing and obligingly gaffe prone.

The only bad news was the possibility of a verdict in the Vicky Pryce/Chris Huhne trial. This afternoon, the trial collapsed in a complete and utter farce, with the judge dismissing the jury and ordering a retrial.

The jury had sent the judge a list of ten questions. One asked the judge 'how he would define a reasonable doubt', prompting the judge to reply: 'A reasonable doubt is a doubt which is reasonable.'

The jury also asked, 'Can a juror come to a verdict based on a reason that was not presented in court and has no facts or evidence to support it?'

Mr Justice Sweeney, the judge, said he had 'never come across' anything like it in thirty years in the criminal courts.

FRIDAY 22 FEBRUARY

Channel 4 News yesterday ran their 'exclusive' about Chris Rennard, the former party chief executive. This accuses him of inappropriate advances on a number of female Lib Dems.

SATURDAY 23 FEBRUARY

Britain has lost its triple-A credit rating. A lot more pressure on the Chancellor in the run-up to his Budget.

SUNDAY 24 FEBRUARY

Two boxes full of work. Rather disturbing to read about the 'Wave Four 2014 free school applications' – some of these have failed on the basis of input from the 'counter-extremism division' within the DfE!

One of the applications is for a school based on 'transcendental meditation and the science of creative intelligence'. Apparently they have an existing free school which is struggling.

I spent half of Sunday morning on a DfE paper about a new skill test for prospective teachers. We're bringing in new maths, English and reasoning tests, but the problem is that the last time these were looked at, it turned out that some of the questions were flawed and unanswerable, and others were taken by Michael Gove, who failed to get them right!

The officials have come back with new papers, which I decided to try.

Some of the punctuation section questions were complete gobbledegook, and on the reasoning tests I got a number of the questions wrong, got very irritated with the answers, and concluded these are wrong! The tests cost £5.2 million, and based on this morning I'm not going to agree them.

I was heading back to London when Nick Clegg put out a statement clarifying what he knew about the Rennard allegations. He has had to acknowledge that he was aware of the broad allegations back in 2008 and asked Danny Alexander, who was then his chief of staff, to investigate.

MONDAY 25 FEBRUARY

Woke up today to an email from Olly Grender at 6.25 a.m. It said simply: 'Argggghhhhhh!' The press is absolutely ghastly today. Rennard, Clegg, Huhne, Eastleigh.

When I went through my box this evening, I found a packet of red liquorice 'laces', which had obviously been inserted by my DfE private office! I mentioned to them on Wednesday my fondness for red liquorice. Very thoughtful.

TUESDAY 26 FEBRUARY

9.15 a.m. Cabinet. Saw Nick Clegg for the first time since last week. He looked very pale and tired, and unusually didn't say much for most of the meeting.

At 2 p.m. to Nick's office for Budget Quad preparation. Danny described how this Budget is going to be a difficult one, with growth still stalled and borrowing higher than forecast. He said that there was very little money around etc. At 4 p.m. we met again over in the House of Commons. Nick looked pretty wiped out and I understand that he hasn't managed to clear his red boxes for the last two nights because of the volume of calls to do with the Rennard situation. Nick sounded pretty bitter about the press, and clearly feels they've turned up the volume massively because it's him and because of Leveson, and of course because of the Eastleigh by-election.

WEDNESDAY 27 FEBRUARY

Attended a meeting with Paddy Ashdown, Nick Clegg and his core team in Portcullis House. The assessment was that the Eastleigh by-election could go any way – either to us or to the Tories or to UKIP. If we lose the by-election, Nick will go down to Eastleigh and be seen to be confronting the issue of our defeat. Frankly, I still think we'll probably squeak home, not least because many postal votes will have been cast before the Rennard storm, but it may well be quite close.

A quick chat with the brilliant Tim Leunig about the new tests for teachers. Tim has attempted some of the questions and also asked the Permanent Secretary to do so. Both of them got a number of the questions wrong! And Tim is an LSE professor!

THURSDAY 28 FEBRUARY

At 2.30, had a meeting with officials about the new skills tests. I challenged them on whether we can reduce the £5.2 million cost, and they eventually acknowledged we could cut this in half. The danger as a minister is that you often spend ages quibbling about the cost of a £20,000 survey, and then suddenly you get a proposal to spend £50 million on something and you wave it through in five minutes. Today I had a meeting with officials about another proposed scheme that could have cost £20 million, and we agreed that it was a bad idea and canned the whole thing. That one decision saved over 50p per taxpayer per year.

I also challenged the quality of the tests. Eventually, I decided that we would axe the reasoning and logic tests.

The whole thing wasn't inspiring, as one assumes these tests have been thought out in great detail and tested in all sorts of ways rather than ministers having to take them in their spare time over a weekend! However, for a half an hour meeting this was quite productive. Getting rid of the logic and reasoning tests will save about half a million pounds a year in perpetuity.

FRIDAY 1 MARCH

Stayed up to see the Eastleigh by-election results. These came in at around 2 a.m. and we'd won by almost 2,000 votes, with the Tories driven into third place by UKIP. A bloody good night, and a massive relief, after what has been an absolutely nightmarish week. Nick is elated but furious with parts of the media.

MONDAY 4 MARCH

Monday ministerial meeting, chaired by Michael Gove. The whip said to Michael that after recent Commons revolts, it was hoped that Cabinet ministers would pay more attention to Conservative backbench MPs, and go on some constituency visits to make backbenchers 'more amenable'. Michael looked dubious: 'I think they road-tested appeasement in 1938. I recall it wasn't a great success!'

In the evening, to an event at 11 Downing Street which was hosted by Frances Osborne, the Chancellor's wife. This was with Henry Winkler, aka The Fonz from *Happy Days*. Nick Clegg looked jealous when I told him later.

TUESDAY 5 MARCH

Vince Cable is proposing to write for the *New Statesman*, making the case for more capital expenditure. Cameron is again pushing Nick to sack or move Vince.

The Cabinet had a pretty thin agenda. On the Justice and Security Bill, Ken Clarke said he was 'really pleased to have got the amendments through before the Liberal Assembly this weekend'. Somebody pointed out there hasn't been a Liberal Assembly for twenty-five years.

At the end, a discussion about the situation in Iran. Obama is clearly not keen on Israeli action against Iran's nuclear facilities, and is inclined to make a 'big offer' to Iran to try to get them to move to a non-nuclear stance.

WEDNESDAY 6 MARCH

There are stories in today's newspapers about Philip Hammond and Theresa May being potential Tory leadership candidates, or even forming a pact to put themselves forward as a leadership team. I find that very unlikely, as both of them are dry as anything, and dull as ditchwater. It would be very difficult to imagine them as any kind of 'dream team'.

It is interesting that we've now got rumours about Philip Hammond, Iain Duncan Smith and Theresa May all having bad relations with Cameron.

Today, attended the Joint Ministerial Committee (Domestic), which is basically a Cabinet committee of UK ministers and ministers from the devolved administrations of Scotland, Northern Ireland and Wales. That ghastly SNP woman, Nicola Sturgeon, who I think is Deputy First Minister or something, turned up fifteen minutes late. She was somewhere else in the building, but obviously didn't think it was sufficiently important to turn up on time. A cold and unattractive character.

The next meeting was the crucial Home Affairs Committee meeting. All of the focus was on immigration. There were three papers: one on migrants' access to benefits and public services, one on biometric residence permits, and one on the communications planning for the lifting of transitional controls on A2 countries – Bulgaria and Romania.

Nick Clegg invited Theresa May to open the discussion and then Ken Clarke came in as the most sceptical person in the room.

Ken was pretty critical and said that the worst thing would be to over-hype all of the problems and then discover we couldn't implement changes because of legal constraints.

Ken said – in his rather overdramatic way: 'The number of Bulgarians and Romanians who actually come to the country for benefit purposes will be unlikely to run into even three figures.' Chris Grayling and Philip Hammond snorted their disagreement.

I was also blunt and warned there is a serious risk that we were going to over-hype all of the problems and then launch a series of half-baked solutions. I said that if we did, this would only help UKIP. I also pointed out that there was a major problem that if we were going to try to find out more about illegal immigrants in this country, then the question was what we were doing to fix things. A recent Implementation Unit report states that there are 620,000 illegal immigrants in the country, and apparently while there are about 40,000 to 45,000 illegals leaving each year, there are about 67,000 new cases that are coming in. In other words, the stock of illegal migrants seems to be going up over time rather than down. I said there was no point in people reporting in illegal migrants to the UK Border Agency if they were not going to do anything about it – we had to urgently improve enforcement.

Later, I went to Nick Clegg's office in Dover House, to meet with Danny and Nick ahead of a Budget Quad.

At Tuesday's Quad, the Chancellor had presented his latest scorecard. He is suddenly proposing a 1p cut in income tax in 2015/16, costing £4.5 billion per annum! He is also suggesting additional cuts to total managed expenditure to pay for the tax cut and fill the previous £5 billion gap in last week's scorecard. Last week's scorecard apparently had the cancellation of the fuel duty increase and an increase in the personal allowance to £10,000. George also wants a cut in corporation tax to 20p.

The Tories look as if they are in a panic after Eastleigh. No doubt Osborne and Cameron are desperate to have a 1p reduction in income tax, which would end up being a dividing line issue with Labour – a trap which would be sprung around general election time. The whole thing is completely ridiculous.

Post-Quad. Nick and his team looked slightly shell-shocked. Both Jonny Oates and I took the strong view that having a Budget where there was a small increase in the personal income tax allowance to £10,000, but accompanied by three very clear Tory things – a 1 per cent cut in corporation tax, a 1 per cent cut in income tax, and a freeze in petrol duties – would not be a good position to end up in.

Danny then sat back in his chair and in a rather relaxed way suddenly said, 'Actually, the thing that I'm slightly more worried about is the proposal to cut the National Health Service budget in order to fund the income tax reduction.' At this, my mouth fell completely open. For about two seconds I thought it must be a joke. Protecting the NHS budget is a key coalition and Tory commitment, and I could not believe that this was seriously being considered.

I said I was 'absolutely gobsmacked' by this proposition and thought it was completely politically and economically mad. The idea that we could then just lop £1.7 billion off NHS spending without anybody noticing or complaining was extraordinary.

THURSDAY 7 MARCH

Vince Cable has published an article in the *New Statesman*: 'When the facts change, should I change my mind?' It's a very well-argued case for a fiscal boost. Needless to say, it doesn't have anything about saving money, so it's totally unsellable to the Tories. By advertising his views so publicly in this way, Vince is making it impossible to change the Chancellor's mind.

I've just seen the emergency motions for the Lib Dem spring conference. The first motion is entitled 'Kick-Starting the Economy'. If this hasn't been written by Lord Oakeshott, Vince's representative on Earth, then I'm a banana. It's short, concise Vince-onomics. The *New Statesman* article and this motion are clearly an organised attempt to change economic policy, and perhaps undermine Nick's leadership.

Emailed Nick my views on the Budget negotiations: 'George's proposal to reduce income tax, funded by a cut to the NHS budget, is the most idiotic and dangerous suggestion anyone has made since the government was formed.'

Had some feedback tonight from the Tories on the 'Freedoms' package in the mid-term review. There is a proposal to allow 'wild swimming' in any river. Apparently Cameron is very concerned that this will get in the way of people fishing! He's also worried about the proposals to allow much more open access to the countryside: 'It will upset landowners.' So much for modern, compassionate Conservatism!

FRIDAY 8 MARCH

Left London for our Brighton conference. When I arrived, Nick had emailed me: 'Osborne has dropped his basic rate income tax cut. He's agreed not to do unfunded tax cuts. He's scaled back on the unspecified future cuts. He's agreed that a corporation tax cut would go no further than 20p.' Thank God.

Nick went on: 'The conference motion is drafted by Matthew Oakeshott. The whole thing was orchestrated by him. We've got a plan to avoid defeat – fingers crossed.'

SATURDAY 9 MARCH

Spoke to Nick. He said that clearly things are on a knife-edge re. Vince and he is 'seriously pissed off at Vince's attempt to bounce us into a full-blown change of strategy on the back of a *New Statesman* article and a cobbled-together emergency motion'.

I've now discovered what the strategy is for dealing with the economy motion. There are many competing emergency motions at this party conference, and generally speaking only two of these can be taken. Some sensible person in Nick's office has managed to persuade the Federal Conference Committee that if the economy motion is taken then, it's so big that it would require an entire hour. This means that unless the economy motion comes top of the emergency ballot, then it will fall. As there is a very critical emergency motion on 'secret courts', the party leadership seems to think there is every prospect of kicking Vince's motion into touch. Loyalists have even been asked to vote for the secret courts motion!

In the meantime, Danny has phoned up Sharon Bowles, who has proposed the economy motion. She admitted that Matthew Oakeshott had asked her to do this and she 'didn't realise' how significant it was.

The results of the emergency ballot came out later on in the afternoon, and the plan worked perfectly. Secret courts topped the ballot and second place was the economy. I have no doubt at all that if the economy motion had been debated there would have been a massive split in the party, and I think that motion would have passed.

SUNDAY 10 MARCH

Before Nick's conference speech, I met up with Danny. The OBR have made their final fiscal forecasts, and they're pretty awful.

Danny started to talk about further caps in public sector pay, further increases in the state pension age, and even another increase in VAT. That really would kill the government and the economy stone dead!

MONDAY 11 MARCH

'How are the mighty fallen!' My Latin teacher, Mr Mitchell, used to recite this phrase whenever any 'smart' pupil failed to translate accurately. In Chris Huhne's case, the fall is rather greater. Ten years ago tomorrow he drove past a speed camera late at night at 69 mph, when the speed limit was 50mph. It must have seemed like an irritation when the speed camera went off, particularly as he had nine points on his licence. But he can never have imagined the ghastly chain of events that would have begun some eight years later. Now, this freezing day dawns with every prospect that Chris and his former wife Vicky will be sentenced to prison.

In the middle of a DfE meeting, the results from the Huhne/Pryce trials came through. Chris and Vicky have both been given eight-month prison sentences. The slow-motion car crash of this personal and political tragedy has finally come to an end. Truly awful.

WEDNESDAY 13 MARCH

Apparently the Tories have now got completely cold feet on their road privatisation/charging plan. What does it say for the Prime Minister that a few months ago this was his major 'ask' from the mid-term review?

The newspapers are also full of an apparent U-turn by Cameron on increasing the minimum price of alcohol. As far as I'm concerned, this U-turn is well overdue. However, it makes Cameron look weak, as he has been the champion of the policy and he has had to back down in the face of resistance from Michael Gove, Andrew Lansley and Theresa May. It's all a bit of a shambles.

THURSDAY 14 MARCH

11.30 a.m. A meeting at the DWP, with Iain Duncan Smith and 'Child Poverty Ministers'. It now looks as if we are going to come up with three child poverty measures – focusing on relative incomes, entrenched poverty and life chances. Oliver Letwin started to go on about how complicated the new measures were going to be and how we were going into this 'helter-skelter'. I interrupted and said it was hardly helter-skelter to suggest new measures that would take four years to introduce.

TUESDAY 19 MARCH

At 8 a.m. Philippa Stroud, Iain Duncan Smith's special adviser, came to see me for her regular fortnightly meeting. Philippa is a tall, leggy, bright, posh blonde who is very open and pleasant and actually seems surprisingly passionate about the social justice agenda – with a definite Tory tinge. I like her and we've struck up quite a good relationship and can talk bluntly to each other.

WEDNESDAY 20 MARCH

Budget Day. The Cabinet gathered at the unusually early hour of 8 a.m. A palpable sense of excitement. George spent quite a lot of time talking the Budget proposals through. He's reducing corporation tax to 20 per cent, the lowest rate in the G20. He's delivering the Lib Dem policy of a £10,000 personal tax allowance (hurrah!), cancelling increases in beer and fuel duty, and introducing a new allowance to reduce employer national insurance contributions.

How has he managed to do all this with a yawning Budget deficit? Well, there's the usual tax avoidance stuff. There's a small reduction in departmental expenditure. And he has also brought forward the introduction of the single-tier pension, which involves a large tax rise on public sector workers, by getting rid of the contracted-out national insurance rebates. In other words, the Chancellor has brought forward tax increases to deliver tax cuts!

George has now announced that current expenditure will be cut by £11.5 billion in 2015/16, so there will be a tough spending round.

Vince said that while there were good things in the package, he really didn't understand why we weren't doing more on capital expenditure. He said that he was now supported in this view by 'Trots' such as *The Economist*, Goldman Sachs, the City, the IMF…' Vince also said that he thought it was going to be very difficult to deliver the departmental expenditure cuts. He finished by saying that although he had all these concerns, he 'would of course be very supportive in public'. This might be regarded either as loyalty or as having your cake and eating it.

Philip Hammond was more positive – he said the Chancellor should be praised for 'finding a few odd bones and cans of soup in the back of the cupboard and turning them into rather an impressive dish'. That was the general view.

THURSDAY 21 MARCH

Going through my box this morning, there is a private note from one of the advisers in Downing Street, talking about the deterioration of A&E performance.

Ten per cent of people are now waiting more than four hours to get into A&E – which is a hell of a long time if you are in pain. There is also a problem with the NHS 111 service. It is likely that a patient in Kent died because their carer was not able to get through to the 111 service for twenty-four hours. As the note says, this could 'shake the public confidence in the new system'. Thank goodness we managed to nail the dotty idea of the Chancellor taking money out of the National Health Service in this month's Budget.

TUESDAY 26 MARCH

The last meeting of the Cabinet before the Easter recess. A discussion about the Home Office growth strategy, with a presentation by Theresa May.

As ever, various people launched into the discussion to criticise the existing situation on issuance of British visas to Chinese citizens. Osborne said that the situation was still 'hopeless' and that Chinese businessmen constantly complained to him about their inability to get visas. Apparently there was some bigwig Chinese businessman who was coming into the UK a couple of weeks ago to sign off on a £1.2 billion contract, but he couldn't get in! Another billionaire was strip-searched at Heathrow!

Danny, Vince and others all piled in to make the same criticism. Theresa May looked defensive and grumpy.

Lord Hill, Leader of the Lords, said he had 'good news to report from the Eastern Front'. Clearly he is becoming more skilled at managing the House of Lords.

Swapped a couple of emails with Nick over the PM's immigration speech. I said we need to persuade Cameron that endlessly launching half-baked proposals before they are seriously ready will do neither the government nor the Conservative Party any good. Nick replied 'You are quite right, of course, but Cameron is acting in an increasingly desperate way to placate his right. I think he knows it, but can't quite help himself.'

WEDNESDAY 27 MARCH

Spent the day in the constituency, canvassing for the local elections. The weather is still bitingly cold – probably the coldest March since 1962.

At four o'clock I called in to the headquarters of the Primary Care Trust in Yeovil. All the PCTs come to an end this Friday – as a consequence of the 2010 NHS reforms. The HQ was in turmoil, with people packing up their belongings in boxes.

I've no doubt that this is one of the worst mistakes the coalition government has made. The senior people in the coalition were occupied with other issues and didn't really understand what Lansley was doing. Crazy.

THURSDAY 28 MARCH

Left on the 6.20 a.m. plane from Gatwick to Nice. Went out for lunch, then fell asleep in the afternoon. My mind is clearly still on work, as I dreamt about 'pupil premium accountability measures' and, in the usual bizarre way of dreams, Nick Clegg suddenly turned up and started cooking burgers for his sons! What this means in terms of dream analysis, goodness knows.

I'm trying to sort out the primary school accountability and assessment consultation document. There's a dispute over whether we need a baseline assessment when children come into primary school – Liz Truss was being very difficult about this.

Dom has now circulated within the DfE a pithy, non-civil-service, Cummings email:

Liz Truss does now support replacing EYFS [Early Years Foundation Stage Profile] with an off-the-shelf alternative like Durham [baseline test]. MG agrees with this in principle. Neither of them support adding another test without whacking EYFS and neither supports the DfE trying to create a new test of its own, so ... MG's view is – before officials do any work on this David L needs to discuss EYFS with Clegg. If Clegg = happy to whack it and replace with off-shelf, hurrah and we can get on with it. If Clegg = not happy, then let's forget the whole thing immediately and never think about it again. It's unclear where the confusion has come from and Liz is confused about DL's views of her views – but hopefully this clarifies things and the ball is now in DL's court vis Clegg...

So that's clear.

SUNDAY 7 APRIL

George Osborne has spent the past few days using a particularly unpleasant case to argue for benefit cuts. A couple of adults were imprisoned for faking a fire which went wrong and which led to the deaths of their six children. It really was a most hideous case, and the person concerned turned out to be living on benefits with vast numbers of children. Osborne has used this as a flagship case to justify cuts. Nasty politics.

MONDAY 8 APRIL

On the way back into London yesterday, James said to me that one of his contacts had recently seen Lady Thatcher, and apparently reported that she looked in 'robust good health'. It came as a bit of a shock, then, that at just after midday one of my private secretaries came in to announce that she had just died!

Met with some of Nick Clegg's special advisers to talk about the Communications Data Bill. This is basically Theresa May's 'Snoopers' Charter'. It was kicked into touch last year after a very critical parliamentary report, but the Home Office is trying to breathe life into it. The Bill is pretty toxic for the Lib Dems. At the end of a 45-minute discussion, we basically all agreed to advise Nick to veto it.

TUESDAY 9 APRIL

I have very mixed sentiments about Lady Thatcher's demise. She is undoubtedly going to be remembered as one of the great Prime Ministers. Unfortunately, it's difficult to escape from the less attractive side of her character – a lack of sympathy for the underdogs in society and those who suffered in the recession at the beginning of the 1980s. She was generally on the side of the rich, the successful and the aspiring – while her record on black rights in South Africa, the Section 28 legislation, and particularly on social justice issues such as education, the Health Service and poverty is not a good one.

THURSDAY 11 APRIL

The Treasury Spending Review letter arrived at DfE today. They're asking for a £2.5 billion cut in our budget – much more than we had been expecting.

MONDAY 15 APRIL

Spent Sunday and Monday looking at the Spending Review papers from the Treasury. These are based on the assumption that the schools budget will be protected in real terms, while all other budgets will decline by 10 per cent.

At 3.30 p.m. we had a DfE ministerial meeting. Lord Nash said he thought we should strongly oppose the settlement – we were the most successful department in government and deserved a good settlement. I spoke strongly in favour of the schools protection. I said I thought the overall budget settlement for the DfE was too harsh.

Michael said that he was minded to try to be a 'good boy'. He felt that we ought to seek to demonstrate whether we could deliver the spending cuts, and then basically show so many 'bloody stumps' that the PM and DPM would decide they didn't want to accept the cuts.

Whether that's a sensible view, I don't know – my instinct is that it probably isn't. This is a battle that I'm going to have to fight in alliance with Nick to make sure that education remains a priority. I can see a tough battle ahead.

TUESDAY 16 APRIL

Cabinet at 9.30 a.m. The agenda today was pretty full, with discussions about Lady Thatcher's funeral, the economy, and a valedictory presentation from the director general of MI5, Sir Jonathan Evans.

On the funeral, Francis Maude expressed some frustration about St Paul's Cathedral. Apparently they don't know how many chairs they have, which is making it rather difficult to decide how many people can be invited!

When we came to the economy, George Osborne said that it was a close call as to whether next week's GDP numbers would show growth or not – clearly if they don't it will be a blow, as we will then be defined as being in a triple-dip recession. George clutched at a few straws, including that 'household incomes have grown over the last year at the fastest rate for around seven years'. After a short pause for thought, Nick Clegg asked: 'Actually, why did household incomes grow last year so rapidly?' Osborne, with a smile and not a little embarrassment, then confessed that the increase had been driven by the government's decision to index pensions and benefits by the full inflation rate of 5.2 per cent. Nick and I laughed. George was a strong opponent of the 5.2 per cent uprating, and this only happened because Nick and I insisted.

The Prime Minister then said that he'd spoken to Mervyn King, who said that 'if you ignore the decline in North Sea Oil output and ignore the decline in construction output, then actually the economy had been growing over the last year'. It is certainly true that if you ignore all the things that are declining, you end up being left with the things that are rising, but this doesn't seem too comforting.

Sir Jonathan Evans estimated that there are around 2,000–3,000 Al Qaeda sympathisers in the UK whom the security services have to keep an eye on. An enormous task.

WEDNESDAY 17 APRIL

Lady Thatcher's funeral. It was interesting to see all the big figures from the past – Lord Howe, whose killer speech had signalled the end of Mrs Thatcher's career, and Michael Heseltine. There was also Lech Wałęsa, the former Polish President, who was the leader of the Solidarity trade union in the early 1980s.

An interminable wait for the service to start. Then, the chiming of the bells and the noise from outside the cathedral that signalled the arrival of the coffin.

The service wasn't emotional or personal, with no speeches from any family members and only a well-judged address from the Bishop of London. Only one element of emotion intruded upon the event, which was when the coffin was carried out at the very end and one could hear very clearly the loud applause from people who were gathered outside the cathedral. It must have been rather like the moment at the funeral of Princess Diana when the noise and cheers of the crowds from outside intruded.

SUNDAY 21 APRIL

I spent the entire day working at home to clear my (record) three red boxes – about eight and a half hours in total.

MONDAY 22 APRIL

Apparently, David Cameron wants to support Steel's Bill on Lords' reform, including a scheme to encourage Lords to 'retire'. This is apparently the only reform that has a chance of being voted through, as with the influx of new peers there are now lots of complaints about how crowded the Lords' Tea Room is!

TUESDAY 23 APRIL

At 9 a.m. went to see Nick Clegg to discuss the Spending Review. He was sitting at his desk clearing paperwork, with his glasses on. He ushered me in and I closed the door. I asked him how he was, and to my surprise he replied, 'Actually, since you've asked, not that well really. It just feels like quite a wearying and difficult period. If the first quarter GDP numbers are bad, then obviously we're back in a triple-dip recession and that's going to be incredibly difficult and there'll be rows later on this year about economic policy at our conference. The local elections still look very challenging, and when I go round the country and talk to party members, they are unhappy about all the things we have to do in government and never focusing on the big picture of what we're achieving. On top of that, there's the constant wearying process of dealing with the Conservatives and Cameron in particular.'

I asked whether he had yet discussed the issue of the Communications Bill with Cameron. 'Yes, I talked with Cameron over the weekend. Predictably, he went totally bonkers and has asked for more time – he was extremely difficult. I have to say that I'm finding it increasingly difficult to deal with

Cameron, who I have rather lost respect for. He's extremely petulant and difficult over issues like this, and utterly shallow in his engagement with policy. Funnily enough, I have more time for George Osborne, who may be an arch-Tory but who at least goes out of his way to understand other people in politics and the way they see things. Cameron is not like that at all. He's thinks he can bully people into things in a rather unattractive way.'

We then discussed the education settlement. I said of the £2.5 billion cuts proposed, we could probably make about half relatively painlessly. But if we have to deliver more, either we would have to cut the two-year-old education/childcare offer for disadvantaged youngsters that he was personally responsible for securing, or we'd have to give up the real protection on the schools budget. I said that the only other alternative was to make massive cuts in 16–19 education, which would undermine sixth forms and colleges.

Nick said, 'I'm more worried about education being cut than almost any other area. I won't go back on our pledge over the two-year offer, and I agree that we shouldn't undermine the schools protection.' Useful.

Cabinet. IDS made a presentation on Universal Credit implementation. He tries to sound incredibly informed, but one gets the impression that the depth of knowledge isn't there, and that if he was to be grilled intensively, it would all fall to pieces in five seconds.

Nick didn't contribute very much, and I noticed that he had his eyes down for most of the Cabinet meeting, not engaging at all with Cameron, and with a rather bad vibe between them. Normally he is very positive and engaged.

We then moved on to a discussion about the terrible situation in Syria, where the loyalist forces are using heavy weapons to blow up the rebels. This is enabling terrorists to take hold, and the situation is deteriorating rapidly. Michael Gove leaned forward enthusiastically. He really does engage with foreign affairs. It is quite clear from this what his dream job would be.

Essentially, William Hague was making the case for a much more activist approach in Syria, and he was supported by Michael and the PM, who is clearly gagging to deploy more military forces. Philip Hammond was a cautionary voice, noting that Syria has one of the most impressive air forces in the Middle East.

To my surprise, Patrick McLoughlin, the Transport Secretary, chipped in at the end to caution against UK involvement: 'The public doesn't believe the

UK should be involved in every single war. Will it be seen by the public as yet another foreign intervention that will cost us money and potentially lives?'

A striking intervention, as it was clearly so unwelcome to David Cameron, who looked rather disdainful. Patrick has nonetheless demonstrated a streak of independence that I didn't think he had.

WEDNESDAY 24 APRIL

Received today a copy of Michael Gove's views on the feedback received from the DfE consultation on the national curriculum. Unusually, I have been sent the note MG received, with his written annotations.

As I read through, I could sense his levels of frustration rising.

On page three, he was already asking, 'Does anyone actually make any constructive suggestions?'

By page four, he was commenting on the 'soft bigotry of low expectations'.

On a section about consultees wanting additional funding to implement the changes, he wrote: 'The story of the vested interest throughout the ages.'

Against a paragraph on the English curriculum, recording a 'desire for reference to media and multimodal text to be included', he had written the single word 'Rubbish', underlined four times.

Under 'Geography', a suggestion for the inclusion of weather and climate change met with the refrain 'Ignore.'

The foreign languages section included reference to 'vocal campaigns for the inclusion of Hebrew and Japanese', prompting the single word 'No.' Next to a suggestion about the need for 'intercultural understanding' was the single word 'Never', and under a bullet point about there being 'some support for a multilingual "carousel" approach' was the comment 'Absolutely not!!!!' underlined five times.

The citizenship section noted support for the inclusion of volunteering and for 'more explicit references to teaching about human rights' ... 'No.'

On mathematics, 'The main concern continues to be that draft content is too challenging.' ... 'Hardly.'

Under the feedback against art and design: 'Very depressing.'

More on animal welfare in the primary curriculum: 'No!!!'

Michael is not a person with weakly held views.

Home Affairs Committee in Conference Room A. This is the most interesting committee of government, since there are real debates that take place in it. It's chaired by Nick Clegg, and includes all the big beasts of the Cabinet, with the exception of the Foreign Secretary.

We discussed a controversial proposal from the Home Secretary to increase the minimum tariff for murdering a police officer, from thirty years to an indefinite life sentence. There is no evidence that increasing the minimum tariff will make the police safer, and there are all sorts of concerns about singling out some groups and not others. The Home Office paper seems to admit the weakness of their case, saying it's all about 'sending a message'.

Ken Clarke didn't pull any punches. He said the whole thing was 'complete nonsense', would not save a single police life, and selecting certain categories of public servant as 'protected' and others as not would be 'ludicrous and laughable'. It would cause outrage amongst the judiciary, and since it was a sentencing guideline and not compulsory it would be widely ignored. Ken went on and on in the most uncompromising way, and I glanced round to the Home Secretary and saw that she was quietly fuming – looking completely daggers and very cheesed off. She was clearly even more upset when Ken finally finished his assault by describing her policy as 'the most appalling populist nonsense'!

The right-wing Tory Cabinet ministers sat looking glumly as Dominic Grieve also launched into the proposals. I then spoke to say that they had no credible policy foundation and we would end up with ludicrous injustices – so that killing police officers and public transport police would receive a tougher sanction than killing a firefighter or a British spy or a police community support officer or somebody from the Border Agency. It really is an insult to the intelligence.

I was then followed by a whole string of right-wing Tory Cabinet ministers who supported Theresa's plan. This right-wing voting bloc all sit on one side of the square-shaped table, facing Nick Clegg. In the middle are Theresa May and Chris Grayling, and to their left are Philip Hammond and Michael Gove. On Theresa's right are Iain Duncan Smith and Eric Pickles. Basically these are the hard men – and one woman – of the Conservative Party.

IDS perhaps gave the game away by saying that really there wasn't a persuasive policy reason for change but it would help to 'buy off the police', who were feeling pretty bruised at the current time.

Even Michael Gove trotted out a load of supportive twaddle. Worse still, Oliver Letwin then chimed in to support Theresa May's position. At least he had the decency to look embarrassed.

I was cheesed off with the whole thing, not least at the end when Theresa pretty much admitted that while police officer killings would attract a minimum life sentence you could shoot a police community support officer and they would get no minimum tariff at all. Barmy!

Later in the day, Nick reported back that he'd had a conversation with George Osborne and the Tories are furious about losing the Communications Data Bill. They are now saying they are willing to 'do' the restrictions on third-party campaigning, but in exchange for this 'Lib Dem policy' they want some anti-union legislation. I reminded Nick that the third-party campaigning proposal was actually George Osborne's idea. This is vintage Tory negotiating – claiming something as a Lib Dem 'win' which isn't, then asking for a Tory policy 'gain' to set against it.

Received a text message from Francis Maude, saying that the PM and DPM had agreed to take forward third-party campaigning, and that Francis and I need to work on a Bill.

THURSDAY 25 APRIL

At 9.30 a.m. meeting with Francis Maude. Francis occupies one of the biggest offices in government – the room once used by Michael Heseltine when he was DPM, and in which the coalition negotiations were held in May 2010.

Francis thinks Nick has agreed anti-union legislation with Cameron. He merely agreed to 'look at it'. I'm determined to ensure this goes nowhere. I suggested to Francis that he should draft a note for me on their priorities.

The first-quarter growth numbers came out at a better than expected +0.3 per cent. We've avoided a triple-dip recession – a massive relief.

SUNDAY 28 APRIL

The Queen's Speech has to be agreed on Tuesday, even though that is a full week before the 'Gracious Speech'. This is apparently because the speech is printed on vellum, and the ink takes a week to dry. We are under strict orders to avoid getting ink stains on the Queen's hands!

MONDAY 29 APRIL

A week ago, Michael Gove was saying he wanted to be helpful to the Treasury and offer them the full saving they were requesting of £2.5 billion. He soon changed his tune. He now wants to offer £1.1 billion, and even more amazingly he then wants the Treasury to give him back £400 million to use for the introduction of a national funding formula! Senior officials and I both agree that the Treasury will regard this as 'taking the piss'.

His latest proposals also involve a massive cut in early years education, and a block on the second-year roll-out of early years education for disadvantaged two-year-olds. He also wants to make a massive reduction in the Education Services Grant – money that goes to local councils to run their school departments. Meanwhile, he wants to protect his own pet academies programme from cuts.

Liz Truss is still ploughing ahead with her plans to allow nurseries to have much worse ratios of staff to children, even though the consultation showed this is mind-bogglingly unpopular. Julian Astle and Matt Sanders believe that we can accept higher childcare ratios for the older children, but not for under-twos. Liz is 'not for turning'.

At 4.30 p.m. I went to Francis Maude's massive office on the second floor of 70 Whitehall. Francis was supposed to have spent the weekend coming up with a shortlist of Tory proposals on trade union reform.

It soon became clear that he had not done his homework. He started in a rather aggressive way, saying, 'As you know, the Prime Minister and Nick Clegg have agreed to put a line in the Queen's Speech about trade union reform, and now we need to agree the broad details.'

'I don't think that's accurate. Nick has said that we're prepared to look at this, but we're not prepared to have some open-ended line in the Queen's Speech without any clear understanding of what the policies are.'

Francis was clearly angry, and asked me what policies I was proposing. I reminded him that he was supposed to have come up with a list. He said that he had not had a copy of the note on trade union reform that had been written by Danny Alexander and George Osborne last August until this Monday morning.

I replied: 'That's not my problem. I have the note and there's no reason your office couldn't have got hold of it.'

The whole thing was now quite frosty and aggressive, and for a moment I considered just walking out.

Francis then said that the only way we could proceed was to go through the list of the possible trade union reforms in the annexe to the note from George and Danny. Francis said, 'Of course a lot of the objections to reform are just a lot of nonsense from officials in the Business Department, who are themselves union sympathisers and union members. We really shouldn't take their objections seriously. We don't need a detailed agreement before the Queen's Speech. All we need is a line in the Queen's Speech saying that we will move ahead with trade union reform.'

I replied, 'No. If we have a line like that in the Queen's Speech, there will then be a huge amount of briefing from both sides about what it means and it will inevitably end up as a confused row. If we're going to do anything in this territory then we're going to have to have a clear agreement on it first.'

Francis then grabbed the policy list and started flicking through it. He listed a variety of apparently randomly selected proposals, including: enhancing the regulatory powers to investigate union membership list discrepancies; imposing an annual audit of union membership; requiring unions to provide evidence of how they would store and monitor membership data; requiring that the voting paper on a strike specify what action and on what dates action would be taken; a statutory requirement that notice to an employer of intention to ballot contains a statement of what is in dispute; limiting the overall lifetime of a strike mandate to three months; and increasing to fourteen days the notification period to the employer following a positive ballot.

I said that this didn't cover either of the two issues that the Prime Minister had actually discussed with Nick: a minimum service agreement for the public sector and allowance for private sector agency workers to cover for striking workers in schools. Francis said the first of these wasn't really workable and would take too long to sort out!

It's quite clear that the Tories aren't remotely serious about particular union reforms; all they wanted to do was a) have a fight with the trade unions and b) get a 'place-holder' in the Queen's Speech so that they could then ratchet in all sorts of much more extreme and difficult measures later.

I said I would discuss his ideas with Nick Clegg and Vince Cable. He grunted his assent. As my private secretary and I descended the stairs to my office, I muttered: 'After that bloody meeting, I'm killing this nonsense stone dead!'

Later on we had a conference call with Nick and Danny. Nick said that Cameron was so furious about the Communications Data issue that he was threatening to call in the head of MI5 to give the Cabinet a security briefing on what the lack of the legislation would mean. Danny very sensibly said that this would be totally unacceptable.

I then came back to the issue of trade union reform. Danny was completely aligned with me on this, and he said that while he'd been prepared to consider this last year, he'd come to the inevitable conclusion that the Tories only wanted this in order to have a fight with the trade unions.

We agreed that the only sensible position was to have nothing in the Queen's Speech, though Nick then said the Tories would be very difficult over reform of lobbying and recall of MPs. Jonny Oates said, 'Well, if the Tories are going to do things like that, why don't we just withdraw our support for the Immigration Bill… Eventually we could just have no Queen's Speech whatsoever!'

In the evening, Nick and the PM had a very fractious call over union legislation and Osborne phoned Danny at 11 p.m. to say that the Tories were expecting a very difficult round of local elections and they 'needed some red meat on trade unions to throw to our troops'. Absurd!

TUESDAY 30 APRIL

Cabinet. A discussion about UK exports, led by Lord Greene. Ken Clarke poured cold water on figures showing large percentage rises to certain countries: 'We really mustn't be too excited – all we're seeing is an increase from pathetic levels to slightly less pathetic levels.'

There were lots of worthy, supportive contributions, then Michael Gove plunged in: 'I don't understand at all our plans to increase exports. This all appears to be about hiring additional bureaucrats in the Department for Business; I don't see how that's going to help. How is hiring an 'internet tsar' going to help the communications business; surely it's going to simply destroy it? There was also a lot of discussion about how ministers can aid exports, but my understanding is the Prime Minister recently had a trade visit to India, which was immediately followed by declining UK exports to India. Governments don't create exports. Businesses do.'

The Prime Minister smiled weakly, but he's clearly addicted to overseas visits and more 'strategies'.

WEDNESDAY I MAY

Breakfast with Oliver Letwin at 7.45 a.m. Oliver is particularly obsessed by examples of over-regulation, and we made the mistake of touching briefly on the planning regulations relating to protected wild animals. Oliver proceeded to ask how many pages of regulations we thought there were on the protection of dormice. I guessed at thirty-eight, but it turned out that there are fifty-five. Oliver started to laugh uncontrollably. Once he gets a joke, he laughs very loudly and in a very high-pitched and incessant way and goes on laughing for more than ten times as long as any normal person would.

The Quad. On the way there, Danny said he had received the spending letter from Michael Gove, offering less than one third of the savings requested. Danny said he's told the Treasury to send back a message saying that he is sure that the DfE must have sent through the wrong letter and could they now see the real one!

When we arrived in the Cabinet Room, it was empty. The Tories were clearly having a longer than normal pre-meeting. The doors to the back garden were open, and it was a beautiful sunny day. We went outside and chatted on the steps.

When the meeting started, Cameron accepted our decision not to have a Bill on union reform.

We then agreed the final Queen's Speech detail. Because we couldn't decide earlier whether to include legislation on third-party campaigning reform, we have apparently had to send off two versions of the Queen's Speech, which have both been printed up on vellum. Danny joked: 'Oh dear – due to coalition divisions, we've ended up having to slaughter two sheep when one would normally do!'

At the end, there was then a discussion about the economy, and George

Osborne mentioned that the IMF 'inspectors' would be over in mid-May to carry out their review of UK economic policy.

Rupert Harrison, the Chancellor's economic adviser, said that he thought the IMF could be persuaded to be 'mildly supportive' given the recent growth numbers. David Cameron looked sceptical, but said that we ought to do all we could to persuade the IMF to come up with a supportive assessment: 'Our best hope, George, may be to take the inspectors out for a nice dinner, then go on to some nightclubs, get them completely drunk, and take some compromising photos!'

THURSDAY 2 MAY

The media is full of stories about how UKIP is going to do well in today's elections. The contribution from Ken Clarke over the weekend, when he called UKIP supporters 'a bunch of clowns', hasn't helped.

FRIDAY 3 MAY

Yeovil. Awoken by a telephone call at 2.45 a.m. from our constituency organiser, James Ludley, who said the county council elections had been 'a bit grim' – we've lost two seats to the Tories and, astonishingly, two to UKIP.

Clearly what's happening is a lot of right-wing Tory supporters are voting UKIP, along with a lot of working-class voters – because UKIP represent the best protest against the current coalition government and are also anti-Europe and anti-immigrant.

I think that this will be a one-term wonder, and we'll get rid of UKIP in four years' time.

TUESDAY 7 MAY

The media is dominated today by an article in *The Times* by former Chancellor Nigel Lawson: 'I'll be voting to quit the EU.'

Significant, as it marks the point where voting to leave the EU enters the mainstream. Lawson's article is magnificently dismissive about Cameron's proposed renegotiation: 'I have no doubt that any changes that Mr Cameron – or, for that matter, Ed Miliband – is able to secure will be inconsequential.'

Cabinet. Boring. Pointless. I've discovered that these Cabinet meetings are really an excellent opportunity to get a lot of paperwork done in a quiet and undemanding setting. Every now and again it's important to glance up and look interested, in case anyone thinks that you aren't paying attention. By the end, I'd cleared about a foot of paperwork.

WEDNESDAY 8 MAY

Queen's Speech Day. We've somehow managed to insert 'My government wants to build a stronger economy … in a fairer society.' As this is the Lib Dem general election slogan, it does sound rather odd to hear the Queen saying it!

THURSDAY 9 MAY

The media is dominated by news about Nick Clegg blocking Liz Truss's childcare proposals. It's unclear who has leaked it, but it looks like the Tories.

Apparently No. 10 have gone crazy. Nick is also particularly angry because he had a meeting with Liz Truss on Tuesday, and apparently said to her that he wasn't happy with the proposals – but he wanted to give her time to come back with some amendments or further evidence. Liz apparently looked downcast, and her head fell and she simply stared at the desk and said nothing for a long period of time. She then went off and within a few hours had written a formal letter to Nick and the rest of the Home Affairs Committee proposing clearance for her existing policies. This is now going to turn into a big stand-off.

Michael Portillo has joined the attack on Cameron over his EU referendum ploy. Like Lord Lawson, he would leave the European Union. Particularly devastatingly, Portillo has said that the PM's promised referendum was a manoeuvre that would lead to 'minimal renegotiation and lacks conviction … You cannot imagine Margaret Thatcher approaching the issue in such an insincere and political way.' Ouch.

In the afternoon, had a DfE meeting with Liz Truss. She seemed pretty relaxed and I suspect that she's rather enjoying all the publicity over her clash with Nick. At the end, I asked the officials to leave. I said that Nick was very angry about what had happened, and he felt that Liz had acted in bad faith by sending her letter to the Home Affairs Committee.

Liz then told me – privately – that she discussed the result of the Clegg meeting with both the PM and Michael Gove. Both told her that she should just ignore Nick Clegg and write straight to the Home Affairs Committee. Extraordinary!

In the afternoon, I had a phone call from MG. Michael was his normal reasonable self, although he somehow forgot to mention his mischief-making on the Truss letter. When there are divisions and rows in the department, it is quite amusing, in that Michael Gove and I will talk to each other in the most civilised, polite and reasonable way, even while both of us are pulling strings desperately behind the scenes in order to get the outcomes we want. We both have sharp elbows but dislike open confrontation.

Nick Clegg told me later that he had spoken to Cameron about the leaks and briefings against him on both childcare ratios and Book Trust. He said he was blaming Michael, and in particular his adviser Dom Cummings – 'Get me the evidence on Cummings,' said Cameron, perking up. 'I would love to sack Cummings. Just get me the evidence.'

FRIDAY 10 MAY

Astonishingly, there is now going to be an amendment by Eurosceptic Tory MPs to the Queen's Speech, calling on the government to hold an immediate referendum on the EU! Even more amazingly, the briefing from the Tories is that they may allow ministers to vote for this amendment! Gobsmackingly, it now seems as if even Cameron may be willing to vote for the amendment – it must surely be unprecedented for a Prime Minister to amend his own Queen's Speech!

A lot of briefing in the media from unnamed Tory sources saying that Nick Clegg has 'stabbed the Tories in the back over childcare', and he 'can't be trusted on it, just as he couldn't be trusted on tuition fees and on a European referendum'. That is really going over the top, and there's no doubt that it will be regarded very bitterly by Nick. Liz's stuff on ratios is dead.

SUNDAY 12 MAY

I knew Michael Gove was going on the *Marr* programme this morning, but I didn't see his performance until around 1 p.m.

What I saw appalled me. Firstly, Michael apparently suggested that if there was a referendum on the EU, he would vote to leave, while at the same time suggesting that he supports the Prime Minister's policy on renegotiation. It's clear that the Tory splits on Europe are widening.

But far more shocking was a gratuitous attempt to attack and undermine Nick Clegg. MG was asked about Nick's resistance to the childcare proposals, and he went out of his way to say this was all about internal Lib Dem politics. When James Landale failed to pick this up, he then came back to it and alleged that Nick was blocking the childcare plan because he was worried about a leadership challenge from Vince Cable, which was being stoked up by Mathew Oakeshott!

I was so furious that I emailed him: 'I accept that you are not happy with the position on childcare ratios but I think it is a rather low blow to link it to leadership issues. D.'

Later I received what I can only take as a slightly tongue-in-cheek response:

> Dear David, I'm sorry that it's been taken amiss. I don't think that Vince has a strong opinion on ratios, as it happens. But I do think that he and his people are manoeuvring. And I also believe that I have to defend my ministers – all my ministers – when their positions are under attack.

MONDAY 13 MAY

11 a.m. Nick Clegg's office in Dover House for the government business meeting. Nick made clear childcare ratios is dead.

The next issue was Europe. It now seems that many Tories are going to vote in favour of the referendum amendment, with ministers ordered to abstain. Yesterday Philip Hammond, Michael Gove and Chris Grayling sent out anti-EU smoke signals. Cameron is in the United States today, talking to President Obama to help secure an EU–US trade deal! As Nick Clegg said: 'You really couldn't make this up! While Cameron's trying to sell an EU trade deal to the US, his fellow Cabinet ministers back home are rubbishing the entire basis of his European policy. No wonder he's so tetchy.'

Later on, Nick said that he wanted to throw a bit of a political grenade into the debate. He said he wondered whether we should do some contingency planning for an early general election: 'All our assumptions when we started this coalition have now proved to be false. Cameron is increasingly plunging off to the right, following his party, and I really wonder whether we would have gone into the coalition if we'd known what the Tories were going to be like, and if we'd known how right-wing they would become. I had a telephone call with Cameron yesterday and frankly as far as I'm concerned he's lost any credibility as Prime Minister of the United Kingdom. The way in which he discusses issues and the superficial way that he deals with important matters is just unbelievable.'

TUESDAY 14 MAY

In the evening, I went over to Paul Marshall's offices in the Adelphi Building in John Adam Street. Lots of wine and food, and a record attendance at this Coalition 2.0 dinner. Michael was there, along with Nick Boles, Matt Hancock and Amber Rudd. As well as Paul and me, there were Julian Astle, Tim Leunig, Norman Lamb and Jo Swinson. The discussion was all about coalition relations, and Nick Boles launched into an incredible attack on the childcare row. He said this was a sign that the Lib Dems had decided they wanted to go into coalition with Labour at the next election and it was all about political differentiation. I came back pretty robustly and said it was about policy and not political differentiation and I pointed out that the Conservative Party was hardly helping coalition relations given its position on the EU and the way that it was lurching off to the right.

Julian and I both made the case that the Conservative Party no longer looked like the party that we had gone into coalition with in 2010. Jo Swinson even told me later that Maria Miller was getting very wobbly about gay marriage, and is trying to prevent Jo Swinson from attending an EU summit on gay rights.

WEDNESDAY 15 MAY

In the evening, we had the votes on the Tory EU amendment to the Queen's Speech, and during one of these I had to go into the toilet on the lower ministerial corridor. While I was washing my hands, in came Tory MP Damian Green, who asked how the Lib Dems were going to be voting.

'We're going for the novel approach of supporting the government and the Queen,' I said. He looked embarrassed.

THURSDAY 16 MAY

Half the Tory backbenchers voted against the Queen's Speech in spite of the Prime Minister's hastily produced draft Referendum Bill. One hundred and sixteen Tory MPs, including thirteen ministerial aides, voted for the EU amendment, while all the rest of the Conservative parliamentary party abstained! Extraordinary! Overall, the Tory rebels were defeated by 277 votes to 131, with Labour and the Liberal Democrats uniting. It is interesting that Ed Miliband has stuck to his position on this and not gone for a referendum. It suggests that Ed is thinking about the realities of being in power, and the last thing he needs would be a referendum on Europe!

FRIDAY 17 MAY

Question marks are now being raised about the coalition's sustainability, and *The Times* leads today on a story about the Tories making contingency plans for an early end to the coalition.

That prime-time right-wing bozo Philip Hammond was on *Question Time* yesterday, throwing buckets of cold water over the proposals for same-sex marriage. He said that he doesn't understand why we're pursuing this at a time when there are so many other problems, of the economy, etc. etc. This is the normal old Tory right-wing tosh. What is astonishing is that he should directly contradict the position of the Prime Minister. Tory MPs of all types are clearly quite mutinous.

Had a discussion with officials about the votes next week on gay marriage. Apparently the Tories are now thinking of tabling an amendment saying that teachers would still be able to teach that they don't believe in gay marriage and that they're opposed to homosexuality. This is absurd, as the right to freedom of thought/speech is already contained in regulations, and all this would do would be to throw the right wing of the Tory Party a bone and imply that it's OK to spread bigoted and prejudiced views. I made clear that I was absolutely not willing to agree government support for such an amendment.

SUNDAY 19 MAY

Drove to Wembley for the League One play-off finals. Alastair Campbell was there with his children, checking out the opposition for next season.

An amazing game, with Yeovil going 1–0 up after just a few minutes and then scoring again towards the end of the half. Brentford came out with all guns blazing in the second half and got a quick goal, but we managed to hold them off for the rest of the match.

Incredible progress from the small semi-amateur team that I first knew back in 1999, to a club that's now in the Championship! A really happy and memorable day – one that I'll certainly remember from my time as Yeovil MP.

TUESDAY 21 MAY

In early to go through the GCSE English subject content before it goes out to consultation. Lots of feedback from Ofqual, including on a proposal from MG that people should be obliged to use 'the Queen's English' rather than the previous wording of 'standard English'. Apparently Ofqual have raised serious concerns about the use of a term that could give rise to 'a variety of interpretations'.

Michael is also suggesting that young children should learn about literary terminology, including 'synecdoche' and 'pathetic fallacy'. Tim Leunig has suggested that Michael 'seems determined to serve up a gift to the sketch-writers'!

9.30 a.m. Cabinet. We were supposed to be having an update from the 'Minister for International Security Strategy', whose name I've forgotten. He wasn't there at the appointed time, and the Prime Minister looked rather embarrassed and then had to go on to the next agenda item. Never seen anything like it.

The PM then closed the meeting and indicated that we would take a short break before starting the meeting of the Inter-Ministerial Group on Migrants' Access to Benefits and Public Services – which civil servants are calling the MATBAPS Group.

Cameron started the meeting by saying that he didn't want us to get 'lost in policy complexities', and we should 'explain your proposals as if you are describing them to people on the doorstep while out canvassing'. That's about the level at which Cameron is thinking about this issue.

IDS started on benefits, which went perfectly well. Jeremy Hunt then made quite a good pitch on health. We then went on to private landlords, where the Prime Minister frankly wants to go much further than Eric Pickles supports.

Eric wants to start off by targeting housing in multiple occupation, but he doesn't want to oblige smaller private landlords to take on responsibility for checking the immigration status of tenants. He's still worried that landlords might simply decide not to take on tenants who are foreign or who look foreign. It was soon clear that the Prime Minister's expectations far exceeded this compromise.

The Prime Minister kept pushing for a maximalist position, and Eric kept pushing back. Cameron was getting increasingly frustrated, and asked other ministers for their views. This didn't help him. Nobody supported his position other than Oliver Letwin, in a relatively limp way.

Vince Cable made a rather blunt contribution in which he said that if he was on the doorstep he'd be rather dismissive of 'people who come up with a whole lot of prejudiced twaddle about immigration' and he'd point out the benefits of immigration – a message the PM clearly didn't want to hear.

I wanted to come in to back up Nick and Vince's views, but I could see that the Prime Minister didn't like the idea of calling another Liberal Democrat, and he ignored me and looked down at the other end of the table, taking a couple of contributions from Tory junior ministers. However, to his evident frustration, they weren't backing his position either. He began to flush red and look harassed.

We only had forty-five minutes for the meeting, and now had little time for the education paper that I was due to present and a further paper from the Treasury.

But just as we were due to conclude the landlords discussion, Cameron suddenly banged closed his briefing folder and said, 'OK, end of meeting.' He then pushed back his chair and walked out of the Cabinet Room.

For a while, no one else moved. The officials looked embarrassed. People glanced at each other, aware that there were still two major agenda items. In government, no meeting ever finishes without the agenda being covered. As I went out of the room with Nick Clegg, he said, 'The problem with Cameron is that he's hopelessly petulant. Can't stand not getting his own way. Childish.'

Julian Astle added, 'That was Cameron at his worst – panicking about UKIP and failing completely to allow a sober analysis of the issues. Just a knee-jerk anti-immigrant position.'

At 7 p.m. the Equal Marriage Bill had its third reading. I went down to vote with Michael Gove. We went up the back staircase behind the Speaker's Chair and came into the Chamber at the rear access. We both glanced to the right at the Aye lobby and, seeing two Labour tellers on the doors, we automatically turned left to go into the No lobby to vote. I said to Michael jokingly that I assumed that we were in the correct lobby, and he laughed. Then we suddenly realised that a) it was rather empty and that b) there were a whole load of head-banging right-wing Tories, such as Bill Cash. We both suddenly realised that we were about to vote against same-sex marriage – something that would look particularly odd for me.

We immediately dashed out before the doors could be locked, and nipped round into the Aye lobby. The vote for the same-sex marriage Bill was overwhelming, but around 135 Conservative MPs voted against and only 125 for the Bill, with the rest abstaining. The Conservative Party has on balance voted against same-sex marriage. So much for Cameron's modernisation project.

WEDNESDAY 22 MAY

Breakfast with Oliver – who said that he had had a meeting with Conservative ministers after the 'shambles' of the MATBAPS meeting yesterday. He is 'knocking heads together' to ensure unity behind Cameron's idiotic position.

SUNDAY 26 MAY

Took me seven hours to plough through my two red boxes. Got to the very bottom of my first box and found a supposedly low-key letter to Andrew Lansley from Iain Duncan Smith entitled 'The Legislative Programme for the Fourth Session'. All in all, not a very interesting subject. I dutifully read on into the letter and was increasingly amazed by the contents: 'This letter outlines a reform agenda that I recommend. I also anticipate that the spending round, and future fiscal events, will mean that further measures must be added to this list.' The letter then went on to outline massive welfare cuts – starting with cuts to child benefit and child tax credits.

I immediately emailed Nick Clegg and Danny to warn them. Nick replied: 'Ridiculous behaviour by IDS – I had a bilateral with him last week and he didn't even hint at this stuff.'

TUESDAY 28 MAY

Down in Yeovil today for an advice centre and various appointments.

In the morning, I went to Yeovil Hospital to see the chairman, Peter Wyman. Before the meeting, I visited our activist Pauline Booth, who is on Ward 6A. She was diagnosed with terminal cancer last July. She is deteriorating rapidly. I stayed with her for fifteen minutes, and she knew who I was, though for the first time she was getting a little confused and eventually she shooed me away when she was too tired.

WEDNESDAY 29 MAY

Off to France today for five days – what a huge relief. Caught the 6 a.m. plane from Gatwick.

The newspapers speculate about IDS and his offer to cut the welfare budget in order to 'protect the police and defence'. It's difficult to know whether this is freelancing on the part of the Tory right or whether this is licensed anti-coalition defiance by Cameron and Osborne.

THURSDAY 30 MAY

Went out for a run. Felt quite healthy when I got to the lake, but as I stopped to catch my breath an elderly lady ran up to me and seemed to be asking me whether I needed help! Did I really look that bad?

MONDAY 3 JUNE

At 8.30 a.m., I met Philippa Stroud, Iain Duncan Smith's adviser at the DWP. I waved the letter from IDS to Andrew Lansley at her, and said that I thought that this was IDS 'on manoeuvres'.

Philippa did her best to look surprised, shocked and hurt and said that 'Iain simply thought it was important that the government should keep going with welfare reform'. She revealed that Iain had discussed some of his ideas with Philip Hammond and Theresa May a couple of weeks ago – and claimed it was not IDS who'd leaked them, but probably Philip Hammond. Interesting. Maybe Hammond is more ambitious than I thought.

At noon, I found myself attending a meeting of the new 'Extremism Task Force', which is the government's knee-jerk reaction to the dreadful murder of a serviceman in Woolwich. The meeting is chaired by the Prime Minister. As is usual with these Prime Minister reactive things, the whole agenda seemed to have been thought out extremely badly. Just as on immigration, there is a rush to 'do something', without even properly defining what we're trying to tackle.

TUESDAY 4 JUNE

A rather bizarre email has come through today inviting me to go on an ITV programme called *Splash*, with the Olympic diver Tom Daley. They are looking for 'celebrities', presumably ones willing to make fools of themselves. Training would apparently start in October. My office staff in London seem very amused. I don't think I'll be rushing to take part.

Nick says that he thinks the Tory Spending Review strategy is to under-deliver on departmental savings so that they force the Liberal Democrats to support more welfare cuts.

THURSDAY 6 JUNE

5.30 p.m. Ministerial meeting in the DfE on the Spending Review. We need to find more savings to satisfy the Treasury.

Added to the £1.25 billion worth of savings that we've already tabled, we've decided to table about £500 million more, including £70 million from the apprenticeships budget, school transport cuts of £25 million, a reduction in spending due to the 'structural underspend' on the schools budget of £300 million, the abolition of the Mayor of London Excellence Fund (worth £12 million), and a reduction in contingency for post-sixteen maths funding of £30 million. That gets us to about £1.75 billion, although it includes scaling back some of the two-year-olds early years offer – unlikely to be acceptable to Nick.

I had to fight very hard to avoid Michael Gove tabling the full £2.5 billion worth of savings. Michael seems to swing from one second wanting to take a very hard line to the next second wanting to concede everything. He and his advisers also seem to have gone wobbly on the real-terms schools protection. I made a strong case for keeping this, and said that this was necessary to make a national funding formula workable. In contrast, the Tories all seemed to think that a national funding formula could be implemented even if we lose our real schools budget protection. Politically naïve nonsense.

Michael also wants to go further with reductions in the Education Services Grant to local authorities. I've made clear that this is not something I will accept.

TUESDAY 11 JUNE

Michael Gove's office sent to the Treasury last night a letter from Michael on the Spending Review. They failed to let me check it first. The letter blames the additional education cuts on the failure of the government to grasp the nettle of additional welfare cuts. All part of the boring Tory strategy to take more from the poor. And clearly designed to be leaked.

As well as offering the agreed £1.75 billion, Michael has proposed two things that I'm massively opposed to. Firstly – and eccentrically – he is proposing to cut the amount of money going to local authorities for their education functions by 55 per cent! Some people might have thought that there was a decimal point missing and that he was merely suggesting a 5.5 per cent cut. But yes, he is actually suggesting 55 per cent cut.

There is a good Michael Gove who is courteous, well informed, reasonable, diplomatic and well educated, and then there is a bad Michael Gove, who is political, mischievous, Machiavellian and manipulative. This letter is very much the bad Michael.

Today's Cabinet was going to be one of the growth implementation Cabinets, where the Prime Minister goes around beating up ministers about their failure to deliver. Theresa Villiers, David Willetts and I joked privately that it would not be long before Owen Paterson mentioned the famous 'nightingales', which are allegedly holding up various housing developments around the country. Sure enough, within minutes of the Cabinet meeting starting, the nightingales popped their heads up.

We came to the issue of Chinese visas, where, by tradition, Osborne normally beats up Theresa May about how it is that rich Chinese can't get into the country. There was some discussion about why it wasn't possible for people to get their visas more easily to come to Britain. Philip Hammond made a rare balls-up when he asked Theresa May, 'Other European countries manage to get their visas out quickly – why don't we simply allow the Schengen country visas to be accessible to the United Kingdom?' Theresa May raised her eyebrows and laughter burst out around the room. Joining the Schengen system of open borders is the last thing that any Tory right-winger such as Philip Hammond should want to do. Ed Davey said, 'This is going to look very strange for you, Philip, in the *Daily Mail.*' Cameron responded – only half-jokingly – by saying, 'If any of the newspapers end up covering this discussion, I will fire whoever briefs them on sight!'

WEDNESDAY 12 JUNE

Apparently Vince spoke to Danny yesterday and said that if he didn't get a decent Spending Review settlement he might well walk out of the government and 'become a backbench critic of the government's economic policy'. Danny said, 'Vince needs to be very careful that we don't just call his bluff.'

At 10.45, I left for the Treasury.

We were given some pretty unpleasant tasting coffee, then a couple of minutes later we walked through into the Chancellor's rather palatial office, overlooking St James's Park.

George was already seated on the sofa on the other side of the room, with his back to the window. To his right was Danny Alexander, and I took the sofa seat on George's left, with Michael Gove sitting next to me and his very bright policy adviser Tom Shinner taking a chair around the edge of the circle. The only other person present was the head of the public spending.

George said, 'Look, I'm keen for us to get a settlement on education. We don't want any narrative about division.' Michael said that was absolutely right and Danny butted in to say, 'Yes, we don't want any more stories like that in the *Mail on Sunday*.' He was referring to a story which had clearly been planted by the DfE, saying that Michael Gove was fighting to protect schools funding in the face of the Treasury's attempt to cut it, and the Lib Dems' unwillingness to cut welfare spending.

What we are now offering is around £1.68 billion of cuts – some way short of the £2.5 billion the Treasury wants.

George said, 'Look, we don't even seem to be close at the moment, and we've got this problem of the two-year offer savings.'

Michael said that he was just trying to be helpful by looking at a massive cut to the Education Services Grant funding and moving off the real schools protection.

I said that I thought it was insane politically to move off the real protection of the schools budget, because to try to redefine this for £100 or £200 million net savings was terrible politics. I said that if we wanted to introduce a national funding formula, this would need to be done with a sensible schools budget because otherwise the story would all be about the losers.

The Chancellor looked unhappy and turned to the senior Treasury official. 'What would we actually settle for?'

'Chancellor, we need at least £2.1 billion or £2.2 billion.'

George said, 'Look, can you two go back and work together to get a sensible coalition settlement on this? We're all pretty pro-coalition people here, and if we can't find a sensible settlement, then nobody can.'

In the evening I called a meeting with DfE civil servants and advisers to think about how we could get a bit more money from the DfE budget.

We racked our brains for about two hours and came up with a list of potential ideas – totalling the £300 million we may need. Left the office feeling we had made good progress.

THURSDAY 13 JUNE

Met with MG and advisers. Michael turned to the list of potential savings. I got the impression that he wasn't enthusiastic about us having gone off to discuss these the night before.

He went through the list of savings in a rather brisk and brusque way, rejecting most of them out of hand. He said he didn't think there was a good case for the £50 million of 16–19 participation funding cuts, there wasn't a good case for saving any money on the military ethos, there wasn't a good reason for saving money on early workforce development, he wasn't prepared to save any money on cultural education or on the school food plan, he didn't think there was any case for reducing money on apprenticeships, he wasn't willing to make funding cuts to music hubs and he wasn't keen to cut school support. He said that he was prepared to make a piddling cut of £15 million to voluntary and community sector grants. But as for the modest cuts that we proposed to academies funding, these were 'totally unacceptable' to him, and would 'compromise the entire academies programme'.

I was pretty irritated, as the list of potential cuts was intended to be a constructive and positive thing and Michael clearly wasn't engaging sensibly. I interrupted and said, 'Look, let me just make clear that if you're saying you're not going to make any savings from academies then I am taking off the table my proposed increase in the Education Services Grant cut from 11 per cent to 14 per cent.' Michael turned to me: 'Why would you do that?'

I said, 'Look, none of this process is going to work if all you're going to do is bank every concession that I am prepared to make in areas that the Liberal Democrats think are important, while defending every single thing that the Conservatives value. The Chancellor challenged us to find compromise solutions. That's not what we appear to be doing here.'

Michael looked pretty irritated and then we had a long debate about the Education Services Grant and the role of local authorities. He said his vision was one where local authorities didn't have any serious role. I said that it was pointless to rehearse our differences on this, but we both knew that we had a different vision of the education system and it would be completely unacceptable for the Liberal Democrats to make cuts of 30, 40, 50 or 60 per cent to the Education Services Grant.

The meeting ended badly. I said I had a dinner to go to and left.

When I got back from the dinner, there was an email from the Secretary of State's office – a draft letter to the Chief Secretary to the Treasury from Michael.

I read through the letter and became more and more angry. The letter started with the agreed savings of £1.7 billion. It then set out two totally different sets of proposals – one of which was Michael's plan for massive further cuts in the Education Services Grant and potentially removing the real schools protection. Then it also set out a whole series of other cuts, which were attributed to me and which were expressed in the worst possible light. The whole thing was clearly written in order to be leaked to damage the Lib Dems. It looked like it had been written by a political hack. I was furious – incandescent. I decided that I wouldn't reply immediately, in case I was so rude that I later regretted it.

FRIDAY 14 JUNE

Woke up at 4.30 a.m., still fuming about the letter. I couldn't get back to sleep, so I got up and wrote a reply to Michael's private secretary:

> I am afraid this letter is not something I could agree to and it does not seem to reflect what Michael and I agreed yesterday. I am actually rather disappointed by it and feel that the time spent to try to find a positive coalition compromise has not been well used. The description of my position is totally wrong and if my view is going to be put, it should both be accurate and explain properly and positively what I am proposing. I am also 100 per cent opposed to reducing the schools budget. I do not think we should be suggesting this in any way. In short, I am truly disappointed that the letter does not do what the Chancellor asked for and give the proper DfE coalition position.

I warned that either we could amend the letter or I could send my own letter to the Treasury, though I pointed out that this was hardly the best way forward.

At 7.40 a.m. I had an email back from Michael:

> Dear David, I am sorry you are unhappy with the letter. I will work hard with the team to secure a letter we can both send – albeit one that acknowledges legitimate differences. If you cannot sign up, I will respect that. And show you my text prior to sending. But if you write separately to Danny, I must see that text and officials would have to tell me what the consequences of any alternative would be.

I also emailed back to say that I hoped that there would be no briefing out of different coalition positions on the Spending Review to the media: 'If there is, there is no doubt that it will prompt a counter-reaction and we will end up doing great damage to each other and to our reputation in education.'

MONDAY 17 JUNE

At 10.10 a.m. I strolled over to the Treasury, and entered the Chancellor's waiting room. Michael Gove and Tom Shinner were already there, and they looked up at me with a mixture of embarrassment and coldness. We managed to find a few things to talk about for a couple of minutes. And then somebody from the Chancellor's office came through and ushered us next door. Everybody was sitting exactly where they sat last time.

George started by saying, 'Look, I'm really keen in all our interests to settle education soon, so we can focus on the last few difficult parts of the Spending Review. If we go on much longer, it's only going to be you and Vince left – and that's not a place you want to be in.'

There was then a rather convoluted discussion of the two options on the table.

George tried to push me on the two-year-old offer, but I said, 'Look, Nick's not even prepared to discuss phasing that. It's a bottom-line issue for him, and I can't make concessions on it. If you want to look at the two-year offer, you'll just have to take it to the Quad.'

George then asked Michael what his top priorities were and he said, No. 1 academies, No. 2 the schools protection. I said that school protection was the No. 1 priority and then the two-year-old offer, but it was important to us that there was some sort of local authority role in education, both to deliver school intervention and also for efficiency reasons – you don't want 23,500 schools all with their own human resource and legal systems. George sighed and said that he wanted us to go away again and see if we could come up with a joint solution, but I pressed him on what amount of cuts he actually needed.

Helpfully, George then said that what he would settle for would be another £200 million of cuts rather than the £700 million implied by reaching the full £2.5 billion Treasury target. I said that there was no way that we could both find £200 million more savings and replace the £380 million of cuts that MG had wanted to make from the early years budget. George sighed again and then said that he was willing to accept this was impossible and instead settle for £1.7 billion of cuts, not £2 billion. This was literally in the last minute of the meeting – a crucial concession.

The truth is that £1.7 billion worth of savings is about where I expected we would end up when the whole process started!

TUESDAY 18 JUNE

I think perhaps that if Michael Gove had been negotiating for the Tory Party in May 2010, we'd never have formed the coalition, because he is clearly a very difficult negotiator who is unwilling to sacrifice anything. By contrast, Osborne wants to know what the fundamental interests and bottom line of each side in the negotiation is and then he seeks to find a solution.

One of the senior DfE officials said to me that I should be quite happy with where we have ended up. I fought more strongly than anyone for the real schools protection. Securing this means we now have a chance of delivering a national funding formula at acceptable political cost. We've also fought hard to protect the two-year-old offer and secured this against considerable Tory opposition. Overall we have got to a good place for the department, for Michael and for me.

This morning, Michael and I went off to the Home Office for a meeting of the Extremism Task Force, chaired by Theresa May. This was a pre-meeting for the next Prime Minister-chaired session.

It was interesting to see the dynamics in this almost wholly Conservative group. We met around a very large conference table in the Home Office, with clocks for different world time zones on the wall. It looked like an emergency-type room for major incident management.

Instead of the other Conservative Cabinet ministers collecting around Theresa May, they all sat as far away from her as possible. It looked like none of them wanted to acknowledge her chairmanship.

The meeting started off with a discussion about extremism in communities and mosques. I have to say that it all seemed a bit airy-fairy. It was one of those touchy-feely conversations where you couldn't understand what people were actually proposing. Things didn't really liven up until we got onto the schools area, although we did have a rather interesting contribution from Baroness Warsi, who started comparing different types of extremist Muslim websites to various Conservative Party websites. She went into the difference between Conservative Home and some other Tory websites, and her colleagues looked a bit uncomfortable.

Michael then intervened to talk about schools, and gave a rather over-the-top analysis of how the department was going to start regulating madrassas all over the country. Since madrassas are mostly in people's private homes, the idea that we can effectively regulate them or pick on one particular religion seems to me to be pretty unlikely. There are thousands across the country.

As Michael spoke, Theresa May raised her eyebrows a number of times and glanced across the table at me. Clearly she thinks that Michael's ideas are politically and practically unwise. I also caught Baroness Warsi's eye and she also looked pretty unimpressed.

The meeting eventually ended and Michael and I left in his ministerial car. Michael turned to me and said, 'Did that all seem rather strange to you? I wonder whether you thought that that was a complete waste of time?' A lot of tension amongst senior Conservatives. I'm not sure that any of them like the fact that Theresa May has recently been on leadership manoeuvres.

THURSDAY 20 JUNE

I had a quick chat with Philip Rycroft, the civil servant head of Nick Clegg's office. He wanted to know about my meeting with Francis Maude last night, about civil service reform. No civil servants were present to take notes, so they are all in a panic!

If there's one thing that petrifies the civil service, it's civil service reform, and I have no doubt that my frank account of my meeting with Francis will have been passed back through the civil service machine fairly rapidly. In any case, I said all the right things and emphasised how supportive the Lib Dems were of the principle of civil service impartiality.

At 2 p.m. I went over for the Parliamentary Business and Legislation Committee, chaired by Andrew Lansley, in that ghastly, airless, windowless conference room on the lower ministerial corridor. The meeting was an opportunity for Secretaries of State to 'bid' for Bills that they want in the last Queen's Speech.

Michael Gove came in to discuss his letter requesting an Education Bill. There was a notable lack of any detail, and Michael took an unconventional approach: 'I have to say to you, Leader, that my general inclination is to be very honest and straightforward with the committee. I've brought this Education Bill forward because of the views of the Prime Minister and Deputy Prime Minister that it would be useful to have an Education Bill in a key area of government policy. However, my own view is that legislation for the sake of it tends to be dangerous. The reform programme is moving in the right direction, and it seems risky to have a Bill in the final stages of the parliament that might actually divide the coalition rather than unite it. Therefore, although I've written to you asking for this Bill, I'm not sure whether I really want it.'

Sir George Young frowned and leant back in his chair. 'Leader, the Education Secretary is adopting a most unusual approach. It's like a student who takes a public examination and starts off by asking the examiner whether he could possibly fail him.'

Next was Iain Duncan Smith, who was late. Iain started off by presenting his proposals for a new Workplace Pensions Bill, which is entirely uncontroversial. He went on to set out a plan for an incredibly controversial Welfare Reform Bill, for which he's got no cross-coalition support.

Sir George said, 'I wonder how much buy-in there is across the coalition for these proposals? I see you are proposing to make parents work even if their children are under five? Presumably you are not proposing that mothers should have to work straight after childbirth – or are you?' Iain, as ever, fumbled his way through a response.

FRIDAY 21 JUNE

I was speaking today at the *Sunday Times* Festival of Education, at Wellington School in Berkshire. Phoned the Yeovil office to see whether it was possible to visit Pauline Booth. Arrived at Yeovil Hospice at 4 p.m. Pauline was, of course, in bed, and looking out over the beautiful gardens. It was soon evident that she has gone seriously downhill, and though she was still pretty lucid she was also clearly tired, uncomfortable and in some pain. I just sat for around half an hour holding her hand, and some of the time we spoke and some of the time she just closed her eyes. After about half an hour, she turned to me and said that she thought it was 'time to say goodbye'. She didn't say it, but I could tell what she meant.

What a relief that I came down this Friday, as I would have been very upset if I hadn't seen her again before she died. We said our goodbyes and I gave her a kiss on the head and then left, pausing in the corridor to wipe away tears. Not easy, as she's been such a good friend and strong supporter over many, many years now. She is too young to die.

SATURDAY 22 JUNE

Following a recent meeting where ministers met departmental staff in the DfE, Michael Gove has decided to write a letter setting out good practice on how letters to the department should be replied to. He's drafted a letter to his private secretary, Pamela Dow:

Dear Pamela,

Thank you for your letter of the 17th asking me on behalf of your colleagues how I like letters to be drafted. Letters should be concise, precise and polite. Concision is itself a form of politeness. Ministers, and taxpayers, lead busy lives. Making points briefly saves everyone time. Of course, on occasion, some factual detail, such as the inadvisability of ending a sentence with a preposition or the folly of using impact as a verb or even the ugliness of behaviours as a usage when behaviour covers a variety of human activity, might require a complex longer sentence. But brevity is always a virtue. As is precision. So read the original letter to which we are replying. List the points raised or questions asked in your notebook. Make sure you are precise in your requests to colleagues as to the information required to address those points or answer those queries. Do not accept general formulaic replies to precise questions. So, when someone asks why the Secretary of State referred to Mr Men in a speech which discussed history, do not send back a standard reply on the national curriculum review, or even the draft history programme of study. Instead, go back to the original speech, check the reference and provide a full and proper explanation of the reference and the underpinning reasoning for using that reference. The more care that is taken to address the direct questions raised in the letter, the less likely the letter is to be sent back with cross annotations. Time spent on reconnaissance is seldom wasted. Politeness requires getting the name of the correspondent correct and maintaining a sympathetic tone. It does not require a writing style modelled on Leonard Sachs from *The Good Old Days* or Sir Humphrey in *Yes Minister*. Using inflated political rhetoric of the 'First may I say how much I care about X' is not polite. It is a time-wasting exercise and self-regarding pomposity. So don't even go there. Instead, use direct, clear and vigorous language. Make the paragraph the unit of composition. Devote one paragraph to each topic. And one sentence to each idea within that topic. Ideally, every sentence should introduce the topic of the paragraph. And the concluding sentence should return to or summarise that theme. Use the active and not the passive voice. Ministers have decided to increase spending on the poorest children. Poorer children are not having a harder time under this government. Cut out unnecessary words. For example, rather than writing 'The policy that we are introducing is intended to drive a change in behaviours on the part of teachers with respect to the poorest and most disadvantaged children and young people', say that 'The policy will change how teachers behave towards poorer students'. And make the most emphatic point at the end of the sentence. For example, instead of saying 'The coalition government, which has been an unprecedented historic success, was formed in May three years ago', write 'The coalition government, formed three years ago this May, has been an unprecedented historic success'. The more care you take over elegant composition, the greater the compliment you pay the correspondent. Some people, of course, prefer bullet points to continuous prose. You should use such a device sparingly. But if it seems appropriate, then remember to keep each point to one idea, as in the following.

Gove's Golden Rules.

1. If in doubt, cut it out.
2. Read it out loud before sending – if it sounds wrong, don't send it.
3. In letters, adjectives add little, adverbs even less.
4. The more the letter reads like a political speech, the less good it is as a letter.
5. Would your mum understand that word, phrase or sentence? Would mine?

6. Read the great writers to improve your own prose – George Orwell and Evelyn Waugh, Jane Austen and George Eliot, Matthew Parris and Christopher Hitchens.
7. Use concrete words and phrases in preference to abstractions.
8. *Gwynne's Grammar* is a brief guide to the best writing style.
9. Simon Heffer's *Strictly English* is a more comprehensive – and very entertaining – companion volume.
10. Our written work should be the clearest, most elegant and most enjoyable to read of any Whitehall department because the Department for Education has the best civil servants in Whitehall.

I hope this reply is helpful. If I can be of any further help, please don't hesitate to get in touch. And thank you for your consistent commitment to the highest standards in public service.

Michael

MONDAY 24 JUNE

At 10.30 a.m. Bob Constantine from ITV West Country came to see me to record an interview about the letter I received back in May 2010 from Liam Byrne, the former Labour Chief Secretary, saying there was 'No money' left. This attracted a vast amount of publicity, but nobody has actually seen the letter. Bob has been pestering me for months to let him do a piece on this. It rapidly became big news – appearing on the main ITV news. Nick Robinson wanted to do a piece for the BBC, but I declined.

Went over to the House of Commons for DfE Oral Questions at 2.30 p.m. It was all going rather well until I relaxed. The Speaker called 'Question 8', and I sat on the bench doing nothing, waiting for either Liz Truss or Edward Timpson. Then someone said, 'I think it's you.' I really must pay more attention in future, but it's pretty easy to switch off, as the Labour front bench is so hopeless.

TUESDAY 25 JUNE

Just before I was leaving for Cabinet at 9.30 a.m. I got an email to say that that Pauline Booth had died overnight.

A dull meeting of the Cabinet, where we discussed the Ministry of Defence growth strategy. If Philip Hammond ever loses his job, there definitely isn't an alternative career for him as a comedian. His presentation was ten minutes too long, and towards the end of it ministers were dipping into the bowls of boiled sweets which are dotted around the Cabinet table, and crinkling their wrappers in a way that always indicates boredom.

WEDNESDAY 26 JUNE

8.15 a.m. Cabinet on the Spending Review. Pretty much as I already understood, with a modest welfare reform package to titillate the Tory right wing, protection for the schools budget, the health budget and the overseas aid budget, and cuts of 5 to 10 per cent for all other budgets.

George announced that he was allocating a small amount of money to improve facilities for people visiting the site of the Battle of Waterloo, for the 200th anniversary of the battle in 2015. There was a ripple of laughter as this was announced, and it's the kind of gimmick that Gordon Brown would have been proud of.

Michael Gove couldn't resist intervening to say that he was delighted to hear the news as it will 'help us to celebrate the victory of a strong and united coalition over attempts to restore a bankrupt former regime'! George immediately jotted the joke down, and used it to good effect later on in the Commons.

Home at 12.30 a.m. A good day at last for the coalition. We have delivered in an impressive and uncontroversial way the spending settlement for 2015/16. As Nick put it at Cabinet: 'The coalition seems to rise extremely well to the challenges of doing the big things; it's often the little things that seem to trip us up!'

THURSDAY 27 JUNE

George Osborne was yesterday snapped before his spending statement in one of those rather posed 'casual' photographs, at his desk in the Treasury, eating a burger. It later turned out that it was a particularly expensive burger, which rather ruined his 'man of the people' pose. After a cheeky comment by George about Eric Pickles and 'lean government' in his spending statement, Eric decided to get his own back today by having an almost identical photograph shot over his shoulder in his office. But this one had Eric eating a small salad, with a pile of carrots and a Diet Coke!

Left Westminster at 1.30 p.m. for a conference centre just outside Milton Keynes, where the parliamentary party is meeting for one of its pointless away days. Arrived at 3 p.m. – ghastly, soulless and bland.

Eventually, and somewhat unwillingly, I made my way to the conference room where our MPs were already meeting. After ten minutes I tried to escape, but Chief Whip Alistair Carmichael caught me in the corridor and said that he'd expect me back in the room for the next subject, which was 'particularly important'. This turned out to be an economy discussion.

Nick made some opening comments, saying there is quite a debate about economic policy, with the Treasury/Danny view that we need to stick with all the fiscal rules, and the Vince view that we should borrow a lot more to invest.

Nick said that he took a middle course. We need to stick to the plan to reduce borrowing, but should do more to stimulate investment, possibly by allowing councils to borrow to fund housing.

Nick said he wanted a motion to settle the debate at the autumn party conference, and he is inclined to put a motion down in his name. Nick said that since Vince had a different perspective, we should hear his view next.

Vince said that he didn't like the Tory narrative about borrowing all being Labour's fault and he thought we ought to acknowledge that there had been a worldwide recession and a banking collapse, not just spending profligacy. He said he thought that the government's fiscal plans were too austere and that we could be borrowing more to invest in productive capital investment, and perhaps flexing the fiscal rules. Frankly, there was a lot of economic sense in what Vince was saying, though not as much political sense.

After Vince spoke, about twenty-five MPs piled in. A handful of not particularly impressive MPs spoke on the Vince side of the argument, but they were drowned out by a ratio of about six to one by other MPs who made the case for sticking with the existing policy.

I emphasised that we couldn't possibly go back on our political narrative over borrowing but that we must not give the impression that our Lib Dem position is just 'Tory economics and Labour social policy'.

My own view is that the government's current fiscal policy is too ortho-dox. But I think Vince is being rather naïve in his proposed strategy, and the trick for us is to stick to the narrative of lower borrowing while doing positive things to boost manufacturing, jobs and infrastructure spending.

Duncan Hames, the chair of the Federal Policy Committee and Nick's Parliamentary Private Secretary, made a particularly brutal intervention where he referred to Clare Short, when she was criticising the government's policy on Iraq while staying in the Cabinet. He said that when she finally left government, she had 'no credibility left'. Vince sat looking glum.

At the end, Nick summed up decisively in favour of his own view, and there was a round of applause and table-banging. The risk is that we may be detaching Vince too much and giving him the impression that he is in such a tiny minority that he's got to either shut up or resign.

FRIDAY 28 JUNE

Had a brief chat with Nick. Said I thought that the debate with Vince had been a bit brutal and we needed to be careful not to marginalise him. Nick said that he totally agreed, and he had meant to sum up in a more constructive way.

TUESDAY 2 JULY

Sent an email to Nick about the McKay proposals, which back English votes for English MPs in the House of Commons, but with the somewhat bizarre addition of a final vote by all members of the UK Parliament, which could then overturn the English MPs. This would be a recipe for political disaster if the next government was a Lib–Lab coalition, with a majority of Conservative MPs in England. The Conservatives would keep on amending all largely English Bills, and the government would then have to overturn these measures using Scottish and Welsh votes. Lunacy of the highest order. I reminded Nick of the old adage: 'The answer to the West Lothian question is not to ask it.'

9.30 a.m. Cabinet. During the discussion on the NHS, a mobile phone went off. This is a major faux pas, as you are not supposed have phones in Cabinet. It was a jazz ringtone, and Cameron quipped, 'That reminds me – today is Ken Clarke's 73rd birthday!'

THURSDAY 4 JULY

To Dover House for a government strategy meeting. At the end, Nick asked all the officials to leave and said he agreed yesterday with Cameron that he can proceed with the favoured Tory marriage tax break, at a cost of £500 million per year. This was in the coalition agreement. However, Nick made clear that in return we would want something in the Autumn Statement that would also spend an equivalent amount of money on one of our priorities. This would need similarly to be a policy which 'eases the squeeze' on household budgets.

Nick also said that Cameron is unhappy about the letters from Vince and me, putting conditions on the immigration control for landlords section of the Immigration Bill. 'Can't you get your guys under control and get your tanks off my lawn?'

SATURDAY 6 JULY

The first incredibly beautiful and hot day of summer. Had lunch by the river.

At around 6 p.m. I went out for a run. At 7 p.m. my phone rang – Switch. It was a conference call that Nick had fixed to discuss party funding reform/ trade unions.

It's funny the way they dial up these conference calls – they line up the most junior person first, and then bring in the increasingly senior people, so that these have to wait the least amount of time. Finally, Nick joins.

Danny said that he'd spoken to George, who had said that we ought to 'put Miliband on the spot' by forcing trade union members to have to 'opt in' if they wanted to donate to Labour. I said that I thought this was very unwise, wouldn't get through the House of Lords, and it isn't in our interests to allow the Tories to be the only the well-funded party in British politics. It would simply free up their resources to come at us harder in the Tory/Lib Dem marginals.

Nick summed up by saying we wouldn't accept 'one-sided' party funding reform – we either have a cap on individual donations, trade union opt-ins and state funding of political parties, or have nothing.

The conference call went on for some considerable time, and I stood by the side of a field as people went backwards and forwards with their dogs. A lovely evening and a truly beautiful British summer's day.

MONDAY 8 JULY

At the political meeting this morning, I teased Nick about the weekend coverage of his dinner with Mick Jagger and girlfriend – photographs of them leaving a top London restaurant! Nick said it was somewhat embarrassing that lots of media 'snappers' had gathered outside the restaurant.

Had to attend a meeting of the Extremism Task Force Coordination Group, chaired by the Home Secretary in the Home Office. Michael Gove, Eric Pickles, Chris Grayling and various junior ministers. Michael had to present a paper on extremism in schools, and he painted a somewhat gloomy picture. He seemed to conclude that we needed to regulate all madrassas and, by implication, all other religious settings, such as Christian Sunday Schools.

Even the right-wing Tories such as Theresa May, Chris Grayling and Eric Pickles looked a bit shocked, and Baroness Warsi was distinctly unimpressed and asked Michael whether she could have a list of all the members of the Muslim community the DfE had consulted. She obviously knew that we had consulted nobody. Michael was quick to admit this, which did create an impression that his proposals had been rather cobbled together.

Chris Grayling noted that it would be very unpopular to regulate Sunday Schools. All in all, Michael's proposals went down like a bucket of cold sick.

At midday, I went over to Admiralty House with Nick Clegg for the first annual Pupil Premium Awards. It is great to see the pupil premium being embedded in the education system, and now there's a serious amount of money being spent in thousands of schools across the country, which I believe is having a real impact in narrowing the gaps between the life chances of young people from disadvantaged backgrounds and the rest. Although the political cut-through of this policy probably isn't huge, it is one of the big successes of coalition.

At 5.30 p.m. I met up with the Tory MP and head of the Policy Unit,

Boris Johnson's brother Jo Johnson, in my office on the lower ministerial corridor. The Tories still aren't giving up on the idea of adding on to our Third Party Campaigning Bill a proposal to force trade union members to opt in to paying the political levy. I made clear that we are not interested. A dream scenario for the Tories would be to undermine Labour funding while ending up with no cap on individual donations and no state funding of political parties.

Jo Johnson asked me whether things would be changed if Ed Miliband, in his speech tomorrow, announced that he was going to move to an opt-in. I said that I couldn't believe that Ed Miliband would be that stupid.

Got home at about 11.30 p.m. and the Miliband speech was being trailed on the wires.

The reports suggest that Ed Miliband is pushing unilaterally for an opt-in approach for trade union members, without any demand for a donations cap on the Tories. Maybe he is that stupid.

TUESDAY 9 JULY

Cabinet, where we had quite a busy agenda including Royal Mail, the national curriculum, tackling bovine TB, civil service reform and Libya.

Vince kicked off by talking about the privatisation of the Royal Mail. I said that I was delighted to see that Vince was taking forward this proposal – one of two key policies in Vince's chapter of *The Orange Book*. I said that the other key proposal from Vince had been the abolition of the Business Department, and noted that progress in this area had been 'less impressive'. Vince looked a little bit sheepish.

Next, the badger cull, and Owen Paterson. There is something about Owen that nobody can quite take seriously. He claims to have a great degree of credibility over the badger cull because when he was young he owned two pet badgers! On that basis, I must be an expert in fisheries policy – I once owned a goldfish. Owen ploughed through a long presentation, mentioning New Zealand, where he said there had been a 'significant investment in possum control'. This turned out to mean that of the 50 million possums in the country, 20 million had been exterminated!

There are going to be trials of the badger cull in England, and instead of the 20 million killed in New Zealand, there are going to be 2,100 killed in

Somerset and 3,000 killed in Gloucestershire. It will be interesting to see what difference this makes, as the science is hugely disputed.

At 7.45 p.m. I headed off for the Coalition 2.0 dinner at the Adelphi Building on John Adam Street. Paul Marshall was yet again a wonderful host and this time he'd arranged a reception out on the terrace on the top floor of the building, with wonderful views over the Thames.

We had a magnificent dinner, which was attended by a couple of Tory MPs as well as Michael Gove and Greg Clark, and from our side Tim Leunig, Julian Astle, Jo Swinson and Norman Lamb. We had a productive discussion about coalition and reflected on the fact that a year ago we'd only just finished rowing over Lords reform – when people were questioning whether coalition could survive. It was a very enjoyable evening, and Michael was on his usual sparkling form.

WEDNESDAY 10 JULY

Got in at 6.30 a.m. and at 7.45 a.m. went down to the Downing Street cafeteria for my regular meeting with Oliver. The weather is still very pleasant, and for the first time we ate our breakfast outside in the courtyard area. The subject was immigration, with the Bill expected soon.

The truth is there is still a lot to be resolved. Nick Clegg has now written to Theresa May on the issue of landlord checks, giving the Home Office permission to proceed but with the largest number of conditions I have ever seen.

Oliver was at his perky best. We went on to discuss entry and exit checks, where both Oliver and I think that the Home Office policy is a complete and utter shambles, with these checks seemingly focused only on major criminals and terrorist risks. I said to Oliver that I was getting quite impatient and I felt that it would be an issue at the next general election if Theresa May didn't pull her finger out. I think Oliver got the message, and if he didn't then the Prime Minister's private secretary, who was attending the meeting, may have.

Had a brief discussion with Nick about the Chequers Cabinet away day next week.

Nick said: 'I can tell you exactly why Cameron is so attracted to this. For him, it will all be about spin, having a nice lunch in the country and going down to Chequers a day earlier so he can stay there for the weekend. Cameron will want to brief out that this is all about the coalition rolling up its sleeves and getting down to action, and he has already tried to convince me that we should put out some very anti-Labour lines, which I don't want to do, as it is not in our interest to be seen to be partisan towards Labour.'

Wandered down to Admiralty House, where Nick was hosting a reception for the Westminster lobby. They were all there and it was really pretty busy, in contrast to the types of drinks parties the Lib Dems used to have when we were in opposition, when we'd be lucky if the odd stray person from the *Western Daily News* turned up by accident. After a while, Nick and I went off to dinner at Il Convivio in Ebury Street.

Nick said he was feeling incredibly good and positive at the moment, and he actually looked quite well and not his normal pasty-faced self. He said that he now fully intends to go on leading the party into the next general election. If we went back into opposition, then he'd stand down immediately as leader. If we stay in coalition post-2015, either with Labour or with the Conservatives, he'll remain leader.

Nick said that the pressure was really on his family, particularly Miriam but also the children, and he didn't want to remain in the intense job of being Deputy Prime Minister for ever, particularly as his children grew up. That all implied to me what I had assumed already, which is that if we remain in coalition after the 2015 election then Nick will probably go on to 2017/18 and then hand over. Nick's view is that if we go back into opposition after 2015, then Tim Farron would be elected, as the 'easy' choice for the party to play to its old-fashioned instincts as a campaigning third party.

Nick said that he'd met up with Vince after the parliamentary party away day. Vince was initially quite grumpy about the ear-bashing, but has now taken it in good heart and decided to knuckle down. Apparently Vince has even agreed to propose the policy motion on the economy at the autumn conference. This is a major breakthrough. We both agreed that Vince has to remain as Business Secretary for the rest of the parliament, as it is difficult to see where else to move him, and we wouldn't want him rattling around on the back benches.

I said I was hugely enjoying my double-hatted role. My ambition was to return to the Treasury at some stage as Chief Secretary. However, I said I quite understood that Nick could not reorder all the Liberal Democrats in government on the basis of what I wanted to do. Nick asked whether I would prefer Chief Secretary to Education Secretary. I said that ultimately I was more interested in being Chief Secretary than any other job as not only was it unfinished business for me, but what is attractive about it is you have huge positive influence over many vital areas – including education. So I felt I could do just as much for education from the Treasury.

Nick said that if we went back into government after the 2015 election, then he would definitely want to have a new Chief Secretary, and I was the obvious person. However, his working assumption was that he would keep his senior Cabinet members as they were until then. He did acknowledge, however, that Danny Alexander really would want to run a department of his own – preferably Business.

Nick went on to discuss the next government reshuffle. He's finally lost patience with Jeremy Browne and will sack him. He said that Tom McNally would retire. He thinks Simon Hughes deserves a job in government, probably in the Justice Department.

Nick also said that he feels increasingly guilty about sacking Nick Harvey, and he is now inclined to bring him back. He wants to move Norman Baker from the Department for Transport to the Home Office, to 'really man-mark' Theresa May and be a 'pain in her backside'.

We agreed that Ed Miliband is a nice guy but not a very convincing Prime Minister – his heart is really on the soggy left of British politics, so when he makes speeches about welfare scroungers or immigration, it just doesn't really have credibility.

Nick said that he found Cameron increasingly unimpressive but has far more time for Osborne: 'With George, he is what he is. He's a liberal on many social issues, he's actually quite pro-immigration, he couldn't really care less for the poor but doesn't disguise it, and he's pretty right-wing on welfare. However, you can deal with him and at least you know that he's got a core of beliefs. The problem with David Cameron is you really don't know where he stands. He's a marketing man, and he doesn't have a strong core of beliefs, other than that the Conservative Party and he personally should be in power. He's obsessed with saying that things must be done "because I have promised it", without actually explaining why the particular thing is important.'

Nick said that Cameron is at the moment increasingly desperate over the risk that the UK courts may require prisoners to be given the vote, and is thinking about some extreme legal opt-out in order to deal with this, which apparently would drive Ken Clarke mad. Nick said that the only reason that Cameron is looking at doing this is 'I've promised that we wouldn't give prisoners the vote, and whatever happens I must keep this promise'. We both agreed that Cameron is at his best when he's chairing meetings and master of a brief, and Nick also said that he has a lot of 'emotional common sense and good abilities as a political leader'.

Cameron is at his worst when dealing with issues such as extremism, terrorism or immigration – where all he cares about is getting a policy sound bite rather than getting the policy right. Nick said that he was sitting on the front bench next to Cameron and asked him whether the new policy on restricting migrant access to private sector rented housing would actually work. Cameron just shrugged his shoulders and said, 'I guess so. We'll just have to try!'

MONDAY 15 JULY

A busy week. We're launching our proposals on primary school account-ability, a big increase in the pupil premium, and the allocation of £820 million for new school places.

I have decided to set the pupil premium for primary schools at £1,300 in 2014 – up by £400 per pupil from the 2013 level, an increase of 44 per cent. The secondary pupil premium will increase by at least inflation. I have also agreed a new higher premium for looked-after children – £1,900 per pupil.

In my red box today was a present from Michael Gove of a book called *The Path to Power* – the first volume of a biography of US President Lyndon Johnson. We discussed this book briefly in the margins of the Coalition 2.0 dinner last week, where I was asking Michael for recommendations for summer reading. He said how great it was, and now suddenly the book turns up on my desk with a note from him! Given that he is one of the busiest people in the country, this is remarkably thoughtful and generous. There is a good Michael Gove and a bad Michael Gove, but the good Michael Gove is generally in the ascendancy.

TUESDAY 16 JULY

At 2.15 p.m. I had a meeting with Glenys Stacey, the head of Ofqual. She is very worried about I-GCSEs. Thinks some of them are too easy, and schools are increasingly using them as an easy way to get better results. I-GCSEs are international GCSEs, which used to be championed by Michael Gove, when the former Labour government would not allow them to be counted in the league tables. Unfortunately, the I-GCSE is not properly regulated, and while the assumption has always been that it's a more serious and rigorous qualification, Ofqual now thinks it's becoming a bit of a joke. Ofqual has written a very blunt letter to MG telling him that I-GCSEs are not as good as GCSEs. Now this is on the record, he will have to act.

WEDNESDAY 17 JULY

Had to get up at the absurdly early hour of 4 a.m. to spend two hours ploughing through my red boxes. Then on the *Today* programme at 7.30 a.m. to talk about the announcement on more challenging attainment targets for all primary schools, linked with a huge increase in pupil premium funding for primary schools. This is great for schools with lots of disadvantaged youngsters, including the one I visited last year in Redcar that has 80 per cent of young people on the pupil premium.

The pupil premium is a policy I developed in opposition, insisted on making a manifesto priority, and am now delivering in government – a real privilege. I'm convinced it's going to make a big impact in improving the life chances of children from poor backgrounds. This really is something worth being in politics for. Provided the Ofsted accountability framework forces schools to use this money for its intended purpose, this policy could be a great success.

At 9.30 a.m. Jo Johnson came up to talk about the presentation that we've got to give at the Chequers away day tomorrow. I can't help liking Jo, and he's the sort of person one can have quite a blunt conversation with. I haven't yet worked out how bright he is.

Jo had been talking about having a final slide after the ones on the economy, the squeeze on living standards, fairness and social mobility/ opportunity. I'd suggested something about keeping the United Kingdom united and winning the referendum in Scotland.

Jo had said he wanted to put in bullet points about how well we'd done in carrying off a successful Olympic Games (just about plausible), how we'd won Wimbledon (not plausible at all to claim credit for), and he then even suggested mentioning the birth of the new royal baby! I said that perhaps we should also claim the credit for the hot summer weather.

Got a text message at 9 a.m. from Michael Gove: 'The Prime Minister's very keen on your primary accountability announcement. He wants you to do an oral statement.'

I was immediately a little bit suspicious – thinking there must be some cynical reason for this. I then received a text from our Whips' Office confirming that there would be two statements today – the first on primary accountability and the second from Jeremy Browne on 'the government's strategy on minimum pricing for alcohol'. I immediately realised why I'd been asked to make the primary statement. Cameron is doing PMQs today, and if the alcohol statement had followed this immediately, then he would have had to walk out just as the alcohol U-turn was being announced.

THURSDAY 18 JULY

The last day before the long summer recess.

Got in my car and drove up the M40 to the village of Great Missenden, where Chequers – the country house of the Prime Minister – is located. It was an absolutely beautiful summer's day, temperature over 30°.

We stopped off in a coffee shop in the village, so we didn't turn up absurdly early. Then to Chequers and arrived at 10.45 a.m.

Chequers is nothing like as impressive a building as Chevening, Nick Clegg's country residence, but the setting is very beautiful, with fields sweeping away from the house and presenting a perfect vision of rural England.

The mood as Cabinet ministers gathered was very positive. The economy is improving, and even the polls. The weather is brilliant, and to cap it all we won Wimbledon for the first time for seventy years. All these things have contributed to the country cheering up, after the long period of miserable austerity.

On the first floor is a huge reception room, looking out over the gardens and fields, with a big table, just like the Cabinet table in No. 10. The Cabinet place cards are set out to exactly mirror where people would normally sit at Cabinet. So, David Cameron was sitting in the middle of the table with his back to the wall, looking out over the gardens. It was so hot that all the windows in the room were open, with air blowing through and fluttering the curtains and papers.

Ken Clarke turned up relatively late: 'I can't believe that David has called an away day when it's an Australia versus England Test match. Utterly crazy!' When he saw me, he shouted across the room: 'At last, I've found a Liberal! I couldn't see any of you lot around, and I'd begun to wonder what had happened to you all.' One gets the impression that Ken Clarke is far happier with a Cabinet that's populated by a few Liberals, as opposed to some of his other colleagues.

The meeting eventually started with a discussion on policy implementation, led by Danny and Oliver. This was terrifically boring and lasted only half an hour. I had the strong impression that it was designed simply to 'justify' us all coming to a Cabinet away day, before moving to political Cabinet. There was a brief discussion, which was instantly forgettable, apart from Michael Gove's quirky contribution: 'As well as the implementation challenges that we need to deliver on, we all need to think about whether the things we're trying to implement actually make sense, so I have a number of questions for the rest of you. Why are we bothering with the Troubled Families Unit – is there really any indication that the money that its spending is worthwhile and shouldn't we just close it down? Some time ago we set up a 'Gangs Task Force' to deal with the problems of gang violence. How is that going? How many gangs have closed down as a consequence? What about cross-government work? Isn't it a complete waste of time? How many cross-government committees are there and what have they ever achieved? Why do we keep on reviewing 16–24-year-old education? We closed down the Education Maintenance Allowance and that was very unpopular, but now all the information shows that we're spending money effectively and in a better targeted way, so does it really make any sense to keep on picking at this sore? Why do ministers bother going on the *Today* programme? Isn't it a complete waste of time? Why do people on the *Today* programme ask stupid questions about where additional money is coming from to fund government projects? Why don't we just say it's coming from the Treasury? What about party conferences? Aren't they a complete waste of time? Why don't we end party conferences and certainly avoid making any policy announcements, which usually turn out to be a complete waste of time?'

Theresa May, Eric Pickles and others stared down sulkily, while others laughed. 'OK, Michael, interesting points,' said Cameron.

We then moved on to political Cabinet, which started off with a polling presentation, highlighting that Labour's narrative over the need for more borrowing isn't convincing people.

Jo Johnson and I then did our presentation. I started by emphasising the coalition still has almost two years to go and the public would expect us to use this time productively. We therefore had to go 'all the way to the wire' rather than allowing the government to fizzle out. I saw Cameron nodding enthusiastically.

We set out our four themes of a stronger economy, and winning the global economic race; easing the squeeze on living standards; a fairer Britain with more rights and responsibilities; and action on creating more opportunity.

At about 1.30 p.m. the conversation closed, and the PM summed up in support of the paper, which will no doubt be briefed out as a pro-coalition moment, with us determined to 'go all the way to the wire'.

We all went downstairs for a buffet lunch, with some rather good white wine and some rather average chicken. All in all, a relaxing 'team-building' event, in a beautiful setting, on a golden summer day.

THURSDAY 25 JULY

Second-quarter growth numbers out – on expectations at +0.6 per cent. The recovery is slowly building momentum. George is on the news today but I noticed there wasn't much of Danny. Looks to me like the Tories have cannily monopolised the airwaves, now that the more positive news is coming through.

TUESDAY 30 JULY

The silly season has certainly started with a vengeance.

Yesterday it was some daft Tory idea from Eric Pickles to allow drivers to park on double yellow lines. This is exactly the type of story that people love – with strong opinions on both sides. Sadly, this also included the Liberal Democrat Party, as our Transport Minister, Norman Baker, was publicly critical, only to be followed by Vince Cable saying he thought it was a very good idea!

Meanwhile, we're continuing to work on the Liberal Democrat 'alternative' to the Tory plan for a marriage tax break. We're looking at various different options: an increase in the tax allowance, a better childcare offer, or – the two front-runners – extending free school meals to all primary school pupils or giving free bus travel to 16–21-year-olds, to help them access education, training or work.

On the 16–21-year-old transport offer, the problem is that Norman Baker has set his heart on a 50 per cent discount. But the statistics show that almost half of 16–18-year-olds already get a 50 per cent discount. So this wouldn't improve education access for many, and there would be large deadweight costs.

On free school meals, we have commissioned some detailed policy work and the cost for all primary school pupils would be £1.2 billion in England, which is about twice the money we have. One option might be to roll free school meals out initially to infant-age pupils.

THURSDAY 1 AUGUST

A conference call to discuss our Lib Dem priorities for the September party conference.

We agreed policies including: the living wage, particularly extending it to employees of all government departments and legislating to require larger companies to publish the number of people who are being paid less than the living wage; tackling zero hours contracts abuses; corporate trust and transparency; a new school building programme; action on tax avoidance; a more generous housing borrowing cap for local authorities; a rail fares package including a lower cap on rail fare price increases.

Goodness knows what the Tories will come up with. More shooting burglars stuff, I suspect.

At 4 p.m. I had a briefing in my diary for 'training' by the security services to allow me to see sensitive documents. It sounded exciting and I was expecting a James Bond-type figure. But when he arrived, he looked more like a junior planning manager from a small district council.

At 5 p.m. I went over to 9 Downing Street to meet up with Oliver and Jo Johnson to go over our proposed conference announcements. We both had a sheet of paper summing up our policy asks, which we rather cautiously exchanged.

The Tories had a list of sixteen policies, and they said that they might have ten, twenty or thirty more to discuss at some stage! They obviously had a sense of humour, since the first policy on their list was 'Earn or Learn'– the policy I had proposed last year as part of the mid-term review, which Nick Clegg then ended up vetoing! Second was 'ending unconditional housing benefit for the under-25s'. Predictable.

Then there was: post-work programme support; child benefit – school attendance allowance; access to GP services; the sale of vacant social homes; single unit pricing for utilities; ending automatic early release of prisoners; changes to deportation rules; more family-friendly tenancies; an aspiration for Britain to be one of the best countries in the world in education in maths by 2023 (why 2023?), which was entitled 'Maths Shock'; a manifesto for improving town centres; a ban on unfair rental fees; part-time season tickets; a cap on rail fare flexibility (exactly the policy that was also on our list); and some kind of tourism campaign entitled 'Great Gets Greater'.

As usual, there were the sensitive Home Affairs policies, including ending automatic early release and changing the deportation rules to make Article 8 Rights to Family Life be more qualified for people who posed a national security threat. Oliver explained that ending automatic early release for prisoners wouldn't actually make much difference to when people were released (parole boards would still decide) but it would give the Tories 'a good right-wing policy to bang on about at the conference'.

FRIDAY 2 AUGUST

I phoned Oliver to tell him that Norman Baker, our Transport Minister, is very keen to announce the lower cap on rail fare increases. Norman says that he's fed up with Cameron 'nicking' his policy announcements. Oliver said the PM really wanted to announce this himself at the Tory conference: 'The problem is that the PM is on holiday, and I'm really not too sure that I want to ring him up on the beach to ask him whether he's prepared to concede to Norman Baker the announcement of a policy on slightly reducing the cap on rail fares!' Probably wise.

TUESDAY 6 AUGUST

At 10 a.m. went over to the Ministry of Justice building to meet Tom McNally, the Lib Dem peer and Leader in the Lords. Tom was a special adviser to James Callaghan, so this is his fifth decade in frontline politics. Tom described the tension between the Ministry of Justice and the Home Office, referring to Chris Grayling and Theresa May as 'two scorpions in a bottle'.

More good economic news – industrial production up 2 per cent. The UK economy suddenly seems to be growing robustly. Nobody can really understand why. I suspect that the simple absence of negative news has been quite a spur – and inflation is now much lower.

WEDNESDAY 7 AUGUST

Left for France at 3 a.m. Drove down from Calais through massive rainstorms. As we got close to the Mediterranean, the temperature soared to 30°, and the rain stopped and gave way to clouds, with sun poking through. Went into the house and opened up all the shutters and let the light come streaming in.

TUESDAY 13 AUGUST

In the evening finished reading the 840-page abridged version of Winston Churchill's *The World Crisis*. Surely one of Churchill's most magnificent works of literature.

WEDNESDAY 14 AUGUST

The newspapers are dominated by the weak position of Ed Miliband and the inactivity of the shadow Cabinet. The press is now getting up a leadership crisis story, on the back of Labour inactivity combined with the recovery of the economy. I think we are seeing a political turning point. Are Labour now on track to lose the next general election?

SATURDAY 17 AUGUST

Spent the morning reading through the papers on autumn policy announcements. The key issue is what policy we're going to select for allowing the Tories to go ahead with their Married Couples Allowance. I mulled the paper from the DPM's Policy Unit, and then sent Nick a note:

1. We should rule out any more on childcare for now, there is already a lot going on.
2. We should rule out Danny's idea of pushing for a freeze in fuel duty. Osborne will do this anyway.
3. I think you were clear that for now you did not want to go beyond £10,000 on the allowance.
4. That leaves free travel for young people and free school meals. Both help with the cost of living and have the strong connection with education, employment and life chances etc.
5. On free school meals, the obvious policy is to pledge them for all primary school pupils, rolling them out first to infants. Schools can start delivering for infants in September 2014. Phasing it in in this way would help schools to adjust. While the policy has dead weight – paying for the meals of children whose parents can afford it – there are a huge number of children in poverty who are not presently entitled to free school meals, and they will benefit. It also has been shown to improve educational outcomes in pilot areas. And it was recommended by the recent School Food Review. It would help many, many families with living costs, including many middle-income families who do not presently feel rich. It would also help us to deal with deterrent effect of losing free meals for families going from benefits into work. We could also afford to end the long-running injustice of low-income students in school sixth forms getting free school meals but not similar students in colleges.

6. The free transport option has a strong policy rationale given the increase in the education leaving age this year and next year, although the bursary is there to target money to those particularly needing help. Clearly we cannot afford free travel for all 16–24-year-olds, so we need to narrow down. A 50 per cent offer isn't enough of an improvement for many 16–18-year-olds who already get a discount of this type.

MONDAY 19 AUGUST

Sat by the pool mapping out the work I need to do on the manifesto and on education over the next year and a half. On the DfE side, I've set myself five main priorities:

1. To bed in the pupil premium and make sure it works to narrow the disadvantage gap.
2. To deliver a national fair funding formula for schools without a political backlash.
3. To deliver a new school rebuilding programme.
4. To deliver a basic need programme to make sure we've got enough school places.
5. To complete the work to help get good leaders into weak schools.

I then set five subsidiary priorities, including doing more work on early years funding and quality and the issue of whether or not we should introduce an early years premium.

SUNDAY 25 AUGUST

The end of our holiday. It's the saddest day of the year, when we have to return to England.

Nightmare journey back into London on the hideously congested, nose-to-tail M25. Next time Norman Baker tells me we don't have any congested roads, I am going to cut his head off and nail it to the last bollard on the A303 Stonehenge bypass.

MONDAY 26 AUGUST

Up at 6.30 a.m. and headed to the Cabinet Office. Greeting me, laid out upon the table, were three red boxes – two from the Education Department and one from the Cabinet Office.

On the top of the Cabinet Office box, a note: 'Update – please read this note first.' Ignored this. I had to plough through something like 200 different policy submissions and updates. Started work at around 7.30 a.m., left for home at 7 p.m. and then worked until midnight.

Amongst the fascinating papers somebody had decided I really needed to see was one listing the officials within the Department for Education who are approved to give authentication for the Secretary of State's seal!

Before going to bed, I reached a memo considering what guidance should be given to schools about Cameron's daft 'school sport premium'.

In one section, a description of best practice in encouraging group sports:

Children need to be encouraged to engage in sport in a progressive and inclusive way. Specific sessions should be delivered by splitting into groups. Each group should then practise the same discipline but with different objectives e.g.: Group 1, bounce a ball to an adult and catch the return; progression – bounce and catch on your own. Group Two, bounce a ball consecutively without catching it; progression – use the other hand. Group Three, bounce a ball consecutively whilst walking forwards; progression – use the other hand to bounce the ball whilst walking.

I hope Michael Gove knows what is being signed off here in his name.

Meanwhile, the news is dominated by Syria, and allegations that the Syrian regime has been using chemical weapons against its citizens.

TUESDAY 27 AUGUST

Met Nick in his office in Whitehall. He appeared very relaxed. He's had the first serious break since becoming DPM.

He gave me an update on Syria. Obama is very unwilling to get involved, but the recent chemical weapons strike has pushed him over the edge and apparently he phoned up Cameron last weekend to say that he'd decided that military action needed to be taken, with a retaliatory bombing strike on key facilities.

Nick said that he has no problems with the conclusion that Obama/ Cameron have come to, but he thinks that this could be quite a difficult issue with the party. He has apparently made clear to Cameron that he thinks we need some kind of 'cover' by going to the United Nations to see if we can get their support.

Nick said that he believes the use of chemical weapons is unacceptable, and that we should have some kind of strike – a very limited operation with Cruise missiles.

Apparently most of the firepower would be US, though we appear to be deploying a submarine that would also fire a modest number of Cruise missiles. Various other European nations are desperate to take part, including France, but it doesn't possess any Cruise missiles. The US administration is trying to find something 'useful' for France and Germany to do, even though they'll be doing no more than 'cooking the burgers'.

I said to Nick that I was sceptical of the value of a big military intervention in Syria but could see the argument that we couldn't simply allow chemical weapons to be used with impunity. I supported a 'fire and forget' missile strike against key Syrian facilities, without putting civilian lives at risk.

Apparently Paddy Ashdown is very much up for a limited strike. Shirley Williams and Simon Hughes are also being sensible and constructive. Ming, however, is apparently obsessed by the United Nations.

Nick said that he was particularly frustrated with Tim Farron, who's positioning himself to be the next leader. Nick said that Farron has suggested that we should consider taking Assad to the International Court in the Hague. Nick pointed out that Assad might not be all that keen to leave Syria!

Nick said he was worried about the party reaction but noted that when Obama finally comes out for military action in a clear way it would be quite influential with many people in the centre/centre-left. Apparently Cameron has spoken to Obama and made clear that as he's in a coalition, that requires some signal that we're going down a UN route.

It sounds as if the military action could be taken this weekend or in the early part of next week.

Nick said he'd spoken to Ed Miliband: 'I can't believe that he's going to play the left-wing card over Syria, as the press will tear him to pieces. Does he want the blame for chemical weapons being used again by Assad in the future?'

In the evening I spoke to Matt Sanders, who said that he'd sat in a lot of meetings with Miliband and his team over the whole press regulation issue. Matt said that the striking thing about Ed Miliband was that he didn't seem to carry a great deal of respect amongst people from his own party, from Harriet Harman down.

WEDNESDAY 28 AUGUST

Advice centre in Yeovil, but had to return to London for a Syria meeting.

Went across to Nick's office in Dover House for 6 p.m. Ryan Coetzee, Nick's strategy director, came in and commented that a lot of the British public and the Lib Dems are still living in a post-Iraq phase, where their attitudes to any military ventures are coloured by the loss of faith in government and security services over Iraq.

My own brief experience in the constituency earlier today confirms this. People are very worried about the parallels between Syria and Iraq, and they also don't seem to understand that what the government's contemplating is a very limited action to stop the use of chemical weapons.

Nick finally came in, and there was quite a contrast with his demeanour when I last saw him on Tuesday. He was again looking quite frayed. He said he'd been in meetings with Cameron and Miliband all day. He said that he and Cameron are completely aligned but it had been a nightmare dealing with Ed Miliband, who was showing himself to be 'weak-willed and hopelessly tactical'.

Every time Miliband had agreed to and secured one particular concession, he would then move the goalposts and start asking for something else. Cameron and Nick have shown him the legal advice from the Attorney General, they've agreed to a UN process of approval, even though the Russians will inevitably veto this, they've taken his views over the motion that's going down in the Commons for debate this Thursday, and they've now finally agreed that there will be a separate second vote after the original vote on Thursday, so that Parliament can have a view after the UN inspectors have reported back.

In spite of this, Miliband is still playing hard to get, and having said yesterday that he was committing the Labour Party to supporting the government, he now appears to be trying to weasel out of the whole thing.

Nick said he really despaired about Miliband and felt that he came across as a very weak and indecisive leader who is constantly looking over his shoulder at his own party and at the potential for creating political mischief.

Nick made clear that the Attorney General has emphasised that the use of chemical weapons is an illegal act under international law and is considered to be a war crime.

He said there was a risk that the US administration would simply get impatient and go ahead with its strikes anyway, probably with the support of France. Nick said he'd be extremely uncomfortable if the US and France went ahead without the UK's involvement, and he also thought it would be extraordinary if the US, France and all the European nations and the Arab League were united in taking action, while the UK ended up in the same camp as China, Russia and a ragtag of nations such as Iran in arguing for no action.

Nick explained in a clear and convincing manner how the action would be carefully targeted – the aim would be to strike a limited number of military targets associated with chemical weapons in use and distribution. Nick said that since Assad seemed to be winning the conventional war, there would be every incentive for him not to use chemical weapons in the future if the West is firm. Nick revealed privately that there are only eighteen targets the military are currently prioritising.

Tim Farron, Ming and others sat very silently. Tim in particular looked quizzical and unconvinced. Shirley Williams was the first to chip in, and she was pretty supportive. Simon Hughes was also helpful, while saying that we had a lot of work to do to keep party members on side.

Tim was much more negative. He suggested that we should be taking Assad to the International Criminal Court even though he must know that this is impossible. He then started talking about how we should try to get Russia on side. Nick listened carefully, frowning.

Tim referred to having asked constituents for their views and having had 400 emails back, only four of which supported military action. God help us if we start running Britain on the basis of self-selecting email surveys.

I supported Nick's position and said that the truth of the matter was that if we took decisive military action in the very limited way described then we would almost certainly prevent future chemical weapons atrocities in Syria. However, I said that we needed to do a lot to convince party members and the public, who are still very influenced by a) the memories of Iraq and b) fear that we're going to get dragged into a wider confrontation in Syria. It could be an uncomfortable discussion at the parliamentary party meeting tomorrow.

THURSDAY 29 AUGUST

Emergency recall of Parliament to vote on Syria.

Newspapers are lukewarm. Ed Miliband has managed to position himself so as not only to table Labour's own amendment, but also to try to vote against the government.

The Cabinet met at 9.45 a.m. Cameron set out the government's position.

Nick spoke, emphasising the steps that both leaders had taken to try to get Ed Miliband on board, finishing by saying he hoped to 'have the support of a number of colleagues in my party'. David Cameron glanced up and said, 'I hope it's going to be more than "a number" of your colleagues, because we'll need the votes!'

Osborne spoke in support and so did I. About half the Cabinet then chipped in, all in support. Towards the end there were some notes of dissent. To my surprise, Theresa Villiers spoke against military action. Owen Paterson, as a Little Englander, also said there were potential problems, and Chris Grayling, while not actually opposing the PM, said he was cautious about getting sucked in.

Got back to the House of Commons at noon to go to Committee Room 11, where our parliamentary party was meeting.

There was, as ever with the Liberal Democrats, a massive debate in which at least half the parliamentary party spoke. Martin Horwood, our foreign affairs spokesman, came out strongly in support. This is about the first time I can ever remember having the same opinion as Martin, and it turned out not to be a good omen.

Lynne Featherstone was neutral. Ming Campbell said he would support the motion but then said a lot of things about how important the United Nations was and how difficult and dangerous the action could be.

Julian Huppert, the Cambridge MP, was the first person who said that he would vote against. Tim Farron was very negative, said that we should go slower, look at all the evidence, there was a risk that we might make matters worse, blah blah blah blah blah. Paddy Ashdown was predictably clear, robust and uncompromising in his support.

Vince was as close to neutral as you could get without toppling over into being negative. Jeremy Browne then spoke and said that it was being portrayed as if the debate within the Liberal Democrats was between 'right-wingers and muesli eaters'. He said that he didn't accept this characterisation, and he thought that the planned military action against Syria was 'a spectacular gesture', which could end up killing innocent people and wouldn't work. I was shocked, not only because I felt that his characterisation of the balance of risk was completely wrong, but also because he spoke extremely disloyally as a member of the government.

The dreadful John Hemmings was negative and unconvinced. A disgruntled Sarah Teather said that 'violence wouldn't help to deal with violence' and we 'couldn't uphold international law by undermining international law'. Sixth form debating points.

At this stage, I had to go to a meeting, so I was looking for a moment to leave quietly. Lorely Burt then indicated that she wanted to speak – she was sitting right next to me so I felt that I couldn't get up and leave at that moment. She said, 'I am really very uncomfortable about what is being proposed. I have never voted against the party on a really important issue before, but on this I think I'm going to have to.' At this, she suddenly burst into tears, and it was a little embarrassing, though also rather sweet. There are some people who couldn't give a damn about stabbing their leader in the back, but when you come across a colleague who does what they think is right even though they absolutely despise letting their leader down, it really is quite moving. Jo Swinson, to my left, handed Lorely a paper handkerchief, and I gave her a squeeze on the arm and a wink as I got up to leave. She really is a lovely, utterly decent person.

Had a brief meeting with Michael Gove. He seemed pretty confident the government was going to win.

2.30 p.m. Cameron kicked off the debate. He was fine but not great, and what was striking was how unsupportive the Tory benches were. Ed Miliband then got up and this was clearly his moment. However, he was also deeply unimpressive, and the impression soon clearly dawned on most people even on his own benches that what he was setting out was a tactical position, to unite his party, oppose the government, but not completely come out against action. A total fudge, in other words. I came to the same conclusion as Nick – that Miliband simply doesn't have the balls to make a great party leader or a great Prime Minister. Even if he wins in the short term, I think he will be the loser in the longer term.

At around 9.30 p.m. I decided that I really ought to go over for the close of the debate, as Nick was summing up. He started off reasonably well, but lost the House because he kept ducking a minor question about whether or not British bases could be used for an attack on Syria if the vote was lost.

Eventually the Speaker called the votes, starting on the Labour amendment. It looked pretty clear that we'd won, and there were 220 in the Aye lobby for the Labour amendment and 332 in the No lobby. I was standing in the Whips' Office, next to Ben Williams, our very experienced staff member who works for Alistair Carmichael. Everybody in the room seemed to think it was a really good result, but Ben immediately looked worried and said that maybe we would end up losing the second vote.

I then voted in the Aye lobby and returned to our Whips' Office to gossip with a few MPs. Ben suddenly shouted out for us to be quiet, as the tellers were going up to stand in front of the Speaker. He winced: 'Oh God, we've lost,' and it was suddenly evident that the tellers for the Labour Party were standing on the right as they faced the Speaker. The Ayes to the right were 272 and the Noes to the left were 285 – and that meant the government was defeated by thirteen on its own motion.

Ed Miliband rose. This could have been his moment to be statesmanlike by making clear that we now needed to follow the process as set out in his amendment, and go down the UN route and have the second vote, but without ruling out action.

Instead, he made some silly little point about asking for a reassurance that action wouldn't be taken without a second vote. David Cameron was clearly better prepared for the defeat. He said that he took the mood of the House of Commons and of the public, and the UK now wouldn't be part of the military action.

Cameron was decisive, but also looked quite shocked and upset. The truth is that this is a huge blow to him as Prime Minister, and it also massively diminishes the UK's position in the world.

Nick texted later: 'It's dismal. Isolation and grubby opportunism in equal measure.' I think that's about right. Essentially the government was defeated by the grubby opportunism of Labour, the isolationism of some members of the Tory Party and, I'm afraid, by the wobbliness of many Lib Dems.

I spoke to Paddy Ashdown. He said he couldn't remember a British Prime Minister losing a vote on such a critical foreign policy issue and he thought that this was permanently damaging to Cameron's leadership and that he might have to resign. Not sure I agree re. resignation. But we're paying the price for the outrageous way Blair acted over Iraq.

FRIDAY 30 AUGUST

The Times leads with 'Cameron humiliated as MPs veto missile strikes on Syria', and *The Sun* has 'Cam down – war vote bombshell – PM humiliated'.

Nick phoned around 9 a.m., just as I'd arrived back in Yeovil. Apparently both Nick and Cameron were expecting Obama to give more leadership. Cameron even asked Obama privately if he would publicly make the case for military action in Syria – but although Obama made this undertaking, he didn't actually deliver. Even today, he still sounds somewhat equivocal and is certainly not going out in front to make the case.

TUESDAY 3 SEPTEMBER

Met Oliver Letwin and Jo Johnson about possible party conference announcements. When they departed, I noticed on my desk a folder that they'd left behind. We looked inside – it was Jo Johnson's briefing pack, setting out the Tory negotiating position on all the conference announcements.

One of my advisers dashed off for a quick read-through, under strict orders not to photocopy anything. Looks like the Tories are also planning to announce some 2015 manifesto pledges – protecting the real NHS budget beyond 2015.

Cabinet. Firstly, an update on the housing market from Eric Pickles: 'Ever since Mrs Pickles and I decided to build ourselves a new patio, house prices and house markets have started to fly!'

As Eric went through his presentation, something kept stroking up against my leg. Originally I thought it was Baroness Warsi, who sits next to me, but I was relieved to find it was the Downing Street cat.

Cameron concluded with a brief discussion about the G20 conference, which is in Russia. He said that he'd recently spoken to Putin, who was calling from the side of a lake in Siberia. They had someone translating. Cameron said that he was a bit baffled when Putin finished by saying something that was translated as 'David Cameron, I hug you!'

In the afternoon, we had a long debate with Nick, Danny and policy advisers, and finally decided to make universal infant free school meals our policy priority, with the money we have secured for letting Cameron's idiotic and wasteful 'marriage tax allowance' go ahead.

WEDNESDAY 4 SEPTEMBER

9.45 a.m. A meeting with Ken Clarke on the Immigration Bill, at his request. He has a wonderful office, which looks right across Horse Guards Parade Ground.

When we arrived, Ken was actually moving through his private office, but at a very slow rate. He's now seventy-three.

He ushered us into his office – not a single piece of paper in view. There then followed thirty minutes of vintage Clarke-ism. Ken said he was pleased that I was looking at the Immigration Bill, as Tory ministers 'couldn't be trusted on this' as they were all 'barking mad and right-wing'.

He said that the Border Agency was a 'complete shambles', and the appeals system was 'ludicrous'.

2.15 p.m. Nick Clegg's office. A prep session on the party conferences Quad. We are going to prioritise: a new priority school building programme, the living wage paid to civil servants, a levy on plastic bags and a consultation on abuse of zero-hours contracts. Polly wants local councils to be able to veto more high street betting shops, though Julian and I see this as rather illiberal.

We would trade some of these policy asks for Tory priorities of: a workfare programme; greater access to GPs, with surgeries open from 8 a.m. to 8 p.m.; the ending of automatic early release for serious offenders; and a couple of other minor things.

I also highlighted with Nick the corporate trust and transparency package, and a package on the national minimum wage, where Vince wants to increase the apprenticeship rate and the under-eighteen rate and ask the Low Pay Commission for advice on removing barriers to a higher national minimum wage.

The Tories are pretending that they don't like the minimum wage stuff, but the newspapers today suggest that Jo and Oliver support this but are facing a Treasury block.

Meanwhile, we're planning to tell the Tories that we are not going to agree their housing benefit or 'Earn or Learn' packages, we're not going to deduct child benefit fines for truancy, and we're not going to proceed with the McKay English votes package.

To Downing Street for the Quad. Oliver, Jo and George Osborne were already seated at the Cabinet table. George was on good form, joking about PMQs today. Apparently Ed Miliband asked all six questions on Syria – a bit excessive, given that his own position is a mess. David Miliband has just published an article about Syria, implicitly critical of his brother's position. George laughed: 'More evidence that Labour chose the wrong Miliband.'

About ten minutes late, Cameron finally came in. He looked a bit over-weight and a bit knackered. He started to go through the list of conference policy announcements, and we agreed the first page quite easily.

We then came on to the category 'probably OK but need more detail'. We questioned whether the town centre manifesto was going to include Eric Pickles's daft idea of allowing cars to park for fifteen minutes on double yellow lines. Cameron laughed: 'Oh no, we certainly don't want to proceed with that completely ridiculous idea.' Jo Johnson blushed, and Cameron added, 'Oh, that was your idea wasn't it?'

We then moved onto the more interesting page of 'difficult but should be discussed' policies, and Nick said that his view is that we should try to do all of these. Cameron said that he was worried about that because there appeared to be six serious Lib Dem ideas but only four serious Tory ideas. Nevertheless, he seemed on for an attempt to get as many things agreed as possible.

Osborne wants a workfare announcement – that once people have been on the work programme for three years and not got a job, they'd then face intensive job search or some kind of compulsory community programme. That all sounds fine, but George was also talking about reducing peo-ple's jobseeker's allowance. Nick said he thought that would be difficult for us.

We then went on to the Lib Dem proposal for a plastic bag levy, where the PM said that we should be cautious for cost of living reasons, but then he conceded that he was actually quite keen on this himself, as the *Daily Mail* supports it!

We've done some polling on the levy and it turns out it's very popular, not least with potential switchers to UKIP! We have given the polling on this to George Osborne, who joked that it was about the first time he'd seen any Lib Dem polling. He said he was 'pretty amazed' that the plastic bag tax was so popular. What we didn't reveal was that the polling sample was only people who were naturally sympathetic to the Lib Dems!

On zero-hours contracts, it was clear that the Tories really don't want to do anything, but we agreed we'd do a consultation focusing very much on banning exclusivity clauses, but without any commitment to take any action until we saw the evidence.

Osborne and Cameron made clear that they were really not keen on the living wage, and they refused to progress this. We agreed instead to ask the Low Pay Commission for advice on barriers to a higher national minimum wage and increasing the apprenticeship rate of minimum wage to the under-eighteen rate.

Our final discussion united Nick and Cameron on the idea of allowing councils to ban high street betting shops. Osborne hated this. Nick tried to push back, by reminding the Tories that it's 'popular with the *Daily Mail*'. Osborne chuckled: 'Since when did the Liberal Democrats start paying attention to the views of the *Daily Mail*?'

'Look,' he said, 'I'm a liberal on these issues – you think that if you ban betting shops you will end up with something nice like muesli shops. I think you'll just end up with empty shops.' I could not help but smile and nod.

The fact is that George is generally pretty liberal and sceptical about government interference. Cameron is far more populist and inclined to chase newspaper campaigns.

THURSDAY 5 SEPTEMBER

The Times includes a devastating article about Ed Miliband by David Aaronovitch: 'Ed Miliband is no leader. He is a vulture.'

He says:

It was being put about this week that Labour would now only back action in Syria if 'there is a very significant change. There are two examples: if Al Qaeda got possession of very large stockpiles of weapons or if there is a direct threat to national security'. By next week it will only be if a member of the Assad family with a pot marked 'anthrax' jumps on the Duchess of Cambridge…

And in this moment of crisis it became clear … what Mr Miliband is. A personable man (and he is a very pleasant companion), politically he is not a presence at all, he is an absence. He is Oedipal Ed, the negator of the unpopular actions of the fathers; the anti-Blair, the non-Brown. His technique for victory is to follow behind the leader, wait for a slip-up and exploit his or her mistakes. He did it to his brother. He hopes to do it to David Cameron. He is neither hunter nor prey, he is scavenger. He is a political vulture … And though you can just about see how in a bad year Ed Miliband could become prime minister, what I cannot any longer pretend … is that he would be a good one. On the contrary, I think he would be a disaster. Strangely, I think both the country and his party already know it.

Spent the afternoon in the DfE. We're getting a dribble of letters from people who've failed the new teacher skill tests. You get three attempts to pass. If you fail them all, you are banned. If they can't do basic English and maths, then they probably shouldn't be teaching.

But there are more complex cases, particularly for people who have already passed their teacher training and then discovered that they've failed the skills test. Had a conference call with officials today about three different cases, where I've been presented with standard letters upholding the test decisions. I wanted to challenge this.

There is one young lady who's been approved as an outstanding teacher and who's been offered a teaching job, but she's failed the maths test by one mark. She's dyslexic and apparently didn't get the support that she needed in the test. I instructed the officials to give the young lady another opportunity. I also asked them to look again at the case of a fifty-year-old who has apparently invested all her time and energy in up-skilling from teaching assistant to teacher, but she has also failed the maths test by one mark. She has got eyesight problems and the test has to be done on a computer, so I have asked officials to see whether they can use a bit of flexibility here. When you are confronted by the personal consequences of these seemingly rational rules, they can seem far too severe – and we may be losing a few really brilliant teachers.

SUNDAY 8 SEPTEMBER

Went to church in the morning for the christening of James's niece. The service was chaotic, and the vicar distinctly odd. He announced that the organist was unwell, and therefore he'd be playing the background music for our hymns on a tape recorder. He warned us to be ready, so that we started the singing as soon as the music began. Unfortunately, on the third hymn, the background music disappeared halfway through, and as nobody really knew the music, the congregation got lost and the singing almost petered out – before the music suddenly surged back on again, in the final verse. I had something of a giggling fit and only just managed not to laugh out loud.

TUESDAY 10 SEPTEMBER

No. 10 cafeteria at 7.30 a.m. to get a coffee, and Oliver Letwin was sitting outside dictating his constituency correspondence. I suppose it's a better place than St James's Park, where he was once photographed by the *Daily Mirror* throwing his constituents' letters into the park bin.

At 8 a.m. Philippa Stroud came to my office for her regular catch-up. I raised the issue of the Tory conference announcement on workfare. She knew nothing about it. It's amazing that No. 10 and the Chancellor barely seem to consult IDS. It's all very different from Michael Gove's department, where Cameron wouldn't dream of announcing a policy without clearing it with Michael first.

WEDNESDAY 11 SEPTEMBER

Vince is all over the newspapers with a gloomy speech on the economy. He's the only person in the country who seems to be miserable now that the economy is turning up.

Went over to the Department for Education and had a confidential chat with a senior official about our plan to make school meals free for infant pupils. We are testing out all the policy detail.

The Quad. More on party conference announcements. While we waited for the PM, George proceeded to joke about Vince's 'helpful' speech. He said he was pretty amazed by Vince's behaviour, as he sent his speech for approval to the Treasury but it turned out that a different speech was briefed out to the press.

Cameron came in: 'Are you lot talking about Vince? Don't criticise the guy. I always say that he's a brilliant economist – he's successfully predicted eight of the last three recessions!'

Cameron then kicked off in his usual way: 'Look, all these Conservative proposals really don't add up to a vast amount for me. The really important things for us are the workfare programme and the tougher stuff on foreign offenders. These are the really interesting things that are going to be front-page news, otherwise the Tory proposals are small stuff. Nick, on your side, the thing that's really going to get you lots of publicity, as well as the Lib Dem cost of living booster, is the levy on plastic bags, which is a front-page-type story.'

George Osborne then spoke, pressing for cuts to benefit rates to pay for his workfare package, but Nick and I resisted. The Tories have a real lack of understanding and interest in finding out about the way poorer people live. Their own experiences just don't include the problems of those who have nothing.

Nick also mentioned that he'd discussed the benefit cuts idea with Iain Duncan Smith, who 'wasn't supportive at all'. Cameron looked pretty dismissive – 'With Iain, unless a policy has got the letters "UC" in it, he's simply not interested.'

But Nick and I dug in, making it clear that we weren't going to accept 10 per cent cuts to unemployment benefit. Osborne and Cameron then started to say that perhaps they couldn't wear the plastic bag levy.

After a while, it became clear what George wanted on this – which was a delay in the levy until after the general election, until 2016. Cameron also started saying that the levy should perhaps only be 2p rather than 5p.

I said that 2p would be ridiculous and wouldn't change behaviour. I also said that the 2016 date for the plastic bag levy coming in was in 'never-never land', and we simply couldn't accept that. We could compromise on autumn 2015. Cameron and Osborne eventually conceded both points.

At the end, Oliver Letwin started to talk about 'rolling friends and family tests out to other public services'. Jo Johnson gave the example of the Chinese airports, which apparently allow passengers to press a button indicating a smiley face or a gloomy face after they've been through immigration control. David Cameron immediately butted in: 'For God's sake, let's not do that – don't forget Heathrow Airport!' Jo looked crestfallen.

FRIDAY 13 SEPTEMBER

Have now read all the consultation responses on the landlords section of the Immigration Bill. Sent an email to Nick Clegg saying we cannot support this. We can either back the Eric Pickles idea of controls for houses in multiple occupation or have some kind of pilot in one small area of the country, with no national rollout until after the general election. Nick came back to say he favours the piloting proposal.

I now have the DfE paper on the free school meals policy, which costs the whole thing at between £500 million and £550 million, and around £42 million extra for the disadvantaged 16–19-year-olds in colleges. I am really quite excited about this. It's going to make a great deal of difference to many families. For an average two-children family with both children in infants' school, this is going to save something like £900 per year. There are also hundreds of thousands of children in poverty who don't receive free school meals and will now do so, and there is the point of ending the injustice between sixth form pupils in schools, who get free school meals if they're from low-income families, and those in colleges, who don't.

Later in the afternoon, the draft party conference speeches began to come through from Lib Dem ministers. These have to be approved by me and the Conservatives, so that we clear any new policy announcements.

The speech from Vince Cable was pretty robust stuff, with sharp attacks on the Tories, who were variously described as 'the hated Tories, the nasty party' and people who have a hostility towards the 'unholy trinity of foreigners, workers and shirkers'. The speech goes on to talk about the Tory friends and donors who 'are at the heart of the greed and recklessness which lay behind the disaster of the early 2000s'. It finishes by claiming the Conservatives have become the 'Tea Party Tories'.

The Vince speech came back from No. 10 later in the day. On the copy which had gone to Tory advisers in the Treasury, the words 'nauseating rubbish' were written, neatly, on the front page.

SATURDAY 14 SEPTEMBER

Our conference in Glasgow starts today, and even though I normally hate party conferences with a vengeance, I feel more optimistic. However, we face difficult debates on tax, defence, energy, tuition fees etc. etc., not to mention economic policy.

The media this morning is good, with the *Daily Mail* splashing on the new 5p plastic bag tax.

On the plane to Glasgow I reread the paper on landlords and immigration control that Eric Pickles sent to the Cabinet committee in February. A searing critique of the PM's present policy:

> It would be disproportionately burdensome, ineffective and intrusive to oblige all private landlords to satisfy themselves as to the immigration status of prospective tenants. It's hard to assess how many illegal migrants this policy would deter in practice as it would be easy to circumvent/evade detection ... Those landlords/agents who are already rogues will not obey the law – and will make more money by exploiting a niche market in illegal tenants by increasing rents/compromising on health and safety for tenants who cannot complain ... The costs and risks considerably outweigh the benefits.

This is a useful defence if the Tories get nasty.

In the evening, a dinner for major Lib Dem donors. Was sitting next to James Palumbo of Ministry of Sound fame.

He's obsessed with fitness and admittedly looks good for someone in his fifties. He told me he had some important advice for Nick and Danny that would help our poll ratings. I leaned forward, expecting a policy nugget: 'Tell Nick and Danny that they are both far too fat. It's not a good public image for the party. They both need to lose some weight. Urgently.'

SUNDAY 15 SEPTEMBER

Up at my usual time of 5.20 a.m. and over to the conference centre to do a round of morning media. All of us are surprised that the announcement on free school meals has remained under wraps.

In the evening, the story came out that Vince has decided he is too busy to attend the economy debate tomorrow and that he will be abstaining. Extraordinary! An act of mutiny.

Emailed Nick late in the evening to ask what was going on with Vince: 'Just beggars belief. It is now essential we win the vote tomorrow.'

This is now getting pretty high stakes, and suddenly from a conference that looked as if it was going to be peaceful is the real risk of a massive final bust-up between Nick and Vince. Nick said that he spoke to Vince at length a few days ago: 'I'm afraid I no longer know what to do – he simply refuses to place his own views below that of a clearly agreed collective position.'

MONDAY 16 SEPTEMBER

The alarm went off at 5.15 a.m. Absolutely knackered, and didn't manage to get up until 6.15 a.m. Jonny Oates had emailed back overnight saying that he thought it would be helpful if I could try to talk Vince Cable round on the vote today, but he thought the chances were low.

Rang Vince's special adviser, Emily, who said Vince is sympathetic to the slightly vague amendment that's being moved by the Social Liberal Forum of more left-leaning party members. Emily said he was upset about the recent media briefing about his 'humiliation' at the away day.

I've got some sympathy with Vince's views about overly orthodox economic policy, but it really isn't the right moment to have a row about this, just as the economy recovers. We agreed that I would meet Vince at 8.45 a.m. in his hotel room.

The traffic was awful and at 8.55 a.m. I got through security and ran over to the conference hotel. However, I got a text message from Vince's team saying that because there were so many media hounding him, he'd gone straight to the parliamentary party meeting, which was due to take place at 9 a.m. I was worried I wouldn't get a chance to speak to him.

When I arrived, Vince and his team of Emily Walsh and Giles Wilkes were already there. Vince came over and said that he was keen to talk and we went into the empty conference room next door. Vince was pretty uptight, and without waiting for me to say anything he said, 'Look, I do understand that this has now become a matter of confidence in the leader, and for that reason I'm going to vote for the motion today, but I can't understand why we haven't compromised with the Social Liberal Forum, and I think that the whole thing is totally unnecessary.'

I said he must realise that not only would it be very damaging to the party to have a split over economic policy, but it would be almost impossible for him to stay as Business Secretary and that he might well be sacked in a reshuffle if he failed to support the party on its economic policy.

Vince and I then went back into the parliamentary party meeting room. Eventually he was called to speak: 'Look, all of this has got very difficult. I'm pretty angry about the way in which things have been briefed out about what happened at the away day, and I also can't see why more effort hasn't been made to come up with a compromise solution on the amendments. However, I now understand that this has become an issue of confidence in the leader, and I will be supporting the motion today.'

The crisis was over.

At lunchtime, I met with *Guardian* journalists Patrick Wintour and Nick Watt. They were disappointed by Vince's surrender. This has been quite a knock to Vince's credibility.

TUESDAY 17 SEPTEMBER

The announcement on free school meals is going to take place today.

Went back to the press office and made some calls to let Russell Hobby, the head of the National Association of Head Teachers, and Martin Doel, of the Association of Colleges, know the news. Both seemed very pleased. Also telephoned the authors of the School Food Plan – Henry Dimbleby and John Vincent. They were delighted, and John – who was out in Ethiopia – said that when he heard the news he burst into tears!

Some people on the liberal right won't like this announcement. But the truth is that four out of ten children in poverty are not entitled to free school meals, and this will have a positive impact on socialisation, educational attainment, healthy eating and living standards. This is one of the best and simplest policies that we've announced.

Bumped into Danny Alexander. He said that Vince's position was beginning to become 'a bit of a joke' and seriously undermining our economic narrative. There is no doubt that Danny covets the Business portfolio and would want to move there if Vince was sacked. I would then return as Chief Secretary. However, we have to do what's in the best interests of both the party and the government, and if Nick asked Vince to move, he would probably end up resigning. That would be immensely destabilising.

Met up with the *Times* journalists in the evening, and they were all grumbling about the fact that the broadcast media got the free meals story under embargo at 5 p.m., whereas the written media couldn't publish it until the next day. As a consequence, they will all be extremely grumpy and they'll probably be determined to be negative.

WEDNESDAY 18 SEPTEMBER

Nick's speech was at 3 p.m. The messages were:

1. That we've achieved a hell of a lot in government.
2. That we stop the Tories doing bad things.
3. That Nick is a strong, confident leader.
4. That we want to be in government after the next election, in a coalition.
5. If we're in government with the Tories, we'll stop them pursuing ghastly right-wing policies and making Britain a more unfair place, and if we're in coalition with Labour, we'll stop them from driving the economy into a ditch.

FRIDAY 20 SEPTEMBER

My roving advice centre in East Yeovil. Met a couple of people living in conditions of real squalor and loneliness. Particularly sad was one young man in a wheelchair in his sheltered bungalow. He has both mobility problems and severe learning difficulties, and he was sitting there surrounded by junk with just a radio playing in the background. These are the types of people Cameron and Osborne just don't seem to understand or even think about.

SUNDAY 22 SEPTEMBER

Ed Miliband has admitted at the start of Labour's conference that he wants to 'bring socialism back'. A gift to the right-wing media.

MONDAY 23 SEPTEMBER

7.45 a.m. breakfast with Oliver Letwin. The summer weather is fading away, and it was cloudy and a little bit cold, but Oliver insisted on us sitting in the outside patio area.

He was in his normal perky mood, and we started on entry and exit checks. Oliver thinks that the Home Office is designing some incredibly expensive IT system that won't work, and he claimed: 'My own daughter could probably come up with a better and cheaper system that could be in place within six months.'

Eventually, I said that it was time for us to discuss the Immigration Bill, at which Oliver looked a bit more serious. We had a detailed discussion, and I left 'landlords' until last. I explained bluntly that we had decided that this was a very bad idea, and when Oliver asked why, I said, 'For exactly the same reason that Eric Pickles set out so clearly in the note that he prepared for the Ministerial Advisory Group.'

Oliver put his head into his hands and looked very gloomy. I said that I thought we ought to work up backstop options, including a one-year pilot. Oliver said that he would be amazed if the PM would even agree to the Home Office doing this type of work, and that Cameron simply wouldn't want to make any concession to us.

I said we were not going to change our minds. Oliver looked a bit crestfallen and miserable and then he dashed off to the 8.30 a.m. Tory morning meeting, to deliver the bad news to Cameron.

News of the German elections is coming through. Angela Merkel and her centre-right party have been returned, but her coalition partners, the German Liberal Party, have been absolutely smashed. They have failed to get over the 5 per cent vote threshold, which means that they don't get any seats in Parliament at all – for the first time since the Second World War. This demonstrates how you can have a coalition that does relatively well but where all the benefit goes to the larger party. This is an omen for 2015 that we really shouldn't ignore.

At the Labour conference we've had a motley variety of policy announcements, none of which will set the world alight. There's some slightly dotty policy, asking every firm that employs an immigrant to also recruit an apprentice. This is the kind of 'great idea' that's dreamt up in Westminster, but doesn't really work with the public or in practice.

Labour is in serious trouble. People don't believe in Ed Miliband as a plausible Prime Minister. 2015 is going to be a grumpy general election in which the Lib Dems will be under huge pressure, Labour will struggle to make any advances, and the Tories are likely to lose a few seats to Labour and gain a handful off us. I think UKIP will continue to poll quite well, but I doubt that they will get many or any seats. I can see another hung parliament, with a weaker Lib Dem contingent, a marginally stronger Labour contingent and a similar size Tory grouping.

TUESDAY 24 SEPTEMBER

Ed Miliband's speech at the Labour Party conference. He announced a 'surprise' new policy of freezing energy prices. This is highly populist, but it could easily unravel. It sounds too good to be true, and it's also likely to undermine investment in the energy sector.

At 8 a.m. Sir Bob Kerslake, the head of the Home Civil Service, came to see me for a meeting to discuss 'Border systems programmes stock-take', which is some kind of Home Office computer system that is supposed to monitor people as they come in and out of the country. The whole thing is ludicrously over budget and isn't going to work. Basically, this looks like an IT system that's been overdesigned, and is supposed to be doing everything from basic immigration control to meeting the requirements of various other arms of government.

All Oliver Letwin and I are really interested in is a proper system of entry and exit checks. The Home Office are just about beginning to understand that we are serious. Up until now they appear to have regarded it as a box-ticking exercise in terms of the coalition agreement.

Oliver said that he'd discussed this with Cameron and warned him that the problem with having an entry and exit system is that we would actually know how many people who should have left the country hadn't done so – which could be pretty embarrassing. Cameron apparently said that he understood the risk, but it was a risk that he was prepared to take. Cameron also knows that the entry and exit check system is something we Liberal Democrats are very committed to, and he won't want to be outflanked by us.

One of the senior civil servants who came with Sir Bob Kerslake explained to us towards the end of the meeting that immigration 'really isn't a high priority in the Home Office'.

I interrupted: 'I'm sorry, did I hear you right?'

Everyone around the table looked surprised. Sir Bob Kerslake explained: 'The Home Office is really institutionally only interested in crime, disorder and terrorism. Immigration has always been a secondary concern for them. They regard all this entry and exit check stuff and immigration control as pretty second order and not a big priority for senior people.' This is all extraordinary. No wonder there is little public confidence in the immigration system, when people in the Home Office don't think that immigration policy and the loss of public confidence is a priority.

Nick is due to have a discussion with David Cameron on the 'landlords' issue before going to the UN conference. Oliver said that Cameron is planning a 'controlled explosion' about our veto.

At 4.30 p.m. I had a meeting with officials in the DfE. The first item was intriguingly called 'The NUT and NASUWT – plotting in relation to'.

The NUT and the NASUWT have supposedly been cooperating for the last few months on strike action. It now seems as if the relationship has broken down. Amusingly, the NASUWT have spoken to the department and said that they are looking for an exit route from the strike, but they don't want the NUT to know. The NUT have also relayed to us the same message that they're looking for an exit route, but they don't want this to be known by the NASUWT!

FRIDAY 27 SEPTEMBER

Last night received an email from Dom Cummings. Dom tends to broker sensitive policy agreements between me and Michael, and he's now trying to do this on the issue of secondary school accountability – which we've been battling on for months. Dom's note suggests a compromise:

> MG has agreed secondary accountability – reluctantly and with grum-
> bling ... but he has one terrorist demand in return. [This is exactly the
> kind of language that Dom loves, and which reflects his destructive and
> revolutionary approach to policy-making.] He wants the double-weighted
> English option to be simply English language and English literature,
> i.e. if you do English language and don't do English literature then you
> score zero on literature and this counts as the double-weighted element.
> He thinks it will strongly incentivise English literature in poorer parts
> of the country that currently swerve it with many poorer children. He
> feels very strongly about this. He thinks it is totally defensible and he
> is entirely happy about any degree of noise from the usual suspects.
> Happy? So – if you live with the English literature proposal then we are
> DONE. If not, then you'll have to have a tricky talk to him because he
> feels he's bent over backwards to be accommodating on everything else.
> Next steps ... He assumes you will square the DPM given that it is your
> plan – this right? Dom.

Tim Leunig is suggesting to me that I should definitely accept this. This will put a good focus on the new 'best eight' measure of accountability, and it will also put a big focus on progress, which will incentivise all schools to do well for all children. Although all these accountability issues seem really dry and boring, they have a massive effect on the subjects that schools encourage young people to take, as well as the way in which schools are held to account, and it's vital that we get this right.

Later on, my office in London sent through to me the first of the Tory Secretary of States' conference speeches. It really is a bizarre process to have to send each other's political speeches out for approval – particu-larly with lots of political knock-about stuff aimed at both coalition parties.

Chris Grayling's speech is the oddest. There's a terrific amount of populist rubbish, which includes how Chris has 'Banned Sky TV across the whole prison estate'. I wouldn't have thought that Rupert Murdoch would be happy about that bit.

SATURDAY 28 SEPTEMBER

Tim Leunig emailed me back about Dom's proposal on English literature. A problem: it requires people to take nine GCSEs! Tim thinks this is not sensible. Currently only 49 per cent of children take nine or more 'proper' GCSEs.

Tim and Tom Shinner are now suggesting that English language is only double counted if you take English literature as well. I phoned Jo Johnson. He hopes to get other Tory speeches through to us today, but said there might be a delay in getting us Theresa May's. Jo said that there was 'a bit of a problem' with the speech and 'the problem is that we are not willing to agree the existing draft with Theresa, and the PM's having to get involved, and there may be a bit of a row'.

SUNDAY 29 SEPTEMBER

Spent the day working on my red boxes. Received a paper on the proposed national fair funding formula which has been drawn up by officials. They seem to have taken too literally my last steer that we should avoid a massive amount of turbulence, and as a consequence they've hugely increased the weighting on deprivation, which means they are proposing that over a third of the lowest-funded authorities should actually lose money! This is political idiocy of the first order. If we are going to deliver fairer school funding, we have to find a marriage of good policy and good politics.

Spoke to Jo Johnson at 3 p.m. I said that IDS's speech wasn't acceptable because he'd included the pilot of the Benefits Payment Card, which we'd already blocked. This is IDS's idea to pay people their benefits on a special card, which means they can't spend money on alcohol, fags etc. Ridiculous nonsense. Jo asked in a rather innocent way, 'Oh, haven't we agreed that?'

Jo said that Iain Duncan Smith was 'difficult', and he said that the Tories suspected IDS had leaked the Osborne announcement about workfare to the *Daily Mail* last week, presumably in anger that George was 'nicking' the issue. Interesting to see that the Tories have as many difficult internal issues with their Secretaries of State as we do. However, on our side it's only Vince we have to worry about, whereas on their side it's Iain Duncan Smith, Theresa May, Chris Grayling...

MONDAY 30 SEPTEMBER

We had Theresa May's speech through last night, and it had a very unpleasant bit in it attacking Nick over immigration, in a grossly misleading way. The official advice was that they considered the wording to represent a direct attack on a fellow minister, which is 'unacceptable under the Ministerial Code'.

They suggested that we forward the speech to Jeremy Heywood, to get him to intervene. Jonny Oates texted Ed Llewellyn, and Ed apparently came back and said that the section attacking Nick had been taken out. Ed claimed that the Home Secretary hadn't even seen it herself, and it had been written by a speechwriter – total balls.

In the late morning I got an email from Dom Cummings. Dom is clearly keen to have the secondary accountability consultation agreed before Michael Gove goes to America. However, I'm still holding up some of the curriculum proposals that Michael wants approved on English literature, English language and maths. Michael has got this absolutely dotty proposal insisting that every pupil should have to read five types of book for their literature exam, and is saying this *must* include both a Shakespeare play and a nineteenth (not eighteenth or twentieth!) century English (not British!) novel.

I have asked what is wrong with somebody doing, for example, The Prologue to Chaucer's *Canterbury Tales* instead?

Pamela, the Secretary of State's private secretary, came back to me this afternoon with his reply. Ominously, her email started: 'I'm sorry if we haven't explained the Secretary of State's position properly, and the reason for his specificity.'

The note went on:

The Secretary of State insists on this prescription because the nineteenth century represents the most important period for the novel as a cultural form. This was the century in which the novel became the dominant form of Western literature. A student of English literature who hasn't studied a nineteenth-century novel is like a student of maths who hasn't studied multiplication.

That put me in my place, since I didn't study an English nineteenth-century novel for my English literature exam! One second Michael talks about the need for school autonomy and the next second he is prescribing the exact texts that people have to read.

On my way back from County Hall in Taunton I heard the coverage of George Osborne's conference speech. Out of nowhere he has inserted a pledge to freeze fuel duty for the rest of the parliament. Outrageous.

George has also made a pledge that in the next parliament the Conservatives will aim to run a surplus on their current budget, in order to start paying down debt. This is all about politics. He will be dying to have some kind of dividing line in which there are deep cuts embedded into the public spending forecast, so that Labour are put on the spot. This is a game we shouldn't help the Tories play, because there is no way that we can keep on cutting public spending in real terms unless we're prepared to see the National Health Service fall to pieces and the education system deteriorate. It's the sort of stupid game Gordon Brown used to play.

TUESDAY 1 OCTOBER

To the Goring Hotel to have breakfast with Lord Nash and Tom Shinner. Tom is a nice guy – very bright and generally sensible on policy.

John and Tom said that they are concerned about the increasing burden on the Department for Education of running the academies system. Now that we have got thousands of academies, it's increasingly clear that the system can't be run from Westminster. They proposed a new model, with 'Regional School Commissioners', who would essentially do the work of the DfE in commissioning academies and performance-managing them. This sounds quite sensible but the risk is that it appears to be a takeover of the local authority role in education, which will upset Lib Dems. I said that I wasn't against the idea in principle, although we had to work out how local authorities and school commissioners would work together.

Nick has now had his phone call with Cameron on the landlords issue. Sounds like it could have gone better. Nick said: 'Cameron was awful – petulant, pathetic and childish.'

WEDNESDAY 2 OCTOBER

12.30 p.m. – a meeting with the authors of the School Food Plan, Henry Dimbleby and John Vincent. At the pre-meeting, Matt Sanders asked the officials how Michael Gove knew Henry and John, and why they were asked to write the Food Plan – rather than Jamie Oliver. The official sheepishly said that Jamie Oliver was regarded more as a friend of the Labour Party. He then, looking even more embarrassed, said, 'Well, I think that the Secretary of State actually bumped into them in a bar in Marrakech, and got talking and then eventually offered them the job!' Anyway, we had a very good meeting with both of them – they seem utterly decent people.

An endless set of education meetings. All my days now seem like this. Half an hour meetings, back to back, to discuss: initial teacher training and closing the gap; free school meal implementation; greater freedoms for governing bodies; the role of the local authority in school improvement; how to get more high-quality leaders to teach in different parts of the country; how to provide better school and college transport for the 16–18s; an update on the Extremism Task Force; an update on how we select free schools; a briefing meeting with an educational research organisation; a discussion about free school pupil numbers and whether or not we've been overfunding some schools; a discussion about whether or not to fund large 16–18 programmes at a higher rate if people are doing large numbers of A-levels, and so on and so forth. Not a single ten-minute session left spare in my diary from 8 a.m. to about 7 p.m.

SATURDAY 5 OCTOBER

Emailed Nick Clegg to say that I looked forward to seeing him in Chevening, for dinner.

He emailed back: 'I also need to update you on the reshuffle – I'm afraid I haven't found a way to move you into HMT this time. Not for want of trying though! Will explain. N.' So that's it on the reshuffle then. Rather disappointing, as I had definitely been hoping to go back to Chief Secretary.

My sadness at getting this news is tempered by the fact that my current jobs in the Cabinet Office and the Education Department are giving me a huge amount of influence and power in areas that are actually very dear to me.

At 6.15 p.m. drove down to Chevening. A lot of traffic on the road, but we were only fifteen minutes late when we entered the lane that leads down to the house, past a whole load of rather feudal-type cottages and the church.

To my mind, Chevening is easily the most beautiful of the three country houses that are used by the Prime Minister and his most senior ministers. You come in through the gate, and an expanse of land opens up to your right which stretches away from the house and disguises the fact that eventually it dips away steeply into a beautiful valley. Meanwhile, on the left you continue through a gate and into the massive courtyard. There is a large circular driveway. A wide and impressive flight of steps leads up to the classically proportioned house.

The reception hall is huge and is hung with large numbers of shotguns and swords. There is a sweeping staircase up to the main part of the house to the left, and in front is an impressive dining room – but we were led off to the right and into the drawing room.

Nick and Miriam were there, with the other guests. The room is impressive, with very large and classical paintings of people such as Pitt the Younger, but there's something about it which is rather homely and if not quite frayed at the edges, then at least resonant of a place in which people live, rather than some kind of museum.

Nick and Miriam were in good form, and Miriam was looking particularly relaxed. You can see why she's regarded as the most attractive and appealing of the three party leaders' wives, and she's somebody who not only looks good but is also sharp-brained and has carved out a high-flying career of her own.

After about half an hour we went through for a dinner of smoked salmon, duck and then a very nice dessert of warm figs with cheese and honey. We chatted about a whole variety of issues, from the situation in Iran and Syria to the prospects for the next election.

Nick mentioned that Cameron is expecting the result of the general election in 2015 to look much like 2010 – i.e. another hung parliament.

Rumi Verjee, a guest of Nick's, spoke quite a lot about Bill Clinton, who's a friend of his. He now expects Hillary to stand in the next set of US presidential elections. I said I thought that Hillary was a rather Marmite figure in the US, and that she might repel some of the natural centre-right vote which is crucial in the US. Personally, I can see Hillary running for the Democrats but losing the election in the same way that Al Gore lost to George Bush the Younger.

After dinner, we went back through to the drawing room for coffee, and Nick pulled me aside to talk about the reshuffle, which he said is going to take place on Monday. Nick said he'd been keen to try to get me back into the Treasury as Chief Secretary, and he'd spoken to Vince Cable to see whether he would be willing to move so that Danny could go to Business. Vince said that he couldn't possibly move from Business, that it was his ideal job etc. etc., and Nick said bluntly that he didn't want to have to sack Vince.

Nick said that he'd phoned Michael Moore to tell him about his sacking and that he'd had 'one of the most difficult conversations of my political life'. Mike obviously couldn't understand why he was being moved, as he's done a pretty good job.

But Nick thinks that Alistair Carmichael would do a better job in engaging Alex Salmond, as he is more of a bruiser.

Nick then said that David Heath will be sacked from DEFRA, and Jeremy Browne from the Home Office. I questioned whether it was sensible to move Jeremy.

SUNDAY 6 OCTOBER

Nick came back to me by email about the reshuffle. He said that he had mulled the situation re. Jeremy Browne but although he saw the dangers, 'It's unfair to keep others blocked out of government.'

So that's it for Jeremy. Pretty bleak news for him. He's gone from the stratospheric promotion to Minister of State at the Foreign Office, sideways and perhaps even down a bit to a fairly non-job at the Home Office, and now he's going to be leaving the government altogether. A sad loss, because he's a very able individual.

MONDAY 7 OCTOBER

Reshuffle day. Up at 5.15 a.m. and in to the office by 6.30 a.m. All regular ministerial meetings are cancelled.

The Conservative reshuffle took place, and it was all below Cabinet level and seemed to consist mostly of promotion of the Chancellor's acolytes. Matt Hancock is upgraded to Minister of State. Liz Truss must be disappointed that she hasn't been promoted.

The Labour reshuffle is more significant, with Ed Miliband unbelievably demoting Stephen Twigg, Jim Murphy and Liam Byrne – all people that one of the top trade union leaders had asked to be demoted or sacked a year ago.

Had a midday text from Norman Lamb: 'David, just been told Nick wants to speak to me in an hour. I'm not about to get sacked, am I?' I texted Norman back to reassure him. For a moment I wondered if Nick's office had muddled Norman Baker and Norman Lamb! In reshuffles, mistakes sometimes get made and people with the same surname have occasionally been given the wrong jobs!

Heard from Tim Leunig that Dom Cummings is going to be leaving the department in January. This is a big change, as Dom is hugely influential, and is really Michael's right-hand man and enforcer. It's interesting that he's moving on, and it's not clear whether he's just bored or frustrated, or maybe he thinks that Michael might be moved from Education in the next reshuffle.

There is due to be one last big reshuffle next spring, and I do wonder whether Michael might at this stage move from Education. If so, that could be an opportunity for the Lib Dems to take over.

TUESDAY 8 OCTOBER

Went to the Cabinet at 9.30 a.m. and it started five minutes late. It turns out that Theresa May was in with Cameron having a full-scale row about Norman Baker being appointed as a Home Office Minister – 'How could you!' Apparently Theresa is spitting blood!

WEDNESDAY 9 OCTOBER

Met Norman Baker, who, I suspect, is rather enjoying all the publicity about his move. Theresa May is said to be pretty furious about him joining the Home Office without her being consulted. Asked Norman how she had behaved: 'Civil, but rather frosty!'

A row over the new planned teacher tests. Tim Leunig has warned that the tests aren't fit for purpose. Apparently even the School Testing Agency has admitted they are a 'bodged job', and that 30–40 per cent of people who are genuine C-grade candidates will not pass the tests while the same proportion of below C-grade candidates will pass! Tim has recommended we abandon the tests. Exactly my view.

THURSDAY 10 OCTOBER

Into the office at the luxuriously late time of 7 a.m.

Ploughed through paperwork and had a meeting with Sir Jeremy Heywood at 8 a.m. Discussed his 16–24-year-olds review. He seemed to have had a rather unproductive meeting with Michael Gove, who seemed to be 'against every one of my ideas'.

MONDAY 14 OCTOBER

An unhelpful article in today's *FT*, claiming that senior Conservatives are trying to steal our key Lib Dem tax policy – of raising the personal allowance to £12,500 in the next parliament.

At 10.15 a.m. I went to Michael's office for a meeting on the national funding formula. Michael eventually expressed himself content with the proposals that I had agreed. We now have a green light to proceed.

Had a call with Tristram Hunt, the new shadow Education Secretary for Labour. Tristram has taken over from Stephen Twigg, who was sacked in the reshuffle. Tristram is a pleasant, modernising Blairite, who's probably been a little over-promoted and who will drive many Labour left-wingers mad.

Went over to the House of Commons to make an oral statement on secondary school accountability. A serious subject but with big consequences – a broader curriculum and better incentives to teach all children. Some very supportive statements from the chair of the Education Select Committee and his Labour predecessor.

To Richmond this evening with Nick Clegg, Richmond Park Liberal Democrats and their new parliamentary candidate.

In the car, Nick said he found it surprising that Dom was leaving, and I speculated on whether Dom might be expecting Michael Gove to be reshuffled. Nick said, 'Well, Cameron did say to me that the next reshuffle might be a bigger reshuffle – but why would he move Gove?'

We got to the event at around 8 p.m. The Richmond party is probably the most affluent in the country, and the items up for auction were not the usual boxes of chocolates, cheap wine and miscellaneous garbage, but exotic overseas properties for short holidays, as well as things like 'afternoon tea for two at Churchill College, Cambridge'.

We sat down to a dinner of green pea and mint soup, followed by 'aromatic chicken marinated in natural yoghurt, ginger and coriander', and finished with a white and dark chocolate truffle cheesecake.

For guest speakers, these are not occasions for much enjoyment – you are endlessly lobbied about party political issues, and even when the food is good you never get a chance to eat it, because somebody's either talking to you or asks you to make a speech just as it arrives.

It was supposed to be a very upbeat event, with only local party members and supporters there, to raise money for fighting the seat at the next general election.

Nick took the first question from the floor and unfortunately picked exactly the wrong questioner. I had warned Nick beforehand that Richmond Park is about the only area in the country where the mansion tax is intensely unpopular, because so many people own homes which are worth more than £2 million.

Well, sure enough, the first question was from an elderly-looking lady with a German accent: 'Mr Clegg, zere is one thing that vee are all really worried about in Richmond. Zer mansion tax! Do you realise that this is really going to hit many of us in zis area, because zer mansion tax really bites at properties worth as little as £2 million?' She made the whole thing sound as if the party would be removing the last crust of bread from her table, and it was one of those ghastly occasions where the more rational the answer Nick gave, the more she continued to chunter on from her seat fifteen metres away.

When Nick went on to explain that elderly people who were close to dying wouldn't actually need to pay the mansion tax, but could leave it as a claim on their estates, she commented loudly, 'Is he really saying that I need to die if I want to avoid zis terrible tax?'

By the time Nick left, he was looking positively pleased to get out.

TUESDAY 15 OCTOBER

Cabinet at 9.30. The first part consisted of some kind of photo opportunity, about cutting European bureaucracy. Cameron went into one of his public relations modes, 'strong leader' etc., for the sake of the cameras, with all sorts of snappy sound bites.

We then had a slightly surreal presentation from Oliver Letwin about national risk assessment – serious hazards and threats facing the UK, including: pandemic flu; large-scale biological attacks; widespread coastal flooding; significant nuclear attack; a civil airliner being brought down; technological failure of the banking system; a crash of a road or rail tanker containing dangerous goods; and – finally – 'severe effusive volcanic eruptions'!

Oliver went into some detail about the risk of coastal flooding, explaining that a lot of our ports are on the east coast, where flooding risk is highest. He then reassured us that 'we shouldn't worry too much because most of the food coming in through these ports is things like avocados, rather than essentials'! There was a ripple of laughter around the Cabinet table and someone mumbled about the 'Great Avocado Shortage of 2014'.

WEDNESDAY 16 OCTOBER

Got back home at 10 p.m. A telephone call from Gabriel, the head of press at the DfE. *The Guardian* have apparently got hold of a fairly toxic report by Ofsted into one of the Muslim free schools. I had a briefing on the report sent through and it was one of the worst Ofsted reports I'd ever seen. Apparently the school is a complete shambles, with unqualified staff and no financial controls. There is going to be fairly bad coverage tomorrow, and this might even prompt an urgent Ministerial Question. Fortunately for Michael Gove, he's away in the United States, so if there is a problem, I'll have to deal with it.

The only good thing is that Labour's own policy on free schools is in turmoil. At the weekend, Tristram announced that Labour are now in favour of free schools. But now that the Muslim free school disaster has been highlighted, Tristram seems to be saying that free schools are a terrible ideological disaster. Totally incoherent.

THURSDAY 17 OCTOBER

Arrived at the House just a few minutes before the Urgent Question. I'd expected Tristram to be fairly measured and forensic. Instead, he went into a rant about free schools. It made it very easy for me to respond and point out the incoherence of Labour's position.

Tory MPs were out in force. In my defence of the government's record I may have been a little dismissive of a Labour question about unqualified teachers, but when you are on a sticky wicket it's natural to use your bat.

Sadly, I missed a meeting with the DPM on his big education speech next week.

FRIDAY 18 OCTOBER

Weekend break in France.

We seem to be in an October 'silly season'. There were a range of daft political stories, including one about the coalition bringing back third-class rail services. There is also a mini-row about a Downing Street spokesman having given advice that people should wear jumpers in order to reduce their heating bills. The whole thing has been picked up by various social networking sites under the hashtag 'Cameron's heating tips'. These now include: 'Have your maid stitch a fine coat of swan feathers after your manservant plucks a swan for Sunday brunch' or 'Simply add a large measure of Courvoisier VSOP to your vanilla latte'.

SATURDAY 19 OCTOBER

Went out for dinner. Unusually for France, the meal wasn't great.

When I got back home I had a series of text messages from Dom Cummings, saying that 'the Clegg office' has briefed excerpts from his education speech, attacking MG over his approach to academies and free schools: 'This has been briefed as "Clegg declares war on Gove".'

This time Dom was in full flow, even claiming that 'hacks' are texting saying, 'After Browne, is Laws next?' Total rubbish but all being stoked up by Dom to imply that there is a split between Nick and me.

Frustratingly, the text of the speech has been changed since I saw it on Friday, and the wording has been hyped up to say the free schools policy is an 'ideologically driven policy'– exactly the words being used by Labour. Unhelpful, because I've only just been in the House of Commons on Thursday defending the coalition's policy on free schools, and criticising Labour for presenting free schools as just being ideologically driven.

Just before midnight I emailed our policy and press advisers: 'Which idiot inserted these words into the speech?'

At around midnight I had a message back from Nick saying, 'David – apologies. I took out direct references to Gove to depersonalise the text but kept in the phrase re. ideology. Of course you should have seen the final wording.'

I explained that I am also concerned that we are trying to agree to announce two new DfE policies in this speech, and unless we have already agreed the wording with the Tories then there's no way they're now going to sign this off, in a speech which attacks them. We've buggered up our chances of getting the Tories to agree to announcements on spreading the best head teachers across the country and raising the bar on qualified teacher status.

SUNDAY 20 OCTOBER

A pretty frustrating day. Nick's advisers have made a complete balls-up of the pre-briefing of his speech. They've briefed what was supposed to be a mid-rank story about the Lib Dems favouring qualified teacher status in academies and free schools into a full-scale outbreak of war.

MONDAY 21 OCTOBER

Nick said that he was going to be having lunch with Cameron today and that he would raise his education speech. We agreed that the announcement on QTS reform is now completely dead, but we should continue to try for an announcement on moving top heads to challenging areas.

Met Dom Cummings to complain about the way he or other Tories have briefed out my position on free schools – exploiting my having to go into bat for Michael in the Commons last week.

Dom said, 'Look I quite understand. It's all the muppets at No. 10. Frankly, I don't care about the politics of these things, as I'm leaving soon. My job is to protect Michael and to look after his back. As you know, I couldn't care less about Cameron and Osborne – I don't owe them anything, and I don't care what happens to them after I leave. They can be chucked out of Downing Street for all I care. In Downing Street they hate me even more than they hate you lot.'

A series of other DfE meetings in the afternoon, including a briefing session for the Education Select Committee about a potential shortage of school places across the country. When the Permanent Secretary recently went to the Public Accounts Committee, he apparently told them that all local authorities were meeting their statutory responsibility to deliver school places, but we have just recently found that there are four places in the country, including three areas of London, where some children in Reception and Year 1 have not actually been allocated places.

We've checked with our legal advisers, and this apparently means that the local authorities are not meeting their statutory requirements. This is really pretty embarrassing and means that if I'm put on the spot by the Select Committee I could be in some difficulty. One of the Tories' political advisers was in the briefing when the officials admitted this and he looked pretty shocked. With the Tories aware of this, I'll have to be particularly careful at the Select Committee, because though I don't want to draw attention to the severity of the problem, nor can I afford to be economical with the truth. This all does emphasise the need to put more money into extra school places rather than an excessive amount into free schools – when most applications are just in places like London.

TUESDAY 22 OCTOBER

A mischievous piece in today's *Times* by Rachel Sylvester, where she reports that according to one 'Whitehall source' – who must be Dom Cummings –

> Mr Clegg has jumped the gun [on middle-tier accountability] because the Department for Education has already drawn up plans to increase the accountability of academies and free schools. Michael Gove and Mr Laws have been working for nine months on a joint coalition proposal to improve the monitoring of and intervention in failing institutions. It will neither return control to local authorities nor leave it in the department; it is due to be in place by the end of 2014.

This is incredibly mischievous, as we certainly haven't been working for nine months on anything, and this is presumably the suggestion that was made to me at the Goring Hotel a couple of weeks ago. Yet another Tory attempt to split me off from Nick and make him look non-reformist and illiberal.

Cabinet. 9.30 a.m. George has come back from a visit to China, excited about how much economic development and business potential there is for UK companies. The theme of his report back appeared to be that wherever he went in China, the Germans had got there first. The Prime Minister described this as 'the beach towel problem'.

Owen Paterson then chipped in with a rather extraordinary intervention where he said that there were huge opportunities to sell things to China including 'the parts of dead animals that we don't like to eat in this country'! Lord Hill, sitting close to me, muttered, 'Oh God, he's not on about badgers again, is he?'

I decided to speak today on an item on winter planning for the NHS. I said that we needed to use information on NHS deficits to project forward figures for waiting times and A&E performance, so that we can act to stop the NHS 'falling off a cliff'. George Osborne listened closely.

A fairly pointless meeting of the Armed Forces Covenant Committee. I had to comment on the service premium, which was introduced at the insistence of the PM. This is £300 per pupil for service families (including the children of admirals, for God's sake!). The problem is that service children actually perform rather better than most other children in schools, so it's not obvious why we're giving this money to them, other than that the Prime Minister thought it would be popular. And his constituency is a big winner.

I went out for dinner with Vince Cable – to the Kennington Tandoori restaurant. Asked him what he wanted to do for the rest of the parliament. To my surprise, he said that the only other place that he'd thought he could go would be the Department for Communities and Local Government.

I was pretty surprised and said that it was possible that there might be a big enough reshuffle next year to secure that job. Vince then backtracked pretty quickly! He went on to say that he'd had a decent clearing of the air with Nick when they got back from the conference. He said Nick had been 'quite charming, as he can often be'.

Vince said that he thought a second coalition with the Conservatives would 'kill the Liberal Democrats' and hollow out the party membership.

He said that it would be very difficult to motivate members in coalition with the Tories for ten years – which is probably true, though I pointed out to him that the prospect of simply flipping from one side of the bed to the other, in coalition with Labour, also risked upsetting one set of voters who hated the Conservative Party and then a second set of voters who hated the Labour Party. Vince acknowledged this risk.

Vince's other big point was that we need to get back to growth in public spending after 2015/16. I agreed with him on this, and he will be a supporter in any battles with Danny over trying to get a sensible Liberal Democrat strategy into the manifesto. However, I will have to handle this carefully, because I don't want to stoke Vince up too much and end up with a massive economic row between him and Danny. We were at dinner an hour and three quarters. He insisted on paying his share of the bill. Always a sign of decency!

WEDNESDAY 23 OCTOBER

We've now agreed with Dom that in exchange for giving Home Affairs Committee clearance to the GCSE curriculum proposals, we will have Michael's agreement for Nick to announce a major initiative in his speech tomorrow, to move some of the best head teachers to schools in some of the most disadvantaged areas of the country. The speech still needs a lot of work and one of the problems is what to call this programme. The DPM's office has come up with a list of unconvincing proposals including 'Titan Heads', 'Super Head Teachers', 'Champion Teachers', 'A-Team Teachers' and, worst of all, 'Rescue Head Teachers'.

Went over to the House at 9.30 a.m. for the Education Select Committee. They should have put me on the spot about the issue of sufficiency of spaces, but instead got fixated on free schools. They wasted two hours and got nowhere. Afterwards there was no publicity – my definition of success.

Nick's latest speech draft opens with a reference to a head teacher of a state-funded school. Nick's speechwriter has now taken the trouble to google this individual, who turns out to have regularly slagged off Michael Gove. Citing him in the first paragraph of Nick's speech doesn't seem a very wise thing to do, and his name has been taken out.

Apparently the Prime Minister dropped a massive bombshell when he suddenly announced to the House that the government is now going to scrap a lot of the environmental levies that are pushing up electricity and gas bills. This was announced without any approval from our side of the coalition. It can only have boosted Miliband's narrative about a freeze on energy prices, and clearly the Tories are in a complete panic. Cameron and Osborne's primary driving force in politics is to get re-elected in 2015, and the last thing they're going to worry about is trampling on the green agenda.

When I got across to Nick's office at 12.45 p.m. he was incandescent. He'd just signed off on an incredibly robust statement trashing the Prime Minister's energy announcement. Nick suggested that at the Quad today he should throw all the officials and other ministers out of the room and have a real 'hammer and tongs' discussion with Cameron about the state of the coalition.

One of Danny Alexander's special advisers then said, 'I don't like to be difficult, but we should think about when you throw that strop, because George Osborne has promised us an update today on the potential sale of the Royal Bank of Scotland and the latest Office for Budget Responsibility economic forecasts. It would be useful to get this information from him before the bust-up.'

We then proceeded to have a rather bizarre conversation about the choreography of the proposed row. Before the Quad was a Growth and Enterprise Committee that Nick also had to attend, with the PM. Would it be a good thing to turn up to the Growth and Enterprise Committee and say very little for an hour and then have a strop at the Quad, or would it be better to simply stay away from the first meeting?

Some people said it would be good to stay away and others said that Nick would have a higher moral credibility if he went to the Growth and Enterprise Committee first and showed that he could still play a constructive part in government before having a row at the Quad.

Jonny Oates pointed out that Vince Cable and Ed Davey would be at the Growth and Enterprise Committee, so it would look odd if they attended but Nick didn't.

Then it was pointed out that if Nick didn't turn up to the Growth and Enterprise Committee but did turn up to the Quad afterwards, he might be waiting outside the Cabinet Room when everybody came out of the Growth and Enterprise Committee – which would look absurd! Perhaps he should turn up three minutes late for the Quad to avoid this?

After ten minutes of serious discussion about the choreography of a row, people seemed to see the funny side of things. I decided I had nothing useful to add, and left.

In the evening I bumped into Stephen Williams, our new DCLG Minister. Talked to him about how he was getting on with Eric Pickles, and he joked that Eric refers to Theresa May as 'Tricksy Belle of Marsham Street'. This reaffirms that the Home Secretary currently has quite a lot of enemies in the Conservative Party.

MONDAY 28 OCTOBER

The day of the 'great storm' that the weather forecasters have been promising. By the time I got up at 5.30 a.m., the winds were very strong. As I came past Downing Street, the police all seemed to be looking up in the air and looking rather nervy, and then as I got about fifteen metres away from the entrance to the Cabinet Office a policeman came running down the street waving at me and telling me to go back.

There was a massive crane which must have been 50–100 metres long on top of the Cabinet Office and it had collapsed in a diagonal line from Downing Street towards the entrance to the Cabinet Office. The end of the crane had smashed onto the balustrade just on top of the entrance, knocking various bricks and other items onto the pavement below. Had I arrived two minutes earlier, I would have ended up being showered by rocks and bits of crane as I waited for the door to be unlocked. It would have been a sad end to my ministerial career if I'd been the only person in London killed through falling masonry outside the Cabinet Office.

Had to leave the weekly government business meeting early to attend an ad hoc ministerial working group on 'Markets for Government Services'. The title of this group is actually to disguise the fact that it is looking at a very sensitive issue – both Serco and G4S have been accused of ripping off the government on various contracts. There could now be a criminal investigation.

Chris Grayling and Francis Maude have been leading on this, but the Treasury have now decided to get involved. I went over to George Osborne's room in the Treasury. Chris and Francis had a pre-meeting with George at around 11.30 a.m. while the rest of us waited. Philip Hammond, Theresa

May and Iain Duncan Smith were also ushered into the waiting room while a vast number of officials and permanent secretaries were kept waiting out in the corridor. Iain said that he'd now discovered what the privilege was of being a Secretary of State – he got to use the Chancellor's waiting room rather than having to stand in the corridor!

At around 11.35 a.m. we were all shown through into the Chancellor's large office. Chris Grayling is worried about the whole thing because he is going to have to make a statement in the House of Commons. He hopes to persuade the companies to avoid bidding for upcoming government contracts, which could be embarrassing.

To my amazement, given that his political sense is normally quite good, George Osborne seemed to be pushing in the other direction. He said it would be incredibly damaging for government outsourcing and for the engagement of government in the private sector if we stopped giving contracts to these types of companies. George seemed to think that we could still go on accepting bids for contracts even if criminal investigations were going on.

I said that given the problems with Serco and G4S, and the problems with Atos with the DWP contracts for Employment and Support Allowance entitlements, there would be a real narrative about private sector companies failing and being bad value for money.

The UK market is currently highly concentrated, with four main suppliers – Atos, Capita, Serco and G4S. Three of these now have big problems. George Osborne and Philip Hammond pointed out that these companies would still be managing extremely sensitive contracts, including being a critical part of the consortium operating the UK's nuclear deterrent. I said I thought it would be simply amazing if we started giving out contracts for things like probation outsourcing when we were in the early stages of a possible criminal investigation. Theresa May said she strongly agreed and that she thought the optics of a bunch of people who were being accused of serious offences managing the escorting of prisoners would be extremely bad. At least she has some political common sense.

TUESDAY 29 OCTOBER

Cabinet. We started off with a dull presentation from the government digital service. Philip Hammond asked why it was that MPs couldn't do more things online, such as their tax returns. George Osborne replied that MPs were in a special category of people who were able to fill in their tax returns on paper, along with 'people on the witness protection scheme, and MI6 agents'!

Don Foster seems to be settling in well as Lib Dem Chief Whip. However, I noticed in Cabinet that although he was sitting in his normal seat at the side of the room, he appeared to have fallen asleep. Don is now getting on a bit, and will just have to make sure that he doesn't start snoring in the middle of Cabinet meetings.

THURSDAY 31 OCTOBER

Had to respond to an adjournment debate in the Commons. Was just reading through the speech when one of the Tory whips suddenly inched along the front bench and gestured to talk. She said that the Deputy Speaker, Eleanor Laing, had mentioned to her that she really was rather keen to catch an earlier train home, and was it possible that I could cut my speech in half!

TUESDAY 5 NOVEMBER

Cabinet. Michael gave a presentation on education and growth. He said there were many other departments that wanted to work with the DfE, but his general view was that of Greta Garbo: 'Please just leave us alone!' Michael said that many people in Westminster tended to attack departmental 'silos' and the 'Balkanisation' of government: 'Why? Silos are terribly important and help protect things like nuclear weapons. Balkanisation has actually been an extremely good thing and better than creating artificial constructs glued together that don't work.'

After Cabinet, I briefly read the presentation on future spending, debt and deficit rules by the Treasury's chief economist.

The Treasury has projected forward into the 2020s to show the impact of various different fiscal assumptions between a balanced Budget or surpluses of up to 1 per cent and deficits of up to 1 per cent. A 1 per cent surplus each year brings debt as a share of GDP down from 78 per cent in 2018/19 to 44.6 per cent in 2029/30, whereas a balanced budget brings debt down from 78 per cent in 2018/19 to 53.2 per cent in 2029/30. A 1 per cent deficit brings debt down only from 78 per cent of GDP to 61.9 per cent in 2029/30.

At the back of the Treasury presentation are some different approaches to fiscal rules in the UK, the EU, Sweden and Canada. My suspicion is that George Osborne is looking at the Canadian example, where the rule that operated between 1995 and 2006 was 'budget balance or better'.

At 2.15 p.m. went over to Nick Clegg's office for a meeting about the Autumn Statement. It's clear that Nick is now embracing my idea of pressing for a further increase in the personal allowance during this parliament – beyond the £10,000 we promised.

Had a DfE meeting about free school meals legislation. Michael is still being incredibly difficult about simply legislating so that all schools, including academies, are obliged to deliver free school meals. He has an obsession about not legislating for academies. However, it's getting quite ridiculous, because the legal advisers have now given us a clear steer that if we want to place a duty on all schools then the only way to do this is by legislation.

WEDNESDAY 6 NOVEMBER

Met Oliver Letwin for breakfast. Another discussion about entry and exit checks.

Oliver said he'd finally concluded that the Home Office doesn't want to have a proper entry and exit checking system, as they would then find out how many people were coming to the country and not leaving when they should. He said that the Home Office clearly didn't have the confidence that they could eject people who were overstaying, so their view is that it was better simply not to have an effective entry and exit check system, and better not to know how many people are overstaying. This is a pretty astonishing view, and I said to Oliver that if the Home Secretary continues to drag her feet over this then we would continue to push hard and if she didn't act, it would become a major issue at the next general election.

Oliver said he thought that Theresa May would rather have a fight over this at the general election than introduce an entry and exit system where people actually knew about the number of overstayers who weren't leaving the country – a pretty awful thing to admit!

Back in Dover House for 12.45 p.m. for a pre-meeting for the Quad on the Autumn Statement. We agreed that Nick Clegg ought to put down a marker at the Quad – telling Cameron and Osborne that we want the allowance raised from £10,000 to £10,500.

At Quad, George spent a huge amount of time talking about the fiscal environment and fiscal rules, and this is clearly what's preoccupying him. He clearly wants us on side for this, with a two against one against Labour at the next election. He also made clear that he's prepared to 'go it alone' if we don't want to have a 'tough' position on fiscal policy and borrowing.

A few officials came to see me today about asbestos in gas masks from the First World War! Apparently the gas masks are full of asbestos and there's a worry that with the anniversary of the war coming up next year, a lot of schools might get old gas masks and invite youngsters to put them on. The official asked me whether I wanted to send out advice encouraging schools to ban gas masks on school property. This might be necessary from a safety perspective, but it could also lead to pretty awful publicity in the *Daily Mail, Sun* etc. – 'Minister mollycoddles young people etc. etc., insult to First World War veterans etc. etc.' I said that we needed to be led by the health and safety evidence.

THURSDAY 7 NOVEMBER

Sometimes Michael Gove is fine to work with, and sometimes he is intolerable. Today he was the latter.

In the afternoon, I went to Newham to look at the implementation of universal free school meals. On the way back, we were trying to fix up for me to see MG, to resolve the issue over legislation. MG does not want to legislate for the duty in academies. This would allow academies to take the money but actually not deliver the meals. This is not acceptable to Nick Clegg or to me. I've therefore unwillingly come to the view that we're going to have to legislate to deliver the obligation on all schools, whatever Michael says.

I can't help but think that Michael is getting himself into a ridiculous situation, because frankly no member of the public will understand why he's trying to resist. I've been trying to see him for the past week, and his office keeps on making excuses. I finally got a message this morning saying that Michael didn't have time to see me and he'd made his own decision that he was not going to apply the legislation to academy schools.

I also got a message that he was irritated that I'd been asking the Treasury through Danny Alexander for capital to fund extra school kitchens. This is pretty breath-taking, since the department has nothing at all to lose from trying to get more capital out of the Treasury – and he was well aware that I was seeking to do this.

Attended the 4.15 p.m. ministerial meeting in the DfE. At the end I thought I would try to stay on to discuss free meals with Michael, but he said that he urgently needed to speak privately to Liz Truss and Lord Nash. His private secretary suggested coming back in ten minutes when Michael was finished.

Ten minutes came, and ten minutes went. Half an hour came, and half an hour went. Forty-five minutes came, and forty-five minutes went, and I still wasn't called.

Eventually Ursula, my diary secretary, came in and said in a rather embarrassed way that she didn't think I was going to be able to get to see Michael as his office were not being very helpful. I didn't say anything, but leapt out of my chair and paced angrily towards MG's office on the other side of the seventh floor. It's only about thirty seconds away. I strode towards his office and past his collection of private secretaries, who glanced up nervously. The meeting Michael had been holding was clearly breaking up. I waited impatiently by the door, saying nothing and determined to see Michael come what may. Eventually the only two people in the room were Henry de Zoete and Michael, and I loomed a few yards away from them.

Henry walked out, and Michael dashed out of the other side of his office into a room I'd never noticed before, but which is apparently the Secretary of State's personal toilet! I was therefore left standing in his room alone, wondering both if the toilet had another exit and how long the Secretary of State was likely to be occupied.

Eventually he came out, making no apology for keeping me waiting and offering no explanation. I said that I wanted to speak to him about the issue of free school meals.

We sat down and Lord Nash joined us. I said to Michael that I had three concerns. Firstly, I needed to be able to send out a letter to schools to let them know that the policy was actually coming in. Secondly, I needed to bid for capital from the Treasury, as we'd estimated that there would be capital costs for schools to upgrade their kitchens. Thirdly, we'd now had definitive legal advice on free school meals that showed that the only way of guaranteeing all children could get them in infant schools was to legislate for both maintained schools and academies.

Michael said that he didn't want to send out a letter to schools because it might imply that we were going to give financial support to them, which we might then not do. On capital, he said he didn't want to spend any on kitchens, and he feared that this might divert from basic need. I said to him that it wouldn't divert from basic need and the risk was that if we didn't get the extra capital for the kitchen upgrades then money that could be spent on basic need/maintenance would be siphoned off to kitchens. I said therefore it was a no-brainer to ask for money from the Treasury.

Finally we got to the nub of the issue – legislation. I said we'd now had definitive legal advice. Michael said that he didn't accept this.

I summarised the situation at the end of the meeting by saying that I'd redraft the letter to head teachers and show it to him. I'd send him a submission on how we could deal with the issue of schools capital, and make a bid to the Treasury, and I would talk to Chris Wormald to see if we could get any other check on the legal advice. Michael looked incredibly grumpy.

Got back at midnight and started work on the red boxes. One of the submissions was about the budget situation in the department. We've got to find money for the national fair funding formula, and I've recently submitted my thoughts about this and how we could avoid the £100 million cuts to early years education, which Liz Truss and I are very worried about. However, Michael has now sent back his own views, and it's clear that he's decided to be confrontational in the extreme.

He wants to reopen the incredibly controversial coalition agreement from the July Spending Review about cutting the Education Services Grant – which is already going to be cut by a mind-boggling 20 per cent in one year. MG is now suggesting 30 per cent!

He's also suggesting raiding the pupil premium budget to pay for spending on non-pupil-premium children. He also knows that that is something the Liberal Democrats won't accept. And he's saying that he's not interested in trying to reverse the cuts in early years education. All this is supposed to be discussed at the board meeting next week, but Michael is not presenting it as his views but rather as the final decision that he has made. This is going to lead to a major row. Bad Michael has been much on display in the past couple of days. I fear it's going to be quite difficult to avoid a major bust-up over this next week or so.

MONDAY 11 NOVEMBER

Over the weekend there has been a certain amount of noise in relation to the great plan to have a joint Nick Clegg, Danny Alexander and Vince Cable launch on the economy. Apparently Nick discussed this with Vince last week and thought he was on side, and then on Friday Vince's special adviser Giles Wilkes attended a meeting with the other special advisers. Giles interpreted the economic plans – perhaps correctly – as making a major announcement on fiscal policy that would commit the party to a 'balanced budget'. He threw a bit of a wobbly and said that this wasn't what Vince had agreed, wasn't economically literate and was all driven by politics. There was quite a nasty row – ending up with Giles walking out. My view is that we shouldn't go out and say anything on fiscal policy until this is straightened out.

At 1.45 p.m. I had a meeting on the lower ministerial corridor with the Permanent Secretary, Chris Wormald, and Claire Johnson, the senior legal adviser. Chris had spent the weekend thinking about the challenge of trying to find a joint coalition position on whether or not we should legislate for the free school meal entitlement. In the past, people used to talk about a Heath-Robinson contraption, meaning something that had been glued together in an implausible and unconvincing way. In the future, I think people will be able to talk about the 'Wormald' – a similarly contrived solution to what otherwise would be a fairly simple problem.

Chris's solution is to change the existing legislation so as to add child benefit to one of the benefits which gives access to free school meals for infant pupils. The problems with this would be: a) that there are some richer families who now don't receive child benefit, and b) that there would be a small group of other children such as those with no recourse to public funds and foster children who also aren't in receipt of child benefit. The legal adviser and other officials all looked slightly embarrassed by the absurdly complicated solution to a non-problem.

TUESDAY 12 NOVEMBER

In early at 6.30 a.m. Very heavy workload at the moment and pretty knackering.

At 8.45 a.m. I went to Nick Clegg's office along with DfE officials and we presented the conclusions of our work on the national fair funding formula. I'd heard that a lot of the DPM's advisers are very negative. This is incredibly irritating. I've put a massive amount of time into making sure that the politics of this work. This is a very politically robust set of proposals as well as being sound in a policy sense.

I pointed out that there is now an expectation that we will press ahead with the new formula, since this was announced in Spending Review. Nick said at the end of the meeting that he was very happy with the technical solutions, but he thought the real issue was about the politics.

At 5 p.m. I attended the DfE board meeting. At one stage, I was thinking about not bothering to attend. However, I decided that it would be better to be there to put my points.

To Michael's obvious amusement, most of the ministers commented on their own policy areas and how these really ought not to be cut. Liz Truss made a strong argument for reversing the £100 million planned cuts to early years.

Liz also made a slightly odd point proposing cutting grants for voluntary groups but expanding the budget for the Communications Department in the run-up to the general election. Michael said in his usual amusing way, 'Oh, that's an interesting idea, Liz. So your proposition is that we should cut some of the charitable grants for vulnerable young people, and use the money to buy more DfE press officers?'

WEDNESDAY 13 NOVEMBER

In my red box tonight there was a note saying that the Chancellor is now planning to block the new measures of child poverty. Apparently what he doesn't like is that the entrenched measure of poverty might rise, making it look bad for the government. He also won't accept a relative child poverty measure.

FRIDAY 15 NOVEMBER

At 11.15, I met an official who has been to the Home Office to have a chat about the sensitive issue of entry and exit checks with Home Office officials and the Permanent Secretary. The view was that the Home Secretary was clear that she didn't want to have fully functioning entry and exit checks. Apparently her view is that this will just highlight the ineffectiveness of the Border Agency and the Home Office and their inability to spot people who have overstayed and need to be ejected from the country. This is exactly what Oliver told me. Theresa May is apparently quite openly saying that this would be a distraction from the Home Office's main job of tracking down 'bad people' and stopping terrorists.

We agreed that the only way of dealing with this is for Nick to escalate the matter with the Prime Minister. Apparently the PM had a meeting with the Home Secretary last week, which was pretty prickly and difficult and didn't make much progress on this issue.

Read a submission about the capital position within the department over the next few years. I was absolutely furious because for the first time I read that we have a massive over-allocation of capital for the next three years.

This is apparently due to a huge projected overspend in the free schools programme, of about £1 billion over the next three years. Unbelievably, the civil servants are proposing the money should be taken out of basic need – for new school places in areas where there are shortages – as well as from the maintenance of existing schools, where we have a massive backlog.

There's no way I'm prepared to agree to this. We have a number of parts of the country where local authorities are failing in their statutory responsibility to provide school places and the idea that we're going to plough vast amounts of extra money into free schools while we've got this situation with basic need is absolutely ludicrous. I scrawled very angry comments all over the paper, and asked for a meeting on Monday with the Permanent Secretary and senior officials.

MONDAY 18 NOVEMBER

12.30 p.m. Nick Clegg's office for the weekly government business meeting, which was dominated by DfE issues. Nick will talk to Cameron about the need for legislation on school meals. Then we talked about the national fair funding formula. Nick's now got a piece of political advice saying the whole thing can't possibly be done. It reports that Lib Dem headquarters privately estimate that we will lose about half of our London councillors in May 2014. The note says as London loses from funding reform, this gives those councillors an alibi for losing.

At 1.30 p.m. went over to the Department for Education and called in the two officials in charge of the capital programme. Put my views 'robustly'.

Our capital budgets are over-committed by almost £900 million over the next three years, with an £800 million projected overspend on free schools. Some of these free schools commitments haven't actually been entered into yet, and therefore could be cancelled, but clearly Michael won't want to do this.

The proposals that we should raid the basic need budget and the maintenance budget in order to put money into free schools are completely potty. The officials admitted that they had known about this for a number of months. They also said that the free schools budget is entirely demand-led, so there appears to be no financial control at all. This is the first time that I'd heard this and I was absolutely appalled.

At 4 p.m. went over to the Lib Dem Cabinet ministers' meeting, where I had to do a presentation on the national fair funding formula. Nick had that glazed look that he has when he's already made up his mind about something and we're really just going through the motions. You can also tell he is uncomfortable having to break the bad news to someone who has slogged away on a policy.

He let me make a ten- or fifteen-minute presentation and then invited other Cabinet ministers to comment – I suspect they all knew what they were supposed to do. Alistair Carmichael was negative. Ed Davey was neutral but questioning. Vince Cable was negative. And then Matthew Hanney came in and said it was all a terrible idea and would lose us loads of seats in London.

Nick said he was very cautious about the whole thing and perhaps we should put it off until after the general election. I said that there was nothing surprising in the national fair funding formula and it was always going to cause a redistribution and if we didn't want that, we should never have embarked on it in the first place.

I also said there would be a political price to pay for letting down the rural and underfunded areas, and if we did this we needed to be pretty damned careful to make sure the Tories didn't land us with the responsibility for this. Left feeling distinctly sulky.

TUESDAY 19 NOVEMBER

Cabinet. Very, very boring and pointless.

David Cameron has apparently just returned from visiting a tribe in Sri Lanka – a vulnerable ethnic minority. His visit caused him to be hailed as a 'god'. Cameron said it was 'very flattering, but if I am a god then I regret to report that Mrs Cameron is still an "infidel"'!

Had a telephone conference call with Oliver Letwin at 6 p.m. over a crackly mobile phone line. Neither of us realised that we were sitting three offices away from each other on the lower ministerial corridor. Oliver said that George Osborne didn't like the new proposed child poverty targets, particularly as they would show that entrenched poverty had increased under the government. Apparently George is not prepared to publish anything that makes it look as if any aspect of child poverty has got worse, and he's asking us to go back and find a measure of child poverty that has fallen! I'm simply not prepared to fix the figures. The Chancellor apparently feels strongly about this and wants to veto the whole thing, so we're heading for a bit of a bust-up.

WEDNESDAY 20 NOVEMBER

At 9 a.m. went over to the Home Office for a meeting, chaired by Theresa May, of the Extremism Task Force.

These meetings are quite interesting, because they include other senior Tories who clearly don't particularly like deferring to her. There is Eric Pickles, who doesn't like May at all; Michael, who clearly isn't a fan either; and Iain Duncan Smith, who I think probably gets on OK with her. There was also Baroness Warsi and a few junior ministers. The meeting started off on the issue of how we could get the Muslim community on side to push for de-radicalisation of extremist groups.

It seemed the kind of subject that ought not to have been that controversial, but quite rapidly it descended into a total bust-up between Michael Gove and just about everybody else. Michael started to be quite aggressive towards May, and then he started to pick on Baroness Warsi and Eric Pickles. Eric is not to be messed with and, sitting immediately to Michael's left, he suddenly turned round and in rather blunt terms said, 'Michael, I object to your hectoring behaviour. Shut up for a minute and let me speak.' There wasn't anything jovial about it, and there was a rather embarrassed feeling in the room, with all of the officials looking on in amazement. Michael flushed red and looked angry. He's picking a lot of fights right now.

At 11.30 a.m. I had a catch up with the free school meals team, and we decided exactly what we wanted to do on revenue and capital. We Lib Dems are going to bid for £150 million worth of capital from the Treasury – regardless of what Michael thinks – and £650 million worth of revenue. I said that I would give these figures to the Treasury later on today, but I wanted Michael to have a chance to look at them first.

At 11.30 p.m. got an email from Nick entitled 'Gove':

Danny and I had dinner with DC and GO this evening.

1. I told them bluntly that I would relish public spats with Gove if he didn't become more accommodating. They accepted that his behaviour was a problem, but they needed time to win him over re. free school meals.

2. Apparently Gove is vehemently opposed to the recommendations in Heywood's 16–24 review.

3. Gove wants to avoid further legislation at all costs in education as he believes that any Bill would be hijacked by the 'educational establishment' in the Lords.

4. I agreed that I would see Gove on my own as soon as possible to resolve things directly.

5. DC was sceptical about the national fair funding formula for schools, saying it was 'the right policy but the wrong time' etc.

THURSDAY 21 NOVEMBER

Lib Dem parliamentary away day, Ramada Inn, Hatfield, just off the A1. These occasions tend to be completely pointless.

At dinner there was an unfortunate lady from the Dutch Liberal Party who'd been asked to make an after-dinner speech. The poor lady had not realised that by the time she got to speak it would be in the middle of a fairly boozy and light-hearted post-dinner session. Instead, she'd come with a rather formal speech about the role of liberal parties in government, and how coalition works, blah blah. She was clearly rather embarrassed and rushed through her speech as fast as she could.

FRIDAY 22 NOVEMBER

DfE ministerial meeting with MG. Definitely a chill in the air.

I raised the national fair funding formula. Michael said he thought that Osborne and Cameron were terribly keen. I said that I'd heard from Nick that the PM was inclined to veto it. Michael looked at me rather blank-faced, probably furious to learn this from me. I said that if both the PM and DPM pushed back then we should consider simply raising the underfunded authorities' base funding level, and delay the national fair funding formula to the other side of the election.

MONDAY 25 NOVEMBER

Some good news from Oliver Letwin, who tells me that he has finally met up with the Home Secretary to talk about entry and exit checks, and hurrah, she has suddenly agreed that she's committed to completing them, and has announced that all of the computer technology which previously couldn't be persuaded to 'talk to itself' can now be connected up so that we will soon have a plan for 100 per cent entry and exit checks. I'll believe this when I see it, but it does look as if Oliver and the Prime Minister may finally have succeeded in moving the Home Office to a more sensible position.

I was supposed to be spending this morning on manifesto issues, but ended up being diverted by the Tory panic over the full entry of Bulgaria and Romania into the EU on 1 January 2014. The Tories are in a complete tizz about this, as a consequence of publicity in the *Daily Mail*, *Daily Telegraph* etc. They have briefed out that they're going to be doing all sorts of things to stop people from Bulgaria and Romania coming here, and they now have a list of policies that they want to announce immediately.

Nick has insisted with Cameron that I vet them. The Tories produced a one-page note on the new policies which included:

1. Strengthening the habitual residence test in order to stop EEA jobseekers accessing certain benefits for the first three months after they arrive.
2. A new minimum earnings threshold that would test whether EEA nationals were in genuine work.
3. No housing benefit for EEA jobseekers, or at least for their first period of time until they have got a first job.
4. Removing rough sleepers and beggars and preventing their re-entry within twelve months.
5. Increasing the sanction for employers paying below the minimum wage.

Advice comes in which indicates that basically most of the measures would be likely to be illegal and that we would be likely or highly likely to lose a challenge. However, it seems we could at least make a decent case for most of the measures, which would apparently mean that they would be stuck in the legal system for one or two years before any judgment was reached against us.

The Tory view is that the imperative is simply to try to deter people coming to the UK, and they really don't care whether we win or lose the ultimate legal cases provided that we can announce these measures now. Nick's view is that we shouldn't stand in the way of any sensible measures to manage the European labour market to stop abuses, and I'm bound to say I agree.

At the Social Justice Committee meeting, I asked IDS what his view was on the EU benefits proposals that were being considered by 10 Downing Street. He didn't seem to know anything about them. I showed him a copy of the paper and he just shrugged his shoulders and said that he wished that Downing Street would occasionally consult him. Astounding!

TUESDAY 26 NOVEMBER

Another day in which my relationship with Michael goes into the deep freeze.

The situation is now getting quite difficult for officials. Usually in a single-party government a difference of opinion between a minister and a Secretary of State may matter, but not all that much – as the Secretary of State gets his or her way. But in a coalition government, things are considerably more difficult, as a coalition partner may still exercise a veto over the head of the Secretary of State.

I seem to be fighting with Michael Gove over a series of issues. Firstly, his decision, or Dom's, to try to sabotage the free school meals policy. Secondly, over budget issues where Michael is trying to cut back on all of the Lib Dem priorities in the department, including the pupil premium and the Education Services Grant. Thirdly, DfE capital, where Michael is trying to funnel away basic need and maintenance capital to fund a massive overspend on his free schools programme. In addition, we have got the Chancellor of the Exchequer blocking the child poverty targets, and the PM and DPM blocking the national fair funding formula, about the only thing MG and I agree on right now.

At the same time I'm trying to sort out a major argument about European policy, as the Tories panic about the prospects of Romanians and Bulgarians sweeping into Britain on 1 January.

Today, all of these policies and issues collided.

At 9 a.m. I went off to Nick Clegg's office to have my meeting about education policy. Nick said that Cameron has promised he will impose free school meals legislation on MG if he won't agree it, but I'll believe that when I see it.

9.30 a.m. Cabinet. Every week the Cabinet agenda gets even thinner. A complete and utter yawn fest.

The only subject that sparked anyone into life was Iran, where William Hague described the international agreement that has just been reached to limit Iranian nuclear weapons. Everyone around the table said what a great success this was.

I could tell that Michael Gove was sitting in his seat brooding and building up to one of his volcanic interventions. He kept on texting away on his mobile phone and eventually the Prime Minister got extremely irritated and waved his hands at Michael rather violently.

Michael then intervened on Iran to say that he was sorry he couldn't join in the praise and he was very critical of the agreement. For once, Michael was deadly serious and didn't even attempt to make jokes – highly unusual and a clear warning sign. He started off on the rather weak point that he didn't think it was a good thing for democracies to make agreements with non-democracies. He then criticised every conceivable part of the agreement. The problem is that Michael really doesn't have a better alternative. I suspect that Michael would probably support military action, but he'd be pretty much alone.

After Cabinet, Nick said that he'd like me to have a chat with Ken Clarke on the emerging Tory ideas on EU immigration. We're fixing a call later.

Next was the Extremism Task Force, which was the last meeting of this rather pointless group.

Michael Gove dismissed the papers that we were reading as 'all waffle', but he was attacked by Baroness Warsi, who was provoked into being quite outspoken about how ill-judged most of the proposals were. Cameron, who is very committed to all this extremism stuff, muttered loudly, in the middle of Baroness Warsi's comments, 'Absurd, completely absurd.' I've rarely heard him so angry and dismissive. Everybody else around the table – Iain Duncan Smith, Theresa May, Nick Clegg and Eric Pickles – all looked embarrassed at the altercation.

Cameron is getting increasingly irritated about people who use their mobile phones in the Cabinet Room. Halfway through the meeting, I was sitting next to Ed Vaizey, who was typing away on his mobile phone. Suddenly Cameron picked up one of the Murray mints on the Cabinet table and threw it very hard across the room at him. It missed Vaizey, but shattered on the window behind. Can't see Churchill doing it.

After the Extremism Task Force, I went back to my office and met officials from the DfE free school meals team. I'd spoken to Danny last night and discovered that the Treasury only thought that we needed £50 million for school kitchens, whereas we need £150–200 million. I'd said to Danny that I would send DfE officials over to the Treasury to go through our figures.

I'd had contradictory advice before about whether Michael Gove was supporting this bid for free school meals capital or not. Firstly, I was told that he was supporting the £150–200 million, and then I was told that he hadn't even allowed the paper to be sent to the Treasury. Later in the afternoon I found out just what absurd lengths he and Dom Cummings were going to in order to block the whole release of free school meals capital from the Treasury. I got a note in my box from officials describing the ludicrous events of the day:

> I thought I should put an email in the system to make sure that every-one is clear about the position on free school meals capital and to enable you to facilitate a further urgent discussion between the Secretary of State and David Laws if you agree that is a sensible – and feasible – next step. To recap, David Laws rang officials this morning to say that he'd been expecting the Treasury to provide around £200 million for free school meals capital in the Autumn Statement but that he'd heard from the Chief Secretary to the Treasury that Treasury officials were pressing for a much lower amount – around £40–50 million. The minister asked Julie to push back hard with the Treasury today and argue for the full £200 million. We understood this to be consistent with an agreed posi-tion between the Secretary of State and Minister Laws as set out in the one-pager which went to the Chief Secretary on Friday. My reading of this was that the Secretary of State wanted the Treasury to fund the esti-mated capital costs of free school meals in full so that capital was not diverted from spending on basic need in order to pay for kitchens and dining facilities – though on reflection I realised that the wording was actually more ambiguous than that … Treasury contacted us separately and asked for a meeting about this issue at 2.15 p.m. today. Mindful of the Secretary of State's clear instruction that all negotiating positions over capital with the Treasury must be agreed with him, we sought clearance to go ahead with the meeting on the basis set out by Minister Laws. In response, the message was that the Secretary of State did not want us to be bidding for any capital at all for free school meals on the basis that any capital available should be going towards basic need.

This is completely absurd since the Tories are trying to pinch all the capital for free schools!

The email went on:

Given the very different positions taken by ministers, we tried to postpone the Treasury meeting, but they had already set off so we met with them briefly in the lobby of the DfE and answered some questions they had about possible allocation methodology assuming some capital were to be made available. However, we made clear that we were not in a position to discuss the total amounts required as we didn't yet have cover from our ministers to do so. They were quite nonplussed by that but accepted it; they did, however, say that their aim had been to lock down the figures today so if we did not clarify urgently what we were looking for, there was a risk the decision would be taken for us. I assume they meant by this that we would get £40–50 million, though they didn't say so explicitly. We are very much on borrowed time here but of course we do not want to negotiate with the Treasury on a basis that either the Secretary of State or Minister Laws would be unhappy with. Just two quick points to raise:

1. While I understand the Secretary of State's desire to prioritise basic need, officials think that tactically we are more likely to get additional capital from Treasury for FSM than for basic need. Given that some schools will inevitably need to incur capital in order to deliver the FSM policy, not putting money in the system for this risks existing capital being diverted from both basic need and maintenance;
2. Secondly, there is to an extent a trade-off between capital and maintenance here. We understand that Treasury officials are taking the view that schools don't need to spend as much on kitchens as we had proposed as they can buy food in rather than cooking it on site. However, depending on models of delivery locally, this may increase revenue costs and we should bear in mind that we have already squeezed our revenue bid.

Clearly the situation has got absolutely ridiculous and I phoned Matt Sanders to update him. To my astonishment, Matt told me that the Treasury officials had come round to the DfE and been refused entrance to the building.

Matt was also sent an email by Michael Gove's private office telling him that his desk in the advisers' office (with the Tory special advisers) was no longer free, and his personal effects would be cleared out and moved to another desk somewhere within the building! Extraordinary behaviour. I was absolutely furious.

Danny eventually said that the Treasury could offer us £70 million and that we ought to take a part of the £157 million worth of unallocated maintenance budget for 2014/15 for kitchens. I said I'd be happy to do this, but that Michael Gove had already tried to take all of this money to cover his massive free schools overspend.

Meanwhile, I received a draft article from the PM's office that he's going to write in the *FT* tomorrow. This includes all the five immigration policies that we agreed today, but in addition to this it includes a long section about the Tory attitude to Europe going into the next parliament. This is precisely what I'd asked Oliver Letwin not to do, i.e. have an announcement that mixed up coalition policy with what the Tories were going to do in the next parliament. What the Tories are apparently going suggest in the next parliament is that individual nations should be able to cap inward EU migration, which will be anathema to most other countries within the EU, and it also suggests more intelligently but less practically that in the future if new countries come into the EU with GDP well below the other nations, then they would have a transitional period where until their economic wealth got up to a higher level, their citizens would not be able to work without restrictions in the richer countries. This might have been a good idea ten or fifteen years ago but it's damn-all use now.

Then later in the afternoon Ken Clarke asked to have a word with me. When Ken finally came on the line I could hear a lot of grumbling and mumbling in the background and then I heard him saying, 'I suppose there'll be a whole load of Liberal advisers listening in too...' then he obviously realised he'd been connected, and he asked me what we thought of all the Tory proposals and the Prime Minister's article. I made clear that Nick had agreed the five policy proposals and that these were going in the article, at which Ken Clarke sounded rather upset and disappointed.

'Does Nick', he asked, 'really want to agree these proposals by the Prime Minister? I read David's article and it all looks to me like a lot of total xenophobic rubbish.'

I said that Nick's view was that it was pointless for us to resist measures which were quite small and insignificant and would deal with minor abuses, rather than fighting the big arguments. Ken said he understood that, but we were signing up to a lot of things that some might consider illegal and wouldn't stand up in court. He said he was terribly worried that this would rebound in 2015/16 or 2017 when the Conservative Party had a referendum. I said that was really a Conservative matter, but I didn't believe that people like Oliver Letwin really wanted Britain to leave the European Union.

'Oh,' said Ken, 'Oliver is really terribly Eurosceptic.'

I said, 'But surely Oliver doesn't actually want us to leave the EU?'

'I wouldn't bet on it.'

Ken then went through the Prime Minister's article, reading out bits to me over the phone and saying how dreadful the whole thing was and how there was nothing about the benefits of immigration or pointing out how British people could benefit from going to other EU countries. He said it was 'all claptrap designed to appease the *Daily Mail* and the *Daily Telegraph*', and it simply wouldn't do that. I said that we couldn't tell the Prime Minister what to say about Conservative policy on the other side of the election; all we could do is decide whether we resisted a number of small policy changes that were being suggested now.

Ken accepted this rather begrudgingly, and I eventually said that if he wanted to impede all this then he was likely to have more influence with the Prime Minister than I was. He sounded rather dubious. As we finished the telephone conversation, he said: 'In any case, if I'm asked, I'm not going to support any of this rubbish. I think this is completely the wrong attitude to the EU, and it just plays into the Eurosceptics and UKIP's hands.'

WEDNESDAY 27 NOVEMBER

Spoke to Nick about yesterday's DfE shambles. Said that I was really upset and irritated that Michael had denied access to the DfE to Treasury civil servants yesterday, so that they weren't able to discuss how much capital we needed for the free school meals pledge. Also mentioned to Nick that Matt had been forced out of the special advisers' office.

Nick replied fairly rapidly saying that he was 'effing furious' about this, and that he would be contacting Cameron immediately. We've got to the point where a lot of difficult coalition issues have built up, and either there's a massive thunderstorm with lots of lightning or the storm breaks and the rain comes down and the pressure is released.

Got to Dover House at 2 p.m. and the pre-Quad meeting had already started. Danny Alexander was going through the Treasury scorecard detailing all of the key Autumn Statement decisions.

I had a quick word with one of Nick's officials about where we were on free school meals legislation. It seems that Cameron was inclined to impose legislation on Michael Gove but he was just trying to 'build up the confidence to do so', as he didn't normally like imposing things on Michael.

Just as I was leaving, Matt Sanders came round and said that he was a little bit embarrassed because Nick Clegg had sent a very angry text to David Cameron after speaking to me this morning about the way Michael Gove was behaving, including removing Matt's desk.

Apparently the PM was really upset when he received the text, particularly as he was preparing for PMQs and was somewhat unsettled by receiving a very angry message from Nick. Cameron immediately rang Michael Gove's office and spoke to his private secretary and said he was really unhappy about what Michael was doing to make life difficult in the coalition. Cameron also mentioned 'Matt Sanders's desk' and what on earth was happening with this Liberal Democrat special adviser. Matt said he was very embarrassed to suddenly be the subject of a prime ministerial call about where his desk should be.

In the evening, I texted Nick to say, 'Don't know what you said to Cameron but MG is behaving better today – somewhat!' Nick texted back: 'I went ballistic – Cameron said: "Gove is a bit of a Maoist – he believes in progress through creative destruction!"' Now I see what David Cameron means. That sounds exactly like Michael.

THURSDAY 28 NOVEMBER

Travelled with my private secretary, Sam, to visit a school in Farnham, Surrey. We must have been allocated the worst driver in the entire government car service pool. All he had to do was drive down the M3, but he managed to get lost on two occasions and I eventually ended up having to do the map reading for him. When we got to the school, he tried to drive in via the exit, and couldn't understand why the barrier wouldn't go up.

He hadn't got any better by the time he took us back. He missed two turnings within the first three minutes, including the turning onto the M3. We went on the A3 instead, where he started swerving all over the road and we were hooted quite aggressively by other vehicles.

I had a meeting with Sir Bob Worcester, the political commentator and pollster. He is chairman of a group which is celebrating the 800-year anniversary of the Magna Carta. He apparently had a meeting with Nick Gibb, the previous Schools Minister, back in 2011. Nick apparently made some kind of rash promise that we should give out copies of the Magna Carta to every schoolchild in England, which has been costed by the department at £3.5 million! The department is absolutely horrified by the idea, and at the meeting I was joined by a rather nervous official, who was clearly there to try to prevent me making any further rash promises.

FRIDAY 29 NOVEMBER

Danny phoned to say that he has done a deal with Osborne over free school meals revenue and capital. He's agreed the full revenue number, and the full capital figure that I wanted too – £70 million from the Treasury and another £80 million from the unspent £157 million worth of DfE maintenance budget.

Danny said that in exchange for funding free school meals, Osborne had asked that I should 'lay off' Michael on the free schools programme. George wants Michael to have 'whatever money he needs for free schools', even at the expense of taking some out of the basic need budget. Hmmm.

TUESDAY 3 DECEMBER

Had a meeting about the leaking of the DfE 'Stop document' about things that the department was considering not doing any longer. The Permanent Secretary has commissioned a leak inquiry. On this occasion they've decided to put the frighteners on, and they've brought in a 'leak expert' from the Cabinet Office, who is going round interviewing everybody and distributing lots of questionnaires. That should be effective! I asked the Permanent

Secretary how many DfE leak enquiries have ever identified the leaker. One day later, the answer came back: 'None.'

Got a text through from Matt Sanders saying that DfE Tory special advisers are briefing the *Daily Mail* that our free school meals policy is a 'shambles', and that we were pinching money from the basic need budget for new school places in order to pay for school kitchens! Of course this is total and utter balls of the first order, and the truth is that what is happening in the Department for Education is that Michael Gove is seeking to pinch around £600 million or £700 million from basic need capital in order to prop up his free schools programme. Because he is so sensitive to this criticism, and because he wants every single penny of capital to go into free schools, he's been opposing our bid to the Treasury for money for school kitchens capital. Now he's found out that I've cut a deal with Danny Alexander.

Apparently the Tory advisers are now trying to block the announcement of the free school meals capital, which is due to be made by Nick and me tomorrow.

WEDNESDAY 4 DECEMBER

At 9.30 a.m. I had a telephone call with Gerald Vernon-Jackson, our council leader in Portsmouth and head of the Lib Dem local government group. At the end of our conversation he insisted on giving me a couple of 'good ideas' about our next general election manifesto. One of them was a 'dog poo strategy'.

Gerald explained that we're now going to microchip all dogs, and that a big issue in Portsmouth is people who allow their dogs to poo in public streets without clearing it up. Gerald said that what we ought to do is take DNA samples of the dog turd and then match it up to the dogs through the micro-chipping process. I said to him: 'Very interesting idea. However, I don't propose to put dog shit in our general election manifesto – there's enough of it already.' He was disappointed.

Today was the day that all of the private rows with Michael Gove over the past few weeks spilt out in public.

Last night we were told that Michael's special advisers were briefing against Nick Clegg and the Liberal Democrats and our free school meals plan.

We were trying to get all the press releases ready for Nick's visit to a school in Lambeth to launch the free school meals policy and the extra capital of £150 million. It then became clear that MG and his advisers were being incredibly unhelpful, saying they didn't accept or know anything about the agreement for £150 million of capital funding.

We got a message from the DfE saying that the Secretary of State was content that the department was receiving the extra £70 million of capital for free school meal kitchens, but he was not agreeing the £80 million should be reassigned to free school meals capital, and his office communicated to the DPM's office that 'no announcement can go ahead which includes the £80 million'.

Michael Gove and Dom were trying a full-scale assault on our announcement.

Eventually we received a very helpful email from the Chancellor's office to Michael's private secretary. This was timed at 10.05 a.m. and said:

> Thanks for your email. I understand your concerns, but this is a Quad agreement and since 50 per cent of the Quad is HMT ministers that means ours have agreed to this. I understand the Chancellor discussed this with your Secretary of State over the weekend. The Quad agreed that in addition to the new money, half the existing underspend on maintenance would be used for this purpose – the rest will go towards free schools.

Nick made clear that he intended to make the announcement on free school meals 'no matter what Gove thinks'.

Nick covered for Cameron at Prime Minister's Questions. Afterwards, we drove over to the school in Lambeth – Walnut Tree Primary School – to launch the free school meals policy and to highlight the extra capital that we'd secured. We met a very friendly head teacher and had a good chat with the kids.

When we finished lunch, my private secretary, Sam, ushered me over into a corner and showed me a *Guardian* online article, which said that Michael Gove and Nick Clegg were 'at war' over the free school meals policy and that Michael's office were briefing that it was a 'gimmick' and that there was a £200 million funding hole in the policy! It also implied that we were raiding basic need and maintenance budgets in order to pay for the policy. I said to our press people that this was totally unacceptable and that we needed to brief back very strongly.

By 5 p.m. stories were running headlined 'Gove officials "lying" over funding'. The story from the Press Association said:

> In a particularly robust counter-briefing, senior Liberal Democrat sources accused the DfE of lying, going rogue, being hostile and 'talking bollocks'. Downing Street then made clear that it was Tory Mr Gove's department that were out of line. 'The position is absolutely the one the DPM's office have set out,' the Prime Minister's official spokesman said.

We were due to have a meeting on basic need with Michael Gove at 4.45 p.m., but there was a vote scheduled at that time, so the meeting was delayed. The Secretary of State's office said that Michael wanted to see me, and that apparently he was 'extremely unhappy'. I said that I was pretty unhappy too!

The vote in the House of Commons was eventually called and I was told that the Secretary of State was waiting for me in his car outside the department. I went down in the lift, and sure enough there was Michael's Jaguar parked outside with him in the back, waiting for me. The car drove off and Michael turned to me: 'David, I've got to speak to you about this free school meals issue. I have to tell you that I'm extremely, extremely angry about the policy announcement today.' He went on: 'I knew nothing about this policy, and I would have thought that the Deputy Prime Minister would have had the courtesy to brief me on this before making the announcement. This surely isn't an acceptable way for two partners in a coalition to behave.'

The driver's ears pricked up, and he turned the radio volume sharply down.

I replied: 'I'm sorry you don't feel consulted about this, but we were told that the Chancellor briefed you over the weekend. I also think that the reason we got into this situation is the poor communications in the DfE, including you blocking access between DfE and Treasury officials to discuss the funding of the free school meals capital pledge. That's not made it very easy to sort this matter out. In addition, we have to have the capital for this, and this was agreed by the Quad, which is entitled to sign off on these matters.'

Michael looked a bit defensive and then he said, 'Well the Chancellor did speak to me over the weekend about the revenue funding, but he mentioned nothing about the capital side or any monies coming from within the department.'

I then said, 'Well we're feeling pretty bruised and upset about this, too. After all, we were told yesterday explicitly by the *Daily Mail* that your special advisers were briefing against the policy and Nick Clegg on this and spinning a line directly contradictory to the government policy to the newspapers.'

Michael looked a bit taken aback, though I noticed that he didn't deny this. Eventually we finished the short journey into Members' Entrance for the vote. As we got out of the car, I finished by saying, 'You'll be pleased to know that I've just met Henry Dimbleby and John Vincent, and they are absolutely delighted with the extra revenue funding and capital funding.' Michael didn't say anything and we went our separate ways.

At 6.30 p.m. we were called to Michael's office for a meeting on capital for new school places. The atmosphere was distinctly chilly when I arrived.

As we came into Michael's office, I spotted some large new sofas that had replaced four older seats. To fill a chilly silence, one of the officials said to Michael, 'Oh, I see you've bought some new sofas, Secretary of State.'

'Yes,' he replied instantly. 'We funded them from the underspend in the maintenance budget!' At least he still has his sense of humour.

THURSDAY 5 DECEMBER

Arrived about thirty seconds before Cabinet. George Osborne was briefing us on the Autumn Statement. This is fiscally pretty neutral, but the key thing is that there's the biggest upward revision to growth forecasts for fifteen years.

FRIDAY 6 DECEMBER

The media should have been wall-to-wall coverage of Osborne's Autumn Statement. Instead, it was wall-to-wall coverage of the death of Nelson Mandela.

Heard George on the *Today* programme. The first question he was asked was about Mandela, and he got about two questions on the economy before he was cut off!

SUNDAY 8 DECEMBER

A lovely crisp, clear, autumn-type day. Felt absolutely knackered and would have liked to have stayed in bed, but we had to get down to Chevening for 11 a.m. Nick had invited me and Danny down to a 'meet the media' event, with George Parker, the political editor of the *FT*, Andy Grice of *The Independent*, Andrew Rawnsley from *The Observer* and Gary Gibbon of *Channel 4 News*.

Chevening was looking at its best, and we had coffee and biscuits for about half an hour, before going for a long walk in the magnificent grounds. Lots of children in tow.

Back in London by 4.30 p.m. Sat down to sign 500 Christmas cards and cleared another box worth of work.

TUESDAY 10 DECEMBER

Had a brief chat with Matt Sanders, who was very amused by a meeting he'd had with Maria Miller at the Department for Culture, Media and Sport. The Tories are apparently in a terrible tizz about when they are going to allow the first weddings for same-sex couples. They wanted to do this in the spring, but felt that they couldn't announce the initiative too close to Easter, because of the religious overtones. Then Maria Miller said they also couldn't announce it early in the New Year because of Christmas! They claimed they might have to delay the entire announcement until June 2014. Later on in the day, Maria Miller came back and said that she'd decided that instead of delaying the announcement until May or June 2014, they would now announce it … at two o'clock this afternoon! An interesting indication of how sensitive the Tories still are about this issue.

WEDNESDAY 11 DECEMBER

In at 6.30 a.m. Started to draft a letter to Michael Gove. I've decided to set out clearly my objections to him cutting back on the basic need allocation to fund his free schools overspend, which now amounts to something like £800 million over the 2013–16 period.

As well as setting out clearly the case for making the full basic need allocation, I've also proposed some constructive suggestions about how we can skew the free school programme to make sure that it's expanded to cover all areas of basic need. I've copied my letter to civil servants, ministers and advisers – that's a wide enough copy list and hopefully it won't get leaked.

THURSDAY 12 DECEMBER

It's amazing what ministers have to approve. One of the papers that came to me in last night's red box was asking for my approval for a school to use an extra ten square metres of land in order to rebuild a prefab classroom!

Before I left the office, got an email from my private secretary in the DfE. She said that she'd got a read-out from the meeting between the Prime Minister and Michael Gove today on the national fair funding formula. Apparently the meeting took twice as long as expected and there were 'raised voices' and 'a bit of a row'.

The Prime Minister and Chancellor have overruled Michael and decided not to go ahead with the fully-fledged national funding formula but to replace this with the type of plan B option that I've pushed, of simply raising the lowest-funded authorities to a basic minimum level. This won't create any losers and will ensure that the most underfunded authorities have some useful extra funding in 2015. This probably isn't a bad solution, but it will leave Michael feeling a bit battered and bruised – as he's now been overruled on school kitchens, on the grammar school expansion in Kent and on the national fair funding formula.

Cameron is apparently desperate for all the rows around Gove to calm down. He has told Nick: 'I know Michael is very unpopular with everyone at the moment. We really don't want to have rows on education, which should be a good area for the coalition. Can't both sides sue for peace?' Michael is driving me mad at the moment. A senior civil servant told me he thinks Michael lost it all after the vote on Syria.

MONDAY 16 DECEMBER

At 10 a.m. I met Philippa Stroud. She said that George Osborne was trying to kick all the child poverty stuff into the long grass because he wants to make big welfare cuts in the next parliament and he doesn't want to be restrained from this by the child poverty measures.

At 12.30 p.m. I had a conference call with Oliver Letwin about the child poverty targets. I told him that the recent paper from the Tories proposing to redraft the child poverty measures was 'a load of old flim-flam'. He seemed a bit taken aback.

TUESDAY 17 DECEMBER

The 'Peace Now' meeting between Nick Clegg and Michael Gove apparently went ahead at midday, but I didn't get any read-out until well into the afternoon.

When I got back to my office, I received separate summaries of the meeting from both Nick's office and Michael's. There were no officials present, so the accounts relied upon the memories of the participants. To my amazement, these accounts were pretty similar.

The email from Julian Astle read as follows:

David, Nick gave me a read-out from his meeting with Michael. A lot of it was in getting-off-my-chest territory that was probably quite helpful. Nick began by running through the charge sheet, at the top of which was the Book Trust thing which he said he knew for a fact came from MG's office. He challenged MG to think how he would have felt if the DPMO had done the same to Mrs Gove. Nick also objected to the negative briefing around the free school meal announcement that MG's office had conducted. He said that he felt a lot of the problems we were experiencing stemmed from MG's dogmatic view of school autonomy and his decision to defend it no matter what. He felt this was leading to some bizarre policy position, such as refusing to consider how schools might play a bigger role in preparing pupils for the life of work (careers advice and guidance). MG then had his turn. Said he felt sore about Nick's speech on free schools/QTS etc., but more generally sore about the way that Nick Clegg and the Lib Dems demonise him in the eyes of teachers and parents and present him as a swivel-eyed ideologue and red in tooth and claw privatiser! Nick said he was struck by how stung by this charge Michael Gove seemed. Nick apologised for the way the speech landed and reassured him that he wasn't against schools reform ... He said he was worried, though, about the decision to take £400 million from basic need for free schools. Michael then suggested that Nick write to him on this and the other policy issues he had concerns about. Nick said he would seek to do this by the end of this week, and that the list would include:

1. Careers advice and guidance.
2. The middle tier.
3. The need to marry a set of minimum standards on the curriculum, teacher qualifications, nutrition etc. with school autonomy.
4. The delivery of the universal free school meals policy for infants.

On this last point, MG claimed that he wasn't just a supporter of the policy, but was in fact the first person in government to suggest we do this … The DPM's conclusion was 'an emotionally cathartic and intellectually clarifying meeting that should result in a more constructive period of engagement with a more accommodating Education Secretary'.

Hmmm. We shall see.

WEDNESDAY 18 DECEMBER

10.45 a.m. Home Affairs Committee.

The major discussion was about a proposal to phase out a scheme which allows Eastern European workers to come in to pick crops, because it's impossible to find British people who want to do the work. We are phasing out this scheme in the year ahead, to coincide with Bulgarians and Romanians being allowed to come into the UK to work, without restriction.

Apparently the agricultural sector is very worried that they won't be able to get all the crops in.

Owen Paterson explained his views on the scheme, managing both to support the phasing out of the scheme and also to worry about the effects on the agricultural sector. Owen then came up with a bizarre suggestion: 'One solution to all of this would be to get more British pensioners picking the fruit in the fields, but there might be an issue with the minimum wage – being too high. If we had more pensioners picking fruit we might need to give them some kind of exemption from the minimum wage'!

Everybody else around the table looked incredulous at this suggestion, and I saw the officials who sit to Nick Clegg's right sniggering as they minuted it. Owen is difficult to take seriously at the best of times.

Ken Clarke then spoke: 'I must say that I regard all of this as a complete load of rubbish. The abolition of the scheme is predicated on the assumption that we are going to be able to find British workers to leave the urban centres of the United Kingdom and go out into the fields to pick crops. I can tell you that people in this country are simply not going to do this. There was a time, I remember after the Second World War, when people did leave some of the big cities and go out into the countryside to do this work. That's over. Instead of all this ridiculous rhetoric about 'shooting Bulgarians' and closing down the borders of our country, we ought to welcome people in from the Eastern European nations who are willing to work incredibly hard and take up the jobs that our people are not prepared to do. But if we are going to do that, we have got to tackle all this ludicrous hysteria about Romanians and Bulgarians, and get the debate back on an even keel.'

In the early afternoon I insisted on having a meeting with senior officials about the capital situation in the department. I said that I wanted to go ahead with maintenance allocations to schools as soon as possible, and I wasn't prepared to top-slice any more of this to pay for free school overspends. Then, to my absolute amazement, officials told me that they'd suddenly discovered another massive overspend in the free schools budget, this time of some £300–500 million for 2014/15 – the year that we're supposed to be allocating maintenance capital.

They said that they'd only just discovered this in the last twenty-four to forty-eight hours, by updating all the estimates of costs. I said that I was absolutely gobsmacked and couldn't believe that they were seriously telling me in the middle of a capital allocation that we were hundreds of millions of pounds over budget. How could they possibly have not done these calculations, and why hadn't they told me the day before about this problem when they knew about it and they knew that I was negotiating with the Chief Secretary to try to get budget exchange in order to go ahead with the capital announcement? Around the table there were a lot of very nervous looks.

Returned from meeting Danny in the Cabinet Office. Went up to the seventh floor and was instantly called into the Secretary of State's office to see Michael and officials. We sat at the large conference room on the far side of Michael's office, away from his desk, and as we came in, Michael was finishing off various things at his desk but said hello in quite a calm way. Then he came over to the table and sat down next to me and looked at officials and said, 'I'm very, very, very angry. Frankly, what's happened on capital is an utter disgrace. A shambles. Total incompetence. It's made me and our department look stupid in front of the Treasury, and undermined our credibility and will reduce our ability to get things done and agreed in the future. It isn't good enough.'

The problem is that nobody really seems to be in charge of the free schools budget, and it seems to be utterly unmanaged. It also seems to be, as I put it, the elephant in the room which is allowed to stampede all over the place, crushing other budget headings. I said I understood that Michael Gove was keen on free schools but we couldn't simply allow free schools to gobble up every single penny of money that was designed for things like maintenance, and I pointed out that the maintenance budget was also used by many local authorities to deal with basic need pressures. I said that part of the problem might also be ministerial responsibilities, as although I am responsible for schools capital, this excludes the free schools programme, which I get no information at all about. I said that it's unacceptable that I'm managing capital budgets such as basic need and maintenance but I have no idea what is going on with free schools.

Got an update this afternoon on Sally Morgan, who is the chair of Ofsted, and former adviser to Tony Blair. I want her to continue as chair of Ofsted, which appeared to be the officials' advice, but I have heard that Michael is now thinking of overturning this and getting rid of her. This may be something to do with the fact that she is a Labour peer. I asked my private secretary to look into this and the feedback came through this evening that actually the pressure was coming from 10 Downing Street. Apparently with the election coming up, they're looking to 'place' Tory-friendly people in jobs such as this, so the latest idea is to let Sally extend her contract to September 2014 and then replace her. All a bit depressing. I asked whether it would be helpful to Michael if I pushed back on this and tried to block it through Nick Clegg.

On the way over to the House of Commons, Michael talked about the 'DfE's Got Talent' end-of-year bash, which took place earlier on this week and which I wasn't able to attend. There was a duet between Matt Hancock and Liz Truss, which sounds quite amusing. Michael said that at the end of next year if we were still both in the department then we ought to do a 'Morecambe and Wise' double act in which he would be Eric Morecambe and I would be Ernie Wise. He said that we should leave the stage doing the famous Morecambe and Wise 'dance', which they used at the end of their performances. I said, 'I'd have to be quite drunk!'

MONDAY 23 DECEMBER

I continue to block the proposal from Chris Grayling to make those people whose cases go to court pay some of the court costs if they are found guilty. This would affect some 1.15 million people, and the latest figures show that about 800,000 of these people are minor offenders who are in court for things like road traffic violations and not paying their TV licence. Ken Clarke is blocking this from the usual liberal Tory perspective, but amusingly, Theresa May is also blocking it because she thinks it's a bad message for rehabilitation! It takes quite something for the Home Secretary to block a policy on liberal grounds!

WEDNESDAY 25 DECEMBER

Christmas Day. I've got a miserable cold. It's going to be a quiet end to this year, I hope, but 2014 is going to be a different matter altogether. A year, I suspect, of tension in the Department for Education, a year of difficult coalition compromises in the Cabinet Office, and a year of preparing the general election manifesto for the Liberal Democrats, while having to spend a lot more time campaigning in Yeovil constituency. Altogether it's going to be a challenging and tiring year, and to be honest I can't wait to get past May 2015.

TUESDAY 31 DECEMBER

South of France. We drove down to Cassis on the coast, and had lunch outside on the sea front. A pleasant sunny day, and just about warm enough to eat outside.

A quiet seeing-in of the New Year. Received various text messages from friends and others, including one from Michael Gove wishing me a happy 2014 and thanking me for my 'forbearance and friendship in 2013'.

I texted Nick to wish him a happy New Year, and joked that we would end 2014 on a poll rating of 22 per cent. Nick said that he'd 'settle for 18 per cent'! The truth is that the polls presently show us at only around 10 per cent or 11 per cent – level pegging with UKIP!

2014

SUNDAY 5 JANUARY

Cameron has opened the 2014 bidding by committing the Tories to continue the 'triple lock' on the state pension – so it goes up by the highest of prices, earnings or 2.5 per cent. This was a Liberal Democrat policy we put into the coalition agreement, but the Tories now seem to want to own it.

MONDAY 6 JANUARY

Osborne has given a very gloomy speech forecasting a) massive amounts of further austerity, and b) £25 billion of welfare cuts. The dividing lines of the 2015 general election are clear.

Simon Hoggart, the *Guardian* sketch-writer, died yesterday. His pithy little columns were always amusing. A sad loss.

TUESDAY 7 JANUARY

Some Tory briefing against the Chancellor, probably from IDS – suggesting that hammering the working-age poor again is unacceptable, if pensioners are not to make any contribution to austerity. One day the IDS/Osborne rows are really going to blow through the roof.

Cabinet. We had a discussion about measures to restrict benefits for EU migrants. Nick and I said that the steps we are taking are sensible, but I warned of the risk of a massive and unquenchable appetite for further, less well-considered proposals. At this, Ken Clarke nodded ferociously. I said the risk is that we launch proposals that haven't been properly thought out, or require us to leave the European Union.

Ken Clarke – probably the most pro-immigration person in the Cabinet – said that addressing immigration is 'like catching a tiger by the tail'. Politicians who think they can control the public and media debate are almost always wrong. Baroness Warsi also made some critical comments about government rhetoric.

Michael Gove then made a rare and slightly sycophantic contribution, saying that all the 'hand-wringing' ought to be ignored, and that Theresa May and IDS should be congratulated for the fantastically successful work to stop Romanians and Bulgarians coming into the country. I don't know whether Michael really believes this, but if he does he's seriously out of touch!

Owen Paterson gave us one of his normal quirky updates about recent flooding. He said that he had personally tested some of the local councils by ringing their general enquiries numbers. He said that two councils he'd called both put him through to an automated operator service, where he had to deal with a voice-activated system – 'Absolutely useless! I asked for "sandbags" and they put me through to "electoral services".' It could only happen to Owen!

WEDNESDAY 8 JANUARY

Bumped into Steve Webb, who told me that IDS hadn't even been informed by Cameron/Osborne about the announcement on the triple lock.

Had breakfast with Oliver at 7.45 a.m. and told him that on child poverty I wasn't prepared to compromise any further. Oliver said that Osborne does not want another child poverty measure that's based on income, as he thinks that the welfare cuts he's going to make are likely to push up poverty after 2015. Absurd, but telling.

FRIDAY 10 JANUARY

Spent the whole day in the constituency. The highlight was an event at the Fleet Air Arm Museum, where the Commodore and I presented the Arctic Star medals to local veterans who served on the Arctic Convoys during the Second World War. Amazing to be able to meet people who had fought on British warships that took on the mighty German battleships *Tirpitz* and *Scharnhorst*.

SATURDAY 11 JANUARY

Advice centres in Ilminster and Crewkerne, then off to see Yeovil Town take on Burnley. Alastair Campbell, Tony Blair's old spin doctor, was there. He likes his football and is certainly competitive. On the two occasions that Burnley scored, he was the first person on his feet, and on both occasions he glanced round and gloated at me, waving his fist. We scored a late goal, but ended 2–1 down.

MONDAY 13 JANUARY

Various meetings on the sensitive issue of free school meals legislation. The latest ludicrous excuse from Dom Cummings is that if we legislate in this area it might be 'an interference with the European Human Rights Act'! You couldn't make it up! The DfE lawyers are privately contemptuous, and told me that they 'couldn't even waste time pretending that this was a serious argument'.

Lib Dem Cabinet ministers' meeting – with junior minister Dan Rogerson, to discuss the Common Agricultural Policy. Dan plunged in with considerable enthusiasm, completely unaware that nobody else had the faintest idea what the issue was. After he'd been speaking for five minutes, Nick interrupted: 'I'm sorry about this, but I've no idea what you're talking about. Could you give me the long version please?'

Nick met the PM today: 'It was a very tense and difficult meeting. I had a major row with Cameron over the Wharton Bill,* where he threatened to just go ahead and push legislation through to guarantee a referendum in the next parliament on leaving the EU. I told Cameron that this was completely outrageous and that he simply couldn't act unilaterally. I said that if he did push a vote on a European referendum, then it would be gloves off and I would feel liberated to back Labour motions on a mansion tax, qualified teacher status, party funding reform etc. etc.'

Cameron is now in a permanent panic about his party and is petrified he's losing control.

One piece of good news: Nick said he'd finally got Cameron to agree

---

*   A Private Member's Bill proposing to legislate for a referendum on British membership of the EU.

to impose free school meals legislation on Gove. Thank God! This painful and pointless row can finally end.

TUESDAY 14 JANUARY

8.15 a.m. A 'breakfast meeting' with Nick, Danny and key advisers at the National Liberal Club. We used one of those bloody miserable rooms in the basement. No windows. Very dull pictures.

This was also a breakfast meeting with a difference – the difference being no breakfast. Only after some pressure did we get a cup of vile-tasting coffee.

These are now going to be weekly pre-Cabinet meetings – to discuss upcoming political challenges.

We spent the whole meeting discussing the European elections, where Nick wants to be very gung-ho about us being pro-European. I pushed back, saying that in large parts of England the EU is unpopular. Needless to say, I was the only one talking sense. Danny wants us to say that these elections are 'a test of national resolve on Europe' – an interesting strategy, given that we seem to be assuming we're going to lose most of our seats.

Cabinet. We started by discussing parliamentary business, and Theresa May raised a problem with the Antisocial Behaviour Bill. It's been discovered that the Bill could end up banning carol singers – who could be whipped away into police custody because of their 'antisocial behaviour'. Theresa said that we might need to amend the Bill. Jailing carol singers is a step too far even for her.

Owen Paterson had virtually lost his voice, but decided to make a long contribution anyway, in which only one word in three was audible. Lord Hill whispered to me, 'It's like listening to the World Service on medium wave in a very poor African country!'

Had a meeting with Steve Webb, our Pensions Minister, about future welfare savings. Asked Steve whether he had any ideas to cut back on the £200 billion welfare budget. He came out with two proposals. One was to spend more money trying to get people off welfare. Hmmm. It might work but it might not. His second idea was to reduce the value of pensions tax relief. Just when you think that Steve is getting used to hard choices, he lapses back into exactly where he was pre-2010. Very bright, but basically an old lefty.

Had a note from officials on the issue of free school meals legislation. Arrrrggghhhh!

> The Deputy Prime Minister has told Michael Gove that he will proceed with legislation, and the Prime Minister has come in to tell Michael Gove to back down. However, Michael Gove is speaking to the Prime Minister and refuses to allow a Home Affairs letter to go out until then. The Deputy Prime Minister's office is now escalating this and the PM may have to intervene.

I like Michael, but he can be an utter pain in the arse at times.

THURSDAY 16 JANUARY

Caught the train to speak at the North of England Education Conference. On the way back, we got the news that Cameron has finally told Michael to stop messing around and to legislate. Hurrah! Michael will be bruised because over the last few months he's:

1. had a massive falling out with Nick over qualified teacher status, where most of the public will think he's in the wrong;
2. been forced to legislate for free school meals;
3. been forced to allocate £150 million for free school meals capital;
4. had his proposals for a national fair funding formula for schools blocked;
5. been forced by the Treasury into making savings on the free schools programme and having greater oversight of this.

Met Oliver, who now wants to go ahead with a 'Social Action and Heroism Bill', which is some twaddle that he's come up with about removing any legal risk that people might be taken to court if they do 'brave things' but inadvertently make matters worse. For example, trying to save a drowning man but diving into a lake on top of him and causing brain damage. Oliver clearly has too much time on his hands.

Oliver handed me his proposed draft Bill, which was half a page in length! I said that in my view this fails the normal 'Oliver Letwin test' – i.e. is it really necessary, and is there any evidence of the problem? Oliver was insistent: 'It happens all the time.' Hmmm.

In the evening, sent Nick Clegg a note advocating the introduction of an 'early years pupil premium' for disadvantaged three- and four-year-olds, to help improve social mobility. I want to see us over-deliver our manifesto promises on both the pupil premium and the personal tax allowance.

This afternoon George Osborne has come out in favour of a big increase in the national minimum wage – so it seems that Matt Hancock has prevailed in his row with Rupert Harrison, the Chancellor's economic adviser. Just shows the effect of an election coming up!

SATURDAY 18 JANUARY

Spent the afternoon going through my red box. Came across an extraordinary submission from the 'Due Diligence and Counter-Extremism Division' of the DfE. The unit exists in part to oversee free schools and make sure they're not taken over by religious extremists. The policy note said: 'We agreed to soft market testing with a small number of potential contractors in order to measure interest in doing extremism work by private investigators … we have identified process and presentational considerations that we now believe favour pursuing a slightly different approach.' Extraordinary to think that the department's contemplating recruiting private investigators to scrutinise free schools operators.

SUNDAY 19 JANUARY

The Tories are continuing to stir the issue of migrant access to benefits. Following Nick's decision last week that he wasn't going to be railroaded into further measures, the Tories have retaliated, with a front-page story in the *Mail on Sunday* entitled 'Speak in English – Or Lose Benefits'. The story says that the policy has been delayed following a Clegg vs. Tories row. It quotes one 'Tory insider' as saying: 'The vast majority of voters will think this idea is plain common sense.'

Nick actually looked at the paperwork on this last night and emailed me: 'I'm a little less concerned on substance than before – there are numerous sensible exemptions to the ending of translation support, and a fair number of other member states don't have any meaningful language support – but I remain intensely annoyed at the slapdash way this has been presented to us.'

I replied:

The *Mail on Sunday* talks of the Tories being under instructions from Lynton Crosby to generate a new policy on immigration every week. We have to calibrate our response very carefully if we're to avoid being screwed ... We cannot just say we will only agree a certain number of measures regardless of their merits. We have ultimately to challenge bad ideas on the basis that they are bad ideas.

Nick replied: 'Yes, but we cannot allow a coalition government in the latter stages of this parliament just to become a press release factory for Lynton Crosby!'

MONDAY 20 JANUARY

Nick had his bilateral with the PM today and insisted that the further measures on immigrant benefits will have to be considered by me before sign-off. One involves scaling back translation services, one requires migrants to work for twenty-four hours per week before being entitled to in-work benefits, and one removes child benefits and child tax credits from migrants who are workless. They've all been cobbled together to meet a political need to be 'tough on immigrants', but the one I'm most worried about is the child benefit one – popular, but it looks illegal within the EU.

At 1.30 p.m. I met up with Sir Howard Davies, who is doing the review into airport capacity. I tested him on whether we shouldn't just build the extra runway at Gatwick given the costs and complexities of Heathrow. Sir Howard pointed out that the transport connections into central London from Gatwick are at present quite poor. However the meeting left me thinking that Gatwick may be the better option.

Had a brief call from Neil Sherlock, who wanted to have a chat about Baroness Sally Morgan. Sally was invited to be chair of Ofsted by Michael Gove, but apparently Michael has seen her today and told her that the Tories want to 'put in one of their people' – so instead of getting a second term in office, she has been told that she is going to have to step down in September. Absurd decision! At one stage Michael would have worked very hard to keep people like Sally, an excellent (New) Labour peer, on side. Not anymore. The Tories now want their people in place.

Still working on the idea of having an early years pupil premium. Meanwhile, Dom Cummings has sent out an email within the department saying: 'All this stuff about early years funding and an early years premium is a lot of rubbish. MG is unlikely to regard this as a priority.' Officials don't seem to be too bothered, maybe because they know that Dom is going soon and maybe because they can see that Michael doesn't always get his own way.

TUESDAY 21 JANUARY

At 8.30 a.m. had a meeting with Home Office officials to discuss the new measures to disrupt extremism, which are planned by Theresa May. Amusingly, I knew, and so did my staff, that none of these measures are going anywhere, because the PM has already agreed with Nick that we're not going to have an Extremism Bill. But Cameron clearly hasn't yet told the Home Secretary, which meant that I had to play along.

9.30 a.m. Cabinet. Michael Gove raised an unexpected point, asking why the MoD has so far failed to deliver a coalition pledge to refocus funding on cadet forces in state schools, away from elite private schools. Philip Hammond gave a pathetically feeble answer, saying, 'It's terribly important that we don't do anything to undermine recruiting the right people to become officers.' I saw Michael's eyebrows rise and twitch. I think if he had been closer to Hammond he might have punched him. Cameron quipped that this was an issue that meant a lot to him as 'an ex-member of the Eton Rifles'.

Not a good performance by the charmless, humourless, right-wing Hammond. His only redeeming feature is that he is the only man in Britain capable of making Michael Fallon look a cuddly, charismatic, generous-minded, progressive, liberal lefty.

At noon, Nick called a meeting on the never-ending Rennard situation. Still major rumblings in the party and press.

Then we met with the Home Secretary, who'd come over to Dover House to talk with Nick and me about exit checks. Theresa is now trying to pretend that the Home Office has actually got a plan to deliver exit checks by 2015. It's going to be quite difficult to get all this done for sea and rail routes by then, though the Home Office is suddenly claiming it can be achieved. Frankly, I will believe it when I see it – and I think the Home Office are just telling us what they think we want to hear, to avoid a political bust-up where they are on the wrong side of public opinion.

WEDNESDAY 22 JANUARY

Set off with Nick for the Home Affairs Cabinet Committee meeting. On the way there, Nick said he'd drunk too much coffee and needed to pop into the toilet. Went on without him, and everybody was there waiting, including most of the major Tory Cabinet ministers. Ken Clarke boomed, 'Where on earth is Nick?' I replied: 'He's in the bog!'

As I sat down, Ken said, 'Oh, we all thought he was detained by dealing with this ridiculous Lib Dem sex scandal about this Rennard chap. What's clear about the Liberals is that they have much lower-quality sex scandals than the other parties. The Liberal Party cannot be considered to be a serious, major political party until it has proper, high-quality sex scandals. In the Conservative Party, if we're going to have a sex scandal, you get the full works – Chelsea football kits, toe-sucking, exotic sexual equipment and the deployment of a wide variety of fruit and vegetables. What do you get from the Liberals? Just a bit of bum pinching!'

The Cabinet Office officials just about managed to suppress their laughter into smirks. Ministers were diplomatically silent.

At 3.30 p.m. went off to see the Attorney General about the legality of Tory proposals on immigrant benefits. Dominic Grieve was treading very carefully, and I got the impression he was under firm instructions from No. 10 not to be too 'unhelpful' to them.

He gave us an extremely clear steer that we ought to see the detailed policy/legal guidance before agreeing anything.

Rather suspiciously, an email came through from Grieve's office a couple of hours later, saying the Attorney General didn't want there to be any confusion and he feared he might have left me with the impression that these policies shouldn't be launched until we had clear guidance and policy rationale from the relevant departments. Apparently this wasn't his position after all, and he now believed that both policies could be launched even if we didn't have this detail! Completely ludicrous, and it's quite clear that he's been sat on.

THURSDAY 23 JANUARY

Travelled to Woodside High School in north London. Shown around by Dame Joan McVittie – an impressive lady. She said, to my great pleasure, that the best thing we had done in government was the pupil premium. The school gains over half a million pounds per year – which they are able to use to help poor children to catch up. When I asked Joan whether the school had any problems, she said, 'Well, not with money...' I was also delighted to hear that. It shows that for schools like this, some of the most challenging schools, the protection of the schools budget, combined with the pupil premium, has really helped them to succeed.

Later on, held a meeting with officials about the idea of having a pupil premium in the early years – I remain enthusiastic about this because it will achieve three main aims: wiping out the early years cuts that are planned in 2015/16; getting more money to disadvantaged youngsters in early years settings; helping to drive up quality.

SATURDAY 25 JANUARY

In the red box today is a copy of a letter Michael Gove has sent to Sally Morgan. This says that the department is not going to renew her appointment. Infuriating. I am the Ofsted Minister, and MG hasn't even consulted me.

Received a copy of a letter Theresa May sent to the Prime Minister last May, discussing the potential authorisation of water cannon for use in England and Wales by the police. I noticed an article in the newspapers about this recently, suggesting that the Association of Chief Police Officers had said they needed these to control continued protests, including 'from ongoing and potential future austerity measures'. That certainly sounded warning bells. I will intervene to make sure they are only used in extreme circumstances.

SUNDAY 26 JANUARY

Woke up to a remarkable story in the *Sunday Times* about a huge clash between Sir Michael Wilshaw and the Department for Education. Michael W is apparently accusing staff at the DfE – doubtless Michael's special advisers – of briefing against his organisation. He's apparently spoken out after *The Times* said that two right-leaning think tanks were about to criticise Ofsted. He says that he is 'displeased, shocked and outraged'. And he calls for Michael Gove to call off his 'attack dogs'. He says he was never intimidated as a head teacher and doesn't intend to be intimidated as Chief Inspector. He also goes on to say that in parts of the country no one is effectively monitoring free schools and academies, and he makes quite clear that: 'If I see things going wrong in an academy chain, I will say so. If people tied to the free school movement think I will not do that, they have another think coming … We will do the job fairly, without fear or favour.'

This is quite extraordinary. Particularly dramatic from somebody who used to be regarded as being a 'place man' for Michael Gove.

Interestingly, my red box contains briefings showing that there are another four free schools that have recently been inspected by Ofsted – and three of them have been put in the 'requires improvement' category, while one has been found to be inadequate.

I sent an email to Michael Gove saying:

> You will be as horrified as I am by the Ofsted stuff this morning. Is this somebody in DfE? I cannot believe that Sir Michael would say that without knowing? This also happens one day after seeing your letter bringing Sally Morgan's position to an end. Is this a good idea? You did not discuss it with me and I was rather of the view that she was doing a good job? Is the decision now final?

In the early afternoon had an email from Lydia in my DfE office, forwarding a message from Michael Gove's private office:

You might have seen the interview with Sir Michael Wilshaw. It appears he thinks the Policy Exchange/Civitas papers were prompted by the Secretary of State and his advisers, and that there is some sort of campaign to discredit Ofsted. Nothing could be further from the truth – whilst there are concerns about Ofsted (notably some inspectors using old methodology to assess lessons), these are dealt with behind closed doors. The Secretary of State knows how important Ofsted is to achieving his reforms so wouldn't try to discredit it in public. The important thing will be for the accusation of dirty tricks to be taken back, and for us to find a dignified way for Sir Michael to smooth things over … It is likely the Secretary of State will speak to Sir Michael today. I wanted to let you know so that you can reassure David and the Deputy Prime Minister's office if they ask what's happening. I've also let Ed Llewellyn know at No. 10 Downing Street.

Spoke to Sally Morgan in the afternoon. She told me that the first she had heard of being replaced was after Michael Gove had spoken to Sir Michael Wilshaw last year and told him. Sally was furious to hear second-hand, and had a chat with MG before Christmas, when Michael apparently said that he was keen to have a Conservative in place as the chair of Ofsted before the general election, and said that this was also the view of No. 10.

Sally also said that Sir Michael Wilshaw was absolutely fed up with the drip, drip, drip of negative stories about Ofsted from the DfE. Sir Michael apparently blames it all on Dom Cummings, whom he regards as an 'arrogant little shit', who he thinks 'looks like a tramp'.

He also feels pressure from the DfE to avoid properly inspecting free schools and academy chains, and to pull his punches in evaluation of them. Sally said that when Sir Michael found out about the *Times* articles last Friday saying that Ofsted needed massive reform and that they were spreading progressive teaching practices, he apparently went completely bonkers and was on the point of calling a full press conference. Apparently MG telephoned Sir Michael this morning and they had an argument. Gove was trying to get Sir Michael to withdraw the suggestion that the DfE were briefing against Ofsted, but apparently he's refused to do so.

This all seems crazy. Sir Michael and Sally Morgan used to be MG's two great reform allies, and he's now managed to fall out with both of them!

There really is something wrong with him at the moment and he's lost all sense of judgement.

In the evening I spoke to MG and asked him to think again about removing Sally. He mumbled something about how important it was to ensure a proper transition into the next parliament. I continued to press the point and eventually Michael said, 'Well, I guess I'd better reflect upon Sally's situation, given everything that's happened today.' Good.

MONDAY 27 JANUARY

Had a brief discussion with DPM adviser Alex Dziedzan about the block that I've put on Grayling's proposals to charge 1.2 million people going through the courts for the cost of their cases. The charges range from about £240 for TV licence non-payment to £540 for mass murder and a court case lasting years!

At 6 p.m. took a call from Ken Clarke: 'I hope you're still blocking these crazy proposals by Chris Grayling. They're not properly thought through at all and they could completely undermine everything we're trying to do on rehabilitation. It really is just populist nonsense from Chris.' I asked whether we could make alternative savings, and we discussed proposals which are apparently currently being blocked by No. 10, to close various under-utilised courts. Ken said, 'Of course, I did a lot of this in my time as Justice Secretary, and the right time to do it was at the beginning of the parliament. The Prime Minister and No. 10 got in a complete tizzy, and thought it would be terribly unpopular with all their golf club voters. Eventually I think I had to make some concession to save one court in Oxfordshire somewhere for David, and after that he allowed me to go ahead, and of course there wasn't any fuss at all amongst ordinary people.'

At 7 p.m. met Chris Grayling in his room on the upper ministerial corridor. I know that Danny and Nick find Chris OK, but there is something rather unpleasant and untrustworthy about him. He sat there listening to my concerns, with snake-like eyes and little evident desire to make any concessions. He made clear that he wants to launch these proposals next week. Not in their present form.

TUESDAY 28 JANUARY

Woke up to a lot of coverage of Vince Cable's speech on the economy, the day before what are expected to be good economic growth numbers. The coverage of Vince's speech reads like a critique of the George Osborne recovery – warning of the risks of a housing boom and more public spending cuts. Nick is pretty irritated: 'Vince seems to be utterly addicted to economic gloom, and is desperate to prove that he has been right about the economy.' Nick has apparently met Vince and warned that his interventions are making it impossible for our party to take any credit for the emerging recovery, but Vince doesn't get the point at all.

8.15 a.m. Our DPM/CST regular breakfast meeting in the bowels of the National Liberal Club. A bit of a whinge-fest about Vince and his speech.

WEDNESDAY 29 JANUARY

Met DfE officials to talk about the budget for 2015/16. We're apparently having to make another £250 million of savings. Michael wants to cut the Education Services Grant that goes to local authorities by another 20 per cent, so it would decline in one year by 40 per cent! I said I wasn't interested in negotiating with Michael at all on this issue and I was simply going to block any consultation changes.

I said that in the meantime I wanted officials to provide me with a very detailed options paper of all the potential alternative cuts. The officials looked pleasingly panicked – they can see a bust-up and another major row. Too bad.

In the afternoon I attended a Quad on 'the fourth session legislative programme' – in other words, legislation by the coalition in the last year of the government. Given all the arguments that Nick is having with Cameron at the moment, not least over the Immigration Bill, it's amazing to see how friendly and relaxed everybody was. The Prime Minister seemed to be in a jovial mood and so was Osborne. You wouldn't really believe that these are two political parties with very different ideologies and attitudes, entering the fourth year of a coalition and beginning to look towards a very hard-fought general election.

Cameron approached things in a more relaxed way than I've seen him do in the past and seemed genuinely to want to come to some solutions, and not do his normal thing of pretending to have deeply entrenched views in order to see whether he can bully us into submission.

We discussed the Small Business Bill. Cameron and Osborne said that they hated the Business Bank and all of the measures that Vince Cable was proposing to tighten the enforcement around dodgy company directors. We said that we hated all the stuff about reducing employment rights, as it was all 'back to Beecroft' stuff. The Tories also raised concerns about getting rid of exclusivity clauses in zero-hours contracts.

The Tories said that they would do the zero-hours contract stuff but provided we restricted our changes to this limited area and did not back any more extreme Labour Party amendments. Nick Clegg said that he was prepared to sacrifice the Business Bank-enabling legislation (the Business Bank already exists) provided the Tories dropped all their proposals on undermining employment rights. Nick said he wasn't willing to give up on tightening the enforcement around dodgy company directors.

George Osborne suggested a 'truce' where 'You give up on bashing company directors and we'll give up on bashing the workers!'

We then went on to the Serious Crime Bill, which Theresa May is trying to stuff full of all sorts of illiberal Home Office stuff. Cameron said that he'd had a row with Theresa May, and insisted on dumping a lot of this.

We then came to the proposed legislation on the recall of MPs and legislation to put in place a binding 0.7 per cent GNP target for international aid expenditure. Nick said he felt very strongly about these two issues – both coalition agreements.

Cameron said, 'Look, the 0.7 per cent on international aid thing is something that I just can't get past my backbenchers. This is going to be even worse than gay marriage. This will unite all the people who think that we shouldn't spend money on foreigners with all the people who think that it's totally arbitrary to legislate for random proportions of GNP to be spent on things like international development.'

Nick said, 'Look, I hoped that you might be budgeable on international development; I know that you'll be quite difficult over recall.'

Cameron said, 'No, 0.7 per cent is just undoable for me but maybe there is some kind of thing we could do on recall.'

We then had a pretty astonishing argument about whether or not we should have a Bill for direct elections to national parks. Danny said that he was 'incredibly passionate' about this – and George Osborne joked that he would be, given that he'd worked for a national park before being an MP! Nick said he also had a national park in his constituency. Cameron said, 'That may be the case but a lot of our lot have got national parks too. William Hague has got two national parks and Patrick McLoughlin has got one, and both of them tell me they don't want elections.' I said that this might be because a lot of the people currently running national parks were the Tory establishment! George Osborne nodded. Unbelievable that we could be spending time discussing whether or not we had direct elections to national parks in the last year of the parliament.

We then went on to Oliver Letwin's 'Social Action, Responsibility and Heroism Bill'. Julian Astle has dubbed this the 'Incompetent Heroes Bill'. It's Oliver's attempt to protect incompetent 'have-a-go heroes' from regulation or court action.

Oliver passed round his Bill, which amounts to one sheet of A4 paper – on one side of which was the title of the Bill and on the other side of which were about five sentences. Everybody started laughing again and teasing Oliver. Nick said he wasn't all that bothered, and if it was that important to Oliver we could go ahead.

By the end, we basically had a legislative session. A Consumer Rights Bill, a Deregulation Bill, a Courts and Sentencing Bill, all of which are carry-overs. An Infrastructure Bill and a Small Business Bill. A Serious Crime Bill, a Modern Slavery Bill, a Childcare Bill, possibly a Service Complaints Commissioner Bill. A Finance Bill and an HS2 Bill, a Defined Ambition Pensions Bill, a Wales Bill, a draft Bill on National Parks and a Social Action, Responsibility and Heroism Bill. The Tories seemed pretty pleased and so were we. This was a rare occasion when everyone got what they wanted.

I then turned to Nick, and said that before things broke up we really need to have a discussion on child poverty. Cameron said, 'Look I'm not sure whether there's really much we can do on this. I think we should just spend more time consulting, and we'll just decide it after the general election.'

Osborne said that it would be useful to have measures on education and worklessness but not on anything to do with income – he clearly wants to cut welfare spending after the next election and is worried that this will drive child poverty rates up. Nick and I put up pretty robust opposition and said we'd already conceded a lot and we couldn't simply let the issue drift on beyond the summer. We left the meeting with some kind of fudge that Oliver Letwin and I would look at it again.

THURSDAY 30 JANUARY

At the DfE ministers' meeting I asked Michael Gove whether he'd been shopping on Sunday at Selfridges when the row with Michael Wilshaw took place. He looked a bit surprised but admitted that he had actually been in Selfridges and asked me how I knew. I said that the *Guardian* article online about the Ofsted row had included various comments from people about the story and one of the people had said that he was in Selfridges in the toy department on Sunday morning when he saw Michael Gove on his mobile phone having a row with somebody else he was referring to as 'Michael' while speaking in a very loud voice. If you are a politician these days, you have to be careful about being monitored wherever you go, and suddenly having your movements appear on social media.

At 6.15 p.m. I had a meeting on Grayling's mad plan to levy massive court costs on offenders. Ken Clarke believes this is very bad for rehabilitation, and it would also multiply by a factor of 200 per cent the fines affecting low-income people. In the meeting was Simon Hughes, the new Justice Minister, who's trying to get on with Grayling but who clearly doesn't agree with this policy. I concluded that we should only let this through if: a) we put a two-year debt limit on so that if people on low incomes haven't paid off the charge within two years it's simply deleted, and b) we insist on a reduction in the charge levels for things like TV licence offences.

FRIDAY 31 JANUARY

Up at 5.30 a.m. to plough through paperwork and then off to the Yeovil Golf Club for a local Chamber of Commerce breakfast. Most of the questions were about things like car-parking charges, clearly a council matter, but the truth is that people regard MPs as responsible for everything.

Frustrating call with Oliver Letwin on child poverty. Spoke to Julian Astle briefly after the call and he told me that he'd spoken to the Chancellor's special adviser, Neil O'Brien, who said the Tories weren't interested in child poverty at all and didn't want any serious measures.

The House of Lords have finally killed off the EU Referendum Bill, but David Cameron is astonishingly now proposing to use the Parliament Act to get it through! This is totally absurd, since he seems to have forgotten that he's in a coalition government and he can't simply do as he likes. Cameron has totally lost control of his party on European matters and many of his MPs are determined to exit the EU and dump Cameron too. He's now the tail being wagged by the Eurosceptic dog. If he's not careful, one day these Eurosceptics will end his political career.

Nick said later: 'Being in coalition with the Tories right now is like being trapped in a cage with a huge, mad gorilla ... Cameron is within an inch of losing control of his party on both immigration and Europe.'

Drove home, and on the way finally realised the significance of an email that had been sent to me late that afternoon by my private secretary. This said that two newspapers had approached Ofsted and the DfE, about a story that Sally Morgan was being removed. Apparently both the DfE and Ofsted have now announced that Sally is not getting a second term, and this has been done in spite of my explicit agreement with Michael Gove on Sunday night that he would rethink the decision.

I am absolutely furious and phoned up Chris Wormald, the Permanent Secretary at the DfE, whom I'd spoken to earlier in the week and told that I expected to be consulted before any final decision. I gave it to him with both barrels and said that I wasn't prepared to defend this in public and that I was furious with MG. Chris didn't even attempt to put up a defence and sounded a bit gobsmacked by my rage. Spoke to Nick, who said that he'd discussed this with Cameron, who said that he was 'under a lot of pressure' to put in Tory placemen before the next election. Pretty astonishing that he should be so blatant about this! Spoke to James McGrory, Nick's spiky press spokesman, and told him to let my opposition to this be made public.

A pretty miserable day. Failure to get the Tories into the right place on child poverty. Failure to block Michael Gove from firing a very good head of Ofsted. The Tories running around like headless chickens over Europe. And Grayling being a complete arse over his courts costs recovery plan.

It's on days like this that I really do wonder whether we want to be in coalition with the Conservatives in the next parliament.

SATURDAY 1 FEBRUARY

Baroness Morgan has gone onto the *Today* programme to claim that she is the victim of a 'determined effort from No. 10' to appoint more Tories. Received a panicky late-night email from Michael Gove, asking me to call him urgently. Ignored it and went to bed.

SUNDAY 2 FEBRUARY

Up at 8.30 a.m. Three messages on my mobile from MG asking me to call him urgently. He's on *Marr* this morning and the shit has certainly hit the fan. Stories about me attacking him over Ofsted lead the *Sunday Times*, *The Observer* and the *Independent on Sunday*.

I was tempted to ignore the calls, but finally phoned him at 8.45 a.m. 'David, as you may know, I'm going on the *Marr* programme in fifteen minutes' time. I think I might possibly be asked about the front-page headlines of the *Sunday Times*, *The Observer*, the *Independent on Sunday*...' Some rustling of papers. '...Oh yes, the *Sunday Telegraph*, *Sunday Mirror*, BBC News, Sky News.'

We then had a calm and very formal conversation. He said that he was very upset that I had expressed my views publicly. I said that I was extremely angry about his failure to consult me on the original decision and then on his failure to rethink the matter or even tell me before the press briefing. He claimed the newspapers came to the DfE on Friday, and they had to give a response. I said that wasn't good enough. I also said that I couldn't understand why people like Sally Morgan were being removed for what looked like political reasons. It was totally wrong to politicise organisations such as Ofsted.

Michael said that he'd talk about that with me later. The discussion only went on for about five minutes. At the end, there was a long silence from Michael, which went on for about fifteen seconds – so long that I thought something might have happened to the phone line. But I said nothing and refused to apologise. Marr was pretty hopeless and failed to push home the charges.

MONDAY 3 FEBRUARY

The newspapers are covered in stories about my spat with MG – they split along fairly predictable lines, with *The Guardian*, *The Independent* etc. taking a critical view of Michael, and *The Sun*, the *Telegraph* and the *Mail* supporting him.

Went to the DfE at 2 p.m., where there was a sense of amused shock amongst the officials.

At 3.15 p.m. I got a call from Michael's office that he was ready to meet. Went through to see him with my private secretary, who I thought paced down the corridor beside me with a detectable sense of relish. Outside Michael's office we met Pamela Dow, Michael's excellent private secretary. The three of us went in and sat down on Michael's leather sofas to the side of his desk. I can't help fearing that he's actually relishing being at the centre of controversy and rows. He's naturally somebody who likes to be in the spotlight and who likes a fight.

Michael sought to explain that although he'd told Sally Morgan that she wasn't being reappointed for political reasons, actually he hadn't meant that at all! He told me that he'd only said that to her because he didn't want to upset her and the real reason was that she really wasn't up to properly managing Michael Wilshaw and compensating for 'all his weaknesses in relation to administration'. So he said the only thing he could have said to me, which is that the decision wasn't politically motivated.

I said that I could only take what he'd said to Sally Morgan at face value, particularly as it had been repeated to Nick Clegg by the Prime Minister.

I also said that part of the reason all this had occurred had been Michael's very poor communication and his failure to rethink his decision after promising to do so. I then widened the complaint to say that since September he had failed to communicate with me over a range of issues – free schools capital, the Education Services Grant, free school meals. He stared at me in his reasonable-but-not-conceding-much mode, and certainly didn't suggest anything that might make the situation any better – such as regular weekly meetings. I feel all we are doing is courteously papering over the cracks.

TUESDAY 4 FEBRUARY

In at 6.15 a.m. Rachel Sylvester has a good article in *The Times* saying that Gove should stop making enemies of his friends, and start to secure the future of education reform. The *Telegraph* cartoon has Michael in a boat in the middle of the sea, having lost both oars.

Cabinet at 9.30 a.m. A briefing by the heads of MI5 and MI6 on the security situation and the terrorist risk. The presentation took longer than it should, and as usual with the security services there is a great hushed sense that we're being told incredibly important and significant things. Somehow, you feel that you're being let in on all sorts of important state secrets, but when it comes to the end you can't actually remember anything new or secret you've learned. There was also a paper summary which we were all told not to take away. I heard Lord Hill mutter, 'There's nothing on the damn thing anyway!'

Interviewed two candidates for my new private secretary post in the Cabinet Office. Have chosen Natalie Perera, a feisty official from the Department for Education whom I have worked with on schools funding. She's very bright, very easy to get on with, and I would say pretty gutsy. I think she'll be absolutely ideal for the post – though I'll be sorry to lose Nick Donlevy, who has Cabinet Secretary potential.

3 p.m. A meeting with Anna Soubry MP, the junior Defence Minister. She was supposed to be discussing a few issues around the government's 'military contract' with me and Lord Nash. Michael Gove had wanted us also to discuss the issue of combined cadet forces, as there's a ludicrous situation where the Ministry of Defence subsidises these cadet forces in private schools but not in state schools. This is supposed to be fixed but Hammond is playing for time.

The meeting took place in my office and we started on the issue of the service premium – the pupil premium which is there for the children of service people. The service premium is one of the things that the Prime Minister insisted on, even though there's absolutely no evidence that it's necessary. Anna Soubry didn't seem to know very much about the policy and she said she couldn't understand the rationale for it and thought it was a rather bad idea! Her MoD officials looked absolutely gobsmacked, and one of them even started chuckling. They obviously think she's wayward and uncontrollable.

I asked her about troops returning from Germany and how many there were going to be and when they would come back etc. She didn't seem to have a clue about that either. I had to ask for a note from officials, otherwise we would have been there until Christmas.

Then, about fifteen minutes before the end of the meeting, Michael

Gove suddenly arrived in my office – which is something that Secretaries of State rarely do. He plonked himself down two places to my right and said that he was there for the discussion about cadet forces. Michael then went into the most astonishing rant. I've seen him get angry at times and it really is quite something. He goes from being very calm and sweet to an astonishing intensity of rage.

He leant forward aggressively and shouted very loudly: 'Anna. I am sorry. It… is… totally unacceptable… for this situation to continue. How can we possibly justify as a government the fact that we are spending tens of millions of pounds on subsidising private school pupils to be in cadet forces when poor children in the state-funded system have to pay for this themselves or don't get it at all? IT IS UN–ACC–EPTABLE! WE HAVE GOT TO DO SOMETHING ABOUT THIS. I AM FURIOUS.'

Officials looked stunned and shocked. Since Anna was sitting to my left, it was all a bit uncomfortable, because the shouting was going on across the front of me. As Michael and Anna traded punches, my head swung back and forth like a Wimbledon umpire.

Anna looked gobsmacked but just about held her own. Michael then started pushing for an immediate meeting either with the general responsible or with Philip Hammond. Gaining confidence, Anna said, 'I'm sorry, Michael, but you'll just have to take this up yourself with the Secretary of State. I'm not a post box. I really don't know very much about this and it's all quite complicated and I'm sure there are some reasons why we're making progress on a slower timetable than you'd like.'

As fast as the hurricane of Michael's anger had arrived, it seemed to dissipate. Five minutes later, the meeting ended. I don't know what I think of Anna Soubry after this meeting and whether she will survive the next reshuffle, but as she went out, I said: 'I think you're going to make a very good Defence Minister – I was impressed with your resilience under fire!' She smiled, weakly.

Worked through my box in the evening and had a chat with Matt Sanders. Matt said that he'd been speaking to Laura, the education adviser in No. 10, who said that David Cameron had been 'scarred' by having to force Michael Gove to retreat over free school meals legislation. Laura apparently said that David Cameron had hated having to overrule Michael Gove, who's incredibly difficult when his advice isn't accepted.

A pretty outrageous submission in my box suggesting that Michael Gove wants to pay £45 million to buy a free school building called Steel House in Tothill Street in Westminster. Apparently the lease would be even more expensive, so they've decided that they might buy the entire building, but £45 million is a mind-boggling amount to pay – and it would be the most expensive free school to date. I've asked civil servants about whether they've really tested the value for money. That will put them into a bit of a spin.

WEDNESDAY 5 FEBRUARY

At 8.30 a.m. did an interview with Andy Grice about the Ofsted rows. Tried to focus on the future, by saying that we wanted to see more independent select committee hearings, as well as an expansion of Ofsted's powers – to allow them to inspect academy chains.

Passed Anna Soubry on the way to a committee meeting: 'That was an absolute disgrace yesterday with Michael Gove. The man really is appalling. I don't know how you deal with him. It was totally inappropriate to do that while the officials were present.'

When I got home, Matt Sanders texted me to say that the interview I'd done with Andy Grice has been completely overspun by *The Independent* as a 'Coalition at War' story. Andy really knows how to spray political petrol around.

FRIDAY 7 FEBRUARY

Spent the day in Yeovil constituency. Serious flooding problems across Somerset and more ghastly weather.

Missed a school visit today because a constituent with mental health problems turned up at our office and refused to leave until he'd spoken to me about his problems. He stood behind my car so that I couldn't reverse out. Had to calm him down for half an hour.

SUNDAY 9 FEBRUARY

The newspapers are full today of the story of the resignation of Mark Harper, the Immigration Minister. His cleaner was not entitled to work in the country! This is ironic because we had many meetings with him where we questioned how easy it was for landlords, employers and others to figure out whether their immigrant labour were entitled to be in the country. Mark told us it was quite easy to discover this. He's acted honourably and resigned, and hopefully he'll be back in the next reshuffle.

MONDAY 10 FEBRUARY

Both my private secretaries asked me this morning whether I employed any domestic staff, and if so whether they were foreign and whether I'd checked their immigration status! The words 'closing', 'door', 'stable', 'after' and 'bolted' spring to mind!

Went across to the Department of Health for a meeting with Norman Lamb MP, the Minister of State, and a couple of the senior finance people. A third of the acute hospitals look like they're in deficit in 2013/14.

The department is worried that the NHS might be heading back into the type of economic crisis seen in 2004/05, which finally prompted Tony Blair to make his big commitment to NHS funding. The problem is that the government was so busy dealing with Andrew Lansley's massive reorganisation of the NHS in the first year or so of the parliament that we didn't take any of the tough decisions to cut excessive hospital numbers in areas such as London, and nor did we tackle things like pay inflation. Apparently the NHS pay budget is going up by 2 per cent a year, even with a total pay freeze! That's because there are automatic increments for so many NHS staff. This is complete insanity in an era of austerity.

The problem is that grasping these types of issues in the last year of the parliament is not going to be easy, and there is going to be a huge political pressure on the NHS not to 'implode' before the general election, while the Treasury won't want to fork out a whole load more money. We need to make a judgement in the next few months as to whether the NHS needs extra funding.

TUESDAY 11 FEBRUARY

9.30 a.m. Nick Clegg's office for a discussion on the Budget. Tediously, Danny started off by saying how hard-pressed the Treasury is and then rather dismissively said that it would be impossible to fund my modest £200 million early years pupil premium. This irritated me even more. The truth is that the Treasury can always find money if it wants to. But for Budgets, the Treasury has all the cards. They know where the underspends are, and what tax loopholes can be closed.

Went off to dinner with Tristram Hunt in the Adjournment Restaurant in Portcullis House. When Tristram arrived, he said we should go somewhere 'a bit quieter', but we looked round and only one other table was taken. Now that the Commons only sits till 7 p.m. from Tuesday onwards, most MPs disappear early. Tristram is an interesting chap. Well-groomed, bright, nice, public school Blairite moderniser. It would be quite easy to mistake him for a Tory. He started off by admitting he likes Michael Gove. Also said that Ed Miliband isn't terribly interested in education. I suspect Ed is probably acting as a restraining force on any modernising instincts that Tristram has.

WEDNESDAY 12 FEBRUARY

Started the day by letting off steam in a note to Nick. Said that I was pissed off with the way Danny dealt with the early years pupil premium, given its importance and my weeks of work. Also said that we had another year to go in government and if we weren't going to deliver good progressive Liberal Democrat policies, then what on earth were we wasting our time in government for.

Added that I was seriously worried about Danny's idea of having a completely balanced budget, as it was obvious that this would require massive cuts in the second half of the next parliament, which would damage public services, lead to a massive tax increase, or drive vast numbers of people into poverty. I said that if we weren't careful we could make a strategic policy blunder in signing up to a balanced budget for the sake of having a simple political narrative which differentiates ourselves from Labour, when this could require us in a Lib Dem–Conservative coalition in the next parliament to make massive cuts that would make our mistake on tuition fees look like a minor faux pas.

Nick spoke later and said he'd had an interesting discussion with Cameron about the Gove situation. Cameron said he was very irritated about my intervention over the Ofsted chairmanship. Cameron said he thought all this was about Lib Dem differentiation. Nick hit back hard and said that this was an issue of substance about the independence of Ofsted. Nick said that for Michael to fall out with both me and Sir Michael Wilshaw was a pretty amazing thing, given that we're natural allies on many areas of reform. Apparently Cameron said, 'Yeah, I have to admit you are right on that.' Nick thinks he will be sensible about the next Ofsted chair.

THURSDAY 13 FEBRUARY

While over at the DfE, signed off a whole load of policy submissions, including probably the least important one that I have seen since becoming a minister. This was a submission of seven or eight pages, with all sorts of maps and detail, but the decision that they were asking for was whether I would give permission to convert ten square metres from playing field land to be used as a new school corridor! It really is unbelievable that decisions of this magnitude require the sign-off of a minister.

FRIDAY 14 FEBRUARY

Heard a very funny story today about a female minister and her department's civil servants.

The minister was going out with a young man who decided to break up with her. For some reason the young man wrote a very long and painful break-up letter, but instead of sending it to her home, he posted it to her – marked 'private' – at her department.

Sure enough, the letter arrived, was opened and date-stamped by minister's office, and was then passed to the ministerial correspondence unit for them to draft a reply! The correspondence team saw the contents of this letter and decided that there were 'no policy issues of relevance to the department', so, two weeks later, they diplomatically passed the letter back to the private office. When the letter returned to them, unanswered, the private office then went into a complete panic, and apparently they ended up having a mini-conference to discuss the various options. Eventually, they decided that the best thing to do was simply to pass the letter to the minister.

Not being willing to risk her wrath by doing so directly, they tucked the letter into a file at the bottom of her weekend red box! It apparently took the minister some time to see the funny side of it all.

Some feedback on the recent reshuffle. Baroness Susan Kramer, the very strong and strident Lib Dem who's gone to the Department for Transport as a Minister of State, is apparently grating up a bit against her Secretary of State. The ever patient Patrick McLoughlin has recently complained to Nick that Susan talks incessantly at the ministerial meetings and speaks over everyone else. According to Patrick, the ministerial meetings are now going on for about twice as long and this is, in his view, 'impairing the efficiency of the department'! Patrick wanted Nick to get Susan to be more concise. Nick has suggested Patrick talk to Susan directly – if he can get a word in!

At 5.15 p.m. I had to take a telephone call from IDS about the child poverty strategy. He said that he was extremely fed up with Osborne and that he is now getting worried that unless we get the child poverty strategy out soon, he is going to get judicially reviewed and we'd have to reveal all the internal discussions about the strategy and targets – which could be extremely embarrassing. I said that I accepted that, but I wasn't willing to publish the strategy with us saying nothing at all about targets. I said that this would mean us having to make a very public Lib Dem statement about where we stood on the child poverty measures and why there wasn't an agreement. Iain said he perfectly well understood that, and he felt as frustrated as I did that we weren't able to get agreement on the three new measures of relative poverty, life chances and entrenched poverty. Iain said that he'd hoped this could have been one of the big achievements of the coalition government. We agreed that Iain would have one last attempt to persuade David Cameron.

SATURDAY 15 FEBRUARY

Today's papers have got a story about the army cadet forces and plans to shift funding from private schools to state schools – so it seems as if Michael is making a little bit of progress with Philip Hammond, but not without kick-back from the private schools, who are whinging about it. For once, MG and I are on the same side!

SUNDAY 16 FEBRUARY

A beautiful, sunny, cloudless day. A respite from the storms and rain. Spent a few hours in the morning going through the red box, and then went for a pleasant walk in the afternoon in the countryside.

MONDAY 17 FEBRUARY

Recess. Nick is supposed to be on a relaxing family skiing holiday, but with the flooding, he's had to cancel it as the optics would not be great! Meanwhile, Cameron continues to do his West Country tour of flooded areas.

In at 6.45 a.m. and at around 8 a.m. went down to No. 10 to pick up a kipper and a coffee. As I left the cafeteria, coming along the corridor towards me was a little white dog bouncing around and yapping. I assumed that it was owned by one of the kitchen staff, but hard on its heels was none other than the Chancellor of the Exchequer. I asked George whether the dog was a Christmas present for his children, and he looked a little baffled and said no, it was just a family dog which they'd got at the end of last year. I asked him whether it bit Liberals, as it appeared to be yapping around me quite a lot, but he said that it was quite friendly and just a 'tame lap dog!' I think it was a joke.

George then moaned that according to him every Lib Dem initiative since the New Year had been an attack on the Tories. He said that in today's media there was a story about Nick hinting at a coalition with Labour after the next election. Of course, it's all wildly hyped up, but he did look quite seriously peeved. I suspect that this is what we're going to see on both sides of the coalition in the last year of the parliament.

Michael Gove apparently spoke to Osborne about our plan for new minimum funding levels for schools and the issue of how much money the Treasury will give us to help deliver this. Apparently George was 'terribly sympathetic' but didn't promise anything and now appears to be holding up the announcement until the Budget. Very, very irritating. No doubt he wants to claim all the credit, rather than allowing it to be a coalition/DfE initiative.

In my red box was a fairly surprising memo from Francis Maude, complaining that in spite of government cuts, departments are still using the same amount of square metres per civil servant. How Francis can put his name to a memo of this type with a straight face I really don't know, since the room he occupies in the Cabinet Office is one of the largest in the whole of Whitehall. You could play tennis in his new office, and he must be using about fifty times more space than the civil service!

THURSDAY 20 FEBRUARY

Michael Gove phoned at 9.30 a.m. and said he wanted to discuss a couple of issues. Firstly, he wanted my advice on how to handle the current negotiations with the trade unions. The NASUWT has now dumped on the NUT, by pulling out of plans for a teachers' strike at the end of March.

I also told Michael that the Lib Dems would be putting in a bid as part of the Budget process for an early years pupil premium, and he acknowledged this and also said that he knew Liz Truss was supportive. He didn't commit himself. He also mentioned the discussions about the Education Services Grant. I wonder whether he's making a bit more of an effort to work with me at the moment.

A letter in my box today from the National Archives, asking me whether I would like to hand over to them the famous note from Liam Byrne – the 'I'm afraid there is no money' letter. Apparently the National Archives consider it an important part of political history!

FRIDAY 21 FEBRUARY

The papers today are full of coverage of the challenge that Nick Clegg laid down yesterday to Nigel Farage, to debate with Nick before the European elections. Personally, I think that this is an error, in that all it does is feed coverage of UKIP and highlight our own rather unpopular message on Europe. It's not going to go down well with what I refer to as 'the man in the pub in Yeovil'.

Still, our Euro MEPs have always wanted a 'fully fledged' pro-European campaign, and now it looks like they're going to get it. I suspect that when they see the results, they won't like them very much.

SATURDAY 22 FEBRUARY

Had a look through my *Times* guide to the 2010 election today to try to decide how many Lib Dem seats I think we'll win at the next election.

Going through the fifty-seven Lib Dem seats one by one, I reckon that we will retain thirty-eight seats. I'm going to take a shot at what I think the result of the next general election will be. With the economy recovering now reasonably robustly, I think the Conservatives will hold on to quite a lot of their vote and finish with around 35 per cent. I think Labour will go up from 29 per cent to 34 per cent. I think we will go down from 23 per cent to around 16 per cent. At the last election, the Conservatives had 306 MPs, Labour had 258, we had 57. I forecast Labour up from 258 MPs to 283, but the Tories would still be ahead on 301. There really is a possibility of another coalition of some kind. It's all only speculation at this stage – but interesting nonetheless.

MONDAY 24 FEBRUARY

Left the house at 6.15 a.m. to get a flight up to Aberdeen. Today we have a regional Cabinet, the first in Scotland since the Gordon Brown government, and apparently only the second since Lloyd George held a Cabinet north of the border back in 1921, partly because he was on holiday in the Highlands and too lazy to come back to London.

We met at the Shell UK HQ in Aberdeen. Total snoozefest. Bloody waste of time.

We were all collected in minibuses for our trip back to the airport – David Cameron and Nick Clegg had their own vehicles, but the rest of us were shoved into minibuses that accommodated eight or nine people. I was in one without any Lib Dems – just Eric Pickles, Lord Hill, Baroness Warsi, Oliver Letwin, Grant Shapps and David Willetts. Oliver spent a lot of the journey telling stories about Margaret Thatcher, and speculated on what would have happened if the Westland crisis hadn't occurred and therefore William Hague hadn't been elected to Parliament – implying Ken Clarke would have become Tory leader in 1997. It all had the makings of a good work of political fiction.

In the evening I had dinner with Michael Gove. He chose The Honeypot in Mayfair – a pretty smart restaurant, but the food was overpriced and not that exciting.

ABOVE Lib Dem allies: Deputy
PM Nick Clegg and David Laws
walk up Downing Street.
© ALAMY

RIGHT Coalition colleagues:
David Laws and Michael Gove
leaving No. 10. © GETTY IMAGES

The Letwin chuckle: Oliver Letwin and George Osborne enjoying their politics. © PRESS ASSOCIATION

Dry as dust: David Laws and Nick Clegg with Tory hardman Philip Hammond. © PRESS ASSOCIATION

Defending the wicket: David Laws in the House of Commons. © PRESS ASSOCIATION

Outspoken: Ken Clarke in action. © PRESS ASSOCIATION

Coalition cracks: *Guardian* cartoonist Martin Rowson on the coalition Ofsted row. © GUARDIAN

David Laws delivering free school meals. © ALAMY

ABOVE Lib Dem leaders: Danny
Alexander, Nick Clegg and David
Laws were the most influential
Lib Dems in government.
© PRESS ASSOCIATION

LEFT Constituency duties:
David Laws lays a wreath on
Remembrance Sunday in Ilminster.
© CHRISTINE JONES
OF YEOVIL PRESS

The Laughing Cabinet: The Queen attends Cabinet for the first time in her reign, and manages to lighten the mood in her coalition team, December 2012. © GETTY IMAGES

English votes? Michael Gove, Alistair Carmichael, Iain Duncan Smith, George Osborne and David Laws debating constitutional reform in the Cabinet room. © PRESS ASSOCIATION

The final appearance: Lib Dem Cabinet ministers pose outside Downing Street before the last Cabinet, March 2015. © GETTY IMAGES

Making the case: Nick Clegg and David Laws setting out their election policies. © GETTY IMAGES

Laws to win? Somerset, May 2015. © GETTY IMAGES

The verdict: Yeovil's returning officer reveals the election result to David Laws and his election agent, Sam Crabb (*centre*). © CHRISTINE JONES OF YEOVIL PRESS

We talked about the political situation, the potential for a Tory reshuffle after the May local elections (Michael is expecting this, but I don't think he believes that it will affect the higher orders of the Cabinet) and education policy work between now and the election.

Michael was rather on his guard. I asked him what job he would want to do once he'd finished being Education Secretary, but he said he wanted to stay where he was through the next election – and that his aspiration would be to fold further education and universities into the Education Department. I asked what he would want to do in ten years' time. I assumed that he might be tempted into saying Foreign Secretary or Home Secretary, but he looked rather guarded and tiptoed his way round the subject and eventually didn't say anything at all. He then responded by asking me the same question, and I said the two areas that I'd already been in were the areas that I was interested in – i.e. the Treasury and the Department for Education.

I also asked Michael whether he would ever want to be Tory leader or PM: 'No, I don't think I'd ever be any good at that, and I don't even look the part.'

I pointed out that no one had ever expected John Major to be PM. It was the first time I have ever thought: 'Maybe, very privately, he can contemplate standing for PM under some circumstances.' No senior politician ever likes being written off for the top job.

Also asked Michael who was going to be writing the Conservative election manifesto. He immediately laughed: 'Oh, it's going to a carefully balanced team – five Etonians and one old boy from St Paul's school! Shocking really!'

I assume the five Etonians are Oliver Letwin, Jo Johnson, Rupert Harrison, David Cameron and Ed Llewellyn. The one 'outsider' from St Paul's would be George Osborne. Hardly a good example of the 'opportunity society'.

It was a pleasant meal, but there was something 'end of season' about it. Michael was saying – which is probably quite sensible – that we should focus on delivering the existing policy agenda rather than inventing new things. While we are on friendly terms, some of our disagreements over the last few months have definitely created a bit of a chill.

When we finished the dinner, his chauffeur-driven car was waiting outside, but I declined his offer of a lift. Called a taxi instead and went into the office and worked for a couple of hours on my red box.

There's a story running that Cameron is going to rule out going into co-alition with the Lib Dems after the next general election if the Conservatives are just short of a majority. Instead, he's going to say that he would run a minority government, as the Tories allegedly think that this will make them more popular since many people don't want a coalition.

Got to bed at around quarter to one.

WEDNESDAY 26 FEBRUARY

A meeting about the badger cull that has been taking place in Somerset and Gloucestershire. This by all accounts has been a bit of a shambles, as for the cull to work it would have to kill 70 per cent of the badgers in each area. It's already clear that we're well below this. Present were Professor Ian Boyd, the Chief Scientific Adviser at DEFRA; the Principal Private Secretary to Owen Paterson; and Nick Joicey, the DEFRA Director General for Strategy.

We started off the briefing with an update on where the pilot culls are. Originally DEFRA had estimated that 66 per cent of the badgers in Somerset are being killed and 40 per cent in Gloucestershire. But they've now changed the estimates massively on the basis of some scientific advisory group. The figures are now something between 37 per cent and 51 per cent in Somerset and between 43 per cent and 55 per cent in Gloucestershire. Under questioning, Professor Boyd said that actually we might have made the disease problem worse by killing such a low proportion of the badgers, so that diseased badgers might move into the area and disease might spread more easily.

Professor Boyd didn't attempt to hide his scepticism. Apparently the Scientific Committee is also going to question the humaneness of the cull.

It looks like we've spent at least £7 million on these two culls, and we've only killed around 1,900 badgers. I reckon that's between £3,500 and £4,000 for every dead badger! The Chief Scientific Adviser, under questioning from me, confirmed that we wouldn't know even if the culls continued for four years whether they were effective in reducing TB, as apparently data collection is such that we wouldn't really know whether the figures had fallen in one area but been offset by a rise somewhere else.

The DEFRA officials and particularly Owen's PPS seemed to be in denial. Professor Boyd looked deeply sceptical about the whole thing, and when I really pressed him to say whether we should be carrying on with the existing culls at all, he said that it was a pretty 50/50 decision.

It's all really like something out of *Yes Minister* or *The Thick of It*, and many of the people round the table rolled their eyes as the DEFRA analysis was described. It's absolutely clear to me that there shouldn't be any new pilot areas, and the only real issue is whether we should allow the existing pilots to continue at all.

At 2 p.m. had to go over to the House of Commons for a meeting in Nick Clegg's office about the Budget. Danny was there and he set out some of the background. Our ask for a £500 increase in the personal tax allowance now looks as if it would cost something like £1.4 billion in the first year but £1.9 billion in the second. Osborne then wants £1 billion worth of tax breaks on savings, and some giveaways to business.

Somewhat bizarrely, the Treasury is considering options such as extending national insurance contributions to redundancy pay over £30,000. In the current environment, a 'tax on redundancy' seems to me strikingly bad politics.

In the evening, had dinner with Alan Milburn in the Cinnamon Club. Always fun, because he's a good old gossip and is still acutely interested in politics and is actually a very nice guy. I was very honest with him about where we are on child poverty and he said he'd be very critical of the government, which I said was perfectly fair. Alan was pretty negative about the prospects of Labour winning the next general election. He basically thinks that Cameron is a better leader than Ed Miliband (in spite of Cameron's lack of any driving vision), and he shared my view that Labour seems to be run by a 'C-Team' compared with the people who were in the Blair era.

He said that Ed Miliband has a problem with economic credibility and as the economy recovers and 'the two Eds' are subject to detailed scrutiny during the general election, he thinks the Tories will pull ahead. Alan said that the public today are equally suspicious of both markets and government, and the political parties needed to position themselves accordingly. I asked him who would be key players in Labour in the event of coalition negotiations. He said he was hard pushed to think of people who were MPs who were close to Ed Miliband and who would be at centre stage in negotiations. He guessed Ed Balls and Douglas Alexander, and he said that he thought Douglas might be the best contact for us. Alan said he would mention this informally to Douglas.

THURSDAY 27 FEBRUARY

To the thirteenth floor of the Adelphi Building in John Adam Street, for what has been put in the diary as the 'policy planning meeting' but is actually the first serious attempt to pin down Nick Clegg and others on what they want in the manifesto.

We were originally supposed to be meeting in the National Liberal Club, and the staff had begrudgingly allocated us a room. However, we'd then got a message saying that halfway through the afternoon they wanted to show some people into the room for a potential future room booking, and at that stage all of us – including the Deputy Prime Minister, Chief Secretary to the Treasury etc. etc. – would have to 'clear the room' so that these people could be shown around for ten minutes. For me, this was the final straw.

7.30 p.m. Dinner with Sir Michael Wilshaw. We met at Roux, directly opposite the Treasury. I was directed upstairs to the bar, where Sir Michael Wilshaw was waiting. He was having a glass of Chardonnay and looked pretty relaxed and cheerful. He said how angry he'd been about the think tanks criticising Ofsted, and how he'd felt pretty sure that this was all traceable back to Michael Gove's office.

I said I thought it was very unlikely that Michael or the Prime Minister would want somebody as Ofsted chair who would be unacceptable to him, and they certainly wouldn't want him resigning just before the general election.

Then we went downstairs and had a very pleasant dinner. Sir Michael said that he thought that free schools are a 'fringe issue' in English education, and he said that he'd told Michael Gove this was his view. He also said that Ofsted was going to be inspecting another lot of free schools in the near future and that he was worried that many of them were going to do badly. He said that they were presently carrying out a review of an inspection of the Greenwich Free School, which is very high-profile. At the moment, it's apparently going to be graded as 'requires improvement', which is going to be a shock to MG and his people, because it was regarded as one of the flagship free schools. Sir Michael also said he thought we ought to be doing a lot more to bolster the middle tier, and to make sure we properly inspected all local authorities and academy chains.

At 10 p.m. I had to go back to the Cabinet Office, as my red boxes were waiting. There is another paper on the bizarre idea of hiring private eyes to assess the new governance and leadership of some free schools. Apparently they want us to pay a company which is based somewhere in Bath and run by an ex-police officer. I do worry about paying public funds to private investigators to spy on sponsors of free schools – certainly it would look pretty awful in the media.

SATURDAY 1 MARCH

Bright sunshine. A beautiful day. Cold, but feels like the start of spring.

The papers are still full of a lot of analysis of Angela Merkel's visit to the UK last Thursday. She disappointed those in the Conservative Party who hoped that the Germans would be a strong force for Cameron-type EU reform after the general election. The immigration figures out on Thursday have also destroyed the Tory narrative about reducing net immigration – as although immigration from outside the EU is falling, immigration from within the EU is rising. This is entirely predictable given how well our economy is doing, but it means there's no way the Tories are ever going to achieve their immigration targets by the next election. This is precisely the point that we made in the election debates in 2010 – i.e. that you cannot guarantee a particular level of net migration while being a member of the European Union. The fact that the Tories have played this issue up so much can only help UKIP, unless the Tory Party wants to become an 'Out of Europe' party.

MONDAY 3 MARCH

Nick mentioned a brief bilateral meeting last week with Angela Merkel. He said Merkel had suggested that she was willing to help David Cameron and the UK a little bit to renegotiate our relationship with the EU, but she said that this would be only 'on the margins'. When Nick said that he didn't think marginal renegotiation would very much help Cameron and the Conservative Party, apparently Merkel just shrugged and said, 'What do they expect me to do about that?' She clearly thinks that Cameron has made an idiotic and dangerous pledge on his referendum.

TUESDAY 4 MARCH

In at 6.45 a.m. and then at 8.15 a.m. walked over to the National Liberal Club for the regular breakfast meeting with Jonny Oates, Ryan Coetzee, Nick and Danny. Danny was very grumpy: 'I'm fed up with the Tories at the moment. Have you seen this story that they've leaked today about Cameron making a speech saying that the Tories are pushing for a higher personal income tax allowance? It's outrageous. They've fought every single increase in the personal allowance during this parliament, and pushed for tax cuts for rich people, and now they want to claim the credit for this.'

Ryan was also worried, and said that Nick is going to do a Q&A after his speech this morning where he will accuse Cameron of trying to claim the credit for a Liberal Democrat policy. Ryan said the problem is that many members of the public don't get the fact that it is the Liberal Democrats that have delivered this tax cut. I said that we had to be very careful not to make this all look like a fight in the playground.

Cabinet. 9 a.m. Maria Miller plodded through a presentation about mobile phone coverage – something that a lot of members of the Cabinet obsess about. Alistair Carmichael said that the only place in Scotland he could get decent mobile coverage was in 'the constituency of the Chief Secretary to the Treasury'. Cameron joked that everything was easier to access and cheaper in the Chief Secretary's constituency, and that was the place to go if you wanted cheap petrol, cheap access to ski lifts etc. So the fact that Danny tends to use every Budget and fiscal event to bung money towards his constituency now seems to have become a bit of a joke.

We then went on to discuss 'fourth session legislation', which was designed simply to be a recap on the agreement that we'd reached at the Quad. However, Cameron took us all by surprise: 'We've got a very good list here. However, I've been looking at this again, and I really do think that we should have a Bill on the recall of MPs. This was a coalition agreement and something that both parties committed to in our manifestos, so I really think it should be in the fourth session.'

This hadn't been discussed with us beforehand, and of course the last time we raised it with the Tories they said it was an absolutely shocking and terrible idea which they could never get through their back benches. Cameron has obviously decided that he doesn't want to be blamed for not taking this forward, and so the Tories have done a bit of a panic U-turn.

It's pretty bad and discourteous not to have told us about this beforehand, but the Tories are guessing quite rightly we are not going to object.

We then had a discussion around the room which was fairly predictable. George Osborne spoke before me and said, 'I'm pleased with the fourth session legislation as we've got some good Bills on the economy and childcare and pensions. However, it's a little bit of a pity that we couldn't have a Bill on a referendum on the European Union!' He said it as a bit of a joke, and the next person to speak was me. I said that I thought that the last thing we needed in the last parliamentary term of the coalition government was something controversial like a Euro Referendum Bill!

I then went off to Nick Clegg's office for a discussion on the Budget. The Quad is meeting tomorrow and we are now getting to the situation where we need to make some final decisions. The centrepiece of the Budget from the Tory side is a 'saver's package', including abolishing the 10 per cent savings tax rate and reducing it to 0 per cent. This is the Chancellor's prime ask for the Budget. We want to increase the personal income tax allowance by £500, and we want an early years pupil premium.

Meanwhile, and astonishingly, the Tories seemed to have briefed out this morning's Cabinet meeting within about five minutes of it having finished. They've briefed that the Prime Minister has now decided to go ahead with recall, and they also claimed that the Chancellor made a 'dramatic move' in suggesting a Euro Referendum Bill in the fourth session legislative programme, which the Lib Dems – specifically Nick Clegg and me – were briefed as having resisted. We gave strong lines to our media people on this, saying how the Tories had persistently blocked the recall measure and had suddenly done a last-minute U-turn, while pointing out that the Tories had never seriously suggested that a Euro Referendum Bill should be in the fourth session in any of our negotiations. Bloody stupid political games from Osborne and Cameron. Nick is furious that a Cabinet discussion has been abused in this way.

WEDNESDAY 5 MARCH

Spent most of today trying to negotiate with Danny/the DfE on making sure we get a decent settlement for schools for 2015/16, so that we can implement the minimum funding level to uplift some of the lower-funded areas, while also protecting the wider schools system from the Treasury plan to increase schools' pension contributions by 2.3 per cent that year. Both Michael Gove and I are very nervous about this, and we've decided that we're going to ask the Treasury to give us £125 million back from the £405 million of extra school employer pension contributions, and then also use £100 million worth of contingency within our own budget – increasing the amount of money that goes in from £180 million to £405 million.

Went over to the Commons for a meeting with Ken Clarke on the issue of court costs recovery. The meeting was only scheduled for fifteen minutes but, as ever with Ken, we were still there forty-five minutes later. Ken just can't resist telling all sorts of political anecdotes, but is great fun. All of this includes a large amount of scorn directed at his colleagues in the Conservative Party. He started off by saying how the whole idea of court costs recovery was 'completely dotty' and 'even Theresa' thought the idea was mad. He said, 'Chris [Grayling] just doesn't know what he's doing here. He wants a populist line in the newspapers by saying that he's going to charge criminals more, but not only will he never collect the money but he will make rehabilitation worse because people will come out of prison with this huge debt. It's completely ridiculous and just shows that Chris doesn't understand at all how the mind of the petty criminal works.'

Ken then said that he despaired about how 'my colleagues in the Conservative Party often come up with these ludicrous, mad, right-wing policies designed to buy off voters'. He referred to Theresa May's policy that anyone who killed a police officer should be imprisoned for life, and that this should only relate to police officers, not other people required to protect the public: 'Of course, Theresa only came with this daft policy because she had to make a speech at the annual police conference and she was very worried about being jeered. So she invented this ludicrous policy and announced it at the conference, and of course nobody even noticed and she didn't get any applause and it didn't even win her any good headlines in *The Sun*. The problem with Theresa is that she hasn't worked out that the way to avoid being booed at the police officers' conference is to make sure you speak in the morning! In the morning, they're all much quieter and they haven't had any booze at lunchtime, so you get a much easier ride. I could have told her that, if she had only asked me. It would have avoided making up idiotic new laws and stuffing the prisons even fuller.'

He then explained how the situation would be much better if he'd been allowed to continue with his policy as Justice Secretary of shrinking the number of people in prisons and closing down unnecessary magistrates' courts across the country – most of which are in Conservative constituencies and 'which for some reason my colleagues don't like to see closed'. He said that when he'd been the Justice Secretary he'd come up with an idea for closing some courts, which had caused a terrible counter-reaction from 'that bloke in shorts in Downing Street' – this turned out to refer to Steve Hilton, the long-departed modernising adviser to David Cameron. He said that Steve Hilton had tried to block the court closure policy on the basis that it 'ran counter to the Tory vision of localism'. Ken said, 'The whole thing is completely ludicrous – people's ideas of localism isn't that they have a local prison and a local magistrates' court.'

Got back to Dover House at around 4 p.m., but the Budget Quad was still going on. Danny and Nick didn't emerge until 4.30 p.m., after a two-hour discussion. To my frustration, they said that George Osborne had opposed the early years pupil premium on the basis that they should just cancel the planned £100 million cut in three- and four-year-old funding. Also heard how Danny is proposing various Budget bungs, including a whisky duty cut for Scotland and (fortunately) a cut in cider duty for Somerset and other places! It sounds as if Danny's also going to deliver Ed Davey's long-cherished vision of moving the threshold for cheap inner-London rail travel out to Surbiton station, in order to advantage commuter travellers from Ed Davey's Kingston and Surbiton constituency. Clearly we are working towards a general election at the current time. But I'd rather that we spent money improving early years education than cutting alcohol duty.

THURSDAY 6 MARCH

Got in at 6.45 a.m., determined to make sure that we keep an early years pupil premium in the Budget. Sent a strong email to Nick and Danny putting a new proposal. Basically this means that we would cancel the plan to cut three- and four-year-old funding, and deliver an early years pupil premium on top of the existing funding, and this would be just £50 million extra – £300 per pupil. On a full-time equivalent basis this is almost exactly the same as the schools pupil premium was when it was introduced in 2011. All areas would be gainers. At 7.45 a.m. Danny texted me back to say that he'd seen my email and both he and Nick like it and will push for it. Thank God! Last night we'd lost the prospect of introducing an early years pupil premium but some good work from officials overnight, combined with my determination not to let this go, has ensured that we are now back in the game.

At a later meeting with Nick, we had a brief discussion about George Osborne's proposal to rename national insurance contributions 'the earnings tax'. Both Chris Saunders and I are deeply suspicious that the reason they want to do this is to make national insurance contributions more unpopular – at the moment, the public associates national insurance with something that goes to pay for health, pensions etc. By renaming national insurance an 'earnings tax', Osborne is hoping to toxify it, which must mean he's thinking about an agenda of cutting national insurance in the general election and afterwards.

Apparently we've now signed off on most of the things in the Budget, including the reductions in savings tax that Osborne wants and our big ask of another £500 increase in the personal income tax allowance. It's amazing that with the tax allowance we've been able to drive the entire tax policy of the government for the entire parliament. We still apparently have things in the scorecard such as charging national insurance contributions on redundancy pay – which I'm very worried about but which apparently raises £0.8 billion over the scorecard period. The package for savers is going to cost around £3.4 billion over the scorecard period, including £1.4 billion to abolish the 10 per cent tax rate, £1.4 billion for more generous ISAs and £0.6 billion for pensioner bonds. We're going to extend the annual investment allowance, costing £1.2 billion, and for some reason reduce air passenger duty to India and the Caribbean.

Had a chat with Jonny Oates, who told me that Tim Farron has been chosen to play Farage in the preparation sessions for Nick Clegg's debate next month. This debate will be quite important not only in terms of the public perception of UKIP versus the Lib Dems, but also in terms of Nick's standing in the party. The worst possible situation would be where he was trounced by Farage in the debates and we then went on to do extremely badly in the European elections.

FRIDAY 7 MARCH

Caught the train and arrived in the beautiful city of York in bright sunshine.

Spent two and a half hours in the afternoon in a manifesto consultation session, and then went back to my hotel room early in the evening and fell asleep for a few hours. I was supposed to be going out in the evening to some political reception, but decided not to bother and watched TV instead. It's such a pleasure to be able to relax at a weekend rather than being 'on display'. I'm staying in a bed and breakfast about a mile out of the town, as I hate wasting money on expensive and often poor-quality conference hotels. The owner of the bed and breakfast seemed a bit surprised to find me checking in. He obviously recognised me, and was trying to persuade me to upgrade to one of his more expensive rooms. The room I'm in is literally two metres by three metres. It's so small that he couldn't even show me around it, because the two of us couldn't get in it at the same time.

SATURDAY 8 MARCH

Journalists are rushing round the place asking senior ministers whether they're employing foreign nannies or domestic staff, following a speech by the new Tory Immigration Minister, James Brokenshire, last week where he slagged off the 'metropolitan elite' for using immigrant labour. Since then, it's turned out that David Cameron and his wife have employed a foreigner in their household, and it now turns out that Danny Alexander has a Portuguese cleaner or something. The whole thing is a bit bizarre and ridiculous, and shows how easily the immigration debate is getting out of control, and how the Tories are also shooting themselves in the foot. Since the only real way of cutting EU immigration is to leave the European Union, you would have thought that the Tories would shut up, as it's only stoking support for UKIP.

Went out to a supposedly decent restaurant in the centre of York for dinner, where they refused to serve us any bread rolls until we'd ordered our main courses! I told them that it was like something out of the Soviet Union.

SUNDAY 9 MARCH

The first real day of spring. London in particular was very warm when I got back later in the day – everybody was walking round in T-shirts and sitting outside the cafés having drinks. Nick Clegg's speech to the Lib Dem conference went down fairly well, but it didn't have any new policy stuff. It was just a fully-fledged defence of liberalism and internationalism. Nick is certainly being courageous by fighting the European elections on an anti-UKIP, pro-Europe agenda. The man in the pub in Yeovil won't like it one bit.

I sat behind Tim Farron and Vince during Nick's speech, and it was interesting to see the reaction of each. Vince clapped only when he had to, and with the least enthusiasm possible. It was also informative to see Tim Farron's reaction when Nick praised our legislation on gay marriage. Tim was obviously quite embarrassed, as he knows this is popular in the party but his Christian views mean that he's actually against it. He made the most token attempt at applause, which nobody could possibly have mistaken for enthusiasm. I wonder whether this is going to be a bit of an issue for him when it comes to a future leadership election.

MONDAY 10 MARCH

Went over to the government business meeting at 11.30 a.m. and there wasn't an awful lot on the agenda. 'Badgers' was there, but we didn't discuss it in any great detail and Nick just rolled his eyes a bit.

Back to Nick's office later for the Quad preparation. Danny said that both Gove and Osborne are still resisting the idea of an early years pupil premium. At this stage I got rather irritated, and tried not to lose my temper. I pointed out to both Nick and Danny that all we're asking for is £50 million, on a Budget scorecard which is going to have £5 billion of revenue and £5 billion of cost. Given that on this Budget scorecard are items such as throwing away £250 million on lower air passenger duty because of some daft pledge the Prime Minister made at a Commonwealth summit, and cutting alcohol duties – and given that these two measures alone are costing £500–600 million – I can't believe that we can't find £50 million to put into such an important policy to boost social mobility.

There was then a very boring discussion about energy pricing and mitigation from higher energy costs, which frankly is not my area of expertise. I just sat there inwardly fuming at the fact that we still can't get this early years pupil premium agreed.

Later in the day we had the Lib Dem Cabinet ministers' meeting, and after this Nick asked me to stay behind to update me on the Quad. I instantly knew it wasn't good news, and he looked at me in that rather sheepish way that he does when he knows that there's a policy issue that I feel particularly strongly about and that he's about to disappoint me on.

As I suspected, he said, 'Well it's good news and some bad news on the early years pupil premium. We've agreed to reverse the planned £100 million cut to three- and four-year-old funding. However, apparently Gove has said that he really doesn't want us to press ahead with the early years pupil premium right now – that he thinks it needs a lot more policy work.'

Of course this is a complete load of balls, and all the Tories want to do is sabotage our idea of extending the pupil premium so that we don't have any good news to announce about something positive that the Lib Dems have delivered.

Nick said that he'd got agreement from the Quad to proceed with the early years pupil premium, but the proposal was now that we should delay it a few months. I said that would be pretty hopeless as the Tories would pick away and try to undermine it, and in addition we would run out of time to implement it in this parliament – since we would need to go out and consult on it very soon and then make the announcements and allocations to local authorities.

In the evening, got a good note from Matt Sanders on the implementation issues if we delayed. Matt and I sent this on to Nick and hopefully it will cause him to put more pressure on Cameron. I intend to send him another one of my stroppy emails tomorrow morning.

Also notified by officials this evening that, unbelievably, the *Daily Mail* is tomorrow leading its entire front-page coverage with a massive splash claiming that the whole free school meals policy is going to be a disaster because of implementation problems. We're absolutely sure that this is being briefed out by the Tories, who are getting their friends in the right-wing media to do a hatchet job on us. We won't be able to kill this until the policy is implemented successfully in September. We're going to have to work hard to build an alliance of people who are going to be positive about the free school meals policy.

TUESDAY 11 MARCH

Woke up at the usual 5.24 a.m., feeling slightly grumpy because I know that this morning I will have to deal with the early years pupil premium and get that back on course, as well as seeing off the attacks on the free school meals policy.

Got in at 6.45 a.m. and sent a note off to Nick on the early years premium, urging him to push the policy.

At 8.15 a.m. went off to a breakfast meeting with Danny and Nick and Tim Gordon, the chief executive of the party, along with Jonny Oates and Ryan Coetzee at the National Liberal Club in the ghastly Lawrence Robson Room in the basement. The usual horrid coffee. We spent much of the discussion talking about increasing the donor base of the party. These days, being in government, we're dealing with an awful lot of rich people who want one thing or another from the party. One potential donor even asked if we could get him a ministerial role in the government of the United Arab Emirates! When Nick looked somewhat surprised at this suggestion, he said, 'Well, you British did found the country, after all.' Nick said he was rather gobsmacked, and changed the subject. We agreed that there are some potential donors we need to keep our distance from! It all makes the case for reform of party funding – if only the Tories would play ball.

After the meeting, we walked over to Cabinet and up Downing Street together. I mentioned to Jonny Oates the article in the *Daily Telegraph* today, written by Ben Brogan, which is rather down on Michael Gove and suggests that perhaps he should be moved department and that he's run out of steam at Education. The media have definitely got a bit of a downer on Michael at the moment. I wonder whether somebody in Downing Street is gently pressing the idea of Michael being moved.

Cabinet started with a discussion about the Ukraine and then a presentation from Ken Clarke on EU–US trade negotiations.

Up at the other end of the Cabinet table and sitting back away from the table and against the wall was Jo Johnson – and I remembered the story that Julian Astle told me about him. Apparently Julian and his wife went out with Jo Johnson and his wife and Ed Llewellyn and Ed's wife and it was really quite interesting. Jo's wife is apparently a Labour supporter who is on *The Guardian* and who's a real old leftie and quite forceful. Apparently they spent half the night arguing, and she stamps on Jo quite often – which maybe explains why he's so quiet most of the time.

After Cabinet, we were contacted by *The World at One*, who plan to run a piece on the free school meals policy today. It then turned out that they've actually got on-the-record attributable comments from Dom Cummings (who has now finally left government), who's apparently slagging off the whole policy and saying the whole thing is a shambles caused by Nick Clegg. It really is the worst kind of lies, and although Matt Sanders was a bit uneasy about me going on to do media, I felt I probably had to. Nick has been getting nervous about us not hitting back on this policy, and he clearly wants me to do so as hard as possible.

Went over to 4 Millbank with Matt Sanders at ten past one, and sat in the studio to listen to an awful lot of tosh being reported from Dom Cummings – who is going on the record but had only emailed his comments over, rather than giving an interview. I couldn't help spluttering with amazement as I sat listening to Dom's comments. He really was laying into the whole policy in the most extraordinary way, and also frankly making stuff up by saying that the department was opposed to the policy, it wasn't costed etc. etc. etc. All rather poisonous. I went in rather hard against Cummings and called his comments 'complete and utter balls of the first order'. The BBC reported it as me knocking down his comments quite hard – and it seemed to set the story back quite a bit given that I came out quite robustly.

Went back to my office and did a conference call about the fair funding formula for schools, which has now been signed off by the Treasury and which it looks as if we're going to announce this Thursday.

While I was in the parliamentary party meeting, I confirmed with Danny Alexander that clearance has now been given to go ahead with the early years pupil premium on Monday or Tuesday next week. This will be announced by both Nick Clegg and David Cameron. Frankly I would prefer that we owned this, but at least the policy will happen, which is the crucial thing.

Sent a text to Michael Gove, who was unwell today:

Dear Michael, I do not want to disturb you while you are unwell, but Dom's contributions today are really unacceptable and they raise a serious risk that both parties will start to brief out all sorts of private stuff against each other. This would be hugely in Labour's interest, but not in ours. It would damage both parties and our education agenda. Can I ask you to intervene privately to stop him please?

Michael replied pretty rapidly, 'I totally agree – I've emailed him and hope to speak to him later.'

THURSDAY 13 MARCH

In at 6.30 a.m. to prepare for the oral statement today on the new fairer funding formula for schools. The department had provided me with a fairly limp draft statement which I made a lot of changes to. Approved the final documents and then had a phone call with Tristram Hunt to brief him on the proposals. Tristram never asks too many questions and he seems pretty light-touch in his attitude to policy matters. I told him that he would be delighted that Stoke-on-Trent was one of the gaining areas of the country, since this is where his constituency is! Interestingly, he replied by saying that 'money really isn't the issue in Stoke-on-Trent – it's the competence of the people in the schools'! Spoken like a true Blairite.

The oral statement went pretty well. There were lots of coalition MPs popping up and praising it. After a while, Kevin Brennan, the Labour shadow Minister for Schools, got very shirty and shouted out a couple of things which caused him to be hauled up by the Deputy Speaker and forced to apologise. He really had lost his temper and it didn't do him any favours. We have finally addressed the significant underfunding of areas such as Cambridgeshire, with the schools there getting an uplift of 7 per cent. I'm proud of what we've done on education funding during this parliament – investing heavily in more money for deprived pupils through the pupil premium, but also dealing with the long-running issue of the underfunding of certain areas such as the rural counties.

After the statement, I had to go straight off to the Ministry of Sound near Elephant and Castle. This was for the first practice session for Nick Clegg for the debates against Nigel Farage. We had a few sandwiches and then went through to the area where a mock debate took place, with Nick Clegg debating against a Nigel Farage in the shape of Tim Farron. We pitched various questions to both Nick and Tim, and Tim made a passable effort of being Farage, though Farage will be much trickier to deal with in the actual debates. It was all a bit flat and seemed to me to be a score draw.

SUNDAY 16 MARCH

The first really beautiful day of spring – indeed, it could almost be the first beautiful day of summer. The temperature touched 20° and in the morning it was not only sunny but warm at 9 a.m. when we went for a run. The sky clear blue, most of the floodwaters around the river had retreated and the river was more or less running back within its own banks. On the surface of the river are elegant swans and quite a few quacking ducks, while under the surface the trout lurk in the shadows or dart rapidly upstream: 'hangs, a fat gun-barrel, deep under arched bridges or slips like butter down the throat of the river'.

WEDNESDAY 19 MARCH

Budget Day. To everyone's surprise, the major package for savers has yet to leak. Osborne will be pleased, because the Lib Dem contribution to the Budget, the personal income tax allowance, is now out and he has an opportunity to lead on the Tory policies.

At Cabinet, George gave a relatively upbeat assessment, including the improved growth prospects. He talked about the increase in the personal income tax allowance, the enhanced capital allowances for businesses, the cuts in beer duty and bingo duty (God help us!), and the big package for savers, including abolition of compulsory annuities, a cut in the lower rate of tax for savers, and new pensioner bonds. It's the sort of Budget that will probably go down quite well, though it's rather difficult to see an economic strategy in the detail.

I suppose one ought to forgive the Chancellor his small political fireworks, which are designed to get the public on our side without changing fiscal policy. However, the big question is going to be what happens beyond the election, and whether the fiscal plans for the next parliament are credible. Osborne's plan is reliant upon huge public spending cuts in the next parliament, and it's difficult to see how those can take place without undermining public services. With the Lib Dems in government, we wouldn't want cuts on this scale.

I welcomed yesterday's early years package and said there were some good measures today for 'workers, savers and people who drink a lot'.

After Cabinet, I went up to Ken Clarke's office to have a chat about some of the measures that Chris Grayling wants to see in the latest Justice Bill. It was a vintage Ken performance, in which he said that David Cameron's decision to make Chris Justice Secretary was 'one of the dafter decisions' that David had made. Ken said that he didn't normally do meetings at this time in the morning, as these days the only reason he got up early was bird-watching.

He also said of Chris Grayling: 'He keeps on inventing these extreme and dotty ideas to increase sentences in a way that will simply fill up the prisons in a desperate search for votes. Of course it's all rubbish, and this sort of thing has just been stoked up by Rebekah and *The Sun* and all these daft campaigns for longer sentences. The whole thing's absolutely crazy.'

THURSDAY 20 MARCH

Just after midnight, I saw the first front pages, virtually all of which lead on the Budget. George will be absolutely delighted, as the headlines are universally congratulatory – including the *Daily Mail*, the *Express*, *The Sun*, the *Telegraph* and *The Times*.

Did a morning media round from 6.15 a.m. onwards and there seemed to be a small negative story running about Grant Shapps, the Tory Party chairman, who put out some kind of tweet yesterday with a mock Tory poster, which talked about the cut in bingo duty and beer duty and then said that this was good news for people who were working class. Danny slammed it on *Newsnight*, saying that it was patronising to assume that working-class people spent all their time playing bingo and drinking beer! The media and the Labour Party have seized on this in the absence of having anything else to criticise the Budget for, and the whole narrative of the Tories being an elitist party is running once again quite strongly.

At midday, went over to the DfE for a meeting with Sir Michael Wilshaw and Michael Gove. Michael Wilshaw is due to make a speech at the ASCL head teacher conference tomorrow, and he wants to talk about the reform of Ofsted inspections. The truth is that neither MG nor I particularly agree with all he's going to propose, but MG is terribly nervous about falling out with him again. MG tried to send out some coded comments, implying that he shouldn't make the announcements, but either Sir Michael didn't pick this up or he decided to ignore it.

A lot of good media coverage about the Budget. Worryingly, most of this focuses on how brilliantly Osborne did. The problem with Budgets and other fiscal events is that Osborne is able to get the full credit for them because he's the Chancellor. Part of our problem is that we don't do the announcing part.

SUNDAY 23 MARCH

A note came through for the Prime Minister and Nick from Sir Jeremy Heywood on the issue of 'badgers', which has taken up an unbelievable amount of time. The Cabinet Secretary has attached three notes from DEFRA, asking for permission to continue the current pilots and to have a new pilot in the Dorset area during 2014. The whole thing's crazy.

MONDAY 24 MARCH

Walked with Danny to his office in the Treasury. Went into the inner Treasury courtyard, and this was the first time that I'd been through this entrance since my resignation in May 2010. It took me back to that late afternoon four years before. As Danny was chatting about the issues we currently face, I was thinking only of that day. We passed the room where I faced the TV camera, alone. Echoes of the past around every corner.

Reached Danny's office, and we were the first two there for the meeting of the 'Matthew Group', which is going to plan for any coalition negotiations which could take place in 2015. I got a coffee from Maria, Danny's lovely diary secretary, who's been managing the office for years. Maria was my diary secretary for that short period of time that I served as Chief Secretary, and there's something warm and reassuring about her, which makes you think that you'd always be welcome back if you ever returned to your old job again. The truth is that this is the job I really want to go back to before I complete my time in politics. 'Unfinished business', and the job my whole life was a preparation for.

Anyway, we had a useful first meeting of the group, but a lot more to do.

Cameron has phoned Nick three times this week on badgers! Paterson and Cameron want the cull to go ahead not only in the existing pilot areas but in additional areas such as Dorset. Nick's own instincts appear to be to prevent the culls from going ahead in other counties, but to allow the existing culls to continue. The truth is the existing culls have been a complete failure, and we've been trying for a week now to get a copy of the independent report on the culls from DEFRA, but they've been resisting this.

Instead, they've given information on all of this to the Cabinet Secretary, who's been writing papers to the Prime Minister and Deputy Prime Minister, basically making the case for the culls to go ahead but probably only in the existing zones. My guess is that the Tories realise that we're not going to authorise culls in new areas, but they certainly don't want to row back on the existing pilots – this is part of their pitch to the farmers. I've said that we shouldn't be rushed into a decision on this when we haven't seen the independent report yet.

At 12 p.m. we had the weekly political meeting, which focused on the preparations for the first debate with Nigel Farage on Wednesday. We discussed how to deal with Farage, and Nick said that he thought that Farage would not be 'the man in the pub', but would try to be measured and calm and focused on facts. I'm not sure whether Farage will be that measured, but certainly he'll be trying to portray Nick as part of the Westminster elite.

To the DfE for 1 p.m. for the Monday ministerial team meeting chaired by Michael. A slight chill in the air, perhaps as a consequence of the interview Nick has given to *The Times*, in which he has talked about all of Michael Gove's 'mad' policies.

Cameron has unbelievably come out today and said that the Tories are in favour of raising the inheritance tax threshold to £1 million – the policy that they fought the last general election on. This is surprising, because the Tories still seem to want to be the party of tax cuts for the rich, and it's particularly surprising in that during the negotiations in May 2010 they dropped the inheritance tax policy without even making any effort to argue it with us. Indeed, they dropped the policy with a sense of relief, with both George Osborne and Oliver Letwin saying, 'Thank goodness we no longer have to persist with this ridiculous policy.' Perhaps we should make that known.

Finally managed to get a copy of the independent report into the badger culls. The culls have turned out to be a complete fiasco. We are supposed to be killing 70 per cent of the badgers, but it looks like we've killed more like 35 to 40 per cent. It's unbelievable that Nick and Cameron have now discussed this issue about four times in the past forty-eight hours. The whole issue is a combination of the tragic and the humorous.

TUESDAY 25 MARCH

In at 6.45 a.m. At 7 a.m. had to do an interview for BBC Radio Somerset about universal infant free school meals. Some whinging head teacher, moaning about how difficult it's going to be to implement this policy in September 2014. Why doesn't she just get on with it, it's hardly rocket science.

Then went off to our weekly breakfast meeting at the National Liberal Club. Nick said that he wanted to spend the meeting talking about the challenge of how we try to get some credit for the economic recovery. The polls show that the Tories have got all the credit for the Budget. I suggested that the problem might be that the Tories fronted up things like the Budget, and perhaps we might want to make sure that some of the key announcements we negotiate for the Budget and Autumn Statement are announced in our own time, for example at party conferences. I said there was also an issue about whether we wanted a big Budget statement with major new announcements at the end of the parliament, which might simply serve to be a launch pad for the Tory general election effort. All of us leaned towards the idea that we might want to make our key announcements at our autumn 2014 conference. This would mean having a minimalist Budget in 2015, rather than allowing the Tories an election launch pad.

Danny came out with some hare-brained idea that there should be two Budget statements in March 2015 – one by George Osborne and one by him. How on the earth would that work? We're all rather sceptical about whether the Chancellor will actually give Danny anything worthwhile to announce.

Then went back to the DfE and at 9.30 a.m. went for a meeting which was billed as being a stock-take with two senior officials, including the new lady who runs some of the areas such as pupil premium and free school meals. I wasn't too sure what we were supposed to be discussing but the lead official, looking nervous, suddenly went into a discussion in which she asked me about the free school meal legislation and whether we still wanted to insist on schools delivering free meals by September 2014. I said that of course I wanted to go ahead with this – that was always the plan. The official then said that perhaps I might want to think again, as if the policy turned out to be challenging to deliver we might want to give schools a bit longer to deliver it – perhaps until January 2015. I was rather shocked and said that I couldn't understand where this idea was coming from. I said that not only would it be extremely embarrassing if we now said that we couldn't deliver it until January 2015, but more importantly I didn't see why we needed a delay. All we would do is send out a message of uncertainty to schools and cause them to go more slowly in delivering the policy that I had been told most schools were perfectly capable of delivering in September 2014.

The two officials looked rather nervous and jumpy. I got the feeling that they'd been set up to have this conversation. They said that they would have to report my decision back to the Secretary of State. I can see where all of this is heading. It's heading to the civil service covering their own arses by telling me that one option is to delay the implementation until January 2015, so if it all goes wrong they can say that they offered me this option and I turned it down. If I choose to delay then all the embarrassment will be with me and Nick Clegg. On the other hand, if I decide to press ahead in September 2014 and anything goes wrong then Michael will be able to land the blame firmly on me and Nick. The officials at least had the grace to look uncomfortable about the proposition they were putting to me, as up until now everyone had seemed to be confident that we could deliver in September 2014. I was very firm with the officials and said no, we had to go ahead with September 2014.

I'm going to have to take the full burden and risk of this.

In the afternoon, went off to the Ministry of Sound near Elephant and Castle for the third preparation debate for the clash between Nick and Farage.

The whole thing was quite professionally arranged, with cameras etc. and with James McGrory chairing as the Nick Ferrari character. Tim Farron started somewhat nervously but got well into his stride. He had some very good lines and certainly did his best to portray Nick as part of the

Westminster elite. Tim also heckled Nick a lot, and James McGrory gave him quite a lot of latitude. Nick looked slightly irritated and discombobulated. Nick was particularly poor on the question about why the Lib Dems weren't giving a referendum on the EU and whether we were going back on earlier pledges. Tim Farron definitely got the better of this third debate, and Nick's team were a little deflated.

At around 11.30 p.m. I had a phone call from Switch. Oliver Letwin, who's presently visiting China, wants to talk badgers! The Tories really seem to have their knickers in a twist about this. They are in a real panic that the cull must continue – and this clearly indicates that they regard this as important for their farming lobby. The one thing you can say about the Tories is they really do look after their own people! Oliver didn't express his own views on the cull but he did ask me where we'd got to. I said there was zero chance that we would allow the cull to be rolled out in other pilot areas, and that the issue was whether or not we would allow continuation in the existing areas.

WEDNESDAY 26 MARCH

Sir Jeremy Heywood came to see me at 9 a.m. We had a chat about the badger cull, which Jeremy is keen should go ahead in the pilot areas, though interestingly he admitted to me that he'd never been in favour of the cull in the first place and didn't really think it would work or be scalable! He also admitted that the Chief Scientist had never been in favour either! God help us.

Jeremy thinks the government is too big, and he'd like to see the number of government departments, ministers and members of the Cabinet shrunk considerably. He's probably right. However, I highlighted to him that the argument for machinery of government changes would need to be quite strong to get them through in the face of the natural desire of Prime Ministers to retain patronage by having lots of people they can make Cabinet ministers. The problem of shrinking your Cabinet/shadow Cabinet is that you have to make lots of people redundant, and then you end up making enemies.

At 7 p.m. the great Clegg versus Farage debate was due to take place on Sky TV/LBC. I couldn't watch it because I had to speak in Nick's place at a fundraising dinner. However, it seemed to go reasonably well. The overall view was that Nick had won on some of the questions and Farage on others. All in all, it seemed to be a score draw, although the early polling is showing that Farage got a majority of the voters, with 54 per cent of the vote against Nick's 36 per cent. Doing these debates can be a fairly lonely thing for party leaders, so I texted Nick to say that although I missed the debate, it sounded like he did well. Nick replied: 'Thanks – it was tough, and the polls have declared Farage the winner, but I think I've got through to our voters.'

FRIDAY 28 MARCH

Was in Horton first thing to deliver European election leaflets in the pouring rain. Umbrella in one hand, leaflets in the other. Had only delivered three of the damn things when I crossed a driveway surfaced with shiny black slates. Slipped over and fell badly, slamming my left elbow onto the stones and throwing leaflets all over the driveway. Embarrassingly, the owner of the house saw it all, and came out to help. She insisted I come in to her kitchen, and started drying my election leaflets on her radiators. I felt awful and suddenly blacked out – ending up lying flat on my back under her kitchen table. When I came around, she was leaning over me, and I think she feared I'd had a heart attack or something. I was very British: 'Absolutely fine … no need to worry … sure it's only a bruise,' etc. But she insisted on calling the paramedics, who took me by car to Musgrove Hospital in Taunton. They diagnosed a broken left elbow.

Texted my DfE private office to give them the news. 'Minister, we are SO sorry to hear that', followed thirty seconds later by: 'Could you tell us which elbow you have broken, and whether it will affect your ability to sign letters and do your red boxes?' Touching!

SATURDAY 29 MARCH

My red box arrived home at 11 a.m. Opened it to find it was two thirds full. On the top were three packets of red liquorice laces – a present from my DfE private office – and a 'get well soon' card. Very sweet!

MONDAY 31 MARCH

Got up very early, and took ages to wash and get changed. I'm really missing the use of my left arm, and the plaster cast weighs an absolute ton. I'm still worried that I may end up having to have an operation; it's going to be weeks before my life gets back to normal. The whole thing is making me feel quite old.

In the afternoon we had a ministerial meeting with Sir Michael Wilshaw. He chose to raise in front of the Secretary of State the fact that over a third of free schools are either 'requires improvement' or in special measures. He said this was 'of concern'. Sally Morgan, sitting to his left, winked across the table at me. Free schools were seen by MG as the great Tory panacea for educational underperformance, but if a third of them are poor-quality schools, that's something of an indictment.

TUESDAY 1 APRIL

Driven back from a meeting by the government car service driver. As he got closer to London, his driving got more and more erratic and he took to swerving the car violently around corners, in spite of the fact that he had somebody in the back with a broken elbow, heavily plastered. Was he secretly doing it on purpose?

Free school meals. I was relieved later in the day when I got the first implementation stock-take paper from our officials, which shows that our reporting back from half of local authorities records a much more optimistic picture than expected about preparations in most of the country.

At 2.30 p.m. went off by car to the European debate practice session at the Ministry of Sound. Tim Farron was still playing Farage, and on this occasion seemed to have lost his drive. Nick had his best practice session so far. He was much more aggressive and had a few good sound bites and the odd joke. One rather corny line was that 'If I'm the leader of the party of in, Nigel Farage is the party of "Put-in!"' This is a reference to Farage's bizarre behaviour in blaming the EU for the Russian-inspired bloodshed in the Ukraine and Crimea. Nick came off looking confident and pleased. The feedback from Paddy Ashdown, Danny and me was very positive.

WEDNESDAY 2 APRIL

Final election debate with Farage. Didn't go brilliantly for Nick. The audience seemed unsympathetic, and all Nick's jokes fell rather flat. A very clear Farage win. Nick won't be pleased.

FRIDAY 4 APRIL

Spent the day in London because of my broken elbow, working on the manifesto. It's not easy to write an election manifesto when you're in pain.

I emailed Nick about an idea I have for the Autumn Statement/Budget. Instead of just proceeding with an increase in the income tax allowance, I'm suggesting that we consider two policies: one is a small increase in the tax allowance perhaps to the level of the pensioner tax allowance, which is £10,660. The second would be to cut the level of council tax for people living in band A and B properties. That would benefit over 10 million households out of the 23 million who pay council tax. It would be quite an attractive policy and it would target young people, pensioners, those in work on low incomes, people in areas of the country where property prices are lower – for example the north. It would have a lesser benefit in London and the south-east. It would cost about £1 billion to cut 10 per cent off the band A and B properties. I like the idea because it makes council tax more progressive, it's probably better targeted than an increase in the personal allowance, and it would have the benefit of being unexpected and 'new'.

SATURDAY 5 APRIL AND SUNDAY 6 APRIL

Emailed Nick Clegg again on my proposal about cutting council tax. Heard nothing back. He's been in something of a radio silence since his Farage election debate. Perhaps my text to him afterwards wasn't suitably upbeat, but I knew that he wouldn't be pleased with the result, given he had a thirty-point deficit in the post-debate polls. No point in being sycophantic on these occasions – though sometimes that's what leaders want! He seems to have spent part of his weekend at the Lib Dem Welsh conference – and anyone thinking that it might be nice to be Leader of the Liberal Democrats or Deputy Prime Minister ought to remember how these people end up having to spend their weekends!

MONDAY 7 APRIL

My broken elbow is still making life a misery.

Got back home at about 8.15 p.m. with a red box which pretty much burst open when I unlocked it. Where the hell do they get all this work from! Felt absolutely cheesed off, as I was tired, arm was hurting, and now I had what looked like about four or five hours' work. In addition, I now have to get up early tomorrow to do a round of media interviews on universal infant school free meals, and it looks like we face another day of Tories throwing stones at the policy. Bad enough having to deliver all these policies, but when you have to do so in the face of whinging head teachers and scheming Tories, it really is quite testing. Got to bed at about midnight and woke up at 2.30 a.m. with my arm feeling like it weighed a ton on top of me. Couldn't get back to sleep so I went downstairs, watched TV and then did some work for a couple of hours.

TUESDAY 8 APRIL

Strolled over to No. 10 with Nick for the Cabinet meeting. On the walk, Nick said, 'Look, just between the two of us, I found the debates rather demoralising. They've knocked me back a bit. I was very disappointed that I wasn't able to produce a better result for the party, but I really don't know what else I could have done. The studio audience didn't seem very friendly from the off, and although there were a couple of questions that I could have answered rather better, the depressing thing is how Nigel Farage can do so well with such right-wing populist nonsense.

'It's really got to me that I wasn't able to deliver for the party on something so important for us, for me, and for the country. It's made me question whether I can turn this thing round before the general election. If there's a plan, there's hope. But I feel at present our only plan is to hope.'

WEDNESDAY 9 APRIL

Went down to breakfast with Oliver, who was in his usual merry good mood. He commented on how strong the economy was at the moment and said it was amazing that Vince Cable didn't seem to want to take any credit for it! I said that Vince didn't really do economic booms. Oliver started chuckling and said, 'It really is quite extraordinary! You really would think that the Lib Dems would want to own the recovery, but Vince just seems to rattle on the whole time about how awful everything is. He's actually done quite a good job of creating an industrial policy, but he just doesn't seem to want to tell anybody!'

And then he went into one of his endless Oliver chuckle-fests, where he started laughing and chuckling for a long period of time, and it is pointless talking to him when he's like this because you just have to allow the waves of chuckling to roll over him and eventually abate.

He didn't seem to have the first clue who would be taking over from Maria Miller, who has been forced to resign from Cabinet this morning, and the thing about Oliver is he's very close to David Cameron as a policy adviser but I suspect not somebody that Cameron listens to at all for political or personnel advice.

I joked with Oliver that I'd just heard that John Redwood had been appointed the new Culture Secretary. Oliver looked rather blankly at me until he suddenly realised it was all a joke!

Later on, I took a car from the DfE with Liz Truss, who would probably have been rather disappointed not to be promoted in the Maria Miller reshuffle. She did her best at sounding completely relaxed about it, and said that her view was that DCMS was a terrible job and Sajid [Javid] was welcome to it. I suspect she was bitterly disappointed.

Had a chat with Nick and Danny about various issues. Nick said that he was rather worried about Alistair Carmichael. Alistair looks absolutely knackered and rather ill and Nick said he really needed to sleep properly. Nick even said, 'Mike Moore is entitled to feel a bit upset at the moment, because frankly Alistair is struggling.' Danny said that he was starting to take a bigger role in the campaign planning for the Scottish referendum.

THURSDAY 10 APRIL

Over to the DfE for 8.15 a.m. for various meetings, the most important of which was my free school meals stock-take. There's now a huge scrutiny of this policy and whether or not we can deliver it on time. There are something like 16,000 schools which have to be ready, and it's going to be a major challenge. Each week I'm going to have to go through all of the local authority areas in the country to assess their readiness and that of every school. So far 120 local authorities have reported back. Basically there are about a quarter of local authorities which are completely ready to deliver, but there are quite a lot where there are delivery problems and challenges or a lot of red-rated schools. In total something like 60 per cent of schools are green-rated, another 33 per cent are amber-rated – which means that they should be ready in time but they have some delivery challenges – but 7 per cent of schools are red-rated. If that's replicated across the whole of the primary/infant school system, then we could well have more than 1,000 schools where the readiness for September 2014 is still in doubt. I'm going to have to spend a huge amount of time to keep this on track.

SUNDAY 13 APRIL

Nothing much in the news today but the opinion polls are ghastly. UKIP on 20 per cent and the Lib Dems on 7 per cent. This is going to be seen as an indictment of Nick's decision to go into the debates with Farage. Nick is bound to be fairly gloomy. He'll also be pretty pissed off with the press coverage yesterday of Jeremy Browne. Jeremy has given an interview to *The Times*, which has generated the front-page headline 'Lib Dems are pointless'.

MONDAY 14 APRIL

In at 6.30 a.m. to rewrite my speech to today's ATL teaching union conference in Manchester. If there's one thing officials are absolutely hopeless at, it's writing speeches for ministers, and they're even worse when there are some policy sensitivities to be picked up on! So the only answer is to write the damn speeches yourself, and I spent about three hours on Sunday night writing the first draft and then another two this morning getting it right. Then went by train to Manchester, met some teachers before my conference performance, and delivered a speech which seemed to be relatively positively received. Part of my aim was to get a positive reception and part of it was to avoid being booed – which is usually the fate of Education Ministers at these conferences! Perhaps I held back a little too much on a modernising and liberal message, but it was more important to focus on areas of agreement. So I majored on the pupil premium, the accountability reforms, the need for a better working relationship between politicians and teachers, and the need for more policy stability. Also emphasised heavily the need for more continuing professional development, and there's now an issue about whether we can deliver this in coalition or whether this will have to go into our next general election manifesto.

The DfE seems to have come to a halt for the Easter recess. David Cameron is out in Lanzarote, and his holiday started with the normal photo opportunity with him and Samantha Cameron looking lovingly at each other over a cup of coffee and a glass of water. The standard picture to satisfy the paparazzi.

WEDNESDAY 16 APRIL

Went back to the DfE for 11.45 a.m. and had a very worrying discussion about the situation in Birmingham with 'extremism'. Apparently all this dates back to November, when a teacher or governor in a school found on a photocopier a strategy paper which talked about a Muslim takeover of large numbers of schools in Birmingham. The suggestion is that Muslims were targeting failing schools or trying to make existing successful schools fail, so that they would presumably be pushed into academisation and then be able to be taken over by independent groups of Muslim governors, who would be free to make the schools more Islamic-friendly. This couldn't really be more combustible, and although there is some fear that this is all being hyped up or that some of the paperwork is false, the officials said they took the allegations very seriously and felt that there was evidence that some of this was actually happening. This is doubly sensitive because of the idea of Muslims taking over 'British' schools, but also because it looks as if they're particularly targeting academisation, as it's presumably easier for more independent schools to be 'Islamified' in this way.

Spent the rest of the afternoon on DfE matters – a pupil premium registration stock-take, a free school meals policy catch-up, a discussion about early learning funding for two-year-olds, a discussion with Matt Sanders about QTS reform, a revenue funding catch-up about the way in which we fund free schools, a monthly capital catch-up particularly over the Academies Capital Maintenance Fund, discussion about the 16–18 performance and accountability tables, a discussion about children from overseas and immigration matters, a catch-up on pupil premium policy, and then a discussion about setting the persistent child poverty target for 2020/21. Quite a lot of serious policy issues, but an absolutely average afternoon in terms of the back-to-back nature of the meetings.

THURSDAY 17 APRIL

I phoned Sally Morgan. She confirmed that Ofsted is worried about ten or twenty schools in Birmingham, as well as potentially some other schools in Bradford and Salford. It looks as if Ofsted will report before the May local and European elections, and that they will put some schools into special measures. This could brew up into a major political row – and it will have lots of different angles, about extremism, about free schools and academies, and about faith schools. Sally said that there was no obvious read-across to free schools and academies because the problem of takeover of schools seemed to be as much an issue for local authority schools as for free schools and academies – but that's not the way the media and the left are going to view the whole thing. Sally also said that one school in Birmingham had actually purchased loudspeakers to call the children to prayer!

I also spoke to Sally about the new chair of Ofsted. Sally said that she didn't have any names in mind yet, but she'd been thinking about some female Tory members of the Lords. She said she'd spoken to Gillian Shephard, but she didn't think that Michael Gove would want to choose Gillian and said in any case that both Ken Baker and Gillian were incredibly dismissive about Michael – with Gillian saying he was 'an ideological zealot' who shouldn't be in charge of the education system! We both agreed that Michael Wilshaw wouldn't tolerate being undermined, and there was a real risk that he might resign.

SATURDAY 19 APRIL

France. Woke up at around 8 a.m. French time, feeling the weight of the plaster cast on top of me. Outside it was rather cold, but not a cloud in the sky. This time of year it soon heats up in the sun.

SUNDAY 20 APRIL

Easter Sunday. France. Cloudy. A quiet day. Read a large chunk of Robert Caro's third volume of the Lyndon Johnson biography.

MONDAY 21 APRIL

A fairly overcast day. Drove down to the beautiful seaside resort of Cassis for lunch. As we got closer to the sea, the clouds parted and we were able to sit outside at Nino's on the sea front, in the sun. I think that this is one of my favourite places in the world. The seafood was absolutely magnificent, and the wine went down well too. The great thing about this place is that no British people appear to have discovered it.

Got back home at around 4.30 p.m. and finished the third volume of Caro's biography. An incredible read. Unforgettably good. Went straight on to the fourth volume.

TUESDAY 22 APRIL

Up at around 9 a.m. Our last full day in France. In a year's time we will be slap bang in the middle of a ferocious general election campaign.

Doing a little simple arithmetic, I reckon there must be something like twenty-five parliamentary weeks left to go, which means twenty-five more meetings of the Cabinet, twenty-five more Prime Minister's Questions and maybe six more Department for Education questions. That isn't all that long, but it's still a good period of time to focus on implementation and making sure that the things we've announced in government are actually delivered.

WEDNESDAY 23 APRIL

Up at 7 a.m. as we need to tidy up before catching the 12.45 flight from Nice back to London.

My mind is already turning to the red box that will be awaiting me. Also thinking about what I ought to be trying to achieve in the last year of government. In the DfE, the pupil premium and sorting out the early years pupil premium come top of that list. Then there's free school meals and making sure that's a success. Delivering on basic need, enough school places in September 2014. The Priority School Building Programme 2, which we want to get up and running before the end of the year. And then there's bedding in all the accountability reforms, and finishing off the fairer funding formula for schools. Then there are three proactive things, which we haven't got agreement on yet: continuous professional development for teachers, and helping to get some of the teaching workforce back on side; agreeing a set of reforms on system leadership; and, thirdly, a piece of work that I've commissioned to allow the department to assess the quality of academy sponsors and local authorities – it's amazing that we don't already have this information, and it will be interesting to see how easy or difficult the Tories make it to deliver.

Meanwhile, there is no doubt it's going to be a very tough year for the Liberal Democrats – and I don't expect to see any inflation of our poll ratings until close to the general election. That's when people will really reconsider whether they want a large Liberal Democrat contingent in the next parliament. I expect some pretty dire results from the European elections, possibly with all our MEPs being wiped out – and if that happens there will certainly be speculation about Nick's leadership.

The competitive nature of politics could propel us back into government in May 2015, with another hung parliament. But if the party does very badly in that election and either the Tories or Labour pull away then we could end up with a majority Labour or Conservative government with a shrunken Lib Dem contingent, consigned once more to the back benches. Essentially we'd be back where we were pre-1997. That would not be something to relish.

On the other hand, if we're back in government again I would really like to go back to the Treasury and finish off the job I started as Chief Secretary in May 2010. The result of the election is going to have a massive impact on determining the future course of my life. Either way, I think by 2020, if I am re-elected, I would have been an MP for nineteen years and would have been working in Westminster for twenty-six years. I think that's probably the time when it would make sense to give way to somebody younger. So whatever happens in May 2015, I'm pencilling in May 2020 for retirement from politics.

TUESDAY 29 APRIL

A worrying note in my box about the deteriorating trend in NHS finances and performance. Attached to the cover note is a letter from Jeremy Hunt to the Prime Minister. This makes clear that Jeremy has 'serious concerns' about meeting the savings targets for the NHS and he is saying that there is a clear risk that we will miss the eighteen weeks waiting target for February. The proposal by the DoH is to scrape together an additional £400 million of funding for 2014/15 to try to relieve pressures on the NHS, but there is a question mark about whether this is going to be enough to halt the deterioration.

The latest poll numbers for the European elections are pretty ghastly, with UKIP on 31 per cent, Labour on 28 per cent, the Tories on 19 per cent and the Lib Dems on 8 per cent. However extraordinary it is that the Tories are only on 19 per cent, it seems very difficult to me to imagine the Conservatives being replaced by Labour in government, given that we've got a recovering economy and that the Labour Party doesn't have much economic credibility. I'm convinced the next general election is still wide open.

Got home at about 10 p.m. and had to work on my red boxes for a couple of hours. An interesting idea that we discussed today with officials in Nick's office was the possibility of having a northern economic triangle of Manchester, Leeds and Sheffield in which we would concentrate growth and infrastructure investment in order to create a competing economic centre with London.

THURSDAY 1 MAY

Announced the new priority school building programme that I have been working on for a year – £2 billion to rebuild hundreds of run-down schools.

Some bizarre story that Osborne wants to move to the Foreign Office after the election, assuming Hague stands down. Cameron will be irritated and Osborne embarrassed.

Had a catch-up with the free school meals team. The latest figures show that of the total of 16,500 schools, 60 per cent are green-rated, 34 per cent amber and only 6 per cent are red. However, 6 per cent is still 1,000 schools, so we can't be complacent.

To Taunton by train for a hospital check-up on my broken elbow. Got up very gingerly from my seat, and an elderly gentleman sitting opposite – aged about eighty – asked me whether I needed help!

To Musgrove Hospital. The NHS has been good, but you don't exactly get the impression you are at the cutting edge of new technology. When I went to the X-ray department, they gave me a small wooden block with a number carved on to denote my place in the queue. It's like a system that might have been devised during the Crimean War, and phased out in about 1923.

FRIDAY 2 MAY

Ever since Chris Grayling started pushing the idea of a minimum mandatory jail sentence for second knife crime offences, we've all been concerned that the Tories would seek to leak against us and accuse us of blocking something popular, however ill-thought-out it is. It's clear that even Tory hardliners don't expect it to have any effect, beyond grabbing the odd headline. The death of a teacher in a Leeds school from a (first-time offender?) knife attack raised the risk of a malicious leak even further.

Well, today the *Daily Mail* has splashed with: 'Clegg bids to block knife crackdown'. The story deliberately links the row with the fatal stabbing of the teacher. It's clear this is a deliberate and very vicious leak, and it names Nick, Danny and me (not Ken Clarke, of course!) as blocking the measure.

The story includes: 'One well-placed source said Mr Clegg, who chairs the Cabinet Home Affairs Committee, declined even to discuss it when it was raised in a meeting of senior ministers on Wednesday.'

Leaking restricted Cabinet committee papers is quite a serious matter. Leaking and interpreting discussions in a Cabinet committee – particularly in an inaccurate way – is also a breach of all government rules. I'm incandescent – and linking this to the teacher murder is both misleading and very unpleasant.

Nick is also spitting blood: 'It is most definitely Gove – Grayling wouldn't risk it.'

Nick has sent a blunt email to Cameron:

David, I was going to have a word with you next week about Gove's increasingly weird behaviour – but his leak to the *Mail* today of Danny's letter re.

knife crime makes it more urgent. Following his office's appalling attack on Miriam (Book Trust etc.) and Cummings' loopy rants against me last week, I thought I'd seen it all. But then Michael – who barely deigns to attend Home Affairs Committee normally – hijacks this week's meeting re. knife crime, writes a bizarre letter complaining about my behaviour to Jeremy Heywood claiming I misused my position as chair, and now turns what is a perfectly serious policy debate (mandatory versus judge discretion, concern re. effect on prison numbers) into a full-blown row cynically timed to coincide with the terrible death of a teacher in Leeds. I think this goes way beyond the normal stresses and strains of coalition politics. Gove's behaviour is personally offensive, an abuse of the rules of the game, and unbelievably destructive of coherent government.

Danny said he thought the leak inquiry would need to be police-led, but both Nick and I are sceptical – it might look over the top. Danny did emphasise that the Permanent Secretary to the Treasury is relaxed about involving the police but thinks Jeremy Heywood won't want to push it that far.

SATURDAY 3 MAY

Advice centres in Ilminster and Crewkerne. Rather an odd bunch of people today, including one mature lady who is on a nurses' course at Yeovil College and has ended up with a dispute over whether she can have access to hot water for tea during the day! She wanted me to write to the Business Secretary about it.

To Huish Park to see little Yeovil Town play Middlesbrough in the last game of the season. Our player budget is just £2.8 million and yet we have been competing with clubs with £75 million budgets. It's amazing we are only six or seven points off staying up.

6.20 p.m. conference call with Nick, Danny and advisers on the knife crime leaks. We settled for a Cabinet Office-led leak inquiry. The clear view of everybody was that we should maintain our position in resisting the mandatory minimum sentence for the second possession offence. Anything else would just look weak.

•

MONDAY 5 MAY

In my box today there's a copy of an extraordinary letter dated 1 May, from Michael Gove to Sir Jeremy Heywood: 'Dear Sir Jeremy, I'm writing to express my concern about the operation of the Cabinet's Home Affairs Committee. I fear the way the committee is currently chaired does not allow for open, collective discussion of government policy, nor for accountable decision-making.' Extraordinary and unprecedented. Neither Nick nor Cameron will be amused.

Sir Jeremy replied on the same day, in what I can only interpret as dismissive terms.

TUESDAY 6 MAY

8.15 a.m. to the National Liberal Club for our regular weekly meeting. Discussed the 'implementation update' which is supposed to be taking place at Cabinet today. I said to Nick that we needed to be aware that the coalition commitment on restoring exit checks by 2015 is now being watered down by Theresa May. The PM's Cabinet briefing note says: 'On track for a decent but not fully comprehensive system by 2015, now aiming for completion by 2017.'

Ryan led a brief discussion about the local and European elections. In short, dreadful! We are expecting to lose most of our MEPs, and 340 out of our 732 council seats. Ryan was saying that perhaps we would only lose 300 seats, which we could then present as a triumph. Interesting view.

We were ten minutes early for Cabinet, and there were only a couple of other ministers there – including Michael Gove. As soon as Nick spotted him, he recoiled and headed in the opposite direction.

In Cabinet, I highlighted two Lib Dem priorities – keeping NHS performance levels up, and delivering on exit checks. I said I had heard a suggestion that exit checks delivery might slip beyond 2015 to 2017. As I said this, Theresa May looked extremely agitated. The Prime Minister didn't comment, but it's obvious that he and May are nervous that we are holding them to account on this.

Lansley announced that Parliament will be breaking for another recess from 14 May to 4 June. One or two Cabinet ministers gasped! Cameron returned yet again to his growing obsession with Labour claims that the government has run out of steam: 'I hear all this stuff from Labour about a zombie parliament. This is complete and utter rubbish, and I'm really not worried about it, and we mustn't be distracted. It really is complete and total rubbish.' Every week he says he isn't concerned; every week he keeps returning to it.

Met Nick for an update on free school meals. His advisers are clearly getting nervous, and he said he was thinking about 'lowering expectations'. I said that lowering expectations was absolutely the last thing that I needed. I want to raise expectations that all schools will deliver a hot meal for every single infant in September 2014. I will micromanage this school by school if I have to.

In my red box tonight is a draft report on the pupil premium from Ofsted, which looks extremely positive. Less positive is a letter from Chris Grayling asking for the knife issue to go back on the Home Affairs Committee agenda. In response, a rather magnificent letter from Ken Clarke:

Dear Nick,

I have previously written to you on mandatory minimum custodial sentences for second knife possession offences, making clear that I do not agree with the proposal. My views on this have since been shared with the newspapers. I hope, therefore, that no one is expecting them to change. Ken Clarke.

Magnificent. Ken is a national treasure.

WEDNESDAY 7 MAY

9 a.m. Sir Jeremy Heywood bilateral. I asked whether a leak inquiry on knife crime had started. Jeremy smiled and said the PM was 'very much against a leak inquiry' and was in favour of just giving Michael Gove a good bollocking! Jeremy said that leak inquiries never actually find the source of leaks. Apparently the PM wasn't that bothered about the knife crime proposal in the first place, and he is very angry with Michael and others for causing the row.

Cameron was also very irritated by the Ofsted chairmanship row, and wants this to be dealt with sensitively – with a 'safe' choice for the new chairman. Helpful.

Two back-to-back meetings with Michael. His adviser, Tom Shinner, is pushing hard for us to reform the granting of qualified teacher status, so that you don't get it automatically at the end of your teacher training but you only get it when you have shown you can be an effective teacher. I said the problem is that Michael had controversially removed the requirement for all teachers to have QTS. Michael then said he'd got a 'trade' to offer me. He knew that I wanted to make faster progress on a Royal College of Teachers, and also move to some kind of CPD entitlement for teachers. If we could make progress on his QTS reform, then we could also go ahead on CPD/a Royal College of Teachers. I said I will consider it.

Nick has now talked to Cameron on knives. Cameron has agreed to have a meeting with Gove and Heywood, in which he will threaten to bring in the police if there are further leaks. Michael is now endangering his own relationship with Cameron, who is apparently furious.

THURSDAY 8 MAY

At 11.15 a.m. had a private political meeting with Matt Sanders, Stephen Lotinga and James McGrory to talk about the Gove issue and how we might deal with it. As we were talking, the news came through that Cummings has leaked further internal DfE papers on free school meals to *The World at One*. I'm now going to have to waste a huge amount of time going through all the documentation to knock down Cummings's lunatic story. Very, very infuriating.

Cummings has also now given an on-the-record quote: 'Clegg has been lying about the announcement from the start to cover up his abuse of taxpayers' money for his personal ends. Gove was trying to safeguard taxpayers' money but Clegg ignored him. All the documents should be turned over to the Select Committee immediately...' Absolutely extraordinary and unbelievable that this little shit is behaving in this way. A pack of lies. Now I'm even more determined than ever to tell people what the Tories have actually been up to and that their objection to the capital for the universal infant free school meals policy was simply that they wanted to siphon off even greater sums of money to put into their free schools programme, which is growing out of control.

There is so much really important work we could be doing in the

Department for Education, but the bitterness over this is going to make it impossible to get anything new done. Worked through my box until about 1 a.m.

FRIDAY 9 MAY

Got into the office at 5.30 a.m. to check the DfE press lines that are to be used on the Cummings story. Needless to say, the proposed lines are pathetically weak. I determined to go through all of the paperwork to knock down every allegation. Absolutely seething that I am having to waste time on this.

By 7 a.m. I had looked at all the paperwork and sent an email to the DfE press office, setting out a robust communications plan.

Then spent the next four and a half hours going backwards and forwards between me, Matt Sanders, the Permanent Secretary and the press office trying to sort out the agreed lines. Tory spads were extremely unreasonable and would not sign off my lines, even though these were all agreed by the Permanent Secretary. I spoke to Chris Wormald and insisted that my lines needed to go out. Chris said that this was 'impossibly difficult' because if there was a difference between the two coalition parties – even though the civil service supported my version of events – the press release couldn't be put out.

I said either the press release had to go out from the DfE or we would release it from the Deputy Prime Minister's office as the government's position, or it should go out from me as Minister of State for Schools.

Chris sounded increasingly panicky and clearly didn't want the press notice to go out from the DPM's office. He came back and said that he'd decided the lines could go out from me as Minister of State for Schools. So, I can comment as Minister of State for Schools, but we can't put out a line from the DfE as an institution! Completely ludicrous.

During the morning I decided that it was time to square up to Michael Gove and emailed him in blunt terms:

Dear Michael, we have always I think got on well … BUT I am increasingly despairing of the campaign of lies, leaks and misinformation over our policy on free school meals … While aware that Dom is independent minded,

I do not believe these leaks would be occurring unless you approved them or turned a blind eye to them. I can only therefore regard them as an attack on the free school meals policy by the Conservative Party. I feel that I am working for a Secretary of State who is trying, or allowing, the deliberate undermining of a key policy which I am charged with delivering. And this is a policy which you have always told me you support … What are you doing to stop this deliberate campaign against the DfE policy by people close to you? I have just wasted two hours this morning, when I could be spending time delivering our policies. This is infuriating for me and demoralising for officials working on this and for Henry and John and those who worked on the School Food Plan. I also fear that it will so reduce levels of coalition trust in DfE that it will be impossible for us to do anything new and productive over the next year. This comes on top of the malicious leaking of the Home Affairs Committee letters on knife crime. If it goes on this way, we are going to damage and diminish both our records. I trust that this is not what you want? If so, I would beg you to:

1. Stop this malicious briefing.
2. Make very clear publicly your support for this policy and your disagreement with the ludicrous claims which are being made.

At 9.15 a.m. Michael phoned me, sounding defensive: 'David, I just don't know where to begin. Look, this is very difficult for me. Dom seems to be in a place where he thinks he's helping me. He often thinks he knows my interests better than I do, but I disagree with him. In fact, it's making our relationship difficult, No. 10 is upset with me, and Henry Dimbleby is also fed up. But I do find this very difficult. Dom is an old friend of mine and it's difficult to control him. However, I must make clear that his position of universal infant school meals is not the same as mine. I will explain my position to Dom and ask him to desist.'

I responded bluntly: 'I understand that Dom is quite an independent-minded person, but frankly he's still your adviser. You have to take responsibility for this. If Matt Sanders left the government and started briefing against everything you'd been doing in the DfE, you would be furious and you would hold Nick Clegg to account. You really have to get a grip on Cummings over this. In addition you need to communicate your support for the policy.'

Michael said he did understand this and he would go back to Dom and try to stop his briefings, and at some stage he would write some kind of article in the newspapers giving his support for the policy. Pretty knackered and got to bed at midnight.

SATURDAY 10 MAY

Yet again up at 5.30 a.m. in order to work on the economy section of the manifesto.

Went to the cinema to see a rather low-grade comedy called *Bad Neighbours*. I was mildly enjoying the film when at 5.40 p.m. Lydia from my DfE office texted:

> Hi, DfE press office, officials and Tory spads are in the process of agreeing lines to give Sunday papers, following reports from a government source that the free schools budget is £800 million overspent and reporting your anger at this. Do you want to clear the lines press office are planning to put out?

Insisted on clearing any DfE lines – blissful revenge over the nonsense re. free school meal lines yesterday. More texts from Lydia: 'Five Sunday papers have approached the press office having been contacted by a government source saying you are very angry as you think that the free schools budget is being protected at the expense of basic need funding.' Emerging signs of DfE panic. Too bloody bad.

I was beginning to rather enjoy this. Endless texts and emails followed. I kept texting back to say I refused to clear the inaccurate proposed DfE lines.

Eventually, to my intense pleasure, Lydia said it had been decided that the lines could not now go out from the DfE press office, but they would have to go out from a Gove spokesman – now the Tories get a taste of their own damn medicine.

After the film, we drove to Chevening for the dinner that Nick had organised to discuss free school meals. Dinner was served at around eight o'clock and afterwards Nick and Miriam gave us the normal tour of the house – which they must be rather bored with by now. Bizarrely, the staircase at Chevening is rather shaky and insecure, having been built in a novel way a few hundred years ago without proper support. Therefore only five people are allowed to go up it at any one point in time, in case their weight collapses the whole thing! Eventually, we were all given a rather clear steer that it was time to go.

The Observer are splashing on 'Gove's "lunatic" £400 million raid to rescue his free schools vision'. I'm guessing that James McGrory has done one of his low-key, understated briefings! The *Telegraph* leads with: 'Michael Gove and David Laws at war over free schools'. And *The Independent* has also splashed with a rather grim picture of Michael and the headline: '"Zealot" Gove diverts £400 million to his pet project'.

Listened to the midnight news from the BBC – the free schools row is the lead story.

SUNDAY 11 MAY

The PM had to deal with the free schools row on his *Marr* interview – it dominates the media today. We put up Malcolm Bruce to call for a Select Committee inquiry.

Meanwhile, there is a shocking new paper in my box on the free schools budget. This suggests that in spite of trying to fill the black hole at the end of last year with a £400 million revenue to capital switch, plus £400 million raided from the basic need budget, the free schools budget is still out of control. The original budget in December last year was £706 million for 2013/14, £1.081 billion for 2014/15 and £1.026 billion for 2015/16.

The paper now forecasts £1.284 billion for 2014/15, followed by £1.356 billion, and then £1.167 billion in 2016/17, and £696 million for 2017/18 – that means that the department is planning to spend £4.385 billion on free schools over four years.

It also means that for 2014/15 and 2015/16, the department will be spending more on free schools than for the entire maintenance and improvement budget for all 24,000 schools in England – crazy. We will also be spending more on free schools than all of the basic need funding for new school places. While it's true that some of these free schools are creating new places, many of them are not in the areas of most acute basic need.

And half of the areas of most acute basic need have not had a single free school application.

MONDAY 12 MAY

Still wall-to-wall coverage of the free schools row. Most of the publicity is favourable to us – and there's even a leader in *The Times* which suggests that Gove needs to get control of the programme.

Gove asked to see me privately today about the rows. War or suing for peace?

Nick said that Gove must 'publicly and unequivocally back the free school meals policy and publicly and unequivocally disown Cummings's views. If he does, that's peace. If not, not.'

Went over to the DfE at around 9.30 a.m. There were TV cameras outside the front, so the driver took me to the rear entrance.

At 11 a.m. I received the call that Michael was ready to see me. His private secretaries looked up nervously as I approached.

Michael was in his office by himself. He looked up from his desk and said, 'Oh hello, David' – he was trying to calibrate the right tone and ending up somewhere between friendly and chilly.

We sat down in Michael's leather sofas to the side of his desk. 'David, I really don't know where to start. Obviously there has been quite a lot of negative publicity over the weekend! The PM has apparently spoken to Nick Clegg this morning and after that spoke to me and said how keen he is that we sort things out and make sure that the DfE doesn't become a dysfunctional department.

'Obviously, I am very supportive of the free school meals policy, but as we discussed last week it's very difficult to control Dom. But I am worried about all the things that have been said about free schools over the weekend, and I have to say that I feel that the whole thing is a bit disproportionate in that what we have had is a few negative stories from Dom, whereas what the Lib Dems seem to have done is the equivalent of a nuclear strike.

'While I can also understand why Nick and the Lib Dems might feel sore, there are some things that I feel sore about as well – including the position that Nick took on childcare ratios, the fact that he constantly accuses me of being in favour of profit-making schools, also the attack on QTS and the fact that Nick constantly says rather rude things about me in the media, even though I am a fellow member of the government.'

I said, 'Look, I know that you and Nick are not necessarily ever going to love each other, and I'm certainly not expecting to get to the point where Dom and Nick can go on holiday together. But what Dom has been doing is appalling and unacceptable. I don't personally mind him saying that he doesn't agree with this use of money. I know that that was always his view. But what he must not do is lie. I have got here the *Mail on Sunday* interview that he gave this weekend and what he said about the origin of the policy, and it's just a pack of lies.'

I then read out the relevant sections of the interview and challenged Michael to say whether they were right or wrong. I continued: 'I also can't understand your own position on this. You have always said that you have supported this policy, but you seem to have done precious little to stop Dom from trashing it. I was very upset over the last few months about the fact that you dragged your heels on legislating for free school meals, and you also got in the way of securing the capital for free school meals to enhance kitchens, even refusing access to the department to Treasury officials. That doesn't seem like the behaviour of somebody who wants to support the policy. I don't know whether your view is that we have got too much money for the free school meals capital, hence diverting money that could have come from the Treasury for other purposes, or is your view that we don't have enough money for free school meals capital, which seemed to be the thrust of some of the things that Dom was saying the other day? It just seems to me to be opportunistic criticism that questions your support for the entire policy.'

Michael replied by saying, 'No, I am actually in favour of this policy, and I do want to support it and I have spoken to Henry Dimbleby about it this weekend, and perhaps we can do something together in the newspapers to confirm that we both support the policy. But my understanding is that Lib Dems support the free schools policy and it is the flagship education policy of the government, and I am keen to make sure that it isn't damaged or undermined by all of this.'

I said, 'You know that I'm a supporter of the principle of free schools, but there is a serious issue about how much we allocate to free schools and whether we are allocating excessive amounts. If we can deal with our disagreements on universal infant free school meals, I am perfectly happy for us to have our disagreements on free schools behind the scenes, but that doesn't mean I will pull my punches. I was very unhappy about the transfer of £400 million away from basic need to free schools at the end of last year. I have seen the other submission that has just come up over the weekend suggesting that free schools expenditure could rise to £1.3 or £1.4 billion over the next couple of years – which is more than the total amount we're spending on the maintenance of 24,000 schools in England, and more than our basic need allocations. I think there is a risk of the free schools budget getting out of control.'

Michael said that he understood that and he was happy for us to discuss these matters behind the scenes. But he kept on emphasising that he couldn't control Dom Cummings. He said, 'Dom will be Dom. You know what he's like. I have spoken to Dom and I spoke to him last Friday, but it's very difficult to get him to do what you want – and as I said to you, I think he believes that he's helping me in some way, even though he isn't.'

We agreed that we would do a joint op-ed in one of the newspapers. Michael also agreed that the DfE press office would be firmer in the future on lines rebutting Dom's attacks. So it's going to be back to public unity, but I suspect that the private disagreements are going to continue, stoked by Dom.

At 3.30 p.m. an Urgent Question in the House to MG on free schools, from Labour. Decided not to attend, but watched in my DfE office. Michael made a brief opening statement and then Tristram Hunt responded – he was absolutely hopeless. This was an open goal for Labour, and if they can't score on this, they can't score on anything.

In the evening, I had a call from James McGrory saying that that prize idiot Dom Cummings has yet again contacted the media. He has sent an email to *Newsnight*:

In government I certainly did stop a great deal of Clegg's interference in school policy. He would routinely call demanding £100 million for an unknown gimmick ... We told him to get stuffed. More importantly, we stopped him corrupting the free school process and setting exam grades by improper interference, which particularly infuriates people.

Complete and utter balls. The man is a maniac.

Got back this evening at around 10 p.m. and did my box work. There is an interesting poll in *The Guardian* tomorrow which places the Conservatives in the lead for the first time for two years. Conservatives 33 per cent, Labour Party 31 per cent, Lib Dems 13 per cent and UKIP 15 per cent. This is going to cheer the Conservatives up a lot. It's quite an achievement for them to be ahead, particularly with a 15 per cent UKIP vote.

TUESDAY 13 MAY

An overnight email from James McGrory is entitled 'Yet more Cummings'. It suggests our line on Dom's attacks should be: 'We're not even going to dignify these absurd statements with a response. Dom Cummings is an ex-government adviser and these fantastical musings show why it should stay that way.'

Cabinet. A presentation on Scotland from Alistair Carmichael, who looks increasingly knackered, and who seems to be giving up leadership of the campaign to Danny – who was lively and on the button, as usual.

Cameron said once again: 'I'm really not worried about this Labour idea of a zombie parliament.' He's obviously obsessed about it.

Later on, I bumped into Ken Clarke in the division lobby and joked with him about the leaked correspondence over knife crime. He said, 'Oh, it's all quite disgraceful isn't it? This is exactly what happened at the end of the John Major era, when everyone started leaking against each other – as soon as you do that, it's absolute chaos. We've all been told by the PM to behave, but whether it will actually happen is another matter.'

At 4 p.m. met with Nick, Danny and Norman Lamb to discuss the increasingly worrying NHS budget position, with the performance indicators and deficit numbers deteriorating. Danny did the traditional Chief Secretary thing, saying that the NHS shouldn't look for more money, that they should drive efficiency savings. However, I'm not sure that the NHS is going to survive the next couple of years unless we inject some more money into it. Nick is worried.

At 5 p.m. went off to see Oliver Letwin in his office on the lower committee room corridor. We were supposed to be discussing how to resolve the issue about zero-carbon homes. Oliver said that he had a 'trade'. He said that his proposal was that on knife crime the Tory backbench amendments that suggest a mandatory minimum sentence for a second offence could be supported by all Conservative ministers and MPs, with Lib Dem ministers abstaining. In exchange, the Conservatives would allow the zero-carbon homes policy to go through.

I said this was 'pretty cheeky'. They were trying to trade zero-carbon homes, which we'd agreed as a coalition for the past two years, for knife crime, which we hadn't agreed at all! Oliver smiled. He was very pleasant about the whole thing and he said that on knife crime he thought the Conservative proposals were 'completely mad'.

Later, I had a meeting with the DfE Permanent Secretary. I said to Chris Wormald that I was very worried about the outbreak of coalition war, and I would be particularly concerned if I discovered that data leaked from the department was only available for the period after Dom Cummings had left.

Chris also said that what had happened on Friday and Saturday was 'unprecedented' – the first time ever that a department hadn't been able to put out an official line itself, with this having had to go out from the Secretary of State as an individual! Chris said that he'd had to take a tough line on it and actually refer the matter to the centre of the government for guidance. This is the sort of thing that civil servants really hate. I made clear that if the Tories are going to play dirty with me, they cannot expect cooperation.

WEDNESDAY 14 MAY

Awaiting me in my in-tray this morning was the draft Gove/Laws article on free school meals. I spent forty-five minutes amending it.

At 10 a.m. went over to the DfE for the usual meeting-fest: fourteen meetings back to back, with decisions required in each. The most significant discussion came at 1.15 p.m., when I had called together officials to discuss the financial implications of the sixth 'wave' of free school proposals.

Lord Nash asked to join – I made clear he was welcome. Outside my office was a vast brigade of civil servants, which is a sure sign of departmental panic. They all trooped in, taking up every chair. Lord Nash sat to my left looking rather suspicious.

I said I was very worried that if we did not control free school expenditure, the maintenance and basic need budgets would be squeezed – and I pointed out that whereas our narrative was that only 8 per cent of capital was going on free schools, it looked as if this would touch 30 per cent in the final year of the parliament. Lord Nash looked rather grumpy and said, 'Free schools are doing rather well, you know – their performance is better than other schools.' Of course, this isn't entirely accurate, and it depends on comparing apples with oranges, but I'd decided that it would be rather unseemly to get into a spat about this in front of officials.

We got to the bottom of the fact that in 2015/16 and 2017/18 the budgets are particularly overspent. A slightly uncomfortable meeting.

I was then handed back the copy of the Gove/Laws article on free school meals for *The Times* tomorrow. It was supposed to have been merely 'fact checked'. The more I read through, the more I realised that somebody in the department had gone through and axed out all of the most important parts of the article that rebutted the ludicrous claims that Cummings had been making. I started by trying to reinsert these into the article and then completely lost my temper, and put a line through the whole thing and shouted very loudly for one of my private secretaries to come in. I told her that the changes were entirely unacceptable. They'd even managed to delete Nick Clegg's name from the article, so that Ed Balls got a favourable mention but nobody from the Liberal Democrats at all! Childish behaviour.

Eventually it took a bilateral with MG to agree the text. Michael was in quite an agitated mood and he said, 'We've had to tell Dom about this article. I really don't want to put anything in that will provoke Dom.' There were a couple of areas where he was particularly prickly – he wouldn't put in wording that categorically implied that we had all the money we needed and nor would he put in wording which said that we thought that all schools could deliver the policy by September 2014.

Towards the end of the discussion, Michael said that obviously he was a passionate supporter of the policy although 'not all the issues surrounding implementation'. Even though our private secretaries were there, I decided I couldn't let this go unchallenged: 'What do you mean, problems with implementation? You haven't told me that there's anything about implementation that you're unhappy with.' Michael looked highly uncomfortable and his left leg jerked out spontaneously from the seat on which he was sitting. I don't think he realised it, but he ended up kicking me in the foot: 'Well, of course it's the issue of whether we've really got the right amount of capital.'

I said, 'Look, I really don't understand your position. When it was the Autumn Statement, you prevented us from bidding for capital. What is your position – that we have too little capital or too much capital?'

Michael replied, 'Both! We should have bid to the Treasury for more capital, and obviously I'm worried about it being diverted from elsewhere in the department, but we really do need enough capital for the free school meals policy.'

Both private secretaries shuffled awkwardly in their seats. Michael obviously feels that he has to stick to the Tory attack lines in this area, even though they are ridiculous and incoherent. No sooner had I got back to my office than the new draft article appeared – unbelievably, without some of the lines that I'd discussed with Michael just ten minutes beforehand. I insisted that they should be put back in. Arrrrrrgggggghhhhhhh.

At 5.30 p.m. had a meeting with Tom Shinner, who is effectively Michael's lead policy adviser. Tom said that he was rather upset by all the chaos in the department over the past week. He confirmed that the DfE internal red-risk rating for free school meals delivery, which was leaked out yesterday, was only available after Cummings left the department. I made clear to Tom that I knew that many of the other parts of the department's work were also red-rated, including free schools, and I implied that it wouldn't be very helpful if this leaked into the public domain. We had a good discussion about teacher training, professional development and the Royal College of Teaching. I like Tom – he's a bright guy.

At 6.30 p.m. I phoned Jeremy Hunt. I said I was worried that the NHS might unravel towards the end of the parliament. Jeremy said, 'Look, as a businessman my first instinct is to try to drive efficiency savings. But I also think that while we should be able to get through to the end of this parliament without a crisis, it could be a close-run thing, particularly if we have a very cold winter.

'There's also this issue of the social care fund, which NHS money is going to be transferred to in 2015/16. There's a real issue about whether the cost of services in acute hospitals is going to automatically reduce in 2015/16 to allow that transfer of costs to the social services departments. More likely there's going to be a transition that will take time where we're going to have extra costs in the social services without reducing the costs in the hospital sector.'

So what Jeremy is essentially suggesting is there should be some kind of transitional fund in the first half of 2015/16, which would therefore effectively boost NHS revenues directly.

In the evening, went to a Hackney Lib Dems fundraiser. There were about eighteen people there. God knows how much money they raised, but I couldn't help feeling that it would have been simpler if I'd just sent them a cheque.

On the way home I saw a copy of the final *Times* article – 'We are not at war over free school lunches'. The article reads:

> To judge from the latest breathless headlines, you might expect the two of us to be crouched under our desks like the last survivors in a Bruce Willis movie, only popping out occasionally to blast each other with shotguns ... In fact, this is that rarest of political treasures – a policy that has true cross-party support.

It finishes:

> Neither of us believes in policy-making simply to secure headlines. This is a comprehensive, carefully worked out and coherent plan to improve the food in our schools and ensure that children eat healthily. Long after the current political spats are forgotten and our own political careers have ended, this policy will be helping create a generation of young people who are healthier, happier and doing better in their studies. There is much that we are proud of in our coalition work at the education department. We are certainly both passionate advocates of this policy and, working together, we are determined to ensure its successful delivery.

THURSDAY 15 MAY

We've now started a second survey of all local authorities to see what their updated figures are on the readiness of schools for free school meals. The number of red-rated schools has dropped by a third. I've made clear to officials that we will need to have a list of those 500–600 schools, and will contact them individually. I'm determined that every bloody school will deliver.

Visited Lilian Baylis School in Kennington. One of the children from the pupil council said that she thought I looked like James Bond. My private secretary, Phil, laughed out loud. Rather undiplomatic.

SUNDAY 18 MAY

Woke at 9.30 a.m. Another absolutely beautiful spring day, with clear skies and strong sunshine.

Large number of ducks, and two graceful swans leading their young down the side of the river, followed by a great trail of Japanese tourists, all taking photographs.

A brief late morning conference call with Oliver Letwin. Oliver sounded like he was sitting out in a garden, because I could hear the tweeting of birds.

On knife crime, I said bluntly that Nick wasn't interested in allowing the Tory Party to go off and vote for the mandatory minimum sentencing amendment. I expected Oliver to be very negative, but he wasn't. I said, 'It's too nice a day to disagree.' And he replied, 'I agree with you!' If everybody in the Tory Party was as decent as Oliver, it would be very easy to make coalition work. He will be one of the people I will be genuinely sad not to work with again if our coalition comes to an end in May 2015. He and Ken Clarke are my favourite Tories.

MONDAY 19 MAY

Recess has started! Yippee!

At 10 a.m. went to the weekly government business meeting. Nick looked on good form, and had soaked up some of the weekend's sun.

Somewhat to my surprise, we're having a Cabinet tomorrow. I assume that this is because the PM is getting nervous about the 'zombie parliament' stuff.

Went home at the spectacularly early time of 9.15 p.m.

Got a sensitive DfE paper this evening about the situation in Birmingham. Ofsted is inspecting around twenty-one schools which seem to have been 'taken over' by Muslim groups who are pushing an extreme Muslim approach to education. Apparently the Chief Inspector is going to be very critical of a number of the academy schools. It also looks as if he's going to criticise the oversight of the academies and the curriculum freedoms, which have been abused. All of this is dynamite for the Secretary of State, and can only worsen the relationship with Ofsted. Bizarrely, No. 10 is proposing that we should publish our new restrictions on madrassas on the very same day that the Ofsted reports are released. This would be a smokescreen.

Interestingly, there's also a paragraph indicating that Michael Gove proposes to try to bypass the normal Home Affairs Committee clearance of the madrassa document, so that he can insert his own wording into it. He's asked for the document to be completed late so that it can bypass cross-government clearance. No doubt the official who put that into a formal note, circulated to ministers including me, is going to be in trouble!

TUESDAY 20 MAY

An interesting observation from the veteran pollster Peter Kellner. He notes that no party has ever won a general election when it has been behind on two separate polling questions – who would make the best Prime Minister, and which party would be best for the economy. I can't see Ed Miliband winning the next general election given he lags on both.

Cabinet. 9.30 a.m. The Queen's Speech is apparently supposed to be written on sheep's hide, but Nick said yesterday that he's discovered they're now using fake sheepskin – the whole thing has been 'modernised'.

Cameron started with his normal introduction about how busy Parliament is, and how much the Queen's Speech is bursting with new legislation. I waited for the phrase that we've all become used to, and sure enough eventually it came: 'Nobody can possibly say that this is a "zombie parliament".' Don Foster and Steve Lotinga, sitting at the side of the Cabinet Room with their backs to the Downing Street garden, laughed to each other.

Michael Gove suggested that we were being unreasonable in asking the Queen to read out 'language which is beneath her dignity' – including a particularly strangulated line about phasing out single-use plastic bags! It's going to be amended.

WEDNESDAY 21 MAY

In my box today a 'Confidential Briefing Note on the Economy for the PM/ DPM'. Opened it with great interest, to read:

Asda semi-skimmed milk – 49p.

800-gram Hovis medium wholemeal loaf – £1.35p.

Heinz baked beans – 68p.

Mars bar – 54p.

The average price of a pint of lager in London is given as £3.60 and the average price of a pint of lager in Sheffield as £2.70.

Finally, in case the Prime Minister or Deputy Prime Minister are quizzed on pop trivia, they are told that this week's No. 1 single is 'I will never let you down' by the Kosovo-born British singer-songwriter Rita Ora. They are also told about the top five films of the week – *Bad Neighbours*, *The Amazing Spiderman 2*, *The Other Woman*, *Rio 2*, and *Pompeii* – just in case they are caught out with the latest cinema news! It must be a pain being a Prime Minister or Deputy Prime Minister in the modern media age, where they are looking to catch you out.

THURSDAY 22 MAY

An 8 a.m. conference call with one of the senior officials in the DfE. Wanted to speak to him about the current Ofsted inspection of schools in Birmingham. The results are due to be announced on 5 June. Michael Gove is trying to put out one of the products of the Extremism Task Force – a voluntary code of practice for supplementary schools. No. 10 were originally pressing for both of these announcements to be made on the same day, but I pushed back, saying it is ridiculous to put out something about extremism on the same day that we are putting out something about the way in which Muslim schools may be behaving in terms of their culture and practices. We really must not muddle up issues of extremism/terrorism with the religious culture of Muslim schools.

Today is Election Day. Our poll ratings are between 6 and 12 per cent, and we could be heading for disaster. Got a text from Norman Lamb. Norman asked whether I had heard a rumour about backbench MPs signing a letter of no confidence in Nick. There is apparently a suggestion of fourteen names.

I texted Jonny Oates. Rather worryingly, he replied, 'What letter?' He said that he had not heard of a letter, but that he had been informed by our Chief Whip, Don Foster, that low-grade barmy MPs like John Pugh and David Ward were trying to stir things up. I would be amazed if more than five or six MPs would sign.

FRIDAY 23 MAY

Election results bad, though not a complete disaster, and the Tories and Labour are not doing particularly well either. The story is all about UKIP success.

SATURDAY 24 MAY

My red box arrived at 11 a.m. It was brought by Royal Mail – by the elderly gentleman who uses a walking stick! He always looks absolutely knackered. It was raining, and I warned him to be careful not to slip on the path. Closed the door and about three seconds later I heard a loud cry and a bang. Rushed outside to find him near the gate, on his backside, with his walking stick half in the hedge.

Read the latest draft of the Queen's Speech and noticed the Tories had inserted a line saying 'An updated charter for the Office for Budget Responsibility will be brought forward to ensure that future governments spend taxpayers' money responsibly and restore the public finances to surplus'. We have pushed back. Goodness knows why Danny and Nick ever agreed to this idea of an updated charter – it is intended to be a trap for the Labour Party, but could easily also be a trap for us.

Election results now in. We have lost over 300 councillors – of 780 seats fought. The Tories have lost a couple of hundred, Labour have gained 200 or 300, and UKIP have gained about 160. A number of the newspapers have led on a 'crisis for Ed Miliband' story.

SUNDAY 25 MAY

The attempted coup against Nick Clegg begins.

The Sunday newspapers report a petition for Nick to stand down, being organised by Sandra Gidley, a complete nonentity who is the ex-MP for Romsey. She appears to have been joined by two idiot MPs – that left-wing numbskull John Pugh, who has made some pompous comments in the media suggesting that we should look at our leader and have a discussion of 'strategy'. I assume that means that he wants a change of leader but hasn't actually got the support to trigger it. He has been joined by the awful John Hemmings. Then there are two parliamentary candidates who are such nonentities that I can't even remember their names but who are standing in Winchester and Dorset West.

Spoke to Oliver on the Queen's Speech. The Tories aren't prepared to support the legislation to disqualify corrupt directors unless we massively water down our proposals to protect low-paid employees on stuff like zero-hours contracts! It's pretty extraordinary that the Tories see a direct read-across between action to protect employees from exploitation, and action to stop corrupt directors from practising! What on the earth does that say about the Tory priorities that they think these two things are equivalent or tradable?

An email from Nick Clegg:

> I'm not too downcast but I am pretty angered about the way the petitioners just repeat the personal vilification of me by the *Daily Mail* et al. I always knew that being leader in the first coalition was going to lead to vile attacks from the outraged left and right – but to see them repeated by fellow Lib Dems is awful. I fear we will be in full-blown leadership crisis territory tomorrow after the Euro results.

As the evening went on, the results came in from the European elections – catastrophic! Just before we were going to bed, the results from the south-east of England came through, and we had the only Lib Dem win of the night – by Catherine Bearder. Even she only sneaked in by a few thousand votes.

Norman Lamb texted me: 'Our complacent uncritical pro-EU position has turned so many of our supporters away. This is a very dangerous week now. Suspect the bandwagon could easily gather momentum!'

I said to Norman that I shared his concern and we had certainly tested to destruction the idea that we should promote our pro-European views in European elections. The truth is that every European election I can remember has been fought by the party on non-European issues, in order to try to win votes, and then once the election is out of the way our Euro

MPs have always been incredibly critical that the leadership has 'ducked out of' the need to take our pro-European views to the electorate. Well, our MEPs have finally got the campaign they always wanted, and now they have got the results that we always feared.

MONDAY 26 MAY

Disaster. We have lost eleven out of our twelve MEPs. Looking on the bright side, at least the meetings of the Lib Dem parliamentary party in Europe are now going to be relatively short. Catherine Bearder will be leader, deputy leader, chair, secretary and minute taker.

Our Euro MPs have plenty of time today to reflect on the old dictum of Oscar Wilde: 'There are two tragedies in life – one is not getting what you want and the other is getting what you want; the latter is the real tragedy.'

Nick called at 10.45 a.m. He sounded tired but not as down as I had feared. He said he had gone through various 'emotional waves' overnight, and had contemplated resigning. But he said he had always known that it was going to be difficult leading the party through five years of coalition government during a time of austerity, and he didn't think it would be the right thing for the party or for the country if he threw in the towel now.

He said he didn't relish the idea of spending another year leading the party, with all of the press vilification, but he felt that it was the right thing to do. He said that we now needed to consider whether there was any way in which we should respond to the message of the European election campaign – and said that Paddy was now saying that we should change our position and go for a referendum on membership of the EU. I said that would look like panic, and we would upset those people in the party who were saying that although we lost, at least we had gone down fighting for a cause we believed in.

I said much more of an issue is whether we should be tacking towards the Tory position on pressing for renegotiation of Britain's position in the early part of the next parliament. This is where the centre of gravity of the British people actually is. In addition, tacking closer to Cameron's position might well serve eventually to split the Tory Party, since a large part of the Tory Party doesn't simply want to renegotiate our membership of the European Union – they want to leave the EU altogether.

Vince Cable, who is currently in China on a trade visit, has put out a statement – rather delayed – saying, 'These were exceptionally disappointing results for the party. Nick did a bold thing in standing up to the Eurosceptic wave ... there is no leadership issue ... now is not the time for infighting and introspection.' A good, supportive, unqualified comment from Vince.

Nick has also gone on the media, looking a bit sad and knackered but killing the idea that he's going to give up. If we can last out the next few days then I think that this attempted coup is going to fail.

Texted Nick to say that I thought his interview was good and struck just the right note. He replied: 'Thanks – it's such a long hard road back!'

TUESDAY 27 MAY

Unhelpfully, there is a poll in *The Guardian* which shows us way behind in a number of our key seats – namely Redcar, Sheffield Hallam, Wells and Cambridge. Intriguingly, the poll has been commissioned by a private individual and leaked to the newspaper, and it shows that Lib Dem chances in these seats would be better (though only slightly better) if Vince was leader. My first thought was: 'This is Lord Oakeshott at work.' Matthew was a former special adviser to Roy Jenkins in the 1970s and he hates the coalition. He has become a close friend of Vince – the 'political wing' of the Business Secretary. The truth about Vince is that he's ambitious but not naturally a plotter. He would be pleased if Nick fell in front of a bus, but he's not the kind of person to do the shoving.

Attended a breakfast meeting with Nick, Danny and political advisers. The general view was that the poll must have come from Oakeshott and that it could be a bit of a self-inflicted wound. It must have cost £20,000, and given that people now know that it's a Lib Dem member who has done it, it will be easy for us to say if this £20,000 had only been spent on campaigning, it might have been possible to save some councillors or an MEP. There is a view that we should go to the polling company – ICM – and insist that they reveal the funder of the poll.

Lots of media comment on how awful Nick looked on TV last night. Tired and funereal. Nick said, 'Maybe I rather overdid it, and I need to look a bit more cheerful today – though I don't want to overcompensate in the other direction like some grinning Gordon Brown character.'

I pointed out to Nick that Lembit Öpik is now calling for his head. 'This is great news – Lembit has been on the wrong side of every single leadership contest in living memory.'

Later, had a text from Kiran Stacey of the *FT*. Kiran said that the putsch seemed a bit half-baked. I said that this was right – 'more a night of the blunt knives than the long knives'. I said that it also helps a coup if you have a leader in waiting and an alternative strategy in waiting. Kiran texted back: 'The leader in waiting is in China.'

Meanwhile, we are under pressure to agree the Queen's Speech, which has to be printed on vellum and left to dry for at least a week – which gives us a deadline of noon tomorrow. The whole thing is completely ludicrous in a modern democracy, and all of our attempts to reach agreement on sensitive issues of policy are being determined by the timeline of how long it takes the ink to dry.

The Tories had inserted a line saying that we would introduce an updated charter for the Office for Budget Responsibility which would help ensure that we 'restore the public finances to surplus'. Danny supports this and Nick is relaxed. I said this is very significant politically, and it implies that George Osborne is trying to evolve our fiscal mandate away from simply aiming for a cyclically adjusted current budget balance, and towards aiming for a surplus. I don't want us to move any further to the right on this.

Had a long discussion on it with Nick and advisers. Eventually Nick said that he took my point.

Meanwhile, it turns out that Vince has made a statement from China strongly condemning Matthew Oakeshott, who has been revealed as the source of the ICM poll in today's *Guardian*.

WEDNESDAY 28 MAY

The media is all about Lord Oakeshott, and his 'botched coup'. Good that this has failed but it's keeping us on the front pages, when the focus could equally be on Labour and the Tories, who didn't do well either.

Went over to the DfE at 8 a.m. and did a series of six or seven calls with the chief executives of local authorities, where we are worried about their capacity to deliver the free school meals policy. Encouragingly, most of them reported good progress.

In the car on the way down to Yeovil I ended up with numerous calls from the Deputy Prime Minister's office about the state of negotiations on the Queen's Speech and on the issue of knife crime. Nick had a telephone call with Cameron at noon, and apparently spelt out that he simply wasn't interested in a compromise. He seems to have agreed with Cameron that the Tory front bench can abstain. In exchange for this, Nick has put his foot down – and the Queen's Speech will contain the pledges on zero-carbon homes and zero-hours contracts, and the 'dodgy directors' legislation.

Lord Oakeshott has now resigned from the Liberal Democrats. Vince dismissively attacked Matthew from his berth in China last night, and it sounds like this was the final straw. Oakeshott has issued an absolutely vicious statement attacking Nick – saying that he's leading a party without any principles and without any values, but also landing Vince in it by saying that he told him about the seat polling. It sounds like the two of them have fallen out in a pretty serious way – probably with Vince trying to cover his tracks a bit.

Ming Campbell was magnificent on *The World at One*: 'Lord Oakeshott has conceived of himself as something of a kingmaker, and has gone beyond his competencies in the matter.' A wonderful Ming-ism.

Got to Yeovil to open a new post office in Stiby Road, when Oliver Letwin phoned, wanting to finalise the Queen's Speech. I said jokingly: 'I have to be quick, I'm doing something really important – opening the new Westfield Post Office.' Oliver didn't sound amused.

I was ushered by the manager into a rather grotty back room, two metres by two metres. There, Oliver and I negotiated the remaining issues in the Queen's Speech. Oliver said that the Chancellor was still keen to put some wording in about running budget surpluses. I said that we couldn't accept this.

Had to dash to South Petherton to have my physiotherapy at the hospital. On the way, Oliver phoned back and said that there was a line in the Autumn Statement about running budget surpluses in times of economic prosperity, and what Osborne is pushing for is that we should simply lift this line and put it into the Queen's Speech. He was sounding unusually desperate.

I said that we absolutely couldn't agree to that and it was taking something out of context to promote what would be a significant new policy.

I said that if we wanted something in there we should just say we were going to adhere to the existing fiscal mandate.

Oliver ummed and ahhed, hummed and hawed and kept on pushing and he said that he could not understand why I wasn't willing to accept the wording from the Autumn Statement, as all they were looking to do was restate and 'clarify' existing policy. Oliver's problem is that he is a really terrible liar – he is far too honest to carry it off credibly.

I said the new words would not 'clarify'. At best, they would confuse. At worst, they would change the entire fiscal strategy of the government. I could tell that Oliver was squirming badly, and he'd obviously been told by Osborne to get this line in at all costs. I'm prepared to bet that the Tories want to brief this out aggressively as the centrepiece of the Queen's Speech – but I'm not falling for it.

In the end, Oliver even said that he was willing to concede some extra Lib Dem policies into the Queen's Speech if I would give way on this supposedly unimportant wording. That made it even more obvious they were trying to pull a fast one!

After three calls, Oliver phoned back to say that he had given up and that the Tories would rather just delete the wording altogether and simply say that we would run responsible economic finances in order to get value for money for the taxpayer, or some such rubbish. He accepted defeat with good grace.

MONDAY 2 JUNE

I have a feeling the Lib Dem parliamentary party meeting on Wednesday, called to discuss the election results and party leadership issues, is going to be particularly unproductive. There is going to be a lot of panic in the air from some MPs and everybody is going to have their magic-wand solutions to our electoral position.

We've delivered a huge number of our manifesto pledges, including the £10,000 allowance and the pupil premium. The economy is recovering and the deficit is closing. Our problems in my view are much more about the fact that third parties in coalitions find it difficult to get the credit for things that are going right, and tend to be eclipsed by their bigger coalition partner. Also a lot of the people who have supported the Lib Dems in the past have done so as a protest vote or because they have seen us as vaguely on the left in politics, whereas we are certainly no longer a protest vote and we've been in coalition with a most decidedly right-wing party.

So in large part our problem is simply a consequence of having gone into coalition in May 2010. We made our bed and now we're having to lie in it. Some Lib Dem MPs were incredibly naïve in May 2010, cheering wildly when we agreed the coalition deal. But I remember Ming Campbell's muttered words as everyone cheered: 'Today they are ringing the bells. Tomorrow they'll be wringing their hands.' I knew exactly what he meant.

TUESDAY 3 JUNE

At 8.15 a.m. over to Dover House for a meeting in Nick's office with Jonny Oates, Danny Alexander and Steve Lotinga. We spent most of the time discussing fiscal policy, where apparently Danny and Nick had a meeting yesterday which didn't go well. Danny is still pressing for a change in the fiscal rules so that we aim for a fully balanced budget – with no borrowing for investment purposes. Nick knows that Vince won't buy that, and also that I don't think it is very sensible.

WEDNESDAY 4 JUNE

The State Opening of Parliament and the Queen's Speech.

Cameron is furious because this crucial day is overshadowed by a vicious public row between Theresa May and Michael Gove over who is responsible for the problems of extremism in Birmingham schools.

In the evening, we had an important meeting of the Lib Dem parliamentary party in the Boothroyd Room. A chance to clear the air over the leadership issue, and for any MPs who want Nick out to speak up.

It was a big anti-climax – thank goodness. Virtually every MP spoke, and most were incredibly supportive of Nick. Even the ringleader of the mutiny, John Pugh, was pretty useless – he made a nervous and lonely little speech, where he said how important it was for him to have stimulated a leadership debate and what a useful service he had provided for us all. Turbo-charged balls!

Quite a variety of contributions from our MPs – Jo Swinson, Bob Russell and Norman Lamb were particularly supportive and effective.

David Ward said that he did not want a change of leader and that it would be a waste to get rid of Nick as he had 'so much to learn from his mistakes'. Somewhat back-handed support.

Jenny Willott said she was passing on a message from her granny that Nick should stay.

The meeting ended with a passionate summing up from Nick, and a prolonged round of 'table thumping' – the way MPs signal their support.

The leadership issue is now settled for the parliament, and the coup attempt is dead.

When we left the meeting after some two hours, there weren't even any journalists outside – they are far more interested in the Gove/May rows.

THURSDAY 5 JUNE

A one-hour catch-up on free school meals – the number of red-rated schools has fallen from 900 to 200.

Went round to Michael Gove's office to have a chat about the Birmingham schools issue. On his table was a large plate of cakes: 'Is this a peace offering from Theresa May?' I said. No response. It's clearly serious!

The row with Theresa May has been running for a couple of days. It turns out that Michael was at a *Times* lunch when he started slagging off the Home Office and accusing them of not doing enough to stamp out low-level extremism. The Home Office have hit back hard by saying that the problems in Birmingham schools are the responsibility of the DfE.

I had a brief chat with Michael about some of the issues coming out of the Birmingham inspection reports – I noted that the debate was bound to lead on to issues such as the oversight of academies and whether there should be a minimum curriculum entitlement and whether unqualified teachers should be allowed in state-funded schools. I said that it might be better to acknowledge that the two parties would have different views.

Michael was all very collegiate but he's delivering a speech on Saturday which seeks to take all the credit for the pupil premium policy, as well as attempting to provoke a row by suggesting that the government may legislate to dock the child benefit of families where the child is truanting. I am sure

Michael is simply trying to create rows to try to distract attention from his problems with Theresa May and the issues around Birmingham schools.

FRIDAY 6 JUNE

Had a chat with Sir Michael Wilshaw about Birmingham. He confirmed that he doesn't believe that any of the schools have been deliberately pursuing an extremist agenda. However, he thinks that the agendas that they have been pursuing make the pupils more vulnerable to extremism. He thinks that local authorities should have full responsibility for oversight of governance in all schools, both local authority and academy. He thinks that there is a risk that academy oversight by the DfE is not strong enough, and believes that all children should have access to a broad and balanced curriculum. He says that academies are at greater risk because of their curriculum freedoms. He says that the Ofsted inspection exemption for outstanding schools might need to end, in case there are governance and other issues going on that are not visible in the attainment scores.

A lot of this is going to be extremely unwelcome to Michael Gove.

SATURDAY 7 JUNE

In Yeovil constituency all day. Advice centres in Ilminster and Crewkerne.

In the afternoon, went out canvassing in Yeovil West. There has definitely been a falling off of support for us in our heartland areas. The bottom line is that there are a lot of people on low incomes who do not like us being in coalition with the Conservatives.

In the evening, had to spend my time at Chard Rugby Club at a dinner for the old boys of a local school. I normally do all I can to avoid social commitments on Saturday evenings. But I couldn't get out of this, because they asked me a year in advance and said that they would be prepared to pick any weekend that was convenient! The dinner was absolutely vile. No starter. A bit of cold meat and a few hot potatoes, and some typically British – i.e. hopelessly dull and undressed – salad. God knows how anywhere in Britain gets away with serving this rubbish in the twenty-first century.

The May/Gove row over extremism has really blown up today, as the Prime Minister has received a report from Sir Jeremy Heywood, and he has responded by forcing Michael Gove to apologise, including to one of the staff in the Home Office whom he was very critical of. In addition, Theresa May's key adviser has been forced to resign. The May/Gove row is leading on all the news programmes and distracting from the Tory narrative after both the Queen's Speech and their by-election win in Newark. The whole thing does quite a lot of damage to both Michael and Theresa. Michael in particular looks accident prone and has been picking unnecessary fights, which I suspect the Prime Minister is irritated about. At one stage it looked impossible that Michael could ever be reshuffled out of Education, but I wonder whether this is now an outside possibility.

Got a note from Nick's office saying that on Monday there is going to be a meeting chaired by the Prime Minister to discuss the Birmingham schools issue.

I suddenly realised that we still hadn't seen Michael Gove's draft statement, and nor had we actually seen the official letter that Michael Wilshaw is sending to Gove. I sent a stroppy email to my office, copied to the Permanent Secretary, saying it was ridiculous that I hadn't had sight of this yet when it had been in the department's hands since last Thursday.

Late in the day, the Gove proposals came through, though not his actual statement, and also the letter from the Chief Inspector. MG seems to be ignoring the proposals about oversight of local authority and academy schools, and he is also ignoring the proposals about curriculum freedoms. Instead, he is focusing on criticising Birmingham local authority, and proposing some sort of gimmick around no-notice inspections of schools – which is a very old chestnut. He is also suggesting that schools should teach 'British values'.

SUNDAY 8 JUNE

I spoke to Sally Morgan from a petrol station on the M4 as I made my way back into London. Sally said that No. 10 and Michael were both pushing the no-notice inspections issue – though she regards it as a 'red herring'. She said that Michael was very resistant to making any moves on the curriculum, even though Ofsted thought this was necessary and even though there is evidence that schools were pushing Islamic studies and dropping things like music. She said she thought there was a need for more geographical oversight, but this didn't meet Michael Gove's prejudices in relation to the academies programme. Sally said that she really thought that somebody at a local level ought to be able to join up the dots, so that they could see what was going on in all schools in the area and not just local authority schools or academies. She said the problem was that for academies there was no supervision between the DfE and individual schools, and that wasn't good enough.

MONDAY 9 JUNE

Met this morning in the Cabinet Room to discuss the Gove statement on Birmingham schools. I had been placed immediately opposite the Prime Minister, in the seat normally occupied by Nick Clegg. This was a little bit baffling. On my right was Michael Gove and on his right was Theresa May, and on my left were Eric Pickles and Baroness Warsi. I then realised that I had been placed in that position to act as some kind of buffer between the warring factions in the Conservative Party. The truth is Michael has a fairly extreme position on extremism, and his view isn't shared by either Pickles or May. The atmosphere was a little tense, particularly after a weekend dominated by the Gove/May row.

The Prime Minister came in ten minutes late, and Nick sat on his left. Osborne was last in and he sat on Nick's left. The meeting started with an explanation from Michael Gove of what was going to be in his statement. Cameron said, 'If I've got any comments to make, it's that your statement is rather long, Michael. You have got to remember that Bercow really is a little shit, and he quite often cuts people off if the statement is too long.'

After Michael had spoken, Nick then laid in: 'It's completely unacceptable that we haven't have been consulted properly on this. My office and David Laws only had the papers on this last night, and that is no way to run a coalition.'

The PM mumbled something about the papers having been circulated on Friday night – it's quite clear that the whole thing has been kept away from us until the last minute. Nick then set out his concerns on the substance of the statement, and I followed up by setting out mine – pointing to the gap between the Ofsted recommendations and what Michael Gove is proposing to say. I said the truth was that while we were all in favour of autonomous schools, sometimes autonomy got used for bad things, and there was evidence of abuse of curriculum freedoms and a lack of local oversight of schools. As I spoke, Osborne passed a note down to Cameron, which Nick saw as it went past: 'David – we need to be careful – we really don't want a coalition division on this today.'

Cameron said, 'Look, a lot of those are very good points, but we've really got to avoid coalition division today. Labour just hate free schools, academies, autonomy etc. etc. and they will see this as an opportunity to attack that. We don't want a big row about autonomy today which puts the coalition parties on different sides.'

The Prime Minister than handed over to Baroness Warsi, who ranted at Michael Gove for about ten minutes and said how damaging his views were on extremism and how polarising they were for ethnic minority communities. Eric Pickles repeated this. I could see the Prime Minister getting a bit fed up with the Warsi critique. Theresa May came in last and made a few sensible, practical points, without putting the knife into Michael any further. She then said there were 'other issues needing addressing'. Cameron somewhat impatiently said, 'Yes, but we've got to finish now, as Michael's got a statement to give. Presumably some of you ministers are quite capable of meeting up by yourselves and resolving these things without having me in the room. I really would have thought that government could run so that major departments talk to each other, rather than relying upon me to broker everything.'

Clearly, he is pretty impatient with the fallout between his own ministers.

TUESDAY 10 JUNE

The media is dominated by follow-up from yesterday's statements on Birmingham. There is also a row going on between Michael Gove and Sir Michael Wilshaw. Sir Michael gave an interview to *Newsnight* last night, saying that he had planned to have no-notice inspections shortly after he was appointed in 2012, but these had been vetoed by Michael Gove. Embarrassing for MG.

Cabinet met in the afternoon. Outside it was sunny and warm, and virtually everybody took their jackets off and there was quite a relaxed atmosphere. The Royal Marine Band was still practising on Horse Guards, and some militaristic tunes came floating in through the windows.

Francis Maude was due to give a presentation about government efficiency savings. In front of us all was a small booklet from Francis's department, entitled 'Efficiency and Reform Group 2013/14 Savings'. When you opened the front page you were suddenly hit by a massive full-page photograph of Francis, smiling, in a casual shirt – it looks like something out of a Saga catalogue. When I had come into the Cabinet, I had found Lord Hill chuckling over the photograph and needling Francis Maude as a bit of an egomaniac.

As soon as Francis started his presentation, everyone opened the first page of his booklet and was faced with the enormous Maude photo. George Osborne instantly burst out laughing. He then nudged Theresa May, pointing to the photograph, and she laughed loudly too. Then, as other ministers opened their booklets, there was a steady ripple of laughter around the whole of the rest of the Cabinet table, which completely disrupted the first minute of Francis's presentation. At one point, George even intervened to ask Francis whether he thought the photograph was large enough! In short, nobody listened at all.

One person who seemed to be particularly enjoying Francis's discomfort was the head of the Home Civil Service, Sir Bob Kerslake, an old enemy of Francis.

At the end of the meeting, Cameron led a discussion on foreign affairs – about the G7 heads of government meeting. On these occasions Cameron comes over well, and the body language between him and Nick is still remarkably positive after over four years of coalition. They have their disagreements, but one detects a mutual respect, and there is something plausible about Cameron as a Prime Minister, which I think is going to be rather difficult for Ed Miliband at the next general election. Ed is somehow weird, left-wing and unconvincing, yet Cameron is, in spite of his Old Etonianism, or perhaps even because of it, somebody who seems to fit rather naturally into the role of Prime Minister. As I listened to him summarising his talks with Merkel, I couldn't help feeling that he will end up being the country's next Prime Minister – he doesn't feel like the sort of PM who is only going to get one term.

Meanwhile, the clash between the DfE and Ofsted continues. The DfE – supported by that idiot Dom Cummings, who has spoken to *Newsnight* – are maintaining that Michael Gove has all along believed in unannounced inspections, and he has never wobbled and they are arguing that the Chief Inspector did wobble and changed his mind.

The Chief Inspector has put out a statement saying he favoured no-notice inspections but decided to go back on it after representations from 'head teacher groups and others'. I have no doubt that the 'others' that he has got in mind include Michael Gove – who made a statement at the NAHT head teachers' conference in spring 2012 which basically said that he believed there was an argument for short notice before school inspections but not for no-notice inspections. This is all being sold by the media as Sir Michael backing off and changing his position.

However, before I went to bed, I saw *Newsnight*, which suggests that Sir Michael has restated his original position on whether it was him or Michael Gove who aborted the no-notice inspections. Michael Wilshaw's statement today was spun by the DfE as Wilshaw admitting he changed his own mind on no-notice inspections. But when *Newsnight* phoned Ofsted to confirm this, they denied it, saying that basically it was Michael Gove who vetoed the no-notice inspections, and claiming that they agreed the earlier statement simply because they think it is petty and pathetic to have a squabble between the DfE and Ofsted. All a bit of a mess and Michael Wilshaw must be seething tonight.

WEDNESDAY 11 JUNE

At 8.30 a.m. had a preparation session for forty-five minutes with the DfE team before my appearance at the Education Select Committee. The Select Committee was really pretty useless – they couldn't hit a barn door three yards away. Most MPs just read the questions written for them by the clerks.

At 2 p.m. returned to the Cabinet Office for a meeting with Douglas Alexander. This had been fixed after Alan Milburn suggested that the two of us should get together. I like and respect Douglas Alexander, and I think he would be a key figure in any Lib Dem–Labour negotiations after the next general election. I have to say, he looked a bit nervous and uncomfortable when he turned up. I said that the point of the meeting was to have a clearing of the air and to make Labour understand that our decision to go into co-alition with the Tories in 2010 was just about the parliamentary arithmetic, and not any values-based or policy-based judgement. We discussed that on issues such as constitutional reform and Europe, a Lib Dem–Labour administration would be on a sounder footing for a policy agreement, and he asked me what the issues would be which would underpin a Tory–Lib Dem administration. I said that really the important thing was continuity of approach about finishing off deficit reduction.

At 8 p.m. went to Roux restaurant opposite the Treasury and had dinner with Nick Robinson, the BBC's political editor. I like Nick, and he is very sharp-edged and clever. Apparently the general view amongst the Miliband crowd is that the 'Balls-Coopers', as apparently the Milibandites refer to them, are waiting for Ed Miliband to lose the next election, when Nick expects a leadership election between Yvette Cooper, Chuka Umunna and Andy Burnham. Hardly inspiring! Labour is really screwed, and their best prospect is probably a hung parliament and getting some Lib Dems involved to strengthen their frontbench team.

THURSDAY 12 JUNE

Travelled down to Carshalton for an education trip with Nick and Tom Brake, the local Lib Dem MP. Answered some questions from sixth form students. Nick was probably expecting the first question to be on tuition fees, whereas they asked: 'If you were an animal, which animal would you want to be?' With the TV cameras recording, Nick didn't seem to be able to think of anything, and turned to me. I said, 'Labrador' – the first thing that came into my mind. Explained myself by saying that Labradors get patted a lot, and that there weren't any other animals that ate them. The students looked satisfied, though perhaps underwhelmed.

SATURDAY 14 JUNE

It ought to be a day of rest and relaxation but instead I have to spend the whole day at a meeting of the Federal Policy Committee to consider the pre-manifesto. A number of other MPs and peers who should have been there were absent, and this is the usual problem that when you hold these key meetings on weekends, the people who turn up are the more extreme party activists, whereas the 'sane voices' – or allegedly sane voices – do not turn up at all. Unimpressively, Tim Farron, president of the party, hasn't bothered to attend. I know he doesn't like doing things at the weekend, but if he wants to be leader one day, he is going to have to do better than this. Nick recently had lunch with Ken Clarke, who apparently said of Farron: 'I met your president recently, Nick. I must say that he is the least remarkable senior politician I can ever remember.' Very true. Tim is a pleasant, populist lightweight, with deeply offensive and illiberal views on issues such as gay marriage – totally unsuitable to lead a liberal party worthy of the name.

WEDNESDAY 18 JUNE

At 9 a.m. met with Jeremy Heywood. He asked for an update on my priorities, and I mentioned entry and exit checks. We discussed a major security data issue, which Nick mentioned to me last week. I only understand this in outline, but basically there has been some legal challenge which means that the existing way in which the security services collect data is now potentially illegal. Apparently the only way we can resolve this is to put potentially controversial legislation through Parliament.

At 3.45 p.m. had a private meeting with Tim Colbourne. He explained the problems with the security services and the collection of data. It is all very tricky, though I said that one possibility was to legislate to preserve the existing powers, with time-limited legislation which would expire in a year's time, when we could debate and discuss the whole thing properly.

At 4 p.m. went up to see Nick and Danny. Jonny Oates was the only other person present and Nick wanted to discuss the security services issue. He said he had concluded that it was an absolute nightmare and we were on a hiding to nothing. He said he would never persuade the party of some of what the security services and the PM wanted to do, and the best thing might be to just stand back and let Labour and the Tories legislate, while remaining on the side-lines. Both Danny and I said that we were extremely worried about this, and that this was not a risk-free solution. Our voters will expect us to make sure that there are proper security arrangements in place to monitor dangerous people, so that there are not terrorist attacks on the country. This is going to be a really thorny issue where the balance between individual freedoms and protection of personal space collides with the desire of the security services to monitor literally everything that is going on in the country so that they can prevent terrorist attacks. We agreed to look at renewing the existing position in law and buying time for a proper review.

In my box tonight was a note from Danny's office about the Apache helicopter contract. Looks like Philip Hammond wants to just buy off the shelf from the USA, claiming that this could save £500 million – a number that seems to be picked out of the air. We have to make sure that Agusta Westland has a proper opportunity to bid on this contract rather than it just being handed on a plate to the Americans. A very big constituency issue for me.

THURSDAY 19 JUNE

Up at 5.15 a.m. and in by 6.45 a.m.

At 8.15 a.m. had a meeting with Jonny Oates, Julian Huppert MP and Norman Baker. Tim Colbourne was also present. The subject: the growing panic over security services data access. There are two separate and painful issues which could require emergency legislation before the summer recess. One issue is about data retention, where an EU legal case has thrown into doubt our ability to ask IT companies to retain sensitive data for up to twelve months for use by the police and potentially the security services. The security services are apparently saying that if they cannot retain this data then it would significantly impede their ability to bring cases to trial, including serious security cases, paedophiles etc. However, this is a sensitive civil liberties issue and it could be very difficult to get through the party – though the general view amongst us was that the data retention issue was the less controversial of the two. The much trickier issue relates to the associated but distinct issue about the RIPA (Regulation of Investigatory Powers) legislation. Apparently the security services have been collecting data, on request, from companies such as Google, Microsoft etc. etc., which is particularly useful in stopping terrorist attacks against the UK. But some of the companies are now playing difficult, and some of them are not really allowed to share data anyway given the US laws which allow the data to be looked at by the US security services but not passed to overseas jurisdictions. The security services are discovering that all of the companies are now opting out of providing this data, and they are in a real panic that this will make it difficult for them to keep an eye on serious terrorists etc. They maintain that they have stopped all sorts of attacks on the UK because of the ability to request this data.

It seems to me that the best thing is for us to pass emergency legislation before the summer recess, which is what the security services want to do, but we should insist the legislation has a sunset clause, so that Parliament has to return to this issue in twelve months' or eighteen months' time, and in the meantime a serious review should be set up, including some people who have credibility in relation to civil liberties issues.

At 9 a.m. I had to go down to the Cabinet Office briefing rooms for my first COBRA meeting. I was one of the last to appear in the room, and a few moments later George Osborne came in and sat next to me. George turned to me and said, 'How are things in the DfE – what is the latest state of the "Education Wars"?'

At that point Cameron came in and sat to George's left. Some very difficult life-and-death decisions. This was a rare glimpse into many of the unenviable decisions that the Prime Minister and senior ministers have to take.

Got home to see the end of England playing Uruguay in the World Cup, while drinking a very cheap bottle of wine from the local petrol station. Just before the end of the game, England let in a second goal, and it now looks as if we are going out of the tournament.

MONDAY 23 JUNE

Up at 5.15 a.m. to work on the manifesto.

Met with the Welsh Lib Dem parliamentarians to hear their manifesto requests. These included Wales having devolved powers over sewerage (!), and wanting a lot more money. There wasn't very much about reform or innovation!

Worked on my red box until around midnight. The excellent Tim Colbourne has sent out a superb email setting out a sensible way forward on the issue of emergency legislation over the data access and security issues. This looked like it would be a political and media car-crash, but Tim and others are doing a brilliant job of coming to a sensible compromise solution.

TUESDAY 24 JUNE

Cabinet. Cameron fed back on the European Council meeting. Humiliatingly, his attempt to block the appointment of Juncker* has now fallen to pieces. Cameron said that the problem is that after the European elections he spoke to Merkel, who apparently said that she was not going to impose Juncker against a minority of other nation states. Apparently she then got back to Germany and the German media went completely nuts, and she reversed her position. Cameron's in a bit of a strop about this and threatening to force a vote at the European summit this weekend, in contrast to the usual low-key approach.

Had an Ofsted meeting with Sir Michael Wilshaw and Michael Gove. Matt Hancock, the Skills Minister, had added an agenda item about the quality of 16–19 education, and Ofsted started with an update on a report they are due to publish shortly. The lady from Ofsted in charge of this area said the report was going to be a terrible indictment of the quality of 16–19 education. Matt bizarrely responded: 'Excellent, excellent, this is all great news. Exactly as I thought myself. I totally agree with you, this is just what I wanted to hear.' Sally Morgan and I glanced across the table at each other, thinking that Matt was completely mad. Ofsted are telling us that the sector that he is responsible for is a complete mess and he is telling us this is great news. Matt is hopelessly, ludicrously ambitious, and I have noticed that his ego is beginning to run away with him.

WEDNESDAY 25 JUNE

Up at 5.15 a.m. Saw Oliver at 8 a.m. and pressed him on whether Iain Duncan Smith is pushing to sort out the 'couple's penalty' in tax credits,

---

*　Cameron vehemently opposed the election of former Prime Minister of Luxembourg Jean-Claude Juncker as President of the European Commission.

which he believes discourages people from marrying, in one of the next fiscal statements. I said I needed to understand whether Iain's pressure to move on the couple's penalty was part of a coordinated Tory position. Oliver thought for a little while and started chortling: 'If you're asking whether George Osborne and Iain have got some sort of coordinated strategy on this, I think it's probably a safe bet to guess that they haven't!' Clearly still no love lost there.

At 10 a.m. I went off to the Corinthia Hotel for the Pupil Premium Awards – to the schools that have used the pupil premium most effectively. An inspirational occasion, and it is exciting to see the impact the policy has had, after all the work we did on this from 2007 onwards. I had to battle hard with Danny and Vince to get this in as a manifesto priority in 2010, and insist on it in the coalition negotiations. Now we are spending £2.5 billion per year on it and it is really giving schools the resources to help disadvantaged pupils. Ofsted is making it a big priority, and therefore schools are really placing a lot more focus on the attainment and life chances of disadvantaged pupils. This is probably the most important piece of policy work that I am ever going to do in my career. Nick Clegg made a speech, saying: 'I would also like to pay tribute to Michael Gove and David Laws, who have worked closely on this policy – if not necessarily on all the other policies in the DfE.' There was a little bit of uncomfortable laughter amongst the audience.

THURSDAY 26 JUNE

Cameron won't be pleased about the newspapers this morning. A lot of coverage of his failed attempt to block Juncker. A particularly scathing article from Cummings in *The Times* entitled 'Cameron's empty Euroscepticism fools no one':

Mr Cameron hoped that the referendum promise would kick the EU issue into next year and prevent him infuriating people now by revealing how little he wants to change. Wrong. People have already concluded he doesn't want to change much. Picking fights over Jean-Claude Juncker won't fool people. He bungled into a referendum promise he never liked that commits him to something he never wanted to do yet doesn't even achieve his aim of persuading people to vote for him ... His MPs do not trust him and may soon set their own red lines ... He rages that his party is making his position untenable ... it is unlikely that we will remove the supremacy of EU law and negotiate a new treaty until we have a prime minister who can articulate inspiring goals in a completely different way to the petulant and hollow Euroscepticism of David Cameron.

Ouch! Cameron now looks a complete fool for thinking that he could block Juncker's appointment, and when the crunch came Angela Merkel has left him high and dry.

At 2 p.m. had a catch-up on free school meals delivery. We are now down to between 100 and 200 schools which are red-rated – not bad out of 16,500 schools. I told officials today that I expect us to get to a position by the end of term – in three weeks' time – where not a single school in England is red-rated. They looked a bit shocked.

FRIDAY 27 JUNE

Today the European Union picked its next President – and to nobody's surprise Jean-Claude Juncker was selected, by twenty-six votes to two, with Cameron supported only by the Hungarians! Cameron has made a fool of himself. If this is the man that Britain is dependent upon to secure our place in the European Union, then God help us. By picking a fight with the European Union and then losing it so decisively, he has reinforced the case for the UK leaving the EU.

TUESDAY 1 JULY

In the afternoon, went with Paul Burstow to visit a school in his south London constituency, where they had originally had problems introducing free school meals. The school is called Cheam Fields Primary School – and they had previously been on *The One Show*, saying that they were not going to be able to implement the policy. Now the local council has paid for a pod kitchen to be installed, and it looks like the whole thing is going to be a great success. It was a really enjoyable visit, with a choir of schoolchildren who sang us a song they have written about how wonderful free school meals are! A lot of the parents stayed on to sample the new meals. They seem to be really good quality, and parents were extremely positive. This is something that is going to affect well over a million young people from September, so it is one of the biggest things we are going to do as a party in government.

WEDNESDAY 2 JULY

Mike Moore has decided that he is going to use his Private Member's Bill to put into law the coalition commitment to spend 0.7 per cent of gross national income on overseas aid. This is a thing that both Cameron and the Lib Dems are supposedly committed to, but Cameron has taken the view recently that he cannot commit his party to it because 'it's even more unpopular on the Conservative back benches than equal marriage'. On this occasion we have really put the Tories on the spot, because there is going to have to be a vote in Parliament.

In the afternoon, had a catch-up to discuss where we are on the 'world-class teachers' package. I am happy with the plan to have a Royal College of Teachers, but the proposals on boosting CPD [continuous professional development] are at present a little bit feeble. Most worrying of all are the details on qualified teacher status, where I fear that the Tories are trying to subvert the whole nature of QTS – by essentially allowing anybody to 'rock up' at a school and start teaching and seek to become a qualified teacher later.

In the evening, we had the first of a series of dinners which Nick Clegg has been persuaded to institute, which I do not suppose will last very long. These are supposed to be quarterly meetings between Lib Dem Cabinet ministers and former Lib Dem leaders and they are going to take place at the National Liberal Club. The idea is to draw more on the 'wisdom' of former party leaders.

I was shown upstairs and onto the terrace of the National Liberal Club, where I expected everyone to be gathered. Instead, the only people there were

Lord Steel, Lord McNally, Lord Bill Rodgers, and Lord Robert Maclennan. The old guard of the party from the 1980s. David Steel said rather pointedly, 'You are the first member of the government to actually turn up – I thought we were in the wrong place!' After a while, various others arrived. Jenny Willott and Jo Swinson. Malcolm Bruce. Then Paddy Ashdown, Danny Alexander, Vince Cable, Nick Clegg and Alistair Carmichael. Charles Kennedy and Ming Campbell were also there so we had all of the leaders of the Lib Dems going right back to the early '80s.

After a drink on the terrace, we were ushered inside to have our meal. There had been something of a cock-up. We were supposed to have a private room, but instead the wise people from the National Liberal Club had decided to give us a massive long table right slap bang in the middle of the main restaurant.

At the end of the meal, we were shown into a side room and we sat around a table to have the chat that Nick Clegg had intended that we should have during the meal.

Shirley Williams said that the European Union no longer had confidence amongst a lot of people in the UK and it really needed to be democratised, with a bigger role for the UK Parliament. She said that we needed to focus on boosting funding for the National Health Service and maybe earmarking all national insurance contributions for the NHS.

Bill Rodgers said that when he had been campaigning in the 1960s and '70s, the main issues that he used to talk about on the doorstep were 'jobs, schools, health and homes'. He said that those were the right issues now, too. He said that Nick should emphasise to the public that we had 'lent our party to the country' in 2010 because of the national interest, and he said that we should now make clear that we are taking our party back.

Bob Maclennan said that we should focus on the NHS and, oddly, on democratising the House of Lords – hardly a priority in the pubs of Yeovil! Ming Campbell said that ten years of coalition with the Tories would be absolutely dreadful, and would be very bad for our party. He questioned whether the party would be willing to accept another five years with the Tories, even if there was a hung parliament in 2015.

Tom McNally said that we needed to focus on bread-and-butter issues. He said that he did not think that Labour could win an overall majority, as they had got an uninspiring leader and message. He said that he saw a small Conservative majority or a hung parliament. He said that there could well be a second Lib Dem–Conservative coalition and he would personally welcome this as it was a good thing to be in government delivering on our policies.

Alistair Carmichael also said that he thought a second coalition government would be a good thing for the Lib Dems and he didn't think we should worry too much about the consequences for our electoral support. Sitting next to him, I noticed Charles Kennedy raise his eyebrows and smile across at me. Charles has a wonderful, conspiratorial smile, which he flashes at you, which somehow says, 'You and I are the only sensible people in the world, having to listen to this twaddle.'

When Charles spoke, he said that he thought it was going to be a very difficult general election and that we would end up fighting 'fifty-seven by-elections', with our usual local 'franchise operation'. Charles said that people viewed Miliband as a geek and that Labour Members of Parliament were pissed off with him. He said that we needed to turn the negatives about Nick into positives. Charles said he thought we were heading for another hung parliament with the Conservatives the largest party.

THURSDAY 3 JULY

The media is full today of stories about the disruption of flights from the UK and US because of intelligence information the Western security services have picked up which means that there are more intensive checks taking place of passengers before they board planes. The exact nature of the threat has not come into the public domain, however, so I cannot write about it.

Started the day with a free school meals delivery catch-up meeting and the figures are looking better all the time. The number of red-rated schools has now fallen to 126. That means that around 99.2 per cent of schools are now on track to deliver. The next couple of weeks are critical.

FRIDAY 4 JULY

There is a story running on Sky News about David Ross, the Tory donor who is on the short list of four to be the next Ofsted chair. The article implies that he is Michael Gove's favoured candidate. He so well fits the 'inappropriate Tory donor' model that I wonder if somebody is throwing his name up in order to attract fire and make it easier for one of the other candidates. There are no women at all on the shortlist, and three of the four men are called 'David'.

MONDAY 7 JULY

At noon, Philip Hammond asked to speak to me on the phone. Highly unusual, as he is such a miserable old bastard that even when you ask to talk to him it is quite difficult to do so. Both Danny and Vince are refusing to agree to Hammond's proposal to simply buy Apache helicopters 'off the shelf' from the US, rather than building them under licence in Yeovil. Hammond left me in no doubt that he thinks that there is no chance of AgustaWestland being able to compete, and he really just wants to go through the motions. I spelt out that Westland must have a serious chance to bid in a real competition. Philip eventually conceded this, but it does not sound like it is going to be all that serious, as he proposes to give them precisely two weeks to put together a complicated bid on a billion-pound-plus contract.

In the evening, had a chat with Polly Mackenzie about the pre-manifesto – she revealed that she had a copy of a letter from George Osborne to the PM, arguing for cutting the winter heating payments out entirely for pensioner households earning above the 40 per cent rate of tax. I suspect that Cameron has completely rejected this, but at least it shows that Osborne is open to this type of thinking and because Polly has taken a photograph of the letter, this means that the document could be leaked during the election campaign if the Tories try to criticise our policy.

TUESDAY 8 JULY

Cabinet at 9.30 a.m. and my God it was a boring meeting. A load of baloney designed to fill an hour and a half, without a discussion of any substance. We had a briefing about the upcoming NATO summit in Wales, which is causing a major security headache and is going to cost £70 million to police. David Jones, the slightly odd Welsh Secretary, said that this was going to be the first time a serving American President had visited Wales – though he dropped in rather oddly that Jimmy Carter often visits the country to play golf!

At 3 p.m. went to the Secretary of State's office for what was billed as an Ofsted 'summit' with the Secretary of State and Sir Michael Wilshaw. Michael was sitting in the comfy chairs to the side of his desk, opposite Sir Michael, who had his press adviser on his right. There were a couple of senior officials, and Tom Shinner and I took the remaining chairs.

Sir Michael is due to go in front of the Select Committee tomorrow to answer questions on the Birmingham schools fiasco. Bizarrely, Michael Gove seemed to be trying to turn the meeting into a prep session for the Select Committee, and he insisted on firing a whole series of very short and sharp questions at the Chief Inspector, as if he were an MP on the committee. Michael Wilshaw looked distinctly uncomfortable as the Education Secretary bombarded him with rapid-fire questions:

'One year ago, Ofsted reported this academy in Birmingham was out-standing. Now you are saying it requires improvement. Why the change? Is Ofsted simply incompetent?'

'What's happened to the incompetent inspectors who wrote this Ofsted report?'

'Is it the case that schools run by Muslim governors are more likely to practise extremism than other schools?' (To this, the Chief Inspector said 'yes', prompting a sharp intake of breath by his press adviser.)

'Are the problems seen in Birmingham schools more likely because they are academies?' (Answer: 'In my view, yes', prompting more, restrained, tension.)

'Do you believe there is a lack of effective oversight by the DfE of academies, and there is a need for stronger local oversight?' (The Chief Inspector's 'yes' provokes a long pause from MG.)

'Do you think Ofsted should extend its role so as to report on curriculum breadth in each school?' ('Yes I do,' prompting an even longer pause.)

I could see Sir Michael's left leg twitching at various points, as the questions got quite aggressive, and it must have been uncomfortable and difficult for him sitting in front of a bunch of officials and the Secretary of State being grilled in this way. I get the impression that there is ever less love lost between these two men.

Michael Gove asked Sir Michael what he would be saying to the committee if asked about the curriculum and whether it should become a fifth Ofsted judgement. Sir Michael said that was exactly his position. Michael Gove looked irritated: 'I completely disagree. The last thing we need is Ofsted inspectors going in and imposing a single view of what the curriculum should look like – we will end up with all schools teaching to a set of Ofsted guidelines.'

Michael Wilshaw became quite impassioned: 'Look, some schools just make excuses over this. I have taken this up with some schools in London. All they were doing in some year groups is teaching English and maths – that's not good enough. That's just a cop-out. I showed at my school that it is quite possible to teach a bit more English and maths, but still have a broad and balanced curriculum, where you teach history, music, the arts etc. I don't think Ofsted inspections spend enough time on this, and we ought to be holding schools to account for the broad and balanced curriculum.'

Michael Gove got quite agitated and fidgety in his chair, and raised his hand, palm out-turned, in a 'stop' gesture: 'No. No. I am not in favour of having any more Ofsted prescription in this area, and I believe in curriculum freedom and letting schools decide for themselves.' It all got rather fractious, and eventually I said that I rather sided with Sir Michael Wilshaw, but it seemed to me that we couldn't proceed on this if there was a fundamental difference between the Secretary of State and the Chief Inspector over what a broad and balanced curriculum actually was – as Ofsted would then be inspecting something that the Secretary of State did not agree with. That would leave schools in a confused position. But I also said that in my view the challenge for the Secretary of State was to explain what a broad and balanced curriculum actually meant in reality, when to Michael Gove it seemed to mean anything that a school wanted to do.

These are two people who increasingly do not see eye to eye – and one wonders how long they can continue to co-exist. All they seem to have left in common is their Christian names!

WEDNESDAY 9 JULY

At noon, went over to the DfE for a series of meetings. Asked how the performance of Sir Michael Wilshaw before the Select Committee had gone today. The officials rolled their eyes. Apparently it had gone extremely badly – as Sir Michael Wilshaw was totally off-message in Gove terms. He said that regional school commissioners were too few and that there should be a middle tier in the schools system and that the obvious middle tier was local authorities (totally contradictory to Michael Gove's views); he suggested that governors should be paid (not government policy) and again said that he wanted the power to inspect academy chains (opposed by Michael Gove). To rub it all in he said he wanted a fifth Ofsted judgement about the curriculum. MG's attempt to steer Sir Michael into 'approved' DfE answers has ended in total calamity! I couldn't help laughing.

I later found out that Sir Michael had had no idea that he was going to be subject to the practice questioning by Michael Gove, and apparently he felt rather bruised by being questioned by the Secretary of State in front of a whole load of officials. Instead of being coaxed by Gove into being more on-message, the meeting had precisely the opposite effect. He also apparently got his office to send a tough email to Gove's office saying he felt it was all totally inappropriate and he was very unhappy about the way he was treated.

Today, over the issue of Birmingham, he raised questions about whether the local authority in Birmingham and the Department for Education were taking their responsibilities seriously in relation to school oversight. And he said, 'There needs to be a middle tier in education and to me that is called the local authority.'

In the afternoon, went over to Portcullis House, where we had scheduled a two-hour open meeting to discuss the manifesto with Lib Dem MPs. If you do not do this type of thing, then everybody complains about too little consultation, but whenever these sessions are scheduled nobody comes. To my enormous relief, only one MP turned up, Alan Reid. Alan raised a number of constituency-related points, one of which was that he wanted our commitment on broadband to be changed from promising '99 per cent broadband coverage' to 'over 99 per cent broadband coverage'. He said that this would make all the difference in his constituency. Hmmmmmmmmmmmmmmmm. Some MPs are very odd.

At 4 p.m. met up with Nick and Danny. Gave Nick an update on free school meal delivery – we now have fewer than eighty schools red-rated, and probably only seventeen of them seriously red-rated. This is very good news. However, the *Daily Mail* is now trying to change the terms of the debate, to put more focus on schools that are only going to deliver cold food, so we have still got quite a communications battle.

Went to a very boring meeting of the Social Justice Committee, where Iain Duncan Smith allowed the chairing to break down altogether and everybody was chipping in left, right and centre, as if it was a discussion in the pub. One of the civil servants who was supposed to be taking notes glanced over at me in an exasperated way and put her pen down.

In the evening, attended an education reform summit at Lancaster House, with lots of education ministers from around the world. The Mayor of London was also turning up and there was little doubt that he would be the star of the show.

I had a good chat with the education ministers of the Netherlands and Spain and an academic from the United States, and I was in the middle of a discussion with them when Boris turned up looking unkempt, with an entourage of people following behind. He was ushered up to our little group. They all seemed to know him!

'Hello Mr Mayor, I am the Spanish Education Minister,' said the lady on my left. I don't know whether it was the background noise, but Boris only half-appeared to be paying attention and replied: 'Marvellous, marvellous, Brussels is one of my favourite places! The food is absolutely fantastic and the architecture too.' The Spanish minister looked baffled, but she clearly is no shrinking violet: 'What's that got to do with Spain? I don't understand why you are talking about Brussels?' Boris replied, 'Yes, Brussels, Brussels, marvellous place, marvellous place, you're very privileged to live there. Must go back there myself sometime.' The Spanish Education Minister persisted: 'Mr Mayor, I am from Spain! Spain! Do you actually know where Spain is?' Boris ruffled his hair and frowned: 'Spain? Spain? Yes, I must have been there recently. Can't remember when it was. Hot place, though, isn't it?'

At that moment, a young female teacher approached me: 'Aren't you David Laws, the Schools Minister? I am such a fan of yours and of the pupil premium. I wonder if I could ask you for a photograph?'

'Of course,' I said, ego appreciably massaged.

'Great. Here's my mobile, then,' she responded. 'Could you take one of me and Boris?'

Behind me, my private secretary chortled, while pretending to have a problem swallowing her wine.

Michael Gove then made a speech of welcome, followed by me. Boris spoke last. He started by saying that he wasn't all that impressed with the wine, and said that there was plenty in the Mayor of London's wine cellar, including 'large quantities of Chateauneuf du Pape, laid down by the previous Mayor'. He then proceeded to insult almost every single borough in London. Referring to Walthamstow: 'What a marvellous place it is, magnificent landscape and architectural qualities, which I notice every time I travel rapidly – rapidly mark you – through the borough.' He suggested the people of Bromley exhibit 'no sign at all of the validity of the theory of evolution'. After insulting various other groups, and opening up the possibility of reintroducing academic selection, he ended his speech – leaving everybody amused, but completely baffled.

THURSDAY 10 JULY

A special Cabinet meeting at 8 a.m. to approve emergency legislation to allow MI6, MI5 and GCHQ to carry out surveillance operations to collect data on phone and internet use.

On this special occasion there were bacon rolls in the lobby outside the Cabinet Room, for those who were missing their breakfasts at the allegedly early hour of 8 a.m. I gave the rolls a miss and had a quick chat with George Osborne while collecting a coffee. He is just back from India. He has lost a lot of weight over the last few months.

At five past eight, Nick Clegg, unusually, was still not in the Cabinet Room and Cameron did not want to start the meeting without him. People were speculating on where Nick was. He eventually arrived at about ten past eight, looking a little harassed.

The heads of MI5, MI6 and GCHQ were there, in case there were any detailed questions that needed answering. Cabinet was over in about an hour, and I set off along Downing Street, ignoring the journalists shouting: 'Mr Laws, is this a new Snoopers' Charter?'

Finally left the office at around 10 p.m. and got home in time for the evening news, where they had a fairly straight package about the emergency legislation today. Emailed Nick Clegg to congratulate him on how it seems to have gone, which is probably a lot better than he thought. He and Tim Colbourne have done a great job.

Various emails from party members, MPs and peers about the manifesto keep on coming in. In the farming section, there is a commitment to take action to help protect the bee population, and we have already had to add the words 'and insects' to keep the Lib Dem insect lobby happy! Now the normally sensible Jane Bonham-Carter has come back asking to add 'and hedgehogs'! Thank God our peers and MPs are focused on the big policy picture, rather than trivial issues like education reform, the future of the European Union, or tax policy!

FRIDAY 11 JULY

Had to leave the house at 6.30 a.m. to go up to the LACA school food conference in Birmingham. Announced that over 99 per cent of schools are now ready. Because this is a good news story, I am not expecting to get a huge amount of coverage – good news isn't news!

There is a wonderful story on the BBC today about the rumoured government reshuffle on Monday. Apparently one of Iain Duncan Smith's special advisers was on a train somewhere when she was overheard speaking very loudly. Magnificently, the person who overheard her and relayed her comments on Twitter reported that she said rather loudly that 'Cameron is hoping to move Iain from the Department for Work and Pensions. Esther McVey, the junior minister, wants to take over, but the question is whether she is too much of a bitch to be considered'! Wonderful!

MONDAY 14 JULY

Today, the Prime Minister is expected to begin his reshuffle. All the logic points to Michael Gove staying put, but I can't help feeling that he might be moved. Michael has done the heavy lifting in terms of new policy work, and he really is not an implementation person. Also, over the past nine months, he has steadily pissed off fellow Conservative ministers and the Prime Minister himself, fallen out with me, and had massive and unnecessary rows with Ofsted. I think Cameron has got increasingly impatient with him. It is just possible that he might be moved, though I cannot for the life of me see where he could be moved to – now that it seems that the Home Secretary, Theresa May, is going to stay in place. Michael would relish being Foreign Secretary, but he has such extreme views on foreign affairs that I cannot see the Prime Minister doing that.

Attended a meeting with MG over Birmingham schools. Michael seemed a little bit fractious, and was not his normal joking self. The meeting broke up after forty-five minutes. [I was not to know, but this would be the last meeting that I attended with Michael as Secretary of State for Education.]

In the evening, spent five hours with the Liberal Democrat Federal Policy Committee trying to secure sign-off for the pre-manifesto. This really is not the way in which any serious political party should behave. The Federal Policy Committee is elected by party members, but only those who go to the Federal Conference. So this is a rather unrepresentative band of people, who are often the most extreme and activist members of the party, rather than the people who actually vote for us. The problem is also that the more sensible members of the committee have got better things to do with their time than spend five hours in policy meetings. They are also often too lazy to turn up.

So, we almost ended up with the party's commitment to ring-fence and protect the schools budget and the NHS kicked into touch, and we only secured the protection of these budgets by eight votes to seven. Insane! The committee took all sorts of other bizarre decisions, including ruling out any airport expansion anywhere in the whole of the United Kingdom, and voting rather randomly to abolish the tolls on the Severn Bridge, even though they have no idea what the cost of this is.

By the time I had got home, the shape of the Cabinet reshuffle was beginning to emerge. The biggest shock is that William Hague has decided to stand down as Foreign Secretary and leave Parliament at the next election, and the rumour is that he is going to be replaced by the dry, ghastly right-wing Tory Philip Hammond.

I try to find something nice to say about most people in the government, but Philip really is a miserable, antisocial, charmless Tory of the type who would drive any sensible, reasonable, liberal person away from the Conservative Party. Meanwhile, there is also a cull of moderate white males of middle age, and this is clearly the narrative that Cameron wants running on this pre-reshuffle evening.

David Willetts, the cerebral universities spokesman, is out, as is Andrew Lansley. The veteran minister Kenneth Clarke has 'resigned' as Minister without Portfolio, and Dominic Grieve has lost his position as Attorney General. David Jones, the invisible Welsh Secretary, has been sacked, and also going are Nick Hurd, the Minister for Civil Society, Oliver Heald, the Solicitor General, and Damian Green, the Policing Minister. Greg Barker is leaving the Department of Energy and Climate Change, which rather completes the 'massacre of the moderates', as the Labour Party are describing this.

The useless Owen Paterson has been sacked as Secretary of State for the Department of Environment, Food and Rural Affairs, and – obscured by all this ministerial reshuffle – Bob Kerslake, the head of the Home Civil Service, has apparently also 'been resigned'. Francis Maude will be very pleased.

Intriguingly, there are some media stories that Michael Gove was invited to see Cameron at the beginning of the reshuffle, early this evening, in his Commons office. This may signal that Gove is being moved, since he is clearly not going to be sacked and there has been no briefing that he is leaving the government. I think a move is plausible given that Michael has pissed so many people off and that he has finished a lot of his major reform work at Education, but I simply cannot see where he would go.

Sent 'good luck' text messages to Liz Truss and Matt Hancock. No reply from Liz, but Matt replied within about three seconds to thank me. I suspect that he has been standing by his mobile phone all night waiting for the Prime Minister to call! I can't help liking Matt, but he is a complete egomaniac and is power mad.

TUESDAY 15 JULY

Writing my diary at 11 in the evening on what has been a rather historic day.

Got up as usual at 5.30 a.m. and into the office at 6.45 a.m.

Cleared some paperwork and was due to have a meeting with Liz Truss. Liz, however, is being reshuffled. She is to be the new Secretary of State for the Environment. The irony is that she used to be a Liberal Democrat and spoke at the 1994 Liberal Democrat conference in favour of the abolition of the monarchy – something she has been trying to get over ever since.

Just before I was about to leave for a meeting, Jonathan, my private secretary, came in to tell me that Michael Gove was being axed from Education and demoted to being Conservative Chief Whip!

I'd had a funny feeling for some months that Michael might well get moved from Education. Indeed, I had given the assessment to George Parker, the political editor of the *Financial Times*, a few months before that whereas Michael had previously been unmoveable, there was now a 30 per cent chance that he might be shuffled. This was particularly because he had upset and irritated so many natural allies. In addition, he has alienated teachers and teacher unions, and he is a very polarising character amongst the public. Many people absolutely loathe him. There is also a sense that Michael has finished his main 'revolutionary' agenda, and he probably is not the man to get on and do delivery. Anyway, the Prime Minister obviously has some balls because he has taken on Michael and got him to move to the Whips' Office, in what appears to be an obvious demotion. Frankly, I am pretty surprised that Michael has taken the job. This shows that Cameron does have a ruthless streak, and that nobody is too big to be cut down to size. But in MG he will now have alienated an ally – and these things are always risky. No one can foresee the long-term consequences.

Got to the DfE at around 11.30 a.m. and the media were encamped outside the building. As I went in, I was asked, 'Has this been a good reshuffle, Mr Laws?' I was tempted to say yes, in a rather loyalist way, but my natural instinct for caution overrode, and I said nothing. Thank goodness, as otherwise it would sound like I was welcoming MG's removal!

Spoke to one of the DfE policy advisers, who said rather brutally, 'Michael has discovered that all political careers end in failure.' Apparently Michael's special advisers all expected him to stay on. The rumour is that that Michael has suffered from the 'Lynton Crosby effect' – as apparently Crosby has polled Michael and discovered that he is the most unpopular Tory Cabinet minister, and has advised the Prime Minister to get rid of him if he wants the Tory Party to be re-elected in the next election. But is this just a convenient cover story? Did the PM just conclude that Michael and Cummings were being too destructive?

There is a strange feeling in the building of both release from Michael's powerful presence and strong opinions and also a sense of disorientation in the department in not knowing the new Secretary of State and in not having a powerful and influential Secretary of State leading the department.

Meanwhile, Lord Hill has apparently now gone on to be the new UK Commissioner in the European Union. This is ironic, because I spoke to Jonathan in the Cabinet meeting a couple of weeks ago and he swore to me that the last thing in the world that he wanted to do was to be European Commissioner.

Nicky Morgan is the new Secretary of State for Education. She apparently arrived in the department at around 10 a.m. Within half an hour of Michael's removal, all of the pictures and other items in his office had been taken down and the office had been stripped bare.

Later in the afternoon I got a read-out from Nick's private office of a meeting between him and Nicky:

> Implementation priorities. The Deputy Prime Minister said he was particularly focused on free school meals and expansion of the two-year-old offer. He asked Nicky to focus on these.
>
> Long-running policy debates. The DPM set out that there are a number of long-running policy issues that we have not been able to make progress on.
>
> They spoke about governance of the schools system and the different views across the coalition on how middle tiers should operate – DPM suggested that he may want to go round this again. They both also talked about Birmingham and the need to agree a response to the Clarke Report. Apparently this was discussed at the Quad lunch yesterday and the PM/ DPM agreed that they might need to meet with Nicky and David later in the week to thrash out any disagreements.
>
> Relationship with teachers. DPM and Nicky agreed that we needed to change the tone of how the government talks to teachers and the educational establishment, without rowing back on what the government has achieved. DPM said he would be happy to work closely with Nicky to make this happen.
>
> Mental health. Nicky explained that mental health is one of her key interests and that she has already been discussing this with Norman Lamb.

Eventually, at about five to seven in the evening, the call came through that Nicky Morgan was ready to see me, and I popped round to her office, passing the civil servants, who looked as if they were all in a bit of a flap adjusting to the new regime. The Secretary of State's office was completely empty. All of the photographs on the walls, the pictures, the vast quantities of books that Michael kept behind his desk and all of the other items that made this a personal office in some way were gone. Nicky and I sat down on the chairs at the side of her desk, with nobody else in the room. I congratulated her and said that I wished her all the best for the future. She was a bit vague about priorities, and to be honest she looked a bit shell-shocked. She said that she wanted to change the 'tone', and signal that there was a new era. She also said that she had an interest in the issue of child wellbeing (oh God, this is exactly the kind of thing that Michael Gove would hate!), and she also said that there was now perhaps an opportunity to do more on 'careers advice and guidance' (certainly the sign of a new regime!).

The problem for Nicky Morgan is that the right in the Tory Party will perceive her promotion as being something of a sell out to the 'blob', and a compromising of educational reform, whereas Nicky's natural desire will probably be to promote herself as a more consensual person in education, reaching out beyond the Conservative Party. I fear that Nicky may end up straddling these two positions, and at times try to prove that she is more Gove-ite than Gove, while at other times trying to signal a new direction. This could end up being something of a policy and communications mess.

Got home in the evening and sent an email to Michael Gove, wishing him luck.

WEDNESDAY 16 JULY

The papers are full of the demotion of Michael Gove – and the ruthlessness of David Cameron in cutting down a friend.

For Cameron to act so boldly does show his confidence, and his determination to win the next election. It also shows that Cameron has a natural desire to run a unified coalition government, and that he does not like the fractiousness that has come out of Gove/Cummings.

MG ended up with his one-time big tent of Blairites, Conservatives and Liberal Democrats becoming a very small tent indeed of basically himself, Toby Young and Dom Cummings – not a great tent to be in.

Michael's departure is still a big loss to the education debate and certainly to the front line of British politics. He has been a charming and amusing friend, a formidable foe, a champion of higher educational standards and aspirations, a doughty fighter for greater equality of opportunity, a formidable example of a politician with clear aims and objectives and the ability to prioritise. The Education Department is going to be a much, much duller place without him.

Meanwhile, this will be a painful blow to Michael. I suspect that beneath the publicly resilient man is a very hurt individual who feels that all his determined work in education has been overlooked and that his legacy may be undermined. The problem ultimately was that he has made some pretty powerful enemies, but the most unwise decision of all was to be oblivious to the views and concerns of the Prime Minister himself. I think the recent attack by Cummings on the PM was probably the final straw. Cameron guards his own brand as the 'strong leader' very assiduously, and he has not allowed his own qualities to be trashed in the same way as Nick Clegg's and Ed Miliband's have been. I view Cameron as a proud man who certainly does bear grudges, and on this occasion he has acted to promote the re-election prospects of the Conservative Party and to take out of circulation a minister who is increasingly accident prone in his personal relations and who is alienating potential allies.

Went over this morning at 8.45 a.m. to the Home Office for a meeting with the Immigration Minister, James Brokenshire. Reviewed progress on entry and exit checks. Frankly, I still do not believe that the Home Office is going to get all of this in place by April 2015, and I think they are just trying to pretend that it is all going to be in place so they do not get politically criticised by the Lib Dems in the coalition. And there is a problem not only of completing 100 per cent exit checks in time but of actually doing something about the data that is collected. It will take some time before the data can be used properly to identify individual overstayers, and in any case the Home Office remain clear that their main enforcement action will be prioritised against foreign national offenders, failed asylum seekers and the more harmful cohorts. This means that in reality 'ordinary' overstayers probably will not be tackled for some time.

Had a meeting of the Matthew Group, to discuss possible coalition negotiations in 2015. This time we discussed a Tory–Lib Dem coalition scenario.

I also presented my recommendations on our role in government:

1. To keep the Quad.
2. To keep the Lib Dem presence in the Treasury.
3. To ensure that we secure at least one of the Department of Health, Department for Education, or the Department for Work and Pensions – in other words, a frontline public service department. I favour Education.
4. Keep the Secretary of State for Energy and Climate Change.
5. Ensuring a stronger Lib Dem presence in a few key departments such as DECC and Education.
6. Ensuring one special adviser for every department.
7. A presence in the Foreign Office, which might be necessary given Europe will be such an issue in the next parliament.

When I got back to the DfE, I had a quick chat with Chris Paterson, who is going to come in from Centre Forum as a policy adviser.

Then a meeting with Nick and Danny to discuss the Autumn Statement. As usual on these occasions, we did not have the most enlightening conversation, because Danny's opening pitch always tends to be, 'Well, of course we have not got any money, blah blah blah blah.' I don't know why Nick still falls for this old twaddle. We go through two fiscal events every year, and before every one of them Danny tells us there is no money, and then surprise, surprise, by the time the actual fiscal statement turns up, we have usually spent four or five billion pounds. If we don't establish Lib Dem priorities, then George Osborne will run off with the money.

When the reshuffle took place, Oliver Letwin was supposed to be becoming the new 'Lord Privy Seal'. This is entirely an honorific title, but was designed to be a pat on the back. But it appears that something has gone wrong, and he is now having to be made the Chancellor of the Duchy of Lancaster instead. Apparently there is already a Lord Privy Seal, who was rather upset to discover that his title was being given to Oliver! Also there has been a balls-up today on Michael Gove's first full day as Chief Whip – he has not only lost a vote, but ended up being locked into the toilets in one of the division lobbies! It could only happen to Michael.

In my red box there are a number of requests for Home Affairs Committee clearance from ministers who have now been reshuffled. Ironically, there is one from Michael Gove – his last request for Home Affairs Committee clearance – asking to approve the 20 per cent cut in the Education Services

Grant. Of course, Michael would have wanted the cut to be even greater, but I suspect he will be delighted that axing local authority grant was effectively his last act as Education Secretary.

THURSDAY 17 JULY

Danny has placed the agreed story in the *Daily Mirror*, explaining our change of position on the 'spare room subsidy'. What we are saying is that people will have their housing benefit docked if they are under-occupying a social rented property, but only if they have first been offered an alternative suitably sized property. We have also said that we will not deny an additional bedroom to a disabled couple, provided the disability means that they need an extra bedroom in order to sleep properly etc. Of course, the truth is that we should never have signed up to this policy with these imperfections in the first place.

Got into the Cabinet Office early and the first thing I did was send an email to Nick Clegg about communications on free school meals. Nick did an interview yesterday and started talking about 'difficulties' in some schools, and needless to say, that was the headline. We have now got to the situation where there are fewer than fifty schools that are red-rated out of 16,400, and if we are not going to get unrelentingly positive about this now, we never will. When we did the daily call at 8.15 a.m., he immediately apologised.

At 10.45 a.m. had a free school meal catch-up session with officials. I was quite demanding of them, even though they looked a bit knackered. They have been working really hard for the past few months, but I am determined to try to get all the red-rated schools amber- or green-rated.

Finally got a reply this evening from Michael Gove to the email I sent him: courteous, generous and suggesting dinner in September.

Michael has picked far too many fights with far too many people over the past year, but he is fundamentally a decent person whose heart is in the right place. I am glad that we are still on speaking terms. However, Michael clearly still has a problem with Cummings. Dom has tweeted this evening: 'For many years I have told MG that Cameron's a lightweight selfish clown. He didn't want to believe it. Now he knows I'm right. Thanks Dave!'

FRIDAY 18 JULY

This is the day when we were supposed to be at Chequers, having a brief and somewhat token Cabinet meeting and then a barbeque outside – with the Prime Minister cooking sausages for his Cabinet. It seemed quite a pleasant prospect, particularly as the weather is so glorious, with temperatures touching 30°.

Unfortunately, our best-laid plans were disturbed by the downing of a Malaysian airliner yesterday by what looks like Russian or Russian-controlled missiles over the Ukraine. A terrible tragedy in which hundreds of people have died. There had to be emergency meetings of the COBRA Security Committee this morning and the Prime Minister quite rightly concluded that having his Cabinet at Chequers enjoying a barbeque might not be very good.

The Cabinet met instead in No. 10. I gave an upbeat summary of the state of readiness on universal infant free school meals. I emphasised the extent to which we were seeking to monitor this from the centre, and I said that most schools were now on track to deliver.

SATURDAY 19 JULY

Travelled down to Yeovil for an advice centre at 8.30 a.m. and then on to Chard for another at noon.

In the afternoon, went to the Guildhall in Chard to see a performance of *Smike* by the pupils of Tatworth School. I have been to many musicals by Tatworth School over the years, and they are always brilliant – organised by a fantastic head teacher called David Knight.

On the way back home afterwards, I had to stop in a lay-by to do a conference call with Nick, Danny and advisers. There was some discussion of a story which is apparently going to be running in the *Mail on Sunday*, seeking to blame the Lib Dems for Andrew Lansley not being Britain's choice of European Commissioner. The Tory briefing is that the Lib Dems refused to help avoid a by-election if Lansley had to stand down. Cameron apparently said to Nick that he would like to use this as an excuse when explaining to Lansley why he was not getting this job – and Nick said he was simply not willing to take the blame for this, and had actually agreed that the Lib Dems would not call a by-election if he went off to be European Commissioner. Cameron is apparently deliberately trying to blame it all on us. Cheap.

MONDAY 21 JULY

12.30 p.m. The first Monday ministerial meeting with Nicky Morgan and the new Education team of Nick Gibb, Nick Boles, Sam Gyimah, Lord Nash and Edward Timpson. A very different style to Michael Gove – no banter from Nicky, and a workmanlike going over of all the issues for DfE Questions. Nicky comes across as inexperienced and a bit uncertain, but not lacking a core of confidence that will ultimately serve her well.

Stock-take again on free school meals. The team are exhausted, but they are doing well because there are only ten red-rated schools left out of 16,400. Hurrah!

Nicky Morgan makes her first Commons statement tomorrow, on Birmingham. One embarrassment is that the draft report from Peter Clarke, which was seen by the department last week and which was leaked by somebody to *The Guardian*, has had one particularly crucial section changed between the leaked and final reports. In the section about DfE responsibilities, there had been a particularly juicy statement implying that the department was guilty of 'benign neglect' in its oversight of academies. Miraculously, that statement has come out in the final report!

When I asked about this at the meeting with Nicky and senior officials this afternoon, they all looked rather embarrassed, and I was told that Peter Clarke himself had insisted on changing this: 'Peter Clarke had not seen the final report before it was sent across to us, and somebody else had written it and as soon as Peter saw it, he decided that he wanted to change it.' I find this explanation totally implausible. Would Peter Clarke really have sent a report across to the Secretary of State for Education without bothering to read it? Unless the media or Labour Party are fast asleep tomorrow (under Tristram Hunt, this is perfectly possible) then there is going to be a bit of a row about this.

Meanwhile, I have seen the Cabinet minutes of my briefing last week on free school meals. It is interesting how the civil servants modify words to make them 'government-friendly'. In the Cabinet meeting, I had said that I was exercising 'Stalinist control' over the delivery of the free meals policy. The Cabinet minutes have altered this to 'very close ministerial oversight'.

TUESDAY 22 JULY

The Cabinet today included an infrastructure audit from Danny Alexander, and a report on Birmingham schools from Nicky. I took the opportunity of Danny's update to make the case for improved transport infrastructure in the south-west – pointing out that the railway line from west of Salisbury is single-track for much of the route, and the A303 from Stonehenge westward has large single-track sections, making for one-hour traffic delays during the summer months. Cameron is never slow to spot a political opportunity, and when he summed up he said that there was a 'coalition consensus' that we needed to do more for transport infrastructure – particularly in the south-west of England. Of course, both we and the Tories have a lot of target seats in this area.

Nicky gave her update on Birmingham schools. She read carefully from a prepared script. Totally different from Michael Gove, who was sitting on her left, eyes focused down onto a notepad on which he scribbled various comments. His body language when Nick Clegg spoke was interesting – he almost physically recoiled from each Nick intervention.

After Nicky finished, a large number of Cabinet ministers spoke out to praise her tone and her 'responsible' comments, which sought to reach out to the majority Muslim community. Every complimentary comment felt designed to be, and was, a stake through Michael Gove's heart. Contributions came in particular from Theresa May, Eric Pickles and Baroness Warsi – all three of whom cannot stand Michael.

At 2.15 p.m. I was back in the DfE for a meeting on free school meals. As it was the end of school term, and as the team has worked very hard, I decided to have a few drinks and nibbles in my office, and I invited the Permanent Secretary in and also got Nick Clegg to phone in on the spider phone to thank the team. The number of red-rated schools has now fallen to just five.

Clearly, the battle between HM Treasury and the Department of Health for extra money to bail out the NHS is heating up quite a bit. In my box this evening were two absolutely blistering letters: one from the Treasury to the Department of Health and another back from the Department of Health to the Treasury.

The Treasury letter was signed by both George Osborne and Danny Alexander and dated 16 July. It read:

Dear Jeremy,

We wanted to take this opportunity before the summer recess to write to you about your department's finances … We have taken tough choices in order to protect your department's budget. It is therefore deeply concerning that you do not appear to be making it your priority to ensure that the Department of Health lives within its agreed Spending Review settlement to the end of 2015/16. We share your commitment to ensuring that the NHS continues to meet the high operational standards that the government has set. It is troubling, therefore, that although the data was already starting to show some deterioration against those key targets, you made new spending commitments towards the end of 2013/14. Consequently, we have concluded that increased Treasury scrutiny of the Department of Health and the NHS spending is now necessary.

Firstly, we have decided to reduce your department's delegated limit for new policy in 2014/15 and 2015/16 to zero, starting with immediate effect. Secondly, by early September, we will need to see a credible plan from you for starting 2015/16 in balance. Your officials will need to work with ours to share detailed analysis of all spending commitments for 2015/16. Thirdly, you must take robust action to tackle deficits in NHS Trusts, and to ensure that Trust Chief Executives maintain financial discipline. Fourthly, now that agreement has been reached about the payment for performance element of a better care fund, we expect you to be clear that there is sufficient funding in 2015/16. This should include refuting the emerging myth that the fund takes £2 billion away from the NHS next year. This has never been intended and we can now demonstrate that it cannot happen.

Finally, we have asked the Chief Secretary's office to speak to yours in order to set up a monthly meeting focusing on Department of Health spending, NHS finances performance and your long-term planning. Sharon White, HMT's second Permanent Secretary, also intends to establish a monthly discussion with your Permanent Secretary and senior officials in order to inform our meetings.

Best wishes,

George Osborne and Danny Alexander.

By Whitehall standards, this is a fairly blistering letter, and Jeremy Hunt clearly took it as such.

On 17 July, the very next day, he writes back:

Dear George and Danny,

Thank you for your letter of 16 July ... I reject totally any suggestion that you have not received full and total commitment from me and my department in making sure that the budget is managed responsibly. Indeed, I am very concerned that given the operational and political pressures I have been trying to manage, there is so little recognition in your letter of the enormous efforts I and my officials have been taking to make sure we balance our budget both this year and next. Over my time in post as Secretary of State for Health I have always lived within the allocated budget and will do so, not just for this year but also 2015/16. You will remember that in 2012/13 I delivered £2 billion underspend at your specific request because of concerns that the government might not meet its objective to continue reducing the deficit year in, year out. I did so on the basis that the underspend would be rolled over, but accepted with good grace when it was not even though it created significant additional pressures to be managed. You will also remember that I was not allocated the additional £250 million for winter pressures I was promised in the Spending Review for 2013/14, again something my department accepted with good grace. But you will also understand that amongst Cabinet ministers I face unique operational pressures caused by rising demand over which I have little control. The NHS is currently doing 850,000 more operations per annum, 1.2 million additional A&E visits, 3.6 million more diagnostic tests and 6.3 million more outpatient visits compared to 2010 – all on essentially a flat real budget.

What I most object to in your letter is the suggestion that HMT and DH have not been working with a shared agenda to make the NHS budget sustainable. I need your support to make this happen and you need mine – a spirit of partnership and mutual support that is totally absent from the tone of your letter. Therefore, I am very happy to agree to regular constructive informed meetings with the CST and HMT officials. But I cannot accept such an unworkable decision on my delegated spending limits. Second-guessing every decision would make it impossible to do my job effectively and to respond swiftly to emerging issues. It would create completely unnecessary bureaucracy for both our departments … I would be very happy to discuss this further with you and the Prime Minister if necessary.

THURSDAY 24 JULY

All day in Yeovil constituency. Did a DfE call in the afternoon to catch up on free school meals implementation – there are now only three red-rated schools left in the country, one in Ealing, one in Kingston upon Thames and one in Richmond. I am going to need to speak to the chief executive of Kingston/Richmond tomorrow. Free school meals now turns into a communications and 'keep on track' challenge – as we now have 75 per cent of schools green-rated and 25 per cent amber-rated. With 25 per cent of schools amber-rated, that is still a lot that could go wrong over the summer period.

As I was finishing canvassing in Yeovil Central in the evening, I received a telephone call from Oliver Letwin. Oliver said he had been looking at the issue of entry and exit checks, and he was not at all convinced by the narrative the Home Office were putting out that they were on track for delivering 100 per cent exit checks by April. Oliver said he felt that they would not deliver on rail and ferry checks. He also said he had been looking into who exactly within the Home Office was supposed to be in charge of this policy and he had discovered that it was precisely nobody. We agreed a stock-take with the Home Office sometime in the next week.

FRIDAY 25 JULY

All day in a sunny Yeovil constituency. The conference call with Nick at 8.15 a.m. was spent talking about the Quarter 2 GDP data, which is coming out this morning. Cameron appears to be trying to monopolise all of the broadcast media, and Stephen Lotinga has had a row with his Tory opposite number, Craig Oliver. Stephen made clear that Nick intends to do broadcast media today, but Craig said that he disagreed and would need to 'escalate the matter'. Nick was fairly angry: 'I'm not going to allow Cameron to dictate who does and does not interview me.'

The GDP numbers showed quarterly growth once again at 0.8 per cent – a healthy 3.2 per cent annualised rate. Most significantly, the economy is now larger than it was when the recession started in 2007/08. No wonder Cameron wants to do all the media.

MONDAY 28 JULY

First day of my annual villages advice centre, when we drive around the fifty villages in my constituency to be available for half an hour or so for constituents. It's a bit old-fashioned in this era of the internet and email, but people like it and it is an opportunity to get out and see every single community at least once a year.

We start the day in the beautiful village of Hinton St George, and end up in Podimore in the east. A beautiful sunny day for most of the time. Both *The Sun* and *The Times* lead today on a growing crisis in the NHS.

TUESDAY 29 JULY

Another beautiful English summer's day, out on my villages advice centre. Got back home at the weirdly early hour of 5 p.m. and then went out to celebrate the twentieth anniversary of my office manager, Sue Weeks, running our Yeovil office. Sue is absolutely brilliant – we could not do without her.

WEDNESDAY 30 JULY

Zig-zagged over the South Somerset countryside visiting seventeen villages. Wayford, Buckland St Mary, Wambrook, Chiselborough and Combe St Nicholas really are quite magnificent. Had lunch with our former county councillor, David Gordon, who lives in a house which looks like something out of the early nineteenth century – all falling to pieces and located in a tiny hamlet called Allowenshay. The villagers were all there to meet us when we arrived, to raise a problem about their local water supply. Had lunch in David's beautiful English garden. Wonderful, fresh food and a glass of white wine. Out in the garden were two very old cars from the 1920s. Always a struggle to leave his house, since it is so relaxing sitting there.

Finished the day in Combe St Nicholas and then set off for London. As we left the village, I suddenly realised that if I am not re-elected in May 2015 then this will be the last villages advice centre. I still think the odds are in favour of us retaining this seat, in which case there are five more years of villages advice centres ahead of me – that is 250 more visits!

THURSDAY 31 JULY

Breakfast with Oliver at 7.30 a.m. To the Downing Street cafeteria, and George Osborne was there with his tiny little fluffy white dog, which he was just about to take for a walk. He really does look rather ridiculous with it. It's certainly not on a par with the British bulldog that Peter Mandelson used to parade on behalf of the Labour Party before the 2001 election, and I doubt we will be seeing a lot of George's dog in the campaign.

Went over to the DfE and held a free school meal catch-up. There is now only one red-rated school left in the country!

MONDAY 4 AUGUST

Got a note giving a read-out of a meeting on the NHS this week between the Prime Minister, George Osborne and Jeremy Hunt. Apparently the PM and Chancellor have 'forcefully communicated' to Jeremy that he will not be getting any extra money for the Health Service for 2014/15 and 2015/16. There is serious concern about operational resilience in the NHS, including the eighteen-week waiting time targets, the A&E waiting time target, and cancer waits. Apparently the A&E target was missed again this week. There was a suggestion that it would be better if the Quad meeting on the NHS took place in October rather than September. There will apparently be more and better data on operational resilience at this point. I am nervous about the fact that the Tories are not suggesting putting any extra money into the NHS. This may be the Treasury view and the Prime Minister's view and it may be Danny's view, but that does not necessarily mean it is right for either the NHS or the country. I need to keep a close eye on this and I may need to give Nick some fairly tough advice. I think that the NHS is heading over the edge of the cliff.

WEDNESDAY 6 AUGUST

The happiest day of the year. The day we drive down from London, leaving at 3 a.m. for the south of France.

Threw open the shutters and let the light in. A beautiful day with temperatures of 32°.

The big news today has been that Boris Johnson has finally stated that he is going to stand as an MP in the next general election. This has caused mass media hysteria. If Cameron loses the general election, then the assumption now is that he will stand down and Boris will fight a leadership battle with Osborne and Theresa May. The more intriguing possibility is if Cameron does become Prime Minister after the next general election, then Boris could be a major thorn in his side – including over the preparations for and aftermath of the EU referendum that the Tories plan to hold by 2017.

Cameron has instantly put out a tweet from his holiday in Portugal (can you imagine Winston Churchill doing something so ghastly?), welcoming Boris back and saying how delighted Cameron is to have 'all his key players on the pitch'. Nobody, of course, believes this for a moment.

THURSDAY 7 AUGUST

Had a good sleep for eleven hours, which was much needed. Awoke to another beautiful day.

FRIDAY 8 AUGUST

The government has used the August recess to slip out news of yet another twenty-two new peers – taking the total number up to 796! The size of the House of Lords is becoming a complete joke.

Meanwhile, Nicky Morgan has made her first speech as Education Secretary, and bizarrely she has chosen to make this about government plans to clamp down on the dangers of extremism in Britain's nurseries! Since government officials have had to acknowledge that there isn't any evidence of extremism in nursery schools, this somewhat deflates the value of the announcement. To be fair to Nicky, this was one of the announcements dreamt up in Downing Street during all the hysteria about Birmingham.

SATURDAY 9 AUGUST

Continuing to read the brilliant fourth volume biography by Robert Caro of Lyndon Johnson. Kennedy has now been assassinated and Johnson has taken over as President and is making something of a success of it. As I read some of the stories of Johnson's initial success, I could not help but think of Gordon Brown taking over from Tony Blair back in 2007. Everything initially went so well and then it all came crashing down.

Finished the Caro book today, and it's now likely to be eight years before I get to read the final, fifth volume of what is perhaps the greatest political biography of all time.

At 6 p.m. UK time, we did a conference call with Nick Clegg – mainly a discussion about Israel and controls on arms exports. Vince Cable is very keen, as is Nick, to impose an arms embargo on Israel, and apparently the legal advice from BIS officials is that we can do this. But the Tories are clearly very against it, and Philip Hammond has been dodging a telephone call with Nick.

Vince has turned out to be unobtainable over the past couple of days, so goodness knows where he is. But he has written a letter which has apparently been partially leaked, indicating that he wants a decision on this by 5 p.m. on Monday. Nick was quite shirty on the call. Eventually he said, 'Look, I am fed up with having to deal with this dipstick Hammond, and I am not going to do so any longer.' Nick said he would email Cameron tonight to make his displeasure known and to say that he was not prepared to mess around with this issue any longer.

MONDAY 11 AUGUST

Another beautiful day with clear blue skies. At 8.50 a.m. I joined the daily conference call with Nick. He sounded as if he had just been woken up. The media seems to be dominated by the story about the Iraqi Christians called the Yazidis, who are in danger of being slaughtered by ISIS. The first calls have been made over the weekend by various Tory MPs to have a recall of Parliament (calls for the recall of Parliament in August are now an annual event!). We will need to watch this, as the atrocities in Iraq are so ghastly and extreme – with stories yesterday of women and children being buried alive – that there could become a real reason for tougher international action, which would involve a recall of Parliament.

WEDNESDAY 13 AUGUST

An impressive thunder and lightning display, this morning, and the rain set in for a couple of hours – and then within another couple of hours all the rain was gone, and there were just a few clouds hanging around.

Finished reading Von Manstein's Second World War autobiography – which lacks colour and was far too dry. Now onto the John Campbell biography of Roy Jenkins – am 200 pages in, but already losing enthusiasm.

THURSDAY 14 AUGUST

The clash over Israel arms export licences seems to have been resolved in favour of the Conservatives – with the government's line now being that we will ban arms exports only if there is significant further armed action by Israel in Gaza. Not very satisfactory. However, the focus has now moved back to northern Iraq and the targeting of ethnic groups by the ISIS extremists.

Labour's much-trailed 'summer offensive' seems to have disappeared or failed to even get started. Labour is still five or six points ahead in the polls, but it is very difficult to see why.

On the way back from a wonderful meal in Cassis, at Nino's restaurant, I got a text from Henry Dimbleby which said: 'I'm sitting in a park in Maldon in Essex. There are a table of mothers next to me who have just said, "I am so glad that they are introducing free school dinners. The amount of money I spend on food!"' Forwarded Henry's message to Nick Clegg, who texted back: 'Why didn't they say "Lib Dems" rather than "they"?!'

When we got back from Cassis, did a conference call with DfE officials over the implementation of universal infant free school meals. There are at present no red-rated schools in all England. All the Cummings/*Daily Mail* predictions that this would be a delivery shambles are being discredited.

More surprisingly, officials also said that their survey is suggesting that only eight schools of 4,500 responses so far will not be delivering hot school meals in January 2015, and only sixteen schools are set not to deliver a hot meal option this September. That is massively better than we had expected, as some people had suggested that as high a proportion as 10 per cent or 20 per cent of schools might only be delivering a cold option.

Sixteen schools out of 4,500 means that we are so far on track for 99.5 per cent of schools to be delivering a hot option. The critical thing now is to deliver well and ensure that the success is communicated effectively.

SUNDAY 17 AUGUST

More sun. Not a cloud in the sky. Correction: the only cloud in the sky is the thought of having to return home in just over a week's time.

Finished the Jenkins book today – not that impressed.

WEDNESDAY 20 AUGUST

Part sunny, part cloudy. Went down to Cassis and had lunch in the fantastic Nino's restaurant. Two tables away from me was the Tory MP Sir Edward Garnier. I did my best to keep out of his line of sight. The last thing one wants on holiday is to bump into a Tory MP!

THURSDAY 21 AUGUST

The media is dominated by yesterday's news of the barbaric killing of James Foley, the US journalist who was captured in Syria. There is a video of him dressed in an orange garment, kneeling down with a black-clothed ISIS militant standing behind him with a knife, about to behead him. The whole thing is barbaric beyond belief. Cameron returned yesterday from his holiday to deal with this crisis – which seemed odd, but is explained by the fact that there are serious concerns that the person who has committed the atrocity is actually a British citizen, God help us.

Meanwhile, Danny Alexander reported that the Scottish referendum campaign is going well. He said that he had spent the last few days 'going around Scotland announcing extra public expenditure and all sorts of different initiatives'. I said it would be very nice if he could occasionally come to the south-west of England and announce some spending there, to which he predictably replied, 'Unfortunately, there is no money left.'

SATURDAY 23 AUGUST

Woke up to clouds. Went out for a run. By the time we had got back, the clouds were parting and we were due for another glorious sunny day – appropriate as it is our last of the holiday.

Asked James to guess the result of the next general election. He had Conservatives 295 seats, Labour 287, Lib Dem 32. This was remarkably similar to my estimate of Conservatives 299, Labour 288, Lib Dems 37. Looking at the bookies, they are predicting a hung parliament, with Labour the largest party on around 300 seats and with the Tories on around 283 and us on around 34.

We have got the launch of our pre-manifesto on Wednesday 3 September. And then, effectively, we have got a six-month campaign going into May 2015. This time next year I could be in any of a variety of situations. I could have lost my seat and be unemployed or in a new profession completely. I could be a backbench MP on the opposition benches, or I could be back in the Cabinet. If I am going to be back in government, I really want to be Chief Secretary. However, Nick is toying with the idea of us taking the Education Department, in which case he might want me to go back as Education Secretary. But as for today, our last in the south of France for some months, I am just going to soak up the good weather and try to finish my book on Harold Macmillan.

SUNDAY 24 AUGUST

That sad day has finally arrived when we have to leave France. Closed up the shutters, reflecting that the next time I am in a swimming pool there will be a new government in the United Kingdom.

MONDAY 25 AUGUST

Back in Britain with a vengeance. We have gone from daytime temperatures of 30°C down to 15°C, and driving rain. The weather is more like a miserable autumn day rather than the height of summer.

Went into the office to clear my paperwork, expecting at least three large boxes. To my surprise, there was only one. Is this because all the civil servants have also been on holiday? Or is it because they are holding work back for my return? Or is it that the civil service delivers an output of paperwork that meets ministers' capability to process it? I rather fear it is a mixture of all three.

Liz Truss has finally landed with a vengeance from the DfE into her new job as Secretary of State for the Department for Environment, Food and Rural Affairs. Although being Secretary of State is a very nice thing, this is the last department that I would ever want to go to. Sure enough, there is a Home Affairs clearance letter from Liz, which seeks permission 'for changes to the regulatory system for the control of small sewage discharges'. Liz must wonder whether the promotion was really worthwhile.

THURSDAY 28 AUGUST

My staff in the DfE have now confirmed that every school in the country is ready to deliver free infant school meals from the start of this school term. Indeed, only 1.5 per cent of schools are not on track to deliver the hot meal option, and those that are not on track will be delivering cold meals. This ought to be a major good news story, but it is still going to be an uphill struggle to get the press to write positive stories, as they have got it into their mind that the whole thing is an implementation failure. We have Cummings to thank for this.

Today, free school meals went live in Leicester, Leicestershire and Rutland, and the DfE telephoned all the schools to see how they were doing. The news is very good – all are delivering the policy, and hot meal options.

Today is a pretty significant day, news wise. Firstly, it appears that Russian troops have now invaded part of the Ukraine – and the UN Security Council is having an emergency meeting. And on the domestic front, Douglas Carswell has defected to the UK Independence Party. This is a massive boost to UKIP, and will probably be a further boost when they win the by-election that Carswell has now triggered. Cameron must have been hoping that the whole Europe/UKIP issue would go away, but it is clearly not going to. What is particularly damaging is that part of Carswell's narrative is that he does not believe that Cameron has a serious renegotiation strategy for Europe, and he is claiming that Cameron just wants to go through the motions of renegotiation and then sign off on more or less whatever deal is on offer. Very true!

SUNDAY 31 AUGUST

Cleared all my red box yesterday, so had a fairly easy day watching *A Bridge Too Far* on TV.

Spent an hour on the evening conference call with Nick over the statement that Cameron plans to make tomorrow on terrorists, particularly those in Syria and the Middle East. It is very tricky territory for liberals, because quite a lot of it is about stopping people who may have been involved in terrorism from coming back to the UK. However, if you do not actually have any evidence to prosecute people, then it is a fairly draconian power that essentially means the Home Secretary can make a decision about stripping UK citizens of their right to return to their own country. After about an hour, we came up with a package which Nick is going to propose to Cameron. It is 50 per cent of what Cameron wants. It will be interesting to see whether Cameron accepts it. But he has got to make a statement tomorrow, so we do have something of a vice-like grip.

MONDAY 1 SEPTEMBER

Went into the DfE for 12.45 p.m. for the first major ministerial meeting chaired by Nicky. A totally different tone to Michael's meetings – no jokes, and a coherent agenda. Nicky somewhat strangely asked us to introduce ourselves to each other. She then went round the table asking us to set out our ministerial responsibilities. Definitely very different from Michael – less fun, but more business-like.

Went to my office to get an update on free school meals implementation, as DfE officials are doing a massive survey of schools – phoning every single school. By the end of the day, the department had surveyed around a third of schools in England, and they had only three schools that were not going to be immediately delivering but would be delivering within a week or so. This suggests that we are going to have a small number of schools, perhaps ten or so, that are not initially delivering the policy, but these schools are likely only to be failing to deliver for a week or so. We will not get any additional data on hot school meals, so a figure of over 98 per cent of schools delivering hot school meals seems to be a good one. This morning *The Independent* had an excellent article on free school meals, reflecting the interview with me last week, saying that the whole policy was on track, and advertising the fact that the Lib Dem pre-manifesto is going to signal our commitment to roll out free school meals to all primary school children in the next parliament.

TUESDAY 2 SEPTEMBER

It is 'go live' day for universal infant free school meals today. Nick Clegg did the major morning media, and I mopped up the smaller stuff. The media narrative about the whole thing being a shambles is finally turning round as people see that the policy is actually being delivered effectively. We have got 98.5 per cent of schools delivering hot meals as from today, and almost 100 per cent of schools across the country are actually delivering either the hot or cold universal offer.

I feel sure that we have taken all the right policy decisions in terms of legislation, securing capital, securing revenue, the small schools grant, the support service etc. etc. It is really exciting to see the policy delivered today, and to see the reaction of parents and children.

There are now more than one and a half million children sitting down for the first time to get a free school meal, and this has made a big impact on schools, on children and on parental budgets. Maybe this policy seems a little bit 'socialist' for me, but I have always thought that it's just common sense to serve a good, healthy, nutritious hot lunch to every child in our schools, rather than allowing them to make do with a few sandwiches and a packet of crisps. It is as logical to 'socialise' this cost as it is to socialise the costs of teaching. This is going to be a great legacy of our time in coalition, which should boost attainment, increase healthy eating, reduce child poverty, improve work incentives and help hard-pressed household budgets.

The other main news today is the closing of the independence polls in Scotland. It is now a 53–47 margin between the 'Yes' and 'No' campaigns, which means that if the SNP get any more momentum, they could win.

Later on, I was sitting down to brief myself for the pre-manifesto launch tomorrow when the tragic news came through that the second US journalist – Steven Sotloff – has been executed by the Islamic State militants. This is grotesque, and the fear now is that the British captives (who so far have been kept secret in the media) may be the next to be executed.

Nick phoned and said that there was no way he felt he could launch our pre-manifesto tomorrow while all the media focus is rightly on this atrocity. We decided to postpone the manifesto launch.

WEDNESDAY 3 SEPTEMBER

A bizarre story popped up on the news websites this afternoon saying that the government is considering preventing any school from being rated outstanding by Ofsted inspection unless it introduces setting for all its pupils! This is complete nonsense and micromanagement of the first order. I phoned the DfE office and said that if it was a Tory manifesto idea, that was one thing, but if it was supposed to be a government policy then I was not going to stand for it.

Later in the afternoon, my private secretary called to tell me that the Ofsted story re. compulsory setting was designed to be Tory manifesto stuff that was apparently going to be announced by Nicky Morgan and the Prime Minister on a political visit this week. It is quite possible that today's story was leaked to *The Guardian* by Dom Cummings.

Spoke to one of our DfE policy advisers, who said that he had spoken to the Permanent Secretary about the Tory 'idea' about setting. Apparently the Permanent Secretary said he thought it was the maddest education idea he had ever heard.

Meanwhile, I had an interesting discussion with Luke, the Secretary of State's new education adviser, about the teacher quality package. Apparently the Tories are in favour of the Royal College and the continuous professional development proposals, but No. 10 is less enamoured about opening up the qualified teacher status debate. Obviously their polling must show the same as ours – that having qualified teachers is actually a very popular thing with the public!

In the evening, went to Admiralty House for the reception on free school meals, with Henry Dimbleby and John Vincent. Nick Clegg was there and made the main speech. It was a really happy occasion after all the work that has been put in over the past year, and everybody is conscious that they have achieved something of real value. Very exciting! My civil servants have done a really fantastic job, including Marc Cavey and Jacquie Spatcher.

THURSDAY 4 SEPTEMBER

Morning conference call with Nick, Danny etc. at 8.15 a.m. Two subjects dominated: Scotland and the situation in Iraq/Syria, with the ISIL terrorists now threatening to kill a British hostage.

There is nervousness about how conflict involving UK forces might play into the Scottish referendum, where the gap between the 'Yes' and 'No' camps is now incredibly small. Nick suggested that Cameron is going to be discussing this issue with Obama. It sounds as if we are hoping to persuade the Americans to delay action until after 18 September, when the Scottish referendum takes place.

Meanwhile, there is unhelpful coverage in *The Guardian* today talking about senior government figures looking into the possibility of whether the existing Parliament could be extended if Scotland votes 'Yes' in the referendum. There is a real sense of concern/growing panic in Westminster about the prospects that the Scots will vote 'Yes'.

The great fear that UK policy-makers are having to deal with now is that everything that we do and say has to be done with great sensitivity given that we have got several more British hostages in Iraq/Syria held by ISIL, who all face beheading over the weeks ahead. We have known about these other British hostages for some time, but the information has been held back. But a British citizen appeared at the end of the video of the recent execution of the American charity worker, so everyone now knows that it is a Brit who is next in line. What people in the country do not yet know is that there are more Brits who are also being held, who could also be the next to face the ghastly prospect of kneeling down in the desert next to a hooded executioner. Sickening barbarism.

SATURDAY 6 SEPTEMBER

Spent all day working on my red box, and in the evening did the regular Saturday night conference call. There is rumoured to be a poll tomorrow which will put the pro-independence camp ahead. A lot of talk about what can be done, but not really many new ideas.

SUNDAY 7 SEPTEMBER

Sure enough, there is a poll in the *Sunday Times* which puts the 'Yes' camp ahead at 51 per cent, with the 'No' camp at 49 per cent. The break-up of the Union is now a real prospect, though I still think that the Scottish people will pull back at the last minute.

MONDAY 8 SEPTEMBER

In the evening, held a reception to thank DfE colleagues for the delivery of free school meals.

When I got home in the evening, John Vincent texted me to tell me that there was a great package on *The One Show* about free school meals tonight. Had a look and it was unremittingly positive – really good news.

TUESDAY 9 SEPTEMBER

Cabinet. 9.30 a.m. A discussion about Scottish independence. Alistair Carmichael was rather subdued, but Danny set out the position well and he is clearly much more in the lead now than Alistair. Alistair, sadly, has not risen to the challenge. Indeed, the only thing I can remember him doing recently is speculating very unhelpfully on what would happen if the 'Yes' vote won the campaign, by saying that he would have to resign as Scottish Secretary and join Alex Salmond's team to negotiate with the UK government! A more unhelpful contribution could hardly be devised. Why on earth didn't we keep the solid Mike Moore as Scottish Secretary? Alistair is all ego and no delivery.

Cameron said that the NATO summit was a great insight into the massive amount of security around the US President – when his own helicopter came in to land in Wales, it was refused permission for about ten minutes, and Cameron had to hover overhead until clearance was finally given by the US President's security detail. Cameron said, 'I felt a bit peeved as the Prime Minister of the United Kingdom to have to get permission from the US President to land in my own country!'

Cameron also said that he found at international summits that when the conversation between national leaders lapsed, people tended to ask the 'how big is your one' question – i.e. 'What is your country's growth rate at the moment?' Cameron said in that regard he was having a more pleasant time than a year ago and 'no longer had anything to be ashamed of'.

After Cabinet, had a meeting on the Autumn Statement. What I have been thinking about is cutting council tax for lower-banded properties, probably cutting council tax bands A and B by 10 per cent and band C by 5 per cent or 10 per cent. This would be very popular, and it would make the council tax system more progressive by helping people in smaller properties. The problem is that it makes local authorities much more dependent upon Westminster grants. In addition, some councils would still raise council tax by 2 per cent, so that our promised cut of 10 per cent would then turn into only 8 per cent.

In the evening, got the good news that Michael Fallon has seen sense over the Apache upgrade contract. It now looks likely that he is actually going to allow AgustaWestland to compete for this contract. That is probably a direct result of my lobbying and the support I have had from Vince and Danny. The first time Fallon has ever been of help on anything.

Can never quite look Fallon seriously in the face after an embarrassing incident in 2013, when I went into the gents' toilets located at the far end of the lower ministerial corridor, right next to my office. I pushed at the door of the left-hand cubicle, which looked only partially shut. I had forgotten the lock was broken, and was confronted by the shocking scene of the Rt Hon. Michael Fallon, Minister of State for Business, squatting in front of me, reading *The Sun*. Quickly closed the door and rushed out.

WEDNESDAY 10 SEPTEMBER

David Cameron, Ed Miliband and Nick Clegg are all heading to Scotland to make their 'passionate pleas' for Scotland to remain part of the Union. The polls are still eye-wateringly close. I have a strong feeling that we have seen the high point of the independence wave, and my suspicion is that over the next week we are going to see a lot of panic about the economic consequences of independence, which will cause the Scottish people to pull back.

Today, I am launching the Talented Head Teacher programme, which is about deploying outstanding head teachers from parts of the country that are doing well to parts of the country that are doing badly. I asked how Tom Shinner's talk with No. 10 officials on the teacher quality package had gone, and the lead civil servant looked at me in a very civil servantish and straight-faced way and said, 'I understand the issue of qualified teacher training is now awaiting the opinions of Mr Lynton Crosby'!

Tomorrow have got to attend the Extremism Task Force, where the Prime Minister will no doubt try to bounce through more ill-considered and half-baked proposals. The latest idea is to regulate all supplementary schools, which are at present unregulated. But the problem is how to define the institutions to be regulated, so that we do not end up with compulsory regulation of Sunday Schools, private tutors etc. etc. As usual, none of this tends to be based on very much evidence, but just on the desire of the PM and the Tories to be seen to 'do something'.

THURSDAY 11 SEPTEMBER

At the end of the day, I received the DfE assessment of risk and performance in all policy areas. Free school meals is now rated ten out of ten for delivery. The pupil premium is rated eight out of ten. Meanwhile, academies, where there are a large number of academies in special measures, remain highly red-risk-rated, and the other red-risk areas are free school delivery and capital!

Nick Clegg apparently spoke to the US Ambassador last night and made clear that the UK did not want to be involved in military action in Iraq/ Syria, until after the 18 September referendum.

SATURDAY 13 SEPTEMBER

Conference call at 6 p.m. – mostly about Scotland. Apparently there are three polls out tomorrow – two of which put the 'No' camp ahead and one of which puts the 'Yes' camp ahead. Danny said that he thought that the 'No' camp was now ahead by somewhere between five and eight percentage points. This confirms my view that the final vote will be something like 55–45 in favour of 'No'.

Just before going to bed, I checked my iPhone and read with very great sadness the news that David Haines, the British charity worker held hostage in Syria by the Islamic State group, has been beheaded. As we feared, it is also the case that the next hostage being lined up for execution is another British charity worker. Ghastly and deeply depressing.

SUNDAY 14 SEPTEMBER

The Queen made her regular visit to Crathie Kirk near Balmoral. For once, after the service, she chatted with some of the well-wishers, in the unusual presence of the media. She told one of the members of the crowd: 'The Scottish people need to think very carefully before the vote next week.' This has, almost certainly correctly, been seen as a direct intervention by the Queen in the independence campaign – to try to nudge things towards a 'No' vote. A very rare intervention indeed, which dominates the evening media.

TUESDAY 16 SEPTEMBER

Home at around 9 p.m. and spent three hours working on my red box. A very good paper by Jon Andrews on assessing the performance of academy chains and local authorities. I would like to publish this before the parliament ends.

I am due to go up to Scotland tomorrow, to Glasgow, to help out in our campaign.

The three party leaders today all wrote an article for the *Daily Record*, promising Scotland a massive further devolution of powers in the event of a 'No' vote. This is all very well and good, but what on the earth does it mean for the rest of the United Kingdom? If we give substantial tax-raising powers to the Scottish Parliament so that they can control their own taxes, then why on earth should Scottish MPs vote on English taxes in England? This really runs the risk of unravelling the whole Union by the back door, if we continue to slice up the United Kingdom and its powers in this way.

WEDNESDAY 17 SEPTEMBER

Up at 4 a.m. for the second day in a row. A rather full flight from Bristol Airport up to Glasgow, and I arrived at around 8.30 a.m. I was picked up by the 'No' campaign, which turned out to be two Tory Party members, who chauffeured me to Jo Swinson's constituency office in a very plush Mercedes, with one of those adjustable seats which changes its position depending upon whether or not you are going round a bend. It has the effect of making you feel that your backside is being massaged by the car seat – which was rather nice but a bit bizarre.

Went out delivering leaflets for about three hours, and then came back to the office at lunchtime.

Later in the day, got an email from the director of strategy in the DfE. He made a strong case against Cameron's plan to regulate supplementary schools, and he said that what we should be banning is the activities that we did not like rather than forcing all institutions to register with us. The problem is that Cameron likes these 'wheezes', so that he can announce that he is 'doing something', even if the 'doing something' turns out to be not much or creates all sorts of other problems. Apparently he has set his heart on announcing this regulation of supplementary schools on the flight back from the UN Assembly at the end of next week. Now that this is in some ghastly No. 10 media grid, all the policy has to be lined up to support the announcement, even though it is not thought through.

Vince Cable was also up in Scotland today, but some media adviser of his had made the extraordinary decision that he should visit the government company that operates the English student loans system! Why we would want to highlight the loans that English students have to take out for tuition fees, God knows. Vince saw this as potentially helpful to the 'No' camp, given that many of the jobs in the Student Loan Company up in Scotland could be lost or relocated to England under independence.

But it seemed to some people in the 'Better Together' campaign like a massive potential own goal and they apparently phoned Vince up in a great strop first thing in the morning, and as he stopped to take their call, he then missed his plane up and therefore could not do the visit. I expect they were delighted.

Vince therefore took a later plane and basically just stood on a street stall all day. I had a brief dinner with him while we waited for our respective planes. Vince is still rather negative about the situation in his constituency, where he thinks the Greens, Conservatives etc. are doing very well at Lib Dem expense. He said the results in south-west London as a whole were pretty bad, and he is worried about his seat and Ed Davey's.

Took off from Glasgow at around 9.40 p.m. and we swung back over the city to turn south. The lights were twinkling up at us. Glasgow is always thought of by the English as being a bit of a dump, but some parts are really quite impressive. Its setting is also quite pleasant, with the countryside close by and a large mountain range in the distance. As we took off, I wondered whether this would be the last time I saw Scotland as a part of the United Kingdom – but somehow I doubt it will be.

THURSDAY 18 SEPTEMBER

The day of the Scottish independence referendum.

Decided to have a bit of a sleep in, and was still in bed at 7.45 a.m. when Switch called for the DPM call.

Not much to report on the Scottish referendum, other than that Andy Murray has apparently tweeted out his support for independence.

Yesterday, Nick was on his radio programme and was talking about the need for English votes on English-only matters once 'devo max' happens in Scotland. However, Danny was also on the media separately saying something about how Scottish MPs would still have to vote on all UK matters, including tax. Jonny raised this. Nick said that this was all OK because he was going to set up a commission to look into the matter and to report back on how English MPs should have separate voting rights in the future. I said that I was very concerned about this because we could not simply set up a commission and wish the problem away. We are going to be asked immediately for our views.

Nick got a little bit snappy and said that we could not resolve this immediately, and it would be fine to resolve it by a commission. I disagreed and said that once you start giving away powers on income tax to the Scottish Parliament it would become simply impossible to defend Scottish MPs voting on matters such as income tax in England, but this could also lead to a slippery slope where a UK government was unable to take decisions for England.

For example, if we had a Lib–Lab government at Westminster, but English votes for English MPs, then we could end up with a separate Finance Bill that only English MPs voted on, and separate votes on the NHS, English laws, policing, schools etc. etc. etc. As soon as you do that, you essentially have the Westminster Parliament split into two – with large numbers of debates which are English-only, and only a few debates on foreign policy/benefits etc. that Scottish MPs can take part in. The problem with this is you could then end up with the Tories losing a UK election but essentially being 'in power' for most matters at Westminster. You could also have a UK government that had very little power over matters in the vast majority of the United Kingdom.

Now, in the panic of wanting to throw the 'devo max' solution to the Scots in order to win the referendum, we are in danger of going down this very slippery slope. Of course, it is quite possible that both Labour and the Tories will resist the substance of 'devo max' or will renege on the offers that have been made to date – but that would bring its own problems. As soon as the call ended, Jonny Oates phoned me up and said that he shared my concerns. He said that we ought to do some fast-track work on what the consequences of 'devo max' would be.

Went over to Redstart School in Chard to see their delivery of the new infant free school meals policy. Redstart is run by a wonderful head teacher called Suzanne Flack, and she has thrown her whole heart into the policy. She has got a great school meal provider and has also made the free school meals compulsory for all children in Reception, Year 1 and Year 2.

The quality of the meals was absolutely fantastic. I sat down with a number of the children, and we had turkey, roast potatoes, beans and carrots, and then a very nice dessert of cherries on shortbread. Some of the catering staff said that on the first few days of the policy they actually had to show children how to use knives and forks – which I fear is all too common in schools across the country.

This school is doing exactly what should be done in every school across the country, and it is a real exemplar. The chair of governors who was there said to me that he could previously only afford to give his child in Key Stage 2 a hot meal twice a week, as otherwise it costs £12.50 per child per week – which he said was too much for him with two or three children. Of course, the Westminster-based media live on their own little planet where everybody can afford hot meals for their children three times a day. Sadly, it is not like that in the real world, which is why this policy is going to make such a difference. Left the school feeling very happy.

SATURDAY 20 SEPTEMBER

As I expected, we won in Scotland by a decent margin. Cameron yesterday put Miliband on the spot by saying that any further Scottish devolution is contingent upon English votes on English matters. There is a very good article today in the *Telegraph* by Charles Moore saying that effectively Cameron has neutered the whole constitutional reform issue by tying further Scottish devolution to English votes on English matters – something he must know will be unacceptable to the Labour Party and possibly even the Lib Dems. This is because it is so much in the interest of the Tory Party in England. They could lose a UK national election, but still effectively be in charge in England.

Nick came back to me in the afternoon having read the Moore article. He said:

> It is interesting, as you say, but far too rosy re. the position the Tories are in – Cameron will come up with an English votes solution which we will not support and then his MPs will refuse to support the devolution package for Scotland. He will have broken a solemn pledge to Scotland and look impotent to UKIP voters etc. The key policy priority for us is to identify, as soon as possible, a McKay-style (English votes) solution which is credible in England – even if it is deemed insufficient by the Conservatives/UKIP, so that we cannot be blamed with Labour for failing to stand up for England. Either way, acrimony and blockage beckons. Nick.

I emailed back to Nick later in the afternoon to say:

> English votes for English matters is utterly logical if things like tax get devolved to Scotland. We just could not have Scottish MPs voting for ever on English matters that are sensitive and have been devolved, without moving on this type of solution. This could become a huge issue in England. There are two risks. One is quite simply that the United Kingdom

becomes less united until it eventually collapses. I consider that as a very serious risk indeed. But also English votes on English matters would hugely empower the Tories. Look at the 2010 election results of England: the Tories had 39.5 per cent of the votes, Labour had 28 per cent and we had 24.2 per cent. But look at the seats: the Tories had 297 seats, Labour had 191 seats and the Lib Dems had forty-three seats. Now I take your point that we cannot just block the logic of English votes. But we surely can and must say that English votes on English matters may well make sense – but only if the Commons is elected by STV. Otherwise it would be one party ruling England on 39 per cent of votes. Just as Cameron thinks he has stuffed Labour by offering them a logical but impossible deal, we would be accepting the logic of English votes but offering DC something totally impossible for him.

Later in the afternoon, Nick sent through an email chain between himself and Cameron. Nick emailed Cameron on Saturday:

David, today's headlines are just so dispiriting. It feels like we have narrowly saved the Union north of the border only to see it Balkanised in Westminster re. English votes! I couldn't think of a stronger argument in favour of separatism. I am interested in finding a cross-party solution based on McKay etc., as per our conversation on Thursday, but I am not signed up to a Dutch auction of piecemeal reform. I will be speaking out on Lib Dem views on all this soon – but since I am supposed to carry the can on constitutional affairs for the government, I am not going to support what looks now just like messy one-upmanship.

Cameron sent back a reply just half an hour later:

Nick, sorry but I do not agree.

1. The decision you and I took for a referendum and one question was brave, right and justified. Separation has been defeated.
2. Labour's convention idea is a totally hopeless talking shop. The demand for a version of English votes is completely legitimate – and I thought one you could and should support.

3. I hope you can be part of this. But if all three parties in May next year say 'We all backed the draft clauses for Scotland but have different ideas for the rest of the devolution agenda', then so be it. Let's talk next week. DC.

After getting this positive feedback from Nick, I had another idea on how we might advance PR in Westminster, deal with the English issue and also trump David Cameron:

Nick, a variation on this PR theme would be as follows:

1. Keep the first past the post system for all MPs until we get support for change.
2. On English-only matters there would be two votes – one of the full Parliament of all MPs and one of a 'grand committee' of English MPs. This grand committee would be made up of existing MPs, elected under whatever the voting system happened to be, but made up in proportion to the party votes in the most recent general election. E.g. in 2010 it would be 50 English MPs which would be twenty Tory, thirteen Lib Dem, fifteen Labour and two others.
3. All English-only legislation would then require the votes of both bodies – both the full Commons and the PR English grand committee.
4. This variation of my earlier proposal has three clear merits. One is that it allows all MPs a vote on all issues. But it means that Scottish MPs cannot impose stuff on England against English MPs' wishes. And it has the merit of us sounding reasonable by not proposing to insist on changing the entire UK voting system – which might seem like a deliberate attempt to scupper reform.
5. Finally, this solution would be a massive Lib Dem win as it would insert a form of PR into Westminster and give us the swing votes on all English issues.

SUNDAY 21 SEPTEMBER

Not much in the newspapers. Went out for a pleasant run in the morning. Warm outside. River is still relatively low, but high enough to run over the top of the stepping stones along the side of the river as it opens out into the valley between Bibury and Coln St Aldwyn.

Got back to finish off my red box. Polly Mackenzie and Matthew Hanney have sent through an incredibly detailed paper about machinery of government issues in a second coalition. It goes into huge detail to the point of describing which office buildings Nick should inhabit and what the arrangements should be for the Deputy Prime Minister's wife!

Meanwhile, both Ed Miliband and David Cameron seem to be in a mess over the whole devolution issue. No. 10 were forced to 'clarify' the Conservative Party's position today – after an interview by Michael Gove in Saturday's *Times* saying that there would only be further devolution for Scotland if the English votes for English matters issue could be resolved at the same time. Cameron has now rowed back and said that Scotland will get its extra devolution whatever happens in England, but that the English votes matter should be taken forward 'at the same time'. Ed Miliband is also in a complete mess, acknowledging that there is an 'English' issue, but totally failing to give any answer to it. This is certainly going to cost the Labour Party votes south of the border.

MONDAY 22 SEPTEMBER

The middle of the Labour Party conference, and today Ed Balls gave his speech. The outline of Labour's economic policy is becoming clearer. Frankly, it is all a bit of a semi-socialist, left-wing Lib Dem, floppy mixture of populism and gimmicks. Ed has announced a 5 per cent cut in ministerial pay if Labour get in – exactly what the coalition did in 2010, and something that saves peanuts. He has also suggested freezing child benefit for an extra year. This saves a couple of hundred million at most. He is saying that he will bring in a 10p tax rate by abolishing the married couples' tax allowance, which shows the paucity of ambition on the 10p tax rate – as he would be able to introduce only a very, very tiny 10p tax band, of gimmicky size at best.

Ed Miliband is expected to announce tomorrow that Labour would boost funding for the NHS by using the proceeds of a mansion tax and a new 50p top tax rate. So it is 'soak the rich in order to spend more money on the NHS'. This will poll extremely well with the public, but it is the antithesis of New Labour. The problem for political parties can sometimes be that individual policies look popular by themselves when you poll them, but when you add up all of these populist policies, they do not constitute a credible and coherent whole.

Caught the 8 a.m. train from Paddington to Bath for a special meeting with our new coalition negotiating team. Travelled down with Danny Alexander and Matthew Hanney.

Ploughed through my box until the early hours of the morning, including having a look at the new Cabinet committee on devolution. The astonishing thing is that we have allowed William Hague to be in charge of this new committee, even though Nick is supposed to be leading on political reform.

I have looked at the list of members of the committee, and the Tories are certainly turning out their top people. As well as William Hague chairing the committee, it also includes George Osborne, Iain Duncan Smith, Oliver Letwin, Eric Pickles, Michael Gove, Theresa Villiers and Stephen Crabb as well as the Tory Leader in the Lords. Set against this, bizarrely, are three Lib Dems from Scotland – Danny Alexander, Alistair Carmichael and Jim Wallace – with just two English Lib Dems – me and Don Foster! Completely barmy.

Heard from an inside source that MG was rather taken aback by his enforced removal from the Department for Education in the recent reshuffle. He apparently came back from No. 10 Downing Street saying, 'My God, I can't believe how much they hate Dom Cummings and how much damage he has done to me!'

Also in my box tonight is a note from a senior DfE civil servant. The department is having to put out a statistical release on free school Ofsted inspection grades. This is as a consequence of Lord Nash and Michael Gove publicly saying that free schools are a great success because 21 per cent of them are rated as outstanding by Ofsted compared with just 10 per cent of all schools. However, it turns out the 10 per cent figure is extremely misleading, because this is only 10 per cent of schools which have been inspected since September 2012 – and these schools are not representative because outstanding schools are much less likely to be re-inspected. When you look at the total stock of all schools and work out how many of these are outstanding, you get about 20 per cent, which is statistically no different from the 21 per cent of free schools.

I pushed back hard against what we propose to put out, since it seems deliberately misleading. Got a reply from the civil servant, saying that the claim about free schools should never have been made, but it had been, by Michael Gove, and they were using their best efforts to get him out of a hole. It finished: 'Unless you want to land your colleagues in a big pile of brown stuff, you need to clear this!'

I decided to clear it, but also to file the information away for future use!

TUESDAY 23 SEPTEMBER

The day of Ed Miliband's speech to the Labour conference. But the media is dominated by US Air Force strikes against Islamic State fighters in Syria.

The truth is that the Labour conference has passed in a very low-key way, with lots of populist tax and spending policies, which don't add up to a credible mix.

Cameron has made a terrible balls-up in New York. He was apparently in conversation with ex-New York Mayor Michael Bloomberg and foolishly said, not realising that he was on camera, that the Queen had 'purred with pleasure' when Cameron told her about Scotland's rejection of independence.

At 8.30 a.m. gathered for the weekly meeting with Nick Clegg, and we talked about what key policies should be on the front page of our manifesto. We finally decided that the key priorities were:

1. balancing the budget on time and fairly;
2. increasing the personal income tax allowance to £12,500 per year;
3. a package of measures on education and social mobility;
4. investing in the NHS, and improving mental health provision.

At 1.30 p.m. I went to Nick's office for a final stock-take meeting on devolution and our new policy on English votes for English matters. At the beginning of the meeting, Nick said that he had had some fresh thoughts on the issue, and I bit my tongue, fully expecting him to change his mind. But to be fair, he stuck with it completely. It is also helpful that *The Economist* magazine has written a similar proposal to mine, entirely by accident, last weekend, where they also propose some kind of proportional representation system for representing English MPs. It will be interesting to see how the Tories handle this.

My Tory opponent in Yeovil constituency seems to have suddenly upped his game and gone from doing nothing to delivering two pieces of paid-for literature within the space of a few weeks. It looks like the Tories could suddenly start spending a huge amount of money in South Somerset – which means that I need to up my game.

WEDNESDAY 24 SEPTEMBER

Up at 5 a.m. to get down to Yeovil for 8.30 a.m. Was supposed to be an entire day in the constituency, but have to come back in the afternoon to attend the first Devolution Cabinet Committee, chaired by William Hague.

The newspapers are full of criticisms of Ed Miliband after what was widely regarded as a pretty lacklustre leader's speech yesterday. Worse still, Ed did the whole thing from memory, speaking for over an hour, but forgot to mention anything about deficit reduction or immigration. That might not have mattered had the Labour Party not released the text of what he planned to say – which included material on deficit reduction and immigration. In other words, it looked like either he forgot this section of his speech because he did not care about it very much, or he deliberately excluded it.

Started the canvassing for the general and district elections today in Winsham. The weather was sunny and pleasant. Did the sheltered housing scheme in the centre of Winsham – Davies Close. This was a good place to be because there were lots of pensioners, but the problem was they all wanted to chat, and invited me in.

Got back to London at around 3 p.m. for the first Devolution Cabinet Committee.

Our press people were sensitive about us all going up Downing Street together, with three Scottish parliamentarians in a five-man team! So Don Foster and I went down Whitehall and up No. 10 Downing Street, while Danny, Alistair Carmichael and Jim Wallace – the Scottish three – cut through the Cabinet Office into Downing Street.

Got to the Cabinet Room. All the Tories were already there – it looked as if they had had a pre-meeting. I was seated slap-bang in the centre. William Hague was sitting where the Prime Minister normally is, and I was opposite him. Hague had invited in a camera crew and a photographer to film the 'great occasion'. The Tories are dying to invite Ed Miliband along and see the Labour Party squirm on this particular hook. Danny also said that it might be useful to have some other parties come along and he mentioned Nigel Farage. I chipped in to suggest Douglas Carswell. Hague and Osborne took this in good grace!

We then had a discussion about connectedness in relation to the Scottish question and the English question. The Tory position is now that the two should be taken 'in tandem', but Danny Alexander, Alistair Carmichael and I chipped in very strongly to say that we could not now insert small print into the pledge made to Scotland before the referendum – and we had to proceed with the Scottish devolution settlement without making it conditional on anything else. Michael Gove spoke out strongly and somewhat aggressively for a different position. He said that whether we liked it or not, the English question and the Scottish question were linked and they had to be taken at the same pace and seen to be connected.

I said that I thought Michael was wrong. We had made a pledge to the Scottish people before the Scottish referendum and we could not be seen to renege on that or put conditions onto it. In addition, I said that solving the West Lothian question about English votes for English issues within a very short period of time was going to be very challenging. I said: 'I distinctly remember Michael Gove telling me just six months ago that "the only answer to the West Lothian question is not to ask it"!' There was some laughter.

Michael then said: 'The important thing in life is to learn from mistakes you have made when you are young, and correct them when you have grown up.' William Hague butted in: 'But Michael, you apparently said these things just six months ago!'

Oliver said that clearly there was now a need to resolve the English votes for English matters issue. He said the issue was 'whether the Liberal Democrats were interested in responding to the Conservative proposals on this, or whether the Conservatives would be the only party to have a proposal on English votes for English matters'.

It is clear the Tory strategy is to embarrass Labour to the maximum over this, not least by inviting them along to the Cabinet committee. The Tories would also then be quite happy to embarrass us, or to get us on side for change if we are willing to do that. I replied by saying, 'Look, there is no question of there being a Tory proposal on this English votes issue and no Lib Dem proposal. In fact, we are probably going to be ready to table a Lib Dem proposal in the next couple of weeks. The issue is not whether the Conservative Party will be the only people who have an idea on this, it will be whether the Lib Dem proposal and the Conservative proposal can be reconciled. But I do agree with Oliver that we should do this quickly.

'I would like, however, to make three points about our approach. The first point is a rather Conservative-friendly point, which is that there is a real risk here that the more we devolve powers, the more we put the United Kingdom future at risk if we do not do that in a very carefully thought-out way.'

I went on, 'We also believe, and Nick Clegg feels strongly about this, that we should use this committee to discuss more English devolution and decentralisation – and it is quite possible that we can make common grounds with Eric over these issues. But clearly the critical issue is over English votes for English laws. We do accept that further devolution to Scotland means that this question now needs to be answered. However, we need to think very carefully about our proposals here. I am one of those who is extremely cautious about the McKay proposals, but it seems to me that they give a voice to English MPs without giving any kind of veto or power.'

I made clear that if you have English votes for English matters, those have to be English votes based on fairness and some degree of proportionality. As I mentioned the fair votes issue and the proportionality issue, Oliver started to smile and laugh a bit. George Osborne also shifted somewhat uncomfortably in his seat. William Hague smiled across at me and said, 'But I thought the Liberal Democrats had tried the fair votes thing – and lost the referendum!'

At the end, Iain Duncan Smith tried to bang on about how important it was to resolve this whole English issue and how we ought to rewrite the entire Barnett Formula etc. George Osborne rolled his eyes. Iain also asked that we should commission work on what other countries do to solve this type of problem, and Hague and Osborne looked a bit despairing. Danny and I immediately seized the opportunity to say we thought that was a wonderful idea.

Hague had been planning to do a piece to camera, summing up the outcome of the meeting, but our press people threatened that if William did this then I would do a clip to camera for the Liberal Democrats. That caused the Tories to back off and it was decided that nobody should speak.

THURSDAY 25 SEPTEMBER

Supposed to be down in Yeovil, canvassing, but the Cabinet is meeting today prior to the recall of Parliament tomorrow. Of course, it is a formality that the Cabinet will approve the plans to take military action in Iraq.

Spoke to Nick on the issue of the NHS, and said I was clear that we could not stick with the current situation where NHS performance is deteriorating rapidly. I said that either we could fix this problem as a government, which would be my own priority, or we could offer a Lib Dem fix in the next parliament.

To my great surprise, Danny seemed to agree and proposed that we consider aligning the dividend tax rates with income tax for higher and additional rate taxpayers – which raises up to £1.7 billion. He said that this was something he had pressed at a number of Budgets without getting anywhere.

1 p.m. Cabinet. Iraq. It was incredibly crowded in the room because we had the heads of MI5, MI6 and the armed services. We also had a number of confidential papers marked 'Top Secret', relating to the intelligence services' assessments of the Islamic State's terrorists, who are trying to form their own Islamic State in the Syria/Iraq area. It seems as if there may be up to 20,000 or 30,000 of these fighters, and as many as five hundred of these may be from the United Kingdom. It was also clear from what we were told confidentially that there is now a real risk of some of these Islamic State fighters bringing their terrorism to the United Kingdom – and indeed, it sounds like the security services have managed to prevent a number of serious attacks on the UK over the last few weeks alone.

It was left to Vince Cable to be particularly awkward over the issue of Syria. The motion we are being asked to approve tomorrow gives us permission for military action in Iraq only. Vince highlighted that it seemed absurd to be attacking the Islamic State terrorists in Iraq but not in Syria.

Vince said he did not think this position was sustainable or logical. A number of the Tories nodded vigorously. George Osborne intervened to say that Vince was absolutely right but the plain fact of the matter was that there was not a majority in the House of Commons necessarily for military action against both Iraq and Syria. It was made clear by David Cameron that Ed Miliband and Labour have been incredibly cautious on this issue and were only supporting the motion tomorrow because it focused on Iraq. In addition, Osborne said that there were many Tory backbenchers who were opposed to military action in Syria and indeed even in Iraq, and he said that 'interestingly, there is a high correlation between Tory MPs who constantly call for higher defence spending and those who did not actually want to use our military assets in Iraq or Syria'.

SUNDAY 28 SEPTEMBER

Oh dear, oh dear, oh dear! The Sunday newspapers are covered with two Tory car-crash stories – the defection yesterday of the Tory MP Mark Reckless to UKIP, and the resignation of Cabinet Office Minister Brooks Newmark, who has been caught out by the *Sunday Mirror* texting rather indiscreet pictures of himself to a female undercover journalist!

The early announcements that the Tories were planning at their conference, about reducing the benefits cap and stopping benefits for young people – have been completely lost in the splurge of media coverage.

Cameron will be furious, and it blocks out all the 'War Leader' stuff, which he was no doubt preparing to deploy throughout this week, as British Tornado jets fly over Iraq desperately looking for a needle in a haystack.

Meanwhile, in my box today is a note from officials in the DfE which says: 'Minister, just to let you know, the meeting re. teacher quality package that the DfE was planning to have with Lynton Crosby was delayed today, so we still have not had a decision about whether or not we can go ahead with this.' Official confirmation that Lynton Crosby is now the person deciding whether or not we have a Royal College of Teaching! Quite unbelievable. Will have to chase this up with the Tories after their conference. We cannot have Lynton Crosby running the government's education policy.

MONDAY 29 SEPTEMBER

The Tories have got favourable blanket coverage for a rather obscure announcement by George Osborne about reducing some kind of very high tax rate of 55 per cent on unspent pension pots. Vintage Tory stuff which helps very rich pensioners, nobody else. For some reason it has got wall-to-wall coverage. I initially assumed that this was a Tory policy announcement for the next general election, but reading the small print it turns out actually to be a government policy announcement! I was pretty baffled, because I am supposed to clear the conference announcements but had not heard anything about this.

Soon clear that Nick knew nothing about it either. Nick suggested that I should make a formal complaint. However, five minutes later I got a telephone call from Stephen Lotinga. He said he had spoken to Danny's special adviser, who said that Danny had agreed this with Osborne late on Friday night – but without bothering to tell either Nick or me.

Danny telephoned me and sounded a bit embarrassed. I suspect he was caught napping by Osborne, and George probably managed to convince him that it was all rather minor and something that they had been consulting on for some time anyway. I bet Danny did not know how much it cost or that it was going to get so much newspaper coverage.

I put in a call to Nick Clegg. We both came to the conclusion that it might be best to signal that we were going to make the NHS the Lib Dem spending priority for the Autumn Statement this year, and possibly we could even get a double policy announcement out of our NHS conference commitment – with Nick announcing that the NHS was going to be our Autumn Statement priority, and then with Danny announcing the additional taxation and spending measures on the NHS that we will put in our own manifesto.

The only other major conference announcement today by the Tories has been on welfare savings, where George Osborne has announced a two-year Tory freeze in spending on working-age benefits. This means that there would be a 0 per cent increase for all benefits in 2015/16 and 2016/17 – which would save around £3.2 billion. Interesting that the Tories have no embarrassment at all about announcing a tax cut for very rich pensioners today, alongside a real cut in incomes for some of the poorest people in society. They really are shameless.

TUESDAY 30 SEPTEMBER

Spent the whole day in Yeovil constituency. Started our canvassing in earnest today – first in the tiny village of Limington, then Combe St Nicholas in the afternoon, and finishing in Chard.

WEDNESDAY 1 OCTOBER

Spent the entire day in the constituency canvassing for six hours. A beautiful day, sunny and warm, even though it is the beginning of October.

Cameron's conference speech, as Nick Clegg feared, has stolen our tax policy on the personal allowance – to the penny! The Tories are now committed to a £12,500 allowance in the next parliament, just as we are. But instead of saying that they will also seek to raise the national insurance contribution level to £12,500 – as we have – they have said that they will seek to raise the point at which the 40 per cent tax rate comes in from around £42,000 to £50,000. That will go down well with many of their upper-middle-class supporters, as well as stealing UKIP's main tax policy.

THURSDAY 2 OCTOBER

Woke up to find a couple of emails from Nick Clegg sent at 4 a.m.! He is obviously thinking about how to respond to the Tory conference, not least the stealing of our £12,500 tax allowance. I suggested we keep our nerve and move the focus to raising the starting level for national insurance.

The Tories will be absolutely delighted with the coverage in today's newspapers – *The Sun*, the *Express*, the *Mail*, the *Telegraph*, *The Times*, and even *The Independent* all splash on their massive tax cut offer. The British media has never been so partisan.

Met Oliver Letwin and Jo Johnson about conference announcements. The Prime Minister is blocking our policy of tougher sanctions for the theft of personal data. He sees this as a potential assault on the press, and he won't do anything to piss off the media in advance of the election. When you see the press coverage that the Tories are getting, you can see why.

On the way to the Devolution Committee, I bumped into George Osborne, who was looking pretty smug. I congratulated him on so much front-page coverage out of his change to pension tax relief: 'Well, by now

I've learnt how to titillate the media, and they certainly like stuff to do with tax cuts and pensions!' Then he said, with his magnificent cynicism, 'It took until the afternoon before one journalist realised that all I was doing was reversing a tax increase which I myself brought in earlier in the government!' and he put his head back and chuckled.

We then started the meeting of the Hague Cabinet Committee, with the usual cast.

Hague has today written to Harriet Harman, inviting the Labour Party to send along some representatives. Somebody suggested that Labour should also be invited to send somebody from the Lords. Oliver Letwin said, 'Oh my God, no! If the Labour people in the Lords send someone, it's bound to be Charlie Falconer, and he doesn't get on with Harriet at all. I've been in a room with the two of them and it was an absolute nightmare!' I looked over at the clerks who take the minutes – one of them stopped writing and looked at me, shrugging her shoulders. The other just put his pen down and looked serious.

We then came on to the whole issue of English votes. I let Oliver kick off the discussion.

I said that I assumed the Tories had concrete proposals, since they were making so much noise about the matter. They all looked rather nervous. George Osborne, who is clearly getting a little bit bored, said that perhaps it was not necessary for us to meet every week, and perhaps Oliver and I could be detailed to go off and bring proposals back to the committee. Everybody seemed to think that was a good idea.

Had a chat with Luke Tryl, the Secretary of State's special adviser. He said that the Tories have now been 'banned from discussing qualified teacher status' by Lynton Crosby. Apparently the Tory policy of having unqualified teachers polls incredibly badly.

FRIDAY 3 OCTOBER

Today is the start of our Glasgow conference. I awake with a heavy heart.

By 4 p.m. I had checked into the Premier Inn. The room is nice enough and I have a massive panorama overlooking Glasgow. I would like to say that it is quite impressive, but down to the right of me is an eight-lane carriageway, and in front are a series of enormous cranes.

I hate party conferences. They are expensive. This one will probably cost me in excess of £600. They are stressful, because often there are votes which the leadership is worried about losing. They are tiring, because you have to get up first thing in the morning, do media and go to bed last thing at night. And they are very tribal events, and I'm not a tribal person.

Tonight at around 9 p.m. the horrific news came through that the Islamic State terrorists have killed the British hostage, Alan Henning – a British charity aid worker – in Syria. Barbaric.

SATURDAY 4 OCTOBER

Today is the first full day of the Lib Dem conference.

Labour does not look like a potential party of government, while the Tory Party is increasingly lurching to the right and looks less and less each day like a potential future coalition partner for us. The Conservatives are now committed to: a referendum to leave the European Union; English votes for English laws in the most extreme and ill-considered way; dumping the Human Rights Act; carrying out the rest of the fiscal consolidation without any contribution from taxation; reducing benefits for people of working age, including those in work, in order to fund tax cuts for the top 10 per cent of earners; and a massive programme of cuts that would be bound to decimate public services.

The more I think about this, the more difficult it is to see a coalition with the Tories after the next election. And do I really want to spend the most important ten years of my political life supporting a Conservative-led government – particularly in its second term when it would have moved well away from the compassionate conservatism that Cameron originally espoused? If the answer to this question is no, then either the Lib Dems are going to be in opposition after the next election, come what may, or we would have to make common cause with a Labour Party led by Ed Miliband – and with the least impressive frontbench team that I can remember since the years of Michael Foot and Neil Kinnock. Neither of these things is a very enticing prospect.

MONDAY 6 OCTOBER

I look out from my hotel room onto another dreary, drizzly day in Glasgow. The weather reflects my mood.

Had dinner with some of the *Guardian* journalists last night, including the very nice Nick Watt. It's clear that he and the others are unimpressed by Miliband – they see him as a soft-left figure who is usually on the wrong side of most major arguments. One said that Ed Balls regards Ed M with real contempt: 'Whatever you think about Ed Balls, he is a serious figure in terms of economic policy, and he regards Miliband as some sort of flaky figure who just wants to "re-invent world capitalism".'

TUESDAY 7 OCTOBER

We debated our entire general election manifesto for May 2015, yet the discussion was pretty uninspiring. The only serious debate was about airports policy!

Summing up of the debate was done by Duncan Brack – who loyally saw off amendments to completely abolish the bedroom tax and to spend even more money on social care. But the problem of Duncan summing up is that he absolutely pounded the amendment that sought to keep open airports policy until after the Davies Commission has reported. Instead, he successfully defended the Luddite position that there should not be a single extra piece of airport capacity anywhere in the United Kingdom. We are now stuck with a completely idiotic airports policy.

Dinner with Paddy Ashdown, Olly Grender and others. Drank far too much. Back at 2 a.m.

WEDNESDAY 8 OCTOBER

Woke up with a terrible hangover, feeling knackered and dehydrated.

The last day of the conference – thank God!

THURSDAY 9 OCTOBER

Very good coverage today of Nick's conference speech – with a lot of praise for the concentration on mental health issues.

I was due to go off to the Roux restaurant in Westminster to have dinner with Sir Michael Wilshaw. However, just when I was preparing to leave, Phil Castle, one of my private secretaries, came in to say that unfortunately there was going to be a *Guardian* story tomorrow about a leaked Cummings email criticising the Chief Inspector and Ofsted.

They brought in a copy of the email, dated 23 October 2013. It was entitled 'Ofsted, quis custodiet ipsos custodes?' It reads:

I am increasingly alarmed about Ofsted … I never hear anybody say they are good.

They have missed massive child abuse scandals under their noses … They are easy to con into giving inflated judgements. There has been an abyss between stated goals and practice and the actual behaviour of their inspectors. Wilshaw himself admitted when he took over that 'about a fifth' of his inspectors are 'no good'.

There is no evidence this has changed substantially.

Despite constant pressure from us and constant assurances, there is no evidence that he is substantially changing the organisation…

In short, I think that Ofsted is a serious and growing problem that requires the urgent attention of senior people in the DfE.

At the very least, MW needs a highly competent COO who can manage the organisation well and remove the x% who need removing.

But beyond that, it is worth thinking about the whole Ofsted approach with a blank sheet of paper.

No element of human life that works well – e.g. Silicon Valley – works on an Ofsted basis. If you want excellence, you hold people accountable effectively for failure and channel incentives well – you do not issue endless instructions and have many subpar performers trawling around with clipboards that don't reflect accurately what the real goals are…

Dom.

I walked over to Roux restaurant, in a light rain, and got there after Sir Michael – who was already upstairs in the bar. He looked a bit downcast and said, 'Well, I have not had a particularly good day – made worse by this Cummings stuff. This is going to be very damaging.' I told him not to overreact and said that he was only one in a line of people including the Deputy Prime Minister who had been slagged off by Dom. I said that the best thing that he could do is not overreact.

We went downstairs and had a very pleasant dinner, covering a lot of ground:

1. He did not seem to me to be getting on well with Nicky Morgan, and said he would quite like me to act as a go-between.
2. He thinks that the reforms that Michael Gove made to qualifications and the curriculum were generally pretty good and necessary.
3. He thinks that too many sponsored academy chains are rubbish, and he thinks the whole converter academy movement has been a waste of time.
4. He is very critical of free schools and largely thinks that they are a waste of time and a distraction from the drive for higher standards. He said that one of the recent free schools is 'absolute rubbish and one of the worst schools I've ever seen'.
5. He is worried that the department and the Conservatives in it have been trying to stop him from holding academies and free schools properly to account.
6. He thinks that the National College has been run down too much and that there is a need for a proper middle tier in English education. He thinks that you cannot possibly run all the schools from Whitehall, and that autonomy does not by itself drive improvements.
7. He thinks that the drive to increase the number of initial teacher training places through School Direct is heavily ideologically driven and may well go wrong.

Have decided that I will put out a strong line of my own tomorrow defending Sir Michael against people who want to muzzle him. I drafted a line saying that Ofsted should be a 'watchdog, not a DfE poodle'. That will rile the Tories, but who cares.

FRIDAY 10 OCTOBER

As expected, UKIP have won the Clacton by-election – with a thumping majority.

Spent most of the day canvassing in my constituency and doing two advice centres. Lots of UKIP-type voters.

MONDAY 13 OCTOBER

In my box today, a letter from Jeremy Hunt to Cameron about the performance of the NHS. This points out that the NHS is facing declining performance against the Accident and Emergency, eighteen weeks, ambulance, diagnostic and cancer standards, all set in a context of unprecedented demand and a tightening financial settlement. The extra demands on the NHS are extraordinary. For example, the NHS is referring 51 per cent more people to a specialist with suspected cancer than it did in 2010 and is doing 3.6 million more diagnostic tests each year compared with 2010. The NHS is also seeing nearly 1.3 million people more in Accident and Emergency in 2013/14 compared with 2009/10.

At 12.30 p.m. went to Nick Clegg's office for the monthly political meeting with Paddy Ashdown, Hilary Stevenson and co. Nick said that he had recently seen Andrew Neil, and Andrew is predicting a huge surge in SNP seats.

We went through the status of a lot of our key seats, and there was some discussion about Twickenham – Vince Cable's seat, and surprisingly shaky.

Interesting to hear Ryan Coetzee say that we have already written off the Berwick-upon-Tweed seat, previously held by Sir Alan Beith. A brief discussion of Somerton and Frome, the seat to the north of me. This seat is also highly likely to be lost.

Ofsted have also been asking the DfE for data on the recent GCSE results, but the DfE hasn't released this. Apparently the department thinks that Ofsted is looking for evidence that the results have deteriorated more rapidly for sponsored academies and converter academies than for maintained schools.

I looked at a brief note that one of our officials was proposing to send to Ofsted, giving them only very high-level data on the GCSE results. The note was rather economical with the truth and I said that it should not be sent out in the form it was in. It implied that academies were actually doing much better than local authority schools in dealing with the recent exam changes. This is not actually true – with sponsor academies being worst hit.

TUESDAY 14 OCTOBER

Cabinet at 9.30 a.m. An update on mental health. This follows Nick's very well-received announcement on improved mental health standards. Cameron went out of his way twice to say, 'This is of course an announcement that Nick made at the Liberal Democrat conference, but it must be seen as a coalition announcement that has full coalition support.' Cameron knows a popular policy idea when he sees one!

At 1.15 p.m. we had a meeting with Nick and Danny and officials about the Autumn Statement. Danny kicked off by talking about the tight fiscal position (yawn!). He then listed his priorities, including: bringing forward the £500 increase in the personal tax allowance; extra money for the National Health Service for 2015/16; infrastructure investment, including upgrading the A303; possible changes to the bedroom tax.

I said that I broadly supported this.

Later in the evening, had a look at tomorrow's newspapers and saw that the Tories are now talking about increasing the inheritance tax threshold again in the Autumn Statement. Unbelievable that they want to push for this type of thing which only favours rich people, but they seem now to be just chasing right-wing votes. Clearly, we cannot support a Budget/Autumn Statement which throws lots of tax cuts at rich people, funded by the kind of welfare cuts that Osborne will want to see.

WEDNESDAY 15 OCTOBER

Today started with breakfast with Oliver Letwin in the basement of No. 10. Had a kipper, tomatoes, mushrooms and a hash brown. We had a bit of banter about what it would be like if the Conservatives were in government by themselves after the next election. I said that the Conservative Party appeared to be making a lot of dotty pledges on things like inheritance tax, and that I assumed the only reason that they were making all these dotty pledges is that they hoped that they would be in coalition with the Liberal Democrats so that we could bail them out by blocking these things. Oliver raised his eyes to heaven at the PM's pledge to raise the inheritance tax threshold: 'Yes, it might be a good deal easier if we were in coalition with you, rather than having to negotiate with some of our own backbenchers – who we have nothing in common with at all!'

Did a couple of interviews live from College Green about Jeremy Browne's resignation as an MP. Feeling rather gloomy at the moment. The evenings are getting dark. The rain is coming down heavily. People like Jeremy

Browne, Don Foster, Malcolm Bruce, Ming Campbell and David Heath are all standing down at the next election. The opinion polls are pretty difficult. The Tories are putting a huge amount of literature out in my seat. It is going to be a long, lonely trudge between now and the general election in May 2015, and it could be a close-run thing even though I had a majority of over 13,000 last time.

SUNDAY 19 OCTOBER

A lovely sunny autumn day, with temperatures touching 20°.

In my weekend box, the news that the PM has dropped the regulation of supplementary schools, and says that nothing should be published on this before the election. Apparently this is because they have been unable to convince Nicky Morgan to go for the model of lower-level regulation that Oliver and I agreed a couple of weeks ago. And apparently they have realised what a political storm the Morgan model would cause with the churches and others.

MONDAY 20 OCTOBER

A lot of publicity this morning about Cameron and the way he is playing with fire over our future in the EU. He has hinted that he is going to renegotiate Britain's position in the EU to put a cap on EU migrant workers. Barroso, the EU official, was on *Marr* yesterday criticising this approach and warning that it could leave Britain without allies and unable to deliver on its reform agenda. In the short term, Cameron is not going to mind an argument with 'some EU bureaucrat', but in the longer term this could be a real headache. The problem is that Cameron is so desperate to win the upcoming by-election against UKIP, and maximise his chances of winning the next general election, that he will promise almost anything to the right. But it is questionable whether it would be possible in the next parliament to renegotiate EU free movement. In that case, an EU referendum could end up being fought against the backdrop of a failed negotiation with the European Union, which could easily lead to Britain's exit from the European Union altogether.

Monday ministerial meeting at the Department for Education. These meetings are terrifically different from the old days, when Michael would chair them in his quirkish way.

On this occasion, we were presented with a large A3 spreadsheet from Nicky and her team, which apparently reflects 'the Secretary of State's new priorities'. There was a slightly sycophantic presentation by the head of press, Gabriel Milland. It was so sycophantic that at one point I thought it was supposed to be a joke – when he said the 'go to' moment of the next week's media was going to be the Secretary of State's appearance in front of the Education Select Committee.

The spreadsheet with the Secretary of State's priorities was then passed around the table and ministers started looking at it while Nicky was speaking. My God, it could not have been more different from the set of priorities that Michael Gove would have listed. Three broad areas were set out, including 'Life in Modern Britain', 'Teacher Engagement', and 'Protecting Vulnerable People'. Under these headings were various items that would never have found their way into a list of Michael Gove's priorities, including 'Body Confidence', 'Women in Work', 'Equalities', and 'The Importance of Careers Advice and Guidance'.

I could feel a chill around the table as rather dry ministers such as Nick Gibb and Lord Nash looked desperately down the list for any mention of the 'old favourites' – academisation, free schools etc. Even Sam Gyimah asked where early years were listed in the table. Nicky replied: 'Of course, there are loads of other things that are priorities, but as Secretary of State I want ministers to feel free to develop these other policy areas themselves, and what is on this list are really my own priorities as Secretary of State.'

The whole list was so strikingly different from Gove's ministerial priorities that I had to choke back a strong desire to burst out laughing. I nudged Lord Nash, who was sitting next to me, and said, with relish: 'I hope that your speeches are going to include strong sections on this area' – jabbing at the paper in front of us, and pointing to the line that said 'Body Confidence'. Lord Nash glanced at me and just frowned.

At 4 p.m. went over to the Lib Dem Cabinet ministers' meeting. Nick said that dealing with Cameron and the Tory Party right now was like dealing with a 'demented gorilla which is charging around desperately all over the place out of control'. Nick said that the Tory Party is simply not thinking rationally – and neither is David Cameron. Nick is particularly thinking of the last few days, where Cameron has plunged into this commitment to renegotiate the principle of open movement within the EU.

At the bottom of my red box tonight I found an extraordinary note from Nicholas Macpherson, the Permanent Secretary to HM Treasury. This was entitled 'Note from Liam Byrne' and it read:

> In July 2013 the chief executive of the National Archives enquired about the whereabouts of the note dated 6 April 2010 that Liam Byrne left for you as his successor in the post of Chief Secretary to the Treasury. At the time, we made clear to them that although we considered the note to be intrinsically a Treasury document, this was currently held by you personally … Given its significance, it would be good to retain the note for posterity as part of the Treasury's records, which will subsequently transfer to the National Archives at the appropriate time (currently twenty years after its creation). However, I recognise that it will be a wrench for you to part company with it. If you felt able to let the Treasury have the original, we can provide you with a high-quality colour copy in its place. But if you are not yet ready to relinquish the original, an alternative might be for us to take a copy for our records on the basis that you agree to return the original to the Treasury at some point in the future.

The Liam Byrne note really has ended up as a part of political history.

TUESDAY 21 OCTOBER

In at 7 a.m. Did a BBC Somerset Radio interview at 7.50 about the A303 – the government is planning to dual this and announce it in the Autumn Statement, and there is going to be considerable competition between the two coalition parties to claim credit.

At 9.30 a.m. went off to the Cabinet meeting, where we were discussing NHS 'winter pressures'. I pointed out rather bluntly that we have now run out of road on the strategy of protecting the NHS budget in real terms. I said that if we wanted to keep on doing that, then we would have to accept a deterioration in NHS standards. The Prime Minister looked, I thought, rather nervous, and when I finished by saying that I was very worried about the state of the NHS in the run-up to winter, he said, somewhat grumpily, 'Well, we can all agree with that!'

Jeremy Hunt looked pleased with my contribution, as it can only help him in his battle with the Treasury. George Osborne and Danny Alexander were rather quiet for a change.

I was texted by Polly Mackenzie in the afternoon, to say there had been a minor communications disaster. Ryan Coetzee had left a meeting about manifesto preparation and walked down Whitehall with all his papers facing outwards, and had been photographed. So, embarrassingly, all Ryan's priorities for the front page of the manifesto are now splashed all over the media, along with his list of fifteen key policy areas. This will all be written up by the media as a bit of a Lib Dem shambles, though the truth is that since the list of policies Ryan has on his pieces of paper are the ones that poll best with the public, this will largely mean that we get quite a lot of favourable publicity.

WEDNESDAY 22 OCTOBER

At 10.15 a.m. attended the fourth meeting of the Devolution Cabinet Committee, chaired by William Hague. George Osborne was not there, presumably because we were 'only' discussing Wales. We agreed a reasonably good paper by Stephen Crabb, the ultra-low-profile Welsh Secretary, whose name most people usually cannot remember. At the end of the meeting, IDS rabbited on about some issue, which I could barely understand. The problem is that IDS talks in utter gobbledegook – in communication terms he is effectively the John Prescott of the Conservative Party. If you literally wrote down what he said, it would make no sense at all, and his brain seems to leap from one point to another in a totally disconnected way. I feel sorry for the civil servants who have to write notes of what ministers are actually saying. I think he is personally quite a pleasant and decent man, but coherent he is not.

Also had a briefing on the Key Stage 4 and 16–19 results that are going to be released tomorrow. The GCSE results are going to show a massive drop in the proportion of young people getting five good GCSEs including English and maths, by five or six percentage points – easily the largest drop since GCSEs were introduced. The headline measure of five GCSEs, including all subjects, is going to drop by a massive twenty percentage points (almost), because of the disallowing of various 'easy' qualifications which used to be permitted under Labour. This is certainly going to attract a lot of media coverage. Even Nick Gibb, the dry-as-dust fellow Schools Minister, who is going to have to front this up in the media, looked a bit shocked.

At 4 p.m. went over to Nick Clegg's office for what is supposed to be the weekly trilateral meeting between Nick Clegg, Danny Alexander and me. Nick said he had just had a long lunch with Ken Clarke, who was in expansive and jovial mood. Ken apparently said that the Tories do not expect to get a majority at the next election, and he thinks it is quite possible that the Tory Party will split after the next general election – as many of the Tories are now so right-wing that they would not want to go into coalition with the Lib Dems, and they are so anti-European that some of them will just splinter off towards UKIP.

At 5 p.m. we had to go to the Extremism Task Force in the Cabinet Room. Cameron appeared a couple of minutes late, and he had been clearly watching the TV news, where there are pictures coming through of a number of shootings in the Canadian Parliament. Some madman on the loose. Because we had the heads of MI5, MI6 and the Metropolitan Police, Cameron started off by asking them what they knew about the matter and whether it was likely to be some kind of Islamic terrorist. The head of MI6 rather stuttered and stumbled and I got the distinct impression that he did not have a clue. People like to think that the security services know everything about what is going on, but I suspect the truth of it is that they are quite often reliant upon what they see on the TV news, along with snippets of information that they get from the CIA and the American security services!

Worked on my box for a couple of hours in the evening and then at 8.30 p.m. caught a taxi to Putney to have dinner with Nick. We met in a restaurant called Alquimia. I had to ask for the table booked in the name of 'Nick Williams' – Nick's current codename for these occasions.

Nick confirmed that he was becoming increasingly worried about the possibility of going in with the Tories after the next election. He thinks that they have such an extreme view on Europe that it might be impossible. Nick said also that whatever we negotiated with the Tories on Europe in the coalition agreement would be 'worthless', as Cameron simply panders to his own party's extremist views – so we could not trust him not to move the goalposts.

I said that this was true, though if we went into coalition with the Tories and they moved the goalposts, we could simply leave the coalition – but I acknowledged that being in coalition with the Tories effectively for a period of a decade would be very difficult.

Labour, on the other hand, we both agreed, is unimpressive and much more tribal than the Tories, and would be more difficult to get on with on a personal level. But Nick and I agreed that in values terms and policy terms it would not be difficult to put together a coalition. Nick said again that he likes David Cameron and finds him a nice and decent person, but also quite superficial. We agreed that if you ask David Cameron what he wanted his legacy to be, he would probably just respond with a load of waffle. Anyway, it was an interesting meeting and the first time that Nick has ever expressed a view on which party we were more likely to be in coalition with after the election. But in his own mind he certainly has not made a final decision not to go into coalition with the Tories, and he is clearly of the view that we have to be seen to be absolutely equidistant.

He said that things are quite tough in Sheffield. He is certainly not taking his own seat for granted. I asked about Danny's seat and Nick said that was a more worrying situation than Danny was inclined to admit. Nick said that Ryan Coetzee's view was that the polling was bad. Nick even let slip that Danny had considered the possibility of leaving the Cabinet before the general election to fight his seat – but Nick said that they both decided that the optics of this for the party were too bad to consider seriously.

We discussed what we would do if we were in coalition after the next election and Nick said he thought that the best thing was for him to retain the Deputy Prime Minister role without taking on a major department, and he agreed with me that we ought to take the Education Department. Nick still appears to want me to be the Secretary of State for Education if we did take over that department, though I made clear that my ambition is still to go back to the Treasury.

FRIDAY 24 OCTOBER

One hell of a row has blown up in the EU, at what was otherwise supposed to be a rather quiet summit focusing on environmental policy. Some EU officials recalculated all the contributions for member countries going back for the last decade, and said that because of differences in the expected size of the European economies there would have to be rebates for some nations and bigger contributions from others.

Needless to say, the only country which is making a significantly bigger contribution is the UK, which is calculated to need to pay another £1.7 billion! Apparently this took the Prime Minister and the Treasury by surprise. Nick said the whole thing would be highly amusing were it not such a tragedy in British political terms. It helps UKIP and nobody else. All the British political parties are saying what an outrage it is, though for the time being it looks as if it is something that has been recalculated in previous years and usually has led to a few hundred million pounds either being rebated to us or paid by us. But this year the amount is particularly large – it is being suggested that they have counted in the black economy for the first time, including areas like prostitution! You really could not make it up.

MONDAY 27 OCTOBER

Labour really are in a dreadful mess and over the weekend the Labour leader in Scotland has resigned, saying that the national Labour Party treats the Scottish Labour Party as if it were a 'branch office'. This type of criticism will be joyous music to the SNP's ears, and could set Labour up for a dreadful general election performance in Scotland in May 2015.

Some of the media carries reports of Tory splits over the European arrest warrant. Apparently Theresa May is trying to stick with the government line of support for the European arrest warrant; Michael Gove is apparently being a 'loyal' Chief Whip, while pushing the boundaries to see whether the position needs to be changed because of Eurosceptic backbenchers.

TUESDAY 28 OCTOBER

Nick said that he had had a pretty interesting discussion with Osborne today about the Autumn Statement. Apparently George is trying to get a whole load of infrastructure investment for Manchester or Manchester/ Leeds, but missing out Sheffield. Nick feels that there should be proper investment in all the northern cities including Sheffield, and he is threatening to veto the extra investment for Manchester unless he gets investment in Sheffield. Apparently Osborne, ever the cynic, offered to drop his proposal to invest in Leeds, so that he would promote Manchester (near his constituency) and Nick would get the investment in Sheffield. Nick said he did not think that was acceptable and that he really needs to get a package of investment for Manchester, Leeds and Sheffield. George then apparently discussed the need for further fiscal consolidation in the next parliament. At the Tory conference he was talking about an extra £25 billion worth of fiscal consolidation, but now he has admitted – as Danny Alexander said at the time – that actually we need more like £33 billion. When Nick questioned him on this, George said, 'Oh, £25 billion and £33 billion are pretty similar – perhaps we can just fudge this, as the figures are always rather complicated at Budget time. We do not need to be too explicit about whether it is £25 billion or £33 billion.' Nick said he teased George and said that he was in danger of losing his reputation for fiscal prudence.

Nick then went on to say that he had discussed the NHS with Osborne, who responded: 'I assume more money for the NHS is a Liberal Democrat demand – after all, I hear Norman Lamb talking about the need for more money for the NHS, and more for mental health.' Nick said that he did not regard the NHS as only a Lib Dem ask, but he assumed that both sides of the coalition would actually want to make sure there was not a crisis before the general election.

My view is that given the NHS is incredibly popular and it is now just about the No. 1 public priority, we should as a party now be going out in a fairly robust way campaigning for more money – whereas we are rather holding back on the basis that we do not want this to be seen as 'our' ask.

Nick apparently said to Osborne that he believes that the Autumn Statement should be a 'big' fiscal moment, whereas the Budget next year should be a small and restrained event: 'Look, George, I really don't think the Lib Dems would gain much ever from fiscal events – when they go badly they tend to hit you and when they go well they tend to benefit you.'

Chris Saunders said that he thought the best fiscal event for the Liberal Democrats had actually been the March 2012 Budget, when there was the 'omnishambles', which did so much damage to George Osborne. Cynical – but it may well also be true.

Then Nick came to the final big proposition that Osborne had made to him. He apparently says that what he really wants to make the centrepiece of his Autumn Statement is a big rise in the inheritance tax threshold – to take lots of wealthier people out of inheritance tax. George is saying that if we would agree to the inheritance tax cut then he would agree to the reversing of the 'bedroom tax', though apparently he is suggesting that we should pay for the reversal of the bedroom tax by other cuts in welfare!

We all said that it would be a very toxic moment, like the cut in the top tax rate from 50p to 45p, particularly as we have made such a thing at our conference about a proper contribution from rich people, and not having tax cuts for the rich. In addition, as Chris Saunders pointed out, the bedroom tax would simply be seen as a U-turn, whereas we would be 'trading' this for a new policy of giving the Tories tax cuts for their rich friends. All of us came out very negatively against it, even the civil servants!

The Tories really are unbelievable. Utterly predictable. They leave us to push for tax cuts for the poor and those on middle incomes, and for extra money for the NHS, and they use all their political 'capital' on right-wing policies such as cutting inheritance tax, freezing public sector pay, cutting welfare budgets and having more unspecified 'efficiency savings'.

WEDNESDAY 29 OCTOBER

Norman Lamb has emailed me today about the Autumn Statement to say:

> Fascinatingly, Jeremy Hunt told me today that he had sent a private letter to Cameron to say that the NHS needed £1.5 billion extra for 2015/16 and that a billion of that needs to come from the Treasury! Sounds familiar? He says that they [the Tories] are moving on this now and he thinks we can get this sort of sum – so the Chancellor wanting to label this as a Lib Dem demand – when the Tories will do it anyway – is Osborne's attempt to be smart! Nonetheless, seems completely daft for us not to identify the Lib Dems with demanding it – and securing it.

Meanwhile, Hague is pressing for an 'English devolution Command Paper', similar in style to the Scotland Command Paper, to set out the conclusions of our Cabinet committee. The idea is that it would set out the way forward on 'English votes' and decentralisation.

THURSDAY 30 OCTOBER

To the Cinnamon Club for breakfast with Andrew Adonis. Andrew cannot disguise the fact that he is not a big fan of Ed Miliband, but said that Ed's best decision was to avoid a referendum over the EU. Andrew asked whether we were likely to change our position on this, and I said that we were not.

Andrew seemed to assume that the outcome of the next election is going to be a hung parliament, and when I got up to leave, he said, 'I suspect we will be working closely together over the next couple of years!' However, the polls show that Labour is getting crucified in Scotland by the SNP, and if they lose twenty or thirty of their Scottish MPs, they may be sunk.

I asked Andrew what he thought the Labour Party's attitude would be to a demand on our part for proportional representation for local government. Andrew's face lit up at this prospect, and he is a lot more positive about the possibility of Labour conceding this than I had expected. Andrew said that PR for local government had been conceded in Scotland, and it could be a way to the rebirth of Labour in the south of England.

FRIDAY 31 OCTOBER

Spent most the day canvassing – in wonderful autumn sunshine. It was so hot that I had to go back to the car and take my jacket off, and just walked around in shirt sleeves. Almost November, yet a temperature of 22°C.

MONDAY 3 NOVEMBER

The papers are full of Cameron's slap in the face from Merkel – who has said that if Cameron tries to block EU free movement then she would not be prepared to concede it and would even be prepared to see Britain leave the EU! Frankly, this is deeply embarrassing for Cameron, but how he did not see it coming, God only knows.

In the morning, we also had a discussion about whether or not we should agree to the Tory demand for publishing a Command Paper on English devolution. The meeting started unpromisingly when I asked firstly Jonny Oates, then Matthew Hanney and then the civil servants, what exactly a

'Command Paper' was, only to discover that nobody really seemed to know. The best answer I got was that it was something between a Green Paper and a White Paper. The Tories apparently want this Command Paper out in the week of 17 November, which just happens to be the week of their latest by-election against UKIP – no chance.

I missed the Lib Dem ministers' meeting because I rushed over to 4 Millbank to do some broadcast media on plans to upgrade the A303 road into the south-west. The Tories have been making a lot about this in my constituency, and I want to make sure that I get some of the credit when this is finally announced. We are worried that the Chancellor is suddenly going to pop up in the south-west and claim all the credit himself. So instead, Nick is going down to Somerset on Friday 7 November, to basically pre-announce the announcement.

TUESDAY 4 NOVEMBER

In the evening, had dinner at Quirinale with the other Schools Minister, Nick Gibb. Nick is a really nice person and a big fan of the coalition. He is very socially liberal, but also very small-c conservative when it comes to schools policy – including the hideous spectre of the 'educational blob'. He is instinctively moderate and measured, but as soon as you get him onto 'progressive education', he turns into a bit of a head-banger. The secret of a good dinner with Nick is to keep him off his pet subjects.

WEDNESDAY 5 NOVEMBER

Met Nick and Danny at 4 p.m. to discuss NHS funding. It finally seems as if Danny and the Treasury have accepted that we are going to need £1–1.5 billion extra for next year.

Throughout the rest of the day I was negotiating with the Department for Education and the Whips' Office to allow me to get away on Friday, when Nick is going to make a 'secret' visit to Yeovil. Unhelpfully, I was put down as Duty Minister in London on Friday. Eventually a Tory whip agreed to cover for me in the House. I was told that Nicky Morgan wasn't happy.

FRIDAY 7 NOVEMBER

When I wake up in six months' time it will be Election Day – it cannot come soon enough! For political candidates, the slog of the general election is very hard work indeed – and stressful, when you do not know whether you are going to have a job at the end or not. And in the current rather anti-political environment it is not necessarily something to cherish that you are going to have to knock on 45,000 doors and deal with everything on the spectrum from rage to extravagant compliments. I feel absolutely knackered today, and the entire weekend is blotted out by advice centres, canvassing and two public appearances on Remembrance Sunday.

Went to Yeovil Junction railway station for 11.30 a.m. to meet Nick – whose visit was designed to highlight poor transport infrastructure. Needless to say, he was thirty minutes late, because his train was stuck on a stretch of single-line track, waiting for a delayed train to pass in the opposite direction! Unbelievable. When Nick got off the train, I was amazed to see that he was with Polly Toynbee – the anti-coalition, anti-Lib Dem, anti-everything, whinging *Guardian* commentator, who was apparently speaking at a literary conference in Yeovil.

Anyway, Nick and I set off in convoy to Ilminster, where we popped into a business park for a slightly dull photo opportunity in front of various maps showing the A303 and the A358.

In front of the assembled cameras, Nick glared down at the maps, to see if he could identify the A303. Slightly embarrassingly, he appeared to be looking at Cornwall, rather than Somerset! I quickly refocused him, and we avoided a media disaster.

After twenty minutes, we set off to a petrol station/Little Chef on the A303/A358 roundabout. Nick pointed at cars and generally posed for the cameras – 'Put it this way – I cannot pre-empt a government announcement, but if the A303 is not dualled soon, I will get a spade and some tarmac and do it myself!' At that, I felt pleased, but a little queasy.

Got back home at around 9.45 p.m. and worked for three hours on the red box. Nicky Morgan apparently wants to make PSHE (sex education) compulsory in all schools. It looks like Cameron has vetoed it. The ghost of Gove lives on.

SATURDAY 8 NOVEMBER

Another bleak, rainy day. It does not help with our canvassing when the weather is so miserable.

The media has a lot about Osborne's supposed 'triumph' at the EU summit, where he has allegedly negotiated down Britain's requested £1.7 billion extra payment to just £850 million. It turns out that all he has done is to delay part of the payment, and offset it against a British rebate that was expected next year anyway. A con which Labour would have been roasted alive for. But the Tory papers turn a blind eye.

SUNDAY 9 NOVEMBER

Remembrance Day services. Yeovil in the morning. Ilminster in the afternoon. A beautiful sunny day, in contrast to yesterday.

I have a strange affection for this day, considering it my most important constituency duty – paying respect to those who made the ultimate sacrifice.

Yeovil Town Band played in St John's Church as usual – the beautiful John Williams theme music from *Saving Private Ryan*. Very moving.

MONDAY 10 NOVEMBER

All three party leaders are going to the CBI conference this morning, and the Prime Minister's speech has been pre-briefed. It is all about infrastructure investment, including the A303. Thank goodness Nick came down on Friday to 'pre-launch' the A303/A358, otherwise I would have been seriously angry that Cameron had stolen our thunder.

At 11.30 a.m. had my fortnightly catch-up with Sir Jeremy Heywood. I do like Jeremy. There is nothing 'grand' about him; he is just a serious, grown-up person with the national interest at heart. Had a brief discussion with him about Universal Credit. For the first time ever, I decided there was a complex policy issue best left to the next government. Significant.

Also talked about the English votes issue. I have finally realised why our civil service team are going so slowly on this issue and the Command Paper – they hate all this, and really think it could all lead to the unravelling of the UK.

Normally, the civil service is careful to serve and be seen to serve ministers' agendas and not its own. But there are very, very rare times when I detect there is a collective civil service opinion, which causes them to drag their feet at best and actively subvert at worst. I think this is one of those times. Personally, I think they are right to act with caution, but it does raise questions about 'the establishment versus the elected government'.

Sir Jeremy is, of course, very diplomatic about all this, but I think his view is that the Tories are all tactics and no strategy on this issue, and I suspect he is worried that they are thinking of short-term party advantage and not the long-term interests of the United Kingdom.

2.45 p.m. The regular monthly political meeting, with Nick and political advisers. All our target seats are now divided up into categories – 1, 2, 3 and 4 – where 4 look as if they are going to be lost, 3 are very much on edge, and 1 and 2 are supposed to be safe.

However, the Tories are now throwing a huge amount of money at category 2 seats – and to my frustration, I now discover that Yeovil has been put into this category. Other seats include Bath, Colchester and Kingston, which we once considered safe.

Some very depressing new polling figures from Ryan on the attitude of elderly voters. They seem utterly self-obsessed. Free bus passes for themselves they are in favour of, but do not ask them to fund free bus passes for young people, which they do not like at all. Ditto childcare, free school meals and anything else that doesn't help them. Very depressing.

Ryan also reported back on some of the recent polling in our Scottish seats – namely Mike Moore's seat. Dreadful! We are massively behind the SNP in a seat we would hope to win comfortably. Ryan said that he thinks we are behind in nine out of our eleven Scottish seats. Only Alistair Carmichael and (possibly) Charles Kennedy are expected to win.

WEDNESDAY 12 NOVEMBER

A Norman Lamb NHS story about us pushing for £1.5 billion extra to fund the NHS in 2015/16 is in the papers today, and I think the coverage is pretty good. Rather to my surprise, Nick moaned a bit and felt Norman's language was a bit over the top.

THURSDAY 13 NOVEMBER

Drove down to Tatworth to deliver some campaign literature. Managed to get rid of most of the letters that I was supposed to be delivering – though I posted some through the wrong letterboxes! Why are all the bloody roads here called almost the same thing?

Took refuge from the downpours in the Lord Nelson pub in Norton at around noon. Had some fish and chips and beer. At the moment, it is canvassing, canvassing, canvassing. We have made 600 canvass contacts in the past two days.

My red box contains a massive amount of work. One of the Cabinet committee clearances is from a minister called Claire Perry, who is proposing to redesign the UK driving licence to include the Union flag! God help us. Apparently this is something Cameron promised to do. The briefing note from the civil service rather undiplomatically observes: 'Clearly this is a complete waste of time and money – it will cost £180,000 – but ultimately we do not think it is worth getting into a big fight with the Prime Minister over.'

FRIDAY 14 NOVEMBER

Did the morning call with the DPM which was fairly low-level and forgettable, and then went out leafleting in Tatworth. It really was a beautiful, sunny day, and the great thing about leafleting is it clears your head. My mind went back to Pauline Booth, our great activist, campaigner and friend, who did so much work for us over the past fifteen years. She would have loved a day like this, and loved the challenge of taking on the Tories in the general election. I miss her as an individual, but also her indomitable spirit and her massive appetite for work. It seems rather lonely without her.

Started leafleting in Watermead, and at the end of the cul-de-sac, I was walking down the driveway of the house on the right when I was stunned to see a badger stuck in the bars of a gate. It had obviously been in the back garden and was trying to make its way to the front, and was trying to get through the metal gate, but had got stuck between the poles. For a horrible moment I thought it was stuck solid, and I might be faced with the awful prospect of trying to pull it out or calling for the emergency services, but, seeing me, it suddenly panicked and wriggled very violently and was free – dashing off into the bushes.

Anyway, the seat poll that they have done in Yeovil constituency has come back today. It shows us level-pegging with the Tories, but when I am then identified as the Lib Dem candidate, we move strongly into the lead.

MONDAY 17 NOVEMBER

The civil servants have produced a version of the English Devolution Command Paper, but I don't like it. The first nine pages are just civil service waffle, and absolutely fine. But where there was then supposed to be a description of each party's position on English votes and English devolution, there is a whole load of historic bumpf.

Apparently Sir Jeremy Heywood has not approved something which would set out the parties' own positions. He thinks this may be too 'political'. Interesting that civil servants are being more assertive now that the parliament is coming towards its end.

When I was leaving the Cabinet Office today, I bumped into William Wallace, our peer. He said he was recently in a whips' meeting with his Tory opposite numbers, and they said that they wanted to be very constructive about whipping arrangements. They then said, 'We don't intend to play the silly games that the Conservatives in the House of Commons are trying to play with people like David Laws, where they are trying to pin David down to be in the Department for Education on Fridays, when he should be back in his constituency.'

Very interesting! That may explain why the Tories were in such a strop about me getting out of being Duty Minister recently. I was told no Tory minister in DfE could cover for me, yet discovered later that Sam Gyimah was in London and could easily have stepped in.

One of those classic civil service memos in my box, where you are steered very firmly towards the conclusion that they want. On this occasion, it was a role on the School Teachers' Pay Review Body. I was being invited to choose between two candidates, on the basis of a short civil service note: 'This is entirely a matter for the Minister to decide, but the Minister might want to be aware of the assessment of the interview panel.' When you looked at the assessment, one candidate is described as 'a very strong and dynamic performer, with high competence and effectiveness and entirely suited to this role'. The other candidate is described as '…only marginally above the line'. So I am being offered a no-choice choice.

TUESDAY 18 NOVEMBER

A quick gossip with Norman Lamb. Apparently Jeremy Hunt was absolutely furious about Norman's freelancing on the need for an extra £1.5 billion.

At Cabinet today, David Cameron was at his collegiate best. Showered praise on Vince Cable, Ed Davey and Danny Alexander. He is at his most impressive, Cameron, in these Cabinet meetings. He chairs them well, is always on the ball, pretty collegiate, and well briefed. When he reports back on foreign visits, he always has an amusing line or anecdote. The problem is he is a bit more chairman than chief executive, and he doesn't have Blair's focus on policy and detail.

WEDNESDAY 19 NOVEMBER

Up at 5.30 a.m. Went downstairs for breakfast in the Downing Street cafeteria with Oliver Letwin at 7.45 a.m. Over kippers, a hash brown and tomatoes, we discussed English devolution, plastic bags and freedom of information.

On English devolution, I spelt out to Oliver that there was no way we were publishing a Command Paper before the Scottish Smith Commission reports on 27 November. Oliver seemed to accept this, and rather amusingly he admitted that the Tories do not yet know what their position is on English votes for English laws. He said that they might have five or six options, because they did not have one clear position! All a bit embarrassing for the Conservative Party really – since they have been making such a big thing about this.

Back upstairs by 8.30 a.m. for a meeting on grammar schools. The Tories have started to get the jitters because UKIP are promoting more grammar schools, and there is now rather unhelpfully an application which has come in from Kent County Council for an expansion of a grammar school in Kent. The problem is that the 'expansion' is really a new grammar school, which would be presented as 'an annexe' of the existing grammar school, but ten miles away. I shall press very hard indeed for us to block it, but it will be interesting to see which way the Tories break on this.

Came back and at 2 p.m. had a meeting on the Autumn Statement with Nick, Danny and advisers. Danny said that Osborne is now thinking, since we blocked his proposal to cut inheritance tax, about reform of stamp duty – to get rid of the slab nature of the existing tax – something which is Lib Dem policy. However, the problem is he wants to subsidise this proposal so that people on as high a property value as possible end up gaining, which could cost quite a lot of money.

THURSDAY 20 NOVEMBER

Today we have one of the dreadful Lib Dem parliamentary party away days at a ghastly hotel in Hatfield. I had been hoping to arrive rather late, but there was too little traffic and I got there on time.

While the Tory parliamentary party goes for away days in country houses in the Cotswolds, we end up going to this ghastly place on an ugly roundabout off the M1. A lot of our parliamentary party were there, but some were not – including grandees such as Ming Campbell and Charles Kennedy. I'm not sure that Ming is a Ramada Hotel type of guy.

Got waylaid after dinner having a drink with Olly Grender and Nick Harvey, and back to my room at midnight. Then worked for a couple of hours to clear the red box. As I was coming back to my hotel room after the dinner, I noticed that Nick was just behind me. Even the Metropolitan Police protection team seemed a bit unimpressed with the hotel. At least nobody can claim that we are being extravagant.

Nick has come back to me about the £1.5 billion extra for the NHS that Norman Lamb and I have been arguing for. Nick says that he is committed to at least £1.5 billion and he will not allow the Treasury to salami-slice this back. He said that Cameron and Osborne at the Quad were very angry, or pretended to be very angry, about Norman Lamb pushing publicly for extra money.

SUNDAY 23 NOVEMBER

Today I was told the inside story about Michael's departure from the Education Department. No. 10 had concluded that Michael was becoming a liability – too divisive and rather out of control. The Prime Minister saw

Michael the week before the reshuffle, and sold very heavily to him how he needed him in the centre of government to run things, particularly in advance of the election. Michael asked for a day to think about it and then went back to the PM the next day to say that while he had some reservations, if this is what the Prime Minister wanted him to do, then he would do it. Interestingly, George Osborne phoned later on that day to say to Michael that he was not convinced that Michael should be moved to the job of Chief Whip, and made suggestions as to what Michael ought to say to the PM in order to avoid being moved! Michael then had to explain that he had already agreed to take up the offer. Michael must then have been particularly hurt when the briefing came through in the media suggesting that he had been removed because he was seen to be an electoral liability by Lynton Crosby.

It also became apparent that nobody had thought through how the job move would be presented in terms of 'demotion', and apparently some of the staff members in No. 10 were even found to be googling the pay of the Chief Whip, because they had not realised that the Chief Whip receives less than an ordinary Secretary of State and therefore that Michael would have to take a rather large pay cut! Anyway, it sounds as if Michael is pretty unhappy in the new job. Understandable that Cameron moved Michael, but there could be a price to pay.

MONDAY 24 NOVEMBER

At 7.45 a.m. went to get the usual kipper and tomatoes. At the cafeteria was George Osborne, getting a coffee. I said I was pleased to see that he had been in Somerset last week – to champion the resurfacing of the A303. George said, 'It's a pleasure! I intend to be down in Somerset quite a lot over the next few months. Actually, I know the area quite well. I used to have a girlfriend in Martock.' I said 'How interesting! I will have to see if I can track her down – no doubt she will have some quite interesting stories to tell. I must put an advert in the *Western Gazette*.' George looked a bit nervous: 'Oh, it was quite a long time ago…' The lady behind the breakfast counter, Alison, chuckled.

Meanwhile, there continues to be a fight over who announces what in the Autumn Statement. George wants to announce the extra money for the

NHS on *Marr* on Sunday, with the announcement on roads on Monday, the announcement on infrastructure on Tuesday, the Autumn Statement itself on Wednesday, and then an announcement about oil and Scotland on Thursday. I am seriously worried that the Tories will walk off with the major prizes – on the NHS, roads and tax – leaving us with all the dross. That includes a speech that Nick is making later on this week on the 'National Cycling Strategy', with a couple of hundred million pounds for cycle lanes. We should not be accepting this type of niche Lib Dem thing in exchange for major announcements.

Lib Dem Cabinet ministers' meeting at 4 p.m., where we again discussed the situation in Scotland. Sadly, it now seems as if the Labour Party have conceded on most elements of Scottish devolution, including on income tax bands and rates. Vince looked as nervous as I did. I pressed Danny and Alistair on what would happen if the Scottish economy contracted after taking over responsibility for rates and bands, and Danny said that the shortfall would be picked up by the rest of the United Kingdom. I then asked what would happen if the Scottish economy expanded more rapidly than the rest of the UK, would it then be the case that the grant to Scotland would be cut back? Danny looked rather baffled, glanced down at the table and said, 'I'll need to come back to you about that one.'

In the evening, had dinner with Nicky Morgan in Strangers' Dining Room. She was in fairly relaxed form and seems to be enjoying being Secretary of State. She came across as quite a moderate figure in a Tory Party with lots of head-bangers – but she is clearly taking her instructions from No. 10, and referred to this on a couple of occasions. On grammar schools, I highlighted that the Liberal Democrats would not be prepared to turn a blind eye to what would basically be a new selective school in Kent. Nicky gave the impression that she was not supportive of an expansion of selective education – but she said it would be an extremely thorny issue for the Tory Party and she would have to refer it up to No. 10.

TUESDAY 25 NOVEMBER

Up at 5.30 a.m. – into the office and redrafted the education speech for Thursday morning. The host think tank, where I am giving the speech, have managed to invite Dom Cummings – Michael Gove's former special adviser. They then realised their mistake and tried to disinvite Dom – which predictably enraged him and made him even more determined to come. To compound matters, after they had disinvited him from the speech, they then sent him a second invitation, confirming his original invitation!

Cabinet. 9 a.m. The Counter Terrorism Bill update took about half an hour. Poor old Greg Clark read out his brief about extremism in universities, defending 'his' sector. But as soon as Greg said, 'Obviously we don't want to imply that the universities irresponsibly invite in extremist speakers,' Cameron immediately shouted, 'But they do!' and Theresa May said the same thing. Poor Greg was a bit surprised to be heckled in this way by the PM and Home Secretary, and he paused and then obviously tried to rethink and slightly water down what he was about to say. By then he had lost the rest of the Cabinet, and I could see the glances of dismay from hard-line Tories.

I had to leave the Quad preparation meeting early, after we had discussed infrastructure and which party is going to announce which particular road upgrade scheme ('I'll swap you the A1 for the A303' etc. etc. etc.).

Had to get back to the DfE for a meeting with Nicky Morgan, which ominously was a bilateral with our two private secretaries and the head of schools capital. Nicky asked for my agreement for looking at options for reducing existing capital budgets, in case the Treasury does not give us extra money we are asking for. I said bluntly that if the Treasury was not going to give us extra money, my strong view was that we should cut back the free schools programme, which I now regard as having increased to a ridiculous scale. Nicky said that she wanted to look at other options, including cutting back on the priority school building programme, basic need and maintenance funding. I made clear that I will not support cuts in these other budgets. We may be heading for a stand-off.

WEDNESDAY 26 NOVEMBER

The Tories have already leaked the fact that the Lib Dems and Conservatives have agreed to a new fiscal target of completing deficit reduction by 2017/18 – all briefed out in the context of putting Labour on the spot in a vote after the Budget.

Fortunately, they have not briefed out their other desire that we should reduce the share of debt in GDP to around 60 per cent by 2025. This would give us very little room to borrow to invest without huge asset sales. I am concerned about signing up to such a target, and Nick and his office are also very worried about the politics of this and whether it would look like we were simply signing up to 'George Osborne's deficit reduction and austerity plan'. Slightly naïvely, Danny is still maintaining that there is a 'huge prize' for us if we sign up to the new Osborne plan – as he claims that this would all be seen to be our great success. Jonny Oates is completely opposed to doing anything on this and has emailed Nick: 'It seems to me that this would be a one-way benefit to the Tories. We know that the media will NOT write "Osborne signs up for Lib Dem plans".'

Nick came back to say that we could not possibly sign up to anything without Vince's consent and the last thing we need is a 'self-inflicted internal row'. It all looks as if this idea is going to be killed off in the next twenty-four hours.

Then back to the DfE for a meeting on work I commissioned measuring academy chain and local authority performance. Great stuff from a guy called Jon Andrews. I want to publish league tables that would show the best and worst school providers in the country. Apparently the Tories are in a bit of a panic, because they are nervous about comparing academy chains and local authorities against each other in one table – because this would show that many academy chains are worse performers than local authorities!

THURSDAY 27 NOVEMBER

Spoke to Luke Tryl, the very pleasant and reasonable new special adviser to Nicky Morgan, about various Autumn Statement issues. He is as fed up as I am about the fact that No. 10 keeps on coming up with all sorts of half-baked policies that they want to put in the Autumn Statement, which they do not propose to give us any money for. There is some mad No. 10 proposal on insisting that every school should provide wraparound childcare from 7 a.m. to 6 p.m., even though we are not proposing to provide them with any funding for it.

FRIDAY 28 NOVEMBER

With the election now looming, the media management of good news announcements is going to be messy, as both coalition parties are trying to get 100 per cent credit – and therefore there is a real risk of us front-running each other on every single announcement. This has already been the case on the fiscal mandate, which the Tories briefed out as soon as we had agreed it in the Quad.

The announcements next week that we need to get some credit for are:

1. The extra £1.5 billion for the NHS.
2. Extra money for mental health.
3. The increase in the personal income tax allowance.
4. The cut in national insurance contributions for apprentices.
5. The restructuring of stamp duty.
6. As much of the road infrastructure stuff as we can manage.

I went out yesterday evening and briefed Bob Constantine of ITV Regional News on the A303 roads package. In exchange, he agreed to do an interview with me, so that I am associated with it. This has apparently irritated the press office a lot, but frankly I don't care.

Nick asked today about the Ashcroft poll. This was on the whole pretty good, but one of the seats that was not was his own. I think the poll put him only a couple of percentage points ahead of Labour. There is a real risk that we could lose both Nick in Sheffield and Danny in Scotland.

Went off canvassing in Ashill – up to a place called Windmill Hill, where there is a collection of council houses and a few private residences. I had never been much aware of this small settlement until dear Pauline Booth, our volunteer activist who did so much but died of cancer last year, took me up there once to deliver leaflets. She was probably the only person in the past fifteen years who would ever have delivered to a settlement that was so remote. I was expecting the people in this area to be rather grumpy, but to my profound surprise everybody was friendly and we had a large number of our own supporters there.

The views from Windmill Hill over the surrounding countryside are very beautiful, and when you are canvassing out in an area like this it is really quite relaxing and calming. Even found a lovely old lady aged ninety-nine in a grand house at the top of the hill who was marked down as a soft Conservative but who said that she always voted for me.

SATURDAY 29 NOVEMBER

Up at 9.45 a.m. after a delicious ten hours' sleep – twice as long as normal. The red box arrived at 10.45 a.m. and it was not overly full – amongst the fifty different papers that I had to go through was a proposal from one school to change the use of 27.4 square metres of playing field to put in a disabled toilet.

Did the usual DPM conference call at 6 p.m. The plan is still for an NHS announcement of extra money by Osborne tomorrow, and then a big mental health announcement by Nick on Monday. There will also be the roads announcement on Monday, with Nick going down to Stonehenge to celebrate the dualling of the A303.

I raised the issue of our need to 'own' the tax allowance. Stephen Lotinga wisely said that we should perhaps discuss this without civil servants on the line!

Watched a film in the evening, and then had a quick look at the previews of the morning newspapers. Predictably, George Osborne has briefed out that he is delivering an extra £2 billion (not £1.5 billion!) for the NHS. This dominates the front pages.

SUNDAY 30 NOVEMBER

My birthday!

In the bath, and watched George Osborne on the *Marr* programme on my iPhone. I rather assumed that Marr would give George an easy ride in exchange for having Budget announcements trailed on his programme. Wrong! Marr kicked off by introducing Osborne as 'the master of pain'. George looked a bit shocked, and he was on the defensive for most of the interview.

Osborne looked particularly uncomfortable when Marr pressed him as to whether he would rule out increasing VAT or income tax rates, and all George would say was 'That's not part of our plan'. At the end of the programme they brought Ed Balls back on and there was a bit of a spat. George looked utterly pissed off.

A text from Norman Lamb: 'How have we so spectacularly managed to avoid being in the NHS funding story?'

MONDAY 1 DECEMBER

Today is Roads Day – and the Battle of Stonehenge started early this morning. Nick was on the morning media at an unbelievably early hour, enveloped in mid-winter darkness, trumpeting the road improvements to the south-west. Vince Cable was sent up to the north-east to announce the A1 upgrade. Both relate to target seat areas – the A303 going right through the middle of Somerset, and the A1 going into Sir Alan Beith's Berwick-upon-Tweed seat.

The Tories were also doing their best to claim the credit, and Cameron visited Stonehenge and the A1 later in the day! Indeed, so competitive was it that the PM was actually 'photo-bombed' by Sir Alan!

I started the day more modestly with BBC Somerset Radio, talking about the A303. Not sure, in truth, that this would have been prioritised without me constantly pushing it. I was interviewed by one of those regional reporters who think they are tomorrow's Jeremy Paxman.

At midday, went over to the DfE for an Oral Questions prep session with Nicky and the other ministers. The whips had been very industrious and phoned every coalition MP on the order paper and asked them all what their supplementary question was going to be. But this week there was a mistake, and one particularly overenthusiastic whip went to every single Labour MP and asked them what their supplementary questions were going to be as well! Unbelievably, about half of the Labour MPs actually told us their question – including Stephen Timms, who is a member of the shadow Cabinet! They are clearly all asleep.

To my intense irritation, the Chancellor phoned Nicky Morgan over the weekend and managed to persuade her not to block his wraparound childcare announcement. This is supposed to give parents the 'right to request' childcare from 8 a.m. to 6 p.m. The half-baked idea has come straight out of the Treasury – it has not been thought through, and we would be announcing this right in the middle of a workload challenge which is designed to strip away unnecessary burdens from schools!

I decided that I would send an email to Nick Clegg to see if I could torpedo this whole thing.

TUESDAY 2 DECEMBER

The newspapers are full of coverage of the roads infrastructure announce-ment – including two photographs taken at Stonehenge – one of Nick Clegg visiting in the morning, and the other of David Cameron visiting in the afternoon!

Started the day by writing a fairly sharp email to Nick rubbishing the Chancellor's idea of a new plan on wraparound childcare. Nick sent back saying he totally agreed and would block it.

Cabinet at 9.30 a.m. A dull affair. It started with a dementia update from the Secretary of State for Health, in which it was announced by the Prime Minister that we were all now 'dementia friends'.

We also had a discussion on women and equalities from Nicky Morgan and the Minister for Equalities, who is Jo Swinson. Jo is allowed to attend the Cabinet when equalities are being discussed, and she did quite a good job. However, the whole thing was a bit embarrassing and tokenistic, because for some reason Jo was not even allowed into the Cabinet Room until the bit on women and equalities came up. And when her presentation was over, she then had to leave.

We finished by discussing the Afghanistan conference, and Cameron said that there was a new two-party coalition being put together in Afghanistan. Cameron said he had recently met the person who was leader of the smaller party. Knowing glances were exchanged across the table with Osborne, but Cameron was too diplomatic to joke at Nick's expense. But he did say that the Deputy Prime Minister from Afghanistan would be in the United Kingdom in the near future and perhaps Nick and he could tell him a little bit about how coalition government works. George could not resist: 'Maybe the two of you could take him down to Stonehenge for the day – you could even go at the same time!'

Went over to the DfE for 11.30 a.m. and had a stock-take with Nicky. Her private secretary came in: 'We have just had a message from the Treasury saying that the whole thing on wraparound childcare has been taken out of the Autumn Statement.' I said that was good news, and Nicky smiled knowingly, probably half irritated with Liberal Democrat interference and half grateful that this rather half-baked policy is not going ahead.

WEDNESDAY 3 DECEMBER

Not as many Budget leaks as normal. Nothing about the increase in the personal income tax allowance, and only a reference to stamp duty reform on the front page of the *Financial Times*. George will be pleased.

Nick is not going to be on the front bench today – but is going to do a political visit in Cornwall. This is bound to attract quite a lot of press attention.

8 a.m. Cabinet meeting to discuss the Autumn Statement. There is no net giveaway, and the only interesting tax measures are a measly increase of £100 in the personal income tax allowance, and the restructuring of stamp duty.

Nick highlighted the future issues around reducing debt and deficits and the importance of there being a tax contribution to fiscal consolidation.

Vince started his contribution in a rather ominous way: 'I am very grateful to the Chancellor for all his cooperation over a variety of issues relating to my department, and I very much welcome lots of the measures in the Autumn Statement. I look forward to campaigning in Twickenham constituency on the basis of the higher stamp duty rates on expensive properties, and I can now form an alliance with George to hit people in extremely expensive mansions.'

Osborne did not even smile.

Then we came to the crunch: Vince went on to question not only the entire coalition economic strategy on deficit reduction, but frankly the entire economic strategy of the Liberal Democrats. He implied that the 2017/18 date for deficit reduction was entirely arbitrary, and said it was unfortunate that it had come across in the newspapers that all of this was about political dividing lines rather than a sensible economic strategy. He then went on to say: 'Even on my own party's plans to have an 80/20 fiscal consolidation, there would have to be swingeing public spending cuts which would be extremely difficult to bear without closing down large parts of the army, the police etc. etc.' Why Vince thinks it is helpful to us to have a massive row and a split in the Liberal Democrats rehearsed in front of Conservative Cabinet ministers just before the general election is beyond me. Cameron and Osborne must have been laughing very loud inwardly – although they did not show it.

When Vince had finished, we moved on to a couple of other people and then I came in to say, 'This is likely to be the last big fiscal event of the parliament.' At this, Michael Gove popped up in his seat and looked at me in a very questioning way and started to mouth something. I continued: 'So, I think we should congratulate George and Danny on the extremely effective way that they have managed Budgets and Autumn Statements over the last four years. However, the focus of much of the debate after the Autumn Statement is likely to be the long-term fiscal outlook and whether the fiscal plans are credible. I think it is sensible that we should aim to eliminate the current Budget deficit by 2017/18, as by then we will be seven or eight years into a recovery and we do need to get our public finances into a more robust position before the next downturn.

'However, where the government, or at least the Conservatives, are on much weaker ground is on relying wholly on spending cuts to complete the fiscal consolidation. That is likely to be extremely challenging, and we have already seen with the NHS that a sensible government has had to recognise reality by allocating more money, rather than having service standards plunge. So my view is the City is likely to be sceptical of these future plans – and as George knows, it is one thing to set out good plans for deficit reduction, and it is quite another thing to deliver. There will need to be some contribution in the next parliament to deficit reduction from taxes on the rich, and without this the planned cuts in public spending are not likely to be politically acceptable or deliverable.'

Cameron looked irritated and hurried the debate towards a conclusion.

When I got outside the Cabinet Room, Vince was there and said he was grateful for the points that I made. I said that I was not quite on the same page as him, but offered to meet to discuss the manifesto. He looked rather pleased with himself and sort of skipped off down the corridor to the front door of No. 10. Vince is always most cheerful when: a) he is being gloomy about the economy and b) he is socking it to the Tories.

THURSDAY 4 DECEMBER

Phone call from Jonny Oates. He is very worried about the row within the party that is brewing over fiscal policy, with Vince questioning the strategy and our MPs getting increasingly nervous as they see the media coverage following the Autumn Statement – all about 'massive cuts' to public services. Apparently the Chancellor has been on the media about it this morning and has got quite catty and defensive about the whole thing – which is going to reinforce the impression that Vince is right and Danny wrong.

The Institute for Fiscal Studies has said that the cuts mean a complete reshaping of the state and a return to public spending levels that would look more like the early 1930s. This is because the Autumn Statement assumes the same rate of reduction of total managed expenditure as we have achieved in the current parliament, but it assumes that all of this will be in departmental spending, with no contribution from welfare.

Voted on the 0.7 per cent GNP for overseas aid issue, to back Mike Moore's Bill. This puts 0.7 per cent into law.

FRIDAY 5 DECEMBER

An important Lib Dem manifesto meeting. We concluded that we were going to need to find about £25 billion worth of savings, welfare cuts and tax rises in the next parliament to complete the fiscal consolidation – assuming that we aim for a balanced current budget. It looks as if about £10 billion worth of spending cuts is going to be necessary over the two years, and we concluded we could probably find up to £5 billion of welfare savings. That leaves about £10 billion from tax increases. That is manageable, but it means a 60/40 ratio of tax increases to spending cuts, rather than the 80/20 that we have been assuming.

MONDAY 8 DECEMBER

Some briefing to the *Telegraph* today about the new grammar school which could open in Kent. Kent County Council have presented this as an 'expansion' even though the 'expansion' is ten miles from the nearest grammar school. The department is taking legal advice. I asked Matt Sanders to find out what was going on and who was doing the briefing. Matt reckons it is 10 Downing Street that are briefing – and apparently Nicky Morgan and her advisers are unenthusiastic.

TUESDAY 9 DECEMBER

We finally got there! After months and months of delay, we are today launching the Teacher Quality proposals – announcing a new Royal College of Teaching and extra support for continuous professional development of the teaching workforce. I'm very pleased, having worked on both these policies since the Gove days – almost nine months now.

WEDNESDAY 10 DECEMBER

A free school meals catch-up at 11.15 a.m. and there is good news about take-up – which is around 85 per cent and may go higher next year. In some parts of inner London, the take-up is 92 per cent.

Also had a briefing on the Key Stage 2 (end of primary school) results, which are due out tomorrow. They show an impressive increase in attainment, but also a statistically significant narrowing of the gaps between disadvantaged pupils and the rest – which could mean that the pupil premium is beginning to have an effect. Really good news!

Went to the trilateral with Danny and Nick – where we were discussing the new fiscal mandate, which the government is publishing next week. To my great surprise, the mandate seems much softer than I was expecting. I reckon that even Labour could sign up to it! As Danny explained it all, I could feel everybody around the room relax – and his adviser, Will de Peyer, even smiled at me conspiratorially across the table, though careful not to let Danny see. Jonny Oates also gave me a 'this is not nearly as bad as we were expecting' look. When Danny had finished his briefing, Nick said, 'Well, that doesn't sound too bad to me.'

I said, 'Frankly, it's a lot weaker than I was expecting – maybe too soft for me!' Nick looked rather horrified, and then realised I was joking. He quickly changed the subject.

THURSDAY 11 DECEMBER

Woke up this morning with quite a hangover after a meal out for my private offices. Why is it on these occasions that you forget the common-sense precaution of taking a bit of water along with the wine?!

At 10.30 a.m. went over to the Home Office to have a meeting with

James Brokenshire, the quite efficient and pleasant Home Office Minister who has the poisoned chalice of immigration, entry and exit checks etc. James seems reasonably on top of things. We tested every single route in and out of the country, and it does seem as if the Home Office is finally getting a grip on this.

Nick was clearly delighted about the Key Stage 2 results today. 'I am so deliriously chuffed – this kind of thing shows politics can be a force for good. Given this goes to the very heart of why we came into government – opportunity for all regardless of circumstances of birth – can we make as much of this as possible. It is also crucial that as many people in the party get to hear about it as possible – it should make all Lib Dems very proud. Without getting too mawkish about it, this kind of moment vindicates all the crap we have to put up with in politics!'

FRIDAY 12 DECEMBER

Up at 4.40 a.m. in order to leave at 5.30 a.m. to get to Yeovil at 8 a.m. Visited the Royal Mail Sorting Centre to wish Happy Christmas to all of the staff.

The first submission out of the evening box was a Cabinet Office request for clearance for a paper by the Home Secretary on the Counter Terrorism and Security Bill. There is an absolutely laughable section about childcare providers, which goes far further than we have ever agreed. It says that we would expect early years and childcare providers to assess the risk of children in their settings being 'drawn into terrorism'! It also says that staff should be able to 'recognise signs of being drawn into terrorism'. Does anyone really believe that two-, three- and four-year-olds are going to be drawn into terrorism? It really is beyond parody. I am going to stop it.

SATURDAY 13 DECEMBER

Did not get to bed until 3.30 a.m. as I worked very late on my red box. Had to get up at quarter to seven to get to the Royal Mail Sorting Centre in Crewkerne for 7.30 a.m. The Crewkerne advice centre was busy.

I got an email today from Paul Marshall, who says that the Michael

Gove dinner group which met this week (without me) included Michael speculating about what the next government would look like. Apparently he said that I would be ideal as the new Secretary of State for Work and Pensions – and was imagining how great a reform programme could be delivered in this area. Paul said that he also thinks that a Lib Dem coalition would still be the Cameron/Osborne preferred outcome without a Tory majority.

MONDAY 15 DECEMBER

Amusing article in the newspapers today, with Dom Cummings taking yet another pop at Cameron. This time Cummings says that the PM is so lacking in interest in education policy that 'he wouldn't even look up from *Country Life* if he was told that every state school was about to fall into the sea'.

Got the copy of the English Command Paper back and it still did not have the changes that I wanted. Still no serious chapter on devolution on demand – trying to imply that the only answer to the English question is English votes for English laws. I made very clear to the officials that I was not willing to accept this, and that unless we got our own chapter on devolution on demand, we simply could not sign off the paper. Also made clear that we needed to have a separate bullet point on English votes for English laws, making clear that there had to be a consideration of the voting system for the English MPs who would constitute the group vetting English laws. Of course the Tories absolutely hate this.

William Hague phoned through at about 11 a.m. in a panic: 'I am really keen to get on with this, as we've got to get the Command Paper signed off by 1 p.m. – and tomorrow really is the last day we can do this before the House rises.'

I made clear that the Command Paper would have been signed off by now if only the officials had made the changes that I had asked for two weeks ago.

At around 1.30 p.m. Hague asked to speak to me again. This time he sounded much more agitated. He said: 'Look, there is a real problem here. The paper still has not been agreed, and we are absolutely running out of time. Unless this is agreed in the next hour, we are simply going to have to bin the English Command Paper and I will publish the Conservative Party proposals by themselves.'

I said that I would give my feedback on the issue as soon as I received the latest draft. Frankly, it is the Tories who want the Command Paper more than we do, and I think Hague is actually bluffing about publishing the Tory proposals. I suspect that they will ultimately back off and sign up to what we want. Everyone else in the DPM's office is pushing for me to concede everything and just sign the document off – but I will not do so. We are still in a very strong negotiating position on this and we should be able to get our own way.

TUESDAY 16 DECEMBER

Spent an eternity signing off Christmas cards and clearing various paper-work – this really is a hideous time of year.

The English votes Command Paper came over this morning in its final version, and I signed it off. The Tories finally backed down on content.

Went to see Nick for a political meeting, with Danny, Paddy and vast numbers of staff – all dedicated to the issue of whether our MPs in individual constituencies need to do more fundraising! I am not sure whether it really makes sense for the Deputy Prime Minister to spend all his time on this. We even discussed whether or not a fundraising dinner in Colchester (Sir Bob Russell) should be a military-themed dinner or not! Arrrgghhh!

At 9.30, a fairly lacklustre Cabinet. Only Matthew Hancock would have remembered this occasion, because in Vince's absence he made his first presentation. He later said to me that he was a little bit nervous, but you would not have thought so! He relished every moment. I expect that he was practising in the mirror all morning.

Went to the weekly government business meeting. Had a brief discussion about Theresa May's ludicrous proposal that early years professionals are supposed to be identifying two-, three- and four-year-olds in danger of being sucked into terrorism. Nick asked for an update and was told that Theresa has agreed to drop the entire section. Nick said, 'Oh! I am rather disappointed – I was looking forward to having the argument!'

In the afternoon, had a meeting with Susan Acland-Hood, Luke Tryl, and Chris Wilkins (another of the Secretary of State's special advisers) on our capital settlement. It is all getting a bit fraught. It sounds as if No. 10 and the Treasury have been getting nervous about Nicky not giving the free schools programme 100 per cent backing. I certainly do not intend to make life easy for the Tories over this. I do not intend to cut back on maintenance, necessary basic need or the priority school building programme in order to deal with the massive free school overspend.

It is always a very bad thing in negotiation to look as if you are desperate for something to be agreed, so I am thinking that I may simply pretend to 'lose interest' in this whole issue. I think that what I may now say is that it does not really matter if we get an agreement on capital until after the general election, and it would be better to have no free schools programme and no long-term capital programme than agree to all sorts of cuts in school maintenance and basic need. That really will put the wind up the Tories, because they will certainly want an eighth-wave free schools programme before the general election.

THURSDAY 18 DECEMBER

Working on my box this morning, I came across a submission of total length five pages, which is a Section 77 – School Standards and Framework Acts 1998 – consent to change the use of school playing field land. This is a wonderful and elegantly presented submission – asking me to grant a school permission to convert seven square metres of land as part of a scheme to provide an extra space for teaching. I wonder whether this is going to be the smallest decision that I will ever be asked to make as a minister!

Did some media on free school meals this morning – the take-up data is excellent: 1.3 million more children are now eating free school meals, of whom 750,000 are children who were not eating school meals before and have switched from packed lunches. The take-up rate is over 85 per cent across England as a whole, and over 90 per cent in parts of London.

Labour have opened up a five-point lead in the aftermath of the Autumn Statement. It is reassuring that the Liberal Democrats climbed three points to 14 per cent – although that only puts us on a par with UKIP. Fifty-five per cent say that Osborne is 'going too far in imposing cuts that would endanger important public services'.

WEDNESDAY 24 DECEMBER

A quiet Christmas Eve in James's parents' house in Hertfordshire. We took Theo and Milly – his nephew and niece – out to feed the village ducks.

THURSDAY 25 DECEMBER

A happy, lazy Christmas Day in Hertfordshire.

SATURDAY 27 DECEMBER

The newspapers are full of a rather old story about Labour's poor poll ratings in Scotland. Suggests they may be wiped out in the general election, along with most of the Liberal Democrats! If the SNP take a large number of seats off Labour, that could lead to the awful scenario where no two major parties have control at Westminster.

SUNDAY 28 DECEMBER

Got up early at around 4.30 a.m. Arrived in a sunny, warm Nice, having left a frozen and cloudy England.

My interview with James Lyons was published on page 2 of the *Sunday Times*, as a big attack on the Tory Party over their right-wing policies on cutting public spending and public services. It came out rather well, with James having used the lines I fed him about the Tories writing the right-wing equivalent of Michael Foot's longest suicide note in history manifesto of 1983. It will please all the lefties and anger all the right.

TUESDAY 30 DECEMBER

The newspapers are full of papers released under the thirty-year rule, most of which seemed to feature Oliver Letwin! They reveal all the papers that he wrote to Mrs Thatcher back in the 1980s, pushing the case for the poll tax. That will not surprise anyone who knows Oliver – as he is wonderfully intellectual, but not always fully in touch with the sensitivities of public opinion or the practicalities of life out in the real world. I could not help teasing Oliver by sending him a text: 'Must you hog all of the late 2014 media!'

WEDNESDAY 31 DECEMBER

An overnight text reply from Oliver: 'This was not what I had in mind thirty years ago! Happy New Year.'

Nick has sent the first serious policy email since Christmas:

As discussed with Paddy, it looks likely that as the election draws near, our core appeal will not lie in being agents of radical change, but instead in being the guarantors of good sense, balance and fairness at a time when political instability and populism are on the rise. This will become increasingly obvious to both the press and the markets as they confront the prospect of a parliament riven with the competing demands from the SNP, UKIP, Green, Plaid et al. and the factionism of both Conservatives and Labour. This is of course new territory for us as some of our members may baulk at the party offering itself as a bulwark of stability rather than as a catalyst of disruption. But it fits with our defensive seat strategy, with the tenor of our strong economy/fair society narrative, and has strong appeal to centre-ground liberal voters who abhor extremism and populism. We have made a good stab recently at accusing the Tories of lurching off in a right-wing direction re. future cuts etc. Osborne has been remarkably helpful. But we're not attacking Labour with the same zeal and we are fitful in characterising the narrow populism in UKIP/SNP/Green, Plaid et al.

I'd like a top-to-toe analysis of what money is available to us and how many seats stand to benefit in the coming five months. As far as I can make out from our weekly seat-by-seat discussions, we're basing much of the support we're providing to our seats on approximately thirty-five total wins next May. While this may be logical, it limits our ability to hold on to a handful more seats which may become winnable if a gentle tide of opinion starts flowing back in our direction, especially in the latter stages of the campaign. I do not in any event want us to plan our resource for an outcome which falls short of the psychologically crucial 40+ barrier.

Another snap election after May? Predictably enough, parts of the commentariat are starting to speculate that the current fragmentation of politics may lead to another election. My own view is that the public can't stand to be asked the same question over and over, so we should have no truck with this kind of speculation.

Today is the last day of 2014. James and I will go out this evening to the wonderful Clos de Vignes restaurant outside Cotignac, and then we will be back before midnight. Tomorrow we are down to Cassis, and then we have two more days' holiday.

Once 2014 has tipped into 2015, the prospect of four months of campaigning will be looming over us. This is going to be a historic general election. Perhaps this is the most uncertain general election and the most important of my life. With the SNP and UKIP potentially doing well, and the Tories threatening a referendum on the EU in the next parliament, this is a general election that could make or break the country. Our future as a United Kingdom, our future in the European Union, and the future shape of public services and inequality in our country are all at stake. There is a lot to fight for next year, and we must use these few days of rest to rebuild strength for what is to come.

2015

FRIDAY 2 JANUARY

I may still be on holiday but my mind is not. Last night I dreamt I was talking to Nick Clegg, George Osborne and David Cameron at the end of the 2015 general election. The Tories had 303 seats, we had only twenty-five. We had held Yeovil by a 3,500 majority, but lost Taunton. Osborne was muttering something about a problem with postal votes in South Somerset. Weird how the mind works.

SATURDAY 3 JANUARY

I reflect on going back to the UK without enthusiasm – four months of political slog, and then potentially all the difficulties of a hung parliament. I cannot help feeling that having the Conservatives back in government – not least by themselves – would be a disaster. We would end up with an EU referendum, which might lead to our departing the EU, precipitating the break-up of the UK. And we would experience worse public services and rising inequality. If we can stop the Conservatives getting an outright majority, then there really is an opportunity to lead Britain in a better direction.

Heading home. An interminably long conference call with Nick at Nice Airport. Discussed whether we want to do a Lib Dem NHS announcement – committing to the £8 billion that Simon Stevens has said is needed over the next parliament. The truth is that Stevens's £8 billion is a massive underestimate. Apparently the real figure he came up with was £15 billion, but the Tory special adviser in No. 10 managed to 'talk him down' from £15 billion to £8 billion – on the basis that this might be more politically acceptable and deliverable.

SUNDAY 4 JANUARY

Back down to earth with a vengeance. At 10.45 a.m. on a very cold morning I was in Tatworth canvassing.

Then drove to Yeovil for the game against Manchester United – a great FA Cup tie. When I got to the Yeovil Town boardroom, there was Bobby Charlton. And about an hour later we heard a helicopter overhead and somebody said, 'That must be Alex Ferguson!' I assumed it was a joke. It wasn't. Yeovil really played their hearts out. But United brought on two substitutes, worth a combined £100 million – a hundred times our annual player budget. Finished 2–0 down.

MONDAY 5 JANUARY

The first meeting of the NHS Winter Performance Cabinet Committee. A&E and ambulance performance has deteriorated very markedly since July. Key targets are being missed – for ambulances, only 56 per cent of Red 2 calls are being responded to within the required time – against a target of 75 per cent.

I was expecting the committee to be productive, but it turned out to be very odd indeed – not really a Cabinet committee. It was chaired by Jeremy Hunt and included Oliver Letwin, Jeremy Heywood and me. Aligned in front of us were all the senior NHS executives. It seemed to be a stock-take meeting for Jeremy. Oddly, there were also hospital chief executives dialling in from around the country, who were then grilled by Jeremy about their situations (always dire!), what they wanted us to do (end bed blocking, deal with staff shortages etc. etc.). When each one finished, Jeremy said how wonderful the local staff were and could the chief executive possibly pass on his thanks. The more I listened, the more worried I was. You cannot run the NHS by making telephone calls to individual hospitals – you have got to get your intermediate management sorting things out. Left the meeting deeply concerned.

Norman Lamb shares my worries. He said that Jeremy Hunt has gone into rather a panic over the past few weeks about deteriorating performance and that at the last stock-take meeting he had seemed to be in 'a complete flap'.

Nick mentioned later that Cameron is putting pressure on him to spend money on an overseas electoral registration campaign, seemingly cynically targeted towards registering 'a lot of Tory voters on the Costa del Sol'. Nick wants to focus on voters from low-income backgrounds and students.

TUESDAY 6 JANUARY

The last Cabinet photograph of the current parliament. Went upstairs to the No. 10 drawing room where the photograph was due to be taken. Standing in an empty outer room was Sir Jeremy Heywood, talking to Vince Cable – in the other corner was Nick Clegg, huddled with Don Foster. It soon became evident that there were not any Tories there – Jeremy said that they were having a political meeting. He joked about having a Cabinet photograph with only Lib Dems, and eventually Nick said, 'Why not – let's go next door.' A nice one for the scrapbook – though the absence of any female Lib Dem Cabinet ministers is notable.

At Cabinet, an implementation update from Oliver and Danny. I highlighted the importance of completing exit checks by the end of the parliament. Philip Hammond nodded furiously. But when the Prime Minister came in, he said that he was not too sure whether the public would give us credit over exit checks, and Theresa May then made an incredibly lukewarm statement in which she said that the importance of exit checks should not be overestimated, and the public should not be encouraged to think that they were the solution. Of course they are not the entire solution, but they will help us to identify people who have overstayed so that action can be taken. Theresa May's views reflect her determined resistance to this policy over the past few years, which is clearly because she does not actually want it known how many people are still in the country who should have left – as this would highlight the total incompetence of her department.

Jeremy Hunt gave a semi-upbeat presentation on the NHS. No Tories spoke. I was blunt: 'I'm afraid I'm a lot more gloomy than Jeremy. The truth is that these are not just winter pressures. The deterioration in NHS performance started before the winter, and the reason so many hospitals are in trouble is that they went into winter with insufficient slack. The key thing now is to do as much as we can to unblock beds. We also have a situation where because of the reforms made at the start of the parliament, the management of the NHS is considerably weaker.' Cameron winced.

Went back to the DfE. The Chancellor has come back with a completely unacceptable response to my plan on school buildings. All he wants to do is protect an inflated budget for free schools. To do this he proposes cutting £0.25 billion off the Priority School Building Programme 2 – designed to rebuild some of the worst-condition schools. He also wants to axe £100 million from school maintenance and £200 million from new school places. Contacted Danny and asked him to block the Osborne strategy – suggested we argue for the free school programme to be brought down from sixty-two schools to about forty, which would save about £350 million. We could then cancel the cuts to PSBP2 and maintenance.

Said to Danny that if we cannot get agreement on this, then we should hold up the whole capital programme until the next parliament – that will put the wind up the Tories, who are desperate to announce more free schools.

Had a meeting on managing asbestos risk in schools – the department has been trying to avoid doing anything, partly because of administrative costs and partly because they do not want to end up 'nationalising' responsibility. They are trying to fob me off with some meaningless consultation or warm words. I said I wanted a paper back next week with a serious proposal. I am not prepared to put teachers and children at risk.

At 3.45 p.m. went over to Nick's office for a discussion with Danny and advisers on fiscal challenges – and funding our manifesto. We sent out last night a long paper from DPMO officials. This covered: deficit reduction plans; cost of major manifesto policies; and how to pay for them.

I was expecting Danny to be prickly, and he was. He thinks he is the only one entitled to have any views about fiscal matters: 'I have only just seen this paper. It seems as if somebody's been doing a full review of all government spending – and I thought that that was my job.' He then went on to question why we needed any detail at all and whether we could just fudge everything.

We had a 45-minute row about how much the deficit should be cut by 2017/18, with Danny pushing for Osborne-type austerity. By the end, nothing was agreed.

Saw Vince in the evening. He has been talking to Ed Miliband, and thinks he has persuaded Ed not to offer to cut tuition fees in the Labour manifesto. I very much doubt he is right. I expect a populist Labour fees policy soon. But interesting to know that communications between Vince and Miliband are still very much open.

WEDNESDAY 7 JANUARY

Up at 5.45 a.m. Breakfast with Oliver at 7.45 a.m.

Four items on our agenda – English devolution, the National Health Service, Ebola legislation, and zero-hour contracts. On Ebola, Oliver thinks that there is a case for the introduction of mandatory screening at airports.

The NHS – I said I thought that the Monday meeting with Jeremy was completely hopeless. Oliver said that it is not actually meant to be a traditional Cabinet committee – just a way of us monitoring what is going on in the Department of Health.

The NHS now threatens to dominate domestic politics for the next few months, with a large number of hospitals effectively in crisis.

Oliver said, 'Look, six months ago Danny and I were very worried about the NHS. We stress-tested things and helped work with the NHS and the Treasury to allocate extra money for winter pressures. The NHS and the Department of Health have been absolutely useless. Goodness knows what they have done with this money, but they have not used it to prepare the system for winter. You have got to understand that the NHS almost collapsed completely over Christmas, and we came close to deaths of patients in unsafe hospitals, and the resignation of Jeremy. We only just survived the Christmas period without these things happening.' Even worse than I feared.

Nick today announced the Lib Dem 'frontbench' team for the general election. He has promoted Tim Farron to be the Foreign Affairs spokesman. Apparently many of the old guard in the Lords are appalled – they think that Tim is unreliable on Europe and pretty lightweight. Nick has confirmed that Danny is going to be our Treasury spokesman. Vince is grumpy, but has begrudgingly accepted it.

At 11 a.m. had a quick chat with Luke Tryl. He is a bright, very decent, straightforward person, who is easy to deal with. A really nice guy. Luke let slip that all of the education papers that go into Nicky's red box are also copied to Michael Gove in 12 Downing Street! Extraordinary.

1.30 p.m. A meeting with Lord Nash, Paul Marshall and Sir Theodore Agnew to discuss school leadership – which Paul thinks is a relatively neglected area within the department. Quite right. I said the main issue was whether we actually have something like a National Leadership Institute to pull together all the threads at a national level. I said that I was very keen on this and had concluded that the existing National College was broken. Lord Nash, Theodore and Paul are all very signed up to the reform agenda, but they understand that you cannot just hope that 24,000 autonomous schools will fix things like leadership and teacher development.

2.30 p.m. The weekly trilateral with Nick and Danny. Osborne has been trying to publish a whole load of 'economic plans' for each English region. At one stage, George was trying to do this without any agreement with us – clearly a Tory election plan. Nick is furious.

Danny also reported that George had raised the March Budget. He knows we want a minimalist budget, but is pleading: 'Ultimately Budget Day is my day, and I would like to have some positive announcements to make on tax and other policies – so are there things that the Lib Dems want that could be "traded off" against the things that I want to do?'

I said we should be relaxed about having a near zero-content Budget, and that the Tories would be the gainers from any big announcements. I suggested we come up with a couple of back-pocket policies that cost a few hundred million, and hold these in reserve.

Jonny Oates said that he thought that we should be very sceptical about any new announcements in the Budget. He said if there was any spare money around, then we should make a virtue about using it to reduce the deficit. We all laughed and noted that this was the first time we had ever heard Jonny Oates push the case for fiscal prudence. But Jonny's point is a good one. Danny said that the Permanent Secretary to the Treasury had approached him recently with some newspaper cuttings about the last Denis Healey Budget, in 1979. Healey presented a Budget which had basically nothing in it, in spite of the looming election. The Treasury clearly want a do-nothing Budget, given the deficit.

We touched on the row yesterday about our fiscal policies. Nick said, 'Look, the two of you are my closest political allies, and I don't want to have to adjudicate between you in this difficult issue over the deficit – though obviously I will do if I have to.'

Later in the day, had a meeting with Ed Davey about the manifesto. We met Ed in his room in the Commons. He was sitting in his office in near complete darkness. Apparently the main office lighting failed a number of weeks ago. '"Energy Secretary in the dark" – it would make a great diary story!' I said.

'Don't you bloody dare!'

THURSDAY 8 JANUARY

Read through Tuesday's Cabinet minutes. This week in Cabinet, Michael Gove talked about Jeb Bush and his advocacy of government setting what he calls: 'Big, hairy, audacious goals'. The civil servant note-takers don't usually like flowery language and tend to paraphrase – not this time. 'Big, hairy, audacious goals' has made it into the Cabinet minutes – for what I suspect is the first and last time.

FRIDAY 9 JANUARY

Mostly the canvassing was good. One grumpy man in West Chinnock claimed that I was not working hard enough now that I am a minister. I smiled to myself as I walked back down his driveway, contemplating the 6.45 a.m. to midnight existence that I have for six days a week, with the seventh day spent working six hours on red boxes! If only these people knew.

SATURDAY 10 JANUARY

Started with a Chard advice centre, then canvassed in Crewkerne for four hours.

In the evening, the regular conference call with Nick – he has been canvassing in Sheffield today, and they were followed around by a *Guardian* journalist who apparently is writing a story about Nick being under pressure in his own backyard. With Danny also spending increasing amounts of his time in his own constituency (I think he is now only in London on a Tuesday and a Wednesday), we really are in election mode.

SUNDAY 11 JANUARY

A very easy day with lunch in the pub in Coln St Aldwyn. At the table behind us a lady talking loudly: 'The children are finally back to school on Monday. The new nanny starts on Tuesday. Then I'm off to Argentina for a couple of weeks.' Her companion asked, 'Oh, Argentina! Is that a holiday?' 'No,' she said. 'Actually, I'm just off there for a spot of polo!' Another world from the way most people live.

TUESDAY 13 JANUARY

Cabinet: Cameron started with another of his rants about how the 'zombie parliament' isn't a zombie parliament and we still have lots to do, blah blah.

The Chancellor announced that inflation has fallen to 0.5 per cent – largely because of falling petrol prices. This is working like a massive tax cut – boosting real incomes. Suddenly, a mobile phone went off very loudly, playing a pop tune. Cameron looked up, visibly irritated. It was Michael Gove, who awkwardly whipped the phone out of his pocket, and tried to stop the music. It was a new phone, and he clearly did not know what he was doing, and started randomly pressing buttons – but the music simply got louder. Cameron said, 'I've heard of chillaxing, but this is ridiculous.' And then: 'Look, people really should not have their phones in here – they are supposed to be left outside.'

Michael's phone problem lasted for about thirty seconds, but eventually he managed to switch it off, without looking too embarrassed. He looked more uncomfortable when we had the presentation from Nicky Morgan on her new plans to improve careers advice and guidance – one of the things Michael absolutely hates. The more people praised Nicky, the more there was an implied criticism of Michael, and I could not help glancing across at him and trying to discern what was going on behind the blank look on his face. He decided to bite his lip, and did not intervene. Instead, he took copious notes and stared intently at the table.

We finished with a brief update on international affairs from the Prime Minister. He said that he had shown Merkel around one of the London museums, where there is an exhibition about the history of Germany. He stopped in front of the display about the 1930s hyper-inflation: 'Ah, Chancellor, you will want to see the Mario Draghi display!' This is a reference to the Italian head of the European Central Bank, who has irritated the Germans by proposing massive monetary expansion. Apparently the German sense of humour was not on display – 'Not a flicker of amusement!'

At 12.30 p.m. to the DfE for the weekly ministerial meeting. These are worthy occasions, unlike Michael Gove's amusing but often irrelevant discussions. It was all rather serious, like the head girl reporting back to the prefects from a meeting with the headmaster. Nicky ran through everything that had been discussed at Cabinet, and then mentioned the fact that Cameron is going to see President Obama in the near future and – repeating what the PM had said to the Cabinet earlier – 'So if anyone wants to put anything on the agenda for the talks between the Prime Minister and President, they should let me know.' Nick Gibb burst out laughing, clearly thinking it was supposed to be a joke. Realising his mistake, he then endeavoured immediately to look as serious as possible.

WEDNESDAY 14 JANUARY

2 p.m. The weekly trilateral – on the fiscal position and our manifesto. Nick asked where we had got to on this, and Danny opened up by saying that he thought that we had got some 'white smoke' – an agreement between him and me.

Nick looked relieved. I am also delighted – it is an awful lot better than the assumptions Danny was making just a week ago, and gives us clarity.

SUNDAY 18 JANUARY

A beautiful, crisp, clear winter day. Bibury at its magnificent best – gleaming under a layer of ice. Last night was the coldest of the year, and I slipped a few times on the ice.

Iain Dale has a rather gloomy piece today, forecasting a hung parliament and the Liberal Democrats losing well over half our seats. At least it means that expectations are being set so low that it is going to be difficult for us to underdeliver!

MONDAY 19 JANUARY

Found out from my private secretary that Nicky Morgan has cancelled a meeting that I was supposed to be having today with officials on the Weald of Kent grammar school – where I was going to get the department's legal advice. This is the plan from Kent County Council to effectively build a new grammar school in Sevenoaks by pretending that it is an expansion of a grammar school which is ten miles away. New grammar schools are not allowed by legislation, while expansions are.

I saw Luke Tryl to express my discontent. About ten minutes later, and to my surprise, Nicky Morgan suddenly appeared in my office – Secretaries of State never visit the offices of their junior ministers. Without sitting down, Nicky said that the whole thing was very sensitive and she was happy for me to see the legal advice, but she wanted to see it herself first. I felt I could not argue over twenty-four hours. Later on, I phoned Chris Wormald and made clear to him that not a single dot or comma of the legal submission must change between it being seen by Nicky and by me. Chris agreed. If you put civil servants on the spot, they will make sure that nothing goes off track.

TUESDAY 20 JANUARY

Danny is meeting the Chancellor to talk about the DfE capital budget. I am sending Danny in to bat with a remit that he must not take a single penny off the Priority School Building Programme 2 – designed to rebuild schools in the worst condition. Officials have provided me with pen portraits of some of the schools that would end up being cut out of the programme if the Chancellor had his way. I am sending across the details of five schools – St John Fisher Catholic Comprehensive School in Chatham and Aylesford, the Baverstock Academy in Birmingham, Brinsworth Comprehensive School in Rotherham, Somers Heath Primary School in Thurrock, and Leventhorpe Business and Enterprise Academy in Hertford and Stortford.

St John Fisher Catholic Comprehensive has a condition summary which says:

> The structural engineer has reported the building as nearing the end of its lifespan. This means that the concrete in the building would begin to deteriorate, resulting in a number of health and safety risks such as falling masonry and window casements ... Several classrooms are undersized and suffer extremes of temperature, with summer temperatures reaching 40°.

Of the Baverstock Academy, it says:

> Most windows are not able to be opened and closed and their seals

are ineffective. This allows water to get in, which regularly leads to costly internal damage. In one block, the present windows have been deemed unsafe by the local authority health and safety adviser. The windows have been deemed a danger to the point where they are screwed shut. On occasion, windows have blown open, smashing glass from a height of 10 metres. The gym and PE areas are a grave health and safety concern.

There is no way that we should be putting rebuilding of such schools on hold.

Went down to the Downing Street cafeteria at 7.30 a.m. Had a chat with Alison, who serves the breakfasts and has been there for ten years. I asked her jokingly what it was like to serve breakfast under a coalition government versus Labour: 'I think to be honest the Conservative and Lib Dem ministers have rather healthier eating habits – I tended to serve large greasy breakfasts under Labour!'

At 3.15 p.m. met with Danny and Nick. Danny reported on his meeting with Osborne – we have protected the whole £2 billion rebuilding programme, and struck a deal over free school numbers. Good news – though the schools that have benefited from my intervention will probably never know!

Danny also mentioned the Budget. George is still pressing for this to be more 'interesting' than we want.

Went back over to the DfE, and had a quick chat with Luke Tryl. I said that Nick and I might well want to launch the priority school building programme. Luke said, 'Oh, you might want to know that the PM also has his eye on launching that!' I replied, 'Cameron and the Tories have got a bloody cheek. They have spent the last month trying to cut this programme, and now you are telling me that Cameron actually wants to launch it himself? He must be kidding!'

We also had a briefing from officials on the Weald of Kent grammar school issue. The advice is quite helpful. Basically, it says that by 70 per cent to 30 per cent the balance of judgment is that this is a new school and therefore would be illegal. As far as I am concerned, this proposal should now be dead in this parliament. What I shall say to Nicky is that if she wants to delay her decision until after the election, I am happy with this, but if the Tories try to go ahead and ignore the legal advice, then we are going to have one hell of a public row.

A good day. I am very pleased and proud that there are going to be lots of schools in terrible condition being rebuilt, which frankly would not be happening if the Tories had got their way. We have saved at least sixty or seventy schools from having their rebuilding projects axed.

WEDNESDAY 21 JANUARY

Saw Oliver Letwin for breakfast. Warned him about the legal advice on the proposed new grammar school, and the likely row if Cameron wants to plough on.

Also raised the timid little package on freedom of information that Simon Hughes was hoping to get through before the election. Cameron has said that he is not interested. There are some uncomfortable issues on FoI at the moment, including a suggestion that the royal family should have to reveal the details of all their wills. Bizarre! The truth is the package is so small that it really is not worth having a row about.

The daily call at 9 a.m. Stephen Lotinga mentioned a strange story that has come up overnight, something about the UK now again allowing the import of mangoes from India! The suspicion is that the Tories have just announced this unilaterally to try to win the Indian vote as we come towards the general election. Apparently mangoes are rather a big thing in India. Odd.

At 11 a.m. went to the Mental Health Task Force that Nick Clegg now chairs with senior Cabinet ministers. Amusing that towards the end, Anna Soubry tore a strip off Chris Grayling by saying that his paper on mental health in prisons was 'absolutely pathetic' and that the MoJ should be doing far more. It is quite irregular for a junior minister to tick off a Secretary of State. Ballsy woman!

At midday, went back to the DfE and had a good meeting on measuring the performance of academy chains and local authorities. Officials have done a brilliant job on this and I hope that we will soon be able to publish league tables showing the best and worst academy chains and local authorities.

THURSDAY 22 JANUARY

Spent time discussing an initiative the Chancellor intends to announce on Monday – giving money to coastal towns. We have been completely blindsided on this, and the Chancellor intends to come to the south-west to announce all the schemes! It is basically an opportunity for the Tories to deliver good news to their target seats.

MONDAY 26 JANUARY

Went up to see Nick at 10.30 a.m. We are having to compete with the Tories on policy 'launches', with the Chancellor popping up all over the country trying to announce government initiatives in key seats. In addition, the Tories are on an offensive today to claim the low-tax ground. We put out a spoiler, with some statistics, claiming credit for the increase in the personal allowance.

When I got home there was a letter from the new Lib Dem parliamentary candidate in Vauxhall – on rubbishy paper, with no party logo. The letter is littered with spelling mistakes – and one particularly unfortunate sentence: 'I am very conscious of the disturbing lack of inequality that exists within our society...' Either a serious error or he is a very right-wing Liberal Democrat!

Some strange submissions in my box tonight – including one Home Affairs Committee clearance request from the Tory minister John Hayes, referring to the 'horizontal working-time directive.' I feared it must be something to do with prostitution – but it turns out to be about the hours of people who work on the waterways. Apparently the rest of the EU are trying to coordinate the regulations so that people who pass from one waterway into another country have the same working hours. The UK asked for an exemption on the basis that there are not many waterways in the UK which connect with other countries, but apparently our reasonable request for an exemption was turned down! Another EU shot in the foot.

TUESDAY 27 JANUARY

Up to Nick's office for the weekly strategy meeting. There was much discussion about the proposed TV election debates. Now that the media have accepted that the Greens ought to take part, Cameron is trying to move the goalposts again. Yesterday, he claimed that the DUP needed to be included as well. Nick sighed: 'Cameron's absurd! Next week it will be the Cornish Independence Party!' Nick revealed that Cameron has told him privately that he is determined to find excuses not to attend: 'I have got Ed Miliband on the floor – why would I allow him to get up again?'

Cabinet. A Regional Growth Fund presentation from Nick. The Tories were all over it, saying how wonderful it was. The Tories have a brilliant ability to 'own' anything that looks remotely like a Lib Dem success – obviously a very deliberate strategy.

We are getting feedback that the Tories don't want to go ahead with the new asbestos management programme that I have signed off, which would involve much more oversight of asbestos in schools. I made clear that I am not prepared to publish any plan which is weaker than this. I have asked Chris Paterson to speak to the very sensible Luke Tryl to see if this can be sorted out.

A very useful meeting on a new performance measure for academy chains and local authorities. The Tories are terribly nervous, and made a case that academy chains and local authorities should not appear in the same table. My priority is just to get the new methodology out. In any case, it would be very easy for a journalist to aggregate the results in one table. So I have told Chris Paterson that I am willing to concede and that the priority should just be to get the work published. In coalition, 'no' is a far more powerful word than 'yes'. And when the other side of a coalition is determined not to do something, there is not much that you can do about it – unless you are prepared to trade something else off against it.

WEDNESDAY 28 JANUARY

Nick managed to persuade Cameron yesterday that the school rebuilding programme launch should be led by the Lib Dems rather than the Tories.

Went back to my office and at 10.30 a.m. met up with Jonny Oates. Jonny is a really nice guy, and extremely sensible, and although he is a little bit on the left-wing side, he does make sure that Nick does not lose connection with the party. And since Jonny's heart beats on the left, he makes sure that Nick is protected from some of the slightly dottier ideas that Danny comes up with. Jonny said that Nick is worrying about his Sheffield Hallam seat. Jonny said, 'Personally, I am not really worried about how Nick will do in Sheffield Hallam. We are putting in plenty of resources. But I can understand why Nick is nervous about the situation, particularly as it is a very tempting target for Labour activists.'

An interesting submission from staff about a dispute in the Ministry of Justice about missing discs, including sensitive personal data. It seems that Grayling is trying to get Simon Hughes to announce the problem. Simon is apparently pointing out that this is a departmental management issue, which should be dealt with by Grayling. The advice to Nick from special advisers is clear: 'Politically, this is very simply Grayling trying to get the junior Lib Dem minister to take flak for him. This is simply not on.' Nick and Danny have always been rather generous about Grayling, but frankly I have never trusted the man.

THURSDAY 29 JANUARY

Ryan Coetzee has sent Nick a political note:

Bluntly and simply, Labour is midway through a slow-motion implosion because they lack credibility on the economy, lack a credible candidate for No. 10 and lack a consistent and credible message. They will shed many seats to the SNP and win fewer seats off the Tories than expected, thanks to the Greens and their own ineffectiveness. In contrast, the Tories are in a much stronger position, their UKIP problem notwithstanding, because they have a credible candidate for PM with a credible pitch – only the Tories can be trusted to finish the job on the economy. Given all of this, the biggest risk we face is a significant shift of voters towards the Tories as Election Day approaches. This is a serious problem in seats we contest with the Tories, a category that accounts for the vast majority of our winnable seats. Therefore the single most important thing we need to get across between now and Election Day is that Britain can secure the recovery with fairness and without a scorched-earth approach to public services and a war on the poor. Also known as a stronger economy and a fairer society. So it is 'Yes to finishing the job; no to finishing it unfairly'.

FRIDAY 30 JANUARY

The new figures on university attendance are out today, and they show that in spite of the higher tuition fees, student numbers have surged to a record high – with a big increase for disadvantaged pupils. Nick's press officers report that the media are not interested. As Nick said: 'Only bad news travels fast...' The statistics also show that student numbers have powered ahead in England, where we have the tuition fees, whereas they have flattened off completely in Scotland, because they are dependent upon central government expenditure.

SUNDAY 1 FEBRUARY

An *Observer* poll has us on 5 per cent – profoundly depressing. I had assumed that our poll ratings would be beginning to recover by now, as people start to reflect on what we have done in coalition and think about who they really want back in power.

But the longer time goes on, the more we have to face the horrible prospect of a really low share of the vote – and a very large decline in seats.

Nicky Morgan was on *Marr* this morning, forced to showcase the latest half-baked Tory education policy – oversold No. 10 drivel, including the proposal that every child should know their twelve times table before the end of primary school. I learned my twelve times table at age seven – in 1972! Have we gone backwards in the intervening forty years?

We Lib Dems are putting out today a document called the 'Gove Files', which I am rather uncomfortable about. It focuses on the past five years, emphasising our differences with Michael Gove – I would much rather be talking about positive policies for the future.

MONDAY 2 FEBRUARY

When Cameron gave his education speech at midday, it turned out to be a massive damp squib. We all thought that the Tories were going to protect the schools budget in real terms, but what they have actually promised is what they were planning to do at the beginning of this parliament – to protect per pupil funding in cash terms. That means that real funding would be squeezed – and Sam Freedman, Michael Gove's former policy adviser, has gone on Twitter to say that this implies cuts of 7–10 per cent in the real schools budget over the parliament.

Went to the NHS performance meeting at 11 a.m., chaired by Jeremy Hunt. The whole thing does not get any more impressive. A&E performance appears to have improved a bit over the past couple of weeks, but only because demand for NHS services has fallen dramatically. The number of blocked beds has risen yet again, to the highest level in the parliament. It was all rather pathetic and I have limited confidence in the Department of Health and its senior management. I don't think they could manage their way out of a wet paper bag.

In the evening, had dinner with Jeremy Browne in Strangers' Dining Room. He is still incredibly grumpy and bitter. He described what a nightmare it was to work with Theresa May, who he said was unimaginative, narrow and squashed any sign of initiative from her junior ministers, whether they were Tory or Liberal Democrat. He clearly absolutely loved the Foreign Office and never got over leaving it or his beloved William Hague.

TUESDAY 3 FEBRUARY

A couple of centimetres of snow this morning.

At 8.30 a.m. went upstairs to Nick's office for the regular strategy meeting. We discussed individual seats. Ryan said that Manchester Withington is now effectively unwinnable. In spite of all the work that has gone on in Ashfield – a marginal Labour seat – it still looks as if Labour's vote is high enough to win. Somerton and Frome, where David Heath is standing down, looks pretty awful. The polling data is better for Taunton. A marked improvement in Montgomeryshire and also in Mike Moore's seat.

Cabinet – a pretty dull agenda – with the exception of an early item about cyber security. Like all of these security presentations, you listen to them in hushed awe, and then at the end realise that you have been told nothing of any significance whatsoever. This is not perhaps a surprise – talking to a room full of thirty politicians is probably not the best way of ensuring that information is kept secret. We were also told by the PM that we absolutely must leave every single mobile phone outside the room – as even when they are turned off it is supposedly possible for the Chinese and Russians to listen in. Cameron said there was a last opportunity for anyone who had a mobile phone to get rid of it outside the room before the presentation took place, and Francis Maude, the Attorney General and then a sheepish-looking Michael Gove got up and walked out. I don't imagine for a minute that the Chinese or Russians are listening in – it would be a complete waste of their time, since nothing of importance is ever discussed.

Matt Sanders contacted me to say that he had just discovered that the Prime Minister is now planning to go to one of the schools in the marginal Lib Dem constituency of Cheadle for the launch of the priority school building programme. Nick said he was pretty furious as Cameron had indicated that he was planning to go to the East Midlands. I said that we should make clear that it was unacceptable for Tory ministers to be sent into our seats to announce a priority school building programme that has been led by Lib Dem ministers.

WEDNESDAY 4 FEBRUARY

New polling data has been released today on Scottish seats. The results are pretty awful for all the parties other than the SNP – who would sweep the board. We would be wiped out in every seat other than Alistair Carmichael's. Danny is twenty-nine percentage points behind in his poll. This would surely make it impossible for Labour to secure a majority.

There had been a bit of a row at the Quad today about the fact that the Chancellor is supposed to be going up to Yorkshire tomorrow and has suddenly tabled a 'Yorkshire package' – £300,000 for something called a 'Tour de Yorkshire' cycling event; £1.5 million on a 'Welcome to Yorkshire festival'; and £1.5 million for some kind of Turner Prize at a gallery in Hull. George wants to announce it all himself. Nick was spitting blood because whenever we want to do something to support the regions, it takes months to get clearance from the Chancellor, yet he is now trying to bounce us into this for tomorrow! The Tories are trying to splatter money all over the country to target their marginal constituencies.

Met Nick and Danny to discuss the launch tomorrow of our new economic strategy and details of tax, spending and borrowing. The announcement is apparently going to be at the top of the Shard, and Nick asked what kind of dress was suitable for the event – did he need a tie? I said that since Nick and Danny were announcing an £8 billion tax rise, they needed to be thinking about 'City backdrop, smart suits, ties which look as if they have been bought by their wives or mothers, and dull background music by Bach or Mozart'. Chris Saunders joked that it was all rather like *Yes Minister*.

Nick said there is a poll tomorrow from Unison about his own seat, claiming that Labour are ten points ahead. I said that everybody in party HQ seemed to think that he would be fine, but he replied: 'In my humble opinion they are all being rather complacent.'

I should also mention today the significant news that the great Gary Johnson has been sacked as manager of Yeovil Town Football Club. Pretty astonishing, since Gary has taken the club from the non-league Conference right up to the Championship, but the problem is we are now anchored firmly at the bottom of League One. Football management can be pretty harsh. One second a club legend; the next second sacked. Bit like politics.

THURSDAY 5 FEBRUARY

Today is the launch of our economic plan – with our most detailed exposition yet of what we would borrow, tax, spend and cut in the next parliament. We have got a sensible package, which may be spun by some right-wing media as a 'lurch to the left', and a victory for Vince, but in reality it is an ambitious plan to cut the deficit but is also deliverable, without unacceptable social impacts.

Arrived slightly late in Chard for the first canvass session of the day. There was good support. But one family of previous Lib Dems are now voting Green, and there was an odd chap who said he might vote Tory because of the risk of a Labour–SNP coalition!

In the evening, I spent about an hour phoning all of the union 'barons' – Russell Hobby of NAHT, Brian Lightman of ASCL, Chris Keates of NASUWT, Christine Blower of NUT and Mary Bousted of ATL. Briefed them all on the results of the Workload Challenge, which we are publishing tomorrow. Russell and Brian seemed fairly relaxed and positive, Mary felt it was a missed opportunity not to do more about Ofsted.

FRIDAY 6 FEBRUARY

My red box includes a paper of potential DfE bids for the Budget – all incredibly weak. The paper notes that the Chancellor is interested in options for grant funding a scheme to support chess competitions in schools! You would have thought that the Chancellor had somewhat more important things to worry about in his spare time.

MONDAY 9 FEBRUARY

Today is launch day for the Priority School Building Programme 2, which I have been working on for eighteen months. As it is a good news story, there is very little coverage in the national media. I visit Cheadle Primary School, Great Moor Junior School and Hazel Grove Primary School – all benefiting from the scheme. I yearned to be in Cornwall, where Nick Clegg was announcing two massive secondary school rebuilds – at £16 million a time!

A note in today's box from my DfE diary secretary points out that I have only got twelve more days in the department and asks me not to agree to any more meetings!

TUESDAY 10 FEBRUARY

12.30 p.m. Nick's office for a discussion about the Budget. Officials have produced a pretty hopeless options paper with a rag, tag and bobtail of ideas, ranging from good things like investment in mental health and the early years pupil premium to 'reducing the VAT rate on bicycles to 5 per cent, having a competition for green council of the year, and planting a tree for every child born in the next parliament'!

Worst of all were the VAT cut ideas – including on tourist attractions, bikes, buggies and pushchairs, spectacles and contact lenses, and empty homes. Nick looked distracted and was not in a particularly good mood. He had just come back from Deputy Prime Minister's Questions, and had been getting a hard time from Labour MPs about his Sheffield seat.

I was particularly dismissive of the dotty idea to cut VAT on tourism services – including on expensive hotels and restaurants.

The PSBP launch seems to have gone very smoothly apart from the fact that a Tory MP called Craig Whittaker – who I have never heard of – is now up on top of a school roof somewhere, protesting that this school was not included in the programme. It turns out that Michael Gove went to his school a couple of years ago and said that it was one of the worst in the country and that it should have been rebuilt under Labour. This sounded to the local MP like a bankable pledge, but the school is way below the cut-off for the programme. Apparently the MP has gone a bit bonkers. I am hoping that some more very cold nights will cause him to come down from the roof.

WEDNESDAY 11 FEBRUARY

Home Affairs Cabinet Committee – an interesting affair, mainly because of attacks by Tories on Tories. Theresa May was presenting a paper on tackling child abuse when she suddenly faced a combined attack from Sajid Javid, IDS, Pickles and Michael Gove. Sajid made quite an aggressive attack on the Home Secretary, saying that her paper completely under-estimated some of the ethnic issues underlying child abuse, including the attitude towards women in countries such as Pakistan. Theresa is always incredibly prickly when attacked, and she hit back fairly hard, saying that people had not read her paper properly and that it was wrong to put all the blame on particular ethnic minorities when there was plenty of sexual abuse amongst the white population. The row rumbled on, and amusingly it took Nick Clegg to intervene to protect the Home Secretary from constant attacks from Sajid. There must be a future leadership thing going on here. Theresa looked pretty unamused – she is a bit charmless, but I cannot help feeling sorry for her, because she seems to have few friends around the Cabinet table.

FRIDAY 13 FEBRUARY

Started the red box at 9.30 p.m. and worked solidly until 1.30 a.m. The truth is I love the serious work of being a minister and making decisions that really count. I just hate all the flim-flam of the media and having to make speeches. Goodness knows what I will do after the general election if we are back on the opposition benches again. It must be like coming off highly addictive drugs and discovering that you are having to go cold turkey. But coming down with a bump is looking increasingly likely, given our plunging poll ratings – down to as low as 5 or 6 per cent in some polls. The problem is that this now has a feedback loop – as all the media want to write about is the likely scale of our losses.

It now really is conceivable that the party could contract back to where it was before the 1997 election – between twenty and twenty-five MPs.

SATURDAY 14 FEBRUARY

Advice centres in both Ilminster and Crewkerne, starting at 8.45 a.m. – both incredibly busy. Some people are very good at getting to the point, and others take an eternity. In spite of having sixteen to twenty cases to deal with, I finished at 12.15 p.m.

WEDNESDAY 18 FEBRUARY

Vince was up in Scotland yesterday and made some extremely unhelpful comments about the SNP – saying that it is possible that we could end up in coalition with them, and even touching on the possibility of a Labour–SNP–Liberal Democrat coalition. That is absolutely toxic, not just in Scotland but in England too. The Tories are already trying to get a 'Coalition of Chaos' narrative up and running. Nick was pretty furious, and said he would contact Vince. Ryan said that perhaps we could get Vince to do some campaigning in his own constituency instead! I got the impression that Ryan feels the campaign in Twickenham could be going rather better.

Canvassed all day. Got back to the office at 6.45 p.m. for a call with Nicky Morgan. The Chancellor is making a speech in East Anglia tomorrow and wants to nick an announcement about placing new middle leaders in struggling schools, which I have been working on for the past six months. I vetoed it.

THURSDAY 19 FEBRUARY

Willie Rennie, the Scottish Liberal Democrat leader, has firmly slapped down Vince – briefing that the Lib Dems are not interested in going into coalition with the SNP.

SUNDAY 22 FEBRUARY

Had a dream about Danny losing his seat. Weighed myself and have lost 2 kilograms since last week – all that canvassing.

The media are now expecting a 'messy' hung parliament in May 2015, with no clear strong government. That is not good for us, because the risk is that as we get closer to Election Day people will get nervous about the prospects of a hung parliament and start to feel that they have got to choose either Labour or the Conservatives.

MONDAY 23 FEBRUARY

Worked for a few hours in the morning on my election addresses. I really find drafting election literature incredibly tedious – by the time you are on the tenth leaflet, you cannot think of anything new to say.

Had a brief chat with Jonny Oates. We agreed that we need to be doing some contingency planning for post-election scenarios – Jonny said he could not see how Danny could lead the negotiating team if he had lost his seat.

In my box this morning is a briefing note on a government proposal about pardoning all those convicted under the laws against homosexuality, following all the attention around a recent film and the pardoning of Alan Turing. Civil servants clearly hate the idea of taking retrospective action of this type, partly for practical reasons, partly for bureaucratic reasons, and partly because of 'precedent'. Their note rather feebly suggests that conceding a pardon would 'increase the pressure for other groups looking for mass pardons, for example witches (pre-1735)'. The argument that if we grant this pardon we will be under pressure to legislate to pardon pre-1735 witches seems rather weak to me.

Bumped into Charles Kennedy in the division lobby: 'If the polls stay anything like now, then it will sweep away an awful lot of us.'

TUESDAY 24 FEBRUARY

Budget planning. There remains some crazy proposal on the table from Nick's advisers to reduce VAT from 20 per cent to 5 per cent on children's bikes! This would cost £40 million. My own view is that this is completely idiotic. It might also be illegal under EU rules – which may be the saving grace!

The School Teachers' Pay Review Body report is due out soon. This is going to recommend a 1 per cent increase for most teachers, but a 2 per cent rise for those at the upper end of the teacher pay spine. The 2 per cent rise would only affect a small proportion of teachers, but would be symbolic and welcomed. Danny is sympathetic, but the Chancellor is now saying that he does not support a 2 per cent increase, because this would break the 1 per cent pay guideline. I want us Lib Dems to back the 2 per cent rise publicly, even if this means having a row.

Other significant news today was the car-crash interview by Natalie Bennett. She went on the Nick Ferrari programme and got in a total muddle about the Green Party's manifesto costings. The whole thing went viral and her credibility is trashed.

WEDNESDAY 25 FEBRUARY

Went over to Nick's office for 1.30 p.m. for a pre-Quad meeting.

Danny said he had a word with Osborne yesterday about the Budget. Amusingly, George has proposed increasing the personal income tax allowance by £100 or £200 – the first time that the Tories have themselves proposed this. He is also considering cancelling the fuel duty rise. According to Chris Saunders, Danny himself is trying to get the fuel duty increase cancelled – because he and our Scottish MPs regard this as a sensitive issue in their rural seats.

George is also talking about going further than the Low Pay Commission recommendation, by raising the national minimum wage not just to the £6.70 level that the Commission are recommending but all the way to £7. And in another move to try to steal Labour's clothes, he is proposing that we increase the free childcare allowance for three- and four-year-olds from fifteen hours to twenty hours or even to twenty-five hours. Predictably, Osborne also wants something for the classic Tory voter – a savers package, which would basically be giving away more money for ISAs. And he is trying to shoot some UKIP foxes too, by talking about cutting hospital car parking charges!

What George is doing is clever – proposing a whole series of things that he knows we will find it very difficult to resist. And trying to shoot the policy foxes of all the Conservative Party's opponents. Danny, Nick and I agreed:

1. That we had to go along with an increase in the personal allowance.
2. That we would not want to be seen to be in the way of a fuel duty cut.
3. That we could not stand in the way of a bigger than expected increase in the minimum wage.
4. That if we are going to do something on childcare, it ought to be to make the two-year-old offer universal.
5. That we wanted a mental health package.
6. That we ought to be cautious about a savers' package – that could only benefit the wealthy.

In the evening, attended a reception at Lancaster House to announce the Talented Leaders programme first cohort – this is school leaders and school deputies who have stepped up to become head teachers in challenging schools. A great programme.

FRIDAY 27 FEBRUARY

Up at 7 a.m. Apparently Labour is going to launch its policy on tuition fees – cutting fees from £9,000 to £6,000. The policy is likely to get a large raspberry from many quarters, because it looks far more like a gimmick that will help middle-class children than a rational policy targeted at those who really need extra help.

SATURDAY 28 FEBRUARY

No advice centres today, just canvassing. Started in Yeovil Without on Eliotts Drive. On about the fourth door, I encountered some particularly unpleasant woman who ranted on about immigration and the generally dreadful state of the country. I did my best to listen patiently, but she went on and on about how she no longer recognised the country, and how everybody was now foreign. At this, I got rather irritated and waved my hand up and down Eliotts Drive: 'As far as I can see, everybody up and down here is British.' But it did not make any difference. She said the problems with immigration were 'absolutely disgusting'.

Two doors down, I had the same from somebody who was visiting his elderly mother. He was perfectly courteous to begin with and then started to engage me in a ranting conversation about how much the country had gone downhill since the days of the empire. 'What on earth would Queen Victoria have to say if she was around today? And what about Winston Churchill and King Henry VIII?' It is difficult to know how to answer a question like this. I felt provoked to say, 'Do you really think that people were better off in Victorian England? A lot of people in England died young of preventable diseases. There was no National Health Service, no pension system and squalid living conditions.' It did not make the slightest difference. He still clearly thought we were better off in 1880. Every time I tried to get away, he went on a bit more. I could feel myself losing my temper, and my right hand in my jacket pocket involuntarily grabbed my pen and tried to snap it in half. Most people are wonderful but there is a minority with quite unpleasant views.

SUNDAY 1 MARCH

We went for a walk at lunchtime. Got back at around 2 p.m. and watched the end of the film *Bridge on the River Kwai* – an old faithful, which I absolutely love. Then England–Ireland in the rugby.

Tomorrow is the final DfE Oral Questions, and then we have just three more Cabinet meetings before Parliament is dissolved on 30 March.

MONDAY 2 MARCH

Conference call with Lib Dem Cabinet ministers at 9.30 p.m. – a brief discussion about the minimum wage. Vince wants to put up the apprenticeship rate by more than the Low Pay Commission was recommending, but is opposed to the Osborne idea of raising the national minimum wage by more than the Low Pay Commission suggested. Vince tried to explain why it was right to overrule the Low Pay Commission on the apprenticeship wage but wrong on the national minimum wage – I suspect it's all about the fact that the latter is an Osborne idea.

TUESDAY 3 MARCH

7.15 a.m. Breakfast with Andrew Adonis at the Royal Horse Guards Hotel.

Andrew kicked off by saying that he was very optimistic about the general election, and Labour was doing well in its target seats. He hinted that he thought that there would be a hung parliament and the need for an arrangement between the Lib Dems and Labour.

Andrew said that he thought it would be possible to get an agreement on economic policy between the two parties, with some kind of compromise on deficit reduction. I said I was inclined to agree, but there was a risk in us having too long a list of tax increases, including on business and the wealthy. I said that we did not want to end up where a new government was painted as anti-business, socialist and left-wing by the media.

On constitutional reform, Andrew thought that it would be possible to make progress on party funding reform, and said he was a strong advocate of PR for local government elections, and if Lib Dems made this a high priority in negotiations it was something that Labour could deliver.

9.30 a.m. Cabinet, a thin agenda, cut to just an hour because the Mexican President is visiting.

We discussed Central and South America, where there was a lot of self-congratulation. At the end, Michael Gove could not resist speaking. 'Prime Minister, I think we ought to record the thanks of Cabinet for one of the previous Liberal Democrat ministers in the Foreign Office who did absolutely splendid work in Latin America – Jeremy Browne, the Honourable Member for Taunton, who sadly is standing down at the election.' Everybody laughed, knowing that Michael had only raised this to irritate Nick Clegg. Cameron said, 'Yes, I do remember that Jeremy rather enjoyed travelling around Latin America!' To which Nick replied, 'Yes – he enjoyed it far too much.' Osborne then added, 'Yes, Jeremy Browne is awfully good on diplomacy, isn't he!' – a snide reference to some of Jeremy's recent interviews, where he has showered criticism on Nick.

Nick bumped into Cameron in the No. 10 toilets afterwards: 'Michael was on good form today!' 'Yes,' said Cameron. 'Of course what you have to remember about Michael is that he is completely mad!'

Nick and Danny seem to feel that George has now gone off the idea of a big increase in the minimum wage. Apparently we have had some useful advice back saying that the VAT cut for children's bikes is illegal under

EU law. Thank God! But apparently the Chancellor is now looking at a VAT reduction for children at hotels and holiday parks – even dafter than the bike idea!

Nick is worried about the potential size of the Budget package. We do need to be very careful, as there is a real risk of us getting sucked into helping George to deliver a budget which is far more exciting than would be sensible.

Went back to my room in the Cabinet Office and decided to clear out my desk so that when the general election comes I am ready. Spent about an hour throwing away vast amounts of paperwork. It feels like crossing a bridge.

WEDNESDAY 4 MARCH

At 3 p.m. met Nick and Danny about the Budget. Osborne is apparently getting cold feet about having an increase in the tax allowance, but is pushing hard for a package for savers, which might even involve abolishing the taxation of savings income. This would cost £700 million or £800 million. This gives Osborne exactly the favourable lines in the Tory media that he would want. Jonny was rather sceptical about the whole thing and clearly thinks that we are ending up getting sucked in too deep.

Eventually, we agreed that what we should suggest to Osborne and Cameron was that increasing the personal income tax allowance should be counted as something being pushed by both coalition parties. We could allocate £250 million for a Lib Dem-inspired mental health support package and £250 million for a Tory package on tax reliefs on savings.

The truth is that whatever policies Osborne puts in to the Budget he is going to get a massive amount of favourable publicity from the Tory media, who are desperate now for the Conservatives to win. So it really is sensible for us to have a minimalist package that does not give Osborne too many cards to play with – though I suspect that Danny is probably more up for a big Budget, and his natural desire to get on with George and to promote something exciting that will be delivered by the Treasury risks undermining our agreed minimalist strategy.

Interestingly, Osborne now wants the total managed expenditure assumption to be *higher* than it was in the last Autumn Statement. Danny is reading this as George being very nervous about the publicity that he got after the last Autumn Statement, which showed departmental spending falling to the lowest level since the 1930s. Apparently they now want a spending figure at the end of the next parliament which would be equivalent to the share of GDP spent on total public expenditure in 1997 – when Labour came to power. Presumably this is for entirely presentational reasons.

THURSDAY 5 MARCH

In the evening, went to an event at the Westland Sports and Social in Yeovil – a grand dinner to mark the 100th anniversary of the founding of Westland Helicopters. Paddy Ashdown was supposed to be the main speaker. Unfortunately, at the last moment, they inserted an additional speaker – a Dr Wang, a helicopter engineer. He came on before Paddy and said he hadn't prepared anything but would speak off the cuff. An hour later he was still talking, while people glanced nervously at their watches.

I began to feel a strong urge to fall asleep. Got back very late. Beware Dr Wangs promising short speeches.

SATURDAY 7 MARCH

Should have been in Yeovil canvassing, but had to be in London to go through the final sign-off of our general election manifesto.

Back home at about 6.30 p.m., and at 7.30 p.m. we did a conference call on Budget communications. On this occasion there were no civil servants and it was just Nick, Danny, Jonny Oates, me, Stephen Lotinga, James McGrory and Ryan Coetzee. Jonny started off by jogging us through what was likely to be the Budget communication strategy. This would start next weekend with the unveiling by us of our mental health package at our party conference. Then Osborne would be on *Marr* on Sunday and, as Danny pointed out, 'He would want something to say.' Then on Monday there would be a release of a consultation on business rates, and on Tuesday there would be whatever announcements we had to make about the minimum wage.

On Wednesday there would be the Budget itself. And then on Thursday Danny hopes to release a Treasury paper setting out the Lib Dem fiscal plans for the future – and contrasting these with the Tories'. We then had a discussion about the tax allowance and any potential increase. This is clearly going to be the most contested area, as the Tories will have their savings package and we will have our mental health package – and the issue will be who manages to associate themselves first with the increase in the allowance. Nick said he felt that we had been through this in every single Budget and Autumn Statement of the parliament, and that he was getting a bit sceptical about how important it was for us to put our imprint on. I said that this was no time to start giving up on our leadership on this issue, and we had to make sure we were off the mark rapidly. Ryan and Stephen agreed. I said, 'Let's not be too nice about this.'

We also had a discussion about the Public Sector Pay Review Body reports. The Chancellor is still blocking the teachers report. Nick said his view was that as soon as the Tories saw that there was going to be a big, public argument about this, they would back off. We agreed to surface the coalition splits in a Monday for Tuesday story. James McGrory will flame this up.

SUNDAY 8 MARCH

It is clear that we have not been nasty enough, because splashing on the front page of the *Sunday Times* is the story that Osborne is going to cut taxes for 27 million people by raising the personal tax allowance in the Budget! The little bastard has got in first! There is now a real likelihood that it will be 'open season' on Budget leaks.

When I got home to Kennington, I had a phone call from Nicky Morgan's special adviser, who wanted me to agree an anodyne media line about the asbestos review – saying that it would come out 'shortly'. I made it clear that I was not willing to put out any line other than that the asbestos review would be released this month – he said he would put this to Laura Trott in 10 Downing Street. He texted me later to say that Laura was not willing to agree to this, so that no DfE line could go out on the issue. I am willing to play hardball.

MONDAY 9 MARCH

Went on the daily call with Nick and Danny at 7.50 a.m. Nick said that over the weekend he and Danny had told Osborne that they were going to veto his plan to abolish the taxation of savings income – on the basis that this was fiscally imprudent and we should focus on increasing the personal tax allowance. Osborne has responded in an 'explosive' way, threatening to veto everything else in the Budget.

At 10 a.m. I went to Nick's office for the first discussion of the day on the Budget. It seems that there are now three issues at stake. Firstly, the Tories have got spooked by all the criticisms of their slash-and-burn approach to public spending and public services. So they want to raise the total managed expenditure assumption.

I am slightly worried about the fact that Danny is planning to publish the Liberal Democrat plans for spending and borrowing the day after the Budget, and I am not sure what he actually intends to use in relation to these plans – but I am worried that he is going to show us over-delivering a current Budget surplus in 2017/18.

The second issue is that we will veto the Chancellor's substantive savings package, and argue that all the money should go into the tax allowance. Then apparently we have made very clear to the Tories that we are prepared to allow them to have a package to boost help for first-time buyers, in exchange for a package on mental health.

Osborne apparently admitted to Nick and Danny that his great wheeze of abolishing the taxation of savings income would not mean much to many people – as they are already sheltering their savings income in ISAs. Instead, George admitted that his tax proposal would really only be helpful to 'stupid, affluent and lazy people', who do not put their savings in tax-efficient vehicles – mentioning by name one of his relatives! Typical Osborne cynicism.

TUESDAY 10 MARCH

The Cabinet agenda was pretty limited – we had an update on the Troubled Families Initiative from Pickles and Louise Casey. Most people praised the scheme, but Michael Gove sat there looking grumpy as he thinks it is all a complete con. He asked some particularly pointed questions – and didn't get very convincing answers.

After Cabinet, we went up to Nick's office for an update on the Budget. Nick looked, I thought, a little sheepish. We started off a few weeks ago determined that we were not going to give the Tories an attractive and exciting Budget, but we seem to have gradually got sucked into something much bigger.

It now looks as if we are going to raise the personal income tax allowance by at least £200. We have apparently agreed to a new childcare policy – that involves giving thirty hours of free childcare to all working parents of three- and four-year-olds – which is Labour's policy, and neither the Tories' nor ours.

Then there is some kind of package on savings tax reliefs, though not the complete abolition of tax on interest that Osborne wanted. We are going to freeze fuel duty again. There is a home-buying incentives package for the Prime Minister, and a mental health package for Nick. There are cuts in alcohol duties, cuts in taxes on North Sea oil. To pay for all these things, there is a new banking tax and a reduction in pensions tax relief. The whole thing is very populist and even though it is a 'neutral' Budget in the sense that there is not a fiscal giveaway, it is going to be quite popular.

Nick and Danny went through, listing all the items. Jonny Oates – across the table from me – looked more and more miserable. He and I glanced at each other and we were both clearly thinking the same thing! I also raised with Danny the issue about him publishing economic projections for Lib Dem fiscal policy the day after the Budget. Danny thinks this is a great wheeze and will be his moment in the sun, but the problem is nobody in Nick's office has actually seen what he plans to publish.

WEDNESDAY 11 MARCH

At 10.30 a.m. I met Will de Peyer, Danny Alexander's adviser, and Chris Saunders and Jonny Oates. After the Budget next week, Danny is proposing to publish a paper which would set out the fiscal plans of the Liberal Democrats compared with the Conservatives'. What Will said shocked me. He said that the Treasury is currently projecting a £13.7 billion current Budget surplus in 2017/18 – and Danny was proposing to deliver exactly the same as the Tories. That would mean that the only difference between the Tories and us up to 2017/18 was that they would do more welfare cuts and we would do more tax rises.

I made very clear that I was not willing to sign up to a £14 billion Budget surplus and that if that was the plan then Nick would have to find somebody else to chair the general election manifesto. Jonny calmed me down a bit by saying that he agreed with me, as did Chris Saunders and pretty much everybody else.

I also said to Jonny that I was deeply unhappy about what we were proposing to do on childcare/early years. This is effectively a negative pupil premium as it means that most disadvantaged youngsters in workless households will only get fifteen hours of early years education while three- and four-year-olds in working households will get thirty – completely bonkers and cuts across our entire narrative on social mobility.

My fortnightly meeting with the Secretary of State was cancelled today, amidst an ongoing row over the School Teachers' Pay Review Body report. Danny has now written round to government ministers asking for agreement to publish the other Pay Review Body reports – but I have written back to say that I am only willing for these to be published on the condition that the School Teachers' Pay Review Body is published and accepted before the general election.

There is also a row brewing over the asbestos report, which I have driven through against resistance from the civil service and Conservatives – and which I am now determined to publish before the general election. People are beginning to know that the Tories are sitting on this, and Cameron was questioned on it at PMQs today. I am intending to give an interview on this later in the week where I am going to put Cameron on the spot and hold him personally accountable for blocking this. Let's see whether the Tories will be willing to sit on the STRB report and the asbestos report if they think it is going to lose them any votes.

At 4 p.m. went over to Nick's office for the weekly trilateral between Nick, Danny and me. Nick had clearly spoken to Danny and made clear that he was not happy with projecting a £13.7 billion Budget surplus. Nevertheless, Danny was at his prickly best, and he went on – boringly – to lecture us all about how a balanced Budget actually was not a balanced Budget and it was only a cyclically adjusted balanced current Budget, and we would still be borrowing, blah blah blah.

THURSDAY 12 MARCH

Not long after I got into the office, my mobile phone went and it was Oliver Letwin. He sounded a little nervous: 'Are you able to talk about this issue of deemed discharge? I think you are holding up a DCLG announcement on this.' To be honest, I could not even remember what the issue of 'deemed discharge' was about, only that I was blocking it in order to get leverage to get my review of asbestos out. I was just going to launch into an attack on Oliver over blocking asbestos, when he said, 'I'm offering you a deal – if you are prepared to unblock the deemed discharge issue then we are happy to go ahead with you publishing the asbestos review today.' I said, 'OK, that's fine. As long as the two things happen simultaneously.'

Nicky apparently wants to speak to me because I am holding up the government's response to the Education Select Committee report on the oversight of academies, free schools and maintained schools. I want to use the leverage of holding up this report to insist on putting out the work we have been doing which measures the performance of academy chains and local authorities. This is really excellent work but the Tories are now getting cold feet because they do not want to put anything out which admits that any academy chain is doing badly.

FRIDAY 13 MARCH

The more I thought about it, the more angry I was about the Quad proposal to increase the number of free hours for early years education from fifteen to thirty for three- and four-year-olds, but only for the children of working parents. To me and to our advisers, this is a completely idiotic policy. What on earth is the point of giving thirty hours of free early years education to the three- and four-year-old children of investment bankers, while we only give fifteen hours of free education to children in non-working households – for example the child of a single mother with mental health problems who is temporarily unable to work. By the time I had left my house, I had decided to stop it – if necessary by threatening resignation.

Just before 7 a.m. I sent Nick an email:

I am simply not prepared to defend a situation where we give a disad-vantaged three- and four-year-old fifteen hours of free early years quality education and they then have to leave the setting while the child of an investment banker stays on for another five or ten hours per week. This is idiotic and immoral and runs directly counter to everything we believe in and have worked for, for the last five years.

I also sent a very blunt email to Jonny Oates:

> I don't think I can continue as the party's Education spokesman if we do something like this next week. There has to be a bottom line of something you will not sign up to and this is it for me. I did not come into politics to cut beer duty, cut savings taxes and widen inequality.

I do feel guilty raising the issue in such a brutal way with Nick when he is probably knackered. I was relieved when a patient email came back from Nick at 8.40 a.m. saying:

> David, Danny – given David's strongly held views on what we should do re. childcare, could you both please together propose to the Conservatives a package which meets David's concerns as soon as possible this morning, i.e. either expansion of the two-year-old offer only or expansion of the three- to four-year-old offer on a universal basis – i.e. not prioritising working parents. If the Conservatives do not accept this then we will then need to decide whether we pull the plug on any childcare package.

Had a couple more conversations with Danny and he said that he would go back to Osborne to discuss this – the whole scorecard for the Budget would be locked down by midday.

I spoke to Nicky at 7.30 a.m. to see if we could resolve the 'league tables' issue. Nicky was her usual cheery self and she said that she understood that the league tables etc. were all quite good but she just felt that it was 'far too late' in the parliament to publish them and that Tristram Hunt would make hay by criticising the academy chains that were low-performing etc. etc. I pushed back and said that this was one of the best pieces of work that the department had done, and that I had been waiting for months for the Tories to sign it off and I had been willing to give them plenty of time to understand it and I had also made quite a number of concessions. However, I said I was not prepared to concede any further.

It was a slightly uncomfortable conversation and Nicky must have said five or six times that she was not prepared to publish, but I made clear that I was not willing to give in either. A frosty discussion, with a frosty and indecisive end.

At 2 p.m. Danny sent an email through which said that he had spoken to Osborne about the childcare issue and Osborne was not willing to budge. There would now be no childcare proposal of any type in the Budget. Frankly I am quite happy with that as I do not know why we were planning to spend £1 billion on a proposal that was neither Lib Dem nor Tory policy, just so that George Osborne could shoot a Labour fox.

Also had another success in that Chris Paterson came back to me to say that the Tories have now begrudgingly agreed to release the league tables of academy chain and local authority performance – alongside the Education Select Committee report.

Did an interview with Andy Grice this morning. Probably laid it on a bit thick on the School Teachers' Pay Review Body and asbestos. Apparently Andy has already phoned No. 10 to ask for a comment. I am hoping that his piece in tomorrow's *Independent* is not too dreadful, otherwise relations in the department are going to go into deep freeze.

It has been quite a difficult day and I have got my way on the school accountability tables in the face of Tory resistance, and have also managed to overturn a billion-pound policy – which might have been popular with some people but which would have widened the opportunity gaps between advantaged and disadvantaged youngsters. So in one sense it has been a good day, though my relations with Nicky certainly will not have been helped, and there is also a risk that Nick will feel that I have been extremely heavy-handed by threatening resignation. You cannot do this sort of thing too often, particularly to friends.

SATURDAY 14 MARCH

Got up at 6 a.m. in my hotel room in Liverpool. Wrote my speech for the policy debate on the manifesto this morning. The weather is still unseasonably cold – only 5° or 6°.

Before I left the hotel, a red box arrived from London – full to the brim. No sign of the workload tailing off yet. The Chancellor of the Exchequer is still – inexplicably – blocking the allocation of the pupil premium under-spend to schools for 2014/15. I am getting totally pissed off with this, particularly as the allocation has to be made to schools by 17 March. Osborne is obviously doing this for some stupid tactical reason to give him leverage, so as a consequence I have decided to start blocking lots of things in return. I am currently blocking a neighbourhood planning measure from the Department of Communities and Local Government, the aviation strat-egy from the Department for Transport, Crossrail 2 from the Department for Transport, and a proposal on designated payment systems from HM Treasury. There is now a new HM Treasury write-around on something that Osborne wants out – so this may give me some added leverage. I am blocking a number of other things for policy reasons – travellers planning guidance from DCLG, a proposal on public service broadcasters from DCMS, the extremism strategy from the Home Office, and a police bail proposal from the Home Office.

Before I did the debate on the manifesto, Danny was speaking on the economy. At one stage he reached out behind the rostrum that he was speaking at and suddenly whipped out a yellow box, within which were the fictional contents of a Lib Dem Budget after the next general election. Danny held the box up and waved it around a bit. It got the photographers shooting their cameras away, but the overall effect wasn't too good.

It was also somewhat unfortunate that earlier on in his speech he pledged himself to 'balancing the Budget by 2010'. Somebody in the audience behind me muttered very loudly, '2010?' Danny stopped, looked up and said, 'Well spotted that man!'

SUNDAY 15 MARCH

Woke up at 7 a.m. feeling incredibly hungover even though Olly Grender and I only had a bottle and a half of wine last night. I think it is the combination of alcohol plus intense tiredness.

To the conference hall for 11.30 a.m. and took my seat in anticipation of Nick's speech. There were the usual items beforehand – including a fundraising speech from Sir Ian Wrigglesworth, which managed to end on a slightly deflating note about legacies – saying that if people were going to die, could they possibly leave some money to the party. This did not seem the best way to raise the temperature for the keynote speech by the Deputy Prime Minister.

Nick came on and gave a rousing speech. He throws 110 per cent into his speeches, and what they lack in polish he makes up for in energy. We have achieved so much in government and how sad it would be if the next couple of weeks are the end of the road. At times over the past few months I have felt strangely blasé about the election outcome – but now I know for sure that I want us to win, and be back in government.

Also reflected that it would be sad if this is Nick's last speech as leader and Deputy Prime Minister. However, there has not been a lot of leadership manoeuvring at this conference, except by that prize idiot Tim Farron, who has given some ghastly interview today parading his religious credentials. This is the man who failed to support equal marriage and who apparently thinks every single word of the Bible is true. Two people who did emerge effectively at this conference were Norman Lamb and Jo Swinson – who gave a remarkably good and serious speech yesterday on women's issues. She really does seem to have developed in her ministerial post, and she seemed to put so much into her speech that it almost felt like a leadership bid – except that she is another person who may not return after the election.

MONDAY 16 MARCH

The next couple of days are going to be dominated by management of the Budget, and making sure that it lands in the right place. I remain nervous that we have conceded too many good news stories to Osborne.

TUESDAY 17 MARCH

To Nick's Commons office for a discussion with the coalition negotiating team. Nick is clearly very worried about the whole issue of legitimacy – he questions whether people would see it as right for us to hold the balance of power and determine the next government if we are seen to have 'lost' the election – i.e. if we have only got twenty-five seats or so. The rest of us said that we could not afford to see things just in this way, as the country would expect us to do our best to form a coalition if no party has a majority.

If a Tory–Lib Dem coalition is possible then the key issue would be the

EU referendum. Nick said it was such a big risk that if we allowed an EU referendum we would need to take something very big in return – maybe a Lib Dem Chancellor of the Exchequer. I said that this could be our negotiating position but that we could settle for two massive mainstream public service portfolios – such as Health and Education. We then had a lot of discussion about the prospects of winning an EU referendum – and Nick said we needed to commission work on it. I pointed out that the only thing it was going to show was that it was basically a coin toss what the outcome would be.

Also had a discussion about the Labour Party. Nick confirmed, privately, that he had discussed the EU referendum issue in person with Miliband. Nick said he firmly believed that the only way that Britain would ever vote to stay in the EU was if the Conservative Party were on side in making this argument.

In the evening was the DPM's end of parliament drinks in Dover House, which I could not attend. But I did get to the House of Commons Chamber for the photograph of all Lib Dem MPs in front of the Speaker's Chair, and another photograph of us all on the government benches, with Nick Clegg standing at the Despatch Box waving his arms at an imaginary Labour opposition. This was a cheery occasion, and everybody ribbed Simon Hughes, who was as usual fifteen minutes late.

I cannot help reflecting on what this photograph of Liberal Democrat MPs is going to look like after the next general election. The sixty or so MPs that we have had over the past couple of parliaments looks like it could be the high-water mark of Lib Dem parliamentary representation, certainly in my political lifetime. Today was an occasion to enjoy and savour – the party has come united through five tough years of coalition government, and it has remained united in spite of the very difficult times for the country and the party. We have achieved an amazing number of things in government which I am incredibly proud of – on the economy, on social policy, and on advancing the agenda of personal liberalism and personal freedom. Whatever happens in the forthcoming election, we can be proud of everything we have achieved and I will always feel grateful to have been a member of this coalition government.

WEDNESDAY 18 MARCH

Budget Day! *The Independent* leads with a splash claiming that Osborne is going to effectively abolish the tax on savings income.

Went on the early morning conference call with Nick and advisers at 7.40 a.m. and Nick mentioned that George Osborne had 'gone bonkers' over the apparent Budget leak.

At 8 a.m. went to the second to last Cabinet meeting of this parliament. We had a film crew, recording the opening comments from Cameron, Osborne and Nick. Osborne spoke third and said how wonderful the coalition was and how we had all worked incredibly well together, and then the TV cameras left and Cameron said, 'Don't worry, George – now you can say what you really think!'

Osborne then described the Budget. Debt falling as a share of GDP. Borrowing lower than expected. Increased public spending in 2019/20 – to shoot Labour's fox. Frozen fuel duty. Cuts in alcohol duty. The mental health package that Nick has fought so hard for. The tax allowance going up to £11,000. And of course the savings package and the package for first-time buyers.

Of all the people who spoke, I was probably the most political. I started by congratulating George and Danny on the job that they have done since 2010. I reminded everybody that George had told us in the coalition negotiations in May 2010 that a personal allowance of £10,000 could not be afforded, and I was pleased that he had proved himself wrong in every Budget and Autumn Statement since then. Some good-natured banter around the table.

I then said that I wanted to make a more jarring point about the credibility of the plans beyond 2016. I said that while the increase in public spending in 2019/20 addressed some of the concerns about public spending plans in the Autumn Statement, it was still undoubtedly the case that what was planned would result in a very big squeeze on public services, along with welfare cuts which would drive big increases in poverty. This was all listened to in silence.

At 9.30 a.m. had to go over to the House of Commons for the Education Select Committee. The chair of the Committee, Graham Stuart, said that I was the last DfE minister to attend during this parliament – definitely now into a phase of 'last things in the parliament'. I am beginning to realise how much I will miss the Department for Education and the job that I have had the honour to do over the past three years.

Went over to the DfE and watched the Budget. It was a Statement that was absolutely dripping in politics – with George shooting Labour foxes and delivering carefully constructed Westminster in-jokes aimed at Ed Miliband. Probably the best of these was a quite convoluted statement about how we were going to do more for mobile phone reception, 'allowing people who have two fridges in two separate kitchens to control both simultaneously with a single mobile phone!' This was a carefully crafted jab at Ed Miliband, who has recently been photographed in some magazine in what later turned out to be his 'second kitchen'!

On and on George went, with his positive economic news and his small initiatives (some incredibly small and aimed at individual constituencies!). The final line was a good one – something about the 'comeback country', which he will also no doubt want communicated as the 'comeback Chancellor'. Probably the most political Budget that I have ever seen, and that is saying something.

One rather striking aspect of George's statement is just how smug he looked when he sat down. I suppose it is too late for him to change this characteristic now, but it is not a very attractive one in a politician – anyone viewing the Budget on television will realise that here is somebody who seems to care more about politics and political game playing than a lot of the bread-and-butter issues that will be worrying the electorate.

Later on, saw some of the early headlines on tomorrow's papers – and Osborne is going to be pleased. The *Daily Telegraph* leads on 'End of Tax on Savings'. The *FT* plumps for 'Osborne eases austerity in bid to spike Labour's election guns'. *The Times* has 'The Comeback King'. *The Independent*: 'Osborne throws the kitchen sink at Miliband'.

THURSDAY 19 MARCH

When I was about half an hour from Yeovil I got a text message from Julian Astle, who had been watching Danny's statement in the Commons – 'Whose idea was that? Everything that is confused, unconvincing and embarrassing about differentiation in one toe-curling piece of botched theatre. Virtually empty Chamber. Overwhelming levels of barracking from Labour. A rebuke from the Speaker for abusing ministerial privileges and wasting the House's time. And the scorn of the commentariat for not knowing whether we supported or opposed the Budget. Apart from that, a triumph.' Oh dear.

FRIDAY 20 MARCH

The media coverage of Danny's Liberal Democrat 'Budget' is pretty awful. A lot of piss-taking in the sketch columns.

In the afternoon, I made a speech to the ASCL conference in London. They gave me a very warm round of applause at the end. I am going to really miss this job. I think this is the last speech that I will make as Schools Minister.

SUNDAY 22 MARCH

James and I decided to go out for a walk – past the Arlington Row cottages, up the hill and out onto the fields. A beautiful spring day. A real feel of the countryside coming back to life. This is the last week of the government. A strange sense simultaneously of a dying government and a reborn countryside.

MONDAY 23 MARCH

Stopped to do a Cabinet ministers' conference call on the outskirts of Farnham.

Nick mentioned tomorrow's final Cabinet meeting – Cameron has got some brewing company in his constituency to produce a special 'Co-aleition Bitter!' to give to all Cabinet members. Nick said that in return he would be presenting packets of crisps. I assumed he was joking. 'Crisps?'

Nick said he was serious, and had got them produced by some company up in Sheffield. Alistair Carmichael was unimpressed: 'Don't they make anything a bit nicer in the way of food in your constituency, you bloody cheapskate, Clegg!'

Decided today to veto the right-wing head-banging proposals on travellers and gypsies that Eric Pickles and that ghastly man Brandon Lewis have come up with. They have been chasing me about it over the past few days. I have finally said no – and sent back a 'leak-proof' letter, referencing the objections of the Association of Chief Police Officers. Because the Pickles proposals would effectively not allow gypsies and travellers to settle anywhere, they would therefore increase the risk of unauthorised encampments. Anyway, the Tories will be furious.

This evening Cameron has given a strange interview saying that he will not seek a third term as Prime Minister.

TUESDAY 24 MARCH

The final Cabinet – we've all agreed to troop over together. Met in Nick's office with Danny, Ed Davey, Alistair Carmichael, Jo Swinson, Don Foster and Simon Wright, Nick's PPS. We then went down to the bike racks – where the Cabinet Office connects with Downing Street. We were kept waiting there by press officers, and eventually Vince joined us, wearing his trademark hat. Nick arrived and we all walked down Downing Street together and were photographed outside the famous front door.

The Cabinet table was covered with beer bottles and round containers of Nick's Yorkshire crisps. Each Cabinet minister had a bottle in front of him from Wychwood Brewery – 'Co-ale-ition' beer. This was described as 'Indispensable Political Ale' and on the back of it was a picture of the Cabinet and a caption: 'An unconventional pairing, this experimental beer has astonished doubters and exceeded expectations. Time for some creative thinking with this carefully crafted beer, hints of oak and zesty lemon deliver a truly distinctive refreshing flavour that lasts the distance.' I noted that the 'best before' date was October 2015! Nick's contribution was Henderson's Yorkshire Sauce crisps – named 'Coalition Crunch'.

A photographer dashed round the room taking photos – goodness knows what future historians will think when they look at the table and see it covered with beer bottles.

Cameron began, talking about how many Cabinet meetings we had had since May 2010, mentioning some of the issues that we had discussed, and then saying how proud he was of the coalition government. Nick spoke next, and made some positive comments about working with the Conservatives. Cameron, realising that he had said little about his coalition colleagues, then said that he would like to thank Nick personally for all that he had done to keep the coalition on the road.

It is pretty staggering that the coalition has not only gone on for five years but done so in a very positive and constructive way, so that we are leaving this last Cabinet meeting as colleagues and in some ways friends, rather than as political enemies dying to get away from each other.

George Osborne made a few comments about the economy – including revealing that today's inflation number had come out at 0.0 per cent! George said this just proved that the Labour campaign on the cost of living had come to 'precisely nothing'. There was a round of laughter – perhaps more than the joke merited.

We then had three debates – the first was a presentation by Nick Clegg and Jeremy Hunt on progress on mental health policy. Then a government implementation achievements presentation from Oliver and Danny.

I said, 'Oliver and Danny's presentation reminds us of how much we have achieved since May 2010. This government was founded to deal with the economic problems that our country faced, but it has done much more than that. We should be particularly proud of the reforms that we have made to education and welfare, and changes such as equal marriage which have done so much to challenge prejudice and discrimination in our society. We should also be proud that we have managed to deliver the 0.7 per cent target on overseas development assistance – in spite of the challenging spending environment.'

I then went on to say, 'I think we should all give credit to the Prime Minister for the fantastic way that he has led this government since 2010.' Tory Cabinet ministers perked up at this apparently striking endorsement. I continued: 'The Prime Minister is to be commended for leading the coalition government so brilliantly, and for proving to the whole country how effective coalition governments can be and how much better they are than unstable single-party governments.' Cue laughter. I finished: 'I hope that this has paved the way for many more coalition governments in the future.' Cameron smiled and said, 'I suppose I will have to take praise, wherever it comes from!'

There was a final, brief discussion on foreign affairs and the progress against ISIS in Syria and Iraq. And then there were some final pleasantries and the whole thing was over.

In some ways, a little bit of an anti-climax. Everybody collected up their papers, beer and crisps. Some thoughtful person provided small bags to hide the beer and crisps from Downing Street snappers.

I normally return to the Cabinet Office through the connecting corridor. But on this occasion I felt it right to leave by the front door, and I strolled down the corridor to the front door of No. 10, and out into the street, with all the waiting photographers.

I had a brief meeting to say goodbye to the excellent civil servants in the DPM policy team, and then headed off to the Commons to sit in on the last Deputy Prime Minister's Questions. It was a rather subdued affair, in spite of a good turnout of Lib Dem MPs. At ten past twelve, the whole thing was over. Nick's last appearance in the Commons as Deputy Prime Minister.

Tomorrow is my last 'real' day as a minister.

It is going to be a sad day, and I am already suffering withdrawal symptoms from the very thought of not having a massive number of decisions on interesting issues to take over the weeks and months ahead. I am desperate for us to get back into government so that we can carry on the work we have started.

WEDNESDAY 25 MARCH

The last 'real' day of the government.

At 7.45 a.m. I walked from the Cabinet Office down the long corridor that looks over the back of Downing Street, and through the connecting door into No. 10. Walked past the Prime Minister's study, and then turned down the main staircase where all the portraits of former Prime Ministers hang. At the bottom of the staircase, you go through some double doors and then you are in the small basement kitchen of No. 10. Got my usual takeaway breakfast and said goodbye to Alison, the always cheery lady who runs the cafeteria.

At 9 a.m. to Drapers Hall in the City, for the Pupil Premium Awards. There is absolutely nothing I would rather be doing on the last day of the government than awarding the Pupil Premium Awards to some of the best schools in our country, which are making massive efforts to close the gap between results for poor children and the rest. A great event and very upbeat, and Nick Clegg and I had photographs taken with some of the winning schools.

Afterwards, went over to the Commons and voted in a deferred division – my last vote of the parliament – and then headed back to the DfE. Had my last meeting with the teachers and teaching group, led by the excellent Marcus Bell. Had quite a serious meeting, and then at the end said how much I had enjoyed working with them all and how I wished them all the best. To be honest, I felt a little bit emotional.

Lydia came in and said that we had just received a very rude letter from Eric Pickles on the travellers issue. It is a very blustery letter, rubbishing the police's response to his consultation, and saying basically that if we do not give way then Eric will leak the whole thing. I drafted a very blunt letter back, saying that I was sorry that he did not regard the views of the police as being important and I was not willing to sign off his ill-thought-out proposals. Not everything can end on a happy note in the coalition!

Finished my time in the DfE with farewell drinks in my office for my private office staff and advisers – Lydia, Sam, Georgina, Ursula, Wilhelmina, Matt and Chris. Thanked them for all their hard work and gave them all a gift. Lydia then kindly made a few really nice comments. A bit emotional, again. I will miss this great team of people.

Finally, drinks and a few crisps with Oliver Letwin, Natalie, Jonathan and Katy from my Cabinet Office staff, with Polly Mackenzie and Julian Astle. Julian asked Oliver about some article that has apparently appeared in today's *Spectator*, saying that Cameron is preparing for a second coalition with the Liberal Democrats. Oliver looked at his toes and did not say anything. Said goodbye to Oliver and went off for a dinner with friends. Slumped into bed at about midnight – feeling tired, but having enjoyed the day.

It has been a magnificent experience being in government, and before I left DfE I managed to finish off all of the list of things that I wrote down at the back of my diary at Christmas time.

THURSDAY 26 MARCH

Up at the ludicrous hour of 4.30 a.m. Feeling rather hungover.

Got in to the Commons at 5.30 a.m. and cleared out my desk – dumping all the paperwork in the bin. Driving down the A303, I discovered there were problems with my car. Stopped in the garage in Ilminster and they fixed it.

FRIDAY 27 MARCH

Spent the whole day canvassing. Started in Crewkerne in bright sunlight. Stopped at Norton for lunch. Then Brympton in the afternoon and Yeovil East in the evening.

Got home at the ludicrously early hour of quarter to eight. It is strange not to have red box work to do in the evening now, and frankly life is a pushover without it.

SATURDAY 28 MARCH

Canvassing! A really horrible, miserable, rainy, wet, damp, windy day. I felt knackered and uninspired and desperate to go home.

Nick and Danny are happy with my proposal to beef up our manifesto pledge on education – so that we will protect per pupil funding in real terms throughout the next parliament.

Got to Bibury at about five to seven and watched *The Voice*. Fairly mindless, of course, but just what I need after a hard week.

At 9 p.m. watched the Channel 4 drama about the formation of the coalition in May 2010. The main characters turned out to be Nick Clegg, me and Paddy Ashdown for the Lib Dems, Cameron and Osborne for the Tories, and Brown and Mandelson for Labour. Danny barely got to speak, and when he appeared he was presented as a very fat, bespectacled, slightly clueless Scottish person. He will not be pleased.

SUNDAY 29 MARCH

A *Sunday Times* poll gives Labour a lead of three points – Labour 36 per cent, Tories 33 per cent and we are stuck on 8 per cent. The election is going to be extremely close. However, the strength of Labour's position could be exaggerated – they are likely to lose quite a number of seats in Scotland. The whole thing still points to a hung parliament.

MONDAY 30 MARCH

Out canvassing in Yeovil Without – quite a few supporters, but also some prickly people – on the edge of Yeovil, where there is new-build into the countryside. You can never account for the spectacular hypocrisy of some people – one gentleman who lives in an absolutely brand new house, with beautiful views over the countryside, took me out of the back of his property to complain about the house building that was due to take place behind him. I pointed out that his house would not exist had the planning department of the council taken the same attitude. That did not seem to impress him.

We canvassed in Chard in the evening, in the rain. Solid, but not spectacular. Then to Ilminster, and canvassed the Herne Rise/Springfield area. Again, not bad, but not great either. A lot of wavering Liberal Democrats.

TUESDAY 31 MARCH

Windy all day today, and bloody cold. It was even snowing up in Danny's constituency – the last thing he needs!

WEDNESDAY 1 APRIL

Another day of eight hours' canvassing beckons – I am dreaming of that day in May or June when I will be able to go out to France and sit in the lovely restaurant in the marketplace and drink cheap rosé wine and eat snails.

A load of Ashcroft polling was released today – some good and some bad. Julian Huppert seems to be doing well in Cambridge. The bad news is that we are still a couple of points behind in Nick's seat.

THURSDAY 2 APRIL

A miserable day of rain and drizzle. We started off canvassing in the Monks Dale area of Yeovil West – which was pretty good. In the evening, we were in the normally solid Glenthorne Avenue – still a good support there, but also a lot of people who basically hate the Conservatives and who don't like us being in coalition with them.

Saw the highlights of the election debates on the BBC. Ed Miliband came across as aggressive and slightly overacting. Cameron seemed OK – but you can see why he wanted to avoid these debates – he looked on the defensive quite a lot. Nick looked confident and performed well, but without any knockout blows. By common consent, the SNP scored.

FRIDAY 3 APRIL

A rainy, cloudy, miserable, drizzly day. Good Friday.

In the afternoon, went to Huish Park to watch Yeovil play Chesterfield. Yeovil are due to be relegated from League One. But I have enjoyed all of the club's success over the past decade, so I felt I should be there when we take the drop as well. We took a 2–0 lead, then blew the game by conceding three goals within fifteen minutes. We are definitely going down now. The chairman said to me that this would be a 'good thing in order to allow the side to rebuild!' It is always a bad sign either in football or in politics when you regard defeat as creating a good basis for future success!

A few nice comments out on the stump today about Nick Clegg and his performance in the debate – and I texted him in the evening to pass these on. Politicians, even senior politicians, are incredibly sensitive and insecure individuals, and they need constant ego-boosting.

In the evening, went over to Yeovil Without to canvass – a mixture of Lib Dem supporters and quite a few UKIP. We really do risk losing support to UKIP – people who would never vote Conservative in a million years but who are quite right-wing on issues such as immigration, and who have voted Lib Dem in the past because we were the ones who could beat the Conservatives. These people are now grumpy and they are willing to vote UKIP in large numbers.

SATURDAY 4 APRIL

To Crewkerne, where we canvassed up in Kingswood Road. Most people were out – which is always depressing. Then headed off to Devon, where James and I are spending the weekend with Caroline and Ben – two good friends.

Arrived in Devon at 5.30 p.m. Ben, James and Caroline were already sitting outside drinking beer. We moved on from beer to champagne, and then we had a wonderful meal of fresh mussels from the estuary, before sitting outside late at night in front of a massive fire. Got to bed at around 11 p.m. and slept all the way through to 9 a.m. – a very rare luxury.

SUNDAY 5 APRIL

An absolutely beautiful early spring day – with temperatures peaking at around 16°. We got up late and went for an early lunch on the coast – in a wonderful little fish restaurant which amounted to no more than a shack. Beautiful views out over the bay. Half a lobster, washed down with a couple of bottles of wine. A real luxury. And then we walked off down the beach where James, Ben and I leapt around in the rock pools as if we were children again – looking for crabs.

In the farm behind their house, new lambs have just been born, and we went up to take a look. A few of them were sick or born deformed – and these were separated from the rest. They were all named after political leaders – 'Cleggy', 'Nigel', 'Dave' etc. 'Cleggy' looked really quite frail and vulnerable. When the milk came, 'Nigel' barged all the others out of the way and drank it all up.

MONDAY 6 APRIL

Up at 9.30 a.m. We had a breakfast specially created for me – bacon with no rind on, and HP Fruit Sauce. Then James and I headed off, with considerable regret.

Difficult getting back on the campaign trail after such a nice 36-hour break. Canvassed in Yeovil from 2 p.m. to 9 p.m.

WEDNESDAY 8 APRIL

A quick chat with Danny. He said that Paddy and Ryan are getting very worried about our polling in Lib Dem/Tory marginals – we were on track to lose a lot more than expected.

Went out canvassing all day – until it got dark at 8 p.m.

THURSDAY 9 APRIL

Labour is leading in three separate polls. Their policy of tightening up on non-dom tax avoidance is obviously very popular, and the Tories have gone rather overboard today, with personal attacks on Ed Miliband from Michael Fallon. If Labour manage to maintain this poll lead for a few days then the Tories will go into hyper-panic – they had an arrogant assurance that Cameron plus economic recovery would sweep them back to power.

FRIDAY 10 APRIL

Nick has decided that we should announce all our manifesto costings on Sunday. Danny cannot come down from Scotland, so Nick and I are going to. Bang goes my Sunday off.

Danny says he has found out from a reliable Labour source that they are currently expecting to lose twenty-five seats in Scotland – which means that they will have to do incredibly well in England to get anywhere near an overall majority.

WEDNESDAY 15 APRIL

Up at 4 a.m.! Manifesto Day. Always hate doing the morning media round. However, I was well prepared, having been immersed in all of this for the past eighteen months. Started with the ITV *Good Morning* programme, then BBC TV, Sky TV, Radio 5 Live, BBC London, and the *Today* programme. I was particularly pleased with the 8.10 a.m. keynote John Humphrys interview – he can be very difficult, but this one went well.

Went off to the manifesto launch in south London, in some kind of cavernous cellar that looked a bit like a nightclub. It went well. Nick delivered his speech in a very punchy way, and his energy and enthusiasm really are pretty boundless. I get the impression that he is relishing this campaign.

I did a quick huddle with journalists afterwards, which seemed to go well. Certainly no signs of the whole thing unravelling.

A cracking day weather-wise – with temperatures soaring to almost 25°. Absolutely clear blue skies without a single cloud, and the centre of London was awash with people in T-shirts and shorts.

SUNDAY 19 APRIL

I am finding myself losing patience a bit on the doorstep, the longer this campaign goes on. The worst people are the ones who babble on about immigration and basically are not going to vote at all or are voting UKIP. In 2010, I even had one couple in Chard say to me: 'Don't bother. We won't be voting. We're so fed up with immigration that we're emigrating.' They had not the slightest sense of the irony.

MONDAY 20 APRIL

The SNP is launching its manifesto today, which seems to be where all the political focus is going to be. Canvassing. Canvassing. And more goddamn canvassing.

One more day scored off on the diary.

WEDNESDAY 22 APRIL

A joint announcement with Nick at the National Liberal Club – that the Lib Dems would have public sector pay at least match inflation over the next two years, and then grow in real terms after 2017/18. A good 'political' announcement, but also good for the public sector – otherwise we are going to end up with serious staff shortages.

THURSDAY 23 APRIL

At 1.30 p.m. went over to 4 Millbank to do the *Daily Politics* education debate with Andrew Neil. Nicky Morgan was already there, as were the spokespeople for the Green Party and UKIP. Tristram Hunt turned up last – a bit snooty and arrogant, I thought. Even though Nicky is a Tory, at least she is pleasant to get on with.

The debate was the usual chaotic free-for-all, with everybody talking over each other. On this occasion I was pretty aggressive, to such an extent that the Green guy got in a bit of a tantrum. Frankly, when he did say something it was all idiotic platitudes and ludicrously unaffordable plans based on some kind of magic money tree or perhaps forest. Utter twaddle. The UKIP chap was just as insane, arguing that there should be a new grammar school in every single town. It is unbelievable that anybody is taking the Greens and UKIP seriously.

FRIDAY 24 APRIL

Today the postal votes are due to go out, and the plan is to do as much postal vote knocking up as possible. Needless to say none of the branches have organised themselves. So I have to re-deploy my whole team onto this. Some people I met today had already voted for me – a significant moment in the campaign.

SATURDAY 25 APRIL

Got up to the *Today* programme and was aghast to hear about an interview that Nick has given to the *FT*. Apparently he has ruled out us going into coalition with Labour if the coalition has some kind of side agreement with the SNP for confidence and supply. Why on earth do that? It is going to be difficult enough after 7 May without imposing additional conditions on ourselves. Nick is also quoted as saying that a coalition would be illegitimate if it was formed between the Liberal Democrats and a party which had got fewer votes and fewer MPs than the other big party. Why say that? Provided a government can command a majority in the House of Commons then it is legitimate. Would we really not want to go into coalition with either the Tories or Labour just because they had got 1 per cent fewer votes than the other party?

Nick texted me:

I have merely repeated what I said before – the largest party has the first right to try to assemble a government, the second can try to do so if that fails, but moving straight to a government which does not include the biggest party looks illegitimate. The key thing is to have clear red lines against UKIP and SNP deals – I even think the man in the pub in Yeovil will agree! Surely we would not ever enter a coalition where we do not command a majority in Parliament without the say-so of the SNP? That would be mad – in office but not in power etc. In that case, confidence and supply is the only and best option surely? Nick.

Got into the office for a conference call with Nick. The main item was his *FT* interview. Nick was a bit tetchy: 'Frankly, what I was saying is no more than common sense. Surely it is unimaginable that we could go into a coalition with Labour if we were reliant in any way whatsoever on the SNP?'

Jonny, Paddy and I all said that while this was *probably* true, it was quite a big call to make – as effectively we would be ruling ourselves out of government in what is now looking like quite a likely scenario in which no two parties have a majority. And this could be a very bad thing to do if it forced a second general election or helped the Tories to win an outright majority. We agreed that the formulation we would use would be that we were not interested in any 'deals' with the SNP.

Not long after the conference call, I had a text message from Andrew Adonis. Labour is clearly in a terrific flap. I explained to Andrew that the first point about legitimacy had been rather overplayed in the interview – all Nick was saying was that the party with the largest electoral mandate was entitled to try to form a government first. On the SNP point, I said that while different people in the party might take the view that being in a minority government was not a good idea for us, our formal position was that we were not interested in any 'deals' with the SNP. Andrew seemed relieved.

The evening conference call. Danny said that the canvassing in his constituency was going very well and 'we are going to win'. That may prove to be rather optimistic, if an article in today's *Times* by Matthew Parris is accurate. Matthew has visited Danny's constituency, and paints a rather bleak picture. The article starts by describing a Danny visit to a local care home where he receives 'encouraging noises' from one of the elderly ladies, only to be told shortly afterwards, 'Don't worry about her, she's got dementia.'

I raised two election concerns. One was that I thought that we were relying too much on a message about 'BLUKIP' – that there is a risk of a Tory/UKIP alliance which only the Lib Dems can prevent. I said I thought it was all far too complicated and had not really cut through with the public, and we needed to scare the public far more in the last couple of weeks about the prospect of an outright Tory government. The Tories are basically scaring voters with the idea that it will be chaos if there is a hung parliament, and it seems to me that the best way of scaring voters back is to paint a clear picture of what would happen if the Tories were in power by themselves. Ryan Coetzee got terribly uppity as he always does and said that that was not our strategy and it was far too late to change, and I could put out whatever literature I wanted in Yeovil, but the BLUKIP message was what was going out elsewhere in the country. God help us!

SUNDAY 26 APRIL

Woke up at 6 a.m.

There is a particularly awful constituency poll which puts us in third place in Bristol West. Most of us have been assuming that Stephen Williams would be OK, particularly as he had a 12,000 or 13,000 majority last time! If majorities like this can be overturned, then we really are in trouble.

Got a text message from Stephen Lotinga. He said he agreed with everything I had said yesterday and thought that the overdependence on this 'BLUKIP' line was completely confusing and muddled and has not cut through with the media or the public. He said he would try to persuade Nick that we should do a lot more to highlight the risk of a Tory majority government.

Sam Crabb sent me the data for my constituency this evening, and the whole thing looked ridiculously optimistic. My own best guess at this stage is that we will be on about 40 per cent, the Tories will be on about 30 per cent and UKIP will be about 20 per cent, with the Greens and Labour sharing 10 per cent. But I admit I have never felt so uncertain about an election.

Norman Lamb phoned. He and Tim Farron seem about the only MPs in the country who are not getting a massive Tory campaign against them. Norman is gloomy, and probably right that although it feels like an electoral tsunami is about to descend on us, there is still a slight lack of appropriate panic throughout the party. It is like a thin red line of 100 British troops standing calmly to receive 5,000 Zulu warriors. But will it be the massacre at Isandlwana, or the brave defence of Rorke's Drift?

WEDNESDAY 29 APRIL

There is a new poll out in Scotland, which gives the SNP 54–34 per cent ahead of Labour! Labour's situation is so bad that they are only now three points ahead of the Conservatives. The conclusion from this poll is that the SNP are set to win every single seat.

I cannot now see how Labour can get to a position where it can form a stable government without being hideously dependent upon the SNP. What is happening in Scotland seems to be a game changer.

THURSDAY 30 APRIL

We seem to have fed to *The Guardian* today details of Conservative proposals in 2012 to save £8 billion by means-testing child benefit, and cutting back some of the rates of child benefit. This is obviously politically sensitive because the Tories have so far failed to explain where about £10 billion of their £12 billion welfare cuts will come from.

The first local parliamentary candidates debate at Wadham School in Crewkerne this evening. To be honest I was dreading it, as there is no upside if you are the incumbent MP.

I turned up at the school at 7.40 p.m. Marcus Fysh, my Tory opposite number, was looking particularly uncomfortable and nervous. The debate went on for about an hour and a half, and the main thing to come out of it was how bloody awful Fysh is. All his answers were flat and uninspiring. It was a shockingly bad performance, and the more of his replies I heard, the more my confidence rose.

FRIDAY 1 MAY

Hurrah! We have finally moved into May. The finishing line is finally in sight.

Conference call with Nick at 9 a.m. The main issue that Nick wanted to discuss was what our final manifesto 'red-line' issue should be. We have already set out: a real increase in education funding; an emergency Budget with action taken to tackle the deficit in a fair way; increasing the tax-free allowance to £12,500. Today we are setting out plans to invest £8 billion more in the NHS. Nick asked whether we should also make an end to real pay cuts for public sector workers a red-line issue.

Nick sounded in pretty good form and he had a confident performance yesterday in the Dimbleby debates – where Cameron seems to have done reasonably well and Miliband slipped up, literally, when coming off the stage. Miliband was also put on the back foot by a couple of particularly aggressive questioners who raised the infamous Liam Byrne note, saying that 'there is no money' left in the Treasury. Miliband is still in denial about Labour's big spending.

Met one person in Legion Road who had voted for me last time, who said that what he was really hoping for was a continuation of the current coalition government: 'I think what we really need is for things to stay the same.' He did not say a lot more, but I suspect that his view sums up that of quite a lot of people. But is he voting for me? Or was he trying to tell me that he's voting Tory because he has bought all their 'coalition of chaos', Miliband–SNP alliance stuff?

The canvass data show that we have now canvassed 42,367 people since our campaign started in October – 51 per cent of the electorate.

SATURDAY 2 MAY

Went out delivering in Yeovil Without and Yeovil West in the morning, and then went canvassing in Mudford Road in the afternoon. Mudford Road can be quite difficult at times and I always assume there are a lot of Tories living in the big houses. But the overwhelming majority were actually supportive, and I was cheered up.

SUNDAY 3 MAY

Got up at 4.45 a.m.! Collected Matt Sanders and we made our way up to Liverpool for the National Association of Head Teachers' Annual Conference. The weather was pretty atrocious, with heavy rain, and I almost lost control of the car on one waterlogged stretch of the M5.

It was by no means a classic speech, but laid out clearly what the Lib Dem priorities on education would be.

Then headed back to London because the Lib Dem coalition negotiating team was meeting at 6 p.m. in party headquarters in Westminster.

All of the negotiating team other than Danny were present at the start – that is, Steve Webb, Lynne Featherstone, Kate Parminter, Sal Brinton and me.

Sal Brinton informed us that the party has already booked a conference hall in Liverpool for the Saturday just ten days after Election Day, in case there needs to be a special conference of members. Danny remarked that that gives us rather limited time for negotiations, and suggested booking the following weekend too. Sal said this was impossible, as we couldn't afford the booking penalty if we had to cancel one of the meetings! Steve asked why we could not delay it to the following weekend only, but Sal said as this was a bank holiday weekend a lot of Lib Dems would be away on holiday and it would be terribly inconvenient for them to postpone! Oh well, it's only the government of the United Kingdom we are talking about. Even Steve looked underwhelmed.

At about ten to eight, we ended the meeting and Danny and I set off for my house in Kennington. We had a glass of wine with James, and Danny instantly tucked into a plate of crisps. Jonny Oates arrived at 8.25 p.m., looking cheery and relaxed, with Nick not far behind.

I had expected Nick to look relaxed and demob-happy, with the campaign almost over. Actually, he looked completely knackered and ever so slightly on edge. We went straight into a conversation about what was likely to happen after the election.

Nick said, 'Look, I have been thinking about this a lot. I just don't now see the scenario where we are going to be able to go into government, and bluntly I expect to stand down and pave the way for a leadership election. If there was a possibility of us going into coalition on an outright basis, it wouldn't be that difficult to strike an agreement with Labour – and I would be in favour of that. That would be my preference over an outright Conservative coalition, because of the risk that their referendum policy leads to our departure from the European Union. That is a massive issue for me, and I do not want to end up leading a party which is in government for seven or eight or ten years out of which we end up leaving the EU. I don't in all conscience know whether I could take a risk on something so important.

'And on Labour, I just can't see the arithmetic in which Labour and we could form a government by ourselves. We would be dependent upon the SNP, and I think that that would be a terrible situation which would do massive damage to our party and totally destroy us in Tory-facing seats at the next election. So I think the chances of us ending up in a coalition are rather remote.'

Danny leant forward: 'Nick, I agree on Labour. But can I challenge your view about the European referendum, and I speak as somebody who is obviously very passionate myself about our membership of the EU. We have got to remember that we have fought this election saying that we want to be in government delivering our manifesto. It is going to be quite difficult after the election to suddenly send a message out to people that we're only interested in going into opposition. And my view is that if all of the main political parties are campaigning for a 'Yes' vote in the referendum, then that referendum can be won. So I am not in favour of ruling out a coalition with the Tories if the two of us could effectively form a coalition, maybe with a few DUP MPs tagged on.

'On the SNP issue, I agree with you that that's much more difficult, and obviously I'm fighting the SNP up in Scotland so I have particularly strong views about what an unpleasant party they are. However, we've got to think very carefully about that before we make any decisions after the election, because we have got to think about what the counterfactual is – in other words, would we end up creating an even worse situation if we did not allow Labour to form a government but ended up with the Conservatives instead, or a second general election, which would be absolutely devastating.'

Jonny chipped in at this point to say he agreed with Danny and that one of our prime objectives after the general election must be to avoid any second general election.

I also agreed with Danny, and said that clearly we would have to set out a number of conditions if we went into coalition with the Conservatives and they insisted on an EU referendum – which they would do, because Cameron would have to deliver that to his party. I said the conditions would have to be:

1. That we delivered a very large part of our manifesto, more than people expected, and that the economic and social strategy of the government looked more Lib Dem rather than Conservative.
2. That we agreed with Cameron at the outset what our red lines were in the negotiations with the EU.
3. That if the Tories recommended that we left the European Union in the referendum, then the coalition would immediately come to an end and the Tories would no longer have a majority. That would concentrate the minds of Osborne and Cameron – who at the end of the day want more than anything to be in power.

Nick said that he was also tempted to insist on us having the Chancellor of the Exchequer so we would be controlling a large amount of the domestic agenda. I am still sceptical about whether the Tories would ever agree that – but there's no harm in us proposing it, and it might be a good way of securing the education and health portfolios.

But Nick was still dubious: 'I have to tell you I find the prospect of being in coalition with the Tories again extremely difficult. I bloody hate these people,' he said, banging the table three times. 'They really think they have a right to rule, and their attitude to the poor and disadvantaged is just something that I can never understand or accept, but I suppose you are right that we must consider this European referendum issue and whether it is manageable and what we could get in return.'

It was now about ten to ten and we had eaten our way through a lot of food from the excellent Kennington Tandoori Restaurant – as well as two and a half bottles of Chablis.

Danny's taxi was due to arrive at 10 p.m. to take him to get the night sleeper back to Scotland. I butted in and said, 'Look, we are running out of time and we haven't discussed some other issues that we need to discuss.'

Nick then said that we had to consider what should happen to the negotiating team if one or more members lost their seats. He nodded at Danny and they had clearly discussed the issue. Danny said, 'Look, my view is that I'd like to be on the negotiating team even if I lose my seat, which I am obviously not expecting to do. However, I accept that I could not chair or be the public face if I'd lost my seat – so I would propose that David at that stage takes over the chairing of the committee, and is the public face.'

I said that I would be happy to do that. I said that it was possible that any of the others of us could lose our seats and if we did so, I did not see that we could have two people on the committee who had lost seats – but I said I thought it was very important that Danny did stay on the group given his experience. Nick and Danny looked rather blankly at the possibility of anybody else losing their seat, but Lynne's re-election is far from certain.

Nick then said, 'There's also the question of my own position. My view is that it is going to be extremely difficult to form any coalition if we have got less than, say, thirty-five seats, and it would be very difficult for me to stay as leader if we had suffered a devastating loss of, say, more than half our parliamentary colleagues.'

I said, 'The truth is that expectations are now that we are going to lose far more seats than that, and I don't think it's at all obvious that opting out of government is good for our party. We'd tell the public that we are going to respond responsibly to try to put forward a stable government that delivers as much of our manifesto as possible. Frankly, with our vote down at 8 or 9 per cent, provided we manage our situation well in government, there's no reason why we shouldn't end up with the same vote share or a higher vote share.'

Nick nodded a bit, but said he still thought it would be incredibly difficult if we had lost a huge proportion of our seats. Danny suggested that if the seat number was above thirty-five then we would have no problem with a coalition, but if the seat number was between twenty-five and thirty-five, a coalition would probably be OK but not definitely. He accepted that if we had fewer seats than say, twenty-five, then it might be difficult to have the mandate at all to go into coalition.

It is clear that both Danny and I are quite eager to make sure the party delivers on its promise to be in government, implementing the Lib Dem manifesto, whereas at the moment I feel that Nick is quite knackered, probably rather demotivated, worried about the scale of our losses, and really worrying whether he and the party can stomach being in power again. That is a bit worrying because we need to gee him up a bit before Election Day.

Nick also said that if we were not in government, his inclination was to announce immediately that he would be standing down as leader in the autumn and that a leadership election should take place. He said, 'I'm not inclined to make it easy for Tim Farron to just be anointed leader, so a good long period might be helpful to give the party a proper choice.' At this exact moment I received a text message, which had clearly been sent to all Lib Dem MPs: 'Thinking of you all. Very best wishes for Thursday. Good Luck! Tim (Farron).'

Nick then said, 'The other thing I wanted to ask you, Danny, is whether you would want to go to the Lords if you lost your seat?' Danny said instantly, 'Look, I am absolutely clear that I don't want to do that. If I've lost my seat, I don't want to come back into Parliament through some other route – I'll just have to get on with other things.'

Danny got up to go, and we all wished him the best. Jonny said: 'They'll be absolutely mad up there if they don't re-elect you. And perhaps you should say to them that if they don't vote you back in, the government might ask for all the money back that you have sprayed all over your constituency – including those extra ski lifts!' I also shook Danny's hand and said, 'If your constituents don't vote for you, then they certainly don't deserve you! Good luck.'

Danny shook hands with Nick, and it was unexpectedly a rather sad moment. None of us really expect Danny to be re-elected, and after all the great work he has done in government it will be rather a shattering blow to be thrown out by the electorate in this way. The media are already billing the 'axing of Danny Alexander' as the 'Portillo moment of the 2015 election' and for many people in Scotland and elsewhere he is the face of Liberal Democrat 'betrayal' that supported a Tory government and oversaw cuts.

But what went unspoken amongst us was a bit more than that. When we all meet again, it could be in circumstances where Nick has already announced his resignation, and where we have lost over half our seats in Parliament. This could very well turn out to be the 'Last Supper' of the core Cleggites – Nick, Danny, Jonny and me.

Nick then said that he also needed to leave and get a bit of sleep. As we reached the door, I said to him: 'You have done a fantastic job in this campaign, and you have performed absolutely to the peak of what was possible given our tough time in government. Please can you make sure that you don't take rushed and precipitate decisions after the results? The party needs you and the country may well need you too. You may well feel tired and disappointed, but you mustn't rush to make judgements and end up making mistakes that you'll regret.'

Nick smiled, nodded a bit, but only half seemed to absorb what I was saying. 'Good night.'

Jonny and Nick left, and James and I cleared up all the plates and rubbish and had another glass of wine.

That's almost certainly the last time I will meet Danny as an MP. As for Nick – who knows? He could be gone as leader within days, or back as Deputy Prime Minister in a new coalition government. I hope so.

MONDAY 4 MAY

There is a poll saying that Nick Clegg has pulled ahead in his Sheffield seat – due to Tory tactical voting. Ed Miliband is getting a hard time for unveiling some huge stone in which his key election pledges have been carved – only the pledges are so vague and waffly that they are completely worthless.

TUESDAY 5 MAY

Oh my God, not long to go! I can finally see the light at the end of the tunnel – let's just hope it is not that oncoming train!

Today we spent all day delivering the final leaflet in Chard – in high winds and frequent showers. Went on the daily conference call at 9.15 a.m. and there was a very positive tone. Nick is starting his tour across the country by coach from Land's End to John O' Groats. He sounded happy with the arrangements and obviously feels that the general election this time has been well run – not least thanks to Paddy Ashdown.

In the evening, another candidates debate at the Gateway Church in Yeovil. Absolutely full, with extra seating brought in. This was probably my best performance. At the end, a lot of people came up to congratulate me and one said, 'I had been tempted to vote Conservative, but after hearing that blithering Tory idiot I have definitely decided to vote for you!' Cheering!

WEDNESDAY 6 MAY

Went off to the radio debate at the Numatic factory in Chard. Marcus Fysh was useless as ever. The Labour candidate is pleasant but a bit out of her depth. The UKIP candidate is pleasant but a bit batty. And the Green candidate came over quite well in the first debate but is now beginning to bore me rigid. Sanctimonious green drivel.

Finished my leafleting at around quarter to eight in Yeovil East, on St John's Road. Then I was home by 10.30 p.m. and saw the first part of *Newsnight*. Most people are expecting the Tories to emerge as the largest party in seats, with Labour losing thirty or forty seats. The question is whether any combination of parties will be able to form a solid government.

Had a good wishes message from Andrew Adonis and a very generous text from Nicky Morgan.

I am dictating this at 11.30 p.m. on 6 May, and we are half an hour from Election Day. Really quite exciting.

Spoke to James this evening and warned him that I had no idea what result to expect. Of course, as soon as I said this he sounded terribly nervous, and I think he thought that I was only saying that because I was expecting to lose. The truth is that I have no real idea what the result is going to be in Yeovil. I am hoping that I will have a reasonably solid majority of say, 6,000, 7,000 or 8,000, but I could not rule out a shock result where I lost or only held on by a slim margin.

Tomorrow's poll is going to shape the future of our country for the next decade and more. And it will also shape the rest of my life. If I lose the Yeovil seat tomorrow, then that is it for me with politics – and I will be looking at a new career. If we go into opposition, then I will be on the back benches and counting down the rest of my parliamentary career. But if we go into coalition, then I could be back at the centre of power – perhaps as Chief Secretary or Education Secretary. Everything for the rest of my professional life rides on the result tomorrow.

GENERAL ELECTION DAY – THURSDAY 7 MAY

Up at 4.45 a.m. to put out 'Good Morning' leaflets to get our vote out.

After the wind and rain of the past few days, the clouds have cleared and it is a beautiful morning. I met up with Alec, Khloe and Graham at the Forest Hill car park in Yeovil, and we put out our leaflets across the estate over the road from Westland Helicopters.

Finished the whole round just before 7 a.m. Only fifteen hours to go now till the polls close, and it is going to be an interesting if somewhat nerve-racking day. The *Times* headline says it all – 'Judgement Day'.

9.15 p.m. Back in South Petherton after a long day knocking-up. From the very early morning, all the reports back were of long queues at polling stations. When turnout is high, this is usually good for us – but what does it mean on this occasion? Is this a surge of Tory supporters because of fear of the SNP; is it an increase in UKIP's vote? Nobody really knows.

Finished my canvassing on Westland Road at 8.45 p.m. Virtually everybody that I spoke to was very friendly and had already voted, and eventually I found a lady three quarters of the way down on the left who gave me a really warm welcome and said she had already voted for me – and I felt that that was a good note to end on.

Got home at about ten past nine. Changed into a suit and tidied everything up and packed my bags into the car. Got a text message through from party HQ saying that Nick Clegg now wanted to do a telephone conference call with all of us at 10.30 p.m.

FRIDAY 8 MAY

I am dictating this twelve hours later at ten o'clock on the morning of Friday 8 May.

On Thursday night I drove round to Joan Raikes's house in South Petherton, looking forward to a pleasant meal while we watched the exit poll. I was expecting the Lib Dems to have between twenty and twenty-five seats, and thought the Tories might surprise people with, say, 295 seats, with Labour south of 250.

I had barely got to Joan's when the exit poll came in. The first headline was that the Tories were close to an overall majority – Conservatives 316 and Labour 239. The SNP were predicted to get 58, and UKIP 2. But the absolute shocker was the projection of Lib Dem seats – 10! Nobody had considered anything remotely as low as this. I immediately started to worry that I might have lost Yeovil.

Paddy was on the BBC general election programme and immediately dismissed the poll, saying that he would 'eat his hat' if it was true. I didn't like the feeling of this, because we went through the same dismissal of polls in 2010, but they turned out to be accurate.

Sam Crabb sent me a relatively reassuring text message, which indicated that we were probably ahead in the postal votes – but only by six or seven percentage points.

Went on a conference call with Nick at 10.30 p.m. – Nick, Danny, me, Ryan, Steve Lotinga and Jonny Oates. Nick said that there was really no point in us having any significant discussion until we knew what the scale of the losses was. We agreed we would have another conference call at 2.30 a.m.

I texted Sam Crabb at the count and asked him how things were going: 'Not good.' The rest of the night was just a nightmare. The more information that came in from Sam, the worse our position seemed to be, and at around 11.30 p.m. he told me that I'd lost. I broke the news to Joan Raikes, and then went out into the kitchen to phone James and my mother. Also phoned Jonny Oates and he was obviously a bit gobsmacked. And then Nick – 'My God, that's terrible. Not just you, but Danny, Vince and Ed.' So by the sound of it, all our senior people are going to lose their seats – and even the arch-campaigner Steve Webb seems to have lost in Thornbury and Yate. Indeed, it looks as if we are going to be completely wiped out in the south-west of the country. A catastrophe.

The results in Scotland were truly dreadful – with only Alistair Carmichael holding on in Orkney and Shetland. Danny fell with a majority against him of 10,000, Charles Kennedy too, and all of our other seats.

I said to Joan that I thought I ought to go into the office in Yeovil, so that I was ready to go to the count. Once in the office, I sat down with my iPhone and watched the results.

Basically, the SNP has run rampant in Scotland, and in England the Tories have succeeded in persuading the middle-of-the-road English voter that: a) Ed Miliband is a socialist maniac, and b) there is a serious risk that he would end up in coalition with the SNP – holding England and the United Kingdom to ransom. I can only think that that is what must have caused so many people to switch allegiance in such vast numbers.

I watched Ed Davey losing Kingston, and Vince Cable losing Twickenham, and a shattered-looking Simon Hughes lose in his inner London constituency. Particularly sad for Simon after thirty-two years.

Then there was Nick's own count from Sheffield. I watched the results and he ended up having won by about 2,500 votes over Labour. His speech wasn't too bad, but given how fluent he normally is, he was clearly somewhat shell-shocked and struggled to communicate. He must have a terrible sense of responsibility for what has happened to the party – thirty or forty years of growth wiped out overnight. It will take years and years, if ever, to rebuild. Meanwhile, the country is going to be run by those bloody awful Conservatives – with possibly the right-wing DUP also playing a part.

I arrived at the count at around 5.15 a.m. and was met by my brilliant office manager, Sue Weeks, and my excellent organiser, Theo Whitaker, and by the fantastic Alec Newton.

Got the results from the returning officer. Paraded up on stage and the Tory candidate made a fairly bog-standard speech.

Then I went forward and said the usual things about the returning officer and the police and all the counting agents, and congratulated the other candidates. Thanked Sue Weeks, Sam Crabb, Theo, Graham, Alec and Khloe, and all the other volunteers and office staff. And then thanked all the people of the Yeovil constituency for having elected me for three terms to Parliament and giving me the honour of serving as a minister in the coalition government.

The bad thing about losing your seat is that the staff who worked for you also lose their jobs. That means breaking up the brilliant team of Sue, Claire, Sarah and Sadye, and also losing Alec.

As I drove away from the count and towards the A303, I started to receive a whole load of supportive text messages. At this stage my emotional control went, and I parked in a siding on the Cartgate link to the A303 and sent some replies.

Danny phoned me later and I pulled in to a service station to take the call. We swapped jokes. I said, 'Frankly, I don't think Nick did a very good job in choosing the negotiating team!' Danny roared with laughter. Not only had he lost his seat but we had lost all of the other members of the negotiating team as well – me, Steve Webb and Lynne Featherstone!

Texted Nick: 'Pleased that you won and didn't give the bastards that satisfaction. But it turns out the negotiation team was not well chosen! Hope you are OK.'

Nick had already told me that he was going to resign. The rumours suggest that Ed Miliband will be resigning as well.

Just before I got home, the news came through that Ed Balls had lost his seat by 300 votes. I felt strangely sad and perhaps even guilty about this. I heard an excerpt from Ed's speech where he said that he was particularly sad not for himself but for what the election outcome meant for the country – and I know exactly what he means. Two progressive parties have taken a massive kicking, and now it looks as if the Conservative Party could be able to run the country by itself.

Life must move on. I don't regret having been Member of Parliament for Yeovil constituency for fourteen years, and somehow I never did think I was going to manage to break Paddy's record of being a Lib Dem MP for eighteen years! I am very proud of having been in government for the past five years – helping to turn the economy around and pushing for progressive policies like the pupil premium and equal marriage. The sad thing is that in spite of the good things we have done, we haven't actually been able to achieve the credit for many of them. Is that our fault? Is it the public's? The media's? Perhaps a bit of each.

As I dictate this, Ed Miliband is just about to resign, and Nick's resignation cannot be far behind. I should be with him, really. I was there at the beginning of his leadership, in that tight race with Chris Huhne. There to prep him for those 'Cleggmania' debates in 2010. There to form the coalition, join the government, leave it and then re-join it. There at the last Cabinet, and the last DPM Questions. How thoughtless of me not to be there at the end too.

There is a silver lining: if Nigel Farage does not win his seat, he will be resigning too. Three party leaders out within the space of twenty-four hours! Politics can be a cruel game, but that comes with the territory. And politics can also be quite simply the best and most inspiring thing there is to do with your life.

For James and me, there is now an opportunity to make a new life without the burdens of constituency advice centres and jumble sales and fêtes on Saturday afternoons.

It's been quite a rollercoaster. Now it's time for a quieter life, and new challenges.

And that is 'The End'.

INDEX

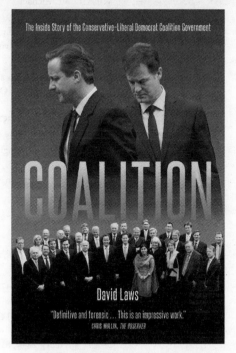

336PP PAPERBACK, £9.99

22 Days in May is the first detailed insider account of the negotiations which led to the formation of the Liberal Democrat–Conservative coalition government in May 2010, along with an essential description of the early days of the government.

David Laws was one of the key Liberal Democrat MPs who negotiated the coalition deal, and the book includes his in-depth, behind-the-scenes account of the talks with the Conservative and Labour teams after the general election, as well as the debates within his own party about how the Lib Dems should respond to the challenges and threats of a hung parliament.

This is an essential account of a historic sequence of events, and the personalities involved, that changed the face of British politics.